USA'S NATIONAL PARKS

Regis St Louis, Amy C Balfour, Anthony Ham,
Lauren Keith, Becky Ohlsen

CONTENTS

Plan Your Trip

The Guide

Camping, Sierra Nevada (p70)

Arches National Park (p128)

Black bear, Great Smoky Mountains National Park (p358)

Toolkit

Storybook

CB_TRAVEL/SHUTTERSTOCK ©

Grand Canyon of the Yellowstone (p303)

USA'S NATIONAL PARKS

THE JOURNEY BEGINS HERE

Some of my earliest travel memories revolve around America's national parks: marveling at Mesa Verde's ancient cliff dwellings, crawling through Mammoth Cave's chilly passageways and watching the fireflies dance around the family tent in the Great Smoky Mountains. Although I've traveled the globe since then, I'm convinced that the world's greatest treasures are right in my own backyard. Every time I've visited a national park, I've fallen in love with a new place.

National parks have always been an important part of the American identity – 'the best idea we ever had' as writer and historian Wallace Stegner put it. Today, those treasured outdoor spaces are more important than ever — both for the ecosystems they protect and the people who visit them.

My favorite experience is tramping through wintry forests in snowshoes while tracing the rim of the **Grand Canyon of the Yellowstone** (p303). Seeing the park under heavy snowfall is magical.

Regis St Louis

@regisstlouis

The son of two Coloradans, Regis has spent two decades exploring the world's wild places. He is the author of more than 100 Lonely Planet guides.

WHO GOES WHERE

Our writers and experts choose the places which, for them, define USA's National Parks

My toughest day hike was a solo trek to the summit of **Half Dome** (p80) from Yosemite Valley. The sense of accomplishment and relief at the summit, shared by all the hikers up there, is one-of-a-kind. And yes, the steep slope of the rock and the steel-cable 'ladder' on the final stretch are as scary as they look, but just keep going. You'll be glad you did.

Amy C Balfour

@amycbalfour

Amy writes about travel, culture and the outdoors. She has authored more than 60 books for Lonely Planet.

The largest subtropical wilderness in the US, the **Everglades** (p387) is a great place to see wildlife, including alligators and birds. I love the diversity of experiences on offer here, from short strolls along a boardwalk to deep backcountry immersion in the 10,000 Islands in a kayak. The Everglades feels like a soul-enriching antidote to Florida's overdeveloped coastline.

Anthony Ham

@AnthonyHamWrite

Anthony writes about wildlife and culture; he is the author of The Last Lions of Africa.

Zion National Park in Utah stirs up every emotion in me. The **Narrows** (p195), where the trail is simply the Virgin River coursing between sheer-cut canyon walls, is one of my favorite hikes I've done anywhere in the world. Wading through the water and wondering what's around the canyon's next corner fills me with pure joy and brings back a childlike sense of awe.

Lauren Keith

@noplacelike_it

Lauren is a travel writer and an avid hiker whose boots have trekked trails all over the world.

It's hard to beat **Crater Lake** (p208) – Oregon's only national park – for the sheer wow factor. The lake itself is breathtaking, but it's also situated in the midst of some of the state's prettiest territory, full of creeks and waterfalls and hiking trails. The best way to experience it is to spend the night at one of the park's campgrounds so you'll have plenty of time to relax into the surroundings.

Becky Ohlsen

@fasterbecky

Becky writes about travel and outdoor adventures in the Pacific Northwest and elsewhere.

Olympic National Park
Towering old-growth rainforests and pristine coastline (p223)

Yellowstone National Park
Legendary place of geysers, hot springs and wildlife (p291)

Rocky Mountain National Park
Scale lofty summits, including 14,259ft Longs Peak (p288)

Yosemite National Park
Granite rock faces, giant sequoias and misty waterfalls (p71)

Death Valley National Park
Wind-rippled sand dunes and fiery views (p109)

Grand Canyon National Park
Jaw-dropping views above and below the rim (p166)

Glacier Bay National Park
Boat past vibrant glaciers and abundant sea life (p236)

Zion National Park
Gaze over red-rock canyons on clifftop hikes (p193)

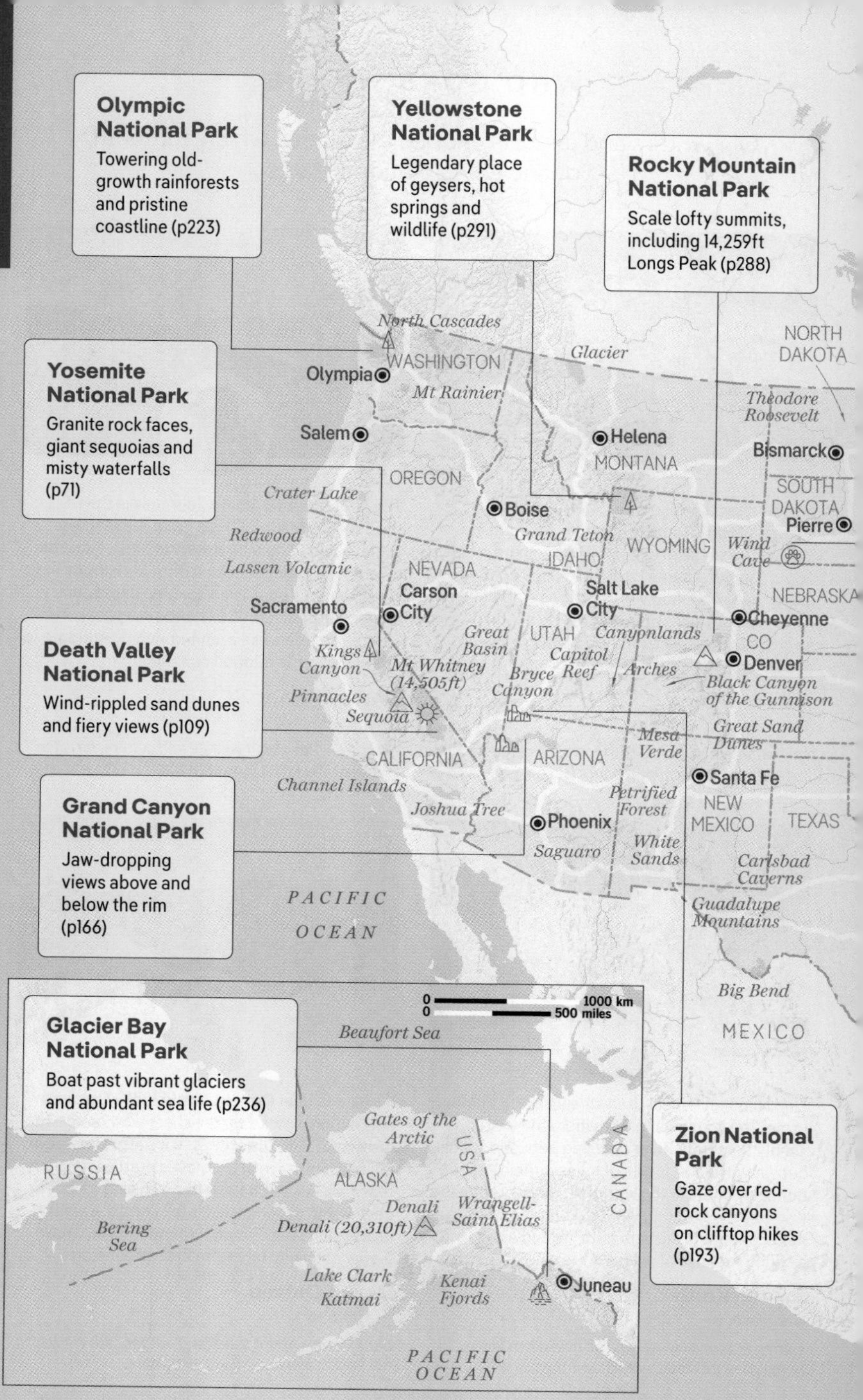

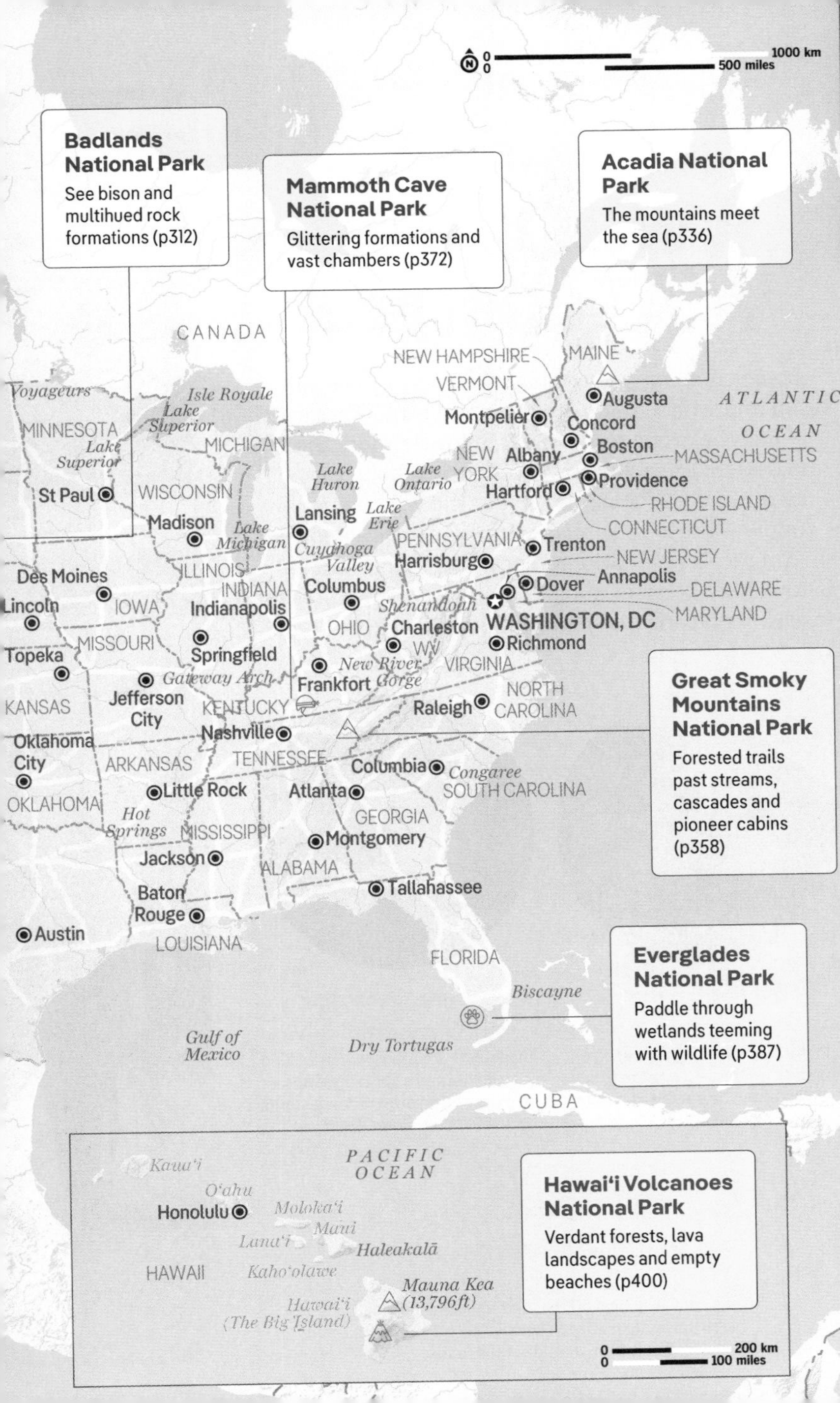

0 1000 km
0 500 miles
Badlands National Park
See bison and multihued rock formations (p312)
Mammoth Cave National Park
Glittering formations and vast chambers (p372)
Acadia National Park
The mountains meet the sea (p336)
Great Smoky Mountains National Park
Forested trails past streams, cascades and pioneer cabins (p358)
Everglades National Park
Paddle through wetlands teeming with wildlife (p387)
Hawaiʻi Volcanoes National Park
Verdant forests, lava landscapes and empty beaches (p400)
CANADA
Voyageurs
Isle Royale
Lake Superior
MINNESOTA
MICHIGAN
WISCONSIN
St Paul
Madison
Lake Michigan
Lake Huron
Lake Ontario
Lake Erie
Lansing
Cuyahoga Valley
NEW HAMPSHIRE
VERMONT
MAINE
Augusta
Montpelier
Concord
NEW YORK
Albany
Boston
MASSACHUSETTS
Hartford
Providence
RHODE ISLAND
CONNECTICUT
ATLANTIC OCEAN
PENNSYLVANIA
Trenton
NEW JERSEY
Harrisburg
Dover
Annapolis
DELAWARE
MARYLAND
WASHINGTON, DC
Shenandoah
Richmond
VIRGINIA
WV
Charleston
New River Gorge
OHIO
Columbus
Des Moines
IOWA
ILLINOIS
INDIANA
Indianapolis
Lincoln
Topeka
MISSOURI
Springfield
Gateway Arch
Jefferson City
KANSAS
Frankfort
KENTUCKY
Raleigh
NORTH CAROLINA
Nashville
TENNESSEE
Oklahoma City
OKLAHOMA
ARKANSAS
Little Rock
Hot Springs
Columbia
Congaree
SOUTH CAROLINA
Atlanta
GEORGIA
MISSISSIPPI
Montgomery
Jackson
ALABAMA
Tallahassee
Baton Rouge
LOUISIANA
Austin
FLORIDA
Biscayne
Gulf of Mexico
Dry Tortugas
CUBA
PACIFIC OCEAN
Kauaʻi
Oʻahu
Honolulu
Molokaʻi
Maui
Lanaʻi
Haleakalā
HAWAII
Kahoʻolawe
Mauna Kea (13,796ft)
Hawaiʻi (The Big Island)
0 200 km
0 100 miles

WILDLIFE WATCHING

Some come to spot the big five: bear, moose, elk, bison and wolf. Others are drawn to exquisite rarities – like the arctic tern, which migrates more than 18,000 miles each year. Whether you hope to spot an animal you've never seen in the wild before or simply want to reconnect with nature's raw power, America's vast national-park system harbors an astonishing array of plant and animal life, with every season offering one-of-a-kind wildlife encounters.

Sunrise & Sunset

Pick a prime viewing spot at dawn or dusk for the best chance to see wildlife, and be patient as nature plays itself out before your eyes.

Visual Advantage

Binoculars are a must when looking at wildlife, and a spotting scope is even better. If you're lacking, stores in the parks are well stocked.

Roadside Etiquette

If you spot an animal off the road while driving, don't block traffic. Instead, pull completely off and view safely from the side of the road.

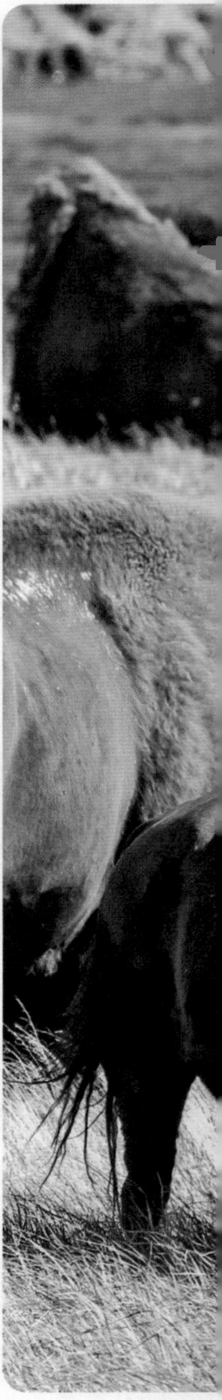

Bison, Hayden Valley (p300), Yellowstone National Park

BEST WILDLIFE-WATCHING EXPERIENCES

Observe huge bison herds and wolf packs on the move from a vantage point overlooking Yellowstone's **Lamar Valley** ❶. (p299)

Look for alligators, manatees and a wide variety of birdlife while exploring the diverse ecosystems of the **Everglades** ❷. (p387)

Scan the banks of ponds and mountain streams for well-concealed moose while hiking Grand Teton trails at **Jenny Lake** ❸. (p280)

Time your visit to see the wondrous display of synchronous fireflies flashing in unison in **Congaree National Park** ❹. (p356)

Enjoy cool early mornings in the Chisos Mountains, a fine time to look for more than 450 bird species found in **Big Bend** ❺. (p134)

Sequoia National Park (p59)

WILDERNESS LANDSCAPES

With thundering waterfalls, snow-covered peaks and chiseled canyons, national parks have been dazzling visitors for centuries. There are countless ways to experience the magic, whether trekking through the backcountry or admiring from an easy-to-reach lookout. Make sure your camera is charged: you're in a photographer's paradise.

Early Risers

Beat the worst of the crowds by getting an early start and hitting key attractions at first light. Alternatively, come in the afternoon, when most visitors have dispersed.

Deeper Knowledge

Many visitor centers help bring the parks to life, with thoughtfully designed exhibitions and films that showcase the geology, wildlife and often-times human history.

BEST WILDERNESS EXPERIENCES

Pace the trails of Yosemite's **Mariposa Grove** ❶, where sequoias rocket to the sky. (p82)

Make the intensely rewarding hike along the top of Zion Canyon's cliffs to **Observation Point** ❷. (p199)

Feel the roar of the Lower Falls as they plunge over 300ft through the **Grand Canyon of the Yellowstone** ❸. (p303)

Step into a forest of verdant splendor in the Hoh River area of **Olympic National Park** ❹. (p223)

Walk trails amid the rock formations, palm-filled oases and desert plants of **Joshua Tree National Park** ❺. (p103)

Grand Prismatic Spring (p294), Yellowstone National Park

GEOLOGICAL WONDERS

America's national parks protect some of the earth's great treasures. You can walk the trails around steaming geysers and gurgling mud pools, or peer back through the eons at billion-year-old rock formations. There are fossilized remnants of ancient forests, jewel-like glaciers and vast, glittering caverns. You could spend a lifetime and not see it all.

Ranger Talks

It's worth timing your visit to coincide with a ranger-led talk. Knowledgeable National Park Service (NPS) staff can give you a deeper understanding of the natural world.

Off the Beaten Track

You can escape overtourism and experience quiet corners of the parks by seeking out lesser-known sites (such as Yellowstone's Fossil Forest trail).

BEST GEOLOGICAL EXPERIENCES

Stroll the Upper Geyser Basin amid numerous spouters in **Yellowstone National Park ❶**. (p291)

See cathedral-sized chambers on a tour through **Mammoth Cave National Park ❷**. (p372)

Walk through trails past logs that turned to stone 200-plus million years ago in **Petrified Forest National Park ❸**. (p185)

Feel like you've left planet earth behind on a wander through **Badlands National Park ❹**. (p312)

Peer back into prehistoric times at the hoodoos, craters and mesas of **Canyonlands National Park ❺**. (p147)

HITTING THE TRAIL

Hiking can mean just about anything in America's national parks. You'll find easygoing paths tracing canyon overlooks, challenging treks to craggy summits and soul-affirming walks through primeval forests. There are accessible trails for all ages as well as remote hikes that draw only a handful of visitors. The benefits of walking for physical and mental health are well documented, and there's no better place for a bit of fresh-air medicine than on a national-park trail.

FROM LEFT: THERON STRIPLING III/SHUTTERSTOCK ©, TUPUNGATO/SHUTTERSTOCK ©, MEXIWING/SHUTTERSTOCK ©

Be Prepared

Many trails are well marked but no matter where you're heading it's sensible to travel with a good map – along with rain gear, sunscreen and other essentials.

Weather Wise

Be sure to check the forecast before heading out. When lightning flashes, take cover – and avoid ridges, isolated trees and exposed areas.

Bear Spray

Unless you're traveling in winter, have a can of bear spray handy on a hike. Keep it within easy reach and know how to use it.

Rim Trail (p168), Grand Canyon National Park

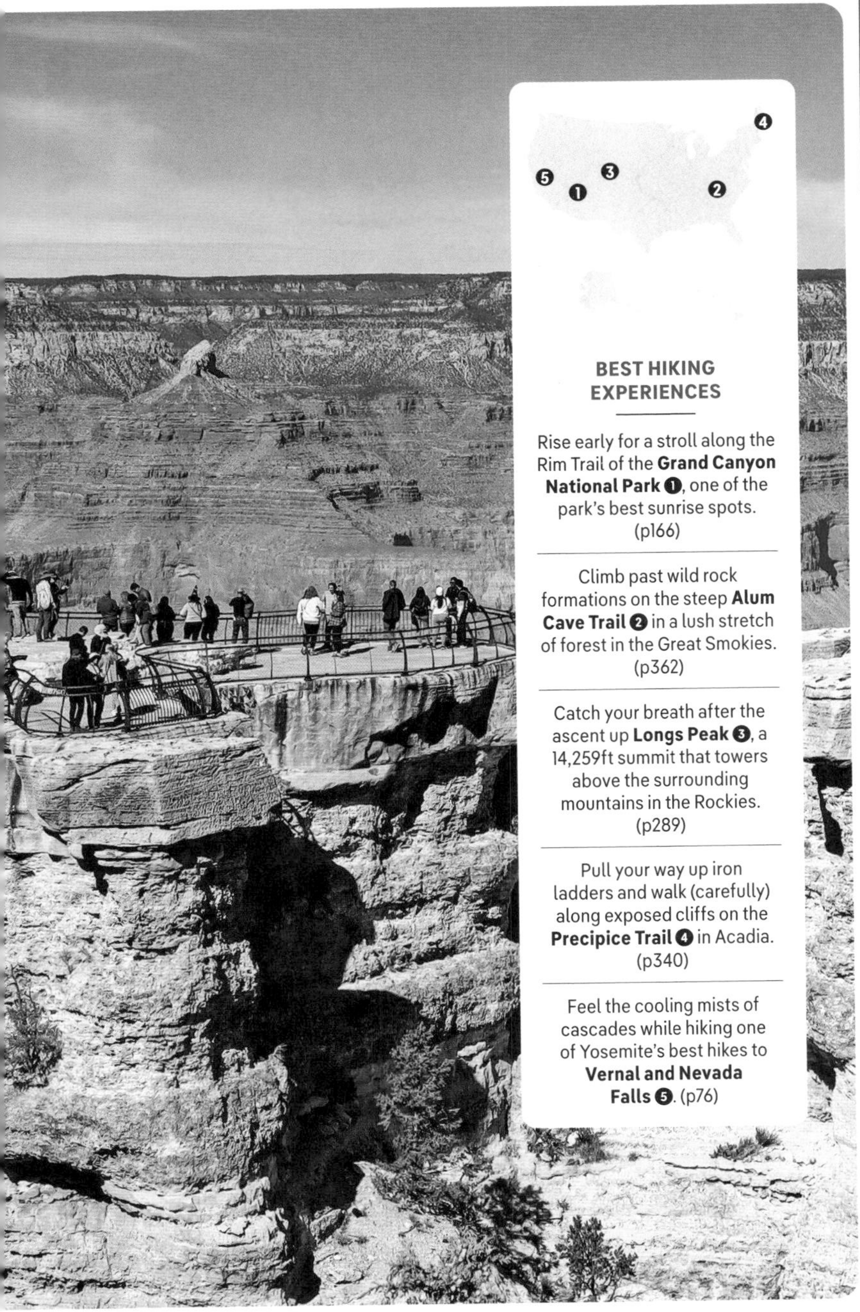

BEST HIKING EXPERIENCES

Rise early for a stroll along the Rim Trail of the **Grand Canyon National Park** ❶, one of the park's best sunrise spots. (p166)

Climb past wild rock formations on the steep **Alum Cave Trail** ❷ in a lush stretch of forest in the Great Smokies. (p362)

Catch your breath after the ascent up **Longs Peak** ❸, a 14,259ft summit that towers above the surrounding mountains in the Rockies. (p289)

Pull your way up iron ladders and walk (carefully) along exposed cliffs on the **Precipice Trail** ❹ in Acadia. (p340)

Feel the cooling mists of cascades while hiking one of Yosemite's best hikes to **Vernal and Nevada Falls** ❺. (p76)

Kayaking (p390), Everglades National Park

ON THE WATER

Whether soloing in a kayak or bundling the family into a canoe, paddling is a great way to glide into nature at your own pace. When your arms tire, shore up on empty beaches for a picnic or a swim. With a permit you can also backcountry camp in appealing spots a few paces from the shore.

Permits

To boat in some parks, you'll need to purchase a permit (available on recreation.gov). This often applies to kayaks and stand-up paddleboards.

Staying Warm

Make sure you have the right clothing: warm layers and a waterproof shell. Things can get chilly on the water even in the height of summer.

BEST AQUATIC EXPERIENCES

Splash along the white water rushing through the **New River Gorge National Park** ❶. (p374)

Paddle across the mirror-like waters in the **Everglades** ❷ amid great blue herons and ospreys. (p387)

Peer out over the edge of a catamaran while gliding past cliffs, icebergs and puffins in **Glacier Bay National Park** ❸. (p236)

Go for a soak at **Hot Springs National Park** ❹ – the perfect ending after a day on the trail. (p370)

Rent a houseboat and spend a few days exploring **Voyageurs National Park** ❺. (p327)

Showshoeing (p146), Bryce Canyon National Park

WINTER WONDERLAND

The parks are mostly warm-weather havens. But you've only really experienced half the action if you haven't been in the winter. After November, the northern landscapes gradually become more snow-covered and challenging (even the bears retire). Skiing is the obvious lure. Snowshoeing, cross-country skiing and fatbiking attract the more adventurous.

Gear Essentials

Make sure your clothing is up to the task: winter here can bring extreme temperatures ranging from just above freezing to well below zero.

Getting There

Plan your route carefully as some roads at higher elevations remain closed for the duration of winter. Get up-to-date weather reports from parks.

BEST WINTERTIME EXPERIENCES

Take in the views while riding in the glass-topped dome car of the **Cuyahoga Valley Scenic Railroad** ❶. (p316)

Strap on your snowshoes on a guided hike at **Taggart Lake** ❷ in the Grand Tetons. (p282)

Escape the frigid winter while taking in volcanic terrain on a visit to **Haleakalā National Park** ❸. (p396)

Enjoy the dramatic contrast of snow on red rocks in **Bryce Canyon National Park** ❹. (p138)

Glide through snow-covered meadows on a cross-country ski outing in **Glacier National Park** ❺. (p266)

SCENIC DRIVES

A head-spinning road snakes up the mountainside to deposit you in a different world, high above the tree line, onto a rolling plateau overlooking topaz lakes and craggy rock faces where marmots sunbathe. Or you might find yourself motoring across desert, through misty forests or along a rocky, wave-kissed shoreline. Wherever you roam, you won't stray far from some magnificent drives – with little-known hikes, remote campsites and charming little towns along the way.

Summer Driving

Plan your road trip carefully as the higher mountain roads open for only a short window during the summer, typically from late May through September or October.

Picnic Supplies

Services are sparse, and many national parks lack food options once you're inside. Prepare for a long drive by bringing plenty of snacks and water.

Fuel Up

Gas stations can be few and far between, so fill up before reaching the park. And try to arrive before nightfall to avoid wildlife on the road.

FROM LEFT: BENNY MARTY/SHUTTERSTOCK ©, OOMKA/SHUTTERSTOCK ©, TRPHOTOS/SHUTTERSTOCK ©

Delicate Arch (p129), Arches National Park

BEST ROAD-TRIP EXPERIENCES

Enter an enchanting world of lush rainforests, glacial-carved lakes and windswept beaches on a trip around the **Olympic Peninsula 1**. (p226)

Photograph the mountain views while driving in **Grand Teton National Park 2**, with roaming pronghorn, deer and moose on the Jackson Hole Valley flats. (p281)

Cruise along a scenic drive in **Arches National Park 3** for views of balanced rocks, delicate arches and the La Sal Mountains. (p130)

Take in the grandeur of Hawai'i Volcanoes on the **Chain of Craters Road 4**, a drive featuring petroglyphs, lava flows and jagged craters. (p402)

Admire ancient giant sequoias as well as waterfalls, lakes and mountain panoramas on the **Kings Canyon Scenic Byway 5**. (p51)

REGIONS

Find the places that tick all your boxes.

Alaska & the Pacific Northwest

A REGION OF SUPERLATIVES

America's biggest state is home to vast national parks larger than some countries. Lush temperate rainforests, iceberg-dotted bays and the highest peaks in North America are all part of the Alaskan allure. Further south, the Pacific Northwest has lush primeval forests, sparkling blue lakes and famous snowcapped summits.

p203

California

EXPLORE WONDERFULLY WILD LANDSCAPES

Home to more national parks than any other state, California offers plenty of ecological diversity. There are gargantuan redwoods and sequoias that are older than the nation, rocky remnants of a volcanic past, biologically rich islands off the southern coast and breathtaking mountain valleys that helped spark early movements in creating national parks.

p41

Rocky Mountains

SOARING SUMMITS AND WILDLIFE WATCHING

Towering snowcapped peaks and wildflower-filled valleys form the backdrop to some of America's most photogenic outdoor spaces. The string of national parks across Colorado, Wyoming and Montana draw visitors from around the globe with wonders including thundering geysers, challenging 14,000ft mountains that day hikers can summit and open range teeming with wildlife.

p258

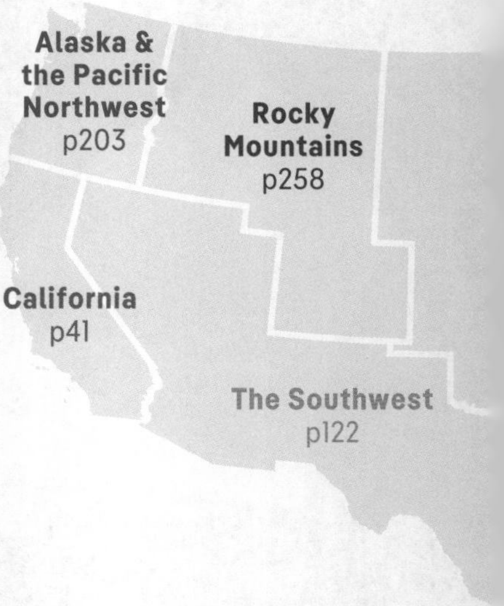

The Southwest

UNTAMED ADVENTURE PLAYGROUND

The Southwest lures travelers with giant arches, desert mesas, canyons and ancient petroglyphs. There are countless ways to get active here, from legendary white-water-rafting trips to mountain biking on world-class single track. The Southwest is also the place to learn more about Native American culture both past and present.

p122

Great Lakes & Great Plains

EXPLORE THE AMERICAN HEARTLAND

Home to howling wolves, shaggy bison and sweeping prairies, this vast northern region is packed with wild spaces. The aptly named Great Lakes, carved by glaciers and dotted with myriad islands, are more like boundless northern seas. Other highlights range from little-known caves to the fantastical buttes of the Badlands.

p307

New England & the Mid-Atlantic

WILD COAST AND GENTLE MOUNTAINS

The eastern US undulates with the weathered summits of the Appalachians, among the world's oldest mountain chains. Along the coast, surf churns against rugged shores watched over by lone lighthouses. Although you'll find only two national parks in this region, it's well worth detouring here for the mix of mountains and coastline.

p332

The South

ADVENTURES ABOVE GROUND AND BELOW

The five national parks found in this corner of the US embody the great diversity found in the six states that contain them. This is a landscape of waterfalls and rolling mountains, swampland and old-growth forest, rejuvenating springs and churning white water – not to mention the biggest cave system on earth.

p351

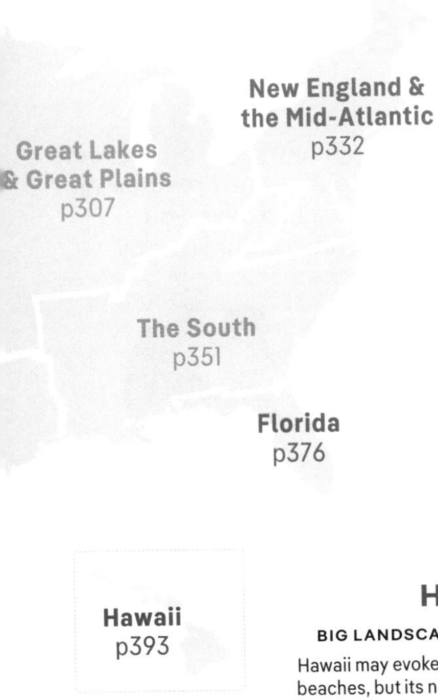

Florida

EXPERIENCE FLORIDA'S WILD SOUTH

Three national parks inhabit the beloved 'sunshine state': the wetland wilderness of the Everglades, the largely subaqueous Biscayne and the splayed keys of Dry Tortugas, which, unusually for a US national park, are guarded by a historic 19th-century fort. Come here for paddling over mirror-like waters, snorkeling on coral reefs and catching legendary sunsets.

p376

Hawaii

BIG LANDSCAPES AND EPIC HIKES

Hawaii may evoke visions of surfboards and beaches, but its national parks reveal a very different side. You can observe creation itself at Hawai'i Volcanoes National Park, with a landscape that's constantly resculpted by dramatic forces. Haleakalā is another volcanic icon, with crater descents and gorgeous trails through the lush surrounding forests.

p393

LINDA HARMS/SHUTTERSTOCK ©

El Tovar Hotel (p168), Grand Canyon National Park

ITINERARIES

California & the Southwest

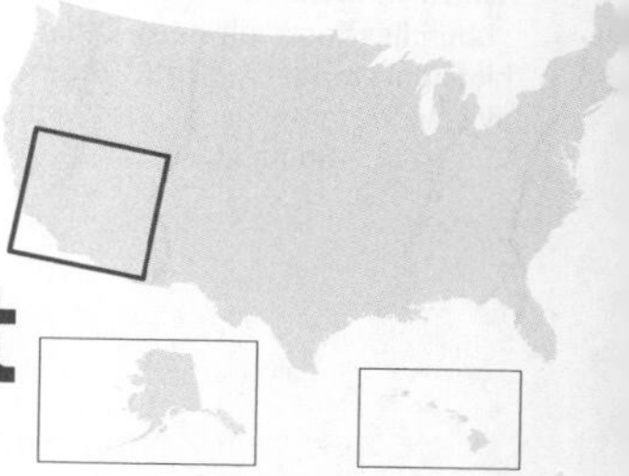

Allow: 7 days **Distance:** 1300 miles

You'll see some of America's most famous western parks on this route that takes in forested valleys, towering sand dunes and breathtaking canyons. While it's possible to do it in seven packed days, you can easily stretch this to two or more weeks, hitting other nearby attractions along the way.

1

YOSEMITE NATIONAL PARK

1 DAY

Start off with **Yosemite** (p71), the park that inspired the great conservationist John Muir in the late 19th century. Take in scenic views of Yosemite Valley and soaring El Capitan, then head off on a hike, either to the lofty Yosemite Falls or the mystical duo of Vernal and Nevada Falls. Later cool off in the Merced River. Spend the night in the historic Ahwahnee Hotel.

2

DEATH VALLEY NATIONAL PARK

1 DAY

Spend the day exploring **Death Valley** (p109), one of America's most captivating desert parks. Enjoy the dramatic panorama from Zabriskie Point. Take a hike amid the rock walls of Mosaic Canyon. When the hillsides are bathed in golden hues, take a spin on the Artists Drive scenic loop road.

3

ZION NATIONAL PARK

1 DAY

The majestic red-rock landscape of **Zion** (p193) provides a dazzling contrast to Death Valley. Get your bearings on the Zion Canyon Scenic Drive, stopping for a snack at the Zion Lodge. Gear up for adventure on a watery walk through the Narrows, or if you prefer to stay dry take to one of Zion's many lofty trails, like Emerald Pools, or for adrenaline junkies, Angels Landing.

MARIDAV/SHUTTERSTOCK ©, DAVID RAJTER/SHUTTERSTOCK ©, GEIR OLAV LYNGFJELL/SHUTTERSTOCK ©

4

BRYCE CANYON NATIONAL PARK ⏱1 DAY

Northeast of Zion, you'll enter the hallowed world of **Bryce Canyon** (p138). See what makes this place so extraordinary on the 17-mile drive up to Rainbow Point, with stops at canyon-rim overlooks along the way. Next up is the Queen's Garden Trail, a memorable hike that takes you down into the canyon. After sundown, spend some time stargazing or taking part in a ranger-led astronomy program.

5

GRAND CANYON NATIONAL PARK ⏱2 DAYS

Whether it's your first visit or your hundredth, it's impossible not to feel the sense of awe while gazing across the **Grand Canyon** (p166). Start day one by learning about geological history on the Trail of Time. Later explore Grand Canyon Village, and have dinner at the storied El Tovar. On day two, head below the canyon rim on the Bright Angel Trail.

6

JOSHUA TREE NATIONAL PARK ⏱1 DAY

Back in California, get your fill of the surreal, iconic Joshua trees while exploring the rocky, sunbaked landscape of the eponymous **national park** (p103). If you're not here for the legendary rock climbing, hit the trail. For an easy 1-mile outing, opt for the Hidden Valley Trail. With more time (and energy) at your disposal, instead go for the Lost Palms Oasis Trail.

ITINERARIES

Across the Northwest

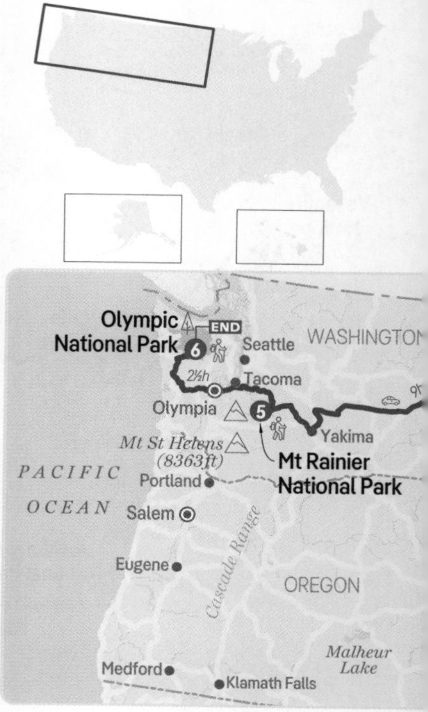

Allow: 7 days **Distance:** 1740 miles

America's northwest is a must for mountain lovers, with a mix of eroded peaks and chiseled summits, as well as the picturesque valleys surrounding them. Other highlights include the dramatic geothermal features of Yellowstone and the lush rainforests of Olympic. There's also great wildlife watching, with bison, bears and moose, among many other creatures.

1

BADLANDS NATIONAL PARK ⏱1 DAY

Start things off in **Badlands** (p312) on a high with a scenic drive along the Badlands Loop Rd. Stop for views over the otherworldly rock formations, then head to the Sage Creek Rim Rd for a look at the prairie-dog towns. Take a hike before calling it a day: though just 1 mile long, the Door Trail immerses you in the rugged landscape of the eroded canyons.

2

GRAND TETON NATIONAL PARK ⏱1 DAY

Shake off the long drive to **Grand Teton** (p277) on a walk along the Jenny Lake Trail. Stop for photos at Hidden Falls and aptly named Inspiration Point. If you're not ready to quit, keep going all the way up to Cascade Canyon, then catch the boat back across the lake. Later, treat yourself to drinks and appetizers at lovely Blue Heron at Jackson Lake Lodge.

3

YELLOWSTONE NATIONAL PARK ⏱2 DAYS

Get an early start at **Yellowstone** (p291) at the Upper Geyser Basin, home to Old Faithful and countless other geothermal features. Afterwards, see more steaming wonders at the Grand Prismatic Spring, Fountain Paint Pot and Mammoth Hot Springs. On day two, see the viewpoints and walk the south rim trail of the Grand Canyon of the Yellowstone. End with wildlife watching in the Lamar Valley.

❹

GLACIER NATIONAL PARK ⏱1 DAY

Drive the Going-to-the-Sun Road to experience some of the best mountain views in northern Montana's **Glacier National Park** (p266). Along the way, stop off at St Mary Lake, dramatically set in a glacier-carved valley. Look for wildlife on the Beaver Pond Trail, then learn more about the indigenous connection to the park in the St Mary Visitor Center.

❺

MT RAINIER NATIONAL PARK ⏱1 DAY

Start in Paradise, one of the best gateways to Washington's beloved mountain. Get insight into **Mt Rainier National Park** (p215) at the Henry M Jackson Visitor Center, then head up the Skyline Trail for a hike that takes in one of Rainier's best views, from Panorama Point. Later on, check out the Longmire National Historic District and spend the night at the delightfully rustic National Park Inn.

❻

OLYMPIC NATIONAL PARK ⏱1 DAY

Make your way to the Hoh River area in **Olympic National Park** (p223), where you can see virgin rainforest featuring massive (and centuries-old) cedars, Sitka spruce and hemlock. Deepen your knowledge at the Hoh Rain Forest Visitor Center, then take in every possible shade of green on the lush Hall of Moss Trail. Afterwards, drive out to Ruby Beach, an enchanting place to explore Olympic's rugged shoreline.

ITINERARIES

Highlights of the Southeast

Allow: 7 days
Distance: 1750 miles

There's ample variety on this road trip that takes you to national parks in seven states in the southeast. You'll see vast wetlands, primeval swamps, the Appalachian Mountains and the biggest cave system on the planet. Adventure takes many forms here, including white-water-rafting trips, summit hikes and lamplit cave crawls.

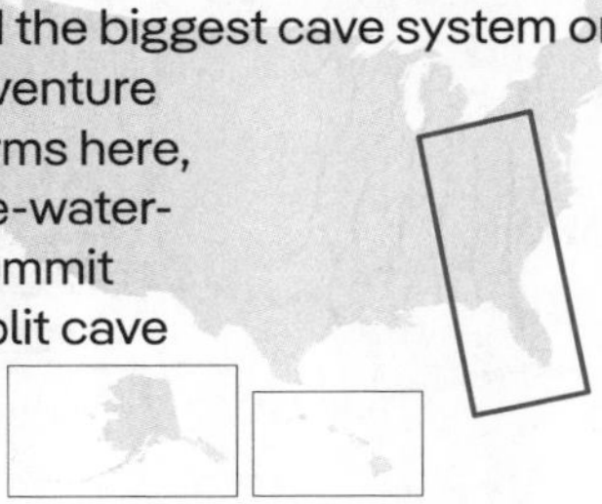

Alum Cave Trail (p362), Great Smoky Mountains National Park

1 EVERGLADES NATIONAL PARK ⏱1 DAY

Just south of Miami, the wetlands of the **Everglades** (p387) immerse you in a watery landscape full of wildlife. Make the most of the park by hiring a kayak or canoe (from Flamingo Marina) and heading off on a backcountry adventure. Nine Mile Pond is a great spot to spy egrets, herons and other birdlife. Afterwards, look for gators along the Loop Road off Tamiami Trail.

2 CONGAREE NATIONAL PARK ⏱1 DAY

You'll find more aquatic beauty up in South Carolina's **Congaree** (p356). After the long drive from the Everglades, stretch your legs on the elevated boardwalk trail. The walk takes you into the heart of the old-growth swampland, with bald cypress trees dripping with Spanish moss and woodpeckers flitting through the forest. If time allows, take a guided paddling trip on the Cedar Creek Canoe Trail.

3 GREAT SMOKY MOUNTAINS NATIONAL PARK ⏱2 DAYS

Leave the flatlands behind as you drive the winding roads into the **Great Smoky Mountains** (p358). On your first day, check out the highlights along the Newfound Gap Rd, a motorway bisecting the park, with hiking trailheads and scenic overlooks along the way. Start day two with sunrise from Clingmans Dome, then hike up the Alum Cave Trail, going all the way to Mt LeConte if you have time.

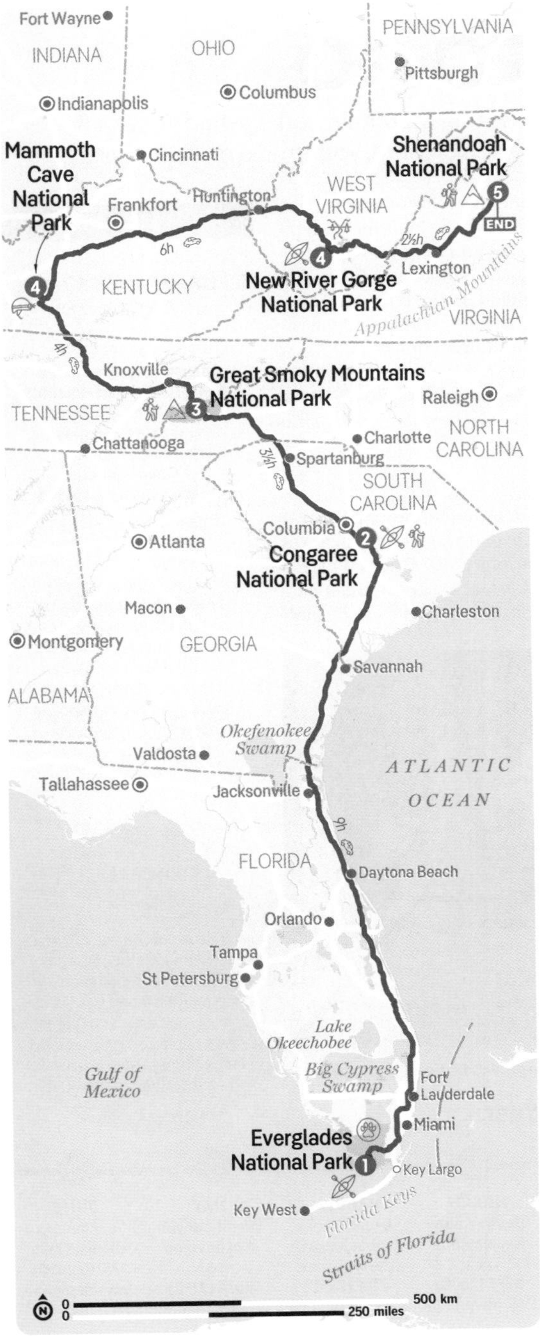

4 MAMMOTH CAVE NATIONAL PARK ⏱ 1 DAY

It's a scenic drive over the foothills of the Appalachians into central Kentucky. There you can spend a day spelunking your way through the subterranean wonders of **Mammoth Cave** (p372). Though there are many different tours, the Violet City Tour gives a fascinating insight into the cave's history. Afterwards, enjoy some above-ground scenery on a forested hike along the Cedar Sink Trail.

5 NEW RIVER GORGE NATIONAL PARK ⏱ 1 DAY

Strap on your helmet, tighten your life vest and prepare to get wet on a thrilling white-water-rafting trip along the **New River Gorge** (p374). After the adrenaline-fueled half-day trip, you can check out some of the great views of the area overlooking the picturesque New River Gorge Bridge. Later, toast the day's adventures over pizza and craft beer at Pies & Pints.

6 SHENANDOAH NATIONAL PARK ⏱ 1 DAY

The final stop takes you back into the Appalachian Mountains amid the forests of **Shenandoah** (p345). Start off at Rockfish Gap at the southern end of Skyline Drive and follow the ridgeline road as you wind past viewpoints on your way north. Stop off at the Hawksbill Loop Trailhead and make the rewarding 2.8-mile hike up to the highest point in the park.

JON BILOUS/SHUTTERSTOCK ©

WHEN TO GO

Seasonality is key when visiting mountain parks, when access is limited outside of summer. Elsewhere, you'll have more flexibility.

From mid-June to mid-September it's high season in most of America's national parks. These are the months when the roads through the Rockies, Sierras and Cascades are guaranteed to be open. It's also when the parks reach full capacity, so you'll need to plan well ahead. If you don't have your sights set on summiting mountain slopes, spring and fall can be lovely times to roam, with wildflowers in April and May, and blazing autumn colors in late September and October.

Winter is a great time to focus on parks like the Everglades in Florida, Big Bend in Texas and the desert parks of the Southwest.

Saving Money

Shoulder seasons (April to mid-May and mid-September to October) are the best time to travel if you want to beat the crowds and higher accommodations costs. Prices typically drop even more during the winter, apart from areas near ski resorts and popular winter destinations such as Florida.

I LIVE HERE

SPRING IN THE EVERGLADES

Founder of Garl's Coastal Kayaking in the Everglades, Garl Harrold is a trusted guide for top media companies including National Geographic. @garlscoastalkayaking

'I came down to southern Florida from Michigan many years ago, fell in love with the place and never left. It's amazing to visit the Everglades in the springtime, especially in April or May. That's when the water level is at its lowest, and you can spot so much wildlife in the cypress domes and freshwater ponds.'

Blue heron and pelican, Everglades National Park (p387)

FIERY FALL COLORS

Peak foliage season can run from mid-September through October depending on the destination, with leaves morphing into shades of yellow, orange and red at higher elevations first. Fall is the busiest time of year at some parks (such as Shenandoah).

Weather Through the Year

JANUARY
Hawai'i Volcanoes Avg daytime max: **75°F (24°C)**
Days of rainfall: 12

FEBRUARY
Everglades Avg daytime max: **78°F (26°C)**
Days of rainfall: 6

MARCH
Death Valley Avg daytime max: **82°F (28°C)**
Days of rainfall: 2

APRIL
Great Smoky Mountains Avg daytime max: **71°F (22°C)**
Days of rainfall: 8

MAY
Grand Canyon Avg daytime max: **70°F (21°C)**
Days of rainfall: 2

JUNE
Yosemite Avg daytime max: **75°F (24°C)**
Days of rainfall: 4

SPECTACULAR WILDFLOWERS

The Great Smokies win Best in Show when it comes to wildflowers, with more than 1500 types of flowering plants – more than any other national park. Thriving at elevations above 3500ft, catawba rhododendrons bloom in June, and you can hike to colorful explosions of flaming azaleas atop the park's balds in early July.

Music, Theater & Fireworks

Various bands gather in the desert for the family-friendly **Joshua Tree Music Festival**, spanning four days in both spring and fall. Pitch a tent in the desert and join the creative-arts-minded community. **May and October**

Fireworks happen all across the country during America's **Independence Day**, so wherever you are on July 4, there are celebrations nearby. If you're in Acadia, it's a short hop to the parades, lobster races and pyrotechnics in Bar Harbor. **July**

Near Zion National Park, Cedar City hosts a summer-long **Utah Shakespeare Festival**, featuring top-notch performances, classes, literary seminars, magic shows and more. **June through October**

The dramatic red rocks near Canyonlands become the backdrop to memorable performances during the **Moab Music Festival**. There are even floating concerts held on the Colorado River. **August and September**

Cowboys, Creatures & Frontier Life

In Furnace Creek, you can join the fun at **Death Valley '49ers**, a historical encampment featuring cowboy poetry, campfire sing-alongs and a gold-panning contest. **November**

Every year the **National Audubon Society Christmas Bird Count** sees thousands of people taking to the wilds to look for and record birds, with some parks organizing events. **December**

East of Yellowstone, cowboys from across the country saddle up at the **Cody Stampede Rodeo** to compete for top honors at this four-day event. Parades, food booths and a craft fair add to the fun. **July**

Just outside of Grand Teton, you can experience a classic slice of Wyoming at the **Teton County Fair**, complete with a farm petting zoo, cornhole tournaments and horse shows. **July**

I LIVE HERE

THE MAGIC OF WINTER

Jeff Henry is the author of numerous books, including *Yellowstone National Park: The First 150 Years*.

'I've always liked the snow and cold weather, which is one reason I was drawn to Yellowstone. In the winter, there's a solitude to the landscape and the scenery is breathtakingly beautiful. The contrast between the erupting geyser with 190-degree water with the 50-below air is staggering. The ice formations are incredible for photography.'

Grand Prismatic Spring (p294)

SNOWED IN

The mountains, especially above 6000ft, experience long snowy winters that last from late October to April. In the spring, crews spend weeks clearing the roads, which requires bulldozers, graders and other heavy equipment to break up the dense snowpack.

JULY
Yellowstone Avg daytime max: **75°F (24°C)** Days of rainfall: 5

AUGUST
Olympic Avg daytime max: **75°F (24°C)** Days of rainfall: 7

SEPTEMBER
Badlands Avg daytime max: **81°F (27°C)** Days of rainfall: 7

OCTOBER
Shenandoah Avg daytime max: **64°F (18°C)** Days of rainfall: 6

NOVEMBER
Zion Avg daytime max: **56°F (13°C)** Days of rainfall: 5

DECEMBER
Big Bend Avg daytime max: **69°F (21°C)** Days of rainfall: 4

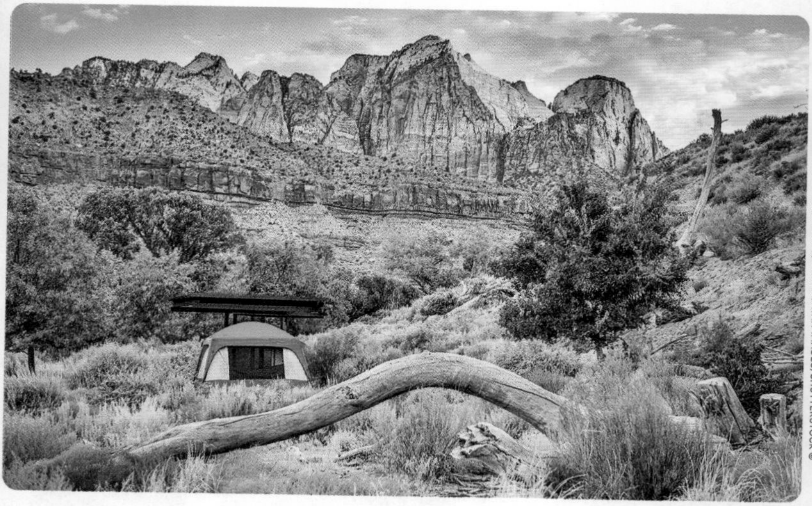

Zion National Park (p193)

GET PREPARED FOR USA'S NATIONAL PARKS

Be prepared when it comes to permits, apps and etiquette, plus inspiring viewing, reading and listening.

Permits

Permits are required for some activities, including canyoneering, overnight backpacking trips, rock climbing and rafting trips. Generally, you don't need a permit to day hike in a national park. Some exceptions are the popular day hikes to Angels Landing (Zion) and Half Dome (Yosemite). Apply well in advance for permits, which are sometimes based on a lottery system. Find more information on individual park websites.

Manners

Be respectful of wildlife. Don't approach animals, and keep a distance of 25yd from most creatures (100yd for bears).

Don't park in the road or block traffic. Use pullouts and get fully off the road if stopping to view wildlife.

On the trail, uphill hikers have the right of way. Cyclists should yield to hikers and everyone should yield to horses.

Maps & Apps to Download

AllTrails Lists of trails, reviews and current conditions. Free, but it's worth paying for AllTrails+ to download maps offline and get wrong-turn alerts.

what3words This company has given every 3m square of the world a unique three-word address. Emergency services are increasingly using what3words to know exactly where to send help.

Recreation.gov Indispensable app: reserve permits, campgrounds and day-use passes for national parks and other federal areas.

Reserve America Book Utah state park campsites.

READ

Our National Parks (John Muir; 1901) Captures the importance of the wilderness and inspired a nation to embrace national parks.

Ranger Confidential (Andrea Lankford; 2010) A former park ranger describes what it takes to fill a ranger's shoes.

Empire of Shadows: The Epic Story of Yellowstone (George Black; 2012) About exploration, American Indian Wars and the frontier.

A Sand County Almanac (Aldo Leopold; 1949) This nature classic embodies the conservation ethic at the heart of the USA's national parks.

Words

Bald A treeless area on top of a mountain in the Appalachians, typically surrounded by forest.

Slot canyon A narrow passageway with towering rock walls. Slots are formed by water cutting through sedimentary rock, such as sandstone.

Flash flood A sudden rush of water that can rise within a few hours – or minutes – of a heavy rainstorm; most commonly occur during the summer monsoon season and are particularly dangerous in canyons, where they sweep away everything in their path.

Hole Used by early settlers in the Rockies to describe a high mountain valley.

CFS Cubic feet per second, ie how much water a river is carrying. One cubic foot is roughly equivalent to 7½ gallons of water. Popular hikes in some areas (eg the Narrows in Zion) are closed when the flow rate rises above a certain CFS.

Wash A dry streambed that fills with water seasonally; called arroyo in some states.

Hoodoo A column of rock sculpted by erosion; also called a fairy chimney. Bryce Canyon has more hoodoos than anywhere else in the world.

Petroglyph Carvings created by chiseling or pecking straight onto a rock surface, often one with desert varnish, a thin and dark mineral coating, which allows the petroglyphs to appear more vividly.

Pictograph Paintings on a rock surface.

WATCH

Into the Wild (Sean Penn; 2007; pictured) Follow Chris McCandless as he hitchhikes to Alaska.

The National Parks: America's Best Idea (Ken Burns; 2009) Captures the challenges of creating the national parks.

Wild (Jean-Marc Vallée; 2014) A woman undertakes a hike of self-discovery on the Pacific Crest Trail.

Vacation (Harold Ramis; 1983) Perfect comedy kick-starter for any family road trip.

Reservation Dogs (various directors; 2021–) Blending drama and comedy, this series sheds light on the lives of present-day Native Americans.

LISTEN

Native Lands (various artists; 1996) Native American music and ambient nature sounds recorded on location in various Southwestern national parks.

The Dirtbag Diaries (Fitz Cahall; 2007) A podcast about adventurers in wild places, with stories ranging from the humorous to the profound.

Volunteer (Old Crow Medicine Show; 2018) Top album by the high-energy, feel-good folk and bluegrass band who celebrate the southern landscapes.

Highway 61 Revisited (Bob Dylan; 1965) The famed album by the legendary singer-songwriter makes a perfect soundtrack for a national-parks road trip.

DAVID SPATES/SHUTTERSTOCK ©

Rocky Mountain National Park (p288)

TRIP PLANNER

HEALTH & SAFETY

Heading out into the wilderness means taking extra precautions to make sure you return safely. This is true whether you plan to be gone for an hour or a week. Make sure you have all the essentials before hitting the trail and have a back-up plan in case things don't go as anticipated.

Before You Go

Some of the walks we cover are physically demanding and most require a reasonable level of fitness, even the easy or moderate walks. If you're aiming for the demanding walks, training is essential.

If you have any medical issues, or are concerned about your health in any way, it's a good idea to have a full checkup before you start walking.

In the Parks

Visiting city dwellers will need to keep their wits about them in order to minimize the chances of suffering an avoidable accident or tragedy. Dress appropriately, tell people where you're going, plan a hike that matches your skills and experience and, above all, respect the wilderness and the inherent dangers it conceals.

Crime is far more common in big cities than in sparsely populated national parks. Nevertheless, use common sense: lock valuables in the trunk of your vehicle, especially if you're parking it at a trailhead overnight, and never leave anything worth stealing in your tent.

Walk Safety: Basic Rules

Allow plenty of time to accomplish a walk before dark, particularly when daylight hours are shorter.

WATER PURIFICATION

To ensure you are getting safe, clean drinking water in the backcountry you have three basic options:

Boiling Water is considered safe to drink if it has been boiled for at least one minute.

Chemical purification You can choose from various chlorine or iodine products on the market. Read the instructions carefully first, be aware of expiration dates and check you aren't allergic to either chemical.

Filtration Devices can pump water through microscopic filters and take out potentially harmful organisms. If carrying a filter, take care it doesn't get damaged in transit, read the instructions carefully and always filter the cleanest water you can find.

Study the route carefully before setting out, noting the possible escape routes and the point of no return (where it's quicker to continue on rather than turn back). Monitor your progress during the day against the time estimated for the walk, and keep an eye on the weather.

It's wise not to walk alone. Always leave details of your intended route, number of people in your group and expected return time with someone responsible before you set off, and let that person know when you return.

Before setting off, make sure you have a relevant map, compass and whistle, and that you know the weather forecast for the area for the next 24 hours. In the Rockies always carry extra warm, dry layers of clothing and plenty of emergency high-energy food.

Alum Cave Trail (p362), Great Smoky Mountains National Park

DANITA DELIMONT/SHUTTERSTOCK ©

HAZARDS ON THE TRAIL

- **Lightning** Getting struck by lightning during a summer afternoon storm is a real possibility, especially if climbing a summit or ridgeline. It's best to undertake long hikes early. If you get caught out, avoid exposed ridges, open areas and lone trees. If camping, crouch on a sleeping pad with your arms around your knees.
- **Rockfall** Even a small falling rock could shatter your hand or crack your skull, so always be alert to the danger of rockfall. Don't dally below cliffs or on trails fringed by large fields of raw talus. If you accidentally let a rock loose, loudly warn other hikers below.
- **Crossing streams** In spring and early summer, streams can turn into raging rivers and make trails impassable, so check your route at a backcountry office. Sudden downpours can also quickly turn a gentle stream into a raging torrent. If you're in any doubt about the safety of a crossing, look for a safer passage upstream or wait.
- **Bears** When hiking in bear country, always stay alert and make plenty of noise on the trail. Never hike before dawn or after dusk. Some shout 'hey bear' when approaching a blind corner. If you do encounter a bear, back away slowly while talking soothingly and avoiding direct eye contact. Do not run. Bears will instinctively pursue a fleeing animal. If a bear charges, deploy pepper spray (p32).

MARIDAV/SHUTTERSTOCK ©

Hiking gear

TRIP PLANNER

GEAR & CLOTHING

Deciding what gear is essential for a trip and what will only weigh you down is an art. Don't forget essentials, but be ruthless when packing, since every ounce counts when you're lugging your gear up a steep mountain or paddling down a steamy mangrove-lined channel in the Everglades.

Clothes

The key to comfortable hiking is wearing several layers of light clothing, which you can easily take off or put on as you warm up or cool down.

Synthetic, silk or wool base layers (not cotton) are the most effective. A waterproof, breathable rain jacket and an insulating fleece are musts. A down vest or light jacket is useful in spring and fall when it can also be good to have thermal underwear and wind/waterproof shell pants.

Light to medium hiking boots are recommended for day hikes, while ankle-supporting sturdy boots are better for demanding hikes or extended trips with a heavy pack. Most importantly, they should be well broken in, with a nonslip sole (eg Vibram).

Sun Protection

In the desert and at high altitude your skin can burn in less than an hour, even through cloud cover. Use sunscreen (SPF 30 or higher), especially on skin not typically exposed to sun, reapplying regularly. Always apply sunscreen to young children and wear wide-brimmed hats and long sleeves.

Bear Spray

Many of the parks' hikes and activities are also in bear country. As a last resort, bear spray (pepper spray) has been used effectively to deter aggressive bears (and other wildlife), and park authorities often recommend you equip yourself with a canister when in backcountry. Be sure to familiarize yourself with the manufacturer's instructions, and

BEAR-PROOFING YOUR CAMP

If you're backcountry camping, you'll need to keep food and fragrant items (eg sunscreen, toothpaste, insect repellent) out of reach of bears. Some parks require backcountry hikers to carry a bear-resistant container. Grand Teton, among various parks, loans you these for free. At other places (such as Yosemite), you'll have to rent or provide your own. In forested parks such as the Great Smoky Mountains, you can also hang your gear from a tree: bring 40–50ft of cord and hang your bear sack at least 10ft off the ground and at least 4ft from the trunk.

only use it as a last resort (ie on a charging bear 30ft away from you). Most shops in or around parks out west sell bear spray (for around $50); some rent it by the day. Keep it close at hand on a belt around your waist.

Backpacking Essentials

If you're going backpacking, you'll be shouldering everything for a few days, so a comfortable pack weight is crucial. Pare down to the essentials, and make sure that what you bring isn't unnecessarily bulky – a clean shirt every morning isn't as important as how your back feels at day's end.

For multiday hikes, you'll need a good backpack made of strong fabric, with a lightweight internal frame and an adjustable, well-padded harness that evenly distributes weight. Wear it before purchasing to ensure it matches your torso length and body type.

A three-season tent will usually suffice. The tent's floor and outer shell (fly) should have taped or sealed seams and covered zips to stop leaks. You can ditch the tent and opt for a fly and ground tarp, or even a hammock system during warm, dry weather.

Mummy sleeping bags have the best shape for warmth and reducing drafts; top bags have a bottom layer of fabric that attaches to a sleeping pad, so you're less likely to roll off.

Air mats, inflated like a balloon, are the best in terms of warmth, packability and thickness, but can be pricey. Cheaper, self-inflating sleeping mats work like a thin air cushion and insulate you from the cold.

Canister stoves are small, efficient and ideal for extended use. You'll need fuel canisters of pressurized liquid propane plus n-butane or isobutane.

FIRST-AID KIT

A few essentials for a first-aid kit:

- acetaminophen or aspirin
- adhesive or paper tape
- antibacterial ointment for cuts and abrasions
- antibiotics
- anti-diarrhea drugs (eg loperamide)
- anti-inflammatory drugs (eg ibuprofen)
- antihistamines (for hay fever and allergic reactions)
- bandages, gauze swabs, gauze rolls and safety pins
- insect repellent with DEET
- iodine tablets or water filter (for water purification)
- moleskin (to prevent chafing of blisters)
- non-adhesive dressing
- oral rehydration salts
- paper stitches
- pocketknife
- scissors and tweezers
- sterile alcohol wipes
- steroid cream or cortisone (for allergic rashes)
- bandages (Band-Aids)
- sunscreen and lip balm

Bear spray

EB ADVENTURE PHOTOGRAPHY/SHUTTERSTOCK ©

Kayaking (p171), Colorado River

THE OUTDOORS

Soaring mountain ranges and vast forests set the stage for a wide array of outdoor adventures, from clambering up rocky summits to kayaking across mirror-like lakes.

Hikers and backpackers could spend many months traipsing the thousands of miles of national-park trails, not to mention the countless paths in the surrounding mountains and forests. Fans of water sports can set their sights on the lakes, rivers and ocean shorelines. You'll find a wide mix of easygoing outings and challenging multiday excursions with portages along the way. When the temperature plummets, do as the locals do and embrace winter: frosty landscapes make a memorable setting for cross-country skiing and snowshoeing.

Hiking

Nothing encapsulates the spirit of the national parks like their hiking trails, which offer access to the most scenic mountain passes, highest waterfalls, deepest canyons and quietest corners. Trails run the gamut of accessibility, from the flat, paved paths of Yosemite's loop trails to the thrilling exposed ascent of Longs Peak in Rocky Mountain.

Detailed trail descriptions and maps are readily available at visitor centers in every park, and they complement this guide well. Know your limitations, know the route you plan to take and pace yourself.

Rafting, Kayaking & Canoeing

Rafts, kayaks, canoes and larger boats are a wonderful way to get to parts of the parks that landlubbers can't reach. River-running opportunities abound in the parks, but none stand out quite like the Colorado River. The most famous trip along the Colorado is a three-week odyssey through the Grand Canyon – arguably the best possible way to visit – though you can also take a heart-thumping multiday excursion further upstream

Alternative Adventures

HORSEBACK RIDING
Climb into the saddle and take an epic ride on the **Maah Daah Hey Trail** (p325) in Theodore Roosevelt.

SAND-SLEDDING
Feel the desert air on your cheeks as you rush down the slopes at **Great Sand Dunes** (p287).

STARGAZING
Look for planets, constellations and distant galaxies amid the dark skies over **Bryce Canyon** (p142).

FAMILY ADVENTURES

Take a family-friendly hike to **Taggart Lake** (p282) in the Grand Tetons. On hot days, everyone can cool off with a dip afterwards.

Explore the otherworldly landscapes of Yellowstone on a walk amid the geothermal features of **Geyser Hill** (p295).

Go rafting or kayaking in Yosemite Valley or just splash around by the sandy shores of the **Merced River** (p80).

Climb ladders and pass an abandoned cowboy camp on the **Cave Spring Trail** (p153) in Canyonlands' Needles district.

Set out picnic blankets and lawn chairs and watch as fireflies light up the night skies near **Elkmont** (p359) in the Great Smoky Mountains.

See bizarre formations on a tour through the subterranean wonderland of **Mammoth Cave** (p372).

through the desert wilds of the Canyonlands. Other great rafting destinations are the Snake River in Grand Teton National Park, West Virginia's New River Gorge and the Pigeon River in the Smokies.

If larger bodies of water are more your speed, one of the best parks to explore in a canoe or kayak is Voyageurs on the Minnesota–Canada border, which consists of over 30 lakes and 900 islands. Another northern park offering kayaking trips is Isle Royale, the largest island in Lake Superior. Many of the campgrounds in both of these parks are only accessible by boat.

BEST SPOTS

For the best outdoor spots and routes, see page 36.

Seal, Channel Islands National Park (p98)

JOE BELANGER/SHUTTERSTOCK ©

In Grand Teton, String and Leigh Lakes are great for family and novice paddlers, and you can rent boats at Colter Bay. In Yosemite, Tenaya Lake makes for spectacular paddling.

Boat Tours & Snorkeling

Both the Atlantic and Pacific Oceans have a handful of marine-based parks – many accessible only by boat, and several perfect for underwater adventures. Boat trips exploring the vast Everglades are de rigueur in the dry season, while only 5% of Biscayne, Florida's largest stretch of undeveloped Atlantic coastline, is land – kayaking excursions, history-themed boat trips and snorkeling tours are obligatory to check out the wonders offshore. South of there, the Dry Tortugas has coral reefs, and getting there by boat (or floatplane) is a memorable part of the experience. On the opposite coast, Southern California's Channel Islands are a prime destination for snorkeling, diving and boat tours.

At the other end of the spectrum, there's Alaska: Glacier Bay's calving icebergs and humpback whales are generally visited on a day boat or cruise, while volcanic Katmai offers innumerable river-running, lake-paddling and sea-kayaking options. Daily boat tours also explore the inlets and islands at Kenai Fjords, Alaska's 'smallest' park.

LADDER TRAILS
Conquer your fear of heights on Acadia's **Precipice Trail** (p340), which is ascended via iron ladders and ledges.

HOUSEBOATS
Rent an easy-to-operate houseboat and head off for an adventure amid the pristine islands of **Voyageurs** (p328).

SNOWSHOEING
Enjoy the serene wintry landscapes on a ranger-led snowshoe walk at **Crater Lake** (p211).

ROCK CLIMBING
Hone your skills by taking a fun and rewarding climbing class with the **Yosemite Mountaineering School** (p92).

ACTION AREAS

Where to find USA's best outdoor activities.

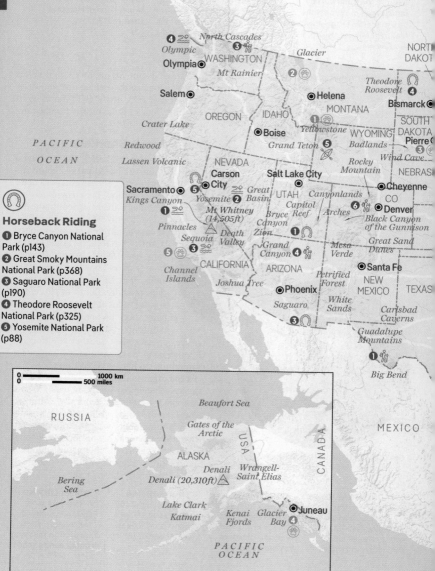

![Horseback riding icon]

Horseback Riding

1. Bryce Canyon National Park (p143)
2. Great Smoky Mountains National Park (p368)
3. Saguaro National Park (p190)
4. Theodore Roosevelt National Park (p325)
5. Yosemite National Park (p88)

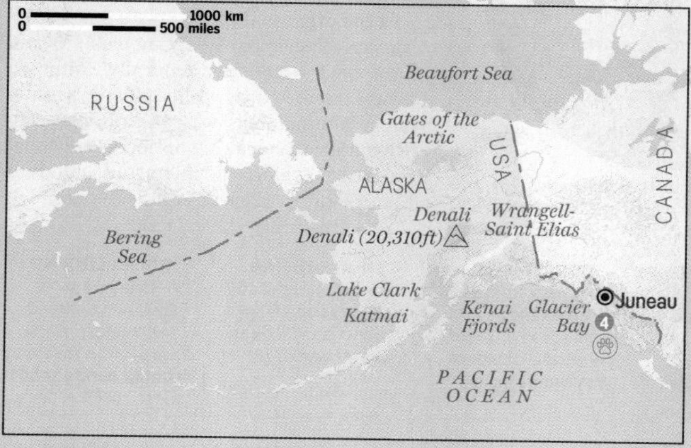

Swimming
1. Kings Canyon National Park (p56)
2. Yosemite National Park (p80)
3. Sequoia National Park (p62)
4. Olympic National Park (p225)
5. Dry Tortugas National Park (p386)

Wildlife
1. Yellowstone National Park (p299)
2. Glacier National Park (p266)
3. Badlands National Park (p313)
4. Glacier Bay National Park (p236)
5. Channel Islands National Park (p99)

Kayaking/Canoeing
1. Everglades National Park (p389)
2. Congaree National Park (p357)
3. Biscayne National Park (p383)
4. Voyageurs National Park (p328)
5. Grand Teton National Park (p283)

Hiking
1. Big Bend National Park (p137)
2. Acadia National Park (p337)
3. North Cascades National Park (p220)
4. Grand Canyon National Park (p166)
5. Shenandoah National Park (p347)
6. Rocky Mountain National Park (p289)

USA'S NATIONAL PARK

THE GUIDE

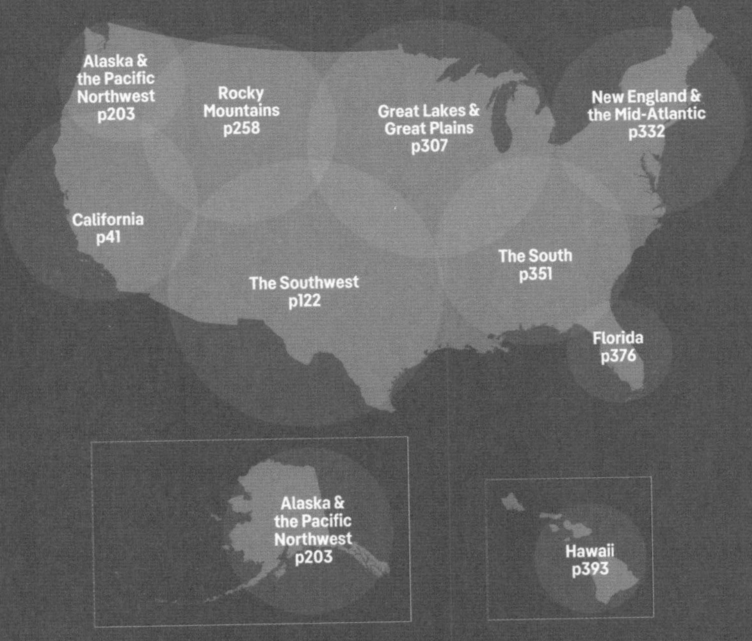

Chapters in this section are organized by hubs and their surrounding areas. We see the hub as your base in the destination, where you'll find unique experiences, local insights, insider tips and expert recommendations. It's also your gateway to the surrounding area, where you'll see what and how much you can do from there.

Jenny Lake (p280), Grand Teton National Park

MARY CAMPO/SHUTTERSTOCK ©

NINA B/SHUTTERSTOCK ©

Above: Joshua Tree National Park (p103); Right: Bumpass Hell (p121), Lassen Volcanic National Park

THE MAIN AREAS

KINGS CANYON NATIONAL PARK
Big Californian adventures.
p46

SEQUOIA NATIONAL PARK
Forest of giants.
p59

YOSEMITE NATIONAL PARK
America's favorite park.
p71

REDWOOD NATIONAL PARK
Walks and whale-watching.
p93

CHANNEL ISLANDS NATIONAL PARK
Get active in California's Galápagos. p98

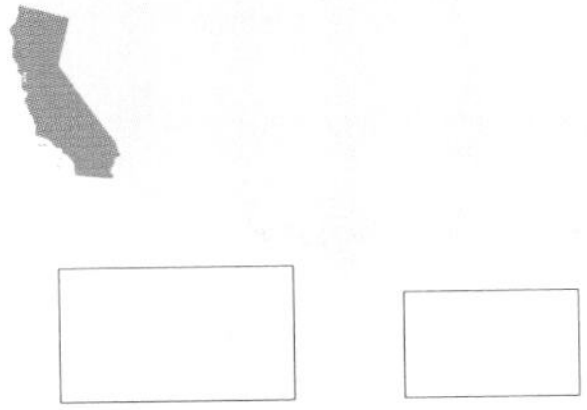

CALIFORNIA

EXPLORE WONDERFULLY WILD LANDSCAPES

California is where America's national parks really take wing. With wildlife and wild places in abundance, the state's parks are wild America at its best.

Any list of America's most beautiful national parks will have a strong Californian flavor about it. Yosemite could just be America's finest park with its astonishingly diverse mix of stirring natural drama and iconic experiences. All of the essential elements that go into making Yosemite such an iconic and quintessentially American experience – superb natural landscapes, large numbers of animals and birds and a rich portfolio of activities – echo out across the state.

JOSHUA HAWLEY/SHUTTERSTOCK ©

California's world-famous redwoods and sequoia trees have the scale and gravitas to match the epic landscapes that dominate elsewhere, from the deserts of Death Valley to the shapely Channel Islands battered by the seas and winds of the Pacific. Elsewhere it's the combination of scale and beauty that so enlivens Kings Canyon, Pinnacles and Lassen Volcanic National Parks. Wildlife, too, defines this remarkable state, from the elk of Redwood and the whales of the Pacific, to the reborn California condors that soar above Pinnacles and Sequoia. And while Yosemite exists at the forefront of the nation's story, other parks such as Joshua Tree tap into cinematic and pop culture from across the last American century: Joshua Tree, for example, has a heritage that's equal part Hollywood Western and U2 album cover.

The result of all this drama and abundance is one of the greatest natural shows anywhere in America.

Find Your Way

Very often in California, the car is king, and you'll certainly find it a whole lot easier to explore the state's incredible parks if you have your own wheels. Boats, plane flights and local buses do the rest.

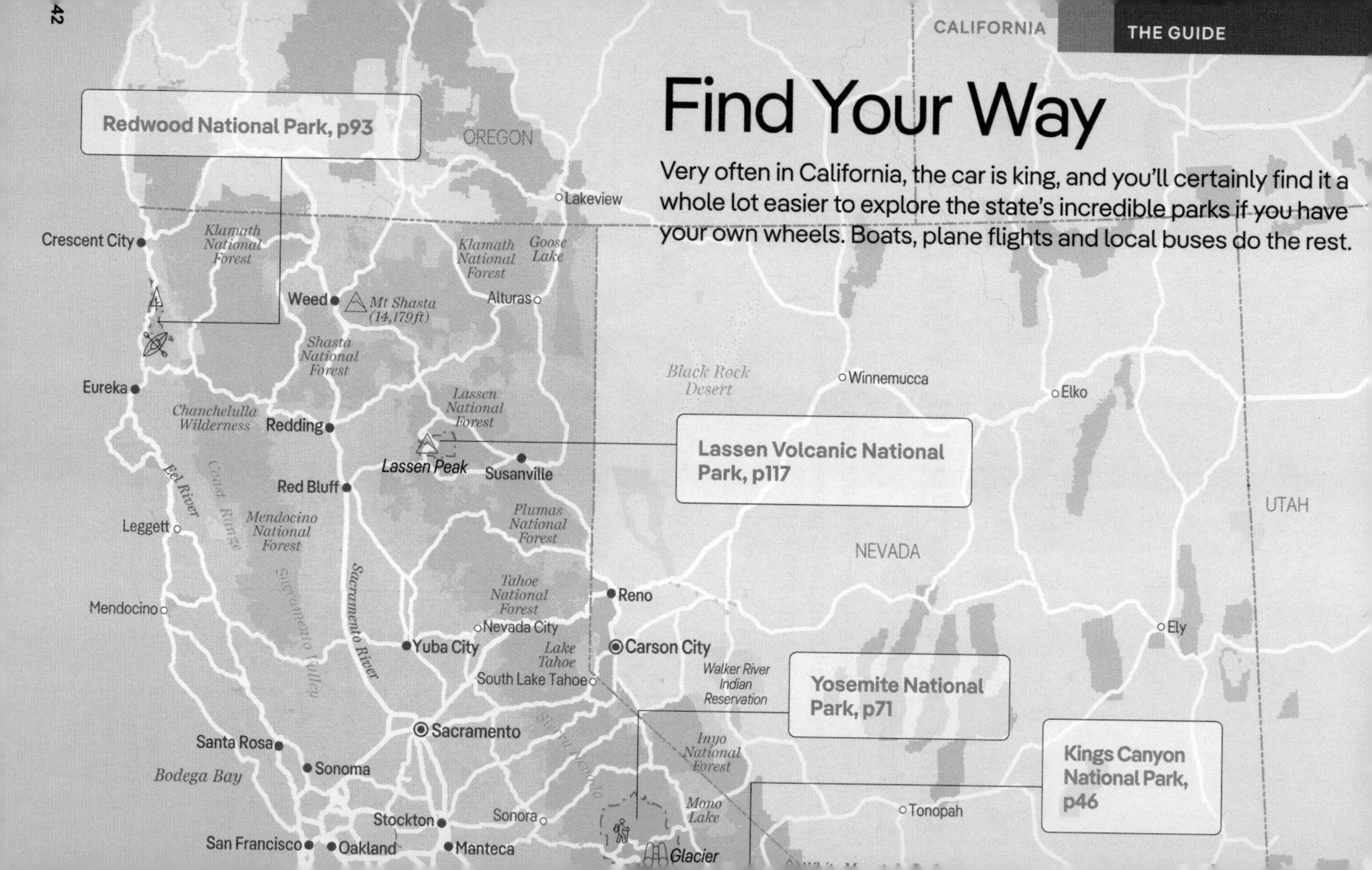

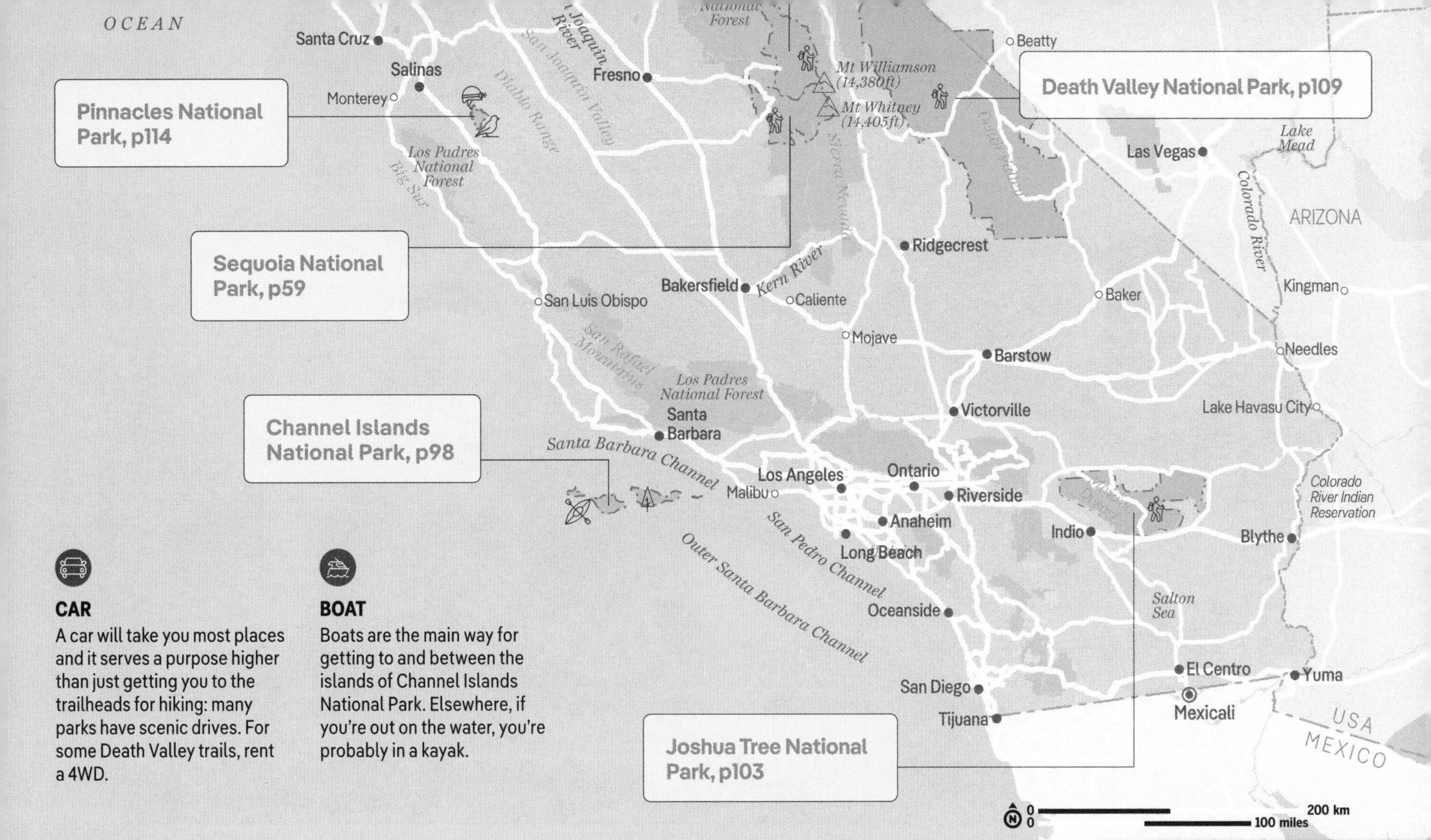

CAR

A car will take you most places and it serves a purpose higher than just getting you to the trailheads for hiking: many parks have scenic drives. For some Death Valley trails, rent a 4WD.

BOAT

Boats are the main way for getting to and between the islands of Channel Islands National Park. Elsewhere, if you're out on the water, you're probably in a kayak.

Pinnacles National Park (p114)

ZHUKOVA VALENTYNA/SHUTTERSTOCK ©

Death Valley National Park (p109)

Plan Your Time

California is a big canvas, and exploring its parks requires careful planning. Stick to the coast or explore inland for star-studded itineraries.

A Coastal Week

Begin out in the Pacific in **Channel Islands National Park** (p98), one of the state's least-visited parks. After a couple of days, track north along the coast to **Pinnacles National Park** (p114) for a taste of California's propensity for arresting rocky formations, then immerse yourself for three days in forests of giant trees in **Redwood National Park** (p93).

Ten Days Inland

So many American national park stories begin in **Yosemite** (p71), and three to four days in this glorious park is a fabulous way to start any journey. **Kings Canyon** (p46) and **Sequoia** (p59) are all about big landscapes and very big trees. Save two or three days at the end for the breathtaking desert scenery of **Death Valley National Park** (p109).

SEASONAL HIGHLIGHTS

SPRING
Spring is not just about milder temperatures and smaller crowds: it's a fabulous time to see wildflowers.

SUMMER
Be careful about hiking at this time: Death Valley, for example, is sometimes the hottest place in America.

FALL
One of the best times to travel in California, with quieter roads and campgrounds and mild temperatures.

WINTER
Winter is generally the best time for hiking in most of California's parks, except in the High Sierras.

KINGS CANYON NATIONAL PARK

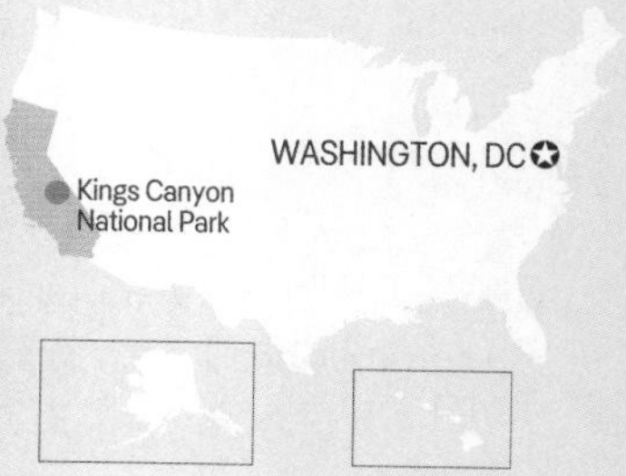

Hold tight for the white-knuckle drive though Kings Canyon, a dramatic cleft deeper than the Grand Canyon that serves up true adventure to those who crave verdant trails, rushing streams and gargantuan rock formations. The camping, backcountry exploring and climbing here are all superb. While its neighbor, Sequoia National Park, gets all the glory, Kings Canyon also has groves of enormous sequoias and its trails are far less trafficked. Grant Grove is where you'll find General Grant, the second-largest tree in the world. Peaks more than 14,000ft high occupy other parts of the park, most of which is designated wilderness, although the main road, Kings Canyon Scenic Byway (Hwy 180; only open end of April to mid-November), is quite the drive – it twists and bends through some of the most astonishing scenery in California. The Big Stump Entrance, not far from Grant Grove Village, is Kings Canyon National Park's only entrance station.

FACTS

Great For Family travel, wildlife, walking
State California
Entrance Fee 7-day pass per vehicle/motorcycle/person on foot or bicycle $35/30/20
Area 721 sq miles

General Grant Tree Trail

MARGARET.WIKTOR/SHUTTERSTOCK ©

BEST PLACES TO STAY

Azalea Campground
Set among stands of evergreens; the nicest of the 110 sites border a green meadow. **$**

John Muir Lodge
Atmospheric building in Grant Grove with homespun rooms and rocking chairs on its wide porches. **$$$**

Sequoia High Sierra Camp
Deluxe tent cabins in Sierra Nevada (1 mile from parking area) in Sequoia National Forest. **$$$**

Admire Sequoias in General Grant Grove

MIGHTY SEQUOIAS TELL THEIR STORIES

Take your time wandering **General Grant Grove** off Generals Hwy. The sequoia trees are simply astounding. The paved half-mile **General Grant Tree Trail** is a good place to start. An interpretive walk, it visits a number of mature sequoias, including the 27-story **General Grant Tree**. This giant holds triple honors as the world's second-largest living tree, a memorial to US soldiers killed in war, and the nation's official Christmas tree since 1926. The nearby **Fallen Monarch**, a massive, fire-hollowed trunk you can walk through, has been a cabin, hotel, saloon and stables.

Follow the more secluded 1.5-mile **North Grove Loop**, which passes wildflower patches and bubbling creeks as it winds underneath a canopy of stately sequoias, evergreen pines and aromatic incense cedars.

The magnificence of this ancient sequoia grove was nationally recognized in 1890, when Congress first designated it General Grant National Park. It took another half-century for this tiny parcel to be absorbed into much larger Kings Canyon National Park, established in 1940 to prevent damming of the Kings River.

Explore Redwood Canyon

ESCAPE CROWDS, HUG TREES

The secluded forest of **Redwood Canyon** has mostly moderate trails. The more than 15,000 sequoias here form one of the world's largest groves of these giant trees. But you won't find any of the California coast's redwood trees – that's what early pioneers mistook these giant sequoias for, hence the erroneous name.

Walk from trailheads at the end of a bumpy 2-mile dirt road (closed in winter) that starts across from the Hume Lake/Quail Flat signed intersection on the Generals Hwy, just over 5 miles southeast of Grant Grove Village.

Nature Walk at Zumwalt Meadow

NATURE WALK WITH THE KIDS

The trails here are extremely scenic, mostly flat loops around a gorgeous meadow beside the Kings River. It's a fun nature walk to do with kids, and the trail flaunts knockout canyon views and excellent chances to spot wildlife.

Sitting a mile west of Road's End along the Kings Canyon Scenic Byway, **Zumwalt Meadow** is best in the early morning,

KINGS CANYON NATIONAL PARK: GETTING ORIENTED

The park's only entrance station is **Big Stump**, which is 53 miles east of Fresno via Hwy 180. You'll find markets, lodging, showers and visitor information at two developed areas within Kings Canyon National Park. **Grant Grove Village** is only 4 miles past Big Stump Entrance (in the park's west), while **Cedar Grove Village**, with a simple lodge, market and cafe, is 31 miles east at the bottom of the canyon. The two are separated by the Giant Sequoia National Monument and are linked by Kings Canyon Scenic Byway (Hwy 180). The byway is closed in winter, typically opening at the end of April and closing in mid-November.

WHERE TO RIDE & RAFT IN KINGS CANYON NATIONAL CANYON

Grant Grove Stables
Pint-sized, summer-only operation offers one- and two-hour guided trail rides on horseback.

Cedar Grove Pack Station
Trail rides along the river inside Kings Canyon and overnight pack trips to mountain lakes.

Kings River Expeditions
Small rafting operator near the park offering one-/two-day trips with Class III rapids.

SIGHTS
1 Big Baldy
2 Buck Rock Lookout
3 Cedar Grove
4 Chimney Rock
see 5 Fallen Monarch
5 General Grant Grove
6 General Grant Tree
7 Grand Sentinel
8 Grant Grove Village
9 Great Western Divide
10 Junction View
see 3 Kings River South Fork
11 Knapp's Cabin
12 Muir Rock
13 Panoramic Point
14 Redwood Canyon
15 Roaring River Falls

ACTIVITIES, COURSES & TOURS
see 3 Cedar Grove Pack Station
see 5 General Grant Tree Trail
see 5 Grant Grove Stables
16 Hume Lake
17 Little Baldy
see 5 North Grove Loop
see 12 Rae Lakes Loop
see 12 River Trail
18 Zumwalt Meadow Trail

SLEEPING
see 8 Azalea Campground
see 8 Crystal Springs Campground
see 8 Grant Grove Cabins

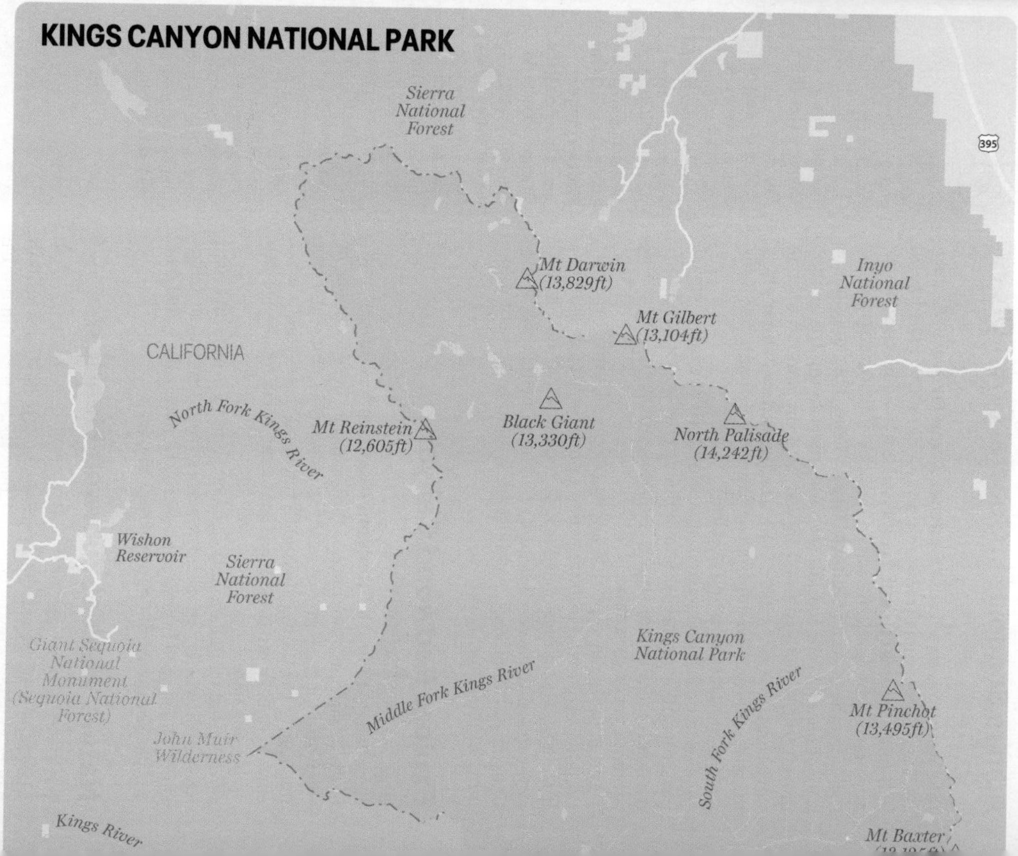

19 Hume Lake Campground
see 8 John Muir Lodge
20 Landslide Campground
21 Princess Campground
see 3 Sentinel Campground
22 Sequoia High Sierra Camp
see 3 Sheep Creek Campground
see 8 Sunset Campground

EATING
see 8 Grant Grove Market
see 8 Grant Grove Restaurant

INFORMATION
23 Big Stump Park Entrance
see 3 Cedar Grove Visitor Center
see 8 Kings Canyon Visitor Center
see 12 Roads End Wilderness Permit Station

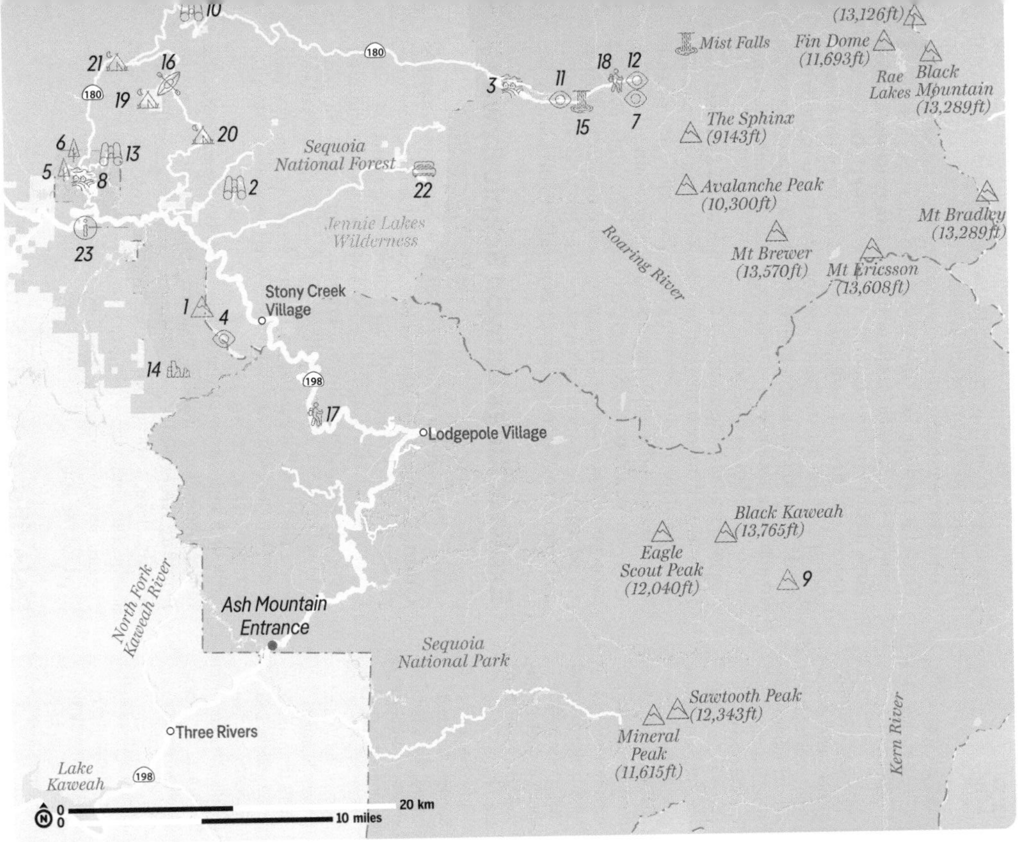

BACKPACKING IN KINGS CANYON & SEQUOIA

More than 850 miles of maintained trails await your footsteps in both national parks. From sun-bleached granite peaks soaring above alpine lakes to wildflower-strewn meadows and gushing waterfalls, it's backpacking heaven. Mineral King, Lodgepole and Cedar Grove offer the best backcountry trail access, while the Jennie Lakes Wilderness in the Sequoia National Forest offers pristine meadows and lakes at lower elevations.

Permits are required for overnight travel in the wilderness. Check the national park websites and recreation.gov for details. Park-approved bear-proof canisters, which are always recommended, are mandatory in some places, especially for wilderness trips (eg Rae Lakes Loop). To prevent wildfires, campfires are only allowed in existing campfire rings in some backcountry areas.

when mist floats above the meadow and birdsong echoes off the canyon's soaring granite walls. Self-guided nature trail brochures ($1.50) are often available at the visitor center in Cedar Grove Village (open between late May and September). From the parking lot, walk parallel to the river then across a suspension footbridge spanning the **Kings River's South Fork**. Behind you to the north is a view of **North Dome**, with a sheer cliff drop of more than 3600ft, higher than Yosemite's El Capitan. At the next junction, go left along the **River Trail**, then keep straight ahead to begin a counterclockwise loop through a forest of cottonwood, willow, black oak, white fir and ponderosa pine trees.

Looking ahead, the granite cliffs of the **Grand Sentinel** cast shadows from more than a half mile above the canyon floor. The trail ascends and continues over a talus slope with great views of canyon cliffs and the lush meadow. At the next signed junction, turn left and follow the Kings River bank through ferns and a carpet of soft pine needles, then traipse across boardwalks that afford panoramic meadow views to close the loop. Turn right and retrace your steps across the footbridge to the parking lot.

Explore: Kings Canyon Scenic Byway

HISTORIC CABIN AND GUSHING WATERFALL

History – and an exceptional sunset view – await at **Knapp's Cabin**. During the 1920s, wealthy Santa Barbara businessperson George Knapp built this simple wood-shingled cabin to store gear in during his extravagant fishing and camping excursions in Kings Canyon. From a signed roadside pullout on Hwy 180, about 2 miles east of Cedar Grove Village, a very short trail leads to this hidden building, the oldest in Cedar Grove. Come around dusk, when the views of the glacier-carved canyon are glorious.

About 3 miles east of the village, slightly closer to Road's End, a five-minute walk on a paved trail (0.3 miles) leads to **Roaring River Falls**, one of the park's most accessible waterfalls. Here, a 40ft chute gushes into a granite bowl. In late spring and sometimes in early summer, the strength of this cascade won't disappoint. Look for the parking lot and trailhead on the south side of Hwy 180.

Relaxing at Road's End

MEADOW, WATERFALL, HISTORIC ROCK

As the name suggests, Kings Canyon Scenic Byway (Hwy 180) stops at Road's End. This remote spot is a pleasant place to relax, splash around (in safe waters), scan for wildlife and hike in a beautiful river valley setting.

WHERE TO STAY IN GRANT GROVE

Crystal Springs Campground
Smallest campground in the Grant Grove area, with 36 standard campsites. **$**

Sunset Campground
Set among evergreens, Grant Grove's biggest campground is a five-minute walk from the village. **$**

Grant Grove Cabins
Aging tent-top shacks, rustic cabins with electricity and outdoor woodburning stoves, and heated duplexes. **$$$**

Environmentalist John Muir called Kings Canyon 'a rival of Yosemite.' This 35-mile scenic drive enters the canyon, traversing the forested Giant Sequoia National Monument and shadowing the Kings River to Road's End.

From **1 Grant Grove**, drive not quite 3 miles to **2 McGee Vista Point** where you can drink in the mountain panorama. Then keep winding downhill through the Sequoia National Forest past the turnoff to Converse Basin Grove, a lonely testament to the 19th-century logging of giant sequoias.

About 6 miles from Grant Grove is the turnoff to **3 Hume Lake**, which offers sandy beaches and coves for summer swims. Keep heading downhill, ever deeper into the canyon. The road serpentines past chiseled rock walls, some tinged by green moss and red-iron minerals, others laced by waterfalls. Roadside turnouts provide superb views, notably at **4 Junction View**, about 10.5 miles from Grant Grove, and beyond **5 Yucca Point**, another 3.5 miles further along.

After countless ear-popping curves, the road bottoms out and runs parallel to the Kings River, its roar ricocheting off granite cliffs. Over 10 miles past Yucca Point is the picnic area by **6 Grizzly Falls**, often a torrent in late spring.

The scenic byway reenters the national park just over 2.5 miles further along, passing the Lewis Creek bridge and a riverside beach. It's less than 2 miles to **7 Cedar Grove Village**, where you'll find a visitor center and market. Over the next 6 miles, don't miss short walks to **8 Roaring River Falls** and pretty **9 Zumwalt Meadow**. More hiking trails and swimming holes (like Muir Rock) await at **10 Road's End** – the only way to keep going across the Sierra Nevada is on foot!

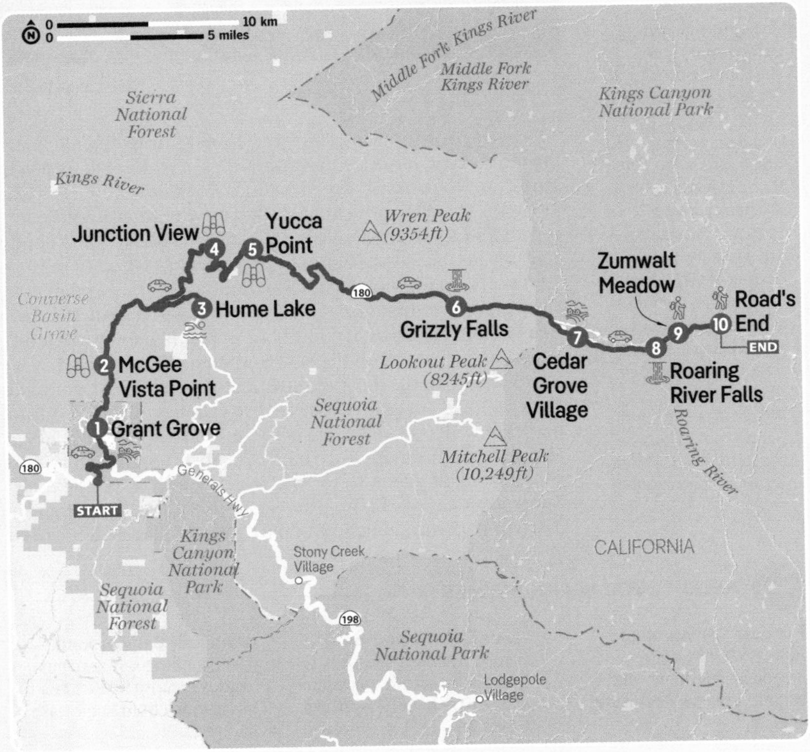

Rae Lakes Loop

FREE CAMPSITES

Potential campers should keep in mind that there are great free, uncrowded and undeveloped campgrounds off Big Meadows Rd in the Sequoia National Forest. They're some of the only empty campsites in the Sierra Nevada during the peak summer season. Free roadside car camping is also allowed near Hume Lake, but no campfires are allowed without a permit (available from the Grant Grove Visitor Center). Wilderness camping permits cost $15 per trip (plus an additional $5 per person in quota season).

On excursions to Kings Canyon, John Muir would allegedly give talks on a large, flat river boulder, now known as **Muir Rock** (not to be confused with Moro Rock in Sequoia National Park). The rock is a short walk from the Road's End parking lot and less than a mile past **Zumwalt Meadow**. A sandy river beach here is taken over by gleeful swimmers in midsummer. Don't jump in when the raging waters, swollen with snowmelt, are dangerous. Ask at the **Road's End Wilderness Permit Station** if conditions are calm enough for a dip.

You can also stroll on the easy and scenic **River Trail**. Near the entrance to the day-use parking lot, you'll find the sign to the trailhead towards the river. After a few minutes on the path, you will cross a bridge over the South Fork Kings River. Head west on the opposite bank. A short 0.5-mile walk next to the glorious green water will join up with a section of the Zumwalt Meadow Loop. Choose to continue along the sandy river pathway, which is a boardwalk in places, but can be

WHERE TO STAY NEAR HUME LAKE

Princess Campground
Almost 90 sites border a meadow near Hume Lake, with sequoia stumps at registration area. **$**

Hume Lake Campground
Busy but feels laid-back. Uncrowded, shady campsites at 5250ft; a handful with lake views. **$**

Landslide Campground
Nine primitive but spacious woody campsites are a few miles uphill from Hume Lake. **$**

unclear in other areas (just follow the river and you'll join up with the path). Alternatively, choose the southern path, away from the river, through boulder-lined trails and then connecting back to the river trail at its western end. If you're quiet, you might spot a black bear here; they love feeding on the flora in the meadow.

The path continues along the river through mostly shaded forest canopy, where flickers of light create a dappled effect on the forest bed, and the occasional exposed section. This section of the path is well worn, leading to the impressive **Roaring River Falls** (p50). The round-trip distance from Road's End to the falls is about 5 miles.

Road's End is open when Kings Canyon Scenic Byway is open, typically from the fourth Friday in April to mid-November.

Backcountry Camping: Rae Lakes Loop

BEST KINGS CANYON BACKPACKING LOOP

A clockwise circumambulation of a cluster of high peaks, the 41.4-mile **Rae Lakes Loop** – which takes five days – traverses some of the most beautiful and picturesque lakes in the Sierra Nevada. The hiking season is from mid-June to September, although early in the season the streams and rivers may be too high to cross. One of the bridges on this trail has washed out, making the loop impossible to complete unless you trek at the height of summer, when the south fork of the Kings River is at its lowest. Construction of a replacement bridge is on the cards.

Get Inspired at Panoramic Point

BIRD'S-EYE VIEW OF KINGS CANYON

For a breathtaking view of Kings Canyon, head 2.3 miles up narrow, steep and winding Panoramic Point Rd (trailers and RVs aren't recommended), which branches off Hwy 180. Follow a short paved trail uphill from the parking lot to the **Panoramic Point** overlook, where precipitous canyons and the snowcapped peaks of the Great Western Divide unfold below you. You'll also have a view of Hume Lake. Snow closes the road to vehicles during winter, when it becomes a cross-country ski and snowshoe route. Hikers may access the road when snow levels are low. From the visitor center in Grant Grove, follow the paved side road east, turning left after 0.1 miles, then right at the John Muir Lodge.

The half-mile trail to the viewpoint is accessible via a moderately sloped path. The cross slopes may be hard for some to navigate.

SEQUOIA & KINGS CANYON: TWO FOR ONE

The two national parks, Sequoia and Kings Canyon, are commonly referred to as SEKI. The seven-day entrance fee covers both national parks and the Hume Lake District of Sequoia National Forest. For 24-hour recorded information, including road conditions, call 559-565-3341.

WHERE TO EAT IN KINGS CANYON NATIONAL PARK

Cedar Grove Grill
Cafe serving breakfast burritos; and trout, rice bowls and steak for lunch and dinner. $

Grant Grove Market
Small grocery store selling camping supplies, sweet treats, packaged food, sandwiches and microwavable pizza. $

Grant Grove Restaurant
Best place for a meal in Grant Grove Village, with local produce and seasonal dishes. $$

HIKING TRIP

Hike to Mountain Cascades: Mist Falls

A satisfying long walk along the river and up a natural granite staircase highlights the beauty of Kings Canyon. The waterfall is thunderous in late spring and possibly into early summer, depending on the previous winter's snowpack. Bring plenty of water and sunscreen. This 9.2-mile roundtrip hike gains 600ft in elevation before reaching the falls. Get an early start because the return trip can be brutally hot on summer afternoons.

1 Road's End Trailhead

The trail begins just past the Road's End Wilderness Permit Station, where you'll find water and a picnic table. The day-use parking lot here fills early in the morning.

The Hike: Cross a small footbridge over Copper Creek. Walk along a sandy trail through sparse cedar and pine forest. The South Fork Kings River runs parallel to the trail.

2 Forest Shade

Eventually the trail enters cooler, shady and low-lying areas of ferns and reeds before reaching a well-marked, three-way junction with the Paradise Valley and Bubbs Creek Trails, just under 2 miles from the trailhead. Veer left onto the Paradise Valley Trail to ascend along the South Fork Kings River.

The Hike: Climbing though the forest, the trail passes a talus pile then meets the river's edge in 20 minutes. Keep an eye out for bears here. The trek up-valley continues.

3 River Waterfalls

After another 20 minutes you'll see the river surging down a series of dramatic and powerful cataracts along the boulder-

STRAYSTONE/SHUTTERSTOCK ©

Mist Falls

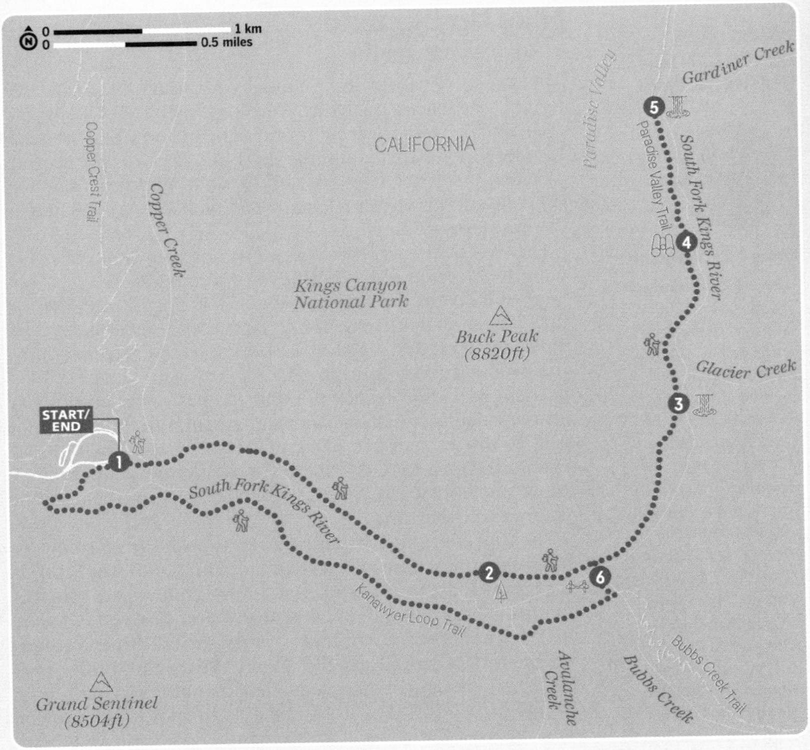

saturated Kings River. These falls should not be mistaken for Mist Falls.

The Hike: Huff and puff around a narrow switchback on a granite hillside.

4 Granite Knob Overlook

Stone-framed stairs lead to a granite knob overlook, with epic southern views of Avalanche Peak and the oddly pointed Sphinx, another mountain peak. You'll want to take photos here.

The Hike: Follow cairns up the rock face and continue briefly through shady forest alongside the river.

5 Mist Falls

Through the trees you'll soon see 5663ft Mist Falls, one of the park's largest waterfalls. Its fine spray cools down warm hikers. Warning: don't wade above the waterfall or swim below it, due to the danger of rockfall and swift water currents, especially during snowmelt runoff. In late summer, the river downstream from the falls may be tame enough for a dip, but use your own best judgment.

The Hike: Retrace your steps, around 2.5 miles downhill, to the three-way trail junction. Instead of returning directly to Road's End, bear left at the Bubbs Creek Trail.

6 Bailey Bridge

Walk a few steps to the steel Bailey Bridge, crossing it over the river.

The Hike: After less than a quarter mile, turn right onto the untrammeled Kanawyer Loop Trail, which is mostly flat as it unfurls along the south bank of the river heading toward Zumwalt Meadow. After crossing Avalanche Creek, the tree canopy opens up to show off sprawling talus slopes along the Kings Canyon's southern walls. The trail eventually recrosses the river then leads to the day-use parking lot at Road's End.

WHY I LOVE KINGS CANYON NATIONAL PARK

Amy C Balfour, writer

Driving Kings Canyon Road is a blast. It starts with sequoias, ends with a waterfall hike and there are curves, drops and big views along the way. What makes the drive one of my favorites? For me, the trip is infused with a sense of mischief, from the swift blast of wind that rips off your cap at the roadside overlook to the knowledge that your last stop is, literally, Road's End. And ah, Road's End. With canyon walls soaring about the gorgeous South Fork Kings River, it's no wonder John Muir was moved to pontificate here. And the hike to Mist Falls? With its variety and large-scale beauty, it is nothing short of perfection.

Hike Up Big Baldy

SCALE A GRANITE DOME

This hugely rewarding hike climbs, via a series of manageable forest switchbacks, up to a granite dome with valley views and epic soaring vistas over Redwood Canyon, the Great Western Divide, Kings Canyon and the foothills. Arrive early in summer months to secure a spot in the small parking lot on the side of Generals Hwy in Sequoia National Forest. The hike is 4.5 miles (round trip).

The trail begins in the woods and continues into the designated wilderness of Kings Canyon National Park. Views appear quickly on the trail, which climbs 632ft to 8190ft via dirt paths, switchbacks, rocky ridges and granite surface. Take your time and watch your footing on the ridge sections; the drop is severe. In early spring, at this altitude, it's likely there will still be snowfall and the path may be slippery on the ridge sections (use your judgment and don't attempt it if it's too dangerous). The path may also be difficult to locate in the forest areas when it's snow covered; either follow snow tracks (it's a regularly traversed trail) or look for the colored tree markings.

The trail continues through mostly exposed sections before making a small descent and then climbing onto **Big Baldy's** big granite dome. Soak up the 360-degree views: spot the picture-perfect alpine forest of **Redwood Canyon**; the jagged (snowcapped in winter and early spring) **Sierra Nevada** mountain range; and the **Great Western Divide** separating Kings Canyon and Sequoia National Parks, with high points of 13,000ft. You'll also be able to spot Kings Canyon and the foothills below in all their glory and the nearby granite dome **Little Baldy** (another similar, but worthwhile, hike if you have time). Continue on for another 0.5 miles for a view of the formation named **Chimney Rock**. Retrace your steps to return to your car.

Chill in Swimming Holes

COOL OFF IN COLD RIVERS

In Kings Canyon, there are swimming holes beside Muir Rock and the Red Bridge in Road's End. In the Sequoia National Forest, **Hume Lake** is dreamy on a hot summer day and you can rent canoes, kayaks and paddleboards at the Boathouse by the beach at Hume Lake Christian Camp. But take note: drownings in the Kings and Kaweah Rivers are the leading cause of death in the parks. Swift currents can be deadly, especially when rivers are swollen and cold with snowmelt

WHERE TO GET INFORMATION IN KINGS CANYON NATIONAL PARK

Cedar Grove Visitor Center
Small seasonal visitor center in Cedar Grove Village selling books and maps.

Kings Canyon Visitor Center
The park's main facility in Grant Grove Village: books, maps, souvenirs and a small museum.

Road's End Wilderness Permit Station
Dispenses wilderness permits, rents bear-proof canisters, sells trail guides. Open seasonally.

NICKOLAY STANEV/SHUTTERSTOCK ©

Hume Lake

runoff in late spring and early summer. Never go in if you see any white water. Get smart advice about current swimming conditions at park visitor centers and ranger stations.

Scan the Forest from a Lookout

CLIMB A FIRE TOWER

To climb one of California's most evocative fire lookouts, drive east of the Generals Hwy on Big Meadows Rd into Sequoia National Forest between Giant Grove and the Giant Forest. Follow the signs to the staffed **Buck Rock Lookout**. Constructed in 1923, this active fire lookout allows panoramic views from a doll-house-sized cab lording it over the horizon from 8500ft atop a granite rise, reached by 172 spindly stairs. It's not for anyone with vertigo. Opening hours may vary seasonally and the lookout closes during lightning storms and fire emergencies.

REDWOODS & SEQUOIAS

California is home to two of the most enormous species of trees on earth: the giant redwood and the giant sequoia. Similarly impressive, there are distinct differences between them. Redwoods are the tallest trees in the world and have slender trunks. They can grow more than 350ft high and typically live 500 to 700 years. Sequoias are the largest trees in the world by volume and have hefty trunks, which can reach 26ft in diameter. Sequoias can live 3000 years. Their habitats differ too. Redwoods stretch along the Northern California coast for almost a continuous 450 miles. Sequoias grow in groves on the western slopes of the Sierra Nevada at elevations between 4000ft and 7000ft.

WHERE TO ENJOY VIEWS OF KINGS CANYON

Junction View
Panoramic roadside pullout on the Kings Canyon Scenic Byway. Soaring views of ridges and mountains.

Knapp's Cabin
Two miles east of Cedar Village, views of the glacier-carved canyon are glorious at dusk.

Panoramic Point
Precipitous canyons and the snowcapped peaks of the Great Western Divide unfold before you.

TRAIL ETIQUETTE IN THE SIERRA NEVADA

Mind Your Manners
Keep noise levels low and cell-phone usage to a minimum.

On the Trail
Stay on the trail. Greet others you meet. Horses and pack animals have the right of way.

Be Courteous
Provide assistance if someone needs help.

Proper Preparation
Prepare yourself for challenging and emergency situations.

Respect Nature
Don't break branches from bushes or trees. Don't remove any fossils or plant (such as pine cones) or animal products from where you find them.

Be Mindful of Animals
Don't feed wild animals and never leave food unattended.

Clean Up
Dispose of waste (human and otherwise) properly.

In the Campground
Respect private property and never leave fires unattended.

Glamp in the High Sierra

LOFTY AND LUXURIOUS TENTS

Luxury feels even better when you've earned it. A mile's hike into the Sequoia National Forest from the Marvin Pass Trailhead, the off-the-grid **Sequoia High Sierra Camp** is nirvana for those who don't think swanky camping is an oxymoron. Canvas bungalows are spiffed up with pillow-top mattresses, feather pillows and cozy wool rugs. Restrooms and a shower house are shared. Reservations and, usually, a two-night minimum stay are required. The camp is typically open from mid-June through mid-September, with prices based on two people per tent. Follow Big Meadows Horse Corral Rd east from the Generals Hwy.

Snow Sports in Kings Canyon & Sequoia

CROSS-COUNTRY SKIING AND SNOWSHOEING

Winter is a memorable time to visit Sequoia and Kings Canyon. A thick blanket of snow drapes giant sequoia trees and meadows, the pace of activity slows, and a hush falls over the roads and trails.

Dozens of miles of ungroomed trails for snowshoeing and cross-country skiing crisscross the Grant Grove and Giant Forest areas (trail maps sold at park visitor centers). There are more tree-marked trails in the Giant Sequoia National Monument. Winter road closures also make for excellent cross-country skiing or snowshoeing on Sequoia's Moro Rock–Crescent Meadow Rd, Kings Canyon's Panoramic Point Rd and Big Meadows Rd in the Sequoia National Forest.

You'll find snow-play areas at Wolverton Meadow in Sequoia's Giant Forest; Big Stump and Columbine in Kings Canyon's Grant Grove; and Big Meadows, Quail Flat and Cherry Gap in the Sequoia National Forest.

Cross-country ski and snowshoe rentals are available at Grant Grove Village and Wuksachi Lodge, which sell limited winter clothing and snow-play gear. In winter, park rangers lead seasonal snowshoe walks (free snowshoe use included), check the online calendar (nps.gov/seki/planyourvisit/calendar.htm) for upcoming walks and activities. Ranger-led activities fill up fast, so reserve a spot in advance in person at park visitor centers or by calling the Giant Forest Museum.

GETTING AROUND

There are no shuttle buses in Kings Canyon. From the west, Kings Canyon Scenic Byway (Hwy 180) travels 53 miles east from Fresno through some bucolic rural scenery to the Big Stump Entrance. Coming from the south, you're in for a 46-mile drive through Sequoia National Park along sinuous Generals Hwy. Budget about two hours' driving time from the Ash Mountain Entrance to Grant Grove Village. The road to Cedar Grove Village (along the eastern end of Kings Canyon Scenic Byway, otherwise known as Hwy 180), with white-knuckle twists and drop-offs, is only open from around April or May until the first snowfall.

SEQUOIA NATIONAL PARK

Making a mad dash from your car to the General Sherman Tree for a quick photo is a time-honored tradition. But picture yourself unzipping your tent flap and crawling out into a 'front yard' of trees as high as a 20-story building and as old as the Bible. Brew some coffee as you plan your day of adventures in this extraordinary park with its soul-sustaining forests and gigantic peaks soaring above 12,000ft. Gaze at dagger-sized stalactites in a 10,000-year-old cave, view the largest living tree on earth, climb 350 steps to a granite dome with soaring views of the snowcapped Great Western Divide or drive through a hole in a 2000-year-old log. All that before you've even walked a trail – where the wild scenes will give you goosebumps, charging waterfalls will leave you awestruck, and epic overnight backpacking trips will lead you to deserted lakes and idyllic backcountry camps.

FACTS

Great For Family travel, scenery, walking
State California
Entrance Fee 7-day pass per vehicle/motorcycle/person on foot or bicycle $35/30/20
Area 631 sq miles

Tunnel Log (p63)

SEQUOIA NATIONAL PARK

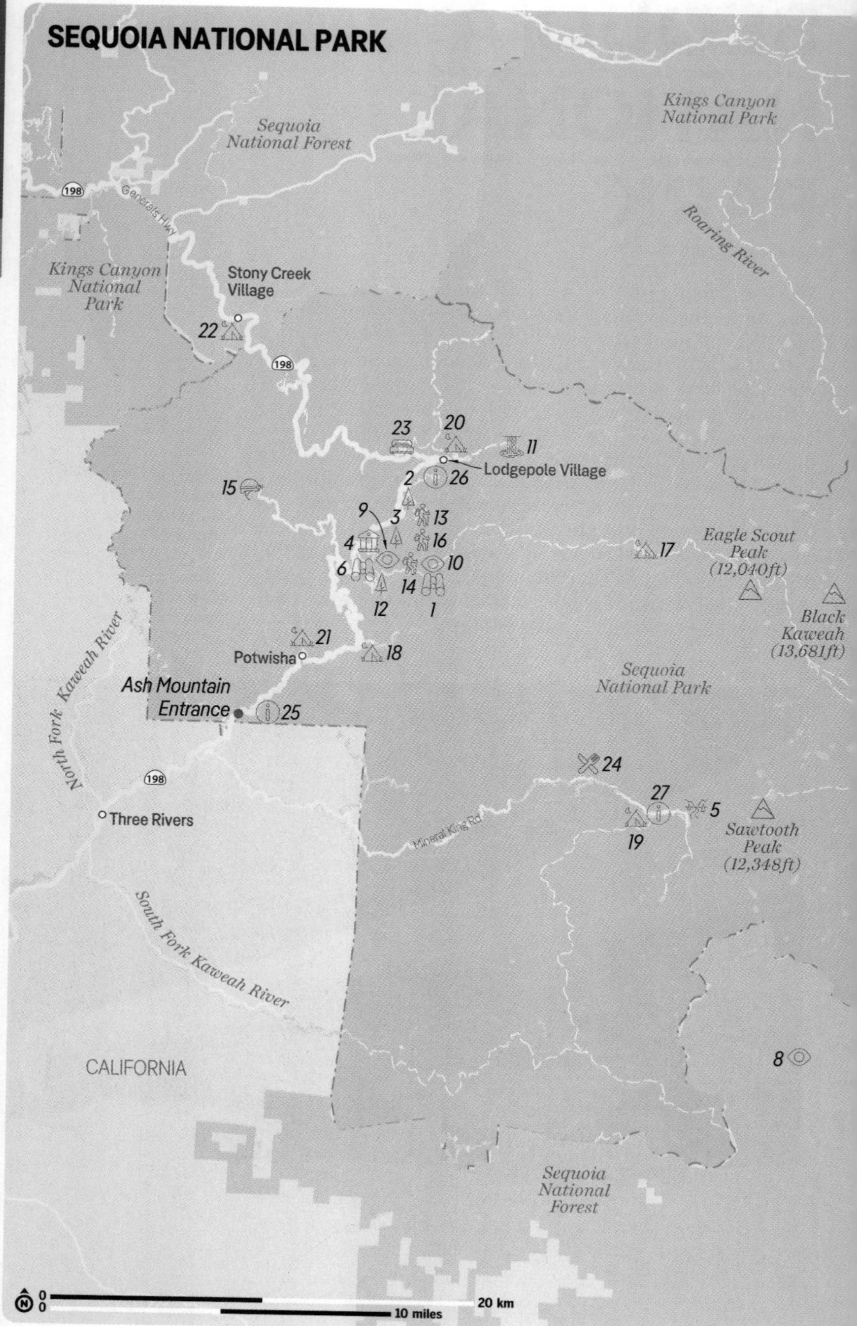
Sequoia National Forest
Kings Canyon National Park
198
Generals Hwy
Kings Canyon National Park
Stony Creek Village
22
198
Roaring River
23
20
11
Lodgepole Village
2
26
15
9
3
13
4
16
6
10
14
1
12
17
Eagle Scout Peak (12,040ft)
Black Kaweah (13,681ft)
21
Potwisha
18
Sequoia National Park
Ash Mountain Entrance
25
North Fork Kaweah River
24
27
5
198
Three Rivers
Mineral King Rd
19
Sawtooth Peak (12,348ft)
South Fork Kaweah River
8
CALIFORNIA
Sequoia National Forest
0
0
20 km
10 miles

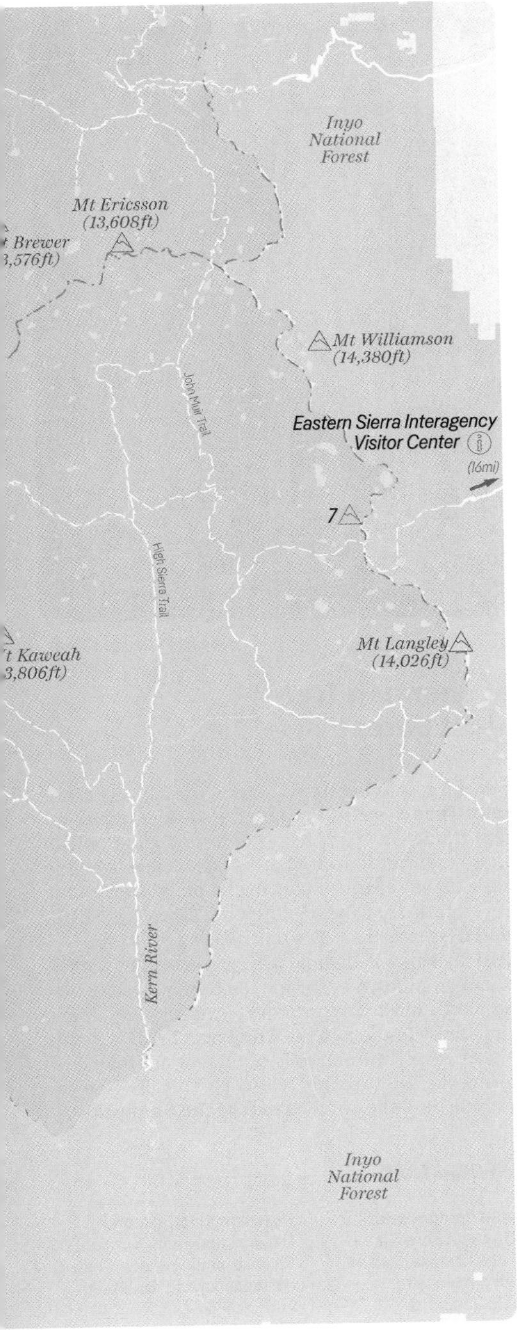

SIGHTS
1 Eagle View
2 General Sherman Tree
3 Giant Forest
4 Giant Forest Museum
5 Mineral King
6 Moro Rock
7 Mt Whitney
8 Sequoia National Forest
9 Squatters Cabin
10 Tharp's Log
11 Tokopah Falls
12 Tunnel Log

ACTIVITIES, COURSES & TOURS
13 Congress Trail
14 Crescent Meadow
15 Crystal Cave
16 Trails of the Sequoias

SLEEPING
17 Bearpaw High Sierra Camp
18 Buckeye Flat Campground
19 Cold Springs Campground
20 Lodgepole Campground
21 Potwisha Campground
22 Stony Creek Campground
see 22 Stony Creek Lodge
see 22 Upper Stony Creek Campground
23 Wuksachi Lodge

EATING
see 23 Peaks Restaurant
24 Silver City Mountain Resort Restaurant
see 22 Stony Creek Lodge Restaurant

INFORMATION
25 Foothills Visitor Center
26 Lodgepole Visitor Center
27 Mineral King Ranger Station

SEQUOIA NATIONAL PARK: GETTING ORIENTED

Hwy 198 runs north from Visalia through Three Rivers past Mineral King Rd to the Ash Mountain Entrance. Beyond here, the road continues as the Generals Hwy, a narrow and windy road snaking all the way into Kings Canyon National Park, where it joins the Kings Canyon Scenic Byway (Hwy 180) near the western Big Stump Entrance (Hwy 180).

Many of the park's star attractions are conveniently lined up along the Generals Hwy. Most tourist activity concentrates in the vast Giant Forest area and in Lodgepole Village just north.

For information about the park's seasonal shuttles see p70.

General Sherman Tree

General Sherman Tree & the Giant Forest

STROLLING BENEATH SEQUOIAS

By volume, the largest living tree on earth, the massive **General Sherman Tree** rockets 275ft into the sky and waaay out of the camera frame. Pay your respects to this giant (which measures more than 103ft around at its base) via a concrete path with stairs from the upper parking lot off Wolverton Rd. The trail cleverly starts at the height of the tree's tip (27 stories high) and descends 0.5 miles to its base.

The General Sherman is the marquee attraction in the **Giant Forest**, a 3-sq-mile grove beside the Generals Hwy that protects the park's most gargantuan tree specimens. A few steps from its base, you can join the **Congress Trail**, a 2-mile paved loop that takes in numerous notable – and named – trees, including the see-through Telescope Tree. To lose the crowds, continue onto the 5-mile **Trail of the Sequoias**.

WHERE TO CAMP IN SEQUOIA NATIONAL PARK

Stony Creek Campground
Spacious and shady sites by a creek a mile north of the national-park boundary. **$**

Lodgepole Campgound
Closest to Giant Forest area: more than 200 close-packed sites, with proximity to Lodgepole Village. **$**

Potwisha Campground
Decent shade near Kaweah River swimming spots; 3 miles northeast of Ash Mountain Entrance. **$**

The top destination in the park, Giant Forest was named by John Muir in 1875. At one point over 300 buildings, including campgrounds and a lodge, encroached upon the sequoias' delicate root systems. In 1997, recognizing this adverse effect, the park began to remove structures and re-site parking lots. It also introduced a convenient, free seasonal visitor shuttle, significantly cutting traffic congestion and reducing the potential harm to these majestic trees.

On your return to the parking lot, take your time on the steep walk back up from the grove – it's 7000ft in elevation and the air is thin. Alternatively, catch the shuttle (summer only) from the lower parking lot (disabled-placard parking only) near the General Sherman Tree and ride it back to the main parking area, about 2 miles south of Lodgepole Village.

For a primer on the intriguing ecology and history of giant sequoias, spend some time inside the pint-size **Giant Forest Museum**, which is located 2 miles south of the General Sherman Tree via the Generals Hwy and various hiking trails. Hands-on exhibits teach about the life stages of these big trees, which can live for more than 3000 years, and the fire cycle that releases their seeds and allows them to sprout on bare soil. The museum is housed in a historic 1920s building designed by Gilbert Stanley Underwood, famed architect of the Ahwahnee. Exhibits will entertain both kids and adults.

KINGS CANYON NATIONAL PARK

Though administered as one unit with the adjacent Sequoia National Park, **Kings Canyon National Park** (p46) is its own unique park, with trails and attractions.

Tour Crystal Cave

ADMIRE UNDERGROUND WONDERS

Stalactites hang like daggers from the ceiling, and milky-white marble formations take the shape of ethereal curtains, domes, columns and shields inside **Crystal Cave**, a popular attraction that is a 30-minute drive west from the Giant Forest Museum. Discovered in 1918 by two parks' employees who were going fishing, this unique cave was carved by an underground river and has marble formations estimated to be up to 100,000 years old. The cave is also a unique biodiverse habitat for spiders and bats.

Tours fill up quickly, especially on weekends, so buy tickets online at least a month before your trip. The museum is crushed with visitors in summer. To avoid parking headaches, take the free in-park shuttle bus. Note that the cave may close during rainy weather (refunds are available). Look for the signed turnoff for Crystal Cave Rd about 2 miles south of the Giant Forest Museum.

TUNNEL LOG

Visitors can drive through Tunnel Log, a 2000-year-old tree that fell naturally in 1937. It once stood 275ft high with a base measuring 21ft in diameter. Regular sedans and small cars fit through the gap, or it's just as fun to walk through the 17ft-wide, 8ft-high arch cut into the tree by the Civilian Conservation Corps (CCC). In winter, the road may be closed due to snowfall – those with winter gear can hike to it from the Giant Forest Museum.

Cold Springs Campground
Short walk from Mineral Springs ranger station. Peaceful, creekside location with a gorgeous forest setting. **$**

Buckeye Flat Campground
Well-maintained, tent-only campground off Generals Hwy. Six miles northeast of the Ash Mountain Entrance. **$**

Upper Stony Creek Campground
Primitive. Accessed off Generals Hwy via unpaved roads in Sequoia National Forest. **$**

HIKING TRIP

General Sherman Tree to Moro Rock

A deviation from the popular Congress Trail Loop, this rolling one-way hike takes in huge sequoias, green meadows and the pinnacle of Moro Rock. Expect stretches of blissful solitude and potential black bear sightings. Keep in mind that hiking this route in one direction is possible only when the free seasonal park shuttle buses are running, usually from late May until late September.

1 General Sherman Tree Plaza

A small plaza and an A-frame shelter mark the start of the trail to the Sherman Tree from the shuttle stop off Wolverton Rd, just east of the Generals Hwy. This spot starts getting busy after 8:30am in summer.

The Hike: A paved trail quickly descends through towering sequoias. The trail starts at the height of the Sherman Tree's tip (27 stories) and descends 0.5 miles to its base.

2 General Sherman Tree

Walk up to the giant's trunk for your photo op. By volume, it's the largest living tree on earth: 275ft tall and measuring 103ft around its base. It is 2300 to 2700 years old.

The Hike: Turn around and walk downhill on the western branch of the Congress Trail Loop. If mistakenly on the eastern branch, jog right then left at two minor trail junctions that appear 0.5 miles south of the tree.

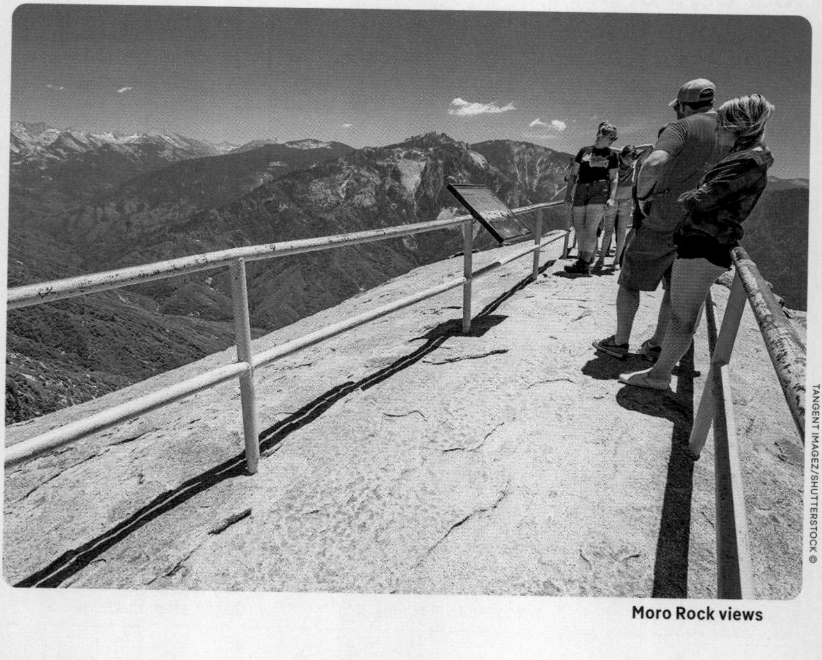

TANGENT IMAGEZ/SHUTTERSTOCK ©

Moro Rock views

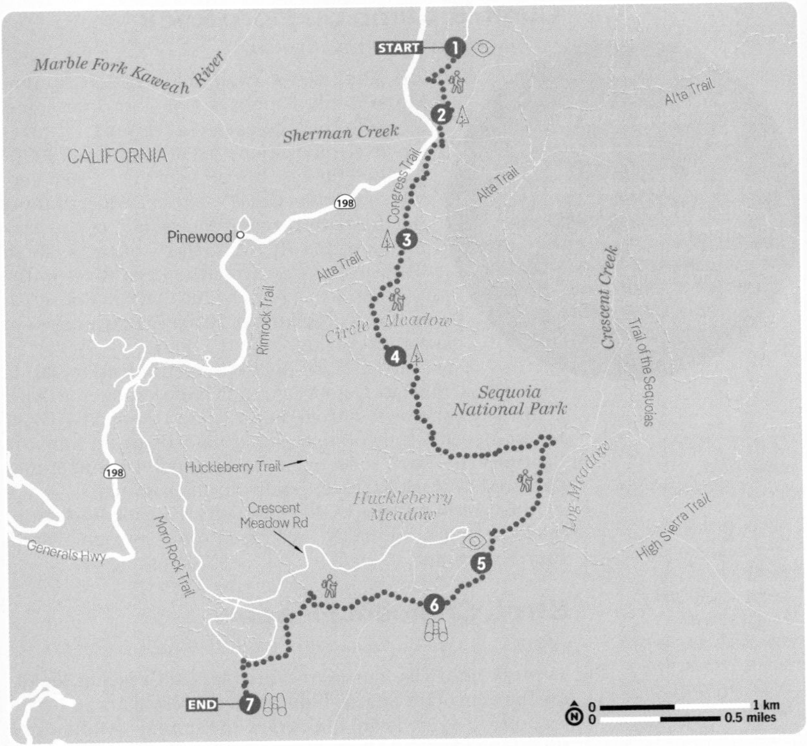

3 McKinley Tree Junction

You'll come to a five-way junction at the McKinley Tree. Continue straight ahead south on the dirt trail toward Cattle Cabin. The hollow-bottom Room Tree is just ahead.

The Hike: Pass the pretty cluster of the Founders Group and walk along the eastern edge of the bright green strip of C-shaped Circle Meadow.

4 Pillars of Hercules

Stand between this well-named tree group – and look up for a heroic view. The trail then passes the huge charred maw of the Black Arch tree.

The Hike: Continue south, veering slightly right and then left at the next two trail junctions. At a three-way intersection, go straight at this junction and the next one.

5 Crescent Meadow

On the north side of Crescent Meadow stands the hollow-bodied **Chimney Tree**. Continue east past **Tharp's Log**, then turn right (south) on a paved trail along the east side of **Log Meadow**.

The Hike: Before reaching the Crescent Meadow parking lot, head left then right onto the signed High Sierra Trail, heading west for more marvelous ridge views.

6 Bobcat Point

Stop at this overlook to take in the Great Western Divide and Kaweah Canyon.

The Hike: In 0.2 miles, cross Crescent Creek on a log to join the Sugar Pine Trail. Go left (west) and follow it for 0.9 miles.

7 Moro Rock

Climb the granite dome for some of the park's best views.

The Hike: Return to your starting point via shuttle buses.

Climb & Climb Up Moro Rock

VIEWS CAN STRETCH 150 MILES

SNOW SPORTS

Winter is a memorable time to visit Sequoia and Kings Canyon. A thick blanket of snow drapes giant sequoia trees and meadows, the pace of activity slows and a hush falls over the roads and trails. For information about winter sports in Sequoia, see p58.

Mind-boggling views await at the 6725ft summit of **Moro Rock**, Sequoia's iconic granite dome. But you're going to earn that reward – it takes a quarter-mile climb up 350 steps (over 300ft) to reach the top. But oh, that view. From here you can see the Great Western Divide, running north–south through the middle of the park and splitting the watersheds of the Kaweah River to the west from the Kern River to the east. The steps, built by the Civilian Conservation Corps (CCC) in the 1930s, end at a railed-in viewpoint corridor atop the dome.

The road to Moro Rock (Crescent Meadow Rd) is closed from late October through late May, but the dome is still accessible on foot from the Sherman Tree and the Giant Forest Museum (p63). Due to pollution drifting up from the Central Valley, this spectacular vantage point is sometimes obscured by thick haze, especially during summer.

Other granite domes in the park include Beetle Rock, Sunset Rock and Little Baldy – which also has awesome views from its summit.

DON'T MISS: SEQUOIA NATIONAL FOREST

Although there's a lot to see just inside both national parks, Sequoia National Forest also has amazingly scenic spots, from ancient sequoia groves to alpine lakes. In fact, driving between the national parks on the Generals Hwy, or from Grant Grove to Cedar Grove via the Kings Canyon Scenic Byway, you'll pass right through the Sequoia National Forest and its Giant Sequoia National Monument, making it easy to stop off and see the sights, score a campsite or hike less-trammeled trails into the wilderness.

Stroll Crescent Meadow

SEQUOIAS, WILDFLOWERS AND – MAYBE – BEARS

They say naturalist John Muir called the lush **Crescent Meadow** the 'gem of the Sierra.' Buffered by a forest of firs and giant sequoias and thick with high grass and summer wildflowers, this is the place for a leisurely loop hike (1.3 miles). And you might just see black bears snacking on berries and ripping apart logs to feast on insects. The meadow environment is fragile, so always stay on established trails.

Several short hikes surround the meadow, including spur trails to **Tharp's Log** (0.8 miles), where the area's first white settler, Hale Tharp, spent summers in a fallen sequoia. Next to Huckleberry Meadow you'll find the **Squatters Cabin** (0.4 miles), an 1880s log cabin that's a ghostly remnant of the failed utopian-socialist Kaweah Colony.

For an impressive view of the Sierra Mountains, walk to **Eagle View** overlook. It's reasonably accessible via a 1-mile walk along the High Sierra Trail from the meadow. Park at Crescent Meadow or the Giant Forest Museum.

The meadow is almost 3 miles down Moro Rock–Crescent Meadow Rd, best accessed by the free seasonal shuttle bus. The

WHERE TO STAY IN SEQUOIA NATIONAL PARK

Wuksachi Lodge
Motel-style, fairly generic rooms in a lovely setting near Lodgepole Village. **$$**

Stony Creek Lodge
Wood-and-stone lodge about halfway between Grant Grove Village and the Giant Forest. Aging motel rooms. **$$**

Bearpaw High Sierra Camp
This canvas-tent village is an 11.3-mile hike east of Crescent Meadow on the High Sierra Trail. **$$**

EXPLORING MORO ROCK TO CRESCENT MEADOW

A narrow, winding and pockmarked road links some of the Giant Forest's popular roadside attractions, with giant sequoias lining the way. This 6-mile road is closed to private vehicles on summer weekends and holidays. On those days take the free seasonal park shuttle, usually running between late May and late September. In winter the road closes to all traffic, but you can still hike (when snow levels are low), cross-country ski or snowshoe along it.

From the **1 Giant Forest Museum**, the Moro Rock–Crescent Meadow Rd swoops into the southwestern section of the Giant Forest. Less than a mile in is the **2 Auto Log**, a hefty sequoia that fell in 1917. For early park visitors, a flat section was carved onto its top and the tree was actually used as part of the road. You can't drive on it anymore, but you can walk on it and imagine.

After more than another half mile, turn into the parking area to gawk at the pale dome of **3 Moro Rock**. Continuing a half mile, the mesmerizing flame-like roots of the 2300-year-old collapsed **4 Buttress Tree** face the road. On the opposite side of the road a bit further along is the **5 Parker Group**, named for the eight-person family of US Cavalry Captain James Parker, the park's superintendent during the 1890s.

In days gone by, the renown of Yosemite's Wawona Tunnel Tree (p83) prompted many visitors to inquire about Sequoia's drive-through tree, but the park didn't have one. So when a 275ft sequoia collapsed across the road in 1937, the park promptly cut a passageway for cars. This **6 Tunnel Log** has an 8ft-high, 17ft-wide opening. From there, it's another mile to verdant **7 Crescent Meadow**.

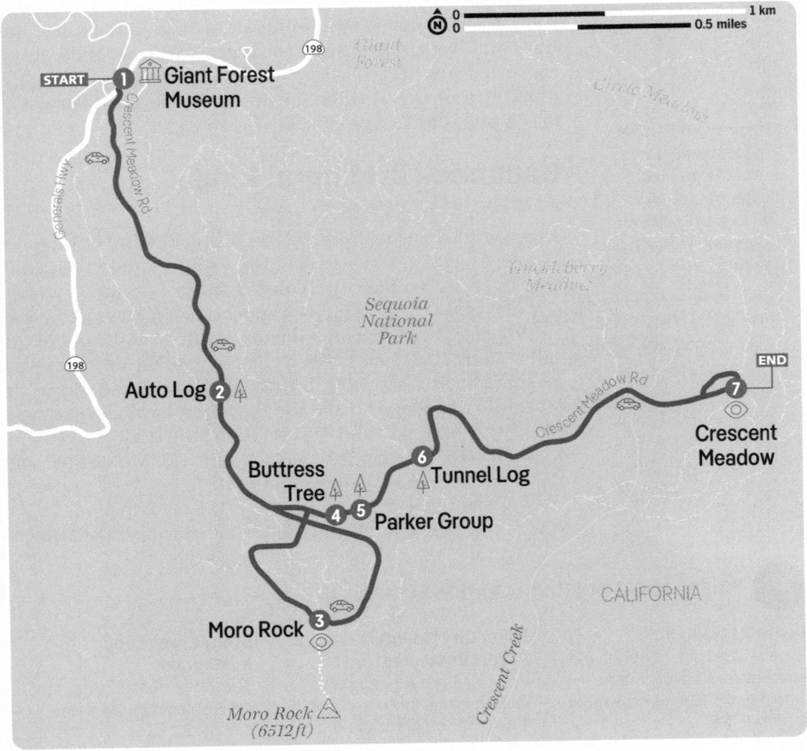

THE SIERRA NEVADA

On the eastern side of the Central Valley looms California's most prominent topographic feature: the Sierra Nevada, nicknamed the 'Range of Light' by conservationist John Muir. At 400 miles long and 70 miles wide, this is one of the world's largest mountain ranges, punctuated with 13 peaks over 14,000ft high. The vast wilderness of the High Sierra (mostly above 9000ft) is an astounding landscape of shrinking glaciers, sculpted granite peaks and remote canyons. This landscape is beautiful to look at but difficult to access, and it was one of the greatest challenges for 19th-century settlers attempting to reach California.

road closes to all traffic after the first snowfall and doesn't reopen until spring, but you can still walk to it, although snowshoes or cross-country skiing may be needed.

Hike to Tokopah Falls

CASCADES AND YELLOW-BELLIED MARMOTS

This easy riverside stroll ends at pretty **Tokopah Falls**, which tumbles down a boulder-lined canyon not far from the Lodgepole Campground. Big rocks along the trail are perfect for scrambling and you'll likely see wildlife hanging out near the trail, making this 3.6-mile round-trip hike a fun one for families. From the trailhead, the path ribbons through a sun-dappled forest beside the Marble Fork of the Kaweah River. Views of the glacier-carved canyon – and the 1800ft granite face of the Watchtower – are exceptional. Look for mule deer, black bears and tiny pikas as you walk. Ferns and wildflowers are also a highlight. The trail eventually leaves the forest as the rocky path climbs past boulders. Don't be surprised at the sight of yellow-bellied marmots sunning and scampering on the rocks.

At 1200ft high, Tokopah Falls doesn't free fall. Instead it bounces off the granite cliffs quite loudly, especially when snowmelt gushes in late spring. Note that the cascades can be disappointing in late summer and autumn. Be careful if you're thinking about swimming. Drownings in the Kings and Kaweah Rivers in Kings Canyon and Sequoia are the leading cause of death in the parks. Swift currents can be deadly, especially in spring. Head to the nearby **Peaks Restaurant** in the **Wuksachi Lodge** for a post-hike meal.

Backpack in Mineral King

SOAK UP SUBALPINE BEAUTY

A scenic subalpine valley at 7500ft, **Mineral King** is Sequoia's backpacking hub and a good place to find solitude. Gorgeous and gigantic, its glacially sculpted valley is ringed by massive mountains, including the jagged 12,343ft Sawtooth Peak. Hiking anywhere from here involves a steep climb out of the valley along strenuous trails, so be aware of the altitude, even on short hikes. Enjoyable day hikes go to Crystal, Monarch, Mosquito and Eagle Lakes. For long trips, locals recommend the Little Five Lakes and, further along the High Sierra Trail, Kaweah Gap, surrounded by Black Kaweah, Mt Stewart and Eagle Scout Peak – all above 12,000ft.

From the 1860s to the 1890s, Mineral King witnessed heavy silver mining and lumber activity. The website of the Mineral

WHERE TO EAT IN SEQUOIA NATIONAL PARK

Peaks Restaurant
Excellent breakfast buffet and soup-and-salad lunch fare, with dinners aiming to be more gourmet. **$$**

Silver City Mountain Resort Restaurant
Country store serving simple fare on picnic tables. Try the slabs of homemade pie. **$**

Stony Creek Lodge Restaurant
The lodge's basic restaurant serves decent pizzas and salads. **$**

SEBASTIEN BUREL/SHUTTERSTOCK ©

Mineral King

King Preservation Society (mineralking.org) has all kinds of info on the area, including its rustic and still-occupied historic mining cabins. In spring and early summer, hordes of hungry marmots terrorize parked cars at Mineral King, chewing on radiator hoses, belts and wiring to get the salt they crave after their winter hibernation. You'll find information on the park website about how to protect your car.

The area is reached via Mineral King Rd – a slinky, steep and narrow 25-mile road not suitable for RVs or speed demons; it's usually open from late May through October. Plan on spending the night, unless you don't mind driving the three-hour round trip. Expect delays related to rehabilitation work on the road, possibly beginning in 2024.

Hiking Mt Whitney

THE LOWER 48'S HIGHEST PEAK

Mt Whitney (14,505ft) captures the imagination. The tallest mountain in the contiguous US, Mt Whitney soars skyward from the fringes of Sequoia National Park on the east side of the Sierra Nevada. The mountain cannot be reached by road from the developed areas of the park, and most people approach from the east, often using Lone Pine, off US 395, as their pre-hike base.

The 10.7-mile hike to the summit is a strenuous, really, really long walk that will wear out even experienced mountaineers.

PIKAS & MARMOTS

That odd 'bleating' coming from jumbles of rocks and boulders on the Tokopah Falls Trail is likely a pika. A careful search will reveal the hamster-like vocalist peering from under a rock with small beady eyes. Pikas typically live on talus slopes above 80,000ft, especially in the alpine realm of mountain hemlock, white-bark pine and heather plants.

Yellow-bellied marmots inhabit rocky outcrops and boulder fields above 7500ft. Sprawled lazily on sun-warmed rocks, marmots will jolt upright and shriek a warning call when closely approached. Ravenous creatures, marmots spend four to five months putting on weight before a long winter hibernation. In spring they have a bad habit: chewing on radiator hoses for the collected salt.

WHERE TO GET INFORMATION IN SEQUOIA NATIONAL PARK

Foothills Visitor Center
One mile north of the Ash Mountain Entrance. Bookstore; maps and tickets for Crystal Cave.

Lodgepole Visitor Center
Off Generals Hwy, offers info plus exhibits about the natural history in both parks.

Mineral King Ranger Station
Small, seasonal ranger station issues wilderness permits, rents bear canisters and sells books and maps.

TREES OF THE SIERRA NEVADA

The Sierra Nevada has three distinct eco-zones: the dry western foothills covered with oak and chaparral; conifer forests starting from an elevation of 2000ft; and a treeless alpine zone above 8000ft. Almost two dozen species of conifer grow in the Sierra Nevada, with mid-elevation forests home to massive Douglas firs, ponderosa pines and, biggest of all, the giant sequoia. Deciduous trees include the quaking aspen, a white-trunked tree with shimmering leaves that turn pale yellow in the autumn, helping the Golden State live up to its name in the Eastern Sierra.

Mt Whitney

However, it doesn't require technical skills if attempted in summer or early autumn. Earlier or later in the season, you'll likely need an ice axe and crampons, and to stay overnight. Many people in good physical condition make it to the top, although only superbly conditioned, previously acclimatized hikers should attempt this as a day hike. Breathing becomes difficult at these elevations and altitude sickness is a common problem. Get a permit at the **Eastern Sierra Interagency Visitor Center** in Lone Pine before visiting.

GETTING AROUND

Highway 198 runs north from Visalia through Three Rivers past Mineral King Rd to the Ash Mountain Entrance. Beyond here, the road continues as the Generals Hwy, a narrow and winding road snaking all the way into Kings Canyon National Park, where it joins the Kings Canyon Scenic Byway (Hwy 180) near the western Big Stump Entrance. Vehicles more than 22ft long may have trouble negotiating the steep Generals Hwy, with its many hairpin curves. Budget at least one hour to drive from the entrance to the Giant Forest/Lodgepole area and at least another hour from there to Grant Grove Village in Kings Canyon.

There are no gas stations in the park proper; fill up your tank before you arrive in the park. Those in need can find gas year-round at Hume Lake (11 miles north of Grant Grove in Kings Canyon).

Gray shuttle buses run every 10 to 20 minutes from the Giant Forest Museum to Moro Rock and Crescent Meadow (between 8am and 6pm). The green route runs between the General Sherman Tree parking areas and Lodgepole Village every 15 minutes. The purple route links Lodgepole, Wuksachi Lodge and Dorst Creek Campground every 20 minutes. A final orange route connects General Sherman to Wolverton every 15 minutes. All routes are free and operate 8:30am to 6pm from June through September. Online route maps can be viewed at www.nps.gov/seki/planyourvisit/parktransit.htm or ask for route info at the visitor centers.

YOSEMITE NATIONAL PARK

WASHINGTON, DC

The astonishing head-turner of America's national parks, and a Unesco World Heritage Site, Yosemite garners the devotion of all who enter – which may take awhile if you arrive after 8am in summer. From the waterfall-striped granite walls buttressing emerald-green Yosemite Valley to the skyscraping giant sequoias at Mariposa Grove, the park inspires awe and reverence – more than 4 million visitors wend their way to the country's third-oldest national park in a typical year. But trouble is afoot in paradise – a controversial reservations system may soon be implemented permanently, and the catastrophic wildfire, drought, floods and severe storms that have come with human-caused climate change are transforming the park's landscapes. Yosemite is more fragile than ever, and its future is uncertain. But lift your eyes above the crowds and you'll feel your heart instantly moved by unrivaled splendors: for now, Yosemite's consummate beauty still abounds.

FACTS

Great For Family travel, scenery, hiking
State California
Entrance Fee 7-day pass per car/motorcycle/person on foot or bicycle $35/30/20
Area 1169 sq miles

El Capitan (p75)

WHEN TO VISIT

Park waterfalls are at peak flow – and quite spectacular – in May and June. Lodging may also be slightly less crowded in May and June before families arrive during summer vacation. You'll find the most sunny and pleasant blue-sky days from May through September, although crowds will be heavy. Crowds are especially heavy in July and August. Good lodging deals and winter activities are highlights from November through April. The enchanting firefall event (p88) – when Horseshoe Falls resembles lava in the evening light – occurs in February.

YOSEMITE NATIONAL PARK

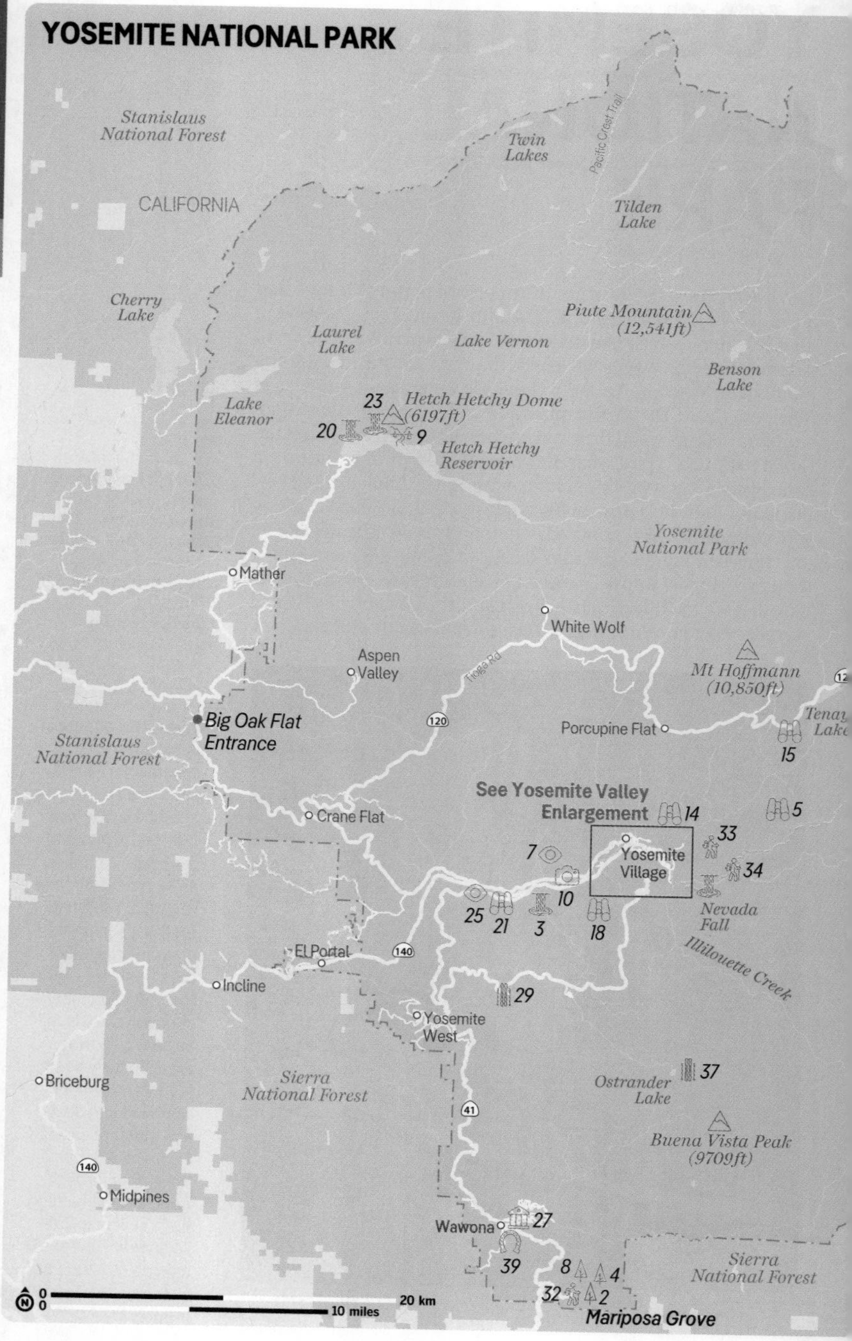

Stanislaus National Forest
Twin Lakes
Pacific Crest Trail
CALIFORNIA
Tilden Lake
Cherry Lake
Piute Mountain (12,541ft)
Laurel Lake
Lake Vernon
Benson Lake
Lake Eleanor
23
Hetch Hetchy Dome (6197ft)
20
9
Hetch Hetchy Reservoir
Yosemite National Park
Mather
White Wolf
Aspen Valley
Tioga Rd
Mt Hoffmann (10,850ft)
Big Oak Flat Entrance
120
Porcupine Flat
Tenaya Lake
15
Stanislaus National Forest
See Yosemite Valley Enlargement
14
5
Crane Flat
33
7
Yosemite Village
34
10
25
21
3
18
Nevada Fall
Illilouette Creek
El Portal
140
Incline
29
Yosemite West
Briceburg
Sierra National Forest
37
Ostrander Lake
41
Buena Vista Peak (9709ft)
140
Midpines
Wawona
27
39
8
4
32
2
Sierra National Forest
Mariposa Grove
0
20 km
0
10 miles

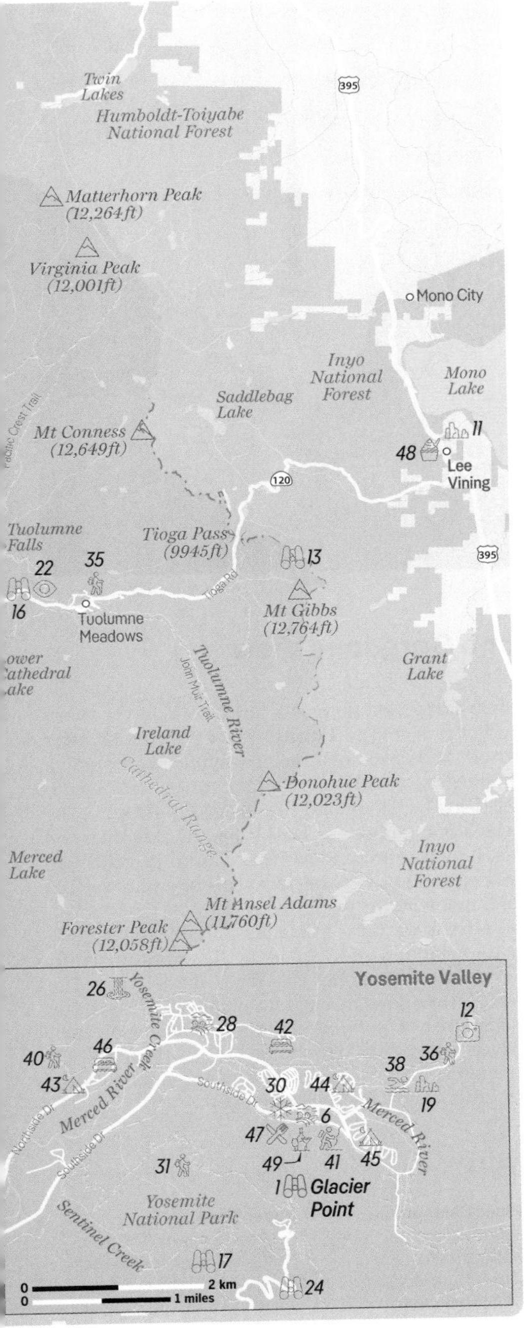

HIGHLIGHTS
1 Glacier Point
2 Mariposa Grove

SIGHTS
3 Bridalveil Fall
4 California Tunnel Tree
5 Clouds Rest
6 Curry Village
7 El Capitan
8 Grizzly Giant
9 Hetch Hetchy
10 Horsetail Fall
11 Lee Vining Canyon
12 Mirror Lake
13 Mt Dana
14 North Dome
15 Olmsted Point
16 Pothole Dome
17 Sentinel Dome
18 Taft Point
19 Tenaya Canyon
20 Tueeulala Falls
21 Tunnel View
22 Tuolumne Meadows
23 Wapama Falls
24 Washburn Point
25 Wawona Tunnel Tree
26 Yosemite Falls
27 Yosemite History Center
28 Yosemite Village

ACTIVITIES, COURSES & TOURS
29 Badger Pass Ski Area
30 Curry Village Ice Rink
31 Four Mile Trail
32 Grizzly Giant Loop Trail
33 Half Dome
34 John Muir Trail
35 Lembert Dome and Dog Lake Trailhead
36 Mirror Lake Loop Trail
37 Ostrander Lake Ski Hut
38 Tenaya Creek
48 Wawona Stable
39 Yosemite Falls Trail
40 Yosemite Mountaineering School

SLEEPING
41 Ahwahnee
42 Camp 4
43 North Pines Campground
46 Upper Pines Campground
52 Yosemite Valley Lodge

EATING
53 Curry Village Pizza Deck
54 Mono Cone

DRINKING
55 Bar 1899

YOSEMITE NATIONAL PARK: GETTING ORIENTED

Visitor activity is concentrated in Yosemite Valley, especially in **Yosemite Village**, which has a revamped central commercial area with a new **visitor center**, a museum, restaurants and other services. Curry Village is another hub. Some of the parks most notable features – Half Dome, El Capitan, Yosemite Falls and Mirror Lake – are in the valley as well as trailheads for popular hikes. Tuolumne (too-*ahl*-uh-*mee*) Meadows, toward the eastern end of Tioga Rd and only open in summer, draws hikers, backpackers and climbers to its pristine backcountry. Glacier Point, another section of the park with no road access beyond summer (except the ski area), offers spectacular views. Wawona, the park's southern focal point, also has good infrastructure.

ZACK FRANK/SHUTTERSTOCK ©

Yosemite Falls

Stop for a Gorgeous View

THE HEART OF YOSEMITE

Yes, you're in a hurry. And there will be a crowd. But the view of Yosemite Valley from the **Tunnel View** parking lot after emerging from the Wawona Tunnel is sublime. And worth a stop. El Capitan rises to the north, pine forests and meadows blanket the valley floor, and Bridalveil Fall drops to the south. A peek-a-boo glimpse of Half Dome ties together the entire scene. It evokes a grand cathedral, and the collective sense of wonder and anticipation is something quite special – if even for a moment.

Yosemite Valley is the hub of the park and its crown jewel. Carpeted with meadows and flanked by sheer granite cliffs, the valley stretches seven miles east from Tunnel View. The rippling Merced River flows through the middle of it. Northside and Southside Drives run parallel across the valley on each side of the river, with four bridges linking the two roads. You'll find the bulk of visitor services, including accommodations, restaurants, stores and a visitor center, here.

WHERE TO CAMP IN YOSEMITE VALLEY

Camp 4
Near base of Yosemite Falls and entwined in climbing history. Reservations late May to September. $

North Pines Campground
Near Mirror Lake and within walking distance of many popular trailheads. Reservations required. $

Upper Pines
Busy and big, with 238 sites. More private spots in the back. Reservations required. $

Watch Climbers on El Capitan

VISIBLE DAY AND NIGHT

Soaring nearly 3600ft from base to summit, **El Capitan** ranks as one of the world's largest granite monoliths. Its sheer face makes it a world-class destination for experienced climbers – one that wasn't 'conquered' until 1958. Since then, it has been inundated. The meadows across from El Capitan and the northeastern end of Tioga Lake (off Tioga Rd) are good for watching climbers dangling from the granite, where they grapple with cracks and ledges, including the famous 'Nose.' The Academy Award–winning *Free Solo* documentary tells the story of Alex Honnold, who was the first person to summit El Capitan using only his hands, no ropes, in 2017.

Bring binoculars and look for haul bags first – they are bigger and more colorful than the climbers and they move around more, making them easy to watch. As part of the excellent **Ask a Climber** program, climbing rangers set up telescopes at El Capitan Bridge from 12:30pm to 4:30pm. (mid-May to mid-_October) and answer visitor questions. At night, park along the road and dim your headlights; once your eyes adjust, you'll easily make out the pinpricks of headlamps dotting the rock face. Listen, too, for voices.

Waterfalls of Yosemite Valley

TIME YOUR VISIT FOR SPRING

Ribbons of water, including some of the highest waterfalls in the US, fall dramatically before crashing in thunderous displays on the valley floor. The falls are typically most impressive in May and June, when snowmelt increases their volume. Some are no more than a very thin stream by August.

At the southwestern end of the valley, **Bridalveil Fall** tumbles 620ft. The Ahwahneechee people call it Pohono (Spirit of the Puffing Wind) as gusts often blow the fall from side to side, even lifting water back up into the air. Peregrine falcons may glide overhead. West of Yosemite Village, **Yosemite Falls** is considered the tallest waterfall in North America, dropping 2425ft in three tiers. A slick trail leads to the bottom or, if you prefer solitude, you can clamber up the **Yosemite Falls Trail**, which puts you atop the falls after a grueling 3.4-mile climb. The falls are usually mesmerizing, especially when the spring runoff turns them into thunderous cataracts, but are reduced to a trickle by late summer. For information about hiking to **Vernal and Nevada Falls**, accessed at the east end of the valley, see p76.

SHUTTLES & BIKE TRAILS

The free, air-conditioned Yosemite Valley Shuttle Bus operates year-round from 7am to 10pm at 12–22 minute intervals, and stops at 19 numbered locations. In winter, free buses also operate between Yosemite Valley and the Badger Pass Ski Area. The seasonal Tuolumne Shuttle Bus runs between Tuolumne Lodge and Olmsted Point in Tuolumne Meadows.

A seasonal shuttle also travels between the Mariposa Grove Welcome Plaza and Mariposa Grove. Two fee-based hiker buses travel once daily to and from Yosemite Valley: the Tuolumne Meadows Hikers' Bus and the Glacier Point Hikers' Bus.

Cycling the 12 miles of paved trails in the valley is a great way to explore the heart of the park.

WHERE TO STAY IN YOSEMITE VALLEY

Curry Village
Mix of canvas cabins, wood cabins and motel-style rooms in a busy park hub. **$$**

Yosemite Valley Lodge
Near Yosemite Falls, with 15 low-slung motel-style buildings, plus pool and cafes. **$$$**

Ahwahnee
Sumptuous historic property with soaring ceilings and atmospheric lounges. Classic rooms and cottages. **$$$**

HIKING TRIP

Vernal & Nevada Falls

If you can only do a single day hike in Yosemite – and it's springtime – make this the one. Vernal and Nevada Falls are two of Yosemite's most spectacular waterfalls, and the sights along the way – a drenching mist, the Giant Staircase, graceful footbridges – are unique. The granite slabs atop Nevada Fall make for a superb lunch spot. This strenuous lasso loop is 6.7 miles and should take five to six hours.

1 Happy Isles Shuttle Stop

You'll find this shuttle stop (#16) at the eastern edge of the Happy Isles Loop Rd in Yosemite Valley.

The Hike: Cross the bridge over the Merced River, turn right at the trailhead and follow the riverbank upstream. Turn left at the informational bulletin board.

2 Vernal Fall Footbridge

This first leg to the footbridge is paved and will probably be the most crowded part of this hugely popular hike.

The Hike: Shortly beyond the Vernal Fall footbridge is the junction of the John Muir and Mist Trails. Turn left onto the Mist Trail. In about 10 minutes Vernal Fall comes into view

BENNY MARTY/SHUTTERSTOCK ©

Nevada Fall

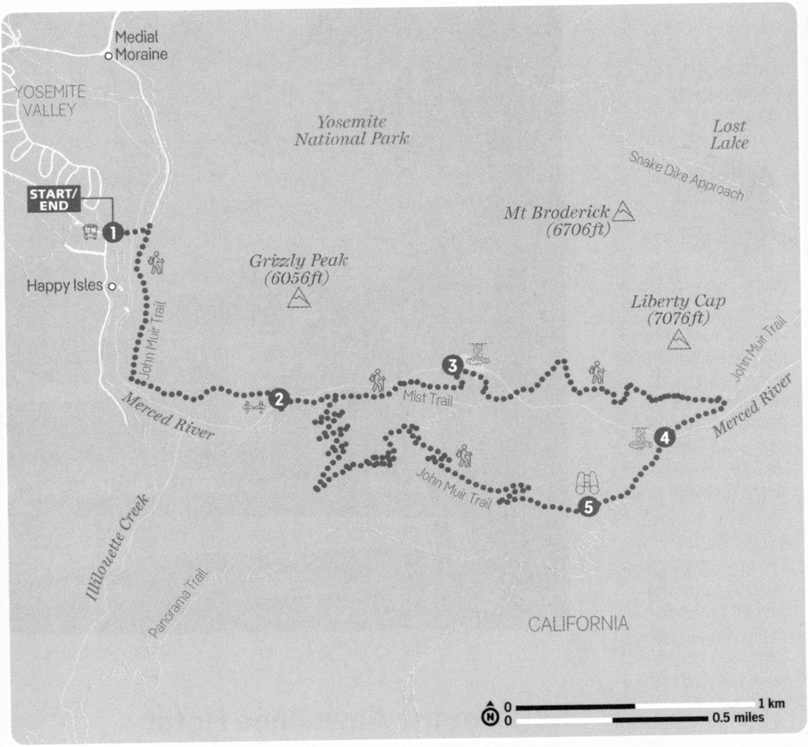

– and you'll be starting an ascent on the Giant Staircase – a steep and narrow series of granite steps – on the aptly named Mist Trail.

3 Vernal Fall Summit

Vernal Fall, which the Miwok people called Pai-wai'-ak, tumbles 317ft over a vertical cliff. The summit is about 1.3 miles from the trailhead – a 1000ft climb. Above the falls, the Merced whizzes down a long ramp of granite known as the Silver Apron into the deceptively serene Emerald Pool before plunging over the cliff. Don't enter the water: underwater currents in Emerald Pool have whipped many swimmers over the falls.

The Hike: It's another 1.3 miles to the top of the Mist Trail, which meets the John Muir Trail 0.2 miles northeast of the falls. From this junction, it's 2.5 miles back to Happy Isles via the Mist Trail or 4 miles via the John Muir Trail.

4 Nevada Fall Summit

Shortly after joining the John Muir Trail, a footbridge crosses the Merced. Beneath it, the river whizzes through a chute before plummeting 594ft over the edge of Nevada Fall. Plant yourself on a slab of granite for lunch and views, and be prepared to fend off Steller's jays and squirrels.

The Hike: A 4-mile return to the valley along the John Muir Trail offers a fabulous glimpse of Yosemite Falls. The trail passes the Panorama Trail junction and traverses a cliff with a stone wall.

5 Nevada Fall Viewpoint

Stop beside the wall to admire the view of Nevada Fall and its majestic neighbor, the 7076ft-tall Liberty Cap.

The Hike: From here, the John Muir Trail switchbacks down the gorge, passing Clark Point and joining the Mist Trail, continuing down through Douglas firs and canyon live oaks to Yosemite Valley.

BACKCOUNTRY CAMPING IN YOSEMITE

Dustin Weatherford is a backcountry split boarder, rock climber and paraglider living in Yosemite Valley and working on YOSAR (Yosemite Search and Rescue). His favorite places to spend the night in the wild include:

Bunnell Point
This old established camp just past the Bunnell Cascade on the Merced Lake Trail is an incredible place to sleep in the backcountry.

Sunrise High Sierra Camp
Accessible from Lake Tenaya or Tuolumne Meadows via the John Muir Trail, this camp offers day hikes to Cathedral Peak, Clouds Rest and Half Dome.

On a Portaledge
The granite walls of Half Dome, El Capitan and Washington Column are all great hosts for a vertical bivvy.

Ahwahnee Hotel

Relax at the Ahwahnee Hotel

HISTORY, BEAUTY, GOOD NIGHT'S SLEEP

A picture of rustic elegance that evokes an era of grand adventure, the **Ahwahnee** has drawn well-heeled tourists through its towering doors since 1927. And you don't need to be a guest to wander its common areas. Built from granite, cement and steel (with hints of pine and cedar), the hotel is adorned with leaded glass, sculpted tiles, Native American elements, German Gothic chandeliers and Turkish kilims. A visit to Yosemite Valley is hardly complete without a stroll through the sumptuous Great Lounge (aka the lobby). If the lobby looks familiar, perhaps it's because it inspired the lobby of the Overlook Hotel, the ill-fated inn from Stanley Kubrick's *The Shining*. And the name? The hotel was built on the site of a former Ahwahnee–Miwok village.

To celebrate an adventurous day, make a reservation for dinner at the **Ahwahnee Dining Room**. The formal ambience

WHERE TO STAY BEYOND YOSEMITE VALLEY

Tuolumne Meadows Lodge
Canvas tent cabins off Tioga Rd with two/four beds and woodburning stoves. No electricity. **$$**

White Wolf Lodge
Two dozen tent cabins, handful of wooden cabins 1 mile off Tioga Rd. No electricity. **$$**

Wawona Hotel
Six graceful, whitewashed New England–style buildings with wide porches and Victorian-style furniture. No TVs. **$$**

may not be for everybody, but most will be awed by its sumptuous decor, soaring beamed ceiling and palatial chandeliers. The menu is constantly in flux, but most dinners have a perfect pitch and are beautifully presented. There is a dress code at dinner, but otherwise shorts and sneakers are okay.

Stroll Around Mirror Lake

PHOTOGENIC MOMENTS

Shallow **Mirror Lake**, which reflects Mt Watkins and Half Dome on its tranquil surface, is one of Yosemite Valley's most photographed sights. Further northwest of the lake, **Tenaya Canyon** offers one of the quietest corners of the valley. Formed when a rockfall dammed a section of Tenaya Creek, Mirror Lake has slowly been reverting to Mirror Meadow ever since the park service stopped dredging it in 1971. Only folks who visit in the spring and early summer see the splendid sight for which Mirror Lake is named. By midsummer it's just Tenaya Creek and by fall the creek has sometimes dried up altogether. Spring is also marvelous because dogwoods are in full bloom and Tenaya Creek becomes a lively torrent as you venture further up the canyon. The Ahwahneechee called Mirror Lake *Ahwiyah*, meaning 'quiet water.' You can follow the easy **Mirror Lake Loop Trail** along Tenaya Creek and the lake. The full loop is about 5 miles.

Taking Guided Tours Through Yosemite Valley

BACKGROUND ON NATURAL SPLENDORS

One favorite for guided tours is **Echo Adventure Cooperative**, a worker-owned outdoor company based in Groveland, offering a variety of sightseeing, hiking and backpacking tours. It also has an outdoor gear store and guest lodgings. Another great company, **YExplore Yosemite Adventures**, offers custom tours with experienced local hiking guides based out of Sonora (it has extensive experience taking guests up the Half Dome cables). Based out of Oakhurst, **Crossroads Tours** does small-group tours in Jeeps, sprinter vans and even a small airplane. **Discover Yosemite Tours** operates bus tours year-round from Oakhurst, Fish Camp and Bass Lake, while **Yosemite 360 Tours** is based at Tenaya Lodge, a family-friendly resort in Fish Camp. The park-affiliated nonprofit **Yosemite Conservancy** offers multiday courses, custom trips and seminars that are great alternatives to tours. The **Sierra Club** has both paid trips and free activity outings sponsored by local chapters. And the park's concessionaire, **Aramark/**

PARK ENTRANCES

Arch Rock Entrance
Hwy 140 runs through the Merced River Canyon before entering Yosemite Valley on the western side of the park.

Big Oak Flat Entrance
Hwy 120 W runs east from Groveland through Stanislaus National Forest before entering the park on its west side.

South Entrance
The southern entrance to the park along Hwy 41 is just north of the town of Fish Camp and minutes to Mariposa Grove.

Tioga Pass Entrance
Hwy 120 E traverses the park as Tioga Rd, connecting Yosemite Valley with the Eastern Sierra.

WHERE TO EAT IN YOSEMITE VALLEY

Curry Village Pizza Deck
Enjoy tasty pizza at this revamped place that becomes a chatty après-hike hangout in the afternoons. **$**

Village Store
Best grocery store in the park is at Yosemite Village: produce, fish, meat and snacks. **$**

Bar 1899
Creative cocktails and bar bites menu of tater tots, artichoke dip and foraged brussels sprouts. **$$**

BEST HIKES FOR FAMILIES

Yosemite Valley Loops
Meander through the valley to admire the park's meadows, waterfalls and granite cliffs.

Mirror Lake
Approach the Half Dome base on this relaxing hike, crossing Tenaya Creek to Mirror Lake.

Vernal Fall
Climb a paved path through the woods in Yosemite Valley to a scenic footbridge below the fall.

Soda Springs
Cold water bubbles out of the ground in Tuolumne Meadows.

Mariposa Grove
Walk through the Tunnel Tree and admire the enormous sequoias near Wawona.

Yosemite Hospitality, runs bus and tram tours, including a wheelchair-accessible Valley Floor Tour.

Swimming & Water Sports

ENJOY LAKES AND A RIVER

On a hot summer day it's hard to beat a dip in the gentle Merced River in Yosemite Valley – but it will be cold! If you'd prefer something less chilly, you can pay to play in the scenic outdoor swimming pools at Curry Village and Yosemite Valley Lodge. With a sandy beach and amazing high country views, **Tenaya Lake**, along Tioga Rd, is a frigid but scenic option. Swimming is permitted in most bodies of water with a few exceptions noted on the park website. Do NOT swim above Vernal Fall – its current is deadly.

From around late May to July, floating along the **Merced River** from Stoneman Meadow, near Curry Village, to Sentinel Bridge, is a leisurely way to soak up Yosemite Valley views. You can rent rafts for the 3-mile trip at the concessionaire (typically in June and July) in Curry Village. Rentals include equipment and a shuttle ride back to the rental kiosk. Children must weigh over 50lbs (23kg). You can also bring your own raft and pay for a shuttle ride back ($5 per person).

Hiking Half Dome

LONG HIKE, EXTRAORDINARY VIEWS

Rising 4800ft above the eastern end of Yosemite Valley is **Half Dome**, the most glorious granite dome on earth and the park's most distinctive natural monument. Climbers come from around the world to scale its legendary north face, but hikers can tackle it too on a 16-mile round-trip hike from Happy Isles in Yosemite Valley. This bucket-list adventure comes with a 600ft climb up an exposed 45-degree rock face, where your only protection is its thick steel cables. The hike is grueling, exciting and potentially fatal.

The summit of this glacier-carved chunk of granite offers 360-degree views, and peering down its sheer 2000ft north face is a once-in-a-lifetime thrill. Advance permits, awarded by lottery, are required. Requiring a permit has helped with the crowds, but unless you get a crack-of-dawn start you'll still encounter people aplenty. This rigorous hike is best done over two days, but fit hikers can attempt it as a demanding 10- to 12-hour day hike. Hiking to the summit is only allowed when the protective cable route to the top has been installed on the rock face, typically between late May and mid-December.

WHERE TO WATCH CLIMBERS IN YOSEMITE VALLEY

El Capitan Meadow
Sit and scan El Cap, or ask questions at the nearby 'Ask a Climber' station (p79).

Swan Slab
On east side of Camp 4, watch how it's done on a low-angled practice area.

Lower Yosemite Falls Bridge
Look right for climbers ascending Sunnyside Bench, a cliff with good cracks and face climbs.

BILL MORSON/SHUTTERSTOCK ©

Merced River

Enjoy Big Views at Glacier Point

BREATHTAKING VALLEY PANORAMA

Glacier Point is the final stop on the 16-mile Glacier Point Rd. From its 7214ft-high perch, the eastern flank of Yosemite Valley spreads before you, from Yosemite Falls to Half Dome to the distant peaks that ring Tuolumne Meadows.

Half Dome itself looms practically at eye level, and if you look closely you can spy hikers on its summit. To the left of Half Dome lies the glacially carved Tenaya Canyon and to its right are the wavy white ribbons of Nevada and Vernal Falls. On the valley floor, the Merced River snakes through green meadows and groves of trees. At the railing, hold tight and peer 3200ft straight down at Curry Village. Overhang Rock is a huge granite slab protruding from the cliff edge at the tip of the point. Though off-limits today, it once provided a stage for daredevil extroverts, who'd perform handstands and high kicks on the rock.

Glacier Point has long been a popular destination, but for years getting here was a major undertaking. That changed once the Four-Mile Trail opened in 1872. A wagon road to the point was completed in 1872 and the current road was completed in 1936.

PEAKS & DOMES

During the Tioga glacial period, just 20,000 years ago, the massive Tuolumne Glacier, a 20,000ft-thick river of ice, coursed from the Sierra Crest through Tuolumne Meadows and completely filled Hetch Hetchy Valley. The contrasting shapes of peaks around Tuolumne are a record of this period – the smooth, dome-like peaks were worn down beneath the glacier while the sharp jagged summits of the Cathedral Range and Sierra Crest remained above the ice that quarried their slopes.

WHERE TO DAY-HIKE TO BIG VIEWS

Clouds Rest
Yosemite's largest expanse of granite, and arguably its finest viewpoit off Tioga Rd.

North Dome
Astounding views of Yosemite Valley, Half Dome and Tenaya Canyon from Tioga Rd trailhead.

Mt Dana
Hike to the top of park's second-highest peak (after Mt Lyell), from Tuolumne Meadows.

GILBERTO MESQUITA/SHUTTERSTOCK ©

California Tunnel Tree

BEST DAY HIKES

Vernal & Nevada Falls Loop (p76) Popular hike in Yosemite Valley with spectacular waterfalls (6.7 miles round trip).

Cathedral Lakes (p90) Hike to gorgeous subalpine lakes with numerous surrounding peaks (7 miles out-and-back).

Elizabeth Lake Steep but short hike (4.8 miles round trip) to superb subalpine lake beginning in Tuolumne Meadows.

Mono Pass Excellent moderate hike (7.4-mile round trip) into the high country near Tioga Pass.

Panorama Trail Connects Glacier Point with Nevada Fall, with 3200ft descent (8.5 miles one way).

The **Four-Mile Trail** climbs from the valley to Glacier Point. Hiking trails along Glacier Road lead to **Sentinel Dome** and its outstanding views of the valley as well as **Taft Point** and its hair-raising viewpoint on a near-vertical cliff. The road is typically open from early May through mid-December. When the road is open, you can also visit the lookout on the four-hour round-trip **Glacier Point bus tour**. One-way tickets are available if you want to hike back to the valley.

Feel Small in Mariposa Grove

GIANT SEQUOIAS, ELEGANT HOTEL, HISTORY

With their massive stature and multi-millennium maturity, the chunky high-rise sequoias of **Mariposa Grove** will make you feel insignificant. The largest grove of giant sequoias in the park, Mariposa is home to approximately 500 mature trees spread over 250 acres. Walking trails wind through this very popular grove, which is 27 miles south of Yosemite Valley. Follow the **Grizzly Giant Loop Trail** to the 3000-year-old **Grizzly Giant**, an enormous beast of a tree with branches that are bigger in circumference than most of the nearby pines. You'll want to walk through the **California Tunnel Tree** and

WHERE TO GET INFORMATION IN YOSEMITE NATIONAL PARK

Yosemite Valley Visitor Center (209-372-0200; Yosemite Village; 9am-5pm) Park's busiest information desk.

Yosemite Valley Wilderness Center (209-372-0745; Yosemite Village; 8am-5pm May-Oct) Permits, maps and advice.

Wawona Visitor Center (209-375-9531; Wawona; 8:30am-5pm May-Oct) In Thomas Hill studio. Issues wilderness permits.

view the **Wawona Tunnel Tree**, which fell in 1969 – its 10ft-high hole was gouged from a fire scar in 1881. You can usually have a more solitary experience if you come during the early evening in summer or anytime outside of summer. The free **Mariposa Grove shuttle** runs between the Mariposa Grove Welcome Plaza and the grove of trees, from about early April to the end of November.

Off Wawona Rd, about 6 miles north, you can explore the manicured grounds of the elegant **Wawona Hotel**. The Wawona area is the park's historical center and home to the park's first headquarters. The original Wawona Rd was completed in 1875 and kick-started tourism for the big trees and wondrous Yosemite Valley. Some of the park's oldest buildings were relocated to the **Yosemite History Center**, which also displays stagecoaches that carried tourists to the park.

Admire Tuolumne Meadows

ESCAPE CROWDS, HUNT FOR WILDFLOWERS

Dubbed a 'spacious and delightful high-pleasure ground' by naturalist John Muir, an early advocate for the park, the verdant **Tuolumne Meadows** are a subalpine dream: a High Sierra landscape of jagged peaks, glacier-polished granite domes, soaring lodgepine forests and alpine lakes that shimmer a dazzling translucent blue. The Lyell and Dana Forks of the Tuolumne River and several creeks drop from the surrounding Sierra Crest to feed the lush meadows, which are dotted with wildflowers for a few glorious months in summer and early autumn.

Bisected by Tioga Rd (Hwy 120), the meadows are about 55 miles north of Yosemite Valley and sit at an elevation of 8600ft. Roadside trails slingshot up the mountains and climb granite domes while gorgeous blue lakes are ready for picnics. The 200ft scramble to the top of **Pothole Dome** – presumably at sunset – gives great views of the meadows. The summit of **Lembert Dome** (p87) is another great overlook above the meadows.

Drive Tioga Road

SCENIC BYWAY, HIGH COUNTRY WONDERS

From Hwy 395 the Lee Vining Scenic Byway, or Hwy 120, shoots west from the chalky-white Great Basin desertscape and Mono Lake to the lush High Sierra in a mere 12 miles – while clinging to the flank of a steep mountain smothered in loose scree. In the morning, the enormous granite mountains flanking the road as it climbs **Lee Vining Canyon** glow a

HETCH HETCHY

In the park's northwest corner, Hetch Hetchy, which is Miwok for 'place of tall grass' gets the least amount of traffic, yet sports two of the highest **waterfalls** in the country: **Tueeeulala** and **Wapama**. Both are easily accessible and the latter flows year-round. The granite cliffs here rival their famous counterparts in Yosemite Valley. The main difference is the Hetch Hetchy Valley is now filled with water, following a long political and environmental battle in the early 20th century. The road to Hetch Hetchy is only open during the day.

Big Oak Flat Information Station
(209-372-0200; 8am-5pm late May-Oct) Has a wilderness permit desk.

Tuolumne Meadows Visitor Center
(209-372-0263; 9am-6pm Jun-Sep) Information desk, bookstore and small exhibits.

Tuolumne Meadows Wilderness Center
(209-372-0309; 8am-5pm late May–mid-Oct) Issues wilderness permits.

HIKING TRIP

Sentinel Dome & Taft Point

This 5.1-mile loop hike along Glacier Point Rd ribbons past two fantastic viewpoints: Sentinel Dome and Taft Point, with a compelling mix of scenery along the way. For those who can't get to Half Dome, Sentinel Dome offers an equally outstanding perspective on Yosemite's wonders. Taft Point serves up a hair-raising viewpoint at the edge of a sheer 4000ft vertical drop. This moderate hike should take about three hours.

1 Sentinel Dome & Taft Point Trailhead

From Hwy 41 (Wawona Rd) turn east onto Glacier Point Rd and drive 13 miles to the signed Sentinel Dome & Taft Point parking lot.

The Hike: Just beyond the parking lot, the trail divides. Take the right fork heading north toward Sentinel Dome. The left fork leads to Taft Point. You'll be looping back here at the end of the hike. Follow the gently rising trail through a mixed forest then walk across granite slabs dotted with manzanita pines. Reenter the forest then bend northwest to reach the shoulder of the dome. Ascend the gentle granite slope from the Glacier Point and Taft Point trail marker, reaching the summit at 1.1 miles.

BENNY MARTY/SHUTTERSTOCK ©

View from Sentinel Dome

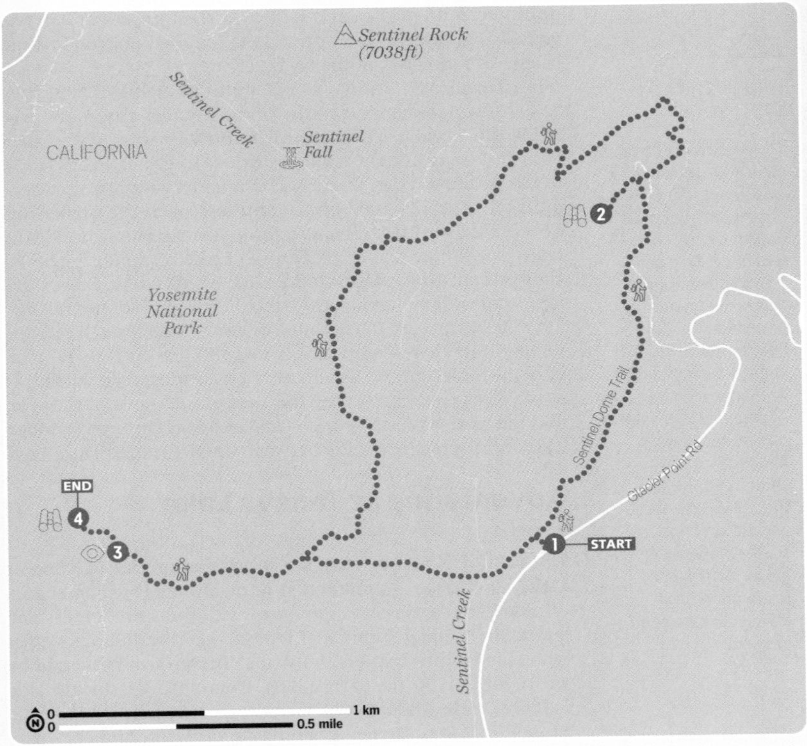

2 Sentinel Dome

The gnarled bleached bones of a Jeffrey pine crown the summit. Soak up the 360-degree views. To the west Cathedral Rock and El Capitan frame the Merced River and Yosemite Valley. Clouds Rest and Half Dome rise dramatically above Tenaya Canyon.

The Hike: Return to the trail sign for Glacier Point and Taft Point and bear left. Walk north descending 300ft toward a radio tower. At the trail junction at 1.8 miles, turn left onto the Pohono Trail. The near-level traverse ahead unfurls through a white-fir forest. You'll pass breathtaking views of the Merced River, lush meadows and Yosemite Falls. After two switchbacks on a soft, conifer-needle-covered stretch of trail, El Capitan is visible. The trail climbs through a mixed forest and joins the Taft Point Trail at about 3.7 miles. Follow the latter through a forest to a rocky slope.

3 The Fissures

Descend and continue past the fissures. These narrow, chimney-like slots drop hundreds of feet to Yosemite Valley.

The Hike: Continue across the rocks to the cliff's edge.

4 Taft Point

The sheer drop at Taft Point (7503ft) is guarded – in only one small area – by a dinky metal railing. Unless you have a profound fear of heights, approach and peer over the edge. The sheer drop is mind-boggling. Looking west through binoculars, you can spot climbers on El Capitan. Be careful near the ledge. People have fallen to their deaths.

The Hike: Return 1.1 miles on the forested Taft Point Trail to the parking lot.

HIGH SIERRA CAMPS

The High Sierra camps are a more relaxing way to experience the backcountry, as you don't have to carry a tent or cooking gear – hearty meals and accommodations are provided. There are five camps in the high country surrounding Tuolumne Meadows. Accommodations are canvas-tent cabins. The seasons are short (roughly June through September) and are very popular, so reservations are by lottery. For reservations visit travelyosemite.com/lodging.

luminous pink in the early light, but their grandeur can feel vaguely ominous – likely due to the harrowing drop lurking beside the shoulder of the road.

The Tioga Pass entrance to Yosemite sits at 9945ft, and Hwy 120 – now dubbed Tioga Rd – is the highest autoroute over the Sierra Nevada. **Tuolumne Meadows** is west of the Tioga Pass entrance. The short ride by car, or free shuttle bus (p75), to the meadows takes you across dramatic, wide open spaces – a stretch of stark windswept countryside near the timberline. Continuing west from the meadows, you can picnic beside the translucent blue waters of **Tenaya Lake** on smooth-granite shores then stop at **Olmsted Point**, which overlooks a stark landscape of glaciated rocks and glacier-carved monoliths.

If you've traveled here from Yosemite Valley, you'll feel the temperature drop – it's typically 15°F (8°C) to 20°F (11°C) cooler in the high country. You may even see widespread patches of snow. Heavy snowfalls keep the road closed most of the year, and the road is typically open from late May through October. Tioga Rd stretches 46 miles between Crane Flat and Tioga Pass.

Adventuring at Tenaya Lake

PICNIC, ROCK CLIMBING, CHILLY SWIM

Just east of Olmsted Point, the shiny blue surface of **Tenaya Lake** (8150ft) looks absolutely stunning framed by thick stands of pine and a series of smooth granite cliffs and domes. The lake takes its name from Chief Tenaya, the Ahwahneechee chief who aided white soldiers, only to be driven from the land by white militias in the early 1850s. Dominating its north side is Polly Dome (9806ft). The face nearest the lake is known as Stately Pleasure Dome, a popular spot with climbers – you may see them working their way up from the road. Sloping up from the lake's south shore are Tenaya Peak (10,266ft) and Tresidder Peak (10,600ft). Stop here for a picnic, canoeing and maybe even a very cold swim. The parking lot has accessible parking, an accessible vault toilet and an accessible path that leads to the lake.

Winter in Yosemite

SKIING, SNOWSHOEING AND PAGEANTRY

The white coat of winter opens up a different set of things to do, as the valley becomes a quiet, frosty world of snow-draped evergreens, ice-coated lakes and vivid vistas of gleaming white mountains sparkling against blue skies. Winter tends to arrive in full force by mid-November and winds up by mid-April. The gentle slopes of the **Badger Pass Ski Area**,

WHERE TO PULL OVER FOR INSPIRING VIEWS

Tunnel View
Offers the best all-around photo op of the valley at east end of Wawona Tunnel.

Olmsted Point
On Tioga Rd: a lunar landscape of glaciated granite and Tenaya Canyon.

Washburn Point
Magnificent view of the Clark Range from Glacier Point Rd; great warm-up for Glacier Point.

PHITHA TANPAIROJ/SHUTTERSTOCK ©

Tenaya Lake

about 22 miles from the valley on Glacier Point Rd are perfect for family and beginner skiers and snowboarders. More experienced skiers can trek 10 miles to the popular **Ostrander Lake Ski Hut** on Ostrander Lake. Operated by Yosemite Conservancy, the hut is staffed all winter and open to backcountry skiers and snowshoers on a lottery basis. There's also an **outdoor ice-skating rink** at Curry Village.

Yosemite's best known seasonal event is the **Bracebridge Dinner**, a traditional Christmas pageant in the Ahwahnee Hotel that's part grand feast and part Renaissance fair. After a multiyear closure during the pandemic and upgrades to the Ahwahnee, the dinners return in 2024.

Tackle Lembert Dome

DOME SCALING, LAKE ADMIRING

For a fun day of exploration and relaxation, with fine views in the mix, make your way to **Lembert Dome** and **Dog Lake** on Tioga Rd. From the trailhead at the Dog Lake parking lot, climb through lodgepole pines for about a half mile to a trail junction. Turn left and walk another half mile to the base of Lembert Dome. Continue west across the gently sloping granite until you see a small summit knob just ahead. Continue to a rise where you'll have sweeping views of the meadows

SLEEPING: CAMPING & LODGING

Reservations for the seven campgrounds within the park that aren't first-come, first-served are handled by recreation.gov, up to five months in advance. Competition for sites is fierce from May to September. Without a booking, your only chance is to hightail it to an open campground or proceed to one of four campground reservation offices in Yosemite Valley, Wawona, Big Oak Flat and Tuolumne Meadows.

Lodging reservations are handled by Aramark/Yosemite Hospitality (888-413-8869; travelyosemite.com) and can be made up to 366 days in advance; reservations are critical from May to early September. Rates – and demand – drop from October to April.

WHERE TO GET GAS

Wawona Chevron
Has high-priced gas, but it's the only option between Oakhurst and Yosemite Valley.

Crane Flat Gas Station
Located in northern end of park beside Tioga Rd, with 24-hour pumps. Sells grocery items.

Mobil
In Lee Vining about 12 miles east of the Tioga Pass Entrance Station.

John Muir Trail

and surrounding mountain ranges. To climb to the summit of the dome (9450ft), swing southwest and approach from the south, where there is a more gentle grade for hiking. From the top, the spectacular 360-degree view takes in the Cathedral Range to the south and Tuolumne Meadows to the west.

After returning to the trail junction, turn left and follow signage to Dog Lake (9170ft). This lovely subalpine lake will likely be busy, especially on weekends, but it's still a pretty place to relax. Return the way you came or follow signs that will loop you around the dome to the Lembert Dome parking lot. From there, cross Tioga Rd and walk east on the Pacific Coast and John Muir Trails to the Dog Lake parking lot. This loop is about 5 miles.

For a delicious post-hike reward, drive east 20 miles to the town of Lee Vining, taking in the vast beauty of **Lee Vining Scenic Byway** along the way. Pull into **Mono Cone** for a burger, fries and shake.

WITNESS THE FIREFALL

In February, the stunning natural phenomenon known as the Yosemite Firefall captivates park visitors. The firefall happens at sunset at **Horsetail Falls**, which tumbles over El Capitan's eastern edge in winter. During the magic hour, the falls resemble flowing lava; glowing yellow, orange and even red. It makes for an amazing video or photograph.

Horseback & Mule Rides

RIDE BENEATH SEQUOIAS

Most trails in Yosemite, except as noted on the park website, are open for horseback riding. The park's concessionaire, Yosemite Hospitality, runs two-hour guided horse and mule trips from the **Wawona Stable** from May through September, as well as all-day rides to Mariposa Grove. Riders must be at least seven years old, 52in (132cm) tall and weigh 52lb (24kg).

WHERE TO FISH

Merced River
Brown trout between Happy Isles and Foresta Bridge in El Portal and in Yosemite Valley.

Lyell Fork
In Yosemite's high country, find brown, rainbow and brook trout – and solitude – in Lyell Canyon.

Tuolumne River
The fish aren't big, but they're still out there. The setting is unbeatable.

Follow in John Muir's Footsteps

NATURALIST, CONSERVATIONIST, SIERRA NEVADA HIKER

John Muir immigrated from Scotland to the US with his father in 1849, and they settled in Wisconsin. After studying botany and geology at the University of Wisconsin, Muir began a lifelong journey through the wilds, and his travels took him all over the world. But more than anywhere else, Muir is synonymous with the Sierra Nevada.

On a weekend trip from San Francisco in the spring of 1868, Muir made his first trip to Yosemite Valley – and found his calling as a naturalist. The following year he returned to begin a monumental experiment in the observation of nature. He wandered, most often alone, into the highest realms of the Yosemite backcountry and explored the area between Yosemite Valley and Mt Whitney, where the 211-mile **John Muir Trail** now pays him tribute.

Though not a scientist by training, Muir looked at the natural world with a keen curiosity. From his prolific and florid writings on nature one might see him as a poet among naturalists, but over time his pen turned increasingly toward the political aims of the growing conservationist movement. Muir's articles and lobbying efforts were the foundation of the campaign that established Yosemite as a national park in 1890. Muir founded the Sierra Club in 1892 and devoted his life to defending California wilderness against the encroachments of dams and urbanization.

After backpacking with Muir in Yosemite in 1903, President Theodore Roosevelt was convinced to preserve additional sections of Yosemite as a national park. Yet despite Muir's passionate objections, Woodrow Wilson commissioned Hetch Hetchy Reservoir in 1913 to funnel water from Yosemite to the Bay Area. In drought-prone California, tensions between land developers and conservationists still run high.

Muir's namesake trail travels through three national parks – Yosemite, Kings Canyon, Sequoia – and offers what many consider to be the very best mountain hiking in the US. Uncrossed by any roads, it is a spectacular and pristine route through continental wilderness. It crosses 11 mountain passes, half of which are higher than 12,000ft and all but one of which are over 10,000ft. As it traverses the timberline country of the High Sierra, the trail passes thousands of lakes and numerous granite peaks between 13,000ft and 14,000ft and takes in the Sierra's highest peak, Mt Whitney.

In Yosemite you can follow the John Muir Trail to Vernal and Nevada Falls (p76) from Yosemite Valley. The trail also runs from Tioga Rd up to the Cathedral Lakes (p90). Tuolumne

DANGERS & ANNOYANCES

Landslides frequently close trails and paths get slippery after rains and flooding. Be mindful of surroundings when taking photos and selfies – there have been fatal accidents near big views in the park.

Avoid direct contact and exposure to animal droppings and never touch a dead animal. Avoid sleeping on the ground; use a cot, hammock, sleeping bag or other surface. Follow park rules on proper food storage and use bear-proof food lockers when parked overnight.

Mountain lion sightings are uncommon, but if you see one, do not run; rather, attempt to scare it away by shouting and waving your arms. Do the same for coyotes, which are more common. Report sightings to park dispatch (209-372-0476).

WHERE TO PICNIC NEAR TUOLUMNE MEADOWS

Lembert Dome
Adventurous picnickers hike to the top of this granite dome for views of Tuolumne Meadows.

Tenaya Lake
Numerous picnicking spots dot this scenic lake, from parking lot to the north shore beachfront.

Olmsted Point
Spread out over glaciated granite with views of Half Dome, Clouds Rest and Tenaya Canyon.

HIKING TRIP

Cathedral Lakes

Easily one of Yosemite's most spectacular hikes, this steady climb through mixed coniferous forest ends with glorious views of Cathedral Peak from the shores of two shimmering alpine lakes. Although it's only about two hours to the lower lake, you could easily spend an entire day exploring the granite slopes, meadows and peaks surrounding it. This moderate round-trip walk, including the stop at Upper Cathedral Lake, is 7 miles.

1 Cathedral Lakes Trailhead

This hike starts at a trailhead on the south-side of Hwy 120 (Tioga Rd), 1.7 miles west of Tuolumne Meadows Visitor Center. Parking for the Cathedral Lakes trailhead is along the shoulder of Tioga Rd, 0.5 miles west of Tuolumne Meadows Visitor Center. Due to the popularity of this hike, parking spaces fill up fast, so arrive early or take the free shuttle. Bring a jacket, because winds at the lower lake keep temperatures a bit cool.

The Hike: The trail heads southwest along the John Muir Trail, rising steadily through lodgepole pines, mountain hemlock and the occasional white-bark pine for the first half mile then levels out. A massive slab of granite – the northern flank of Cathedral Peak – slopes up from the left side of the trail. You'll soon see Fairview Dome through the trees to your right.

EVER GONZALEZ/SHUTTERSTOCK ©

Cathedral Peak

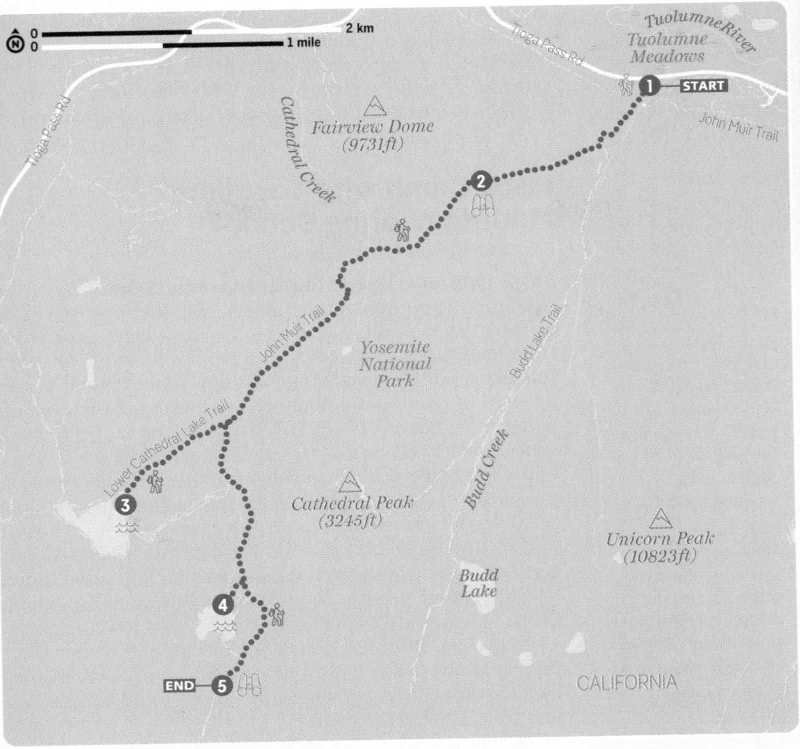

2 Views of Cathedral Peak

Before long the trail begins its second ascent, climbing nearly 600ft. It again levels off and you'll soon reach outstanding views of Cathedral Peak, which rises to 10,911ft.

The Hike: The trail becomes a pleasant forest stroll as traffic noise disappears and quiet descends. Turn right at the trail junction at 2.8 miles. Walk a half mile then bend right to cut through a vast meadow.

3 Lower Cathedral Lake

You'll emerge to a gorgeous glacial bowl, or cirque, at 9289ft, with the pointed spire of Cathedral Peak at your back and the lake glistening before you. Take a seat on a rock to admire the subalpine beauty then walk along the lake's edge for the perfect view of the peak.

The Hike: Return to the junction and turn right to continue south on the John Muir Trail. Continue about a half mile then look for an unmarked side trail on your right. Follow it a short distance.

4 Upper Cathedral Lake

The smaller of the two lakes, this tranquil subalpine jewel sits at 9585ft. The east aspect offers impressive views of the craggy Echo Peaks.

The Hike: Return to the John Muir Trail. Cap off the day by walking another half mile south.

5 Cathedral Pass

Stop to admire the high country's beauty from Cathedral Pass (9700ft), which offers stunning views of the Cathedral Range.

The Hike: Return to Tioga Rd trailhead. Note that mileage can easily bump up a mile or two if you explore the shores of the lakes.

BEST HIGH COUNTRY DOMES

North Dome
Perhaps the best vantage point along Yosemite Valley's rim and Half Dome, this dome sees relatively few hikers.

Sentinel Dome
Unable to visit Half Dome's summit? Sentinel offers an equally outstanding 360-degree perspective of Yosemite's wonders.

Pothole Dome
At the west end of Tuolumne Meadows, with a 200ft climb to the top, offering great views of surrounding meadows and peaks.

Lembert Dome
Easily one of Yosemite's finest places to watch the sunset, with a steep western face.

Meadows was a favorite spot of Muir's and he called it a 'spacious and delightful high-pleasure ground.'

The trail frequently descends from the Sierra Crest into forested areas of the western Sierra, with 5000ft-deep canyons. Visit the Pacific Crest Trail Association website (pcta.org) for more information.

Rock Climb with Yosemite Mountaineering School

KIDS AND BEGINNERS WELCOME

Since 1969 **Yosemite Mountaineering School** has been teaching and guiding rock climbers, mountaineers and backcountry skiers of all levels. While you can learn everything from basic backpacking skills to building a snow cave, the school's specialty is teaching folks how to move their bodies up slabs of granite. Whether you're a 12-year-old who wants to learn the basics of climbing, belaying and rappelling or a sport climber who wants to learn the art of big walls, you'll find this school a gold mine of opportunity. Beginners over the age of 12 can sign up for the **Welcome to the Rock** seminar ($195 per person), which is pretty much guaranteed to inspire participants to go on for more. For parents, it's a great and constructive way to turn the kids loose for a day. Beginners who are 10 and 11, with a supervising adult, can also sign up. Private lessons are available for those under 10 years of age.

Other class offerings include anchoring and crack climbing, for which Yosemite is famous. You can even create your own custom-climbing trip or hire guides to take you climbing (from $205 per person).

The school is based out of the **Yosemite Mountain Shop in Curry Village** from April through November; it relocates to the **Badger Pass Nordic Center** in winter. The friendly and knowledgeable staff will offer suggestions based on your skill level and objectives. The school can be reached at 209-372-8344 or at yms@aamark.com.

GETTING AROUND

Yosemite is accessible year-round from the west (via Hwys 120 W and 140) and south (Hwy 41), and in summer from the east (via Hwy 120 E). Roads are plowed in winter, but snow chains may be required at any time. Rock slides have periodically shut down sections of road for weeks or months at a time.

Yosemite is one of the few parks that can be easily reached by public transportation. Greyhound buses and Amtrak trains serve Merced, west of the park, where they are met by buses operated by Yosemite Area Regional Transportation System (YARTS).

Within the park, free shuttle buses (p75) operate year-round in Yosemite Valley and seasonally in Tuolumne Meadows (usually mid-June to early September) and Mariposa Grove (early April to November). Fee-based hiker buses run seasonally between Yosemite Valley and Tuolumne Meadows and between the valley and Glacier Point (p75). It's easy to explore the valley by bike on its 12 miles of paved trails.

REDWOOD NATIONAL PARK

Hidden away in the upper reaches of California's northwestern Pacific coast, Redwood National Park encompasses some of the world's tallest and most ancient trees, along with a luxuriantly verdant mix of coastal, riverine and prairie wild lands. Its massive stands of old-growth California coastal redwoods *(Sequoia sempervirens)*, draped in moss and ferns and towering up to 379ft tall, are managed in conjunction with three neighboring state parks – Prairie Creek Redwoods, Del Norte Coast Redwoods and Jedediah Smith Redwoods State Park (the latter famed as a backdrop in the *Return of the Jedi* movie).

Collectively the parks constitute an International Biosphere Reserve and World Heritage Site, yet they remain little visited compared to their southern brethren such as Sequoia National Park. It's worth contemplating that some of the trees standing here predate the Roman Empire by more than 500 years. Prepare to be impressed.

DANITA DELIMONT/SHUTTERSTOCK ©

Prairie Creek Redwoods State Park (p96)

FACTS

Great For Family travel, wildlife, walking
State California
Entrance Fee Free
Area 172 sq miles

SCENIC DRIVES

If you're unable to explore the park on foot (and even if you are), you can see a whole lot without leaving your vehicle. Just north of Orick is the turnoff for the 8-mile **Newton B Drury Scenic Parkway**, which runs parallel to Hwy 101 through untouched ancient redwood forests. This is a not-to-miss short detour off the freeway.

Just south of the Klamath River, off Hwy 101, is the scenic **Coastal Drive Loop**, a narrow, winding country road that traces extremely high cliffs over the ocean for six photogenic miles. Sections of the loop are one way, so do it in a clockwise direction.

SIGHTS
1 Del Norte Coast Redwoods State Park
2 Jedediah Smith Redwoods State Park
3 Prairie Creek Redwoods State Park

ACTIVITIES, COURSES & TOURS
4 Fern Canyon
5 James Irvine-Miner's Ridge Loop
6 Lady Bird Johnson Grove
7 Rhododendron Trail
8 Tall Trees Grove
9 Trillium Falls

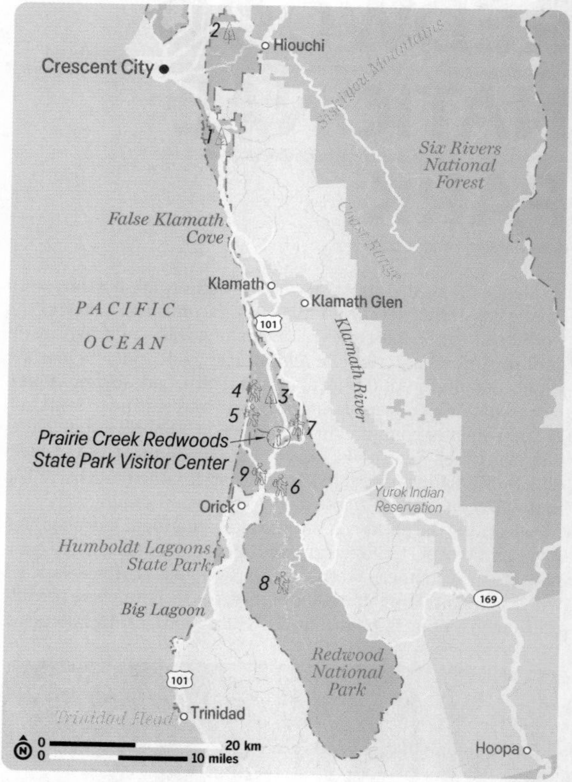

Walk Amid Tall Trees

HIKE AWAY FROM THE CROWDS

Redwoods is a fabulous hiking destination. Pick up a map at the Thomas H Kuchel Visitor Center and start with something easy. A few miles north along Hwy 101, a trip inland on Bald Hills Rd will take you to **Lady Bird Johnson Grove**, with its 1-mile, kid-friendly loop trail, or get you lost in the secluded serenity of **Tall Trees Grove**.

To protect the Tall Trees Grove, a limited number of cars per day are allowed access; get permits at the visitor center in Orick. This can be a half-day trip in itself, but you're well rewarded after the challenging approach (a 6-mile ramble on an old logging road behind a locked gate, then a moderately

WHERE TO STAY IN REDWOOD NATIONAL PARK

Elk Prairie Campground
Elk roam this campground with sites under redwoods (book sites 20 to 25) or at the prairie's edge. **$**

Gold Bluffs Beach
Gorgeous campground set between 100ft cliffs and wide-open ocean, with windbreaks and solar-heated showers. **$**

Jedediah Smith Campground
West of Hiouchi Information Center, this place has gorgeous sites tucked through the redwoods beside Smith River. **$**

strenuous 4-mile round-trip hike). Another recommended hike is to **Trillium Falls** – a 2.5-mile trail leading to a small waterfall, accessed from Davison Rd at Elk Meadow.

Note that during the winter, several footbridges crossing Redwood Creek are removed due to the high waters. If you are hiking at this time of year, be sure to check with a ranger regarding the current situation before striding out.

The park's network of other trails passes through a variety of landscapes, offering hiking experiences for all fitness levels. Most popular is the 0.7-mile loop into **Fern Canyon** along a creekside path framed by fern-covered cliff faces. The 6.3-mile **Rhododendron Trail** is especially scenic between mid-May and early June when flamboyant pink and red rhododendrons tower as high as 35ft above the trail.

Giants of Sea & Land

WATCH ELK AND WHALES

Wildlife-watching opportunities abound in Redwood National Park. One key attraction is the park's resident population of **Roosevelt elk**, which can be seen grazing in the prairie lands at the heart of Prairie Creek Redwoods and along the coast near Gold Bluffs Beach. The males are especially impressive from late summer into the fall, when they sport massive antlers for the rutting season.

The mouth of the Klamath River is a dramatic sight. Marine, riparian, forest and meadow ecological zones all converge and the **birding** is exceptional. For the best views, head north of town to Requa Rd and the Klamath River Overlook and picnic on high bluffs above driftwood-strewn beaches. On a clear day, this is one of the most spectacular viewpoints on the North Coast, and one of the best **whale-watching** spots in California. Your best chances of seeing California gray whales are from December to March, while humpback whale sightings usually occur from August to October.

Kayak the Smith River

TAKE TO THE WATER

The Smith River, part of America's National Wild and Scenic River system, runs through pristine scenery in the park's northern reaches. There are some exceptional kayaking opportunities here. In summer, park rangers lead half-day trips along a 3.5-mile, Class I and II section of the river, which includes minor rapids interspersed with moving flat water. During the rainy season (December through April), independent boaters can pit their skills against more challenging rapids, rated up to Class V.

JEDEDIAH SMITH REDWOODS STATE PARK

Part of the overall network of Redwoods protected areas, the northernmost park, Jedediah Smith, is 9 miles northeast of Crescent City (via Hwy 101 north to Hwy 199 east). The redwood stands are so thick that few trails penetrate the park, but the outstanding 11-mile Howland Hill Rd scenic drive cuts through otherwise inaccessible areas (take Hwy 199 to South Fork Rd; turn right after crossing two bridges). It's a rough road, impassable to RVs, but if you can't hike, it's the best way to see the forest. Stop for a half-mile stroll under enormous trees in Simpson-Reed Grove. There's a swimming hole and picnic area at the campground. Jedediah Smith doubled as the planet Endor in the film *Return of the Jedi*.

Hiouchi Motel
This renovated motel offers clean, straightforward rooms, with friendly, obliging owners. **$**

Mill Creek Campground
Right on Mill Creek, this excellent campsite has 145 sites for tents and RVs, as well as firepits and restrooms. **$**

Elk Meadow Cabins
These cabins with kitchens and mod-cons are in a perfect mid-parks location. Expect to see elk in the mornings. **$$**

LOCAL TOUR OPERATORS

Redwood Adventures
For hiking, kayaking, fishing or other tours, Orick-based Redwood Adventures (redwood adventures.com) has knowledgeable guides who will take you to places you may not otherwise find.

Redwood Creek Bukarettes
Guided horseback rides through the redwoods range from 1½ hours to 2¼ hours, with plenty of interpretive information along the way.

Klamath Jet Boat Tours
Book jet-boat excursions and fishing trips run by the Yukon people.

Explore Prairie Creek Redwoods State Park

A SPECTACULAR MOVIE SET

Famous for some of the world's best virgin redwood groves and unspoiled coastline, the Prairie Creek Redwoods State Park, a 14,000-acre section of Redwood National and State Parks, has spectacular scenic drives and 75 miles of mainly shady hiking trails, many of which are excellent for children. Kids of all ages will enjoy the magnificent herd of elk here, which can generally be spied grazing at the Elk Prairie, sign-posted from the highway – the best times to be sure of seeing the elk are early morning and around sunset.

There are 32 mountain-biking and hiking trails through the park, from simple to strenuous. A few easy nature trails start near the visitor center, including **Revelation Trail**, **Elk Prairie Trail** and **Prairie Creek Trail**. You can also stroll the reforested logging road on the **Ah-Pah Interpretive Trail** at the park's northern end. The most rewarding hike is a spectacular 12-mile loop from the visitor center following the **James Irvine Trail** to Fern Canyon and Gold Bluffs Beach. Return on **Miner's Ridge Trail**, rising from the Pacific Ocean coast into primordial redwoods.

Unpaved Davison Rd provides access to the park's only fee area ($8 per car). Just past the Gold Bluffs Beach Campground the severely potholed road dead-ends at **Fern Canyon**, the second-busiest spot in the park, where 60ft-high, fern-covered, sheer rock walls are so unusual that they were used in scenes from Steven Spielberg's *Jurassic Park 2: The Lost World*. This is one of the most photographed spots on the North Coast – damp and lush, all emerald green – and totally worth getting your toes wet to see on the 1-mile loop trail.

Hike, Drive & Ride Del Norte

DISCOVER REDWOODS AND A WILD COAST

Marked by steep canyons and dense woods north of Klamath, **Del Norte Coast Redwoods State Park** contains 15 miles of hiking trails and several old logging roads that are a mountain biker's dream. Many routes pass by branches of Mill Creek (bring your fishing rod). The park also fronts 8 miles of rugged coastline.

Highway 1 winds in from the coast at dramatic **Wilson Beach** and traverses the dense forest, with groves stretching as far as you can see. Picnic on the sand at False Klamath Cove. Heading north, tall trees cling precipitously to canyon walls that drop to the rocky, timber-strewn coastline.

WHERE TO STAY IN KLAMATH

Flint Ridge Campground
Four miles from the Klamath River Bridge, this tent-only, hike-in campground sits in a wild, overgrown meadow. **$**

Ravenwood Motel
Spotlessly clean rooms are individually decorated with furnishings and flair; it's friendly and great value. **$**

Historic Requa Inn
On bluffs overlooking the Klamath River, the creaky 1914 inn is a favorite, with a carbon-neutral commitment. **$$**

Damnation Creek Trail

Serious hikers will be most rewarded by the **Damnation Creek Trail**. It's only 4.2 miles round trip, but the 1100ft elevation change and cliff-side redwoods make it the park's best hike. The unmarked trailhead is at a parking area off Hwy 101 at Mile 16. Don't worry about signs warning of a broken bridge near the end of the trail; the tiny creek it traverses is easily crossed any time of the year.

At the park's northern end, watch the surf pound at **Crescent Beach**, just south of Crescent City via Enderts Beach Rd. **Crescent Beach Overlook** and picnic area has superb wintertime whale-watching.

VISITOR CENTERS

Hiouchi Information Center
A very useful center (nps.gov/redw) for anyone planning to explore the area, offering maps, directions and plenty of additional information.

Prairie Creek Redwoods State Park Visitor Center
Pick up maps and information and sit by the river-rock fireplace at this state park visitor center (parks.ca.gov). Outside, elk roam grassy meadows.

Thomas H Kuchel Visitor Center
On Hwy 101, 1 mile south of tiny Orick, this beachside visitor center offers ranger talks, tide-pool walks and beach access.

GETTING AROUND

Redwood National Park is most easily reached (and explored) with your own vehicle. The park's attractions are scattered along a 60-mile stretch of Hwy 101 and Hwy 199 between Orick and Gasquet.

Public transport is limited: Monday through Saturday, Redwood Coast Transit bus 20 passes through the park three times daily on its run from Crescent City to Arcata. There are scheduled stops at Klamath, Prairie Creek Redwoods State Park and the national park office in Orick – on request, drivers may drop passengers at other park locations.

Humboldt County Airport in McKinleyville (28 miles south of Orick) is the closest commercial airport.

CHANNEL ISLANDS NATIONAL PARK

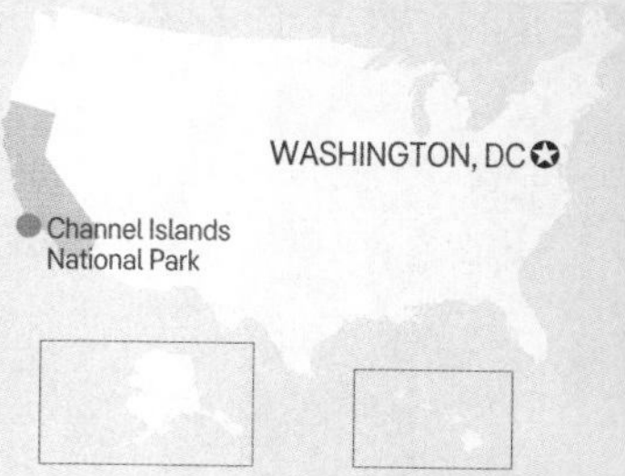

Don't let this off-the-beaten-path national park loiter for too long on your lifetime to-do list. It's easier to access than you might think, and the payoff is immense. Imagine hiking, kayaking, scuba diving, camping and whale-watching, all amid a raw, edge-of-the-world landscape. Rich in unique flora and fauna, tide pools and kelp forests, the islands are home to 145 plant and animal species found nowhere else in the world, earning them the nickname 'California's Galápagos.'

The Channel Islands is an eight-island chain lying off the coast from Newport Beach to Santa Barbara. The four northern islands – San Miguel, Santa Rosa, Santa Cruz and Anacapa – along with tiny southern Santa Barbara make up Channel Islands National Park. There are extensive tide pools and kelp forests, and one of the highest number of endemic plants anywhere in the US national park system. Access is by boat from Ventura or Oxnard.

FACTS

Great For Wildlife, scenery, photo ops
State California
Entrance Fee Free
Area 390 sq miles

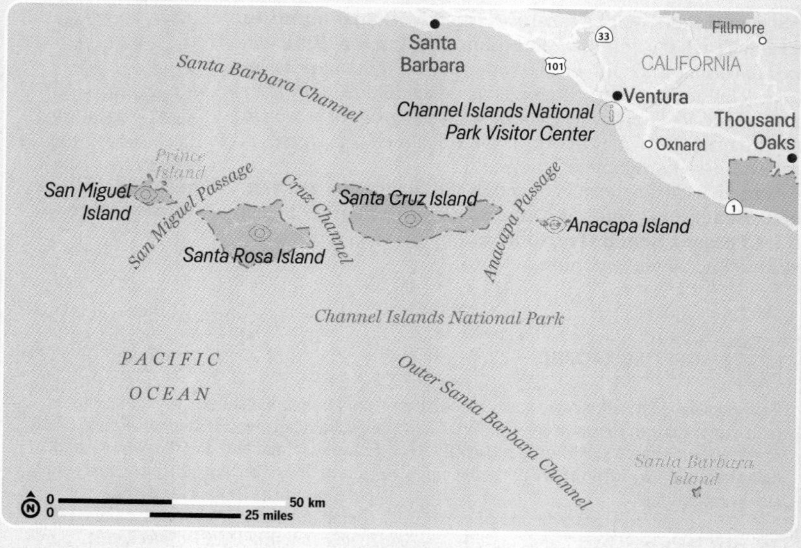

Sea lions, Anacapa Island

Explore the Islands by Boat

GO ON A BOAT TOUR

Anacapa and Santa Cruz, the park's most popular islands, are within an hour's boat ride of Ventura. Both are doable day trips, though much larger Santa Cruz is a good overnight camping option. Bring plenty of water, because none is available on either island except at Scorpion Campground on Santa Cruz. Before you cast off from the mainland, stop by Ventura Harbor's National Park Service visitor center for educational natural-history exhibits, a free 25-minute nature film and, on weekends and holidays, family-friendly activities and ranger talks.

Actually three separate islets totaling just over 1 sq mile, **Anacapa Island** gives a memorable introduction to the Channel Islands' ecology. It's also the best option if you're short on time. Boats dock year-round on the East Island, where, after a short climb, you'll find 2 miles of trails offering fantastic views of island flora, a historic lighthouse and rocky Middle and West Islands. You're bound to see western gulls, too – the world's largest breeding colony is here.

Kayaking, diving, tide-pooling and watching seals and sea lions are popular outdoor activities, while inside the museum

ISLAND OF THE BLUE DOLPHINS

For bedtime reading around the campfire, pick up Scott O'Dell's Newbery Medal-winning *Island of the Blue Dolphins*. This young-adult novel was inspired by the true-life story of Juana Maria, a woman from the Nicoleño tribe who was left behind on San Nicolas Island during the early 19th century, when her people were forced off the Channel Islands. Incredibly, Juana Maria survived mostly alone on the island for 18 years, before being discovered and brought to the mainland by a hunter in 1853. However, fate was not on her side, and she died just seven weeks later.

WHERE TO STAY IN CHANNEL ISLANDS & SANTA BARBARA

National Park Campgrounds
Each island has a year-round campground with pit toilets and picnic tables. Bring your own water and reserve in advance. **$**

Santa Barbara Auto Camp
Ramp up the retro chic, bedding down with vintage style in one of six shiny silver Airstream trailers. **$$**

Agave Inn
Mexican pop meets modern with a Frida Kahlo painting, flat-screen TVs and other mod cons. **$$**

CHANNEL ISLANDS NATIONAL PARK INFORMATION

Channel Islands National Park Visitor Center
Trip-planning information, books and maps are available on the mainland at the far end of Ventura Harbor. A free 25-minute video, *A Treasure in the Sea*, gives some background on the islands, and weekends and holidays see free ranger-led tide-pool talks at the center at 11am and 3pm.

National Park Website
Other than this guide, there's no better planning tool for Channel Islands National Park than a visit to nps.gov/chis. Apart from detailed information about each of the park's islands and activities, it also details closures and extreme weather updates.

NATALIEJEAN/SHUTTERSTOCK ©

Scorpion Canyon Loop

at the small visitor center, divers with video cameras occasionally broadcast images to a TV monitor you can watch during spring and summer.

Santa Cruz Island, the Channel Islands' largest at 96 sq miles, claims two mountain ranges and the park's tallest peak, Mt Diablo (2450ft). The western three-quarters is mostly wilderness, managed by the Nature Conservancy and only accessible with a permit (nature.org/cruzpermit). The rest, managed by the NPS, is ideal for an action-packed day trip or laid-back overnight stay. Boats land at either Prisoners Harbor or Scorpion Anchorage, a short walk from historic Scorpion Ranch.

You can swim, snorkel, dive and kayak here, and there are plenty of hiking options too, starting from Scorpion Anchorage. It's a 1-mile climb to captivating Cavern Point. Views don't get much better than from this windy spot. For a longer jaunt, continue 1.5 miles west, along the North Bluff Trail, to Potato Harbor. The 4.5-mile Scorpion Canyon Loop heads uphill to an old oil well and fantastic views, then drops through Scorpion Canyon to the campground. Alternatively, follow Smugglers Rd all the way to the pebble beach at Smugglers Cove, a strenuous 7.5-mile round trip. From Prisoners Harbor, there are several more strenuous trails, including the 18-mile round-

BOUTIQUE HOTELS IN SANTA BARBARA

Hotel Californian
Beachside Hotel Californian is a winning architectural mix of Spanish Colonial and North African Moorish styles. **$$$**

Pacific Crest Hotel
Remodeled rooms at this family-run motel are spotless, spacious and come in cool, neutral tones for a soothing retreat. **$$$**

Spanish Garden Inn
Casual elegance, first-rate service, a central courtyard and luxury balconied rooms make this feel like a private villa. **$$$**

trip China Pines hike – your efforts will be rewarded by the chance to see the rare Bishop pine.

There's little shade on the island, so avoid midday summer walks and bring plenty of water (available at Scorpion Anchorage only). Make sure you're at the harbor in plenty of time to catch your return boat, otherwise you'll be stuck overnight.

If you're looking for a quieter island experience, look no further than **San Miguel**. While this 14-sq-mile island can guarantee solitude and a remote wilderness experience, its westernmost location in the Channel Islands chain means it's often windy and shrouded in fog. Some sections are off-limits to protect the island's fragile ecosystem, which includes a caliche forest (hardened calcium-carbonate castings of trees and vegetation) and seasonal colonies of seals and sea lions. Peregrine falcons have been reintroduced, and some of the Chumash archaeological sites date back almost 12,000 years.

Speaking of the Indigenous Chumash people, they called the island of **Santa Rosa** 'Wima' (driftwood) because of the redwood logs that often came ashore here, which they used to built plank canoes called *tomols*. Evidence of prehistoric life on Santa Rosa comes in the form of thousands of Chumash sites, dating back some 13,000 years, while the most complete skeleton of the ancient, extinct pygmy mammoth was found here in 1994.

This 84-sq-mile island has rare Torrey pines, sandy beaches and hundreds of plant and bird species. Beach, canyon and grasslands hiking trails abound, but high winds can make swimming, diving and kayaking tough for anyone but experts.

Both San Miguel and Santa Rosa can be accessed by Island Packers boat services from Ventura on the mainland.

CHANNEL CROSSINGS: BE PREPARED

The open seas on the boat ride out to the Channel Islands may feel choppy to landlubbers. To avoid seasickness, sit outside on the lower deck, keep away from the diesel fumes in the back and focus your vision on the horizon. The outbound trip is typically against the wind and a bit bumpier than the return. Over-the-counter motion-sickness pills (eg Dramamine) can make you drowsy. Boats usually brake when dolphins or whales are spotted – always a welcome distraction from any nausea.

Scenic Flights, Kayaks & More

TAKE A GUIDED TOUR

There's so much to do in the Channel Islands that it can be difficult to know where to begin. Why not start with a scenic flight and look down on it all from above? In fact, the only way to get to the Channel Islands without sailing is on a flight with **Wingly** (wingly.io), and this functional purpose can be combined with a joy flight. Wingly offers day trips to Santa Rosa and San Miguel, plus overnight camping from its base in Camarillo.

Having taken it all in from on high, it's time for you now to hit the water. **Channel Islands Kayak Center** (cikayak.com) rents out kayaks and SUPs, although the latter are restricted to use in the harbor. The center can also arrange a private guided kayaking tour of Santa Cruz or Anacapa Island.

WHERE TO EAT IN VENTURA

Beach House Tacos
Varied tacos, a fine location on Ventura Pier with beach and Channel Island views, and a brewery next door. Bliss. $

Paradise Pantry
Grab a sandwich, soup or cheese or meat plate in the cafe, or supplies from the deli for a Channel Island picnic. $

Lure Fish House
Go nuts ordering sustainably caught seafood, organic regional farm produce and Californian wines. $$$

PARADISE LOST & FOUND

Human beings have left a heavy footprint on the Channel Islands. Erosion was caused by the overgrazing of livestock, and rabbits fed on native plants. The US military even used San Miguel as a practice bombing range. In 1969 an offshore oil spill engulfed the northern islands in an 800-sq-mile slick, killing thousands of seabirds and mammals. Meanwhile, deep-sea fishing has caused the destruction of three-quarters of the islands' kelp forests, which are key to the marine ecosystem.

Despite this, brown pelicans – reduced to one surviving chick in 1970 – are now off the endangered list, with healthy populations on West Anacapa and Santa Barbara islands. On San Miguel Island, native vegetation has also returned a half-century after overgrazing sheep were removed.

BRIAN SWANSON/SHUTTERSTOCK ©

Kayaking, Santa Cruz Island (p100)

Island Packers Cruises (islandpackers.com) may be the main boat operator for exploring the islands of Anacapa or Santa Cruz, but it also offers kayak rental. Ask also about its seasonal wildlife cruises, which include whale-watching trips from late December to mid-April (gray whales) and mid-May through mid-September (blue and humpback whales). Another wildlife highlight is the island of **Santa Barbara**. Only 1 sq mile in area, it's the smallest of the islands, but is a jewel box for nature lovers. Big, blooming coreopsis, cream cups and chicory are just a few of the island's memorable plant species. You'll also find the humongous northern elephant seal here, as well as Scripps's murrelet, a bird that nests in cliff crevices. For more information, visit nps.gov/chis/planyourvisit/santa-barbara-island.htm.

For wildlife of a different kind, certified and experienced divers can head out with **Raptor Dive Charters** (raptordive.com) for some underwater action, including night dives, off Anacapa and Santa Cruz islands. Equipment can be rented for a surcharge, and plenty of snacks, sandwiches and drinks are available on board.

GETTING AROUND

Island Packers offers regularly scheduled boat services to all the islands, mostly from Ventura, but with a few sailings from Oxnard. Anacapa and Santa Cruz are closer to the mainland and so less expensive to visit than other islands. Day trips are possible; overnight campers pay an additional surcharge. Be forewarned: if you do camp and seas are rough the following day, you could get stuck for an extra night or more.

JOSHUA TREE NATIONAL PARK

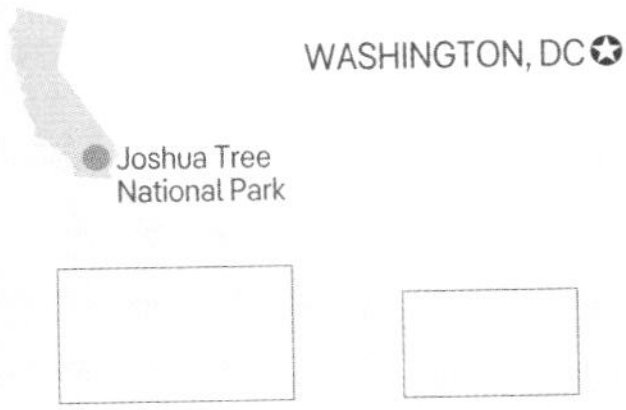

Looking like something from a Dr Seuss book, the whimsical Joshua trees welcome visitors to this 794,000-acre national park right where the low and dry Colorado Desert bumps into the higher, moister and cooler Mojave Desert. Rock climbers know 'JTree' as the best place to climb in California, hikers are hypnotized by desert vistas and hidden fan-palm oases, and mountain bikers find solitude on dusty back roads.

The mystical quality of this stark, boulder-strewn landscape has inspired many artists and musicians, including U2's 1987 *Joshua Tree* album. More recently, communities along the park's northern perimeter – Yucca Valley, Joshua Tree and Twentynine Palms – have drawn a wave of city slickers keen to ditch go-go for slo-mo under starry desert skies. The town of Joshua Tree, in particular, is a hub of creativity with a plethora of galleries, live-music venues, quirky boutiques, a coffee roastery and artistic lodging options.

FACTS

Great For Hiking, wildlife, scenery
State California
Entrance Fee 7-day pass per car/motorcycle/person on foot or bike $30/25/15
Area 1235 sq miles

FOTIMAGEON/SHUTTERSTOCK ©

Joshua Tree National Park

WHAT IS A JOSHUA TREE?

Only found in the Mojave Desert, the Joshua tree (*Yucca brevifolia*) is one of America's best known botanical forms. It is a member of the agave family and easily recognized by its prickly branches reaching towards the sky. It was Mormon settlers who named the whimsical plant, which reminded them of the biblical prophet Joshua pointing the way to the promised land. If conditions are right, the Joshua trees send up a huge single cream-colored flower in springtime.

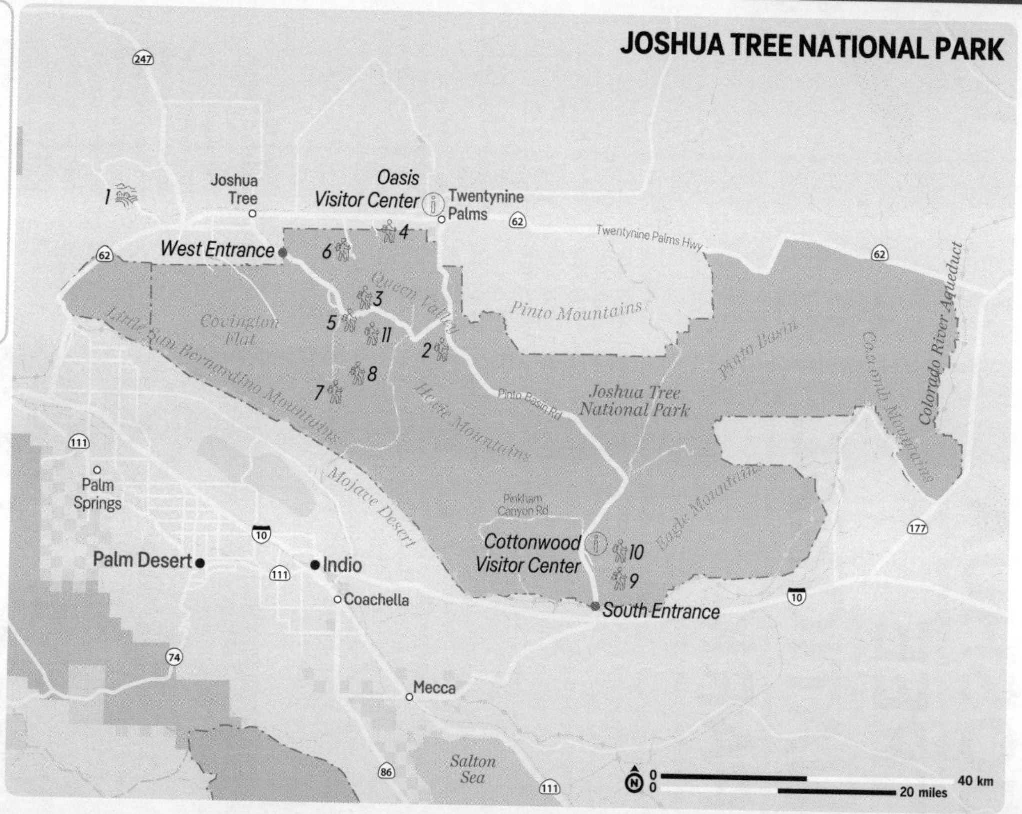

SIGHTS
1 Pioneertown

ACTIVITIES, COURSES & TOURS
2 Arch Rock Nature Trail
3 Barker Dam Loop Trail
4 Fortynine Palms Oasis Trail
5 Hidden Valley Trail
6 Indian Cove Trail
7 Inspiration Peak (Keys View) Trail
8 Lost Horse Mine Trail
9 Lost Palms Oasis Trail
10 Mastodon Peak Trail
11 Ryan Mountain Trail

Arch Rock Nature Trail
ANASTASIA _ PHOTOGRAPHY/SHUTTERSTOCK ©

Cycle the Best of Joshua Tree

EXPLORE ON TWO WHEELS

There's no better way to see the park than on two wheels, under your own steam.

Popular routes include the challenging 20-mile **Pinkham Canyon Rd** starting south of the Cottonwood visitor center and the long-distance **Black Eagle Mine Rd**, which begins 6.5 miles further north. **Queen Valley** has a gentler set of trails with bike racks found along the way, so you can lock up and go hiking. It tends to be busy with cars, though, as is the bumpy, sandy and steep **Geology Tour Rd**. There's also a wide-open network of dirt roads around **Covington Flat**.

Bikes are only allowed on public paved and backcountry roads that are also open to vehicles. They are not permitted on hiking trails.

Easy Walking, Great Scenery

GO FOR A SHORT WALK

Leave the car behind to appreciate Joshua Tree's trippy lunar landscapes. And you don't have to go far to have a wonderful time.

For the quintessential Joshua Tree photo op, take the short and easy **Arch Rock Nature Trail** to an amazing 30ft-wide arch behind the White Tank Campground. There are plenty more formations around here, including the equally impressive Heart Rock, so keep clambering to discover other hidden gems. The trailhead is at the Twin Tanks day-use area, about 2 miles south of the junction of Park Blvd and Pinto Basin Rd.

Another excellent short trail is **Hidden Valley Trail**, an easy 1-mile loop that meanders between whimsical rock clusters to a hidden valley where cattle rustlers once hid their hoard. Feel free to veer off the beaten path and clamber over the piles of smoothly rounded boulders for different perspectives and more solitude. It's a lovely hike for families.

The **Indian Cove Trail** is another winner. Rock hounds love Indian Cove's hulking caramel-colored formations, while birders are drawn by feathered friends hiding out among the yuccas and shrubs along the half-mile nature trail. Access is via Indian Cove Rd off Hwy 62 between Joshua Tree and Twentynine Palms. There's also a campground with more than 100 sites for tenters and RVs.

And don't miss **Inspiration Peak (Keys View) Trail**. This paved 0.25-mile trail leads to an overlook where – on clear days – you can enjoy a panoramic view of the Coachella Valley, Mts San Jacinto and Gorgonio, and the Salton Sea. Also seek out **Barker Dam Trail**, an easy 1.1-mile loop along the

OFFBEAT ATTRACTIONS NEAR JOSHUA TREE NATIONAL PARK

Integratron
This is an electrostatic generator for time travel and cell rejuvenation. Yup!

Noah Purifoy Desert Art Museum
The 'Junk Dada' assemblage of sculptures by Noah Purifoy (1917–2004) can be seen at his former outdoor desert studio.

Pioneertown Beauty Bubble Salon & Museum
Jeff Hafler's *Steel Magnolias*-type home salon brims with vintage beauty paraphernalia.

World-Famous Crochet Museum
A vintage, lime-green photo booth is the home of Bunny, Buddy and hundreds of their crocheted friends collected by Shari Elf.

WHERE TO STAY IN JOSHUA TREE

National Park Campgrounds
Of the park's campgrounds, only Cottonwood and Black Rock have potable water and flush toilets. None have showers. **$**

Kate's Lazy Desert
Owned by Kate Pierson of the B-52s band, this desert glamp-camp has half-a-dozen artist-designed Airstream trailers. **$$**

Pioneertown Motel
Bed down where yesteryear's silver-screen stars slept while filming at Pioneertown. **$$**

BEST FOR A DRINK IN JOSHUA TREE

Joshua Tree Coffee Company
This spotless outfit makes some of the best coffee in JT. It's roasted right here in the little hipster cafe with outdoor seating.

Joshua Tree Saloon & Grill
This whistle-stop has a jukebox, pool tables and cowboy flair. The draws are open-mike Tuesdays and karaoke on Wednesdays and Fridays.

Landers Brew Co
Landers Brew Co has a big local following for its roster of craft beers on tap, convivial beer garden and local musicians on Saturday night.

southern edge of the Wonderland of Rocks, passing a small lake dammed by pioneer cattle ranchers that now serves as a water source for birds and bighorn sheep. It starts at Barker Dam parking lot.

Hike the Joshua Tree Backcountry

TREK LONGER TRAILS

There's almost no end of fun to be had along Joshua Tree's medium to longer hiking trails.

Let's start with some of the short options. Along **Fortynine Palms Oasis Trail**, you can escape the crowds along a moderate 3-mile up-and-down trail to a fan-palm oasis scenically cradled by a canyon. The trailhead is at the end of Canyon Rd, which veers off 29 Palms Hwy (Hwy 62) just east of the Indian Cove turnoff.

For something similar, **Ryan Mountain Trail** promises bird's-eye views of the iconic Wonderland of Rocks formations, Ryan Ranch ruins and the vast desertscape beyond along a well-trodden 3-mile in-and-out hike up 5458ft Ryan Mountain. Be sure to pack water, sunscreen and stamina – although not terribly long, the trail's 1000ft elevation gain will likely make your thighs burn.

Also moderately tough is the **Lost Horse Mine Trail**, an in-and-out 4-mile climb that visits the remains of a prolific Old West silver and gold mine, in operation until 1931. It can be extended into a 6.5-mile loop via Lost Horse Mountain.

For a similar length hike, **Mastodon Peak Trail** brings views of the Eagle Mountains and Salton Sea from the top of 3371ft Mastodon Peak, which crowns the 3-mile loop that also skirts an old gold mine.

Offering a longer challenge, **Lost Palms Oasis Trail** is a rewarding 7.5-mile round-trip trek leading to a hidden desert-fan-palm oasis from Cottonwood Spring near the park's southern edge. The path starts out fairly moderate, weaving through various washes, before descending steeply into a canyon to an overlook and from there down into the oasis. Enjoy the shady palms before embarking on the tough return slog back out of the canyon. For a greater challenge, add the 2-mile detour to the top of Mastodon Peak on your way back.

The Lost Palms Oasis and Mastodon Peak trails share a trailhead – it's 1.2 miles past the Cottonwood Spring Visitor Center.

Enjoy California's Best Rock Climbing

CHOOSE BETWEEN 10,000 CLIMBS

JT is considered California's rock-climbing hub, with more than 10,000 routes in quartz monzonite granite that's famous

WHERE TO EAT IN JOSHUA TREE

JT Country Kitchen
This been-here-forever roadside shack gets a big thumbs up for its scrumptious home cookin'. **$$**

La Copine
Enjoy farm-to-table cuisine with globally inspired dishes in the perky dining room or on the breezy patio. **$$**

Restaurant at 29 Palms Inn
This restaurant does lunchtime burgers and salads, and grilled meats and pastas for dinner. **$$$**

Hidden Valley Trail (p105)

BDLANE/SHUTTERSTOCK ©

for its rough, high-friction surfaces. Trad climbing is tops here, although there are also bouldering and sport-climbing routes. Some of the most popular climbs are in the Hidden Valley area.

Take the Scenic Route

EXPLORE JOSHUA TREE BY ROAD

Exploring under your own steam is a must in Joshua Tree, but adding a scenic drive or two greatly increases how much you'll see while you're here.

Joshua trees grow throughout the north of the park, but some of the biggest trees are found in the **Covington Flats** area accessed by La Contenta Rd, which runs south off Hwy 62 between Yucca Valley and Joshua Tree. For killer views as far as Palm Springs, head up to Eureka Peak (5516ft) from the picnic area. Most passenger cars can usually handle this network of dirt roads, but check at a park visitor center to be safe.

Geology Tour Rd is another fine option. On this 14-mile backcountry drive around Pleasant Valley, the forces of erosion, earthquakes and ancient volcanoes have played out in stunning splendor. There are 16 markers along the route – pick

BEST FOR CLIMBING

Joshua Tree Outfitters
This trusted outfit (joshuatreeoutfitters.com) rents high-quality camping gear (reserve ahead) and bouldering pads (first-come, first-served).

Nomad Ventures
This locally owned store (nomadventures.com) has brand-name gear for rock climbing and hiking. Staff knows the local terrain and can provide tips and advice.

Vertical Adventures
Top-rated climbing school (verticaladventures.com) gets you onto the rock walls during beginner and advanced courses.

Uprising Adventure
Certified climbing guides (joshuatreeuprising.com) offer private instruction for all levels. Rates depend on group size.

WHERE TO SHOP AROUND JOSHUA TREE

Funky & Darn Near New
In Yucca Valley, this boutique sells preloved clothing from campy to classy along with upcycled and fair-trade goodies.

Ricochet Vintage Wears
Great assortment of recycled clothing, including cowboy shirts and boots, along with neat accessories and knickknacks.

Coyote Corner
From Joshua Tree shirts to locally made jewelry, and books to cactus candy, this cute shop has all your souvenir needs.

up a self-guided interpretive brochure and an update on road conditions at any park visitor center. The turnoff from Park Blvd is about 2 miles west of the Jumbo Rocks campground. Two-wheel-drive cars can usually handle the first 5 miles, but beyond Squaw Tank (marker 9) a 4WD is necessary. At the end, you can either backtrack or pick up the Berdoo Canyon to Dillon Rd outside the park boundaries.

To see the natural transition from the high Mojave Desert to the low Colorado Desert, wind down **Pinto Basin Rd** to Cottonwood Spring, a 30-mile drive from Hidden Valley passing by the Cholla Cactus Garden en route.

Discover a Hollywood Movie Set

VISIT PIONEERTOWN

Turn north off Hwy 62 onto Pioneertown Rd in Yucca Valley and drive 5 miles straight into the past. Looking like an 1880s frontier town, **Pioneertown** was actually built in 1946 as a Hollywood Western movie set. Gene Autry and Roy Rogers were among the original investors, and more than 50 movies were filmed here in the 1940s and '50s. These days, it's fun to stroll down 'Mane St', perhaps popping into the little shops, the film museum or the honky-tonk. Weekends are best for visiting; weekday hours are erratic. Mock gunfights and a Wild West show kick up their spurs at 2:30pm on alternate Saturdays from October to June.

For local color, mesquite-wood BBQ, cold beer and kick-ass live music, drop by legendary **Pappy & Harriet's Pioneertown Palace**, a textbook honky-tonk. Monday's open-mike nights (admission free) often bring out astounding talent. From Thursday to Saturday, local and national performers take over the stage.

Within staggering distance is the atmospheric **Pioneertown Motel**, with its nostalgic echo of the era of great Westerns. You could also stay at the similarly themed **Rimrock Ranch**, 4.5 miles away.

ICONIC NATURAL LANDMARKS

Big Morongo Canyon Preserve
Recognized by the Audubon Society as one of California's important birding areas (250 species), with its own spring-fed desert oasis.

Oasis of Mara
A half-mile loop trail behind the Oasis Visitor Center leads to the original 29 palm trees that gave Twentynine Palms its name.

Skull Rock
Skull Rock stares out over Park Blvd from eye sockets hollowed out by rainwater over eons.

Wonderland of Rocks
This labyrinth of whimsically eroded rocks and boulders extends from Indian Cove to Hidden Valley.

GETTING AROUND

Joshua Tree National Park is flanked by I-10 in the south and Hwy 62 (29 Palms Hwy) in the north. The park is about 140 miles east of Los Angeles via I-10 and Hwy 62, and 175 miles from San Diego via I-15 and I-10. From Palm Springs, it takes about an hour to reach the park's west (preferable) or south entrances.

Joshua Tree has three park entrances. The main access point is the west entrance via Park Blvd from the town of Joshua Tree. To avoid long wait times on busy weekends, arrive well before noon or enter the park via the north entrance from Twentynine Palms or the south entrance from I-10.

Bus 1, operated by Morongo Basin Transit Authority, runs hourly between 6am and 10pm along Hwy 62, linking Yucca Valley and Joshua Tree with the Marine Base in Twentynine Palms. Single tickets cost $2.50, and a day pass is $3.75 (cash only, exact fare required). Buses are equipped with bike racks.

DEATH VALLEY NATIONAL PARK

The very name evokes all that is harsh, hot and hellish – a punishing, barren and lifeless place of Old Testament severity. Yet closer inspection reveals that in Death Valley nature is indeed putting on a lively show: sensuous sand dunes, water-sculpted canyons, rocks moving across the desert floor, extinct volcanic craters, palm-shaded oases, stark mountains rising to 11,000ft and plenty of endemic wildlife. This is a land of superlatives, holding the US records for hottest temperature (134°F/57°C), lowest point (Badwater, 282ft below sea level) and largest national park outside Alaska (5270 sq miles).

Furnace Creek is Death Valley's commercial hub, home to the national park visitor center, a gas station, ATM, post office and lodging. There's also a Mission-style 'town square' with a general store, restaurant, saloon and ice-cream and coffee parlor. Facilities at Stovepipe Wells Village and Panamint Springs also include gas, food and lodging.

Death Valley National Park

DAN SEDRAN/SHUTTERSTOCK ©

FACTS

Great For Scenery, hiking, wildlife
State California
Entrance Fee 7-day pass per car/motorcycle/person on foot or bicycle $30/25/15
Area 5270 sq miles

ICONIC VIEWS

Aguereberry Point
Sits 6433ft above the desert floor and delivers fantastic views to the Funeral Mountains.

Badwater Basin
The lowest point in North America (282ft below sea level) is eerily beautiful.

Dante's View
At 5475ft, the view from the top of the Black Mountains is absolutely brilliant.

Mesquite Flat Sand Dunes
Death Valley's most accessible dunes are a gracefully curving sea of sand rising up to 100ft.

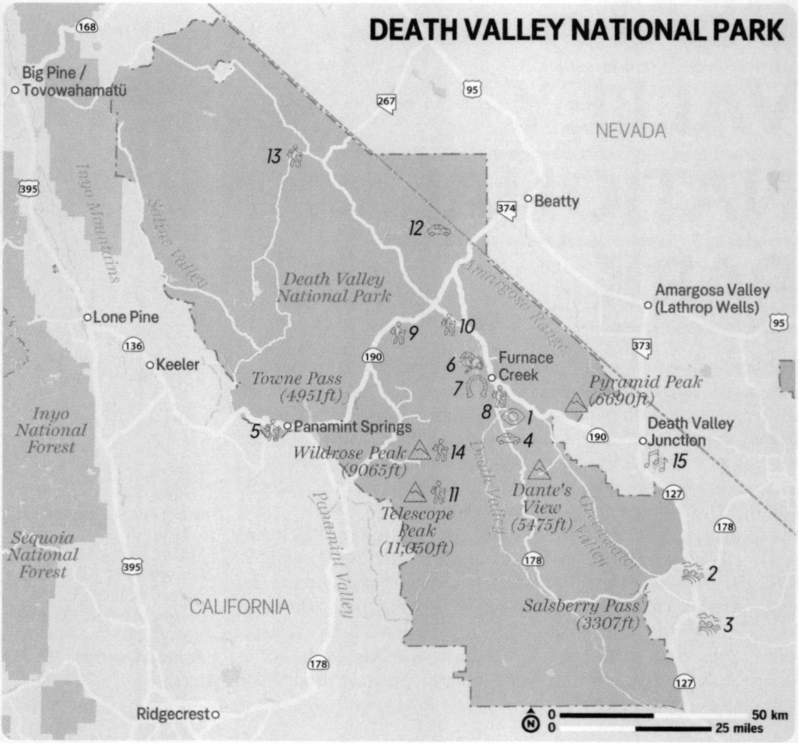

SIGHTS
1 Artists Palette
2 Shoshone
3 Tecopa

ACTIVITIES, COURSES & TOURS
4 Artists Drive
5 Darwin Falls
6 Furnace Creek Golf Course
7 Furnace Creek Stables
8 Golden Canyon
9 Mosaic Canyon Trail
10 Salt Creek Interpretive Trail
11 Telescope Peak
12 Titus Canyon Rd
13 Ubehebe Crater
14 Wildrose Peak

ENTERTAINMENT
15 Amargosa Opera House

Hike Death Valley in Winter

WALK ACROSS THE DESERT

The best time for hiking in Death Valley is November to March. Stay off the trail in summer, except higher-elevation mountain trails, which are usually snowed in during winter. Constructed paths are rare in Death Valley and all but the easiest hikes may require some scrambling or bouldering. An adequate water

WHERE TO CAMP IN DEATH VALLEY NATIONAL PARK

Mesquite Spring Campground
This first-come, first-served campground has 40 spaces and is handy for Ubehebe Crater. **$**

Mahogany Flat Campground
With only 10 spaces, it serves as basecamp for Telescope Peak. At 8200ft, it's the park's highest campground. **$**

Thorndike Campground
With only six sites, Thorndike is in the Panamint mountains at 7400ft and offers tranquility galore. **$**

supply is essential; one gallon per day per person in summer and half a gallon in winter are recommended.

For something really short, begin with the **Salt Creek Interpretative Trail**, an easy half-mile nature trail that's good for bird-watching. It's best in late winter or early spring when rare pupfish splash in the small stream alongside the boardwalk.

Also good if your idea of a hike is something quick and easy but picturesque, the natural-spring-fed, year-round **Darwin Falls** are a good choice. They plunge into a gorge, embraced by willows that attract migratory birds in the spring. Look for the (unmarked) turnoff about 0.75 miles west of Panamint Springs, then follow the dirt road for 2.5 miles to the parking area. The 1-mile hike to the waterfall requires some rock scrambling and crossing of small streams.

Another intriguing possibility involves one of the most impressive geological features in the north of the park: 600ft-deep **Ubehebe Crater**. Believed to have formed some 2100 years ago in a single eruptive event by the meeting of fiery magma and cool groundwater, its Martian beauty is easily appreciated from the parking lot, but for closer inspection embark on the 1.5-mile trek along the rim (not recommended if you're vertigo-prone).

Those looking for something a little longer might consider **Golden Canyon**. Whether a short stroll or strenuous trek, don't miss a spin around this winding wonderland of golden canyons between Badwater Rd and Zabriskie Point. The most popular route is a 3-mile in-and-back trek from the main trailhead off Badwater Rd to the oxidized iron cliffs of Red Cathedral. Combining it with the Gower Gulch Loop adds another mile. Alternatively, kick off at Zabriskie Point for the 2.7-mile Badlands Loop.

West of Stovepipe Wells Village, a 2.3-mile gravel road dead-ends at the mouth of Mosaic Canyon, from where the 4-mile in-and-out **Mosaic Canyon Trail** meanders past polished marble walls carved from 750-million-year-old rocks. About 0.25 miles past the trailhead, the canyon narrows dramatically; about 1.3 miles in, a pile of boulders blocks the passage but it's possible to squeeze by on the left and continue the trek.

We've saved Death Valley's best (and most strenuous) hikes for last. The 8.4-mile round-trip **Wildrose Peak** hike, with a sweat-inducing 2200ft elevation gain, begins near the charcoal kilns off Wildrose Canyon Rd and threads past piñon pines and juniper to a lofty 9064ft. Grand views of the Panamint Valley, Badwater Basin and all of Death Valley National Park start about halfway. It's best in spring or fall. The final mile below the summit is the toughest stretch.

The park's highest summit is **Telescope Peak** (11,049ft), with views that plummet to the desert floor, which is as far

WHEN TO VISIT DEATH VALLEY

Temperatures
Death Valley is sunny, dry and clear year-round, but don't assume it's always hot: temperatures fluctuate hugely, from an average of 38°F/3°C in December to 116°F/43°C in July. Dress accordingly.

Wildflowers
Peak visiting seasons are winter and the springtime wildflower bloom.

Summer
In summer, a car with reliable air-con is essential, and outdoor explorations in the valley should be limited to the early morning and late afternoon. Escape the heat by heading to the mountains.

Winter
Winter rains are a possibility and flash-flood damage or snow in the mountains regularly leads to road closures.

WHERE TO STAY IN DEATH VALLEY NATIONAL PARK

Ranch at Death Valley
This rambling resort has rooms with patios or balconies, and a full portfolio of resort facilities. **$$**

Stovepipe Wells Village Hotel
The rooms at this private resort have beds draped in quality linens and cheerful blankets. **$$**

Inn at Death Valley
This 1927 Spanish Mission–style hotel offers all the expected 21st-century comforts along with languid valley views. **$$$**

TURTIX/SHUTTERSTOCK ©

Artists Drive

below as two Grand Canyons deep! The 14-mile round trip clocks 3000ft of elevation gain from its trailhead at the Mahogany Flat campground. Summiting in winter requires an ice axe, crampons and winter-hiking experience. By June, the trail is usually free of snow.

Go on a Scenic Drive

DRIVE DEATH VALLEY'S BACK ROADS

About 10 miles south of Furnace Creek is the turnoff for the 9-mile, one-way **Artists Drive** that offers 'wow' moments around every turn. About 5 miles in, you'll pass the main stop called **Artists Palette**, where oxidized metals tinge the mountains into hues from rose to green and purple; view them at their luminous best right before sunset. The road is well paved but winding, with the occasional fun rollercoaster-style dip.

Check road conditions at the visitor center before tackling grandiose but tricky **Titus Canyon Rd** by vehicle or mountain bike. For a rough 28 miles, it climbs, dips and winds to a crest in the Grapevine Mountains, then slowly descends back to the desert floor past a ghost town, petroglyphs and canyon narrows. The turnoff is about 2.5 miles northeast of the park boundary. The best light conditions are in the morning. High-clearance vehicles are highly recommended. The last 3 miles are one way.

QUIRKY DEATH VALLEY EXPERIENCES

Palm-fringed **Furnace Creek Golf Course** is the world's lowest-elevation golf course (214ft below sea level). It's been certified by the Audubon Society for its environment-friendly management.

Saddle up at **Furnace Creek Stables** to see what Death Valley looks like from horseback. One-hour rides stay on the sunbaked desert floor while two-hour rides head for the Funeral Mountains.

An opera house in the middle of nowhere? Yes, thanks to the vision of New York dancer Marta Beckett, who fell in love with the 1920s colonnaded adobe **Amargosa Opera House** when her car broke down nearby in 1967. Visiting performers continue to keep her legacy alive in the fall and winter.

WHERE TO STAY IN SHOSHONE & TECOPA

Shoshone RV Park & Campground
This park has hookup sites, tent spaces, showers, flush toilets, a pool and a laundromat. **$**

Shoshone Inn
This roadside motel has contemporary rooms with comfy beds, a shaded courtyard and its own mineral-spring-fed pool. **$$**

Villa Anita
Staying at this artist-run B&B feels much like bunking with good friends. It's eccentric and supremely comfortable. **$$**

We strongly recommend that you rent a 4WD for the Titus Canyon Rd. **Farabee Jeep Rentals & Tours** (farabeejeeps.com) rents Jeeps for off-road trips. Drivers must be 25 years or older and have a driver's license, credit card and proof of car insurance. It also organizes Jeep tours for those who don't want to go it alone.

Explore Shoshone & Tecopa

DISCOVER NEARBY TOWNS

On the southern stoop of Death Valley, about 60 miles from Furnace Creek, blink-and-you-miss-it **Shoshone** stakes its existence on being an early 20th-century railroad stop. The railroad disappeared in 1941, but the village still caters to travelers with a gas station, general store, restaurant, lodging and small tourist office. It's a delightfully sleepy place, with a couple of attractions to anchor your visit.

Shoshone Museum consists of a rusted Chevy parked next to antique gas pumps and exhibits on bootlegging and the railroad that evoke Old West spirit. Curators of this modest museum are especially proud of the display of mammoth bones found in the area. Staff also dispense free maps and handy tips about Death Valley National Park and its surrounds.

While you're here, don't miss atmospheric **Crowbar Cafe & Saloon**. Shoshone's only restaurant, it has fed locals and travelers since 1920. Its main stock-in-trade is burgers and sandwiches, but it also serves breakfast, Mexican dishes and something called 'rattlesnake' chili (sorry, there are no actual snakes in it). The attached saloon can get lively on weekend nights.

Also close to Death Valley is **Tecopa**, an old mining town named after a peacemaking Paiute chief. Its desolate looks belie an artistic undercurrent and an unexpected number of fun spots. Soak in hot natural mineral springs, explore a hidden, lush, date-palm oasis, fuel up at excellent restaurants and get oiled up at not one, but two craft breweries. **Death Valley Brewing** is the brewpub star and was the first craft brewery in this dusty desert outpost. It's not a mirage, but is instead the pint-sized operation of artist and beer-meister Jon Zellhoefer in a restored railroad tie house. Brewmaster Dan uses water from the local mineral spring to whip up small-batch cold ones, from IPAs to Belgian ales, stouts and wheat beers. Tecopa is about 70 miles from Furnace Creek.

CALLING DEATH VALLEY HOME

Timbisha Shoshone tribespeople lived in the Panamint Range for centuries, visiting the valley every winter to gather acorns, hunt waterfowl, catch pupfish in marshes and cultivate small areas of corn, squash and beans. After the federal government created Death Valley National Monument in 1933, the Timbisha Shoshone were forced to move several times and were eventually restricted to a 40-acre village site near Furnace Creek. In 2000 President Clinton signed an act transferring 7500 acres of land back to the Timbisha Shoshone, creating the first Native American reservation inside a US national park. Today, a few dozen Timbisha live in the Indian Village near Furnace Creek. Pop by to sample the filling and tasty Timbisha taco, made with fried bread in place of a tortilla.

GETTING AROUND

The park's main roads (Hwys 178 and 190) are paved and in great shape, but if your travel plans include dirt roads, a high-clearance vehicle and off-road tires are highly recommended and essential on many routes. A 4WD is often necessary after rains. Always check with the visitor center for current road conditions, especially before heading to remote areas.

Gas is available 24/7 at Furnace Creek and Stovepipe Wells Village and from 7am to 9:30pm in Panamint Springs. Prices are much higher than outside the park.

PINNACLES NATIONAL PARK

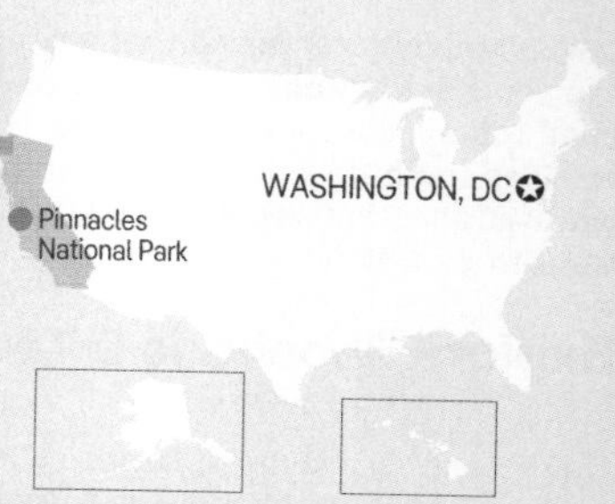

Named for the towering rock spires that rise abruptly out of the chaparral-covered hills east of Salinas Valley, this off-the-beaten-path park protects one of California's most unusual and striking landscapes. Formed by the movements of tectonic plates over millions of years, the rocky spires at the heart of the park are the eroded remnants of a long-extinct volcano that originated in present-day Southern California before getting sheared in two and moving nearly 200 miles north along the San Andreas Fault.

Initially established as a national monument in 1908, Pinnacles earned national park designation in 2013. The park, divided into eastern and western sections, with no through road connecting them, preserves forests of oak, sycamore and buckeye, wildflower-strewn meadows, caves and dramatic rock formations. Endangered California condors still soar overhead, and the park's remote beauty makes it popular with hikers and climbers.

FACTS

Great For Wildlife, scenery, walking
State California
Entrance Fee 7-day pass per car/motorcycle/person on foot or bicycle $30/25/15
Area 42 sq miles

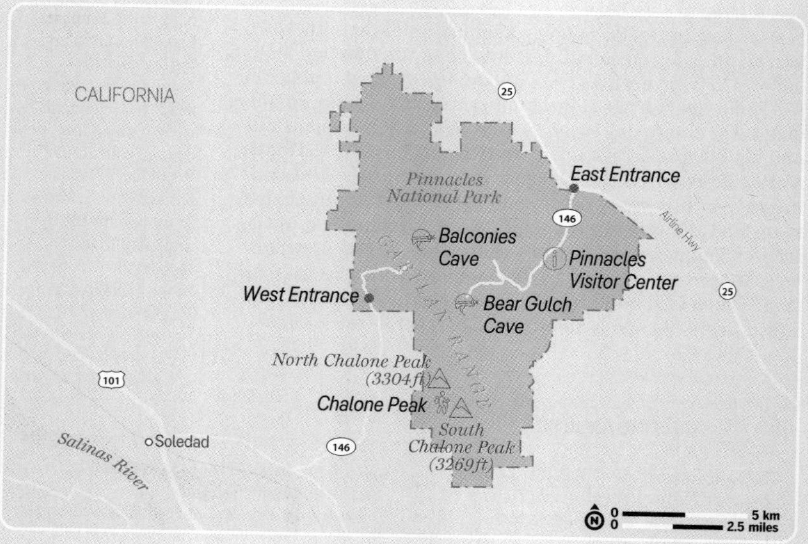

Hike Between the Pinnacles

WALK FOR VIEWS AND WILDLIFE

To really appreciate Pinnacles' stark beauty, you need to hike. Moderate loops of varying lengths and difficulty ascend into the **High Peaks** and include thrillingly narrow clifftop sections. In the early morning or late afternoon, you may spot endangered California condors soaring overhead. Get an early start to tackle the 9-mile round-trip trail to the top of **Chalone Peak**, granting panoramic views.

Rangers lead guided full-moon hikes and star-gazing programs on some weekend nights, usually in spring or fall. Reservations are required: call 831-389-4485 in advance, or check for last-minute vacancies at the visitor center.

Discover an Underground World

EXPLORE PINNACLES' CAVES

Among the park's biggest attractions are its two talus caves, formed by piles of boulders. **Balconies Cave** is almost always open for exploration. Scrambling through it is not an exercise recommended for claustrophobes, as it's pitch-black inside, making a flashlight essential. Be prepared to get lost a bit, too. The cave is found along a 2.5-mile hiking loop from the west entrance. Nearer the east entrance, **Bear Gulch Cave** is closed seasonally, so as not to disturb a resident colony of Townsend's big-eared bats. The opening dates change depending on bat movements, but the lower cave usually opens mid-July to mid-May.

Explore Some of California's Best Climbs

GO ROCK CLIMBING

Pinnacles is a top destination for rock climbers. The most popular areas for climbing are **Bear Gulch**, **Discovery Wall** and the **High Peaks**. Spring and fall are the best seasons, with dry, comfortable weather. Winter climbing can also be good, but expect chilly conditions in the shade. Summer tends to be oppressively hot.

For route information, visit the Friends of Pinnacles website (pinnacles.org).

Rock climbing, Pinnacles National Park

STELLAMC/SHUTTERSTOCK ©

PINNACLES NATIONAL PARK PRACTICALITIES

Pinnacles National Park – East Entrance
The park's east entrance sits at the crossroads of Hwys 146 and 25.

Pinnacles National Park – West Entrance
The west entrance is reached via Hwy 146 from Soledad.

Pinnacles National Park Visitor Center
Information, maps and books are available on the park's east side from the small NPS visitor center inside the campground store.

Pinnacles Campground Store
The place to stock up on supplies along the Pinnacles Hwy. It sells bottled water, snacks and sundries, and also contains the NPS visitor center.

WHERE TO STAY IN PINNACLES & SALINAS

Pinnacles National Park Campground
On the park's east side, this family-oriented campground has good facilities. $

Howard Johnson Inn
A warm welcome at reception and surprisingly stylish rooms lift HoJo's ahead of the pack. $

Laurel Inn
If chain motels don't do it for you, this sprawling, family-owned cheapie has cozy but spacious rooms. $

WHEN TO VISIT & WARNINGS

Spring and fall are the best seasons to visit Pinnacles. Try to avoid weekends and holidays, when the park is extremely popular. The park is remote and blisteringly hot in summer, and there are no water sources on trails.

Remember that although no permit is required to climb in the Pinnacles, conditions can be challenging and solo climbing is strongly discouraged. The park's volcanic breccia is softer than granite and provides less reliable holds for climbers. Climbing routes are periodically closed to protect local wildlife, including nesting falcons and eagles.

Look for California Condors

SPOT AN ICONIC BIRD

Pinnacles National Park offers excellent opportunities to view the California condor, which remains one of America's most iconic birds.

That's because the California condor (*Gymnogyps californianus*) is one of the state's biggest endangered-species success stories. These gigantic, prehistoric birds weigh more than 20lb, with a wingspan of up to 10ft, letting them fly great distances in search of carrion. They're easily recognized by their naked pink heads and large white patches on the underside of each wing.

This big bird became so rare that in 1987 there were only 27 left in the world, and all were removed from the wild to special captive-breeding facilities. Read the whole gripping story in journalist John Moir's 2006 book *Return of the Condor: The Race to Save Our Largest Bird from Extinction.*

There are more than 500 California condors alive today, with increasing numbers of captive birds being released back into the wild. It's hoped they will begin breeding naturally, although it's an uphill battle. Wild condors are still dying of lead poisoning caused by hunters' bullets in the game carcasses that the birds feed on.

The Big Sur coast and Pinnacles National Park offer excellent opportunities to view this majestic bird. In Pinnacles, check out the park's website (nps.gov/pinn/learn/nature/condor-viewing-tips.htm) for tips on where to see condors. They're present across the park, but your best chance seems to be up on the High Peaks in the early morning or late afternoon, or from the spotting scopes near Pinnacles Visitor Center.

If you're exploring beyond Pinnacles, in Big Sur, the Ventana Wildlife Society (ventanaws.org) occasionally leads two-hour guided condor-watching tours using radio telemetry to track the birds; for sign-up details, check the website or ask at the Big Sur Discovery Center.

MORE ROCK CLIMBING IN CALIFORNIA

Pinnacles is a world-class climbing destination, but it's not alone in California. Other excellent places include **Joshua Tree National Park** (p106) and, of course, **Yosemite** (p75).

GETTING AROUND

There is no road connecting the two sides of Pinnacles National Park. To reach the less-developed west entrance, exit Hwy 101 at Soledad and follow Hwy 146 northeast for 14 miles. The east entrance, where you'll find the visitor center and campground, is accessed via lonely Hwy 25 in San Benito County, southeast of Hollister and northeast of King City.

LASSEN VOLCANIC NATIONAL PARK

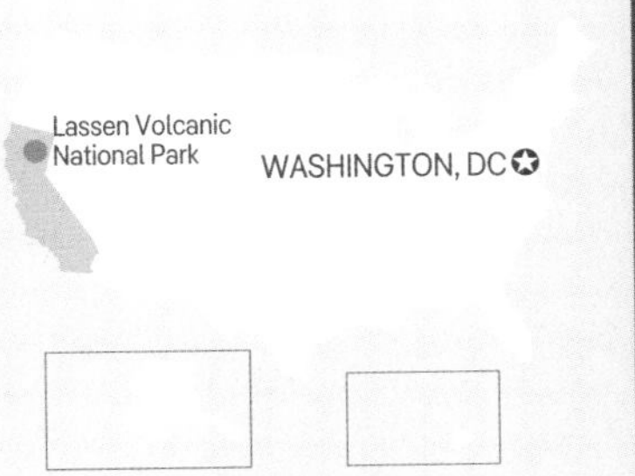

The dry, smoldering, treeless terrain within this 106,000-acre national park stands in stunning contrast to the cool, green conifer forest that surrounds it in summer – in winter, tons of snow ensures you won't get too far inside its borders without some serious gear. Still, entering the park from the southwest entrance is to suddenly step into another world. The lavascape offers a fascinating glimpse into the earth's fiery core. In a fuming display, the terrain is marked by roiling hot springs, steamy mud pots, noxious sulfur vents, fumaroles, lava flows, cinder cones, craters and crater lakes.

In earlier times, the region was a summer encampment and meeting point for the Atsugewi, Yana, Yahi and Maidu Native American tribes. They hunted deer and gathered plants for basketmaking here. Some Indigenous people still live nearby and work closely with the park to help educate visitors on their ancient history and contemporary culture.

FACTS

Great For Photo ops, scenery, walking
State California
Entrance Fee 7-day entry per vehicle $30 ($10 December to mid-April)
Area 166 sq miles

Lassen Volcanic National Park

SIGHTS
1 Devastated Area
2 Lassen National Forest
3 Lassen Peak
4 Manzanita Lake
5 Sulfur Works

ACTIVITIES, COURSES & TOURS
6 Bumpass Hell
7 Lassen Peak Trail
8 Mill Creek Falls

LASSEN VOLCANIC NATIONAL PARK

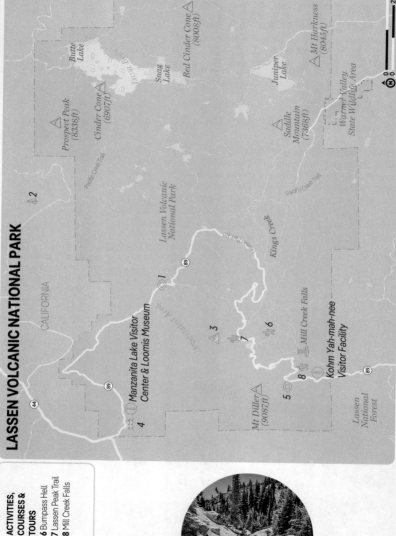

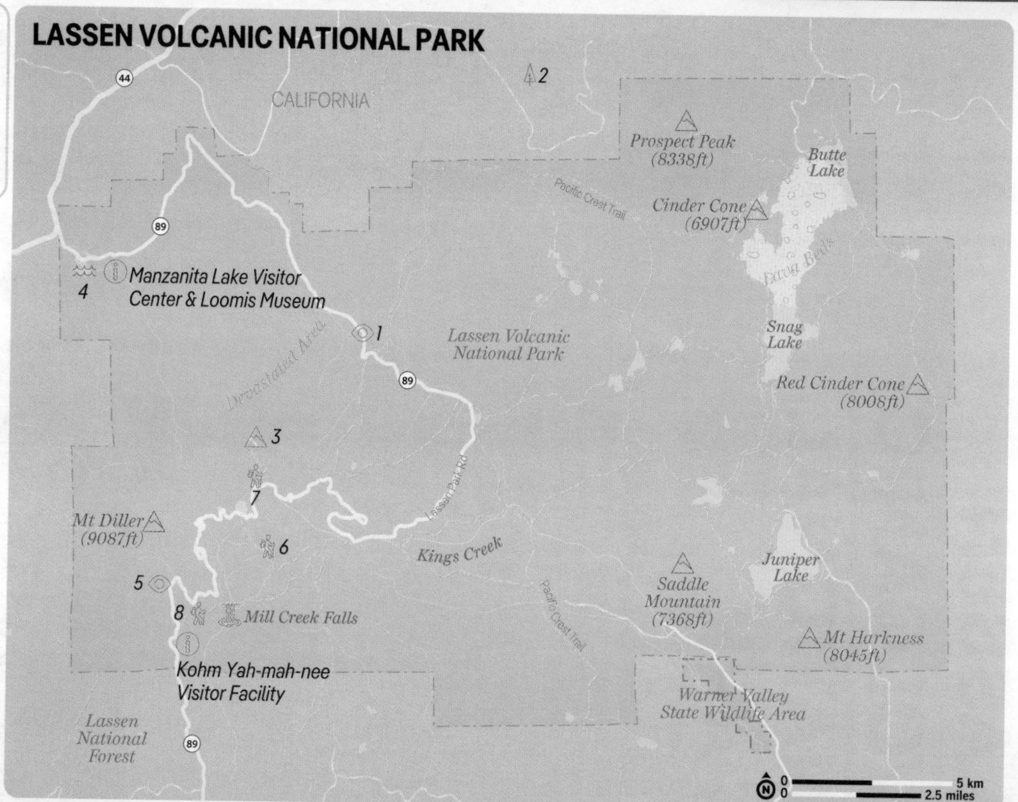

Bumpass Hell (p121)
LOST_IN_THE_MIDWEST/SHUTTERSTOCK ©

Drive Through Scenic Northern California

DRIVE THROUGH AND BEYOND THE PARK

Lassen Peak, the world's largest lava-dome volcano, rises 2000ft over the surrounding landscape, reaching a height of 10,463ft above sea level. Classified as an active volcano, its most recent, sizeable eruption was in 1915, when it spewed a giant cloud of smoke, steam and ash 7 miles into the atmosphere. The national park was created the following year to protect the newly formed landscape. Some areas destroyed by the blast, including the aptly named **Devastated Area** northeast of the peak, are recovering impressively.

Hwy 89, the road through the park, wraps around Lassen Peak on three sides and provides access to dramatic geothermal formations, pure lakes, gorgeous picnic areas and remote hiking trails.

The road and trails wind through cinder cones, lava and lush alpine glades, with views of Juniper Lake, Snag Lake and the plains beyond. Most of the lakes at higher elevations remain partially and beautifully frozen in summer. Leave time to fish, swim or boat on **Manzanita Lake**, a slightly lower emerald gem near the northern entrance.

To take all of this magnificence a little further (and beyond the park's boundaries into the surrounding countryside), consider taking the **Lassen Scenic Byway** in its entirety. Even in the peak of summer, this byway is rarely busy. The long loop though Northern California wilderness skirts the edge of Lassen Volcanic National Park and circles Lassen Peak. It mostly covers the big green patches on the map: expansive areas perfect for hiking, fishing, camping or just getting lost. This is a place where few people venture, and those who do come back with stories.

The launching point for this big loop could be either Redding or Sacramento, but there are few comforts for travelers along its course. The only towns in this neck of the woods – little places such as Chester and Susanville – aren't all that exciting on their own; they're mostly just places to gas up, buy some beef jerky and enjoy the week's only hot meal. But the banner attractions are visible in every direction – the ominous, dormant volcanic peak of Lassen, the windswept high plains and the seemingly endless wilderness of the Lassen and Plumas National Forests. On Hwy 89, watch also for the roadside **sulfur works**, recognizable by its bubbling mud pots, hissing steam vent, fountains and fumaroles.

LASSEN VOLCANIC VISITOR CENTERS

Kohm Yah-mah-nee Visitor Center
In the park's southwest, this center has a topographical volcano relief map, augmented reality sandbox, bookstore, auditorium, gift shop and cafe. Visitor information and maps available.

Manzanita Lake Visitor Center & Loomis Museum
In the park's north, with exhibits and an orientation video. During summer, rangers and volunteers lead programs on geology, wildlife, astronomy and local culture.

Park Headquarters
About a mile west of the tiny town of Mineral, the park HQ is the nearest stop for refueling and supplies.

WHERE TO STAY AROUND LASSEN VOLCANIC NATIONAL PARK

Manzanita Lake Camping Cabins
These log cabins sit lakeside. Shared bathrooms and coin-op hot showers nearby. **$**

Village at Child's Meadow
Nine miles outside the park's southwest entrance, sits this good mountain resort with cabins, camping and a cafe. **$**

Drakesbad Guest Ranch
Seventeen miles northwest of Chester, this secluded place lies inside the park's boundary. Rates include meals. **$$$**

LASSEN VOLCANIC CAMPGROUNDS

The park has eight developed campgrounds that are variably open between late May and late October, depending on snow conditions. Manzanita Lake, the only campground with hot showers, is the biggest camping area in these parts and has lake access, views of Lassen, and 160 campsites with fire rings, picnic tables and bear boxes. There's a store and kayak rentals here, too.

Privately run campgrounds operate outside the park. **Mt Lassen/ Shingletown KOA** has all the standard KOA amenities: a playground, deli and laundry facilities. It's off Hwy 44 in Shingletown, about 20 miles west of the park. **Hat Creek Resort & RV Park** sits along a fast-moving, trout-stocked creek. Stock up at the convenience store and deli, then eat on a picnic table by the river.

SALLIBHATT/SHUTTERSTOCK ©

Lassen Peak

This loop is formed by Hwy 36, Hwy 44 and Hwy 89 (see nps .gov/thingstodo/driveparkhwy.htm). It's best to do the drive between late June and mid-October. At other times, some of these roads close due to snow.

Hike Through an Otherworldly Landscape

HIKE LASSEN'S TRAILS

In total, the park has 150 miles of hiking trails, including a 17-mile section of the **Pacific Crest Trail**. Experienced hikers can attack the **Lassen Peak Trail**; it takes at least 4½ hours to make the 5-mile round trip, but the first 1.3 miles up to the Grandview lookout is suitable for families. The 360-degree

WHERE TO STAY AROUND EAGLE LAKE & SUSANVILLE

Eagle Lake Campgrounds
On the south shore, you'll find several busy campgrounds for tent and RV camping, including Merrill, Aspen and Eagle. **$**

Red Lion Inn & Suites
The best motel in Susanville is central and has friendly service and a fitness center. **$$**

Roseberry House B&B
This 1902 Victorian house has striking dark-wood antique headboards, armoires and fantastic breakfasts. **$$**

view from the top is stunning, even if the weather is a bit hazy. Early in the season you'll need snow and ice-climbing equipment to reach the summit. Near the Kom Yah-mah-nee visitor center, a gentler 2.3-mile trail leads through meadows and forest to **Mill Creek Falls**. At **Bumpass Hell**, a moderate 1.5-mile trail and boardwalk leads to an active geothermal area, with bizarrely colored pools and billowing clouds of steam.

Escape the Crowds in Lassen Forest

IMMERSE YOURSELF IN FOREST WILDERNESS

The vast **Lassen National Forest** (fs.usda.gov/lassen) surrounding Lassen Peak and Lassen Volcanic National Park is so big that it's hard to comprehend: it covers 1.2 million acres (1875 sq miles) of wilderness in an area called the Crossroads, where the granite Sierra, volcanic Cascades, Modoc Plateau and Central Valley meet.

The forest has some serious hikes, with 460 miles of trails, ranging from the brutally challenging (120 miles of the **Pacific Crest Trail**) to ambitious day hikes (the 12-mile **Spencer Meadows National Recreation Trail**) to just-want-to-stretch-the-legs-a-little trails (the 3.5-mile **Heart Lake National Recreation Trail**). Near the intersection of Hwys 44 and 89 is one of the most spectacular features of the forest – the pitch-black 600yd **Subway Cave** lava tube. Other points of interest include the 1.5-mile volcanic **Spattercone Crest Trail**, **Willow Lake** and **Crater Lake**, 7684ft **Antelope Peak** and the 900ft-high, 14-mile-long **Hat Creek Rim** escarpment.

For those seeking to get far off the beaten trail, the forest has three wilderness areas. The two high-elevation wilderness areas are the **Caribou Wilderness** and the **Thousand Lakes Wilderness**, best visited from mid-June to mid-October. The **Ishi Wilderness** (named after Ishi, the last surviving member of the Yahi people, who walked out of this wilderness in 1911), at a much lower elevation in the Central Valley foothills east of Red Bluff, is more comfortable in spring and fall, as summer temperatures often climb to more than 100°F (38°C). It harbors California's largest migratory deer herd, which can contain upwards of 20,000 animals.

RANGER INFORMATION FOR LASSEN FOREST

Eagle Lake Ranger District
Friendly and helpful ranger office along Eagle Lake Rd in Susanville, with lots of maps and pamphlets.

Hat Creek Ranger District
Not in Hat Creek as you'd expect from the name, but in Fall River Mills, just beyond the Old Station Junction.

Almanor Ranger District
About a mile southwest of Chester, this place offers information about Lake Almanor and the surrounding forests.

GETTING AROUND

There's virtually no way to visit Lassen Volcanic without a car, though all the two-lane roads around the park and the ample free national-forest camping options make for excellent, if fairly serious, cycle touring.

The park has two entrances. The northern entrance, at Manzanita Lake, is 50 miles east of Redding via Hwy 44. The southwest entrance is on Hwy 89, about 5 miles north of the junction with Hwy 36. From this junction, it's 5 miles west on Hwy 36 to Mineral and 44 miles west to Red Bluff. Heading east on Hwy 36, Chester is 25 miles away and Susanville about 60 miles. Quincy is 65 miles southeast from the junction on Hwy 89.

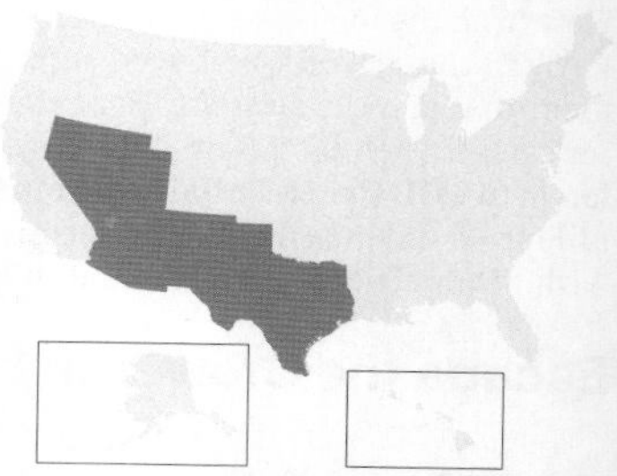

THE SOUTHWEST

UNTAMED ADVENTURE PLAYGROUND

The Southwest lures travelers with giant arches, desert mesas, impossibly vast canyons and ancient petroglyphs carved by Native hands.

THE MAIN AREAS

The Southwest earns its reputation as the country's land of adventure with a dizzyingly diverse landscape of plunging canyons, snowcapped peaks, prickly deserts and red-rock formations. Tracing the Colorado River, you'll find a string of desert jewels: Arches, Canyonlands and the Grand Canyon. Further west are neck-craning Zion and Bryce Canyon's surreal hoodoos.

In this region, beauty and adventure are a fun-loving team. They crank up the rapids, unleash singletrack mountain-biking routes, add wildflower blooms to hiking trails and drape sunsets across red rocks. This captivating mix of scenery and possibility is a siren song for visitors wanting to rejuvenate physically, mentally and spiritually.

The big draw is the Grand Canyon, a two-billion-year-old wonder that shares its geological treasures through hearty hikes and white-water thrills. Next door in Utah and Nevada, the canyons, otherworldly formations and bold red rocks simultaneously blow your mind and nourish your soul. In Texas, everything really is bigger – one of its national parks is nearly the size of an East Coast state.

Underpinning many of the Southwest's national parks is the deep-rooted history of the Native people who lived – and continue to live – here. Fremont-culture petroglyphs decorate rock walls, and Ancestral Puebloan cliff dwellings are tucked safely under the high plateaus of Mesa Verde National Park in Colorado, surviving against the elements for more than seven centuries.

Horseshoe Bend, Colorado River (p171), Grand Canyon National Park

CAR

A car is essential for getting around the Southwest. Make sure you have a 4WD vehicle – and the proper know-how to drive it – to access some remote backcountry trailheads and campgrounds.

TOUR

Companies offer bus tours of the Southwest's most popular national parks, either as standalone visits or grouping together several parks that are in close proximity, such as the Grand Canyon, Zion and Bryce Canyon.

Find Your Way

Many of the Southwest's national parks are huge and extremely spread out, requiring a car to reach them and to get around. Some parks have free shuttle-bus services in the high-traffic seasons.

G B HART/SHUTTERSTOCK ©

Guadalupe Mountains National Park (p179)

Lehman Caves (p178)

Plan Your Time

Visiting all of the Southwest's national parks on a single trip is ambitious, but some spots are clustered together and easy to link up.

The Grand Circle

Perhaps the most famous national-park road trip in the country, the Grand Circle takes in the best of the Southwest. From Las Vegas, head to **Zion** (p193) for unforgettable hikes, and **Bryce Canyon** (p138) for out-of-this-world hoodoos. Loop through **Capitol Reef** (p156) before hitting **Arches** (p128) and **Canyonlands** (p147). Wrap up with the iconic **Grand Canyon** (p166).

Caves, Dunes & Canyons

Savor the solitude of Texas' parks before heading north to New Mexico. The Rio Grande runs through the limestone canyons of **Big Bend** (p134). Get even more off-grid at **Guadalupe Mountains** (p179). Let the gaping caves and enveloping darkness of **Carlsbad Caverns** (p164) absorb you before reemerging in the unique desert dunes of **White Sands** (p191).

SEASONAL HIGHLIGHTS

SPRING

Wildflowers usher hikers along trails, but lingering snow can mean some areas are inaccessible.

SUMMER

Temperatures soar above 100°F (38°C), and parks are at capacity; higher elevations bring cool relief.

FALL

Fall is the best time to visit, with scenes of colorful foliage, cooler temperatures and lighter crowds.

WINTER

Parks in Utah and northern Arizona clear out as the snow arrives; visitors will see a different perspective.

ARCHES NATIONAL PARK

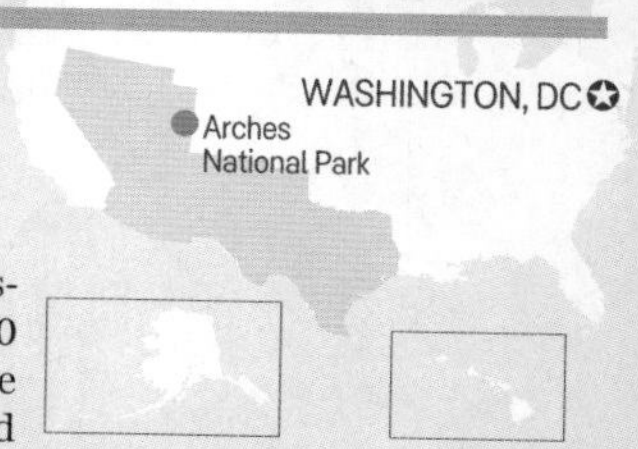

Giant arcs of sandstone frame snowy peaks and desert landscapes at Arches National Park, home to 2000 rock arches, the highest density on earth. You'll lose all perspective on size at some, such as the thin and graceful Landscape Arch – among the largest in the world – which stretches 306ft across. A scenic drive through the heart of the park makes the spectacular arches accessible to all. Arches has many short trails, but this park is geared more toward drivers than hikers, with most of the main sights close to roads.

The wildly popular park saw a 73% rise in visitors between 2011 and 2021, hitting a high of 1.8 million in a year, leading officials to implement a timed entry system. If you're planning to visit between 7am and 4pm from April through October, you must reserve an hour-long entry window on recreation.gov. It costs $2 and does not include the park entry fee.

FACTS

Great For Family travel, photo ops, walking
State Utah
Entrance Fee 7-day pass per car/motorcycle/person on foot or bicycle $30/25/15, plus $2 for a seasonal timed-entry reservation
Area 119 sq miles

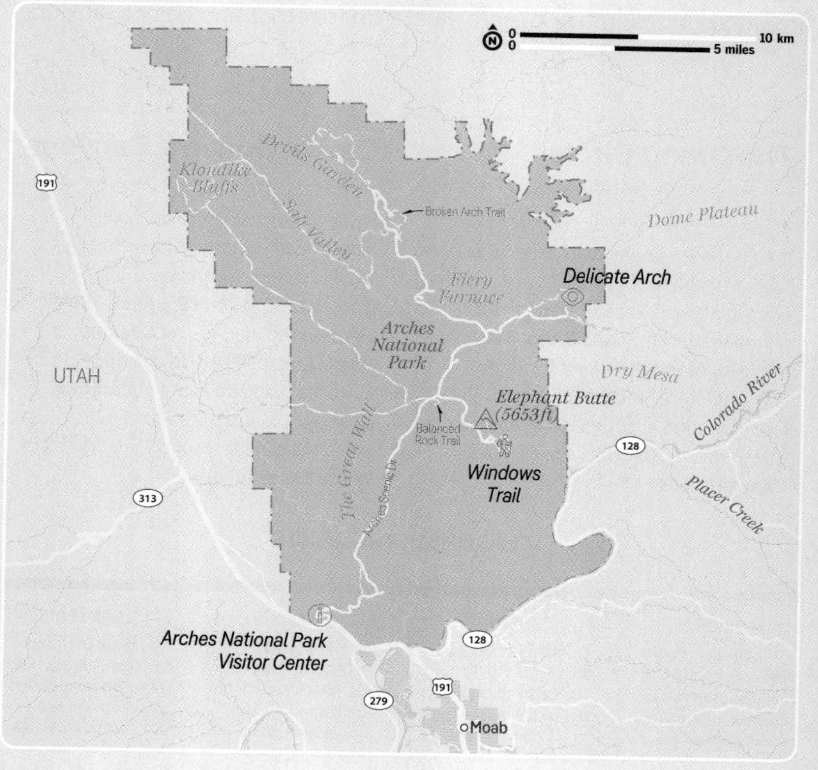

Delicate Arch

Picture-Perfect Delicate Arch

HIKING TO A UTAH ICON

You've seen **Delicate Arch** before: it's Utah's unofficial state symbol, stamping nearly every tourist brochure and gracing license plates. While two viewpoints provide perspective (and an easier hike) from below, the best way to experience the arch is close up.

The trail to Delicate Arch may seem interminable on the way up, but the rewards are so great that you'll quickly forget the toil, provided you wear rubber-soled hiking shoes and drink a quart of water along the way – there is zero shade. This hike is the most popular long trail at Arches, and it's best tackled early in the day when you'll feel less like an ant under a magnifying glass.

AN ARCH IS BORN

The magnificent formations in Arches National Park and throughout southern Utah are created by the varying erosion of sandstone, mudstone, limestone and other sedimentary layers. When water freezes and expands in cracks, it forms fins – thin, soaring, wall-like features. When portions of the rock break away underneath, an arch results.

These formations are forever in flux, and they all eventually lose out to gravity, breaking and disappearing. The most recent notable collapse happened in 2008, when the 71ft-wide Wall Arch thunderously fell to the ground overnight. As you stroll beneath these monuments to nature's power, listen carefully, especially in winter, and you may hear spontaneous popping noises – it's the sound of the future forming.

WHERE TO CAMP IN & AROUND ARCHES NATIONAL PARK

Devils Garden Campground
The only place to stay inside the park. Extremely popular; book months in advance. **$**

Goose Island Campground
These first-come, first-served BLM campsites, the closest to the park entrance, fill by morning. **$**

North Klondike Campground
Opened in 2022, these sites have few facilities (no toilets) but are close to top-notch mountain-biking trails. **$**

ROAD TRIP

Admiring the Arches on a Desert Drive

Hitting all the highlights, this paved drive on the park's main road visits Arches' strange forms and flame-colored desert landscapes. The route is packed with photo ops and short walks to arches and iconic landmarks. We've included the six best stops here, but geology nerds and eager hikers have plenty more viewpoints and information panels from which to pick. They're well signed along the road from the visitor center.

1 Park Avenue

You might not need to stretch your legs yet, but hop out of the car to stroll Park Avenue – or at least visit the viewpoint. While it doesn't have any arches on display, it's a good geological showcase. At the end of the hike (or from the road as you drive onward), look for the Three Gossips, a towering rock trio sharing a secret.

The Drive: Go on for 5.5 miles, stopping as you'd like at the scenic viewpoints.

2 Balanced Rock

Balanced Rock, a 3600-ton boulder as big as a naval destroyer, teeters on a spindly pedestal that shoots from the ground like a fist. The 15-minute loop trail helps you grasp its actual size (128ft to the top of the rock) and provides a good look at the

TOM TIETZ/SHUTTERSTOCK ©

Balanced Rock

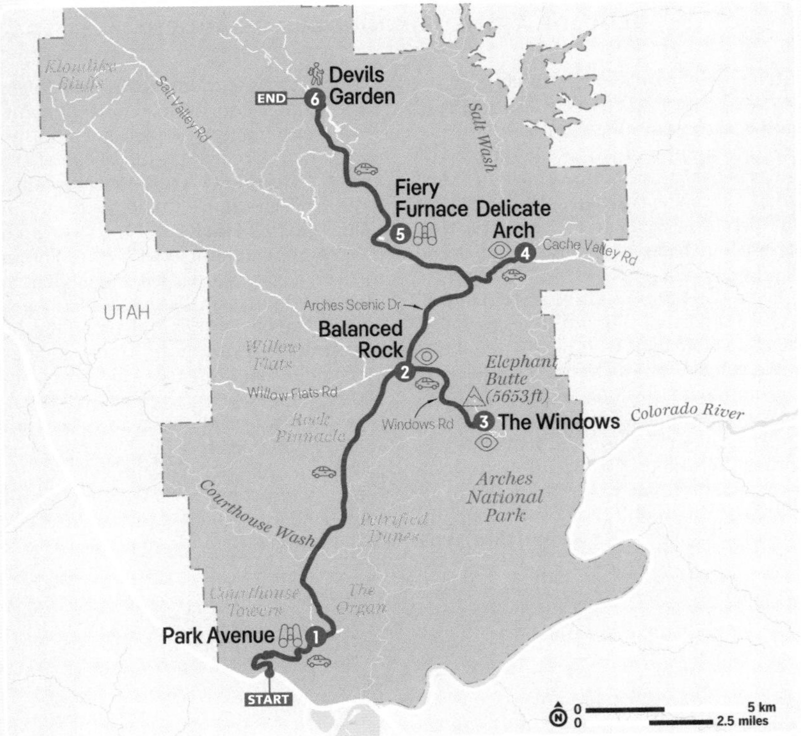

forces of erosion at work. There is wheelchair access to the viewpoint.

The Drive: Turn right onto Windows Rd, which ends at two trailheads.

3 The Windows

Get up close to the arches on this short trail to a rock fin with two ginormous openings (p133). From a separate trailhead across the parking lot, you can clamber around the base of Double Arch.

The Drive: Head back to the park's main road and turn right. After 3 miles, turn right at the intersection with Delicate Arch Rd.

4 Delicate Arch

Delicate Arch (p129) is an unofficial state symbol of Utah. A 3-mile hike leads to it; otherwise, two viewpoints further along the road allow a glimpse. The Lower Viewpoint is an easy 150ft walk, or you can bear left for a moderately strenuous 0.5-mile hike and 200ft ascent to the better Upper Viewpoint.

The Drive: Return to the main road, turning right. After 2.5 miles, turn right at signs for Fiery Furnace.

5 Fiery Furnace

A permit is required to hike Fiery Furnace, but the viewpoint is open to all. A short walk between split-rail fences leads to the overlook of giant fins of Entrada Sandstone. At sunset, they resemble flames in a furnace.

The Drive: Follow the main road to its end, where it loops near the Devils Garden trailhead.

6 Devils Garden

The Devils Garden Trail (p132) takes in a huge number of arches. Tunnel Arch and Pine Tree Arch are closest to the parking lot, while a moderately easy walk goes to Landscape Arch, the span of which is longer than a football field.

DEVIL OF A TIME: HIKING DEVILS GARDEN

At the paved road's end, 19 miles from the visitor center, Devils Garden trailhead marks the beginning of a hike that passes eight arches. Most people only go 1.3 miles to Landscape Arch, a gravity-defying, 306ft-long behemoth that's the largest arch in North America. Further along, the trail gets less crowded as it grows rougher and steeper.

From the **1 Devils Garden trailhead**, the route passes through large rock fins before an offshoot trail heads to **2 Tunnel Arch** and **3 Pine Tree Arch**. Back on the main path, the long and thin **4 Landscape Arch** appears. Beyond this arch, the trail becomes more difficult, sometimes requiring scrambling and route finding, so most hikers choose to turn back. The trail climbs through and then over a rock fin, reaching a spur trail to **5 Partition Arch** and low-to-the-ground **6 Navajo Arch**. Back on the main route, continue gaining elevation and lofty views before dropping down and around the backs of the fins to **7 Double O Arch**, where a much larger arch sits atop a smaller one. Add on a side trip to **8 Dark Angel**, a 150ft-high rock column standing on its own. For an extra dose of adventure, those confident in their way-finding skills should head back toward Double O Arch and set off on the **9 Primitive Trail**. This route wiggles through fins and is marked by cairns, but it's helpful to have a map pre-downloaded. If you're not arched-out, head to the quiet **10 Private Arch** before working your way down fins and back onto flat ground. Soon you'll reconnect with the main trail near Landscape Arch, which leads back to the trailhead.

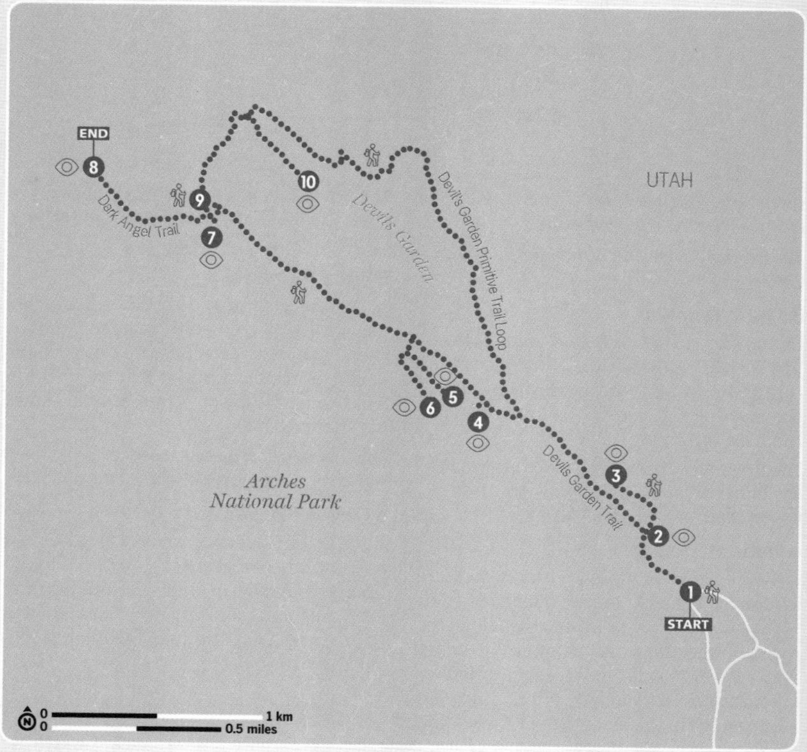

From the parking lot, take the short, easy walk to **Wolfe Ranch**, a one-room cabin built in 1907. Cross the footbridge over Salt Wash for a look at a small **petroglyph panel**. Likely carved by the Ute after 1600 CE, the markings show people on horseback. The trail is wheelchair-accessible to this point.

Past the panel, the trail climbs a series of small switchbacks, soon emerging onto a long, steady slickrock slope. This hill is visible from the trailhead, where you'll see tiny figures trudging up the slickrock like pilgrims.

Delicate Arch remains hidden as the trail skirts behind a narrow slickrock ledge. As you round the final corner, a broad sandstone amphitheater opens up below, with Delicate Arch crowning its rim, framing the 12,700ft La Sal Mountains in the distance. Circle the rim to the base of the arch, which sits atop a saddle that drops precipitously on either side.

Windows on a Sandstone World

SEEING DOUBLE

The **Windows Trail** is an easy 1-mile loop that gently climbs to three massive photogenic arches: North Window, South Window and Turret Arch. It's hard to grasp the immensity of these gigantic marvels until you're beside them.

This hike is one of the busiest in the park, but you can leave some of the crowds behind by returning on the longer **Windows Primitive Loop**, with a beautiful back view of the two windows. The primitive trail is less obvious and doesn't have as many trail markers.

The trail forks about 500ft from the parking lot. Take the left fork and head to the **North Window**, which measures 51ft high and 93ft wide and frames the distant desert. A spur trail (part of the Windows Primitive Loop) heads to the **South Window**, sitting higher above the ground than the North Window. The main Windows Loop Trail then circles to the castle-like **Turret Arch**.

For a bonus arch, head back to the parking lot and set off on the 0.6-mile **Double Arch Trail**. Double Arch is the tallest in the park at 112ft, and you're allowed to walk and scramble underneath the arch (but not on the arch itself).

The National Park Service (NPS) considers parts of these trails 'barrier free,' and some wheelchair users can access them with assistance. The Double Arch Trail has a hard-packed surface, and the first 300ft of the Windows Trail is flat before it arrives at stone steps and other uneven surfaces.

OUTSTANDING ARCHES

Karen Garthwait, acting public affairs specialist at Arches, has worked at the national park for more than a decade. These are some of her favorite features.

Double Arch
This arch in the Windows section is the tallest in the park. You can see it from your car, but it's worth the half-mile walk to stand beneath and gaze up in wonder.

Baby Arch
Most arches aren't labeled on the park map. This one, near the Courthouse Towers, is a great reminder to keep an eye out for hidden treasures.

Delicate Arch
The park's most famous feature. I recommend the easy Lower Viewpoint walk; the long hike up is like climbing 50 flights of stairs.

GETTING AROUND

Driving is the best and easiest way to get around Arches National Park. There is no shuttle system or public transportation. Some companies in the gateway town of Moab run bus tours through the park.

BIG BEND NATIONAL PARK

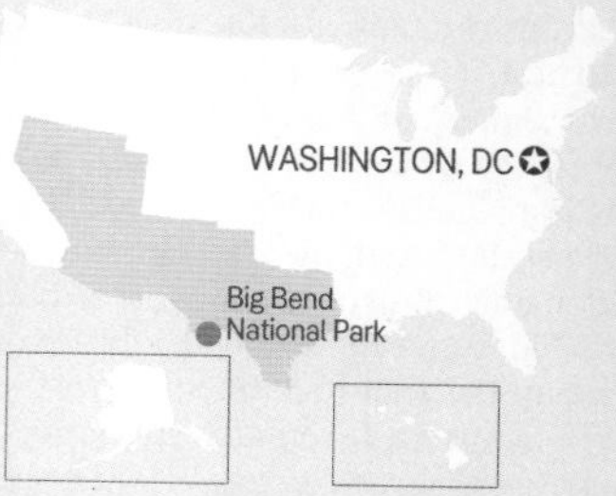

The Spanish dubbed it *el despoblado* – the uninhabited. When you're traversing Big Bend's 800,000 acres, you come to appreciate what 'big' really means. These mountains, desert and river are so lonesome and otherworldly that it can feel like you've stumbled into a moonscape. It's vast enough to allow a lifetime of discovery, yet laced with enough well-placed roads and trails to permit short-term visitors to see a lot in a few days.

Big Bend is dense with alien-like geological diversity. Mountains carpeted with oak and juniper soar above the floor of the unforgiving desert. Steep canyons of limestone and volcanic ash look like the creations of a brutal god. Ocotillo plants spring out of the ground like imposing, wiry sculptures. Adventurous travelers have ample opportunities for hiking, backpacking and rafting, but the best thing to do is sit in silence and soak up the awesome vastness of it all.

JIM AND LYNNE WEBER/SHUTTERSTOCK ©

Santa Elena Canyon

FACTS

Great For Walking, scenery, wildlife
State Texas
Entrance Fee 7-day pass per car/motorcycle/person on foot or bicycle $30/25/15
Area 1252 sq miles

CROSSING THE BORDER TO MEXICO

From inside the national park, you can venture across the border to the colorful Mexican village of **Boquillas del Carmen** – bring your passport. After passing through the port of entry, hop in a rowboat for a small cash fee to get across the river. From the Mexican side of the Rio Grande, walk to Boquillas or pay to ride on a donkey, horse or in a vehicle. Embroidered quilts, textiles and local handicrafts are for sale throughout town. Tacos and margaritas from the two local restaurants are the perfect way to cap off an afternoon before crossing back to Big Bend.

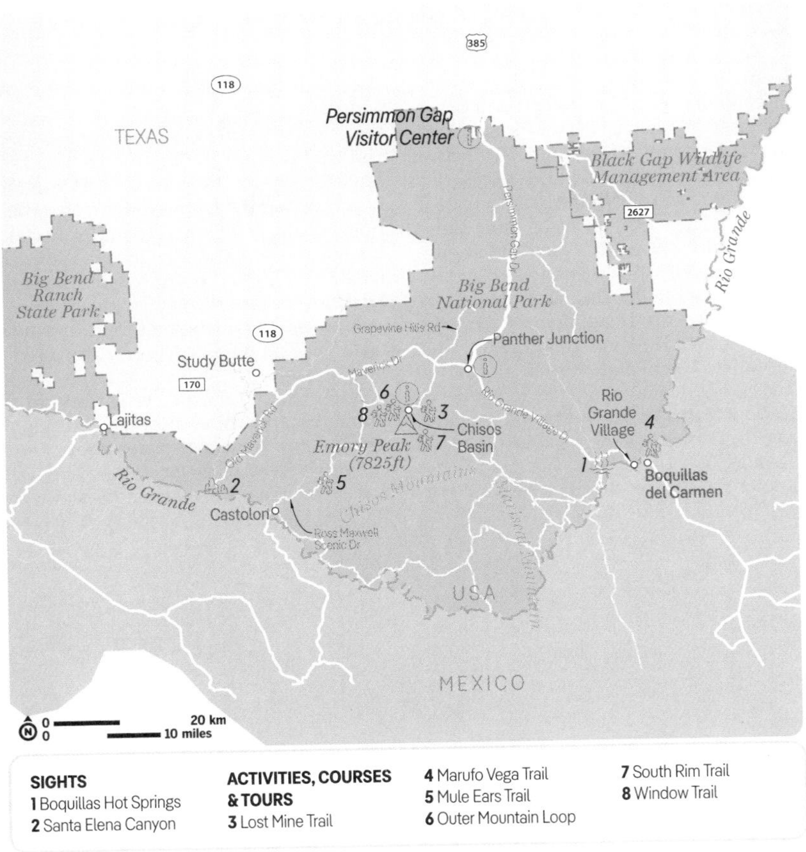

Into the Water

AQUATIC ADVENTURES IN BIG BEND

Santa Elena Canyon is one of the most well-known and impressive natural features in Big Bend National Park. This deep gorge, cut by the Rio Grande, has red-streaked walls that tower well above 1000ft. To get into the thick of things, set off on the 1.7-mile round-trip trail that leads straight into the mouth of the canyon, where you can luxuriate in the thick, cottony silence.

WHERE TO EAT AFTER A HIKE IN BIG BEND NATIONAL PARK

Mountain View Restaurant
The park's only full-service restaurant has a commanding view of the Chisos. **$$**

Bad Rabbit Cafe
Generous portions of mouthwatering Americana cafe food at Terlingua Ranch Lodge. **$$**

Big Bend Pizza
Trek to Marathon for stone-baked pies with handmade crust that hit the spot. **$$**

HITTING THE HIGHLIGHTS ON ROSS MAXWELL SCENIC DRIVE

Everyone knows Texas is huge, but you can't really appreciate just how big it is until you visit Big Bend National Park, which is almost the same size as Rhode Island. This driving tour hits all of Big Bend's high points.

The Ross Maxwell Scenic Drive skirts the western slopes of the Chisos Mountains, climbing to staggering vistas and eventually running parallel with the Rio Grande. Pull over for trailheads, overlooks and interpretative sites. Heading south from the Ross Maxwell junction, the first noteworthy stop is **1 Sam Nail Ranch**, one of the many homesteads once active in Big Bend. At the **2 Sotol Vista Overlook**, gaze out over the gorgeous view of the park's western side. Take the 1.5-mile side road to the base of the cliffs of **3 Burro Mesa**. From here, you can hike along a half-mile trail that leads into a hidden box canyon with a high, dry waterfall. Back in the car, head south to the **4 Mule Ears Overlook**, where you can glimpse the distinctive-looking Mule Ears Peaks. Next up, **5 Tuff Canyon** is a deep, narrow slot that's easily observed from a couple of different viewing platforms, though you can also hike into the canyon itself. Stop by the **6 Castolon Historic District**, once a cavalry outpost, to look around the old adobe buildings and fuel up on snacks and cold drinks from La Harmonia Store. End at the road's showstopping pinnacle, **7 Santa Elena Canyon**, a dramatic gorge with walls that tower more than 1000ft above the water. From here, you can either backtrack on Ross Maxwell Scenic Dr or continue ahead on Maverick Rd, which leads to the park's western gate.

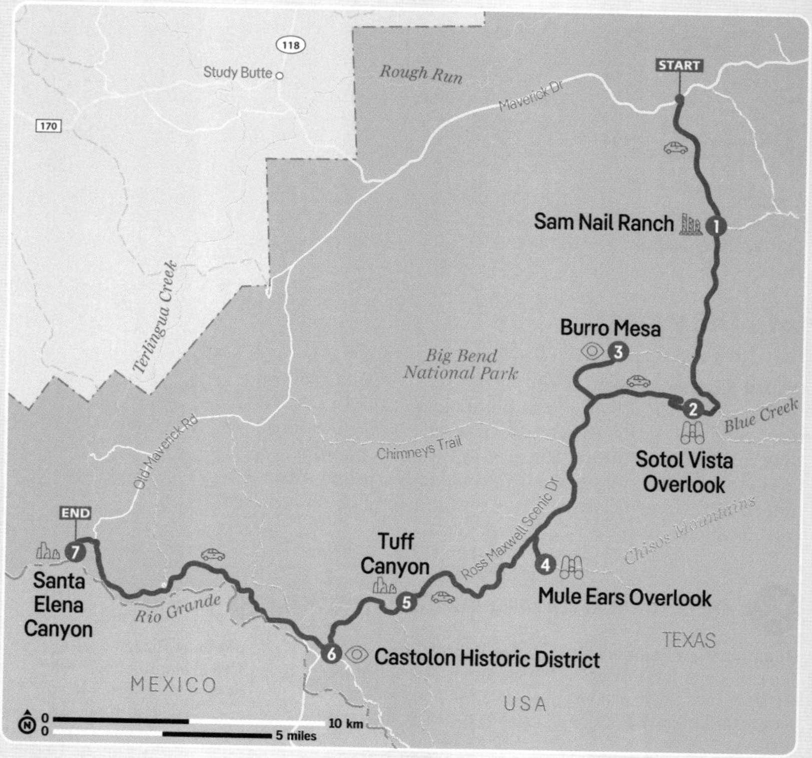

Better yet, plan to raft or canoe the **Rio Grande** through the canyon. Nothing beats seeing the canyon and its wildlife from a kayak or canoe and feeling the deep sense of contentment that comes from drifting along the river. Trips can range from several hours to several days. Several local outfitters provide shuttles, equipment rental and guided trips, including Angell Expeditions (angellexpeditions.com), Big Bend River Tours (bigbendrivertours.com) and Far Flung Outdoor Center (bigbendfarflung.com). A river permit is required for all trips on the water, and they are available in person up to seven days in advance at the Chisos Basin and Panther Junction visitor centers.

The Rio Grande isn't the only water in this desert park. Cap off a sweaty hike in Big Bend by soaking in piping-hot mineral water at **Boquillas Hot Springs**. The shallow 105°F (40.5°C) pool is pressed directly against the river in the remains of an early 1900s bathhouse. When you get too hot, dip a toe or dangle an arm in the chilly river waters. If you want to have the springs all to yourself, go early in the morning or late at night.

Best Hikes in Big Bend

GET TO THE HEART OF THE PARK

With more than 150 miles of trails to explore, it's no wonder hiking is big in Big Bend.

Hikers who tackle the strenuous **South Rim** (12.5 miles to 14.5 miles round trip) are rewarded with the best view in all of Texas. From your perch atop the cliffs of the Chisos Basin, you can see hundreds of miles into Mexico on a clear day.

Less challenging than other hikes in the High Chisos, the **Lost Mine Trail** (4.8 miles round trip) provides an excellent introduction to the park's landscapes. Gently sloping switchbacks climb more than 1000ft through a cool, shaded forest of juniper, oak and pine trees, and then you're treated to awe-inspiring views of Casa Grande Peak and Juniper Canyon. The grand finale is a wide stone saddle, from where you can stare out in all directions at jutting cliffs, craggy peaks and lush canyons. If you're not up for the full climb, you can get a pretty good payoff with impressive views just 1 mile along the trail.

Aside from Lost Mine, signature day hikes include the 1.7-mile **Santa Elena Canyon Trail**, which traverses deep into its namesake canyon. The 3.8-mile **Mule Ears Trail** is a hike through the desert to a historic corral and spring, and the 5.6-mile **Window Trail** boasts panoramic desert vistas.

For serious hikers, the **Marufo Vega Trail** (14 miles round trip) is a grueling but rewarding trek that crosses remote, relatively unshaded and incredibly beautiful terrain. The **Outer Mountain Loop** is a 30-mile backpack through a variety of habitats and scenery. You're unlikely to see many people on these trails.

LODGING IN & AROUND BIG BEND

Big Bend has four campgrounds: Chisos Basin, Cottonwood, Rio Grande Village and Rio Grande Village RV Park. If you get a permit in advance, you can also camp in the backcountry: 42 designated sites in the Chisos are available up to six months in advance online (recreation.gov), and six more backpacking sites are available for permitting in person up to 24 hours in advance at the Chisos Basin and Panther Junction visitor centers. The Chisos Mountains Lodge is the only lodging inside the park. Book as far in advance as possible. If the park is full, the towns of Terlingua, Marathon and Study Butte offer everything from roadside motels to luxury casitas.

GETTING AROUND

The only way to explore Big Bend National Park is by driving. There is no public transportation to, from or within the park. The closest buses and trains run through Alpine, 100 miles northwest of Panther Junction Visitor Center. The nearest gateway town is Terlingua.

BRYCE CANYON NATIONAL PARK

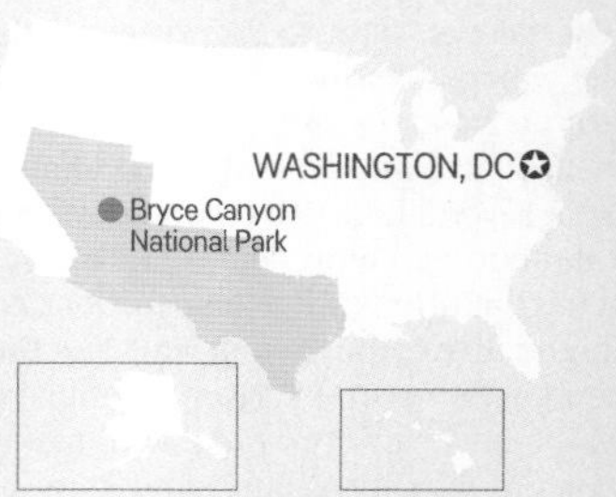

The sight of Bryce is nothing short of otherworldly. Repeated freezes and thaws have eroded soft sandstone and limestone into a landscape that's utterly unique: sandcastle spires known as hoodoos, jutted fins, windows and deep narrows. Though it's the smallest of Utah's national parks, Bryce Canyon stands among the most prized.

Despite its name, Bryce is not actually a canyon but rather the eastern edge of an 18-mile plateau (a canyon is formed by flowing water). The Pink Cliffs mark the top step of the Grand Staircase, a giant geological terrace reaching to the Grand Canyon in Arizona. Trails leave from the rim and descend thousands of feet into the maze of hoodoos in the stunningly sculpted high-mountain desert.

High altitude means Bryce has cooler temperatures than other Utah parks. Clean, dry air also means excellent visibility, reaching all the way into the Andromeda Galaxy 2.5 million light-years away.

FACTS

Great For Scenery, walking, family travel
State Utah
Entrance Fee 7-day pass per car/motorcycle/person on foot or bicycle $35/30/20
Area 56 sq miles

Hoodoos

IRINAK/SHUTTERSTOCK ©

VIEWPOINTS

Paria View

Two miles off the main road, this is *the* place to come for sunset. Most of the hoodoo amphitheaters at Bryce face east and are best viewed at sunrise, but Paria View looks west.

Inspiration Point

Sits lower than Bryce Point and provides much the same view, but Silent City is most compelling from here. The hoodoos feel closer, and you can make out more details on the canyon floor. It's a great place for stargazing.

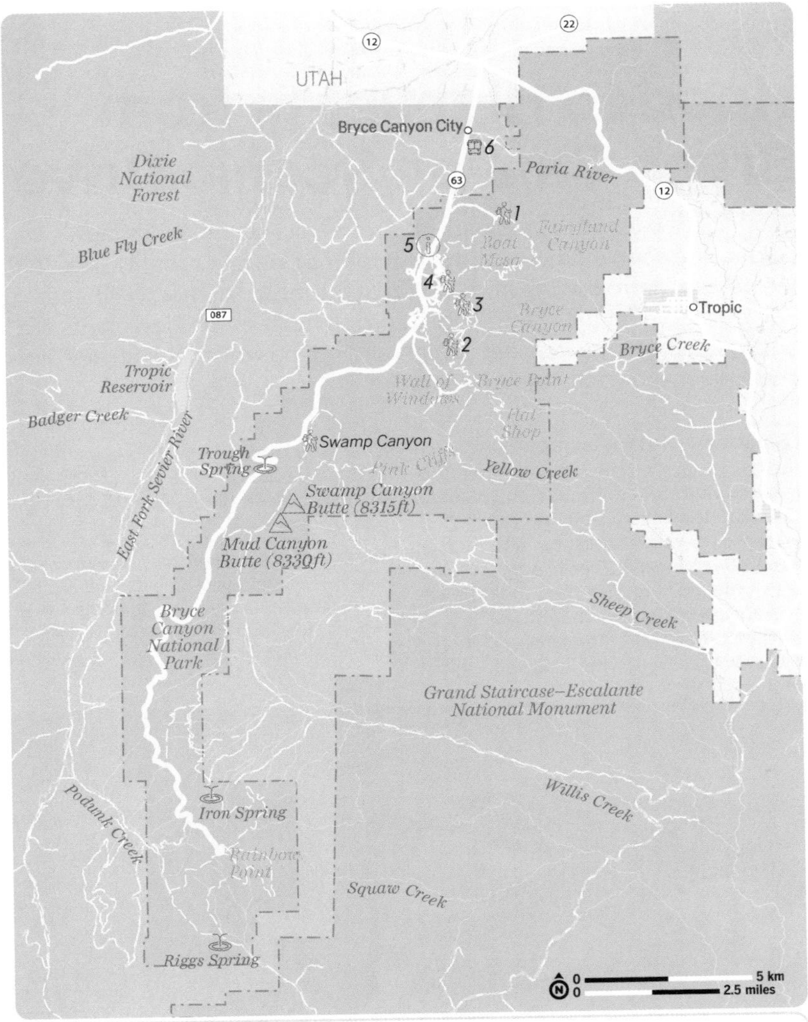

ACTIVITIES, COURSES & TOURS
1 Fairyland Loop Trail
2 Peekaboo Loop Trail
3 Queen's Garden Trail
4 Rim Trail

INFORMATION
5 Bryce Canyon National Park Visitor Center

TRANSPORT
6 Bryce Canyon National Park Shuttle

WHERE TO EAT IN & AROUND BRYCE CANYON NATIONAL PARK

Bryce Canyon Lodge Restaurant
The only restaurant in the park; standard American menu with nice regional additions. **$$**

Bryce Canyon General Store
Grab-and-go pizza, sandwiches and ice cream, plus a good selection of drinks, including Utah craft beer. **$**

Ebenezer's Barn & Grill
Big dinners of grilled meat and all the fixings come with live country music. **$$**

ROAD TRIP

Hoodoo Highlights from Bryce Canyon Scenic Drive

Spanning the length of the park, this route hits all the park's high points. The scenic drive winds south for 17 miles and roughly parallels the canyon rim, climbing from 7894ft at the visitor center to 9115ft at Rainbow Point at the road's end. Because most of the viewpoints are on the eastern side, it's best to hightail it all the way to Rainbow Point and then make your way slowly back.

1 Rainbow Point & Yovimpa Point

On a clear day, you can see more than 100 miles from Rainbow Point. Giant sloping plateaus, tilted mesas and towering buttes jut above the vast landscape. On the north-eastern horizon, look for the Aquarius Plateau – the top step of the Grand Staircase – rising 2000ft higher than Bryce.

At the other end of the parking lot, another short, paved, wheelchair-accessible trail leads to Yovimpa Point, one of the park's windiest spots. The southwest-facing view reveals more forested slopes and less eroding rock.

The Drive: Heading north, you pass overlooks nearly every mile. One of the best stops at this end of the park, the Agua Canyon Overlook eyes two large formations of precariously balanced, top-heavy hoodoos.

Rainbow Point

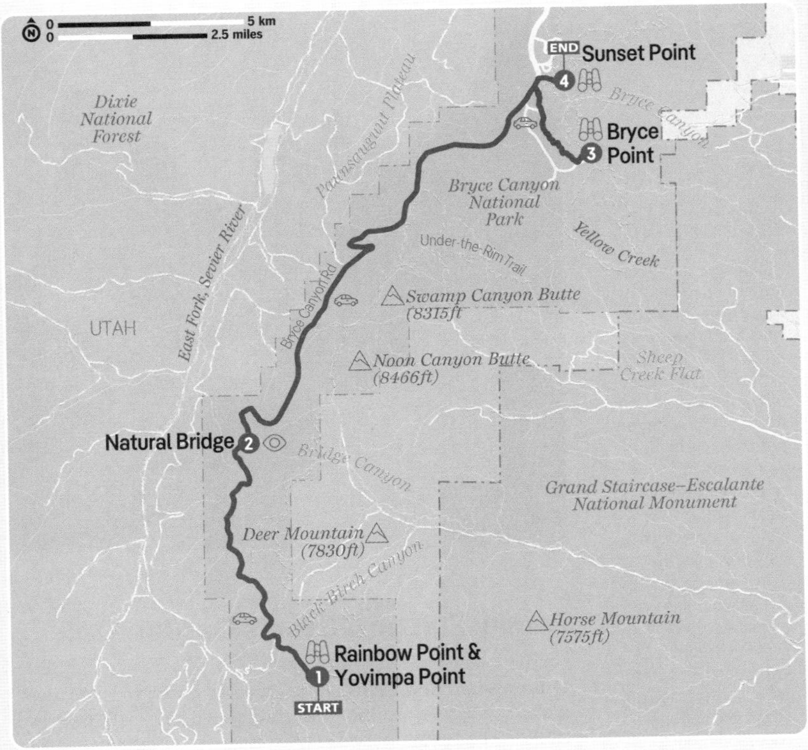

2 Natural Bridge

The parking lot at Natural Bridge is the biggest since Rainbow Point, and with good reason: a stunning span of eroded, red-hued limestone juts from the edge of the overlook. Though called a bridge, it's technically an arch. A bridge forms when running water, such as a stream, erodes the rock. In this case, the freezing and thawing of water inside cracks and crevices, combined with gravity, shattered the rock to create a window formation.

The Drive: Continue north for about 10 miles and turn right on Bryce Point Rd.

3 Bryce Point

Perhaps the best viewpoint in the park, the stretch of landscape seen from Bryce Point is gasp-worthy. Walk the rim above Bryce Amphitheater for awesome views of Silent City, an assemblage of hoodoos so dense, gigantic and hypnotic that you'll surely begin to see the shapes of figures frozen in the rock. Follow the path to the actual point, a fenced-in promontory that juts out over the forested canyon floor 1000ft below, allowing a broad view of the hoodoos.

The Drive: Back on the main drive, turn right. Look for parking around Bryce Canyon Lodge.

4 Sunset & Sunrise Points

Views into Bryce Amphitheater at Sunset Point are as good as they get, but don't expect solitude. It's at the core of the park, near campgrounds, the lodge and all visitor services. Aside from great views of Silent City, this point is known for Thor's Hammer, a big square-capped rock balanced atop a spindly hoodoo.

Walk for 10 minutes along the paved Rim Trail to Sunrise Point. This southeast-facing spot offers great views of hoodoos, the Aquarius Plateau and the Sinking Ship, a sloping mesa that looks like a ship's stern rising out of the water.

CB_TRAVEL/SHUTTERSTOCK ©

Fairyland Loop

SEEING STARS IN BRYCE CANYON

Amateur astronomers are in for a treat at Bryce Canyon. All of Utah's national parks are certified as dark sky parks, but Bryce offers the widest range of star-studded programs, activities and events for visitors who are astro-curious. The National Park Service puts on some 100 astronomy programs a year, including an annual Astronomy Festival in June, full-moon hikes and regular ranger talks. Check the national park's calendar online (nps.gov/brca/planyourvisit/calendar.htm) and stop by the visitor center when you arrive to see what's happening while you're there.

The park is open 24 hours. Time your visit for the new moon, when the skies are darkest, and watch as the Milky Way shimmers all the way to the horizon.

Family Fun on Queen's Garden Trail

ROCK OF ROYALTY

Queen's Garden Trail is the easiest route into the canyon, making it a good trail for kids. It makes a gentle descent over sloping erosional fins and passes elegant hoodoo formations, but stops short of the canyon floor. Queen's Garden Trail is not a loop but an in-and-out hike. If you decide to go further, add on the **Queen's Garden Connecting Trail**, part of the Queen's Garden–Navajo Loop Combination Trail.

From Sunrise Point, follow signs to the trailhead off the Rim Trail. Views of the amphitheater as you descend are superb. A maze of colorful rock spires extends to Bryce Point, and deep green pines dot the canyon floor beneath undulating slopes seemingly tie-dyed pink, orange and white. As you drop below the rim, watch for the stark and primitive bristlecone pines, which are thought to be about 1600 years old. The dense needles of these ancient trees cluster like foxtails on the ends of the branches.

After a series of switchbacks, turn right and follow signs to the Queen's Garden Trail. The short spur from the main trail passes through a tunnel and emerges among exceptionally

WHERE TO STAY IN BRYCE CANYON NATIONAL PARK

Bryce Canyon Lodge
The 1920s park lodge exudes rustic charm; cabins are a better pick than the generic motel-style rooms. **$$**

North Campground
Large campground a short walk from showers, a coin laundry, the general store and visitor center. **$**

Sunset Campground
First-come, first-served, 102-site campground with more shade than North Campground but fewer nearby amenities. **$**

beautiful hoodoo castles in striking colors amid the pines. After looping around a high wall and passing through two more tunnels, bear right and follow signs to **Queen Victoria**. The trail's namesake monarch peers down from a white-capped rock, perched atop her throne.

Return to the rim the way you came, or link with the **Navajo Loop Trail** via the Queen's Garden Connecting Trail, which drops to the canyon floor.

The Magic of Fairyland Loop

A HIKE ON THE QUIET SIDE

Fairyland Loop is a great 8-mile day hike and a good workout, with 1900ft of elevation gain. Fairyland is spared the Bryce Amphitheater crowds, and the trail is difficult primarily because it meanders in and out of the hoodoos, down into washes, and up and over saddles.

This trail begins at Fairyland Point and circles the majestic cliffs of flat-topped, 8076ft Boat Mesa, emerging on the rim near Sunrise Point. The last 2.5 miles of the loop follow the Rim Trail back to the trailhead. Note that the park shuttle doesn't stop at Fairyland.

From **Fairyland Point**, the trail dips gradually below the rim. To the south, **Boat Mesa** stands between you and views of the park. A short walk leads past ancient bristlecone pines, some clinging precariously to the ragged cliffs, their 1000-plus-year-old roots curled up like wizened fingers. Looping around hoodoos that rise like castle turrets and towers, the trail soon drops to the canyon floor and a seasonal wash. Much of the north-facing terrain holds its snowpack until May or June.

At **Fairyland Canyon**, 600ft below your starting point, towers of deep-orange stone stand like giant totem poles. The trail rises and falls before traversing a ridge toward Campbell Canyon. Zigzagging up and down, the trail eventually reaches a seasonal wash on the floor of **Campbell Canyon**. Keep an eye out for **Tower Bridge**, which connects three spires to two windows. To reach the base of the formation, take the clearly marked dead-end spur from the wash. From Tower Bridge, it's a 950ft climb over 1.5 miles to the Rim Trail.

Hiding Out on Peekaboo Loop

HOODOO, I SEE YOU

An ideal half-day hike, the **Peekaboo Loop Trail** sees the most variety of terrain and scenery in Bryce, with 1560ft of elevation change. The Peekaboo Loop Trail is also a horse trail, so expect to see occasional riders. If you don't want to

PEEKABOO ON HORSEBACK

See Bryce Canyon from the saddle on a guided horse-riding tour of Peekaboo Loop. **Canyon Trail Rides**, the park's official concessioner, has a corral near Bryce Canyon Lodge and offers two- and three-hour rides on horses and mules through the hoodoos from April through October. Seeing the sights from this angle promises another perspective, even if you've already ticked many of the hikes off your list, and the 'cowboy' guides add amusing commentary, telling stories and pointing out rock formations along the way.

Horse owners are also allowed to bring their own stock into the park, but only in certain areas and at specific times. None of the park's backcountry campgrounds are suitable for stock animals.

Ruby's Inn
This gargantuan hotel complex is your one-stop shop for accommodations, activities, groceries and more. **$$**

Bryce Canyon Grand Hotel
The large, clean rooms are a step up from other hotels clustered outside the park entrance. **$$**

Bryce Canyon Resort
Definitely more motel than resort, but has good-value, kitschy rooms 4 miles from the park. **$$**

CALM IN THE CANYON

Peter Densmore, park ranger at Bryce Canyon, shares his recommendations for finding solitude in the park.

The Rim Trail
One of the park's easiest hikes, the Rim Trail follows the canyon edge as it connects Bryce Canyon's popular viewpoints. While these viewpoints can sometimes become crowded, a short walk on the Rim Trail is a great way to get some space. The section from Bryce Point to Inspiration Point is my favorite.

When to Visit
Peak visitation is typically from April through October, with spikes on major holidays, but August is often a quieter summer month. A winter visit requires packing more clothes, but the profound quiet and vivid contrast of snow on red rocks makes it a favorite season for a hardy few.

navigate around horse droppings, choose another route, but the views here are among the park's best.

From **Bryce Point**, follow signs to the Peekaboo Connecting Trail east of the parking area. Bear left at the fork and descend for 1.1 miles, passing through mixed conifers and swooping out along a gray-white limestone fin beneath the Bryce Point overlook. Further down the trail, hoodoo columns take on a bright-orange hue. After passing through a human-made tunnel, look for the **Alligator** in the white rock ahead. As you work your way down the switchbacks, watch for the **Wall of Windows**, which juts above the hoodoos atop a sheer cliff face perpendicular to the canyon rim.

At the loop trail junction, bear right. As you pass beneath healthy fir and spruce trees, you'll spot a few blackened snags. They're victims of lightning, not forest fires. Look for ancient bristlecone pines, too. An inch of these trees' trunks represents a century of growth.

Climbing a saddle, you rise to eye level with the hoodoo tops before dropping over the other side to the cluster of delicate red spires at **Fairy Castle**. Just past the turnoff for the Navajo Loop, the trail climbs again to spectacular views of **Silent City** and passes beneath the **Cathedral**, a majestic wall of buttress-like hoodoos. The rolling trail skirts the Wall of Windows, threads through a tunnel and switchbacks down. As you approach the Bryce Point trail, take the spur on the right to the lush rest area near the horse corral for a cooldown or picnic before climbing out of the canyon.

A Full View of Bryce on the Rim Trail

CIRCLING THE CANYON

The easiest hike in the national park, the 0.5- to 5.5-mile (one way) **Rim Trail** outlines Bryce Amphitheater from Fairyland Point to Bryce Point, promising an entire journey of incredible views. Several sections are paved and wheelchair accessible, the most level being the half mile between Sunrise Point and Sunset Point. In other spots, you'll ascend moderately steep, wooded rises to seek shade beneath the pines, watch wildlife, or delight in vibrant displays of spring wildflowers. The colors in the rock pop most when lit by the morning or afternoon sun.

When the park shuttle is running (April to mid-October), you can easily take it to any point along the trail and return from another instead of backtracking to your car. You can join the Rim Trail anywhere along its route, though note that shuttle buses don't stop at Fairyland.

Remember that Bryce sits atop a sloping plateau. The north end of the Rim Trail is lower than the south end, so it's downhill

WILDLIFE TO LOOK OUT FOR

Utah Prairie Dog
These burrowing rodents pop up from their colony between the visitor center and Bryce Canyon Lodge.

Uinta Chipmunk
Don't feed these cute striped critters that often hang around picnic areas and overlooks.

Pronghorn
The fastest land animal in the western hemisphere, and likely the largest you'll spot in the park.

Wall of Windows

from Bryce Point to Fairyland Point, though the trail rises and falls in a few spots.

From **Bryce Point** to **Inspiration Point**, the trail skirts the canyon rim atop white cliffs, revealing gorgeous formations, including the **Wall of Windows**. After passing briefly through trees, it continues along the ridgetop to the uppermost level of Inspiration Point, 1.3 miles from Bryce Point. The leg to **Sunset Point** drops 200ft in 0.75 miles, winding its way along limestone-capped cliffs. Below the rim, **Silent City** rises in all its hoodoo glory.

At Sunset Point, you may wish to detour along the Navajo Loop Trail for a taste of the canyon. You can reemerge on the Rim Trail further ahead by adding the Queen's Garden Trail. Otherwise, stay the course and look for **Thor's Hammer** as you continue the 0.5-mile stroll along a paved path to **Sunrise Point**, the most crowded stretch of trail in the entire park. The views are worth it.

Past Sunrise Point, crowds thin as the trail climbs 150ft toward North Campground. Fork left at the Fairyland Loop Trail junction, unless you'd like to follow the moderately difficult, 3-mile round-trip spur into the canyon (950ft elevation loss) to see the window-laced **China Wall** and **Tower Bridge** –

WHY I LOVE BRYCE CANYON NATIONAL PARK

Lauren Keith, writer

Even if you've seen photos of it, nothing quite prepares you for the sight of Bryce Amphitheater as more hoodoos come into view with every step. My body never lets me stay up too late, so on this trip, I set an alarm for 4am to squeeze in as much stargazing as I could before sunrise. I walked through pitch-black forest to Sunrise Point, switched my flashlight off and let the darkness settle. After 20 minutes, I thought I saw a cluster of stars, but they were at ground level and coming toward me. Soon, a few fellow stargazers appeared, and our little constellation swapped stories and travel tips until the sun came up.

RANGER PROGRAMS AT BRYCE CANYON NATIONAL PARK

Hoodoo Geology Talk
This hoodoo FAQ will give you the answers you seek; daily at 11am at Sunset Point.

Rim Walk with a Ranger
Hour-long interpretive hike that sets off from Sunset Point at 2pm from Memorial Day to Labor Day.

Evening Program
A grab-bag of topics is up for discussion in the auditorium of Bryce Canyon Lodge.

twin arches between chunky rock spires. Otherwise, watch for these features from the Rim Trail.

Topping out near North Campground, the path ambles across gently rolling hills on the forested plateau before rejoining the canyon rim at **Fairyland Point**, 2.5 miles from Sunrise Point.

Multiday Hikes in Forests & Meadows

THE BEAUTY OF BRYCE'S BACKCOUNTRY

If you seek solitude, head into Bryce Canyon's backcountry for a multiday adventure. Only 1% of visitors venture into the park's remote areas. You won't walk among many hoodoos here, but you will pass through forests and meadows with distant views of rock formations.

Backcountry permits are required and can be booked in advance (recreation.gov) for trips during the busy months of March through November or purchased at the visitor center if spaces are still available. Permits for December through February are available on a walk-in basis. Campsites are assigned as part of your permit.

Bryce Canyon has black bears, mountain lions, coyotes, snakes and other wildlife that might be around backcountry campsites. You must have a bear canister or rent one for free from the visitor center. If you bring your own canister, a ranger will inspect it. Water sources in the backcountry aren't reliable and need to be filtered before drinking.

Most backcountry trails are covered with snow from late October to March or April. Even in May, snowpack sometimes obscures sections of trail. June and September are ideal times to hike, while in July and August, you'll have to contend with thunderstorms.

Both of Bryce's backcountry trails are strenuous, with lots of elevation change. The 23-mile **Under-the-Rim Trail**, south of Bryce Amphitheater, skirts beneath cliffs, wanders through amphitheaters and walks amid pines and aspens. The 11-mile stretch between Bryce Point and Swamp Canyon is one of the hardest and most rewarding. The 8.8-mile **Riggs Spring Loop Trail** goes from the tip of the Paunsaugunt Plateau, descending beneath the spectacular Pink Cliffs through spruce, fir and aspen, and then through ponderosa pines to a desert habitat of sagebrush and scrub oak. Fit hikers could finish it in a day, negating the need to get a permit and campsite.

WINTER IN BRYCE CANYON

With an average elevation of 8000ft, Bryce Canyon is a high-altitude park that is blanketed by snow in winter. The snowcaps on the formations are stunning, and the cycle of freezing and thawing water is responsible for shaping the hoodoos. Most roads are plowed, while others are designated for **cross-country skiing** and **snowshoeing**. The best cross-country skiing and snowshoeing trails are on the Paria Ski Loop, the Rim Trail and Fairyland Rd. Rangers lead free two-hour snowshoeing hikes – and even hikes in the snow during the full moon.

Rent snowshoes and cross-country skis from **Ruby's Inn** in Bryce Canyon City, which also has miles of groomed trails.

GETTING AROUND

During the busy season from April through October, free buses shuttle passengers around the park. Visitors are still allowed to drive into Bryce Canyon when the shuttle is running. The shuttle has 15 stops, nine of which are in the park; it also stops at some hotels in Bryce Canyon City outside the park entrance.

Private vehicles are the only transportation option from fall through spring.

Cycling is a great way to get around the park, and you can bike to every major trailhead. A paved multiuse path, perfect for families, goes through the park to Inspiration Point and connects with the Red Canyon Bicycle Trail, which ends 15.5 miles from the visitor center.

CANYONLANDS NATIONAL PARK

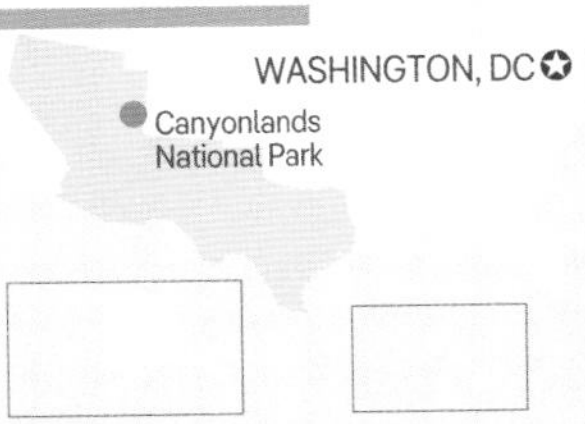

An expansive vision of ancient earth, Canyonlands National Park is Utah's largest – and least visited – national park. Vast serpentine canyons tipped with white cliffs loom 1000ft over the Colorado and Green Rivers. Skyward-reaching spires, deep craters, swirling tie-dye mesas and majestic buttes dot the landscape.

The two rivers form a Y that divides the park into four separate districts, inaccessible to one another from within the park. Cradled atop the Y, Island in the Sky is the most developed and visited district because of its proximity to the town of Moab, about 30 miles from the visitor center.

The thin hoodoos and sculpted sandstone in the Needles district offer an excellent backcountry experience, but you'll need serious skill and equipment to traverse the 4WD-only roads of the Maze, the park's remotest frontier. Northwest of here, Horseshoe Canyon features spectacular Native American rock-art paintings.

FACTS

Great For Scenery, cycling, walking
State Utah
Entrance Fee 7-day pass per car/motorcycle/person on foot or bicycle $30/25/15
Area 527 sq miles

Great Gallery (p154), Horseshoe Canyon

SIGHTS
1 The Maze
2 Horseshoe Canyon
3 Upheaval Dome

ACTIVITIES, COURSES & TOURS
4 White Rim Road
5 Aztec Butte Trail
6 Cave Spring Trail
7 Chesler Park Loop
8 Pothole Point Trail

CANYONLANDS NATIONAL PARK

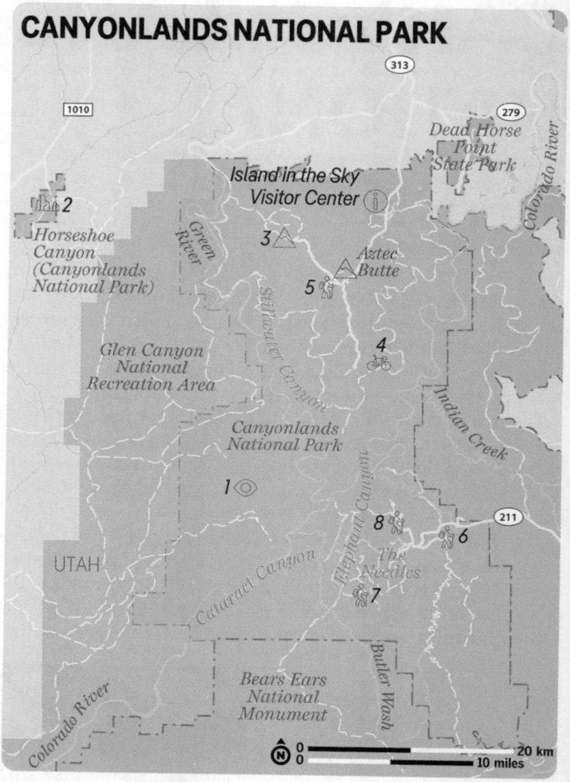

PERMITS FOR CANYONLANDS

In addition to the park entrance fee, permits are required for day use of White Rim Rd, as well as overnight backpacking and river trips. Designated camp areas abut most trails, and open-zone camping is permitted in some places.

Each day, 100 day-use permits are issued for White Rim Rd (50 for motorized vehicles and 50 for mountain bikes). These permits cost $6 if reserved on recreation.gov, or they are free if picked up at the visitor center on the day of your trip.

Reservations are recommended for overnight backcountry permits, which often book out quickly in spring and fall. Some are kept open for first-come, first-served walk-ins. Permits cost $36, plus $5 per person per night.

Historic Storage at Aztec Butte

HIKING TO AN ANCESTRAL PUEBLOAN GRANARY

Shortly after the turnoff on Upheaval Dome Rd, the moderate 1.4-mile round-trip **Aztec Butte Trail** climbs slickrock to stellar views and an ancient granary ruin. (Despite the name, the structure was built by Ancestral Puebloans, not the Aztecs.) It's the only archaeological site at Island in the Sky.

This short ascent of a Navajo Sandstone dome yields fantastic views; it's a steep hike over slickrock to the top. Parts of the hike require going up and down high ledges that might require scrambling. Wear rubber-soled shoes or hiking boots for traction. Stay on the trails, as fragile cryptobiotic crust is widespread atop the dome. In summer, bring plenty of water

WHERE TO SEE CANYONLANDS' BEST VIEWS

Grand View Point
A humble name belies the park's best overlook at the end of the paved road.

Green River Overlook
Get a glimpse of one of Canyonlands' great carvers; less busy than some other viewpoints.

Shafer Trail Viewpoint
Watch as Jeeps and 4WD vehicles navigate the hairpin turns that unfurl down the canyon.

and wear a wide-brimmed hat because the exposed butte offers no shade.

A little more than a quarter mile from the parking area, a spur trail leads to a **granary** built around 1200 to 1300 CE, tucked below an overhang on the butte's northern side. Native people stored food and medicine in this structure, sheltered from the elements. Head back to the main trail and carry on to Aztec Butte. Use the cairns and switchbacks to follow the route up. The butte levels off at the top, revealing views and endless sky. Circle the top of the butte to soak in the sights before returning the same way to the parking area.

Upheaval Dome: History's Mystery

A GEOLOGICAL MARVEL

Was Upheaval Dome created by salt or something from outer space? Scientists disagree over how the feature formed. Some suggest it's a collapsed salt dome, while more recent research posits that it was the site of a meteorite strike some 60 million years ago. Scope out the geological drama on the moderate **Upheaval Dome Trail**, which leads to two overlooks that gaze out at the 3-mile-wide crater.

It's an easy 0.3 miles one way to the **first overlook**. From the parking area, climb to the fork in the trail, bear right and ascend the slickrock to the viewpoint. If you find yourself on switchbacks, you've made a wrong turn. To reach the **second overlook**, return to the fork in the trail and bear right, descending over slickrock before clambering to a final steep ascent. From here, you have a broader panorama of the surrounding landscape. The afternoon light is magnificent, and this viewpoint adds only 1 mile to the trip.

Hikers up for a strenuous trek can take **Syncline Loop**, a difficult 8.1-mile hike around the dome (but without views of it). It's the district's most challenging route, and most park rescues happen on this trail, so make sure you're prepared for steep switchbacks, scrambling through boulder fields and navigating with few markers. Tackle it clockwise for more shade in the afternoon.

Driving & Biking Through Canyonlands' Backcountry

MAKING A GETAWAY

Canyonlands has hundreds of miles of unpaved roads, inviting mountain bikers and drivers with high-clearance 4WD vehicles and off-grid know-how into the park's hidden and more remote corners. Blazed by uranium prospectors in the 1950s, the primitive, 100-mile **White Rim Rd** encircling Island in

WHO WERE THE ANCESTRAL PUEBLOANS?

The Ancestral Puebloans were a Native people who lived across the Four Corners region (modern-day Utah, Colorado, New Mexico and Arizona) from as far back as the 12th century BCE. They farmed and built a variety of homes and communal spaces, such as pit houses, ceremonial underground kivas and multiroom and multistory complexes tucked under cliff faces. Prime examples of their impressive architecture can be found at Mesa Verde National Park (p181) in southwestern Colorado. Their modern descendants include the Pueblo, Hopi and Zuni.

Ancestral Puebloans have been referred to as Anasazi, a Navajo word that's sometimes translated as 'ancient enemies.' Some Pueblo people today consider this word derogatory. The Hopi call them Hisatsinom, which means ancient people.

WHERE TO CAMP IN & AROUND ISLAND IN THE SKY

Willow Flat Campground
The first-come, first-served, 12-site Willow Flat campground has vault toilets but no water or hookups. $

Dead Horse Point State Park
Two campgrounds for RVs and tents, plus nine gorgeous glamping yurts with wraparound decks. $$

Horsethief Campground
BLM-run spot with no-reservation sites atop a mesa in a piñon-juniper forest. $

ROAD TRIP

Cruising Island in the Sky

From the visitor center, the paved road through the Island in the Sky district leads past numerous overlooks and trailheads, ending after 12 miles at Grand View Point, featuring one of the Southwest's most sweeping views, rivaled only by the Grand Canyon and nearby Dead Horse Point State Park. This scenic drive takes in the best of the viewpoints and short hikes in this part of the national park.

1 Shafer Canyon Overlook

About 0.5 miles south of the visitor center, pull off to the left at the Shafer Canyon Overlook, where you can peer down 1500ft. Watch as Jeeps snake down the switchbacks of Shafer Trail, once used by cattle ranchers and later by the Atomic Energy Commission to truck uranium to Moab for processing.

The Drive: A quarter mile ahead, you'll cross the Neck, where the ridge narrows to 40ft across – eventually this strip will erode away, further isolating the mesa. Drive on for another 5.5 miles.

2 Mesa Arch Trail

This easy 0.6-mile round-trip hike is worth every step. The 27ft-long arch, perched right on the cliff edge, makes a beautiful frame for the distant La Sal Mountains, and it's particularly popular at sunrise when its underside glows a fiery red.

The Drive: Head south, turning right on Upheaval Dome Rd. Follow it for 5 miles to the parking lot at its end.

SEAN XU/SHUTTERSTOCK ©

Upheaval Dome

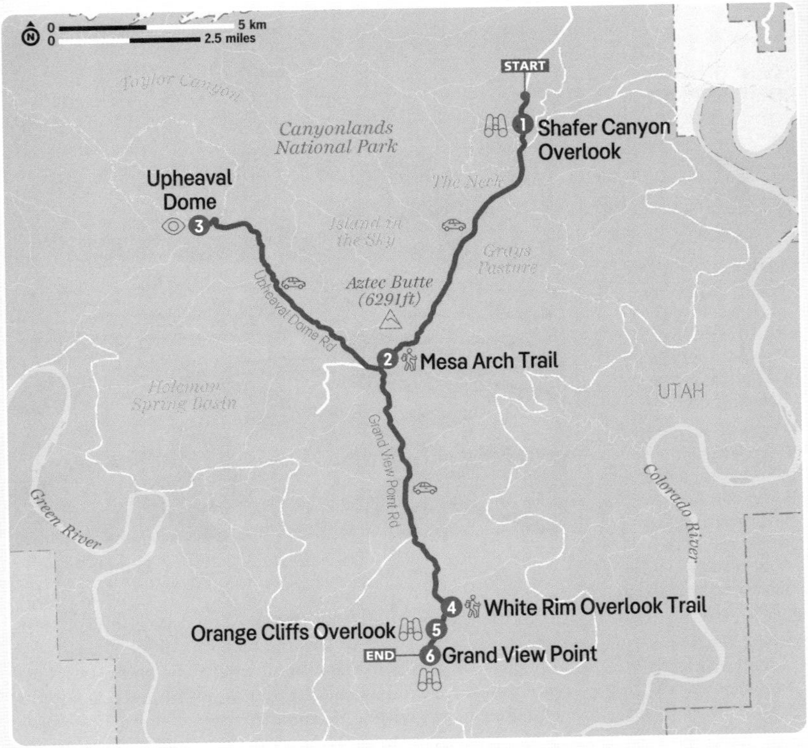

3 Upheaval Dome

Can you solve the Island in the Sky's geological mystery? While most of this district has systematic layers of rock, Upheaval Dome jumbles them. Was this caused by 'salt bubbles' that deformed the rocks, or from the impact of a meteor? Hike the steep quarter mile to a viewpoint and decide for yourself.

The Drive: Return to the main park road, turning right to continue heading south.

4 White Rim Overlook Trail

Enjoy your packed lunch at the picnic tables around the parking lot before setting off on this 1.8-mile round-trip trail that skirts the canyon edge before peering down into the depths. This east-facing overlook has a similar vantage point as Grand View, but fewer visitors.

The Drive: Continue driving south for 1 mile.

5 Orange Cliffs Overlook

This turnoff offers views west to the Henry Mountains, the last-charted mountain range in the Lower 48. The Orange Cliffs lie southwest, beyond the Maze district of Canyonlands. At sunset, the canyons glow orange in the waning light.

The Drive: Carry on until the end of the road, which loops in a parking lot.

6 Grand View Point

The name says it all: Grand View is one of the Southwest's most sweeping and beautiful scenes. Hundred-mile panoramic views are easily earned by walking the short distance to the cliff edge, but for more of a leg stretch, set off on the easy 1.8-mile round-trip stroll to the overlook for a better perspective of the massive mesa underfoot.

CANYON CONTEMPLATION

Cadence Cook is the district interpreter at Canyonlands' Island in the Sky. These are her favorite viewpoints in the national park.

Green River Overlook
This viewpoint showcases stunning views of the Green River and the vast wilderness of the Maze district. Light in these canyons is best in the morning.

Grand View Point
A short walk leads to stunning views toward the south, east and west. From here, you'll see a myriad of canyons and beautiful red-rock layers. Check at the visitor center to see whether any ranger talks are happening here.

Big Spring Overlook
This viewpoint in the Needles district is a great spot to see unique geological features, including hoodoos and terraced canyons.

Pothole Point

the Sky is the top choice for 4WD and mountain-biking trips. It generally takes two to three days in a vehicle, or three to four days on a mountain bike. Because the route lacks any water sources, cyclists should team up with a 4WD support vehicle or travel with a Moab outfitter.

Day-use permits for one-day trips, or overnight permits for trips on White Rim Rd, are required. Overnight permits can be hard to come by in spring and fall. Permits become available four months before the start of the season (eg fall permits for September to December open in May). Walk-in permits are sometimes available. Check with rangers at the visitor center the day before or the day of your trip.

Potash Rd and the iconic switchbacks on **Shafer Trail** do not require permits and make a thrilling dirt-road drive between the park and Moab, passing below Dead Horse Point State Park and the spot where the final scene of *Thelma & Louise* was filmed.

All-terrain vehicles (ATVs), utility terrain vehicles (UTVs) and off-highway vehicles (OHVs) are not allowed anywhere in the park. If you're bringing a rental car, make sure you've read the agreement closely as most do not allow drivers to take their car off paved roads.

4WD & MOUNTAIN-BIKE ROUTES IN THE NEEDLES DISTRICT

Colorado River Overlook
Jaw-dropping views of the canyon. Park and walk the final, steep 1.5-mile descent. No permit needed.

Elephant Hill
One of the most technically challenging routes in the state. Permits required for day and overnight use.

Salt Creek (Peekaboo) & Horse Canyon
Archaeology junkies love the rock art here, but it's often impassable. Permits necessary.

Human History on Cave Spring Trail

DRAWN TO THE WATERING HOLE

Cowboy artifacts, historic pictographs, ladders and slickrock scampers: **Cave Spring Trail** is a fun-filled hike for history buffs and kids of all ages.

Pungent sagebrush marks the trailhead at the end of a well-maintained, mile-long dirt road. Hikers first reach an abandoned **cowboy camp** with miscellaneous remnants from the 19th and 20th centuries. The trail continues beneath a protruding rock lip to Cave Spring, one of the few perennial water sources in the Needles. Look for the rust-colored **pictographs** painted on the walls more than 1000 years ago.

From Cave Spring, you climb two ladders up slickrock for wraparound views of rock formations, steppes and mesas. The trail has awesome views of rock spires and the La Sal Mountains. After crossing the undulating sandstone, the trail drops into a wash and returns to the trailhead.

Pools of Life at Pothole Point

HERE TODAY, GONE TOMORROW

The 0.6-mile **Pothole Point Trail** loop across slickrock explores the microcosmic ecosystems of potholes – naturally occurring dimples in the rock that collect water during rainstorms. The hike features views of distant cliffs, mountains and rock formations.

To the naked eye, these potholes appear to be nothing more than mud puddles, but closer inspection reveals tiny organisms that must complete their life cycles before the water evaporates. Keep hands and feet out of the potholes because these organisms are fragile. Though this is an excellent walk for contemplative souls and the scientifically inclined, it does lack drama, unless the potholes are teeming with life (which isn't always readily visible).

Connecting the Dots Around Chesler Park

LOOPING THROUGH CANYONLANDS' BACKCOUNTRY

Get among the namesake 'needles' formations on the **Chesler Park Loop**, an awesome 11-mile hike across desert grasslands, past towering red-and-white-striped pinnacles and between deep, narrow slot canyons, some only 2ft across. Elevation changes are mild, but the distance makes it an advanced day hike. Make sure you plan your route and download maps in advance because this area has a number of intersecting circular trails.

Park at the **Elephant Hill trailhead**, 3 miles from Squaw Flat Campground on a gravel road that's suitable for sedans

'HALF THE PARK IS AFTER DARK'

Canyonlands National Park is an incredible sight to behold by day, and by night the landscape is blanketed by some of the darkest skies remaining in the US, making it perfect for stargazing. On some nights, it's possible to see 15,000 stars twinkling overhead, compared to fewer than 500 stars visible in urban areas.

The night sky at Canyonlands is so astounding that the International Dark Sky Association named the park a Gold-Tier International Dark Sky Park in 2015.

The park is open 24 hours a day, 365 days a year, so stargazers can have a DIY dark-sky session, or rangers occasionally lead evening astronomy programs.

RANGER PROGRAMS AT CANYONLANDS NATIONAL PARK

Geology Talk
Remember all the rock layers after this lesson at Grand View Point; 10am and 10:30am daily.

Patio Talk
Rangers pick from a mixed bag of topics at 1pm daily at the visitor center.

Night Hikes & Stargazing
Set off on a bright night hike (around full moon) or see the stars (around new moon).

SHORT HIKE TO 'ROADSIDE RUIN'

The easiest hike in the Needles district is the 0.3-mile round-trip walk to the 'Roadside Ruin,' a remarkably well-preserved Ancestral Puebloan granary tucked into a hidden gap in the rocks. The trail takes only about 20 minutes to walk and starts out across uneven gravel before finishing over slickrock.

Ancestral Puebloan and Fremont people lived in this area, farming the locations that had enough water, such as nearby Salt Creek. Although the name 'Roadside Ruin' has appeared on national park maps since 1985, tribes today object to calling it a ruin, saying these places are still living and that their ancestors continue to use them.

but in places is wide enough for just one car. From the parking area, the trail climbs to a bench and then undulates over slickrock toward rock spires. The next section is typically where people make a wrong turn. Cross the wash at the T-junction and follow signs to Chesler Park (not Druid Arch), descending 300ft along switchbacks into Elephant Canyon. Continue to follow signs along the canyon floor.

The final 0.2 miles to the **Chesler Park Viewpoint** climbs 100ft, topping out on the rocky pass amid spires. This marks the beginning of the 5-mile Chesler Park Loop. Five campsites lie southeast of the junction for backpackers.

If you're camping, leave your backpack at the campsite the next morning and explore the claustrophobia-inducing **Joint Trail**, where the fractured rock narrows to 2ft across in places. Pause just east of the Joint Trail for stellar views of the towering pinnacles that ring Chesler Park. On the southwest section of the loop, you'll follow a half-mile stretch of a 4WD road. If staying two nights, take the side trip to **Druid Arch**.

Hidden Art of Horseshoe Canyon

THE 'LOUVRE OF THE SOUTHWEST'

Part of Canyonlands National Park, but detached by road from the park's other sections, **Horseshoe Canyon** shelters one of the most impressive collections of millennia-old rock art in North America. The centerpiece is the 200ft-long **Great Gallery**, where about 80 haunting human figures were painted in red, white and brown on the high rock wall between 2000 BCE and 500 CE, though they might be older. Similarly styled clay figures found in the vicinity date back more than 7000 years, meaning that this rock art could be twice as old as the Great Pyramid of Giza. The heroic life-size figures are magnificent, especially the 7ft-tall painting at the center of the scene, known as the Holy Ghost.

The Great Gallery is only one of four rock-art sites along this trail. Don't miss the other spots at **Horseshoe Shelter**, **High Gallery** and **Alcove Site**, which aren't well signposted on the ground.

This area was previously called Barrier Canyon, which hints at how difficult it is to get here. The Great Gallery lies at the end of a 7-mile round-trip hiking trail that descends 780ft from a dirt road, built by the Phillips Petroleum Company in 1929 to supply its oil wells. Plan on six hours. Rangers lead guided hikes most weekends in April, May, September and October; check Canyonlands' park calendar for specifics (nps.gov/cany/planyourvisit/calendar.htm). You can camp on BLM land at the trailhead, though it's really a parking lot. There is a vault toilet, but no water.

WHERE TO CAMP IN & AROUND NEEDLES DISTRICT

The Needles Campground
Some of the 26 in-park sites are reservable from spring to fall; otherwise, it's first-come, first-served. $

Needles Outpost
Campsites, tipis and treehouse tents plus an on-site store just outside the park entrance. $$

Superbowl Campground
This BLM-administered spot has 37 sites with picnic tables, fire rings and vault toilets. No water. $

The Maze

Getting Lost in the Maze

LEAVE IT ALL BEHIND

A 30-sq-mile jumble of high-walled canyons, the **Maze**, part of Canyonlands National Park, is a rare preserve of true wilderness for hardy backcountry veterans. The colorful canyons are rugged, deep and sometimes completely inaccessible. Many of them look alike, and it's easy to get turned around, hence the district's name.

The rocky roads absolutely necessitate reliable, high-clearance 4WD vehicles. If you're at all inexperienced with four-wheel driving, stay away. Be prepared to repair your 4WD and, at times, the road. There may not be enough money on the planet to get you towed out of here. Most tow trucks won't even try.

Plan on spending at least three days out here, though a week is ideal. Before you set off, contact the **Hans Flat Ranger Station** for conditions and advice. It has a few books and maps, but no other services. The closest towns are Hanksville and Green River. The canyons are three to six hours' drive beyond the ranger station. The few roads into the Maze district are poor and often closed when there's rain or snow; bring tire chains from October to April.

WHAT IS BARRIER CANYON STYLE?

Formerly known as Barrier Canyon, Horseshoe Canyon is home to a handful of rock-art sites with a style so distinct it has its own label. Barrier Canyon style shows front-facing human-like figures with broad, rounded shoulders but often no arms or legs. Many are painted in red, which was made from ground hematite (iron oxide).

The pictographs in Horseshoe Canyon are the oldest on the Colorado Plateau, and their meaning isn't fully known. Some researchers think the larger figures, such as the Holy Ghost, are shamans or spirits. The spirit figures have over-sized eyes and are sometimes depicted with headdresses or horns. The torso shows life-giving symbols of water, such as waves, dots, zig-zags or parallel vertical lines.

GETTING AROUND

You need a car to get to and around Canyonlands. Make sure you have a 4WD and a permit if you're planning to venture into the backcountry. Moab is the closest town to the Island in the Sky district, and Monticello is nearest to the Needles district.

CAPITOL REEF NATIONAL PARK

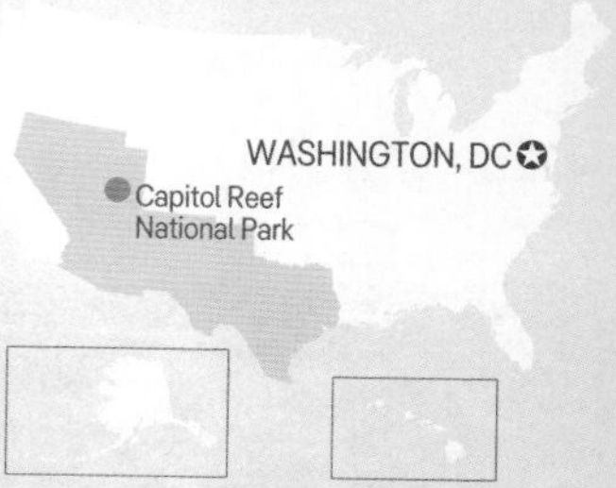

In this forgotten fold of the Colorado Plateau, slot canyons appear as cathedrals cut from the earth, and giant cream-colored domes arc into perfectly blue skies that hold fluffy clouds.

Capitol Reef doesn't always make it onto travelers' Utah national park itineraries, lending it a carefree air that promises wide-open vistas, limited crowds (relatively speaking) and plenty of adventurous activities, from hiking through canyons and up to overlooks, to dusty-bottoming your way out on rugged 4WD tracks. Or you can simply take in the history and geology that reveals itself in petroglyphs and early Mormon settlements, sandstone streaks and hidden arches, and a labyrinth of canyons that stretch back millions of years.

This narrow park runs north–south following the Waterpocket Fold. Unlike most national parks, there's no entrance station. Just follow Hwy 24, which cuts through the park, to the visitor center where you can pay the entrance fee and pick up information.

FACTS

Great For Photo ops, scenery, walking
State Utah
Entrance Fee 7-day pass per car/motorcycle/person on foot or bicycle $20/15/10
Area 378 sq miles

AMEHIME/SHUTTERSTOCK ©

Road to Capitol Gorge (p159)

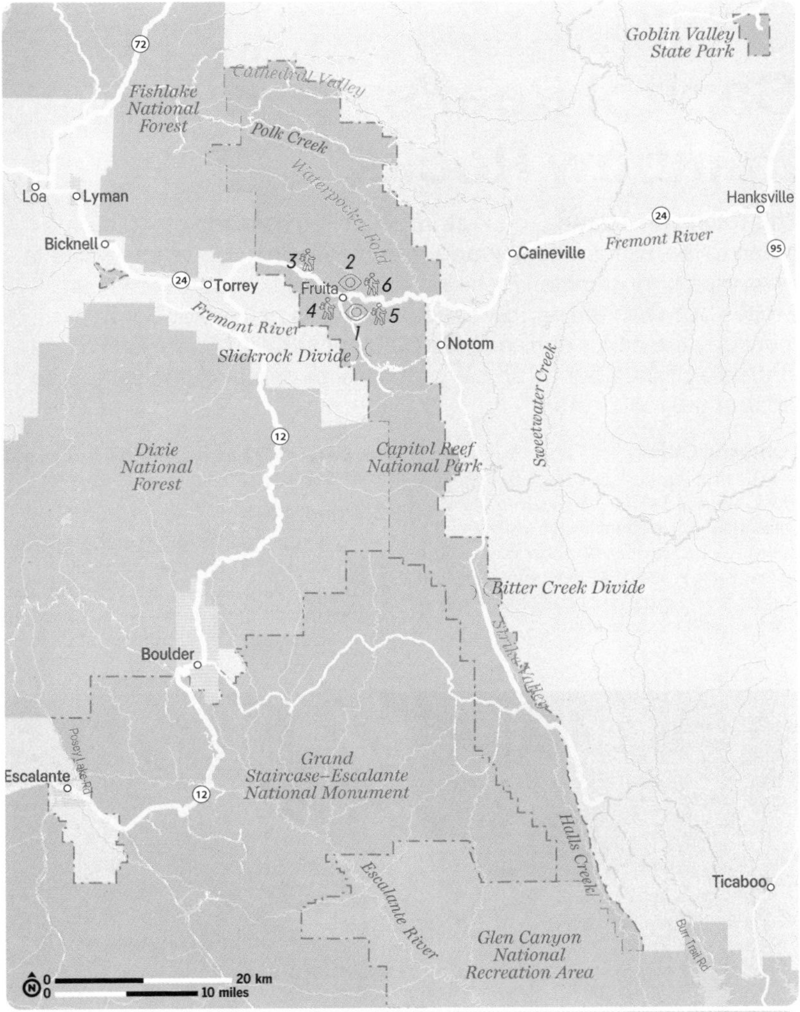

SIGHTS
1 Cassidy Arch
2 Petroglyphs

ACTIVITIES, COURSES & TOURS
3 Chimney Rock Trail
4 Cohab Canyon Trail
5 Grand Wash Trail
6 Hickman Bridge Trail

WHERE TO CAMP IN & AROUND CAPITOL REEF NATIONAL PARK

Fruita Campground
Terrific 71-site campground under cottonwood trees beside the Fremont River, surrounded by orchards. Book well ahead. **$**

Singletree Campground
Closest non-park option to the visitor center, with lots of space and even wi-fi (extra fee). **$**

Sunglow Campground
Six first-come, first-served sites with good facilities (flushing toilets, sinks) on Forest Service land. **$**

ROAD TRIP

Capitol Reef's Rainbow Rocks

This rolling drive along the Waterpocket Fold is a geology diorama come to life, with arches, hoodoos and canyon narrows easily within view, plus opportunities for hikes. The best of the route is the last 2 miles between the narrow sandstone walls of Capitol Gorge. You must pay the park's entrance fee ($20 per vehicle). There isn't a staffed entrance booth, so pay at the visitor center or the self-serve kiosk at the road's start.

1 Colorful Cliffs

For the first 2 miles after the self-serve pay kiosk, the road skirts the bottom of gorge walls that are striped in bands of colors, including layers of red-brown shale of the 225-million-year-old Moenkopi Formation and gray and purple volcanic ash. Stop at the pull-off to take a photo.

The Drive: After 2 miles, turn left on the dirt road to Grand Wash.

2 Grand Wash

Stretch your legs on the stunning Grand Wash Trail (p160), an easy hike that winds through a canyon that gets progressively narrower as you carry on. If you're up for a more active trek, hike up to Cassidy

Grand Wash

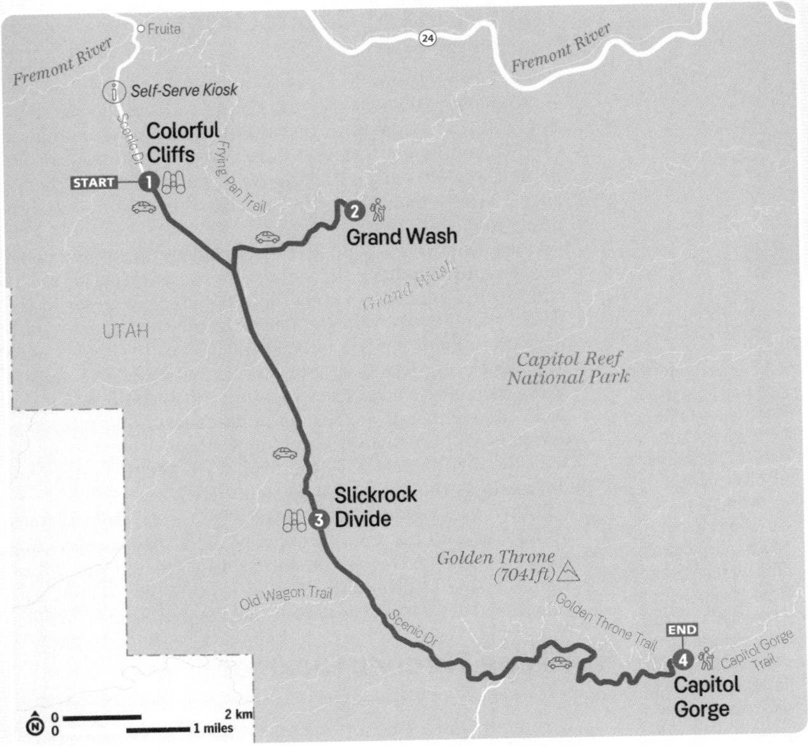

Arch for vertigo-inducing views of the canyon floor below.

The Drive: Head back the way you came to Scenic Dr. Stop at the information panels near the intersection to read about the abandoned Oyler Uranium Mine. It opened in 1901, long before the nuclear bomb and the Atomic Age. Uranium was used to 'cure' arthritis, rheumatism and similar ailments. The metal doors closing off the entrance to the mines are visible from the road.

3 Slickrock Divide

Scenic Dr winds on past soaring sandstone. About 2.5 miles after your last turn, a small pull-off marks the boundary between two major drainage systems in Capitol Reef: north to Grand Wash and south to Capitol Gorge.

The Drive: In 2 miles, the road curves to the northeast, leading to Capitol Gorge, and switches to gravel after the sheltered picnic area.

4 Capitol Gorge

From 1884 to 1962, before Capitol Reef was a national park, you could drive – your car or wagon – through Capitol Gorge (p161), the primary route through the Waterpocket Fold until Hwy 24 was built in the 1960s. It took Mormon pioneers more than a week to clear the first road through the gorge, a process they had to repeat every time a flash flood blitzed through with more boulders and debris.

For a fascinating history lesson, hop out of the car and hike to the panels of Fremont petroglyphs and the names and dates of 19th-century pioneer passersby. Another 3.5-mile round-trip trail from the parking lot heads to the Golden Throne Viewpoint. The top layers of Capitol Gorge are part of the Navajo Formation. These white domes reminded early settlers of the US Capitol building, giving the park the first part of its name.

The Drama of Capitol Reef

A WALK IN THE WASH

Grand Wash, Capitol Reef's most captivating canyon, is worth visiting just to walk between the sheer walls of the Narrows. This flat, easy hike with just 200ft of elevation change is sandwiched inside a Navajo Sandstone canyon that at one point towers 80 stories high but with walls that are only 15ft apart. Avoid this hike if rain threatens because the wash is prone to flash floods.

Along Scenic Dr, a good dirt road leads to the 2.2-mile one-way **Grand Wash Trail**. Start from the parking lot at the end of the Grand Wash spur road. It's an easy stroll up the packed-sand wash from the parking area. An offshoot path near the start of the Grand Wash Trail leads to Cassidy Arch and the Frying Pan Trail, but stay in the wash. The canyon walls inch closer and closer together until, about 1.25 miles from the trailhead, you reach the **Narrows**, where the skyscraper-height canyon is barely more than two arm-lengths wide – a thrilling sight. The canyon walls shrink and spread out again as the flat trail approaches Hwy 24.

Return the way you came or arrange for someone to pick you up on Hwy 24, 4.5 miles east of the visitor center. Look for a trailhead marker on the south side of the highway, where there's a small gravel pull-off. It's also possible to start this hike from Hwy 24, but the parking area is significantly smaller.

SIDE TRIP: CASSIDY ARCH

A 3.3-mile round-trip side trail from Grand Wash leads to Cassidy Arch, a natural red-rock formation that you can walk on. With 670ft of elevation change, this hike is much more difficult than Grand Wash, switchbacking up the cliffside and traversing some sheer drops before flattening out on slickrock, but the views into the side canyons and from the arch are absolutely worth it.

The arch is named after Utah-born Butch Cassidy, one of the West's most notorious outlaws, who robbed banks and trains in the late 1800s. It's said that Cassidy hid out from the long arm of the law high on these cliffs, which provided a good view of any action going on below.

Hiking Through Hickman

NATIVE HISTORY AND A NATURAL BRIDGE

If you only have time for one hike, make it Hickman Bridge. Capitol Reef's most popular trail is diverse, offering a canyon and desert-wash walk to a natural bridge, plus long sky views and spring wildflowers.

This popular hike is easy enough for anyone from kids to grandparents to enjoy. Because the route is largely exposed, it's best to hike it in the early morning. Cairns mark some of the route, which starts off the same way as the longer, more strenuous hike to the Rim Overlook and Navajo Knobs. Pick up a nature trail brochure at the trailhead, which corresponds to numbered signposts along the way.

Starting from the Fremont River, the trail ascends a red-rock cliff via a few easy switchbacks. As you cross an open area of desert vegetation strewn with volcanic black rocks, the highway vanishes behind giant white sandstone domes. A short spur leads to a tiny archaeological site where you can inspect the foundations of **Fremont pit houses**. A short

RANGER PROGRAMS AT CAPITOL REEF NATIONAL PARK

Geology Talk
Understand the many layers that make up Capitol Reef at this daily, year-round 30-minute talk.

Archaeology Talk
Summertime half-hour chat about the people who have lived on this land.

Evening Program
Hour-long conversation about various topics, including the night sky. Meet at Fruita Campground.

WRITING ON THE WALL IN CAPITOL GORGE

At the end of Scenic Dr (p158), leave your car behind for the easy 2-mile round-trip Capitol Gorge Trail, a historic wagon, and later automobile, route that leads past petroglyphs, 19th-century pioneer names carved into the rock and giant water pockets known as the Tanks. The sheer canyon walls are stained with desert varnish, which stands out in dramatic contrast to the red rock. Keep your eyes peeled for bighorn sheep. Avoid this flood-prone route if rain threatens. The **1 trailhead** is at the parking lot. Just a quarter mile later, you reach a scoured panel of ancient **2 Fremont petroglyphs**. About 300ft further on, you'll spot signatures on the right-hand wall. These date to 1911, when a US Geological Survey team lowered its leader over the wall to incise the party's names – vandalism by today's standards. A quarter mile further, look up to see the **3 Pioneer Register**, a collection of carved names and dates. Despite more recent graffiti, you can clearly make out many of the historic carvings. Two gold prospectors, JA Call and Wal Bateman, etched the earliest names on this panel, in 1871. Look up to see the remnants of an early 20th-century telephone line. Just over 0.8 miles from the trailhead, bear left and follow signs to the **4 Tanks**, which lie atop a fairly steep 0.2-mile spur. These giant potholes hold significant volumes of water for much of the year. They were invaluable to early settlers and remain so for animals, so don't drink from or disturb them. When you're rested and ready, head back the way you came – the onward wash trail crosses park boundaries onto private land.

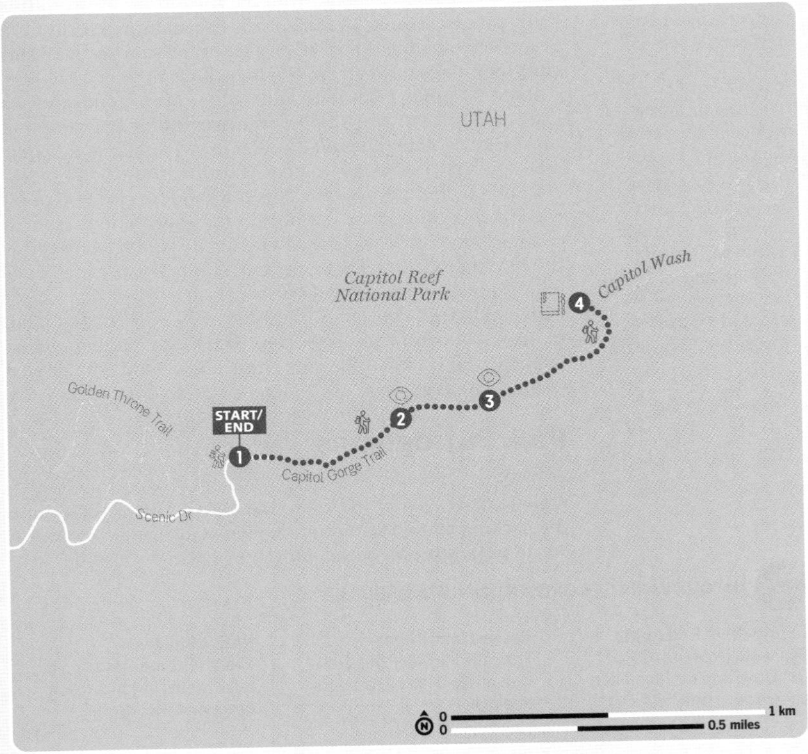

distance further, look right to see the remains of a 700-year-old **granary** in a cliffside alcove.

The trail soon drops into a wash, where you can rest in a shady alcove before ascending over slickrock to **Hickman Bridge**, having gained 400ft in elevation from your start. While this chunky yellow arch can be tricky to spot from afar, the trail loops right beneath it for a marvelous appreciation of its mass. Hike counterclockwise and bear left beyond the arch to keep following the trail's loop. Pause to look over the rim and downriver to Fruita, an oasis of green.

CAPITOL REEF IN A DAY

Shauna Cotrell, park ranger at Capitol Reef, shares how to make the most of one day in the park.

Hike
One of the best ways to experience the park is hiking. Trails immerse you in the landscape while you explore at your own pace.

Visit an Orchard
Get a taste of Fruita and learn some of its history in the historic orchards. In season, you can pick and eat fruit fresh from the trees, including heirloom varieties you won't find at the store.

The Park After Dark
Enjoy the changing light on the cliffs near sunset and then stay until the stars come out. Marvel at the sky in one of the darkest places in the country.

The Curious Story of Cohab Canyon

HIKING TO A HIDEAWAY

Often overlooked, the moderate 3.4-mile round-trip **Cohab Canyon Trail** deters crowds with a steep climb at the beginning, but with the chance to explore a hidden canyon and the views from atop Capitol Reef it's worth every sweaty step.

Utah outlaw Butch Cassidy wasn't the only one who was said to hide out in the secret folds of Capitol Reef. Early Mormon settlers in the area were polygamists, also called cohabitants, shortened to 'cohab.' After Congress passed the Edmunds Act in 1882, which made plural marriages illegal, US marshals were empowered to pursue them as felons.

Starting across the road from the Gifford Homestead, this trail makes a steep 0.25-mile initial ascent atop a rocky cliff. From there, it levels out through a desert wash with small **slot canyons**, nicknamed 'the wives,' branching off from both sides.

About 1.1 miles from the trailhead, a short but steep spur trail veers off left to climb to two **overlooks** of Fruita and the orchards. After about 0.25 miles of switchbacks, this spur trail splits into separate branches heading toward the southern and northern overlooks. This is a good turnaround point if you'd rather do just a 3.2-mile out-and-back hike, instead of a one-way shuttle hike to Hwy 24. The trail to the right is the **Frying Pan Trail**, a moderately difficult route that leads to Cassidy Arch and Grand Wash.

The main trail continues threading its way through Cohab Canyon, going down switchbacks to Hwy 24, ending almost opposite the Hickman Bridge trailhead, around 2 miles east of the visitor center.

Park Petroglyphs

CARVINGS IN THE CLIFFS

A short drive east of the visitor center on Hwy 24, pull into the parking lot and stroll the wooden boardwalks to see dozens of **petroglyphs** pecked into the nearby rock wall. These

UNIQUE VARIETIES GROWN IN FRUITA ORCHARD

Capitol Reef Red Apple
Similar to Golden and Red Delicious apples; found as a unique variety in 1994.

Potawatomi Plums
From the Midwest, but likely brought to Utah by pioneers and miners.

Native Pecans
These nuts are small and have thick shells, but also a rich flavor and a lot of oil.

EDMUND LOWE PHOTOGRAPHY/SHUTTERSTOCK ©

Hickman Bridge

rock carvings convinced archaeologists that the Fremont people were a group distinct from the Ancestral Puebloans. The shorter boardwalk leads to a panel of human-like figures wearing headdresses and surrounded by bighorn sheep. The longer boardwalk runs closer to the cliffs, but the petroglyphs here can be more difficult to see. Bring binoculars for a better view. The longer you linger, the more you're bound to notice. The boardwalk is wheelchair accessible.

Getting a Close-Up of Chimney Rock

LAYERS ON LAYERS

The 3.6-mile **Chimney Rock Trail** loop is a textbook of Capitol Reef's geology and is named after the magnificent red-rock formation that towers near the trailhead. Even though the trail skirts below Chimney Rock, you'll get the best photos of it before you set off on the hike. The route climbs steeply to its namesake – stacks of banded Moenkopi Formation rock layers crowned with a beige capstone – with 590ft of elevation change across the whole hike. Panoramic views of Waterpocket Fold, the volcanic Boulder Mountain plateau, mesas and canyons unfold, and their colors positively glow in the waning light just before sunset.

The trailhead is off Hwy 24, between the Capitol Reef Visitor Center and the town of Torrey.

STARGAZING AT CAPITOL REEF

You're bound to be tired from all the hiking, but when it gets dark, it's not quite time for bed yet. Stay up late to watch the twinkling stars over Capitol Reef, which was awarded the status of a gold-tier International Dark Sky Park in 2015, an accolade acknowledging the highest quality of night sky.

Thanks to its remote location, Capitol Reef has pitch-black skies cut only by the Milky Way and the confetti of a million stars. Ranger programs occasionally include star talks, and **Heritage StarFest** is an annual astro event in September that heralds the beauty of the area's night sky.

GETTING AROUND

Public transportation does not travel to or around Capitol Reef, so you need your own vehicle to get around. Aside from Hwy 24 and Scenic Dr, park routes are dirt roads that are graded only a few times a year.

CARLSBAD CAVERNS NATIONAL PARK

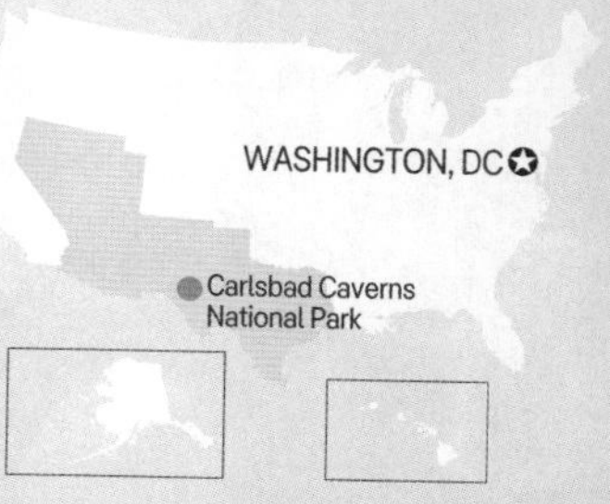

Elaborately carved by the slow hand of time, the magnificent underground rooms and passageways of Carlsbad Caverns feel like they belong in another realm. The portals to this magical place? An elevator that drops the length of the Empire State Building or, more enjoyably, a spooky 1.25-mile subterranean walk that goes down and down (and down) from the cave mouth into the yawning darkness. It's hard to imagine a more dramatic transition than leaving the desert air behind and stepping through the cool, utterly silent tunnels. Adding to the sense of enchantment are the nightly feeding migrations of thousands of Brazilian free-tailed bats. From May through October, the winged nocturnal mammals, which roost in the cave, take to the skies just after sunset. Tucked in the furthest reaches of southeastern New Mexico, far from any major cities, the national park is also a fine dark-skies destination for stargazing.

FACTS

Great For Family travel, photo ops, scenery
State New Mexico
Entrance Fee adult/child $15/free, plus $1 timed entry ticket
Area 73 sq miles

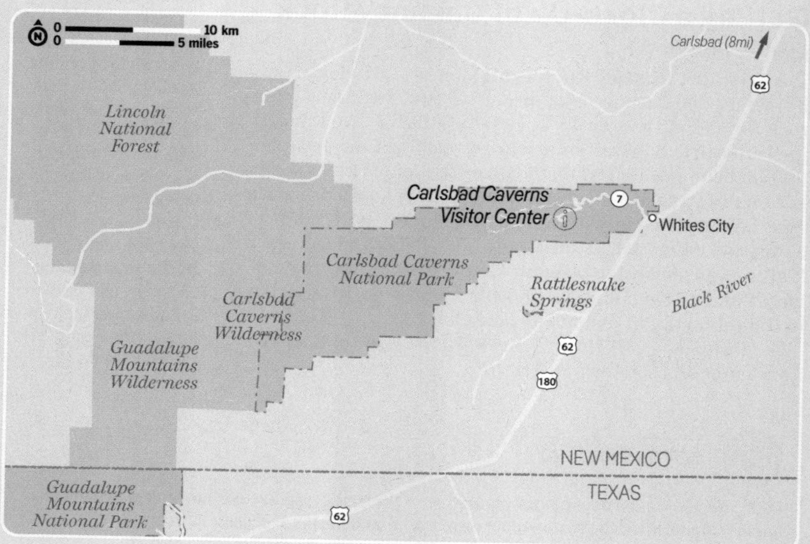

Big Room

Enter an Underground Universe

CREEPING INTO THE CAVE

This gargantuan, 30-mile-long cave descends into a world of bizarre stalagmites and stalactites devoid of plant life and sunlight. For a century, Carlsbad Caverns has been lit up (more recently by a theatrical light specialist who worked on Broadway), with paths for the public to explore.

Reserve a time slot online more than 24 hours in advance (you will be turned away if you show up and it's at capacity) and pick up an informative audio guide at the gift shop. Put on a sweatshirt before you descend into the depths: the temperature is 56°F (13°C) year-round. Whether you take the elevator or walk down, you'll find yourself in the aptly named **Big Room**, an underground limestone room larger than six football fields where you're free to stroll another 1.25-mile loop trail. The rock formations formed over millions of years of water dripping from the surface are truly amazing.

Rangers lead guided tours of **King's Palace** that last 1½ hours, taking you through three chambers in the deepest part of the cave system that's open to the public, 830ft below the surface.

While Carlsbad is massive, consider this: it's only one of 120 known caves within the park's borders, and the largest, Lechuguilla, extends for more than 145 miles, dropping to a depth of 1604ft. Unfortunately, it's only open to research and exploration teams.

BATS TAKE FLIGHT

Now this is a show you certainly won't find at any theater. Every evening from May through October, watch as hundreds of Brazilian free-tailed bats pour out of Carlsbad Caverns to hunt for their dinner. The program is free, and you don't need reservations – seats at the **Bat Flight Amphitheater** are first-come, first-served. Before the show begins, a ranger will do a five-minute presentation to provide context.

Throughout the year, **Bat Flight** is reserved for sunset (check the website as times change across the year), but on the third Saturday of July, it's a tradition to watch the bats return to the cavern in the morning. **Dawn of the Bats**, as it's called, is also free.

GETTING AROUND

Carlsbad Caverns National Park is located in the southeastern corner of New Mexico. The tiny town of Whites City sits at its entrance.

The closest major airport to the park entrance is El Paso International Airport, which is 145 miles southwest in Texas.

GRAND CANYON NATIONAL PARK

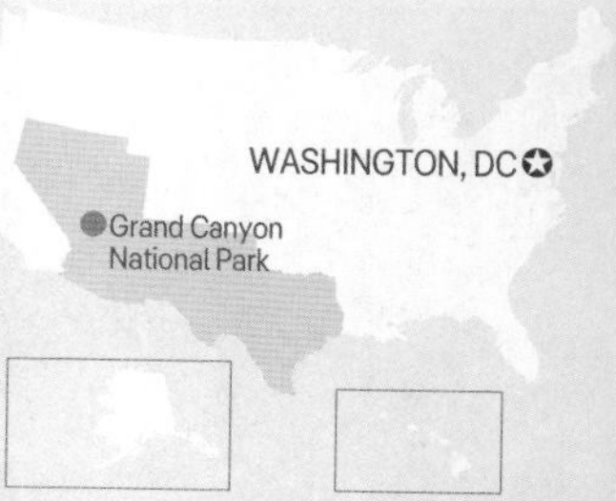

It's big. It's wild. It's dangerous. The Grand Canyon is both an American icon and a world wonder, the site of incredible achievements of the human spirit and unintended consequences, generations of conflict and timeless beauty. The epically sized hole in the ground crumbles away for more than 275 miles from east to west – so massive that it is visible from space, from where it appears to twist like a giant hummingbird etched into the face of the earth.

The second most popular national park in the country, its ringside views of nature's awesome and transcendent power leave no person untouched. Whether you linger for an hour, a day or years, whether you gaze from the rim, trek to secret waterfalls or run the rapids past basement rock that is 1.84 billion years old, the Grand Canyon is an experience that will remain with you for a lifetime.

FACTS

Great For Scenery, family travel, walking
State Arizona
Entrance Fee 7-day pass per car/motorcycle/person on foot or bicycle $35/30/20
Area 1904 sq miles

North Kaibab Trail (p175)

SIGHTS
1 Cape Royal Road
2 Grand Canyon Lodge
3 Point Imperial
4 Yavapai Geology Museum

ACTIVITIES, COURSES & TOURS
5 Havasu Canyon
6 Bright Angel Trail
7 North Kaibab Trail
8 Trail of Time

DRINKING
9 Phantom Ranch

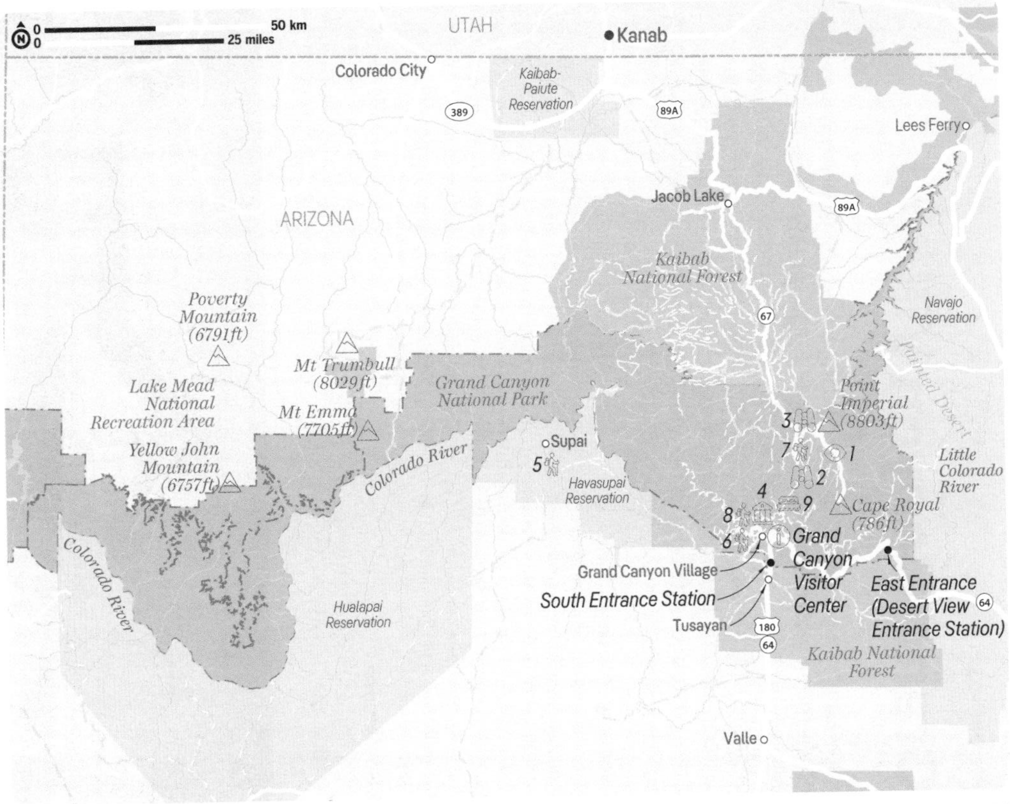

Point Imperial (p173)
DOUG LEMKE/SHUTTERSTOCK ©

WALKING TRIP

Grand Canyon Village

Early entrepreneurs set up camp along the South Rim in the late 1800s, but it wasn't until the arrival of the Santa Fe Railway from Williams in 1901 that the area now known as Grand Canyon Village became the primary tourist hub. The Fred Harvey Company (the railroad-centric chain of hotels and restaurants) and architect Mary Colter established some of the Village's most iconic buildings, which can be visited on a walk along the Rim Trail.

1 Verkamp's Visitor Center

One-time canvas-tent souvenir shop (1898), then the Mission-style Verkamp's Curios building (1905), today this historic structure holds a small but compelling history exhibit and is a good place to start exploring the Village.

The Walk: Follow the Rim Trail 500ft west to the Hopi House.

2 Hopi House

A beautiful Mary Colter–designed stone building, the Hopi House has been offering high-quality Native jewelry, basketwork, pottery and other crafts since its 1905 opening. The structure was originally built to house Hopi artisans and was inspired by their traditional mesa-top dwellings to the east, which are among the oldest structures still standing in North America.

The Walk: Cross the traffic circle to the main entrance of the El Tovar Hotel.

3 El Tovar

Built in 1905 as a railroad hotel, the El Tovar was designed by Charles Whittlesey

CARL DEABREU PHOTOGRAPHY/SHUTTERSTOCK ©

Kolb Studio

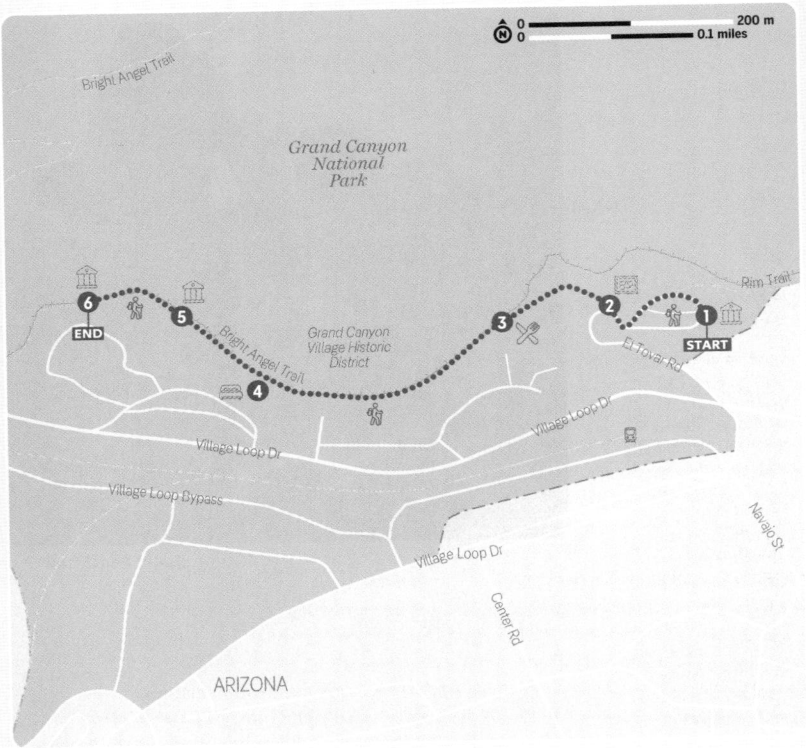

as a blend of Swiss chalet and the more rustic style that would come to define national-park lodges in the 1920s. With its unusual spires and dark-wood beams, it remains a grande dame of national park lodges.

The Walk: Follow the Rim Trail 0.25 miles west, passing the Kachina and Thunderbird Lodges.

4 Bright Angel Lodge

Designed by Mary Colter and completed in 1935, the log-and-stone Bright Angel Lodge offered canyon travelers alternative accommodations to the luxurious El Tovar. Just off the lobby is the History Room, while outside, a few steps west, is the Buckey O'Neill Cabin (1895), the oldest building still standing on the rim.

The Walk: Just past the Buckey O'Neill Cabin is the Lookout Studio, perched dramatically on the rim's edge.

5 Lookout Studio

Like several other Mary Colter designs, the Lookout Studio (1914) was modeled on the Ancestral Puebloan ruins found throughout the Southwest. Made of rough-cut Kaibab limestone, with a roof that mirrors the lines of the rim, the studio blends into its natural surroundings. Inside is a small souvenir shop and a tiny back porch with spectacular canyon views.

The Walk: Continuing along the Rim Trail for another 100ft will bring you to Kolb Studio.

6 Kolb Studio

In 1905 Ellsworth and Emery Kolb built a small photography studio on the edge of the rim, which has since been expanded and now holds a bookstore and a museum. The brothers arrived at the canyon from Pennsylvania in 1902 and made a living photographing parties descending the Bright Angel Trail, which begins just outside the studio's entrance.

DAVID MALAMENT/SHUTTERSTOCK ©

Bright Angel Trail

GRAND CANYON BY MULE

Mule rides into the canyon have a long history: the first recorded trip was in 1887, and by the early 20th century, the Kolb brothers were turning their photos of tourists on mules into iconic souvenirs. Visitors today who want to view the South Rim by mule have two choices: a two-hour above-the-rim day trip to a canyon overlook, or a multiday trip to the bottom of the canyon, which includes sleeping at Phantom Ranch. On the South Rim, trips are popular and fill quickly; slots, available 15 months in advance, are awarded through an online lottery (grandcanyon lodges.com). Otherwise, make tracks to the North Rim, where rides are usually available the day before the trip.

Follow the Trail of Time

MIND-BENDING TIME MACHINE

What if every step you took sent you back one million years? That's the idea behind the ingenious **Trail of Time**, which helps visitors come to grips with the enormity of the Grand Canyon's geological time scale. Taking in over two billion years in 1.3 miles, it's the most educational way to get between the visitor center and the Village. If you begin at the Yavapai Geology Museum, you'll be walking from the present day into the past; if you begin at the Village, you'll be walking forward through time into the present.

Regardless of the direction you take, you'll pass large samples of each rock type found within the canyon (go ahead, touch them), beginning with Elves Chasm gneiss, which clocks in at a cool 1.84 billion years of age and is the oldest rock here. Walking past the metamorphic Vishnu Basement Rocks brings you up through the sedimentary layers of the Grand Canyon Supergroup (middle canyon) to the Paleozoic strata (top), with a handy reminder at 630 million years (over two-thirds of the way along the trail) that it was only at this point that multicelled animal life began to appear on earth. Your final (or

WHERE TO STAY ON THE SOUTH RIM

El Tovar
The public spaces of this 1905 lodge perched at the canyon edge exude Western charm. **$$$**

Bright Angel Lodge
This historic lodge on the Rim Trail delivers simple charm and cabin accommodations at affordable prices. **$**

Kachina & Thunderbird Lodges
Amazingly ugly on the outside, but modern and comfortable inside. Steps from the rim. **$$$**

first) six steps represent six million years, roughly the time it took the Colorado River to carve out the Grand Canyon.

The trail concludes at the **Yavapai Geology Museum**, where the views don't get much better than those framed by the plate-glass windows inside. Handy panels identify and explain the various formations before you, and displays tie together the canyon's multilayered geological history with the samples you've passed along the trail. It's a further 0.7 miles from the museum to Mather Point and the visitor center.

Hiking the Bright Angel Trail

VENTURE BENEATH THE RIM

The most well-known trail to descend beneath the rim, Bright Angel's gentle grade, shade, access to water and convenient trailhead – it begins right in the Village – make this the most popular descent for first-timers.

While the full trail winds 7.8 miles and 4460ft down from the rim to the Colorado River, day hikers have a number of shorter options. The most obvious options are two stone rest houses, located at the 1.5- and 3-mile marks, meaning that the full hikes are 3 and 6 miles respectively.

The trailhead itself (6840ft) is both exhilarating and intimidating, as the canyon unfolds before you in all its glory. After some serious switchbacks, the trail soon passes through two tunnels – look for the red Native American pictographs beneath an overhang just past the first. Just after passing through the second tunnel, you'll reach **Mile-and-a-Half Resthouse** (5720ft), about an hour from the trailhead. Continuing downward through different-colored rock layers, more switchbacks finally deposit you at **Three-Mile Resthouse** (4720ft). Down below, you'll see the iridescent green tufts of Havasupai Gardens, a campground 1.6 miles away, as well as the broad expanse of **Tonto Platform** – a visual reward before beginning the ascent back to the rim.

After the Three-Mile Resthouse, you'll soon hit a demanding set of switchbacks known as **Jacob's Ladder**, which twist through Redwall limestone cliffs into the cool leafiness of Havasupai Gardens (3800ft). The Havasupai farmed here until a century ago, and these days it's one of the park's most sought-after backcountry campgrounds.

HISTORY OF THE BRIGHT ANGEL TRAIL

The pathway known today as the Bright Angel Trail, which follows a major fault line through the canyon, has been in continuous use for thousands of years. The Havasupai used the trail to access present-day Havasupai Gardens, where they grew crops and farmed until the early 20th century. In the early 1890s, prospectors Ralph Cameron and Pete Berry improved the trail, eventually extending it to the river. In 1903 Cameron imposed a $1 toll, a widely criticized decision. In response, the Atchison, Topeka & Santa Fe Railway and others constructed toll-free alternative trails to draw the burgeoning mule tourism trade. In 1928 the park service took over the Bright Angel and lifted the toll.

Rafting the Colorado

RIDING THE RIVER

A journey down the river is a once-in-a-lifetime experience – a virtual all-access pass to the Grand Canyon, in all its wildness, peace and ancient, mighty glory.

WHERE TO EAT ON THE SOUTH RIM

El Tovar Dining Room
Classic national-park dining at its best; windows frame the Rim Trail and canyon. Reservations required. **$$$**

Arizona Steakhouse
Steaks, fish and tamales for dinner, and burgers and sandwiches for lunch. In Bright Angel Lodge. **$$**

Bright Angel Bicycles & Cafe
Grab-and-go sandwiches, wraps, salads and coffee from the bike-shop cafe beside the main visitor center. **$**

DAY TRIPS ON THE COLORADO RIVER

If you're really short on time, you can always sign up for a half- or full-day river trip, though not on sections within Grand Canyon National Park. Operating out of Peach Springs, about 2½ hours west of the South Rim, Hualapai River Runners offers one- and two-day motorized raft trips in the canyon's west end. Don't want a motorized white-water experience? Check out the kayak and SUP float trips on the smooth 16-mile stretch of the Colorado through the legendary Horseshoe Bend, above Lees Ferry. You can camp on the river here if you want the full overnight experience.

Despite their thrills, the river's 160 galloping rapids aren't the only attraction on this ride. One of the great rewards of floating the river is the opportunity to hike to all those places that are extremely difficult to access from the rim, such as the Ancestral Puebloan granaries at Nankoweap. Side canyons reveal cool, verdant grottoes like Elves Chasm and swirling rock formations as in North Canyon. Set aside your pride and strap your personal flotation device to your bum to bump down the warm, turquoise waters of the Little Colorado. Be sure to stop for a cold lemonade and scribble a postcard at Phantom Ranch, your one brush with civilization. And don't miss the otherworldly blue-green waters of Havasu Creek.

As you fall asleep on a sandy beach under the stars, you'll feel connected to the people who lived here long before and inspired by the tales of intrepid explorers who ran the river when it was still uncharted.

The Grand Canyon stretch of the Colorado sees on average 22,000 annual visitors and is run year-round. Most commercial trips operate between April and October, with June, July and August being the peak months. Park regulations stipulate that individuals may take only one recreational river trip per calendar year, whether private or commercial. Remember, most commercial tours sell out a year in advance. However, a small percentage of cancellations do occur, so it's sometimes possible to get in on a trip at the last minute.

If you're interested in running the Colorado River, the first question to ask is: How much time do you have? With six to 18 days, you can run most or all of the canyon between Lake Powell and Lake Mead. You can also raft a shorter section in as little as four days and still have an amazing experience. Grand Canyon trips are usually broken up into three types: the Full Canyon, the Upper Canyon (Lees Ferry to Phantom Ranch) and the Lower Canyon (below Phantom Ranch).

Just because a trip is advertised as 'full' doesn't mean it runs the entire 280 miles. There are three main take-outs in the Lower Canyon – Whitmore Wash, Diamond Creek and Pearce Ferry – so a Full Canyon trip may only run 226 miles. The shortest Grand Canyon trips run the Upper Canyon only, putting in at Lees Ferry (mile 0) and taking out at Phantom Ranch (mile 88), followed by a 9.5-mile, 4340ft climb up to the South Rim. On Lower Canyon trips, you'll join the raft at Phantom Ranch (mile 88); this involves a 9.5-mile, 4340ft descent from the South Rim. There are a variety of take-outs on Lower Canyon trips: Whitmore Wash (mile 188; rafters are helicoptered out), Diamond Creek (mile 225; rafters are driven out via Route 66) and Pearce Ferry (mile 280; rafters are ferried by jetboat to Lake Mead).

BEST DAY TRIPS ON THE COLORADO RIVER

Thunder Spring
Huff 1400ft up Tapeats Creek to a 100ft waterfall gushing out of the side of a cliff.

Deer Creek
One of the inner gorge's finest hikes, with waterfalls and pictographs in a curvy slot canyon.

Elves Chasm
Ferns, orchids and scarlet monkeyflowers drape the walls of this idyllic grotto.

Colorado River from Bright Angel Trail (p171)

The Upper Canyon and Lower Canyon are equally stunning, with a similar number of rapids and side trips.

Going Rim to Rim

LEGENDARY CROSS-CANYON TREK

The two-to-four-day South Kaibab to North Kaibab trek is the classic Grand Canyon **rim-to-rim hike** and one of the finest trips in the canyon. Most hikers beginning on the South Rim descend the South Kaibab trail (6.9 miles) and cross the Colorado River on the Black Bridge to Bright Angel Campground or Phantom Ranch. From Bright Angel Campground, it's 7.2 miles up the North Kaibab to Cottonwood Campground for the second night, and a final 6.8-mile climb up to the North Rim.

Because the North Rim is 1000ft higher than the South Rim, many people suggest it's easier to go north to south – it all depends on what you think is harder on your body: uphill or downhill. Either way you go, it's a minimum 20.7 miles total, and a hot 10,000-plus feet of elevation change.

You'll need a backcountry permit to camp below the rim, and you'll also need to arrange a ride back to your starting point. Between mid-May and mid-October, the Trans-Canyon Shuttle departs twice daily from Grand Canyon Lodge on the North Rim for the 4½-hour drive to the South Rim.

WHEN TO GO

There's no perfect time to run the river. Rather, just be aware of the different weather patterns you'll encounter throughout the year. If side hikes are important, opt for early spring (April) or fall (mid-September to October), as the daytime temps are comfortable – 80°F (27°C). On the flip side, early morning on the river will be *brrr* chilly (50°F/10°C). Summer temps (June to August) top 100°F (38°C), with lows around 75°F (24°C); afternoon thunderstorms are common and the river is typically running faster and higher. One other factor to consider is that there is less daylight in spring and fall, which means trips may take longer. Commercial trips do not run from November through March.

Beaver Falls
Havasu Creek plunges over breathtaking travertine formations; book for Havasupai Lodge or campground.

Nankoweap
This steep climb rewards hikers with Ancestral Puebloan granaries and awesome views.

Little Colorado River
The confluence can be a striking juxtaposition of turquoise and coppery green waters.

FRANCISCO BLANCO/SHUTTERSTOCK ©

Grand Canyon Lodge

From South Rim to North Rim, it departs Bright Angel Lodge. There is only one shuttle daily, weather permitting, from mid-October through mid-November.

Facilities on the North Rim are closed between mid-October and mid-May (or later), and the weather is unpredictable – you could leave warm, sunny skies on the South Rim and walk into a blizzard on the North Rim.

Sunset at Grand Canyon Lodge

SIMPLY SPLENDID

You've hiked all the trails, seen all the viewpoints and driven all the scenic roads. But sitting on the stone veranda behind the **Grand Canyon Lodge** at sunset, cold beer in hand? That just might be your favorite memory of the North Rim.

Built in 1937 out of Kaibab limestone, the lodge features spacious rim-side dining rooms and porches lined with Adirondack chairs. A National Historic Landmark and an architectural delight, the lodge's natural materials blend unobtrusively into the landscape. Architect Gilbert Stanley Underwood designed the original lodge in 1928 for the Union Pacific Railroad (the nearest train station was 100 miles away, in Cedar Ridge, Utah; the railroad then provided motor-coach tours that took in Zion, Bryce and the Grand Canyon). His vision – of a rustic central lodge surrounded by guest cabins – remains unchanged, even though the original building tragically burned down on September 1, 1932.

The centerpiece of the design is the Sun Room. Past the lobby and down a set of stairs brings visitors to a massive

SLEEPING AT PHANTOM RANCH

When most people think of spending the night in the Grand Canyon, their first thought is usually Phantom Ranch, the coveted stone cabins located deep in the canyon at the confluence of Bright Angel Creek and the Colorado River and the intersection of the park's three most popular backcountry trails. Built in 1922, Phantom Ranch consists of 11 cabins and four dormitories. All things considered, it's very plush, with running water and two meals a day provided in the cantina. But to get a bed here, you literally have to win the lottery. Reservation requests are taken from 15 months before the stay date at 12:01am on the first of the month until 11:59pm on the 25th of the month.

WHERE TO STAY ON THE NORTH RIM

Grand Canyon Lodge
Reserve far in advance to nab a rustic log cabin; the larger ones sleep as many as six people. **$$**

North Rim Campground
Reserve six months ahead for a shaded site among the ponderosas. **$**

Kaibab National Forest
Drive down any forest service road before the park entrance and you can pitch a tent for free. No water. **$**

50ft-high stone and timbered room, with three giant windows framing the canyon view in all its majesty. If you don't make Bright Angel Point your first stop, then a seat on one of the couches here is a good second choice.

For a meal, the timbered rim-side dining room can't be beat (reservations are required for dinner only). For beer, cocktails or morning coffee, step inside the Roughrider Saloon. Adorned with Teddy Roosevelt memorabilia, it honors his role in the creation of the park.

Driving Cape Royal Road

MUST-DO NORTH RIM ROAD

The scenic Cape Royal Rd is a must for any North Rim visitor. Climbing to 8800ft at Point Imperial before a gradual descent to 7865ft at Cape Royal Point, the road ribbons for 20 miles through ponderosa forest and stands of aspen. Easy and paved, it passes overlooks, picnic sites and an Ancestral Puebloan site. There are some excellent hikes to be had along the way, often leading to solitary outcrops.

Point Imperial is the highest viewpoint in Grand Canyon National Park (8819ft) and the first can't-miss stop on Cape Royal Rd. To get here, look for the Y intersection 5.5 miles into the drive and turn left on Point Imperial Rd, climbing 2.5 miles past the Fuller burn site (2016). The overlook takes in the entirety of Marble Canyon to the east as it cuts into the Painted Desert beneath the imposing Vermilion Cliffs. Directly below, Nankoweap drainage seems impossible to access, but 1000 years ago it housed a bustling community of Puebloan farmers. The prominent pinnacle to the southwest is Mt Hayden, named after prominent Arizona pioneer Charles T Hayden, who helped found the city of Tempe.

At the end of Cape Royal Rd, a 0.4-mile paved path lined with piñon, cliffrose and interpretive signs leads to a thrilling climax: **Angels Window**, a dramatic natural arch that falls away into the canyon. Venture on top for the photo of your dreams, but take care – you're surrounded by sheer cliff faces on all sides. Despite the crowds, people tend to use hushed tones while talking, overcome by the reverence this awesome place demands.

Falling for Havasu Falls

HIDDEN TREASURES

The blue-green waterfalls of **Havasu Canyon** are among the Grand Canyon's greatest treasures. Tucked in a hidden valley, the five stunning waterfalls and their inviting azure swimming

HIKING THE NORTH KAIBAB TRAIL

The only maintained inner-canyon trail on the North Rim is the North Kaibab Trail, featuring strenuous switchbacks, raging waterfalls, a cottonwood-fringed campground and long creekside stretches. At 14.2 miles (one way) and with an elevation change of nearly 6000ft, it usually takes a few days to complete, but the first few miles also make for popular day hikes.

The sandy trail begins at 8241ft and quickly descends to **Coconino Overlook**, a flat ledge that offers clear views of Bright Angel Canyon and Roaring Springs. A mile later, **Supai Tunnel** – blasted through the rock in the 1930s – is just beyond a tree-shaded glen. On the other side of the tunnel, views open to an intimidating set of switchbacks beside a knuckle-biting drop-off.

WHERE TO EAT ON THE NORTH RIM

Grand Canyon Lodge Dining Room
Bison steaks and vegetarian options, but the view is the thing. Reserve for dinner. **$$**

Roughrider Saloon
Coffee and breakfast burritos pre-hike; beer, wine and pizza post-hike. **$**

Deli in the Pines
Not a deli but a cafeteria, serving takeaway salads and sandwiches, plus ice cream. **$**

Havasu Falls (p175)

GET YOUR KICKS ON ROUTE 66

For a classic American road trip, nothing beats good ol' Route 66. Nicknamed the nation's Mother Road by novelist John Steinbeck, this string of small-town main streets and byways once ran all the way from Chicago to Los Angeles. In Arizona, you'll find an isolated strip here and there – in downtown Flagstaff and Williams, for instance – but it's in the western portion of the state where the longest intact stretch in the country runs for 158 miles.

As a road trip, it's got it all: roadside kitsch, spectacular winding mountain ascents and even wild burros. Whether you just want a slice of retro Americana in a neon-lit diner, or you're feeling the lure of the open road, Route 66 will take you there.

holes sit in the heart of the 185,000-acre Havasupai Reservation. Parts of the canyon floor, as well as the rock underneath the waterfalls and pools, are made up of limestone deposited by flowing water. Known as travertine, these descending limestone terraces give the famous turquoise water its otherworldly hue. Cascading through the red-rock landscape, the area's photogenic mystique is such that it attracts visitors – and even the occasional celebrity – from around the world.

To visit Havasu Falls, you must have reservations at either Havasupai Lodge in Supai or at the campground. Day hikes are not permitted; expect multiple paperwork checks along the way. Getting a reservation at either the campground or the lodge is the crux of any potential trip: in the past, the process would begin every year at 8am on February 1 and available spots would be snapped up in a matter of hours. Havasupai was closed to tourists during the pandemic, and at the time of writing a new permitting process was still being ironed out, so our best advice is to go to havasupaireservations.com, create an account, and check in regularly for the latest updates. All campground and lodge reservations are for three nights.

GETTING AROUND

A car is indispensable for travel to the Grand Canyon, but on the South Rim you'll find it quickly becomes a hassle for getting around. Aim to enter the park before 9am or after 5pm to avoid the two-hour lines at the south entrance. Once you've got a parking spot, take the free public shuttles to get around. Alternatively, park in Tusayan and take the free shuttle from there.

It's only 10 miles as the crow flies from the South Rim to the North Rim, but walking from one to the other is a grueling 23 miles. Driving rim-to-rim in a car, meanwhile, covers nearly 200 miles, taking four hours.

GREAT BASIN NATIONAL PARK

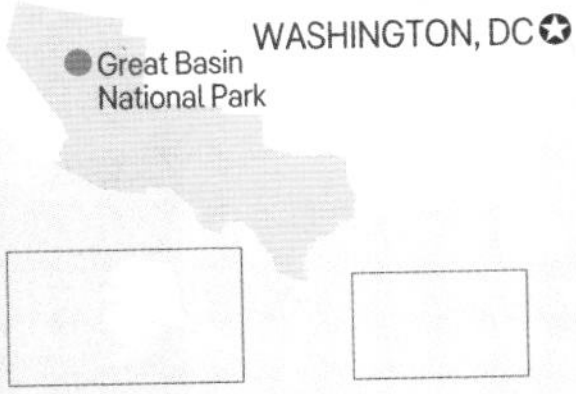

With rugged mountain slopes and ancient trees, the uncrowded Great Basin National Park is a gorgeous place to ponder your insignificance. Its bristlecone pines began growing when Egypt's Great Pyramid of Giza was still under construction. You'll also find formation-filled underground caverns and a corkscrew-curved scenic drive with views of the 13,063ft ice-sculpted horn of Wheeler Peak and the small but tenacious glacier that clings to its side. Perched 1 mile above sea level in the craggy Snake Range, the park marks the eastern endpoint of the Loneliest Road, which stretches across the white-hot center of Nevada along Hwy 50. It's one of the country's least-visited national parks, ranking 54th out of 63 with fewer than 143,000 travelers in 2022.

The dripping Lehman Caves are home to a colony of Townsend's big-eared bats and feature a staggering collection of formations, including stalactites, stalagmites, helictites, flowstone, popcorn and more than 500 rare shields.

FACTS

Great For Photo ops, scenery, walking
State Nevada
Entrance Fee Free
Area 121 sq miles

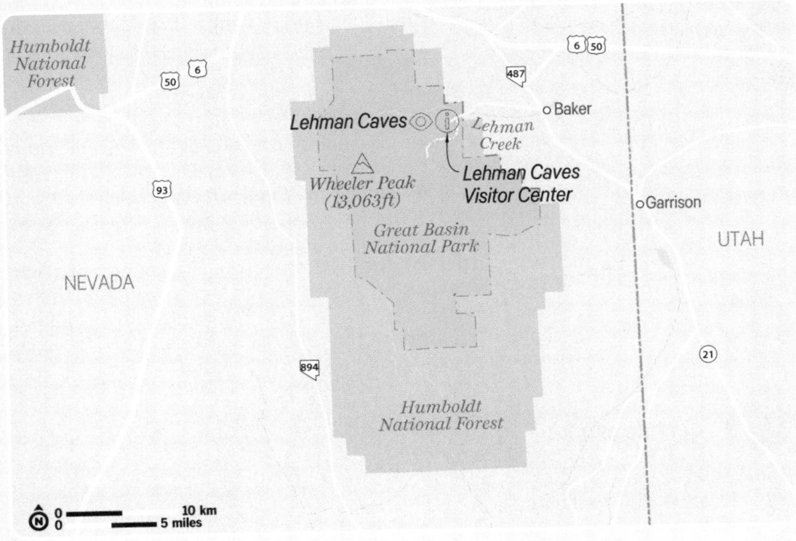

Great Basin National Park

BEST PLACES TO STAY & EAT NEAR GREAT BASIN NATIONAL PARK

Great Basin National Park Campgrounds
The park has five campgrounds with vault toilets, grills, picnic tables and tent pads. $

Stargazer Inn
Spruced-up motel rooms with wood floors, comfortable beds and a warm welcome; pet-friendly. $$

Sugar, Salt & Malt Restaurant
The menu of lamb burgers, Asian tacos and pizza punches above its weight for such a small town. $$

Caves & Peaks of Great Basin

UNDER THE GROUND AND IN THE SKY

The colossal marble caverns of **Lehman Caves** are the main feature of Great Basin National Park, named after local rancher Absalom Lehman, who is credited with discovering them in 1865. To visit the caves, you must join a guided tour. It's best to book through recreation.gov (the website or the app) in advance, lest you drive all this way to miss one of the park's main attractions. The NPS offers two tour options: the longer **Grand Palace Tour** (90 minutes) takes in all accessible areas of the cave, while the hour-long **Lodge Tour** follows the same route but doesn't go as far. The temperature inside the caves is a constant 50°F (10°C), so bring a jacket. Prepare to be screened for white-nose syndrome, a fungus that is harmless to humans but can be lethal to the bats that live in the caverns.

Wheeler's slopes are home to a compact but diverse range of landscapes and life zones, which can be explored along the paved 12-mile **Wheeler Peak Scenic Drive**, which rises more than 10,000ft. This road is open only during a short summer window, usually from July through October.

Hiking trails off the drive take in superb country of glacial lakes and ancient bristlecone pines. On clear nights, a panoply of stars dances overhead. The tiny gateway town of Baker, population 36, sits at the entrance to the park and has a visitor center with exhibits and information.

GETTING AROUND

You must have a car to get to and around Great Basin. It's a 300-mile drive from the airport in Las Vegas, or 240 miles from Salt Lake City, Utah.

GUADALUPE MOUNTAINS NATIONAL PARK

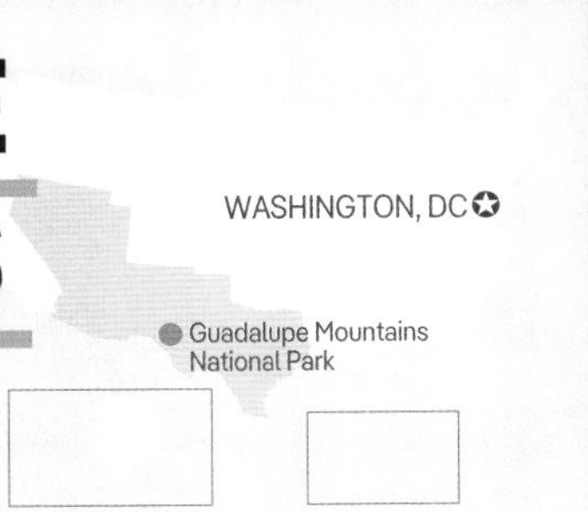

Guadalupe Mountains National Park is a Texas high spot, both literally and figuratively. At 8749ft, Guadalupe Peak is the highest point in the Lone Star State. More than half the park is a federally designated wilderness area, and the fall foliage in McKittrick Canyon is the best in West Texas.

We won't go so far as to call it Texas' best-kept secret, but even many Texans aren't aware of the Guadalupe Mountains National Park. It's just this side of the Texas–New Mexico state line and a long drive from practically everywhere in the state.

The NPS has deliberately curbed development to keep the park wild. To visit Guadalupe is to see the landscape as it's been for hundreds of millions of years, untouched by modern conveniences. There are no restaurants or indoor accommodations and only a smattering of services and programs, so plan ahead to keep your gas tank full and your cooler stocked.

FACTS

Great For Scenery, walking, photo ops
State Texas
Entrance Fee 7-day pass per adult/child $10/free
Area 135 sq miles

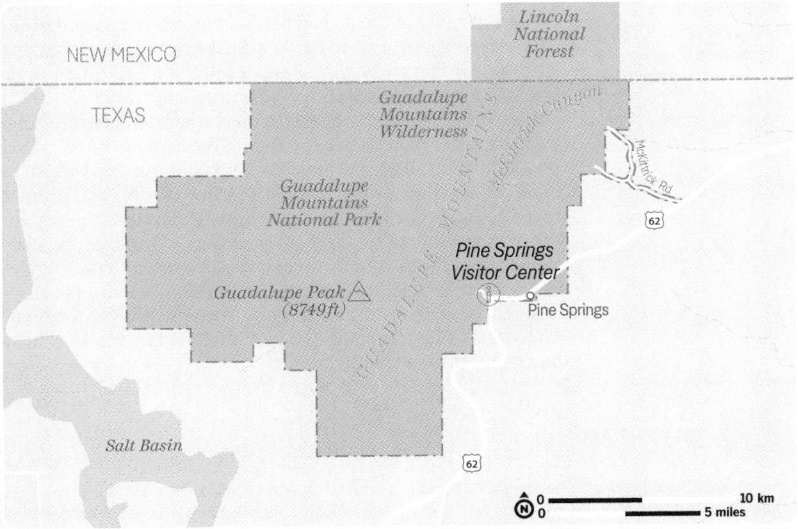

BEST HIKES BEYOND GUADALUPE PEAK

The Grotto
McKittrick Canyon is one of the loveliest places in Texas, especially in fall when it becomes a kaleidoscope of brilliant colors. Tucked inside the canyon, the Grotto is a small limestone alcove with cavern-like features.

Devil's Hall
Scale the Hiker's Staircase to reach this narrow corridor squeezed between 100ft limestone walls.

Permian Reef Geology Trail
This 8.5-mile round-trip trail climbs to the top of Wilderness Ridge and showcases Permian-era geological and fossil features.

Guadalupe Peak

Embracing the Isolation

TRULY UNTAMED WEST TEXAS

Guadalupe Mountains National Park is one of the least-visited national parks in the United States, thanks to its isolated location and relative lack of infrastructure. The park has no real roads and, aside from three bare-bones campgrounds (one of which can only be used by groups with horses), it has no accommodations either. It takes patience and time to get here, but if you're up for the journey, you'll be rewarded with the kind of extreme nature that feels extraterrestrial: 86,000 acres of stark, sublime mountain desert. Geological time converges with the present.

The highest point in Texas, 8749ft Guadalupe Peak is the park's primary attraction. The views are spectacular for much of the way up, and the jagged peaks, spires and canyons of the Guadalupe Mountains will take your breath away, along with that 3000ft elevation gain. Snap a selfie with the steel pyramid at the top before making your way back down.

Regardless of where you plan to hike, stop by the Pine Springs Visitor Center to get a permit and let the rangers know where you're headed. Reservations for backpacking trips must be made at least two days in advance but can be made up to three months ahead. All water must be carried (there's virtually none out here), and backpackers should carry a detailed topographic map. You can explore more than 80 miles of trails, but to sample all of the park's diversity (scrubby desert, sheer mountain cliffs and canyons), head from the McKittrick Canyon trailhead to Pine Springs. It's 19.1 miles on the most direct trails.

GETTING AROUND

Guadalupe Mountains National Park is 110 miles east of El Paso and 55 miles southwest of Carlsbad, New Mexico. The closest gas stations are 35 miles in either direction on Hwy 62/180, and the closest services are in Whites City, New Mexico, 45 minutes northeast of the park entrance.

MESA VERDE NATIONAL PARK

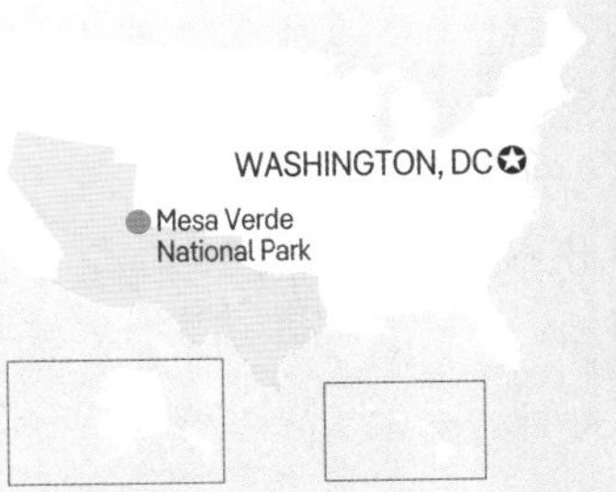

Mesa Verde National Park is one of the largest Native American archaeological sites in the US and certainly the best preserved. Nestled into a stunning landscape of canyons and mesas, it contains more than 5000 ancient structures and 600 elaborate cliff dwellings. The site was inhabited by the Ancestral Puebloans for more than 750 years before being abruptly abandoned in 1300 CE. No one knows exactly why.

Mesa Verde sat undisturbed until 1888 when it was 'discovered' by two white ranchers following a tip from a Native Ute. Their family, the Wetherills, sold artifacts from the site and served as guides. In 1906, with increasing visitor numbers, it was designated a national park and eventually became a Unesco World Heritage Site. Today, Mesa Verde is an archaeological wonderland and a sacred site to the descendants of the Ancestral Puebloans. It is a place to respect, explore, learn about and delve into the mysteries of ancient America.

FACTS

Great For History, photo ops, family travel
State Colorado
Entrance Fee 7-day pass per car/motorcycle/person on foot or bicycle $30/25/15; $10 less for cars and motorcycles from mid-October through April
Area 81 sq miles

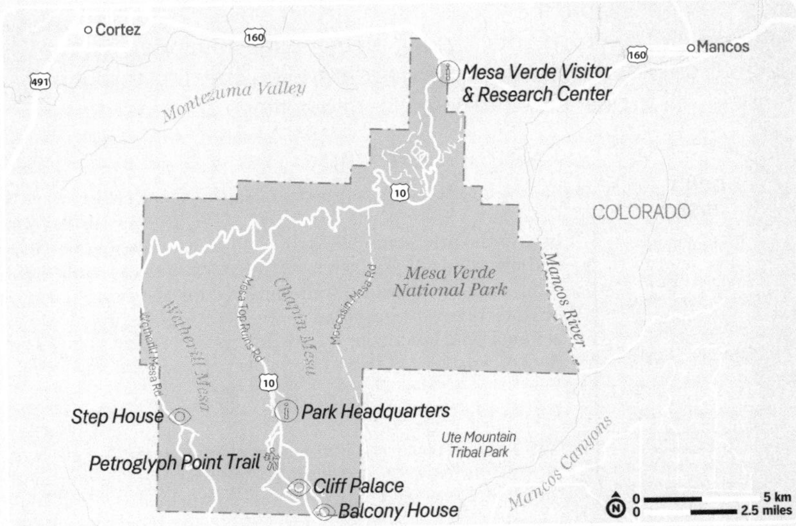

STEPHEN MOEHLE/SHUTTERSTOCK ©

PRACTICALITIES

Scan this QR code to visit the park's website.

TOP SIGHT

Experiencing Mesa Verde

Mesa Verde National Park covers two broad mesas, each rife with Ancestral Puebloan dwellings. Some are on the mesa tops, but the most compelling are those built into high cliff walls. While you can see many from vista points, touring them means adventure at great heights, clambering up and down ladders, even crawling through tunnels...all to peer into the magnificent dwellings up close.

DON'T MISS

- Cliff Palace
- Balcony House
- Step House
- Petroglyph Point Trail
- Mesa Top Loop Rd
- Long House
- Cultural Performances

Ranger-Led Tours

Taking a ranger-led tour is one of the most rewarding ways to experience Mesa Verde. You'll deep dive into the history and lives of the Ancestral Puebloans and have access to otherwise restricted dwellings such as Cliff Palace, Balcony House and Long House. But these tours are not for the faint of heart. Most involve walking along cliff edges, climbing up and down wooden pole ladders and crawling through tight spaces, but they're worth it. Plan on taking two tours if you have time.

Cliff Palace

Cliff Palace (pictured) is the largest-known cliff dwelling in the Southwest USA, a grand engineering achievement with 151 rooms and 23 kivas (ceremonial enclosures) that once housed 25 families. It's remarkable for its fine construction and efficient design. Check out Cliff Palace on an hour-long tour, retracing the same paths taken by the enclave's original inhabitants. In the summer, twilight tours are offered, too.

Balcony House

The Balcony House tour requires you to descend a 100ft staircase, climb a 32ft ladder and crawl through a 12ft tunnel – and that's just to get there. There are even more ladders and steps on the way out. But it's well worth the effort. The 38-room village is built in a cliffside alcove with a long arching roof and offers panoramic views of Soda Canyon, 600ft below.

Step House

Wetherill Mesa has the park's only self-guided cliff dwelling: Step House. A short but steep 0.8-mile trail leads to a two-in-one village, with 7th-century pit houses standing alongside 13th-century multistory dwellings. Informational booklets are available at the entrance, and a ranger is typically at the site to answer questions.

Mesa Top Loop Road

A complement (or alternative) to scrambling through the park's cliff dwellings is a 6-mile driving tour along the Mesa Top Loop Rd. At various pull-offs, you can enjoy magnificent overlooks of Cliff Palace and other cliff dwellings, or take short paths to a dozen different surface sites (no teetering ladders on this route). A free audio tour, played on any smartphone, leads the way.

Petroglyph Point Trail

This 2.4-mile loop trail follows a leafy footpath once used by the Ancestral Puebloans. Dropping below the canyon rim, it's occasionally steep and rocky before it makes a short scramble back to the top of the mesa. Look for the petroglyphs at the 1.4-mile mark – a 35ft-wide wall with almost three dozen human and animal figures, spirals and handprints. A gate at the trailhead is locked in the evenings. If you arrive in the early morning, begin the trail in reverse.

Cultural Dances & Demonstrations

Come summer, the park hosts cultural performances and demonstrations by Native peoples with ancestral connections to Mesa Verde. Fascinating and educational, the demonstrations are a way to learn about Mesa Verde's ancient inhabitants and their modern-day descendants. Performances are in the Morefield Campground Amphitheater, typically in the evenings.

Overnight Stays

Stay overnight in the tasteful Far View Lodge (reservations recommended) or car camp at Morefield Campground, just steps from the park's general store and gas station.

GETTING ORIENTED

The park entrance is off Hwy 160, midway between Cortez and Mancos. From the entrance, it's about 21 miles to park headquarters, Chapin Mesa Museum and Spruce Tree House. Along the way are Morefield Campground (4 miles), Park Point (8 miles) and the Far View Lodge (about 11 miles). Towed vehicles are not allowed beyond Morefield Campground.

TOP TIPS

- Visit from May to October. Several park areas and amenities are closed in winter and spring, and tours are suspended.
- Fill your tank before you arrive – you'll be driving a lot. In a pinch, there's a gas station at Morefield Campground.
- Ranger-led tours can be reserved online. Buy tickets 14 days in advance to assure a spot – they sell out fast.
- The museum is closed until 2025. Pick up informational booklets around the park to learn more about each site.
- Cellphone service is limited; download audio tours and maps ahead of time.
- Morefield Campground almost always has walk-up availability. On holiday weekends, expect a party zone.

MESA VERDE MAPS & INFO

Good maps are issued to visitors at the national park gate on entry. Quality topographical maps can be bought at the visitor center and the museum, as well as in stores in the towns of Durango and Cortez.

The huge **Mesa Verde Visitor & Research Center** at the park entrance has water, wi-fi and bathrooms, in addition to information desks selling tickets for tours of Cliff Palace, Balcony House and Long House. It also displays museum-quality artifacts. Attached to the visitor center, the nonprofit **Mesa Verde Association** sponsors research activities and exhibits. It has an excellent selection of materials on the Ancestral Puebloans and modern tribes in the Southwest, plus related books and souvenirs for sale.

ANITA WARREN-HAMPSON/GETTY IMAGES ©
Mesa Verde

Winter at Mesa Verde

SKIING AND SNOWSHOEING

Winter is a special time in Mesa Verde. The crowds disperse, and the cliff dwellings sparkle in the snow. The skies are often blue and sunny, and you may be the only person around. In some years, there's enough snow to ski or snowshoe after a winter snowstorm, although Colorado's dry climate and sunshine cause the snow to melt quickly. Keep an eye out for wildlife, which is easier to see when the trees are bare. Before setting out, check the current snow conditions on the national park website (nps.gov/meve/planyourvisit/winter_trails_report.htm). Snowshoes are available to rent for free at the visitor center.

Two park roads have been designated for cross-country skiing and snowshoeing when weather permits. The Cliff Palace Loop Rd is a relatively flat 6-mile loop located off the Mesa Top Loop Rd. The road is closed to vehicles after the first snowfall, so you won't have to worry about vehicular traffic. Park at the closed gate and glide 1 mile to the Cliff Palace overlook, continuing on past numerous other scenic stopping points. The Morefield Campground loop roads offer multiple miles of relatively flat terrain. The campground is closed in winter, but skiers and snowshoers can park at the gate and explore to their heart's content.

Walkers are not permitted on skiing and snowshoeing trails, but parts of the Petroglyph Trail and Chapin Mesa Rim Trail are open for winter hiking.

GETTING AROUND

There is no public transportation in Mesa Verde. The roads are steep, narrow and winding, so even a short distance can be slow going. Plan on an hour to drive from the highway turnoff to sites on either Chapin Mesa or Wetherill Mesa, and 45 minutes between the two.

PETRIFIED FOREST NATIONAL PARK

Driving into Petrified Forest National Park feels like a journey into the land that time forgot – sunbaked trails, crimson badlands, tufts of scrubby grass blowing on a desolate plain and swaths of gigantic logs so old they've morphed into crystallized rocks that predate the dinosaurs. Up to 6ft in diameter, they're strikingly beautiful, with extravagantly patterned cross-sections of wood glinting in ethereal pinks, blues and greens. Souvenir hunters filched thousands of tons of petrified wood before Teddy Roosevelt made the forest a national monument in 1906 (it became a national park in 1962). Scavenge today and you'll be looking at fines and even jail time.

Petroglyphs and pueblo remnants tell of the park's human history. At Puerco Pueblo, you'll find interesting rock art and a partly excavated 100-room structure that might have been home to as many as 200 Ancestral Puebloans at the outset of the 14th century.

FACTS

Great For Scenery, walking, wildlife
State Arizona
Entrance Fee 7-day pass per car/motorcycle/person on foot or bicycle $25/20/15
Area 346 sq miles

Blue Mesa Trail (p186)

SIGHTS
1 Blue Mesa
2 Jasper Forest Lookout
3 Kachina Point
4 Newspaper Rock
5 Painted Desert Inn

ACTIVITIES, COURSES & TOURS
6 Crystal Forest Loop
7 Giant Logs Trail
8 Long Logs Trail

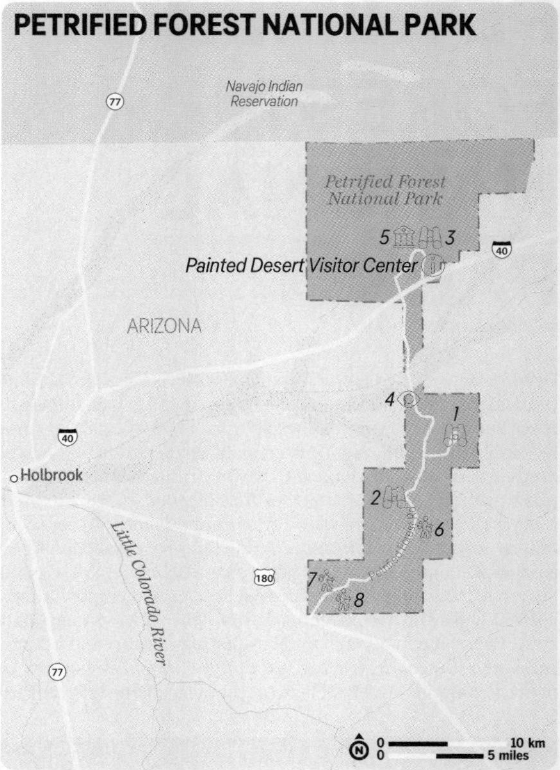

Fossils of the Petrified Forest

HIKES IN AN ANCIENT LANDSCAPE

The 28-mile scenic drive through Petrified Forest National Park has more than a dozen pullouts with interpretive signs and short trails. Start at the more interesting south entrance, which has the highest concentration of petrified wood. Several trails near the southern entrance provide the best access for close-ups of the petrified logs: the 1.6-mile **Long Logs Trail**, the 0.4-mile **Giant Logs Trail** (with the park's largest log behind the Rainbow Forest Museum), the 0.75-mile **Crystal Forest Loop** and the **Jasper Forest lookout**.

A highlight in the center section is a 3-mile loop drive to **Blue Mesa**, where you'll be treated to 360-degree views of spectacular badlands, log falls and logs balancing atop hills with the leathery texture of elephant skin. The 0.9-mile **Blue Mesa Trail** leads scenically into the badlands. Nearby, at the bottom of a ravine, hundreds of petroglyphs are splashed across **Newspaper Rock** like a prehistoric bulletin board.

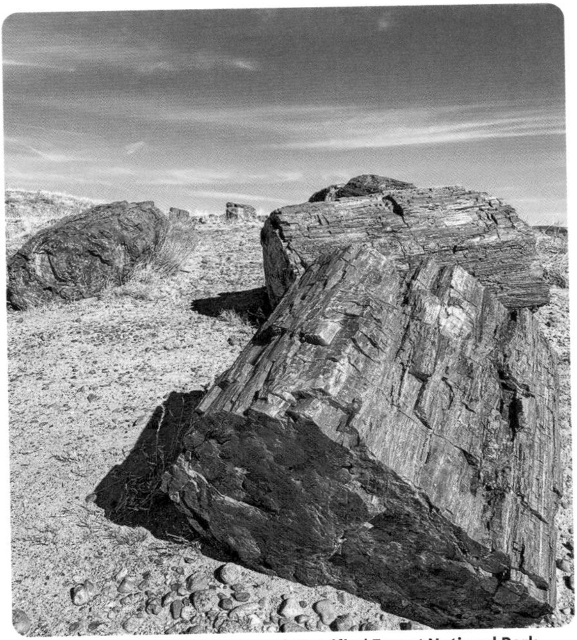

Petrified wood, Petrified Forest National Park

North of I-40 lies a Route 66 interpretive marker and an especially brilliant section of the Painted Desert. Nature puts on a kaleidoscopic show here at sunset: the most mesmerizing views are from **Kachina Point** behind the historic **Painted Desert Inn**, a 1930s adobe lodge turned museum decorated with murals by Hopi artist Fred Kabotie. It was redesigned in the 1940s by Mary Colter, the architect behind similar Hopi-style buildings in Grand Canyon Village. After narrowly avoiding demolition, it was made a National Historic Landmark in 1987.

Kachina Point is also the trailhead for hikes and wilderness camping, and the Painted Desert is a beautiful place for it. A free permit is required.

WHAT IS PETRIFIED WOOD?

The Painted Desert at Petrified Forest National Park is strewn with fossilized logs predating the dinosaurs. The 'trees' are fragmented, fossilized 225-million-year-old logs scattered over a vast area of semidesert grassland. Many are huge – up to 6ft in diameter – and at least one spans a ravine to form a natural bridge. The trees arrived via major floods, only to be buried beneath silica-rich volcanic ash before they could decompose. Groundwater dissolved the silica, carried it through the logs and crystallized it into solid, sparkly quartz mashed up with iron, carbon, manganese and other minerals. Uplift and erosion eventually exposed the logs.

GETTING AROUND

You need a car to visit Petrified Forest National Park. Straddling I-40, the park has an entrance at exit 311 off I-40 in the north and another off Hwy 180 in the south. A 28-mile paved scenic road links the two.

SAGUARO NATIONAL PARK

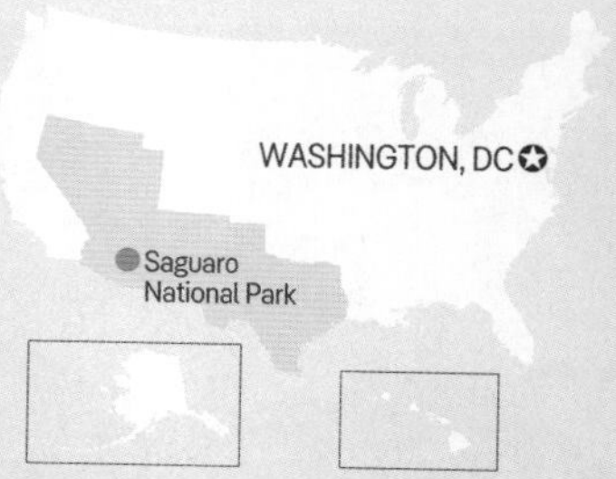

Saguaros are an iconic symbol of Southwest USA, and an entire army of these majestic cactus plants is protected in this two-part desert playground. Established in 1933, Saguaro National Monument was the first federal monument created to protect a specific plant. President Bill Clinton confirmed this mission in 1994 when he signed a bill upgrading its status to a national park. What's so special about this cactus? For starters, its habitat is limited to the Sonoran Desert, which stretches across southern Arizona, southeastern California and northern Mexico.

The park is divided into two distinct sections on either side of the city of Tucson. Petroglyphs, nature trails and saguaro groves grab the spotlight in the Tucson Mountain District on the western edge of Tucson. Thirty miles east, the Rincon Mountain District unfurls across six eco-zones, stretching from low-lying desert to the summits of isolated mountain ranges known as 'sky islands.'

FACTS

Great For Walking, cycling, photo ops
State Arizona
Entrance Fee 7-day pass per vehicle/motorcycle/person on foot or bicycle $25/20/15
Area 143 sq miles

NATE HOVEE/SHUTTERSTOCK ©

SIGHTS
1 Bajada Loop Drive
2 Cactus Forest Loop Drive

ACTIVITIES, COURSES & TOURS
3 Desert Discovery Trail
4 Douglas Spring Trail
5 Freeman Homestead Trail
6 King Canyon/ Gould High Loop
7 Signal Hill Trail
8 Tanque Verde Ridge Trail
9 Valley View Overlook

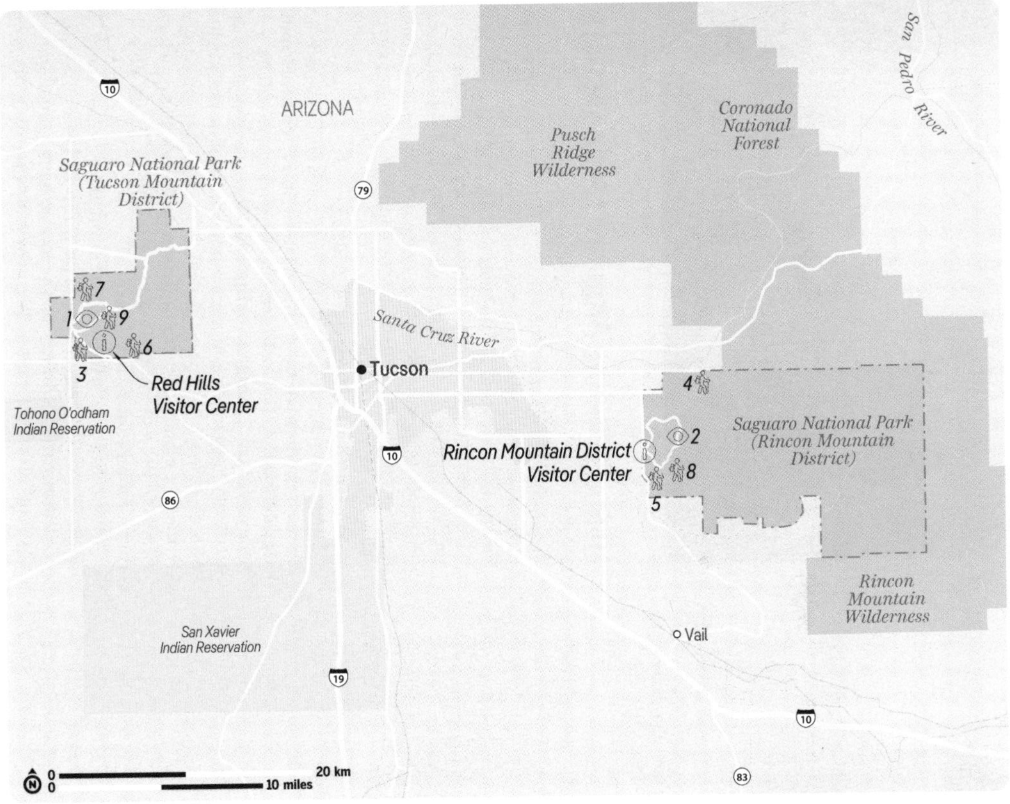

Cholla cactus, Saguaro National Park
COMG/SHUTTERSTOCK ©

SAGUARO STATS

Saguaros (sah-*wah*-ros) grow slowly, taking about 15 years to reach a foot in height, 50 years to reach 7ft and almost a century before they begin to take on their typical, many-armed appearance. In April, the cacti begin blossoming with lovely white blooms – Arizona's state flower. By June and July, the flowers give way to ripe red fruit that local Native Americans use for food. It is illegal to damage or remove saguaros. They only grow in the Sonoran Desert.

Cactus Forest Loop Drive

Hiking & Biking Saguaro National Park

THORNY DESERT BEACONS

Pedaling past saguaros as the rising sun illuminates the mountains is an experience bordering on sublime – smooth pavement, clear skies and the dangerous thought that life is, perhaps, good. Yep, the 8-mile **Cactus Forest Loop Drive** in the Rincon Mountain District east of Tucson is special, and its beauty is open to drivers and cyclists alike. The scrubby desert scenery here also evokes the Old West. To embrace the John Wayne vibe, saddle up for a horseback ride with family-run **Houston's Horseback Riding**.

More than 165 miles of hiking trails crisscross the park. In the eastern district, the 1-mile, round-trip **Freeman Homestead Trail** leads to a grove of massive saguaros. The 5.6-mile round-trip **Douglas Spring Trail** ascends from saguaros to desert grasslands and a seasonal waterfall in the Rincon Mountain foothills. For a full-fledged desert adventure, tackle the steep and rocky **Tanque Verde Ridge Trail**, which climbs to the summit of Tanque Verde peak (7049ft) and returns, for an 18-mile adventure.

West of town, the Tucson Mountain District has the Red Hills Visitor Center. The **Bajada Loop Drive** is a 5-mile, graded dirt road through cactus forest that begins 1.5 miles north of the visitor center. Two easy and rewarding hikes on the loop are the 0.8-mile **Valley View Overlook** (awesome at sunset) and the half-mile **Signal Hill Trail** to ancient petroglyphs. The 7-mile **King Canyon/Gould High Loop** is a more strenuous trek. The informative, 0.5-mile **Desert Discovery Trail**, which is 1 mile northwest of the visitor center, is wheelchair accessible.

GETTING AROUND

The park is divided into east and west units, separated by 30 miles and the city of Tucson. Both sections – the Rincon Mountain District in the east and Tucson Mountain District in the west – are filled with trails and desert flora. Rincon is the larger section, about 15 miles east of downtown.

WHITE SANDS NATIONAL PARK

New Mexico's newest national park appears like something out of a dream, and these ethereal dunes are a highlight of any trip to the state. In White Sands National Park, snow-white dunes roll on as far as the eye can see, one gently merging with the next, and yet it's nowhere near the ocean. The dunes are actually made from powdered gypsum crystals that blew over from the San Andres and Sacramento Mountains 4000 to 7000 years ago.

This place is a must on every landscape photographer's itinerary. Try to time a visit to White Sands with sunrise or sunset (or both), when the dazzlingly white sea of sand is at its most magical.

From the visitor center, drive the 16-mile scenic loop, which circuits through the heart of the world's largest gypsum dune field. Don't forget your sunglasses and sunscreen – the sand's as bright as snow.

FACTS

Great For Family travel, photo ops, scenery
State New Mexico
Entrance Fee 7-day pass per car/motorcycle/person on foot or bicycle $25/20/15
Area 228 sq miles

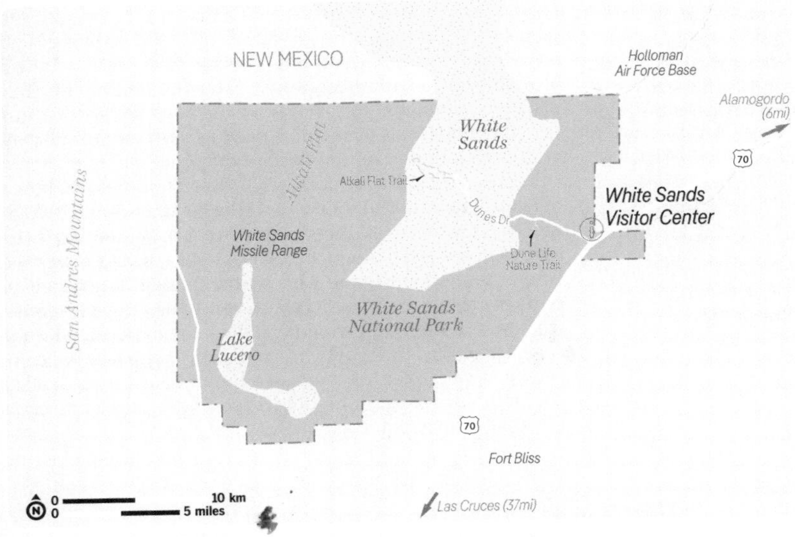

WHITE SANDS MISSILE RANGE

Look on Google Maps and you'll see a large swath of southern New Mexico – some 2.2 million acres – grayed out. This forbidden, government-controlled area is called White Sands Missile Range and has been used as a weapons testing site since 1945 when the atomic bomb was detonated at Trinity Site. The government continues to use the range to test weapons, though there hasn't been a nuclear test since WWII.

Visit the **White Sands Missile Range Museum**, 26 miles from Las Cruces behind the Organ Mountains, to learn more about the world's first atomic bomb detonation as well as other missiles tested at the site. Expect high security and thorough screenings.

White Sands National Park

Sea of Glistening Sand Dunes

GET OUT AND PLAY

Walking the dunes is almost a spiritual experience, especially at sunrise or sunset when the sea of sand sparkles. From the visitor center, drive the 16-mile scenic loop and stop along the way to sink your toes into the sand (be careful, it can get hot!) and tumble down the dune or slide down on a sled – plastic saucers are sold at the visitor center gift shop for $20 (you can sell it back for $5 at day's end), or save money and bring your own. Some accommodations in the gateway town of Alamogordo let overnight guests borrow saucers for free. It's a long, long way to the ocean from here, so don't be surprised to find locals picnicking, playing, sunbathing and generally enjoying the full-on beach experience.

Escape the crowds by doing your best Timothée Chalamet in *Dune* impression and hike the **Alkali Flat**, a 5-mile round-trip backcountry trail through the heart of White Sands (be sure to follow the markers because it's easy to get lost), or the simple 1-mile loop **Dune Life Nature Trail**. Rangers lead **sunset strolls** daily and **full-moon hikes** once a month from March through November; check the park calendar for specific timings (nps.gov/whsa/planyourvisit/calendar.htm). Interpretive ranger-led tours also run to Lake Lucero, called the birthplace of the dunes for its thousands of selenite crystals that form gypsum sand.

GETTING AROUND

You need a car to get to and around White Sands National Park. The gateway town of Alamogordo is 16 miles northeast. The road into the park occasionally closes at short notice for up to three hours for missile tests.

ZION NATIONAL PARK

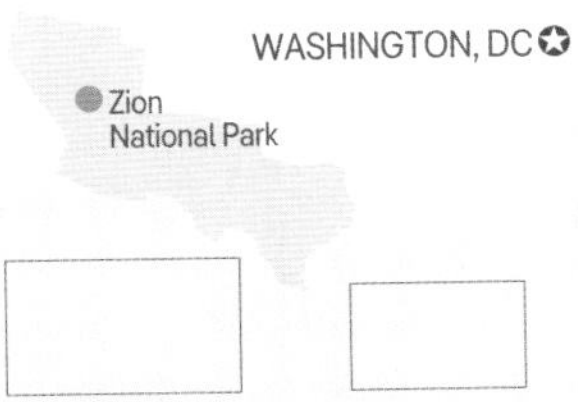

Get ready for an overdose of awesome. The soaring red-and-white cliffs of Zion Canyon, one of southern Utah's most dramatic natural wonders, rise high over the Virgin River. Hiking in the water through the Narrows, or peering beyond Angels Landing after a 1500ft ascent, is indeed amazing. But for all its awe-inspiring majesty, the park also holds more delicate beauties: weeping rocks, tiny grottoes, hanging gardens and meadows of mesa-top wildflowers. Lush vegetation and low elevation give these magnificent rock formations a different feel from the barren parks in the east.

Most of the park's nearly five million annual visitors enter along Zion Canyon floor, and even challenging hikes become congested between May and September. But Zion has quieter corners. Up-country, on the mesa tops (7000ft), it's easy to escape the crowds – and the heat. The Kolob Canyons section, 40 miles northwest by car, sees a fraction of the visitors.

Zion Canyon

FACTS

Great For Walking, scenery, family travel
State Utah
Entrance Fee 7-day pass per vehicle/motorcycle/person on foot or bicycle $35/30/20
Area 229 sq miles

PARK MUSEUMS & RANGER TALKS

Zion Human History Museum
Modest exhibit of the geological and human history of Zion. Ranger talks at 10:30am and 2:30pm daily.

Ride with a Ranger
Two-hour bus ride through Zion Canyon with a ranger. Free and accessible but limited seats.

Zion Canyon Visitor Center
Talks at 1pm daily on a range of subjects.

Zion Lodge
This 4pm talk is a good option after a morning hike.

Watchman Evening Program
A 9pm talk at the campground from May to October.

ZION NATIONAL PARK

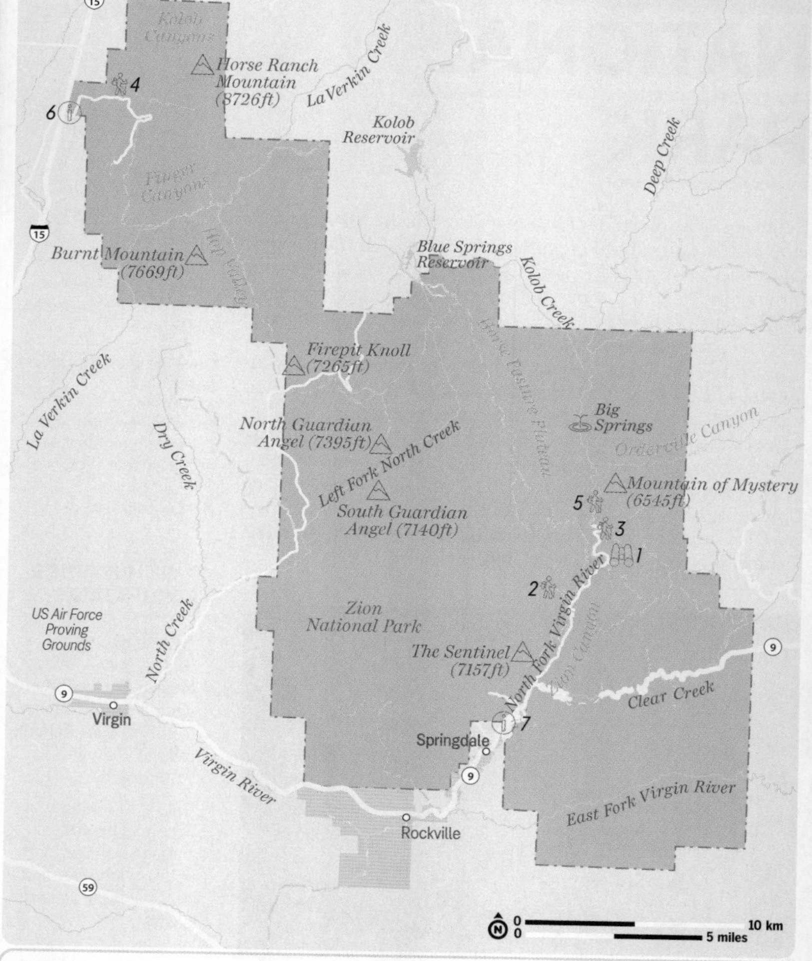

SIGHTS
1 Observation Point

ACTIVITIES & TOURS
2 Emerald Pools Trails
3 Riverside Walk
4 Taylor Creek Trail
5 The Narrows

INFORMATION
6 Kolob Canyons Visitor Center
7 Zion Canyon Visitor Center

WHERE TO STAY IN ZION CANYON NATIONAL PARK

Zion Lodge
More motel than magnificent, but having Zion's domes on your doorstep is sublime. **$$$**

Watchman Campground
175 sites in a prime location south of the visitor center. Reservations required year-round. No showers. **$**

South Campground
Sites sandwiched between the visitor center and the Zion Human History Museum along the Pa'rus Trail. **$**

The Narrows: Zion's Classic Hike

WADING THROUGH THE WATER

Hiking through a rocky river in ankle-to-chest-deep water as the canyon walls grow up to 1000ft tall and close to just 20ft in width – this is the **Narrows**, the quintessential Zion. This wet and wild 'trail' is actually the Virgin River itself. At the end of the Riverside Walk (p198), stairs descend to the water, and the adventure begins. Hordes of hikers visit the Narrows, but many don't walk more than a mile or two. Quieter sections await the further you trek.

The best part about hiking the Narrows is that you can walk as little or as long as you'd like and still have a great time. This out-and-back route is not about reaching a specific spot, but simply soaking up the scene. Day hikers are allowed to go as far as Big Spring, though few do. Don't underestimate the distance (9.4 miles round trip; about eight hours) or the difficulty: it's a long way to hike against the current.

Around the first river bend, you might catch canyoneers on their final rappel at **Mystery Canyon**. About 2 miles in, the **Orderville Canyon** tributary flows from the east. You can explore it for a quarter mile, but to go further, you have to do the top-down hike. The bottom-up route continues north through **Wall Street**, where the sheerness, nearness and height of the cliffs shatter whatever remains of your perspective. After this section, the canyon opens slightly, and the water gets deeper, usually requiring swimming.

Tackling the Narrows Top-Down

GOING THE DISTANCE

One of Zion's most famous backcountry routes takes on the unforgettable Narrows from the Chamberlain's Ranch trailhead in East Zion to the Riverside Walk in Zion Canyon. This strenuous 16-mile journey meanders through the towering slot canyon along the North Fork of the Virgin River. Plan on getting wet: most of the hike is in the river, and full swims are sometimes required. Soaring walls, scalloped alcoves and chest-deep wades with your backpack lifted over your head make it truly memorable.

Some hikers complete this trek as a one-day through-hike, which can take 12 hours or longer. In shuttle season, you must make it to the Temple of Sinawava stop before the last bus out of the canyon, lest you add another 9-mile walk to the visitor center. The better experience is an overnight backpacking trip. No matter which way you tackle the top-down Narrows hike, permits are required and are some of the park's most sought-after.

CAUTIONS & CLOSURES

Preparation and timing are the keys to a successful Narrows adventure. Always – and we mean *always* – check conditions and the flash-flood forecast with rangers before setting off. A sudden rainstorm miles away can send down a surge of rock- and log-filled water that sweeps away everything in its path.

The park service closes the Narrows hike when the Virgin River runs more than 150 cubic feet per second, which is sometimes the case during spring snowmelt. Some years there is little change in the water level, but in other years, the Narrows could be closed in April, May or June. Getting the right gear is imperative for a safe and fun trek.

The Narrows

STEPHEN MOEHLE/SHUTTERSTOCK ©

EASY HIKES IN ZION CANYON NATIONAL PARK

Pa'rus Trail
The only park path open to bicycles and pets on a leash; paved and wheelchair accessible.

Watchman Trail
Ascend 368ft to a short loop providing fine views of the park's formations, best seen at sunset.

Grotto Trail
This half-mile trail connects Zion Lodge with the Grotto picnic area.

ROAD TRIP

Zion Canyon Scenic Drive

Discover the heart of Zion National Park on a journey along its scenic drive, which threads along the Virgin River between towering sandstone cliffs. If you have time for only one activity in Zion, this route is it. North of Canyon Junction Bridge, the road is closed to private vehicles from March through November, so use the excellent park shuttle instead, or go by pedal power on a bicycle or e-bike.

1 Zion Canyon Visitor Center

Get your bearings with a quick intro at the Zion Canyon Visitor Center, near the park's south entrance. Outdoor exhibit panels provide a quick lay of the land.

The Drive: Jump on the shuttle from the visitor center (stop 1) to the Court of the Patriarchs (stop 4). Cyclists can pedal the river-hugging Pa'rus Trail – the only path in the park open to bikes – before heading north on Zion Canyon Scenic Drive.

2 Court of the Patriarchs

A steep 150ft path leads to a view of magnificent peaks named after men in the Old Testament. Christened by a Methodist minister in 1916, from left to right are Abraham (6890ft), Isaac (6825ft) and Jacob (6831ft), while crouching in front of Jacob is Mt Moroni (5690ft), named for a Mormon angel.

The Drive: Take the shuttle one stop to Zion Lodge (stop 5).

DENIS UM/SHUTTERSTOCK ©

Court of the Patriarchs

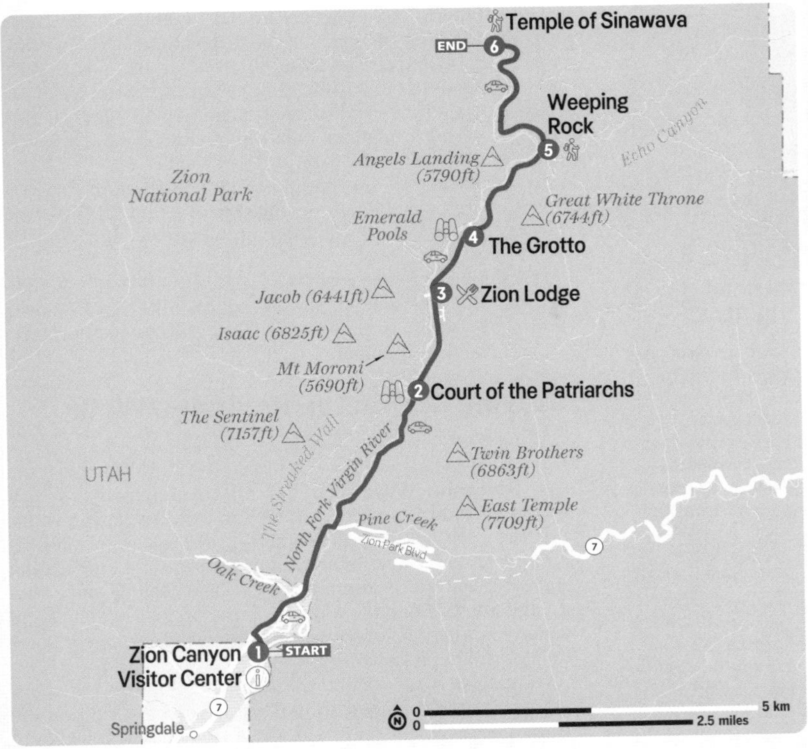

3 Zion Lodge

Zion Lodge houses the park's only hotel and restaurants. The wide front lawn, shaded by a giant cottonwood tree, is a favorite place for a post-hike ice cream and nap. Stretch your legs on the Emerald Pool trails (p198) to investigate Zion's incredible hanging gardens, where plant life clings to the cliff walls.

The Drive: Ride the shuttle one stop to the Grotto (stop 6). If you hike the Emerald Pool trails, take the Kayenta Trail to the Grotto instead of returning to Zion Lodge.

4 The Grotto

The hike to Angels Landing (p200) starts from this large, cottonwood-shaded picnic area. To admire Angels Landing rather than climb it, stroll the first flat quarter mile of the West Rim Trail for a perfect vantage point.

The Drive: Take the shuttle one stop to Weeping Rock (stop 7).

5 Weeping Rock

The steep, 0.4-mile Weeping Rock Trail ends at a large dripping rock alcove. As water percolates through the Navajo Sandstone, it's pushed out by the less permeable layer of Kayenta Sandstone underneath, causing the water to seep, feeding a large hanging garden – and dripping on your head.

The Drive: Ride the shuttle to the end of the line (stop 9).

6 Temple of Sinawava

Zion Canyon's dramatic conclusion (by way of concrete at least) is a natural amphitheater known as the Temple of Sinawava. From here, you can take the popular Riverside Walk (p198) to the ultimate Zion experience, the Narrows (p195).

Only 40 permits per day are issued. At 10am on the 5th of each month, reservations for the next month become available online (zionpermits.nps.gov). Reservations cost $5 and are often booked out within minutes. An additional fee of $15 to $25, depending on your group's size, is paid when picking up your permit in person. Last-minute and walk-in reservations are possible – check online for specifics.

Backpackers can stay in one of 12 campsites in the canyon. Six are bookable online, and the other six are reserved for day-before walk-ins at the Zion Canyon Visitor Center's Wilderness Desk.

Permits aren't issued when the Virgin River flow rate is higher than 150 cubic feet per second, so this hike may be closed at times between April and June. The best time to hike is late June through September.

GETTING THE GEAR

As an almost entirely water-based hike, the Narrows isn't your standard walk in the park. Outfitters in Springdale, near Zion's south entrance, rent canyoneering shoes, neoprene socks, wooden walking sticks and dry suits or bibs. You might balk at the price ($30 to $75 depending on the season), but what you wear will greatly influence your enjoyment.

The Narrows is cooler than elsewhere in Zion because of the tall canyon walls, and hypothermia can be a risk in colder months. A walking stick helps you navigate the fast-moving currents on slippery rocks, and you'll want to put your phone, camera and anything else you don't want to get wet in a dry bag.

Staying Dry on the Riverside Walk

WATERSIDE WANDER

If you don't want to take the plunge into the Narrows, the easy **Riverside Walk** is the dry and paved part of the journey. Shadowed from the slanting sun by lofty canyon walls, this fun path parallels the slippery cobblestones of the Virgin River and rambles by seeps, hanging gardens and wading spots. Interpretive signs explain the local geology and ecology, and points along the way give access to the riverbank and water, making it a family favorite. The water is a great place to play, though it can be chilly.

The canyon walls around the Temple of Sinawava are popular rock-climbing sites, so look up as you set off. From the start, the pavement undulates close to the canyon wall and past water-carved alcoves. Park maps describe the walk as 'wheelchair accessible with assistance.' We think someone fairly strong would have to be doing the pushing, but strollers work fine. The paved trail ends where the Narrows begin, at a raised cul-de-sac with benches. Steps lead down to a rocky fan at the river's edge. Wear shoes you don't mind getting wet – you may not be able to resist the river, which beckons even those not hiking further up-canyon.

The trail is 2 miles round trip and starts at the Temple of Sinawava shuttle stop at the end of Zion Canyon Scenic Drive.

Path to the Emerald Pools

ZION'S HANGING GARDENS

Short and sweet, the Emerald Pool trails are a superb introduction to Zion's unique ecology and microhabitats. These

ENDEMIC PLANTS IN ZION NATIONAL PARK

Zion Daisy
White or light-pink flower with a yellow center that grows in small bunches.

Crimson Monkeyflower
Four eye-catching, lipstick-red petals give riparian habitats a burst of color.

Zion Milkvetch
These delicate purple flowers are some of the first to bloom in spring.

popular paths lead to a series of bucolic ponds, stunning desert-varnished rocks and a beautiful example of Zion's hanging gardens. The pools fill with water that seeps from the sandstone, augmented by seasonal rains, creating oases in the desert ringed with algae and ferns. The water is ecologically sensitive, so getting into the pools is not allowed.

The paved **Lower Emerald Pool Trail**, the easiest of the three trails, gradually rises and falls for 0.6 miles before reaching the first pool. Waterfalls cascade down a multicolored, mineral-stained overhang in a long arc, misting the trail (and you) as you pass beneath. If that was enough walking for you, this is a good spot to turn around. Otherwise, follow the dirt trail as it ascends 150ft to the less dramatic **Middle Emerald Pool**, which feeds the waterfalls below.

From here, a steep, rocky half-mile spur leads to the **Upper Emerald Pool**. It's the loveliest grotto of all, surrounded by the sheer-walled skirts of Lady Mountain.

The round-trip hike to all three pools is roughly 2 miles. You could return to Zion Lodge the way you came, but we recommend continuing in the opposite direction, on the **Kayenta Trail**. This path affords spectacular views down the valley. Expect to be picking your way among rocks along the mile-long trail before you descend to the Grotto picnic grounds and shuttle stop.

Surveying the Scene from Observation Point

THE BEST VIEW IN THE PARK

It feels deliciously like cheating to wander along a mostly flat woodland path and then descend to **Observation Point**, which towers more than 700ft above Angels Landing – you get all the rewards with hardly any of the work.

The trailhead, also called East Mesa, is at the end of a small parking lot off a 4WD road in East Zion. The parking lot fills early, and the road is often too rough for standard sedans. Instead, book a spot on a shuttle ($8.50 per person round trip) run by East Zion Adventures (eastzionadventures.com), which leaves from nearby Zion Ponderosa Ranch Resort.

The first 2 miles of the hike meander through open stands of tall ponderosa pines, which may show signs of the periodic park-prescribed burns. In May and June, keep an eye out for showy up-country wildflowers. To the right, canyon views open up in the distance. From there, the main trail turns southwest and starts gradually descending, with glimpses of Echo Canyon on your left and Zion Canyon on your right. A further descent down slickrock and loose

PERMITS FOR ANGELS LANDING

In 2022, the National Park Service started requiring hikers to obtain permits to climb Angels Landing (p200), one of the most popular spots in Zion. Permits are awarded through seasonal and day-before lotteries. In the seasonal lottery, you pick seven days and times in the next three-month season (eg if you want to hike from June to August, the lottery takes place in April). Apply for day-before permits from midnight to 3pm.

It costs $6 to apply for a permit. If you're successful in the lottery, you'll be charged an additional $3 per registered person. Without a permit, you can still hike as far as Scout Lookout.

Trail to Observation Point
MARIDAV/SHUTTERSTOCK ©

WILDLIFE TO LOOK OUT FOR

California Condor
Crane your neck near Big Bend to spot the bird with the largest wingspan in North America.

Mule Deer
Large-eared deer frequently spotted near Zion Canyon Visitor Center and the lawn of Zion Lodge.

Bighorn Sheep
Reintroduced in the 1970s; keep an eye out near the east entrance and the Zion–Mt Carmel Tunnel.

HIKING TO THE HEAVENS AT ANGELS LANDING

A must-do in Zion Canyon, Angels Landing offers an exhilarating half-day hike with a jaw-dropping payoff. The 5-mile round-trip hike hugs the face of a towering cliff, snakes through a cool canyon and climbs a series of sharp switchbacks before finally ascending a narrow, exposed ridge where steel chains and the encouraging words of strangers are your only friends. Your reward after the final scramble to the 5790ft summit? A lofty view of Zion Canyon and some unreal photos of your vertigo-defying adventure. A permit (p199) is required for the full hike, but you can go as far as Scout Lookout without one. The **1 trailhead** is on the west side of Zion Canyon Scenic Drive from the Grotto shuttle stop. At the **2 intersection** with the Kayenta Trail, turn right to follow the West Rim Trail, which meanders along the desert floor before ascending gradually but relentlessly, becoming steeper as you begin climbing long, paved switchbacks up the canyon wall. Beyond a rock overhang, the trail levels out, running deep into the narrow, slightly cooler **3 Refrigerator Canyon**. You'll ascend a few more switchbacks before reaching the engineering marvel of **4 Walter's Wiggles**. Built in 1926, this set of 21 steep stonework zigzags is named after the first superintendent of Zion. Huffing and puffing, you emerge at **5 Scout Lookout**, a sandy area with stellar views. If you have a permit, carry on to **6 Angels Landing**, where the ridge along the razor's-edge traverse is just 5ft wide and the sheer cliffs plummet 1000ft. Pull yourself along the chains for the final 488ft elevation gain. At the hike's dramatic conclusion, take in the stunning 360-degree view of Zion Canyon. You've earned it.

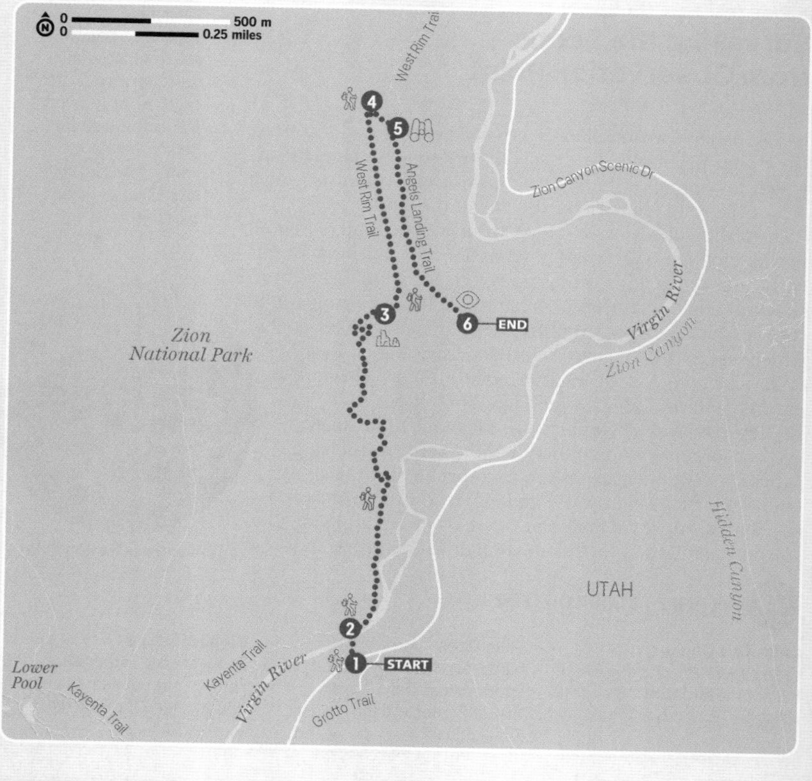

stones shaded by juniper and piñon leads past some sandy sites to the Observation Point spur at 3 miles. Sit and soak up the panoramic vistas and see if you can spot the intrepid, and much more tired, hikers on Angels Landing.

For a longer and more challenging hike, you can tack on **Cable Mountain**, descending the spectacular East Rim Trail through Echo Canyon on the backside of Mt Baldy before climbing to the flatter trail out to the viewpoint. This full route is a little more than 15 miles, and you'll need to use a shuttle service to get back to your vehicle.

Splashing Through Taylor Creek

HOMESTEADER HISTORY AND AN ARCHED ALCOVE

This refreshing 5-mile out-and-back hike crisscrosses **Taylor Creek** dozens of times, passing through juniper, sage and piñon to get to two historic cabins. But keep walking for the real payoff at the end: views of Double Arch Alcove, a natural amphitheater ringing with birdsong and dripping with spring water.

From the parking-lot start, the path quickly drops down a set of stairs and sand to creek level. The overall elevation change is 450ft, but the walk is mostly flat beyond this point. From there, trail and water interweave like strands of DNA. Though the creek is small, expect to get a little wet and muddy, and harassed by bugs in the warmer months.

After about a mile, you come to the 1930 **Larson Cabin**, a homestead started by a state historian that had to be abandoned when the area was declared a national monument in 1937. As the trail enters a finger canyon, the walls narrow, and your steady ascent grows steeper. A mile further, **Fife Cabin**, another homesteader structure, appears. Both buildings are too fragile to enter, but you can peek through the windows to see the remnants of furniture and the floor.

The trail's last half mile leads to **Double Arch Alcove**, where the seep-stained red rock glows and echoes with dripping water and swirling wind. It's a cooling break before your walk back.

IS ZION SUFFERING FROM OVERTOURISM?

US national parks are busier than ever. Visitor numbers to Zion have doubled in the last two decades, and the park had its most-visited year in 2021, reeling in five million travelers – only the fourth national park ever to reach that figure. New permits have limited numbers on some trails and, with flexible plans, you can more easily find a quieter corner. May, June and July are the busiest months, while winter sees just 25% of peak visitor numbers. Zion Canyon is the park at its finest, but hikes in Kolob Canyons are still stunning and less trodden. Afternoons see fewer visits and, in summer, sunset is still hours away, allowing enough time for a trail or two.

GETTING AROUND

From March through November, private vehicles are not allowed on Zion Canyon Scenic Drive while shuttle buses are in operation. The Zion Park Shuttle makes nine stops along the canyon, from the visitor center to the Temple of Sinawava. The Springdale Shuttle stops along Hwy 9 between the park's south entrance and the Majestic View Lodge in the gateway town of Springdale. You can ride the Springdale Shuttle to Zion Canyon Brew Pub and walk across a footbridge into the park. The visitor center and the first stop for the Zion shuttle lie on the other side of the kiosk. Both shuttles are free to ride.

Limited free parking is available inside the park; arrive as early as possible. Otherwise, it costs $20 to park in Springdale.

North Cascades National Park (p220)

ALASKA & THE PACIFIC NORTHWEST

A REGION OF SUPERLATIVES

The deepest lakes, the highest peaks and the greenest forests: welcome to the untamed wilderness in Washington, Oregon and Alaska.

THE MAIN AREAS

Lush rainforests, snow-covered peaks and rugged, wave-battered shorelines are the hallmarks of the Pacific Northwest. Glacial snowfields emerge from a sea of clouds, and virgin stands of massive Douglas fir and red cedar serve as reminders of what the continent's ancient forests must have once looked like. Mt Rainier and Crater Lake steal the limelight in the Lower 48, but far to the north lies wild, remote Alaska with its staggering collection of glaciers, volcanoes and fjords.

You can get wonderfully lost wandering among the moss-draped trees of the thick, wet Hoh Rain Forest of Washington state's Olympic Peninsula, or look for sea creatures amid the tide pools of nearby Ruby Beach. Photographers can click to their hearts' content at the stunning springtime wildflower meadows surrounding Mt Rainier, the peak so iconic that everyone in Washington just calls it 'the Mountain.' Hikers can get into some seriously rugged backpacking in Washington's North Cascades, surrounded by glaciers, jagged peaks and alpine lakes, the deepest and bluest of which is at Crater Lake, Oregon's only national park.

In Alaska, America's largest wilderness preserves offer a lifetime of adventures. Among the many highlights, you can watch massive brown bears catching salmon at Katmai or paddle among icebergs, sea otters and puffins in Glacier Bay. There are magnificent treks over rugged terrain, and wilderness lodges reachable only by floatplane. The hardest part is deciding where to begin.

Find Your Way

You can make a rewarding road trip out of visiting the four national parks of the Pacific Northwest. Alaska's remote parks require more planning (and money!), with access to some places limited to bush plane or boat.

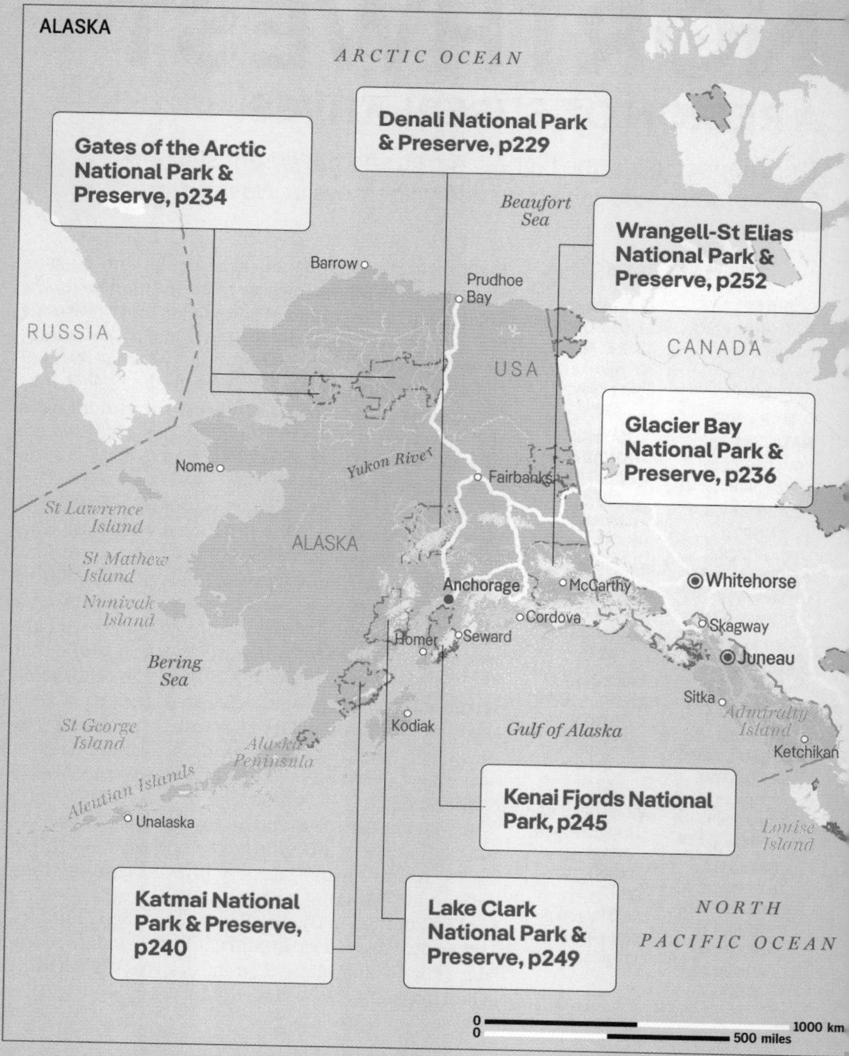

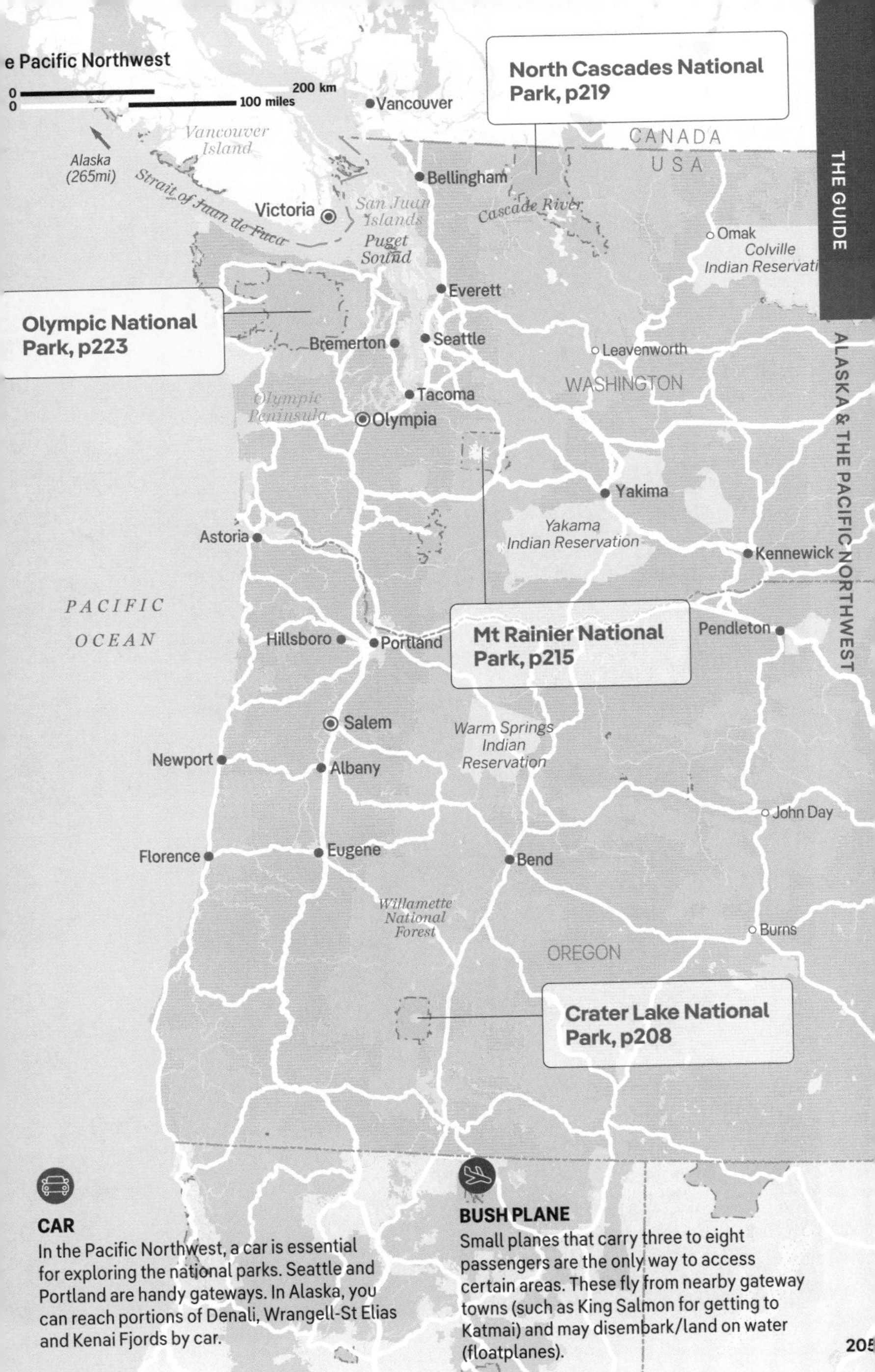

CAR

In the Pacific Northwest, a car is essential for exploring the national parks. Seattle and Portland are handy gateways. In Alaska, you can reach portions of Denali, Wrangell-St Elias and Kenai Fjords by car.

BUSH PLANE

Small planes that carry three to eight passengers are the only way to access certain areas. These fly from nearby gateway towns (such as King Salmon for getting to Katmai) and may disembark/land on water (floatplanes).

NAYADADARA/SHUTTERSTOCK ©

Nisqually River, Mt Rainier National Park (p215)

PATRICK CIVELLO/SHUTTERSTOCK ©

Canoeing, Aialik Glacier (p246), Kenai Fjords National Park

Plan Your Time

Careful planning is essential, especially in Alaska, where you may need to book well in advance for limited spaces in campgrounds and on transportation (like water taxis and bush planes).

Pressed for Time

After flying into Seattle, make the two-hour drive to **Mt Rainier** (p215) for a day of exploring in the Paradise section of the park. Get a park overview at the Henry M Jackson Visitor Center then hike the Skyline Trail for magnificent views of the famous mountain. From there, head over to **Olympic** (p223) for rainforest walks amid massive cedars, followed by some downtime on the coast.

Five Days to Explore

Fly into Anchorage and drive north to **Denali** (p229). Get an overview of the park on a narrated bus tour, then hike the Savage Loop Trail or the more challenging Savage Alpine Trail. Next up is **Wrangell-St Elias** (p252), where you can stay in an old mining village while planning trips into the wilderness. Afterwards, make your way to Seward for glacier-filled adventures in **Kenai Fjords** (p245).

SEASONAL HIGHLIGHTS

SPRING

At lower elevations, there are wildflowers and early animal sightings. Higher up, snow covers mountains.

SUMMER

July to September are the prime months for outdoor activities. It's also the best time for spotting bears in Alaska.

FALL

Summertime crowds disperse and lodging prices fall. It's also a fine time to see the fall birds migration.

WINTER

You'll have the parks largely to yourself, with snowfall making a magical backdrop to skiing and snowshoeing.

CRATER LAKE NATIONAL PARK

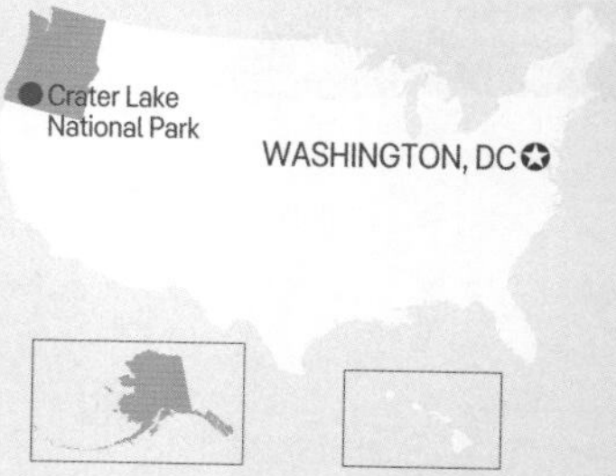

The gloriously clear waters of Crater Lake reflect surrounding mountain peaks like a giant dark-blue mirror, making for spectacular photographs and breathtaking panoramas. Crater Lake is Oregon's only national park and the USA's deepest lake (1943ft).

The lake sits inside a 6-mile-wide caldera created when Mt Mazama erupted nearly 8000 years ago. It has no inlet or outlet; the water comes from snowfall. Protruding from the water and adding to the drama of the landscape is Wizard Island, a volcanic cinder cone topped by its own mini crater, called Witches Cauldron. In summer you can gaze upon the splendor from every angle via the 33-mile Rim Drive, which winds around the edge of the crater with more than 30 viewpoints.

Cleetwood Cove Trail, at the north end of the crater, provides the only water access to the lake. You can also camp, ski or hike in the surrounding old-growth forests.

FACTS

Great For Family travel, photo ops, scenery
State Oregon
Entrance Fee $30 per vehicle ($20 Nov–May)
Area 287 sq miles

Wizard Island

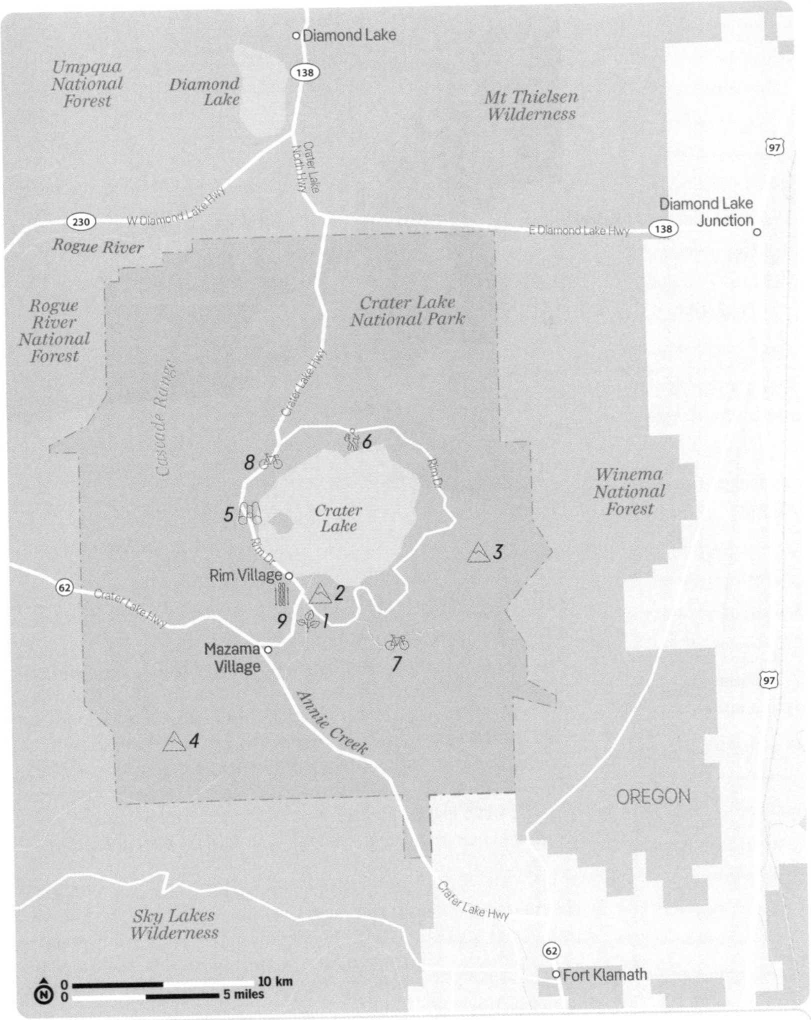

SIGHTS
1 Castle Crest Wildflower Garden
2 Garfield Peak
3 Mt Scott
4 Union Peak
5 Watchman

ACTIVITIES, COURSES & TOURS
6 Cleetwood Cove Trail
7 Grayback Drive
8 Rim Road
9 Rim Village

MT MAZAMA

The ancient mountain that collapsed to form Crater Lake was Mt Mazama, a roughly 12,000ft volcanic peak. The mountain was heavily glaciered and inactive for thousands of years until it came back to life around 7700 years ago. A catastrophic eruption scattered ash for hundreds of miles as flows of superheated pumice solidified into massive banks. The eruption emptied the magma chambers at the heart of the volcano, and the summit cone collapsed to form the caldera.

Snowshoeing

Hiking the Park

ABOVE AND AROUND THE LAKE

Crater Lake has over 90 miles of hiking trails, though some aren't clear of snow until late July. From the eastern edge of the Rim Village parking lot, a 1.7-mile trail leads up 8054ft **Garfield Peak** to an expansive view of the lake; in July the slopes are covered with wildflowers. A strenuous 4.5-mile round-trip hike takes you to an even better lake vista atop 8929ft **Mt Scott**, the highest point in the park; this is an excellent place to catch a sunrise, if you're an early bird, but it's often snowed in until August.

For a steep but shorter hike, trek up 0.7 miles to the **Watchman**, an old lookout tower on the opposite side of the lake that boasts one of the park's best views. For flower enthusiasts, there's an easy half-mile nature trail loop near the Steel Visitor Center that winds through the **Castle Crest Wildflower Garden**. The popular but very steep and sketchy 1-mile **Cleetwood Cove Trail**, at the northern end of the crater, provides the only water access at the cove. It's also where you can hop onto a boat tour (reserve ahead).

Avid hikers can spend some time on the beloved Pacific Crest Trail on their way toward **Union Peak**, a 10-mile round trip

WHERE TO STAY IN CRATER LAKE NATIONAL PARK

Crater Lake Lodge
Historic park lodge with views of the lake and rustic decor.
$$$

Mazama Campground
Large, well-equipped campground just inside the park's south entrance; open in summer. **$**

Lost Creek Campground
Primitive 16-site tents-only campground along on the road to Pinnacles Overlook; first-come, first-served. **$**

that starts out through mellow forest and ends in a steep climb up another volcano. Union Peak (7709ft) is the worn-down nub of an eroded volcano; you can't see Crater Lake from here but you'll get views over the surrounding forest. The trailhead is south of the lake on Hwy 62.

Skiing & Snowshoeing Around the Lake

A WINTER WONDERLAND

Crater Lake can get more than 50in of snow in winter, and keeping the roads clear is an enormous project. The short drive from the south entrance to the rim is usually the only section of road that's drivable between November and May, if not later (and heavy snow can close even this section). You might find yourself feeling very small indeed as you drive between two massive walls of piled-up snow the length of the road. When you reach the parking lot at the top, you might see just the roof of the lodge peeking out from beneath its snowy blanket. Nothing is open and no one's around.

But there's a silver lining: several feet of snow and no traffic on the road makes this an ideal setting for snowshoeing or cross-country ski touring.

Parking at **Rim Village** (the only option) gives you access to several **Nordic skiing trails**. None of the routes are groomed, and you may be breaking trail. The unplowed **West Rim Drive** makes for the most scenic route; it's just over 2 miles from Rim Village to the Wizard Island Overlook.

On snowshoes, you can simply tromp around the lodge, sneaking peeks at the lake below. But the two-hour **ranger-led snowshoe walks** starting from Rim Village on weekends (reservations required) are recommended.

The entire 31-mile **loop around Crater Lake** is an undertaking for serious backcountry skiers and snowshoers only – it takes an average of three days and can be dangerously prone to avalanches. It also requires getting a backcountry permit from park headquarters.

WHAT ABOUT WINE?

For a quick primer on the wines of southern Oregon, visit restaurants and tasting rooms in Ashland and nearby Jacksonville on the **Crater Lake Circuit road trip** (p212).

Cycling the Rim Road

TOUGH BUT REWARDING

Bicycling around Crater Lake is a spectacular way to take in the landscape. The 33-mile paved **Rim Road** around the crater's edge is gloriously scenic, though demanding. It's hilly, with high elevation. It's often narrow, with no bike lanes or

PHANTOM SHIP

Near the lake's south shore is a craggy rock island that resembles a ship sailing away, especially when fog hangs over the lake. It looks small but is actually the height of a 16-story building. The 'ship' is made of lava and is the oldest exposed rock inside the caldera. To see it, hike the 0.8-mile loop to Sun Notch or drive to the Phantom Ship viewpoint.

WHERE TO EAT IN CRATER LAKE NATIONAL PARK

Rim Village Café
Grab-and-go snacks, sandwiches and light meals year-round, with a patio available in summer. **$**

Annie Creek Restaurant
Casual hangout in Mazama Village serving burgers, pizzas and pub fare, with beers on tap (May to September). **$$**

Crater Lake Lodge
Upscale meals using local ingredients, in a grand lodge. Open for breakfast. Make reservations for dinner. **$$$**

ROAD TRIP

Crater Lake Circuit

Serene, mystical Crater Lake is one of Oregon's most enticing destinations, but it's also surrounded by worthy sights and lovely scenery. This 365-mile route takes you on a heavily forested, waterfall-studded loop adjacent to the national park.

1 Ashland

A favorite base for day trips to Crater Lake, Ashland is bursting at the seams with lovely places to sleep and eat (though you'll want to book your hotel room far in advance during the busy summer months). Home of the **Oregon Shakespeare Festival**, it is the cultural heart of southern Oregon, packed with galleries, shops, restaurants and wine-tasting rooms. Ashland's historic downtown and Lithia Park encourage a leisurely stroll.

The Drive: Medford is 13 miles north of Ashland on I-5.

2 Medford

Southern Oregon's largest metropolis can also be a convenient base. Check out nearby **Table Rocks**, impressive 800ft mesas that speak of the area's volcanic past and are home to unique plant and animal species. Flowery spring is the best time for hiking to the flat tops, which were revered Native American sites. Aim for TouVelle State Park, then fork either left to reach the trailhead to Lower Table Rock (3.5-mile round-trip hike) or right for Upper Table Rock (2.5-mile round-trip hike).

The Drive: The drive along Hwy 62 isn't much until after Shady Cove, when urban sprawl cedes to forest. Your next stop is 45 miles northeast in Prospect.

3 Prospect

The real treat at **Prospect State Scenic Viewpoint** is hiking down to the Avenue of Giant Boulders, where the Rogue River crashes dramatically through huge chunks of rock and a little bit of scrambling offers the most rewarding views. Take the trail from the southernmost of two parking lots on Mill Creek Dr. Keep left to get to the boulders. From the upper parking lot, another short hike leads to the lovely Pearsony Falls.

The Drive: Follow Hwy 62 for another 28 miles to get to the Crater Lake National Park turnoff at Munson Valley Rd.

4 Crater Lake

Arguably Oregon's most beautiful body of water, **Crater Lake** is filled with some of the clearest, purest water you can imagine – you can easily peer 100ft down. The lake and surrounding national park reward exploration.

The Drive: When you're ready to exit the park, head north on Hwy 138 for 41 miles and turn right on Rd 34.

5 Umpqua Hot Springs

Set on a mountainside overlooking the North Umpqua River, this is one of Oregon's most splendid **hot springs**. Springs are known for soothing weary muscles, so earn your soak at Umpqua by starting with a hike through lush, old-growth forest punctuated by waterfalls. Half a mile from the parking lot is the scenic North Umpqua Trail.

The Drive: The turnout for Toketee Falls is right on Hwy 138, 2 miles past the Umpqua turnoff.

6 Toketee Falls

More than half a dozen waterfalls line this section of the Rogue-Umpqua Scenic Byway, but the one that truly demands a stop is the stunning, two-tiered **Toketee Falls**. The falls' first tier drops 40ft into an upper pool behind a cliff of columnar basalt, then crashes another 80ft down the rock columns into yet another gorgeous, green-blue pool below. A staircase of 200 steps leads down to the viewpoint.

The Drive: From here, the scenery tapers back down to only moderately spectacular as you

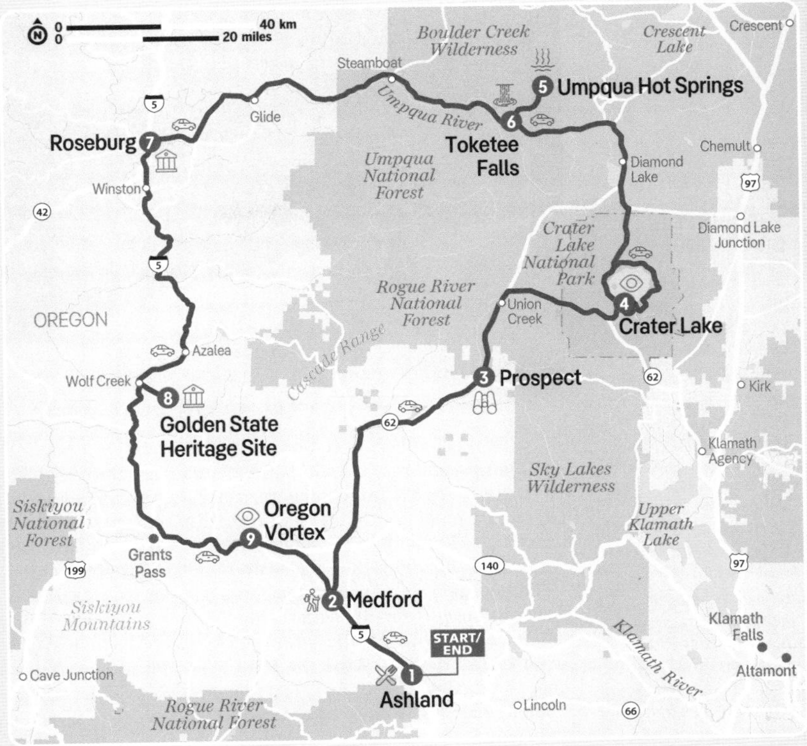

leave the Umpqua National Forest. It's just one hour to Roseburg.

7 Roseburg

Sprawling Roseburg lies in a valley near the confluence of the South and North Umpqua Rivers. The city is mostly a cheap, modern sleepover for travelers headed elsewhere (such as Crater Lake), but it does have a cute, historic downtown area and is surrounded by award-winning wineries. Don't miss the excellent **Douglas County Museum** (umpquavalleymuseums.org), which displays the area's cultural and natural histories.

The Drive: Go south on I-5 for 47 miles and take the Wolf Creek exit. Follow Old State Hwy 99 to curve back under the interstate. Golden is 3.2 miles east on Coyote Creek Rd.

8 Golden State Heritage Site

Stop off in the ghost town of **Golden**, population zero. This former mining town was built on the banks of Coyote Creek when gold was discovered there. A handful of weathered wooden buildings remain, as well as some newfangled interpretive signs that tell the tale of a curiously devout community that eschewed drinking and dancing. Fun fact: the town was once used as a location for the long-running American Western TV series *Gunsmoke*.

The Drive: Go south another 45 miles on I-5 and take exit 43. The Oregon Vortex is 4.2 miles north of the access road.

9 Oregon Vortex

Just outside the town of Gold Hill lies the **Oregon Vortex** (oregonvortex.com), where the laws of physics don't seem to apply – or is it all just an optical illusion created by skewed buildings on steep hillsides? However you see it, the place is definitely bizarre: objects roll uphill, a person's height changes depending on where they stand, and brooms stand up on their own... or so it seems.

JOHN ELK/GETTY IMAGES ©

Cyclist, Crater Lake National Park

THROUGH THE GRAPEVINE

A warmer, sunnier climate has helped create some of Oregon's fledgling wine regions within easy striking distance of Crater Lake National Park. Grapes in the Umpqua and Applegate Valleys, and around Jacksonville, Grants Pass and Medford, are transformed into big reds and oaky whites. Ashland is a good place to try several local wine producers and see what you like; from here it's easy to visit the wineries themselves.

shoulders. Hazards include sudden weather changes, fallen rocks, potholes, blind corners, scurrying animals and, of course, automobiles. In other words, riding the rim is not for beginners. You should be experienced at riding in two-way traffic and in good physical condition before attempting it.

For two days a year, usually in September, the East Rim Drive is closed to motorized traffic, giving cyclists, runners and walkers about 25 miles of this epic road all to themselves in a free event called **Ride the Rim** (visit ridetherimoregon.com to register).

There are also usually brief times in spring and fall when the road is snow-free but closed to cars, and cyclists again have it to themselves. Single-file riding is the general rule, but during these car-free periods you're allowed to ride abreast.

Park officials caution against cycling up to the Rim Road from the park entrance, because the steep, narrow road has poor sight lines and heavy traffic. But cyclists are allowed on park roads whenever motor vehicles are allowed, and must obey all the usual traffic rules, including stop signs and speed limits. Helmets are mandatory for those under age 16 and encouraged for everyone.

Mountain biking is allowed on gravel **Grayb1ack Drive**, but no bikes are allowed on trails – there's no singletrack in the park.

GETTING AROUND

You'll need a car to reach Crater Lake; carry chains in winter. Once inside the park, you can drive, bicycle, walk, or take a trolley/bus tour to explore.

The north entrance and most of the roads inside the park are closed in winter (usually November through June). The park's popular south entrance is open year-round and provides access to Rim Village, as well as the park headquarters at the Steel Visitor Center. In winter you can only go in as far as the lake's rim and back down the same way; no other roads are plowed.

Top up your gas tank before arriving at Crater Lake. The closest pumps are in Prospect, Diamond Lake and Fort Klamath.

MT RAINIER NATIONAL PARK

Emblazoned on every Washington license plate, iconic Mt Rainier is the contiguous USA's fifth-highest peak and, to some, its most awe-inspiring. It stands 2000ft higher than anything else in the Pacific Northwest, in the middle of a 368-sq-mile national park. Locals call it simply 'the Mountain.'

Mt Rainier is notoriously shy, often hiding under a blanket of clouds. But when wildflowers cover the meadows in spring, it's a photographer's dream. The forested foothills around the snow-capped summit are prime territory for hiking and backpacking.

The Nisqually entrance in the southwest corner of the park is open year-round; you can usually get as far in as Longmire in winter. The northeast White River entrance to Sunrise is accessible July through September. In the southeast, Ohanapecosh (o-ha-nuh-peh-kosh) – the name means 'at the edge' – is reachable via the small settlement of Packwood on US 12 from May through November.

FACTS

Great For... Wildlife, photo ops, walking
State Washington
Entrance Fee 7-day pass per vehicle/pedestrian $30/15
Area 368 sq miles

Mt Rainier National Park

MOUNTAIN IN THE MIRROR

If you have a postcard image of Mt Rainier in your mind, it probably came from **Reflection Lake**. On calm cloudless days, the mountain gets to admire itself in the mirror of this glassy pool, formed during a violent volcanic eruption nearly 6000 years ago. Wildflowers frame the scene like they were installed by a set decorator. To get here, take Stevens Canyon Rd just east of Paradise. You won't be the only one stopping to take a photo, but don't even think about passing it by. Sometimes visual clichés exist for good reason.

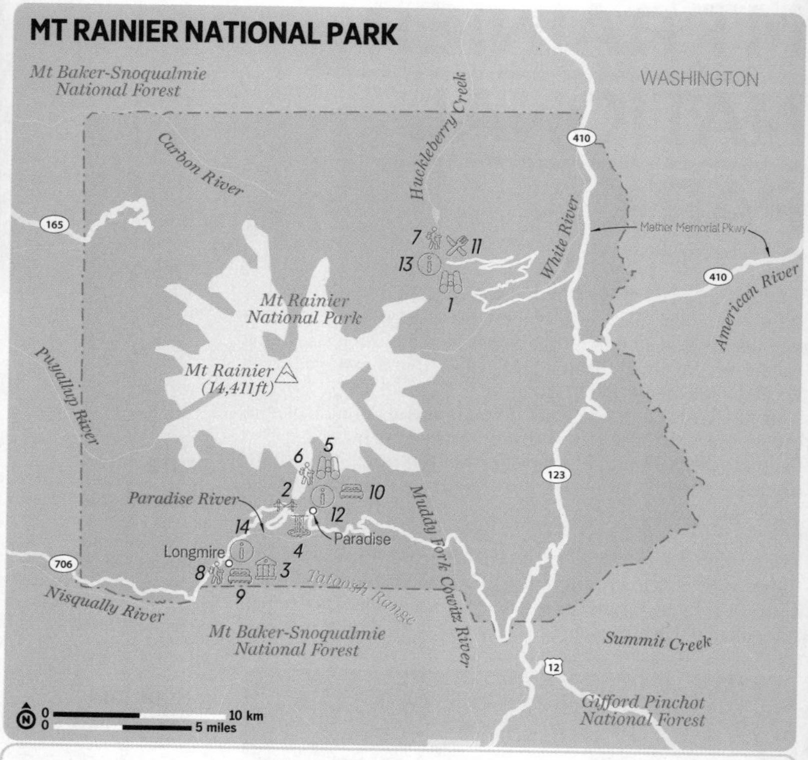

SIGHTS
1 Emmons Vista Trail
2 Glacier Bridge
3 Longmire Museum
4 Narada Falls
5 Panorama Point

ACTIVITIES, COURSES & TOURS
6 Skyline Trail
7 Sourdough Ridge Trail
8 Trail of the Shadows Loop

SLEEPING
9 National Park Inn
10 Paradise Inn

EATING
11 Sunrise Day Lodge

INFORMATION
12 Henry M Jackson Visitor Center
13 Sunrise Visitor Center
14 Wilderness Information Center

Exploring Paradise

THE NAME SAYS IT ALL

Home to a cluster of trailheads and the starting point for most summit hikes, Paradise is the section of the park where you'll find the historic **Paradise Inn** and the large, informative **Henry M Jackson Visitor Center**, open 10am to 5pm daily May to October and weekends from November to April. An excellent entry

WHERE TO EAT AROUND MT RAINIER NATIONAL PARK

Mountain Goat Coffee
A traditional refueling stop for coffee and pastries to bookend your mountain hike. **$**

Sunrise Day Lodge Cafeteria
A snack bar with epic views serving burgers, sandwiches, ice cream and other casual fare. **$**

Paradise Inn Dining Room
Feast on buffalo meatloaf and homemade berry pie in the glow of a giant fireplace. **$$$**

point for any venture into the park, the visitor center holds a cutting-edge museum with hands-on exhibits on everything from local flora to glacier formation and shows a must-see 21-minute film entitled *Mount Rainier: Restless Giant*.

The daughter of park pioneer James Longmire unintentionally named this high mountain nirvana, when she exclaimed what a paradise it was on visiting this spot for the first time in the 1880s. She wasn't wrong. One of the snowiest places on earth, at 5400ft elevation, Paradise can be hard to get to sometimes, but it's the park's most popular area. Flower-strewn meadows are backed by dramatic Rainier views on the days (a clear minority annually) when the mountain decides to take off its cloudy hat. Winter activities keep the place busy from October through May.

The Paradise area is crisscrossed with trails, of all types and standards, some good for a short stroll (with the kids), others the realm of more serious hikers. For something in between, hike the 5-mile **Skyline Trail**, starting behind the Paradise Inn and climbing approximately 1600ft to **Panorama Point**, with good views of Mt Rainier and the neighboring Tatoosh Range.

Park rangers lead interpretive hikes from the visitor center daily throughout the summer and snowshoe hikes on weekends in winter.

Looking Around Longmire

A LANDMARK HISTORIC DISTRICT

Once the homestead of park pioneer James Longmire, who first came here in 1883 and noticed the hot mineral springs that bubbled up in a lovely meadow nearby, this site became park headquarters in 1899. The village has been designated a National Historic District, and a short, self-guided walking tour lets you study its buildings, prime examples of what today is known as National Park Service Rustic architecture.

An epitome of the style is the **National Park Inn**, which has stood here since 1917. It's complemented by park offices, the tiny, free **Longmire Museum** (open May to July) and several important trailheads providing access to the backcountry. The park's **Wilderness Information Center** (WIC; open daily May to October) is where hikers pick up wilderness permits and information about backcountry camping.

Sightseers are spoiled for choice. Get a laid-back look at some old-growth forest and pastoral meadows on the **Trail of the Shadows Loop**, a 0.8-mile circuit that begins across the road from the museum. Five miles east of Longmire is **Glacier Bridge**, with views of the Nisqually Valley; the Nisqually Glacier once reached the location of the bridge, but has

PANORAMIC VIEW

Photographers of all skill levels count the scenic overlook at **Ricksecker Point** as one of their favorite viewpoints in the park. You can drive right to the overlook, no hiking required – so go ahead and bring the big lens. The overlook makes a fine place to study a handful of Rainier's rapidly disappearing glaciers. Fun fact: what looks like the summit from here is actually a false one (Point Success); the obscured true summit is 257ft higher. Equally majestic to the southeast is the sawtoothed Tatoosh Range. The road out to the point begins 6 miles east of Longmire.

WHERE TO SLEEP AROUND MT RAINIER NATIONAL PARK

National Park Inn
Built in classic 'Parkitecture' style, this rustic inn at Longmire was built in 1917; it's open year-round. **$$**

Paradise Inn
The larger of the two historic lodges in the park, impressive Paradise is open May through October. **$$$**

Cougar Rock Campground
Of the three car campgrounds in the park, this is the most convenient, located between Longmire and Paradise. **$**

retreated up the valley. Further east, a parking area marks the starting point for a steep 0.2-mile trail that leads down through flowers and ferns to the misty **Narada Falls**. The falls, often embellished by brilliant rainbows, carry the Paradise River over a basalt cliff. In high season, expect to get a face-full of water spray along with an earful of oohing and aahing, as this is the park's most popular waterfall.

CLIMBING MT RAINIER

Close to Puget Sound's urban areas and unobstructed by other peaks, Mt Rainier is an iconic peak to bag, but climbing it is no picnic; old hands liken it to running a marathon in thin air with crampons stuck to your shoes. Approximately 9000 people attempt it annually, but only half of them make it to the top. Hazard Stevens and PB Van Trump made the first documented Mt Rainier summit in 1870. The most popular route starts at Paradise and involves an overnight at Camp Muir before you rise between midnight and 2am to don crampons and ropes for the climb to the summit. All climbers going higher than Camp Muir must register at the Paradise Ranger Station.

Spectacular Sunrise

TOP OF THE WORLD

Mt Rainier's main eastern entrance, White River, is the gateway to Sunrise, which at 6400ft marks the park's highest section of road. Thanks to the superior elevation here, the summer season is particularly short and snow can linger well into July. The area is also noticeably drier than Paradise, resulting in an interesting variety of subalpine vegetation, including masses of wildflowers. The views from Sunrise are famously spectacular and – aside from stunning close-ups of Mt Rainier itself – you can also, quite literally, watch the weather roll in over the distant peaks of Mts Baker and Adams. Similarly impressive is the glistening Emmons Glacier, which, at 4 sq miles in size, is the largest glacier in the contiguous USA.

For a closer look at the glacier, a trailhead directly across the parking lot from the **Sunrise Day Lodge** takes you to **Emmons Vista**, with good views of Mt Rainier and Little Tahoma as well. Nearby, the 1-mile **Sourdough Ridge Trail** leads to pristine subalpine meadows with stunning views over other volcanic giants. At the end of this trail, hikers with more in the tank can continue on to either the **Mt Fremont Lookout Trail**, which leads to a historic fire lookout; or **Burroughs Mountain Trail**, with awesome views and access to the fragile tundra of the Cascade Range.

The **Sunrise Visitor Center**, usually open from early July through September, has information on other hikes that start here, as well as ranger-led interpretive hikes and other activities. There's a cafeteria in the Sunrise Day Lodge serving the basics.

GETTING AROUND

Your best bet for getting to and around Mt Rainier is with your own wheels. The Nisqually entrance in the southwestern corner of the national park is its most developed (and hence most visited) area, and the only one open year-round. Here you'll find the gateway settlements of Ashford and Copper Creek, which offer plenty of useful park-related facilities. Hwy 706 enters the park about 1½ hours' drive southeast of Seattle. After the entry tollbooth, a well-paved road continues east, offering the first good views of Mt Rainier, weather permitting. At the 7-mile mark you'll reach Longmire. From here the road climbs steeply for 12 miles, making numerous hairpin turns and passing several viewpoints until it emerges at the elevated alpine meadows of Paradise.

The northeast White River/Sunrise entrance is open in summer via Hwy 410, and in the southeast, the Ohanapecosh entrance is reached via the town of Packwood on Hwy 12, also summer-only. The Mowich Lake and Carbon River entrances in the northwest, off Rd 165, are the least accessible due to road conditions.

NORTH CASCADES NATIONAL PARK

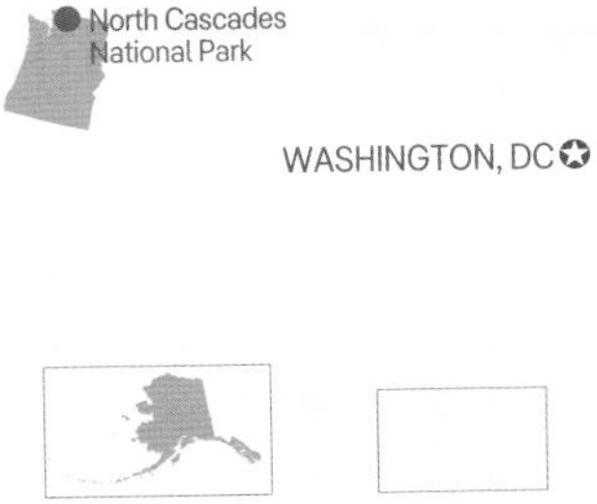

North Cascades National Park feels like Alaska transplanted into the lower 48 – 789 sq miles of dramatic, daunting wild country strafed with mountains, lakes, glaciers (over 300 of them) and wildlife, but with almost no trace of civilization.

Erratic weather, massive precipitation, thick rainforest and vertiginous cliffs have long ensured the remoteness of the park's mountains: steep, alpine behemoths with names like Mt Terror, Mt Fury, Mt Despair and Forbidden Peak. Approach with caution, but don't be afraid: there are many ways to make inroads into this wild area, whether you're inclined to view it from the window of a car or backpack for days to a remote campsite.

The North Cascades Hwy (Hwy 20) crosses the middle of the park, skirting Diablo Lake and Ross Lake and paralleling the Skagit River. You can get an overview of the area at the North Cascades Visitor Center, on the southwest side, before going deeper.

Diablo Lake (p222)

FACTS

Great For... Wildlife, scenery, walking
State Washington
Entrance Fee Free
Area 789 sq miles

EAGLE EYE

Along the Skagit River, including the area around the North Cascades Visitor Center near Newhalem, bald eagles can be seen feeding on the riverbanks throughout the winter months. The visitor center is closed in winter, but you can follow interpretive trails to the river's edge and try your luck. The **Bald Eagle Interpretive Center** (skagiteagle.org) in nearby Rockport offers two-hour guided eagle-spotting walks on weekends in December and January. If you prefer to watch your eagles from a boat, several local companies offer eagle-watching float tours in the area.

NORTH CASCADES NATIONAL PARK

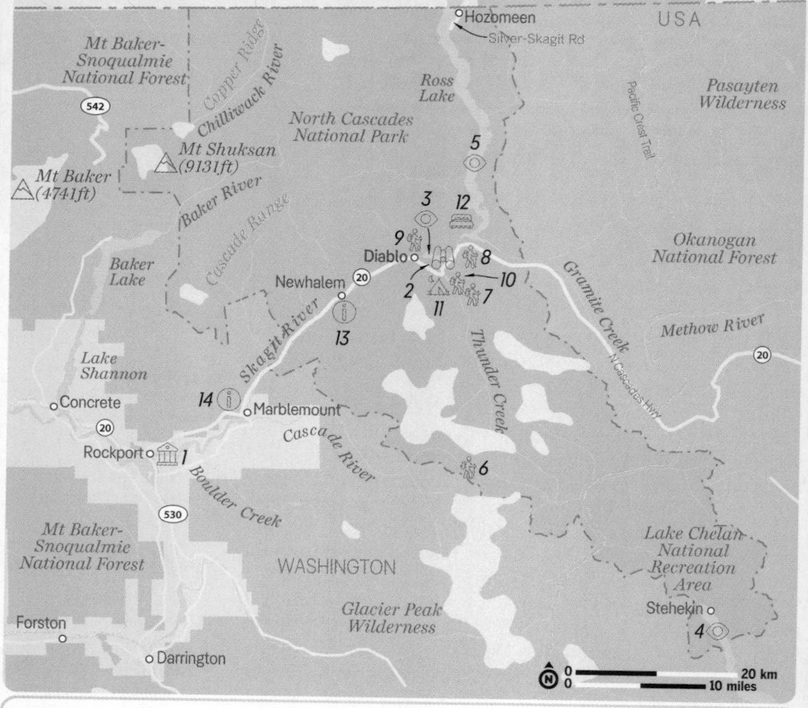

SIGHTS
1 Bald Eagle Interpretive Center
2 Diablo Dam Overlook
3 Diablo Lake
4 Lake Chelan
5 Ross Lake

ACTIVITIES, COURSES & TOURS
6 Cascade Pass
7 Fourth of July Trail
8 Happy Creek Forest Walk
9 Sourdough Mountain Trail
10 Thunder Creek Trail

SLEEPING
11 Colonial Creek Campground
12 Ross Lake Resort

INFORMATION
13 North Cascades Visitors Center
14 Wilderness Information Center

Hiking the Cascades

THE BEST WAY TO VISIT THE PARK

It's possible to get a basic overview of this vast alpine wilderness by motoring through in a car on Hwy 20, making use of the numerous pullouts and short interpretive hikes that are scattered along the route. But to get at the park's

DRIVE-IN CAMPSITES AROUND NORTH CASCADES NATIONAL PARK

Colonial Creek North Campground
This campground is just off Hwy 20 on Diablo Lake, with a fishing pier and boat launch. **$**

Goodell Creek Campground
In old-growth forest on the banks of the Skagit River – a good choice for fishing and floating. **$**

Gorge Lake Campground
A primitive campground in the Ross Lake section, near Diablo Lake with access to Stetattle Creek. **$**

essence you'll need a tent, a decent rucksack and a gung-ho sense of adventure.

Hiking and backpacking in the North Cascades is legendary, and there are about 400 trails to choose from. The 3.7-mile hike to 5384ft **Cascade Pass** is the best loved in these mountains. It gets you very quickly up into a flower-carpeted, glacier-surrounded paradise that will leave you struggling for superlatives. It's an excellent day hike, but if you're backpacking (with a permit) you can spend the night at one of the nearby campsites and continue further into the park from here.

For day hikers, one of the most challenging but rewarding routes is the strenuous **Sourdough Mountain Trail**, which gains a mile in height over its length of 5.5 miles (one way). Most say it's worth the effort; the views of Cascadian peaks and turquoise Diablo Lake 5000-plus feet below are some of the best in the park.

From the southern end of the Colonial Creek Campground (Mile 130, Hwy 20), the long **Thunder Creek Trail** leads along a powerful glacier-fed river through old-growth forest and clumps of wildflowers. After 2.5 miles the **Fourth of July Trail** branches left to a pass of the same name and makes a good early season hike (10 miles round trip from the campground). Alternatively, for a multiday adventure, you can continue along Thunder Creek over Park Creek Pass and, ultimately, all the way to Stehekin.

Looking for something more bite-sized? Near the Ross Dam trailhead off Hwy 20, the wheelchair-accessible **Happy Creek Forest Walk** (0.5 miles) gives you an up-close look at the forest on a raised boardwalk.

North Cascades Visitor Center, open daily June through September and weekends in May and October, is a good place to get an overview of hiking options. Rangers can advise you on where to spot wildlife or wildflower meadows, and there are frequent short guided hikes departing from here in summer.

Staying overnight anywhere in the park requires a backcountry permit, which you can reserve online in an early-access lottery (see recreation.gov) each spring if you're lucky, or, failing that, try to score on the day of your visit. Either way, collect your permit in person at the **Wilderness Information Center** (open daily May to September). About 40% of the backcountry permits are reserved for walk-ups.

Lake Life

SPARKLING WATER SURROUNDED BY MOUNTAINS

Come for the backpacking, stay for the lakes. The three main lakes that are part of North Cascades National Park – Ross,

SKAGIT WHITE WATER

Although it doesn't offer the heart-in-the-mouth white-water runs of less-tamed waterways, the dam-controlled **Upper Skagit River** in the Ross Lake section of the park makes for a good introductory trip for beginners or families. You'll float through old-growth forest, surrounded by craggy peaks, with plenty of opportunities for wildlife watching. The approximately 9-mile stretch is rated Class II to Class III. About halfway through the run are the S-Bends, a set of three Class III rapids in a row, after which the river is calm enough to look around and enjoy the scenery until the takeout.

Access the river via a boat launch near Goodell Creek Campground at Mile 119 on Hwy 20. The takeout is at Copper Creek near Mile 112.

BOAT-IN CAMPSITES AROUND NORTH CASCADES NATIONAL PARK

Ten Mile Island
One of several amazing sites on Ross Lake, all of which require backcountry permits. $

Thunder Point
One of three small boat-in sites on Diablo Lake. Launch from Colonial Creek Campground. Permits required. $

Weaver Point
This campground across from Stehekin Landing requires no backcountry permit but there's a dock fee for motorboats. $

CONTINUING EDUCATION

If your time in the park has sparked an interest in learning more, or if you want to take your wilderness skills to the next level, look into the educational programs offered by the **North Cascades Institute** (ncascades.org). There are courses, tours and excursions for children, adults and families, including day and weekend courses on geology, wildlife and art. Educational tours by boat deliver cultural history along with an exploration of Diablo Lake. Family getaways include guided hikes, treasure hunts, trivia, stargazing, and navigation classes for all ages. Overnight stays feature organic meals and lodging at the **North Cascades Environmental Learning Center**, an ecofriendly campus on the north shore of Diablo Lake.

Diablo and Chelan – attract boaters, campers, hikers and anglers, and getting here really is half the fun.

Ross Lake stretches 23 miles long, its north end crossing the border into Canada. (It's sometimes possible to reach the lake by road from Canada, but weather damage had closed the road at the time of writing.) Ross Lake was formed when the Ross Dam was built in 1937 as a hydroelectric project to generate power for a growing Seattle. To get a good look at it, follow the Ross Dam Trail from the trailhead on Hwy 20; after descending steeply for about a mile, the trail forks left to cross the dam.

Lining the shores of Ross Lake are 19 boat-in campsites, with fire pits, picnic tables and vault toilets. You'll need to secure a backcountry permit to stay in them. And to get out on to the lake, it's necessary to portage across from Diablo Lake, as there's no boat launch on the south end of Ross Lake. (Portaging is only possible for smaller boats that can be carried along the 1.2 mile gravel road.) Sound like a pain? **Ross Lake Resort**, the only other place to stay on the lake, will portage your boat for you for a fee; call 206-386-4437.

Like Ross Lake, **Diablo Lake** was created by a dam. From the **Diablo Dam Overlook** off Hwy 20 you can get incredible views of the turquoise-green lake framed by glacier-capped peaks. The water's otherworldly hue is a result of powdered rock ground down by glaciers. Diablo Dam was the world's highest arch-type dam when completed in 1930.

There's a boat launch for kayaks and canoes in **Colonial Creek Campground**, and three boat-in campgrounds on the lake. As with Ross Lake, securing a backcountry permit is required to camp.

Lake Chelan, at the park's southeastern corner, has three boat-in campgrounds, available first-come, first-served, from Stehekin Landing – doubly remote, as you can only get to Stehekin by ferry or on foot.

GETTING AROUND

You'll need your own wheels to get into and around the national park, but even so, the only road is the 30-mile section of the North Cascades Hwy (Hwy 20) that bisects the park.

For administrative reasons, the park is split into two sections – north and south – belted in the middle by the Ross Lake National Recreation Area. Along the park's southern border around Stehekin lies a third region, the Lake Chelan National Recreation Area, a 97-sq-mile protected park that hugs fjord-like Lake Chelan.

There's no road access to Ross Lake Resort or to Stehekin. They can only be reached by hiking in or arranging to get there by boat. The best way to get to Ross Lake Resort is to park at the Ross Lake/Dam trailhead off Hwy 20, hike 1 mile down the trail and use the pay phone to call for a shuttle across the lake. To reach Stehekin, take the *Lady of the Lake* boat or Stehekin Ferry from the town of Chelan.

OLYMPIC NATIONAL PARK

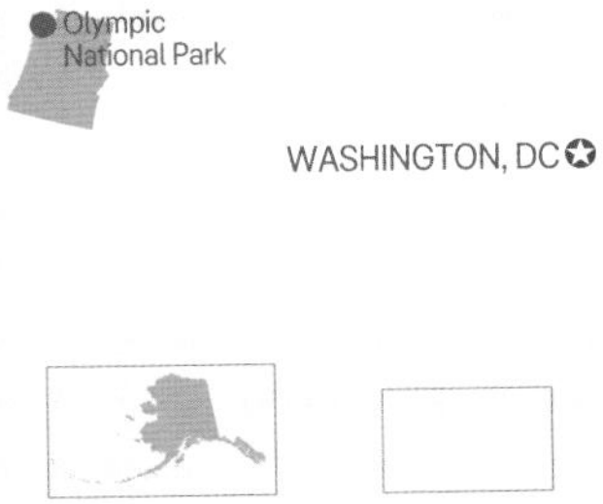

Olympic National Park shelters a rainforest, copious glaciated mountain peaks and some of the wildest beaches on the continent. One of North America's great wilderness areas, most of it remains relatively untouched by humans, with 1000-year-old cedar trees juxtaposed with pristine alpine meadows, clear glacial lakes and a roadless interior. Those last words should provide a clue about the best way to see this magical place – definitely on foot. The untrammeled woods and pristine coast are a hiker's dream. Whether you like long walks on the beach, overnight treks through misty forests or a short stroll to natural hot springs, this park fits the bill.

Most of the park occupies the middle of the Olympic Peninsula, including the impressive, white-topped Olympic Mountains. But just for contrast, there's also a long stretch of coastline along the peninsula that's included in the park. Hwy 101 loops around the peninsula to provide what road access there is.

FACTS

Great For... Family travel, scenery, walking
State Washington
Entrance Fee 7-day pass per vehicle/pedestrian $30/15
Area 1406 sq miles

Lake Quinault (p225)

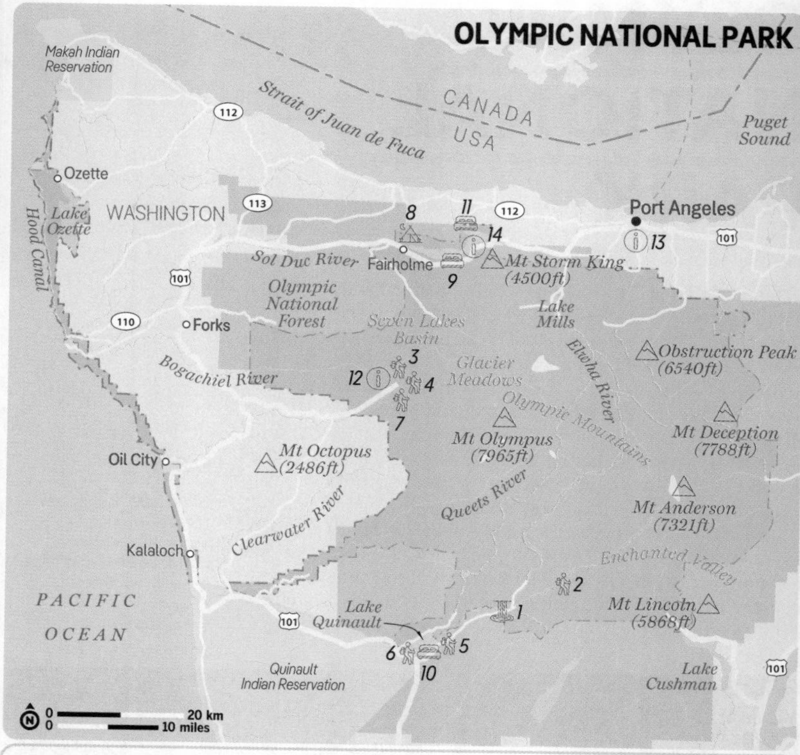

SIGHTS
1 Bunch Falls

ACTIVITIES, COURSES & TOURS
2 Enchanted Valley Trail
3 Hall of Moss Trail
4 Hoh River Trail
5 Quinault Loop Trail
6 Quinault Rain Forest Nature Trail
7 Spruce Nature Trail

SLEEPING
8 Fairholme Campground
9 Lake Crescent Lodge
10 Lake Quinault Lodge
11 Log Cabin Resort

INFORMATION
12 Hoh Rain Forest Visitor Center
13 Olympic National Park Visitor Center
14 Storm King Ranger Station

Hiking the Hoh

WALK IN THE WOODS

If you can only make one stop on the western side of the park, this should be it. The Hoh River area offers magical rainforest scenery and hikes of varying levels. To get here, follow the paved Upper Hoh Rd for 19 miles from Hwy 101

REFUELING TOWNS NEAR OLYMPIC NATIONAL PARK

Port Townsend
Great architecture, good food and drink, cool old hotels.

Port Angeles
Unpretentious and functional, but with some nice restaurants and decent hotels.

Olympia
The state capital has an indie spirit, vegan cafes and plentiful parks.

to the **Hoh Rain Forest Visitor Center**, where you'll pick up required permits for backpacking. Along the way you'll pass a giant Sitka spruce tree, 270ft high and over 500 years old.

The visitor center has displays on the ecology of the rainforest and the plants and animals that inhabit it. Rangers lead free guided walks from the center twice a day during summer. Several excellent day hikes into virgin rainforest start from here, the most popular of which is the 0.8-mile **Hall of Moss Trail**. The 1.25-mile **Spruce Nature Trail** and a short, wheelchair-accessible nature trail both make interpretive forays through the woods.

Backpackers can hike the **Hoh River Trail** toward Hoh Lake (about 16 miles), turning north to explore the Seven Lakes Basin, where a campsite-rich loop follows the Sol Duc River and briefly joins the Pacific Northwest Trail. Or you can choose to continue east past the Hoh Lake turnoff to reach Elk Lake and on to Glacier Meadows and Blue Glacier on Mt Olympus. Part of the trail to Glacier Meadows is washed out and requires the use of a rope ladder to descend, so it's not for everyone.

Note that bear canisters are required for backpacking trips in most parts of the park. Wilderness backpacking permits are required for all overnight hikes.

Exploring Lake Quinault

LOOP TRAILS THROUGH ANCIENT FOREST

The enchanting Quinault River Valley is one of the park's least crowded corners. Clustered around the lake's deep-blue waters lie forested peaks, a historic lodge and some of the oldest Sitka spruce, Douglas fir and western red cedar trees in the world. The lake itself offers plenty of activities such as fishing, boating and swimming, while upstream both the north and south branches of the Quinault River harbor a couple of important trans-park trails.

A number of short hiking trails begin just below **Lake Quinault Lodge**; pick up a free map from the USFS office on the lake's south bank. The shortest of these hikes is the **Quinault Rain Forest Nature Trail**, a half-mile walk through 500-year-old Douglas firs. This short trail adjoins the 3-mile **Quinault Loop Trail**, which meanders through the rainforest before circling back to the lake.

The Quinault region is renowned for its huge trees. Close to the village is a 191ft Sitka spruce (purported to be up to 1000 years old), and nearby are the world's largest red cedar, Douglas fir and mountain hemlock trees. Beyond the lake, both N Shore Rd and S Shore Rd continue up the Quinault River Valley before merging at a bridge just past **Bunch Falls**.

LONG WALKS ON THE BEACH

There are two long-distance beach hikes along the isolated coast. The more northerly is the 32.7-mile stretch between the Makah Shi Shi trailhead near Cape Flattery and Rialto Beach near La Push, which commonly makes up a moderate five-day, four-night trek. This hike stays close to the shoreline, meaning that a good understanding of tidal charts is imperative. There are 14 campgrounds en route, eight of which take reservations. If you're contemplating a trek along the coast, get info from the National Park Service (NPS), buy good maps, learn how to read tide tables and be prepared for cold and rainy weather year-round.

CAMPGROUNDS IN OLYMPIC NATIONAL PARK

Hoh Campground
Year-round campsites in a rainforest full of ancient trees. $

Kalaloch Campground
A large and popular cliffside campground where some of the sites have ocean views. $

Staircase Campground
Open year-round, in old-growth forest next to the Skokomish River. $

ROAD TRIP

Olympic Peninsula Loop

Freakishly wet, fantastically lush and chillingly remote, the Olympic Peninsula looks like it has been resurrected from a wilder, pre-civilized era. This 435-mile trip is best from June to September, when heavy rains are less likely. Highlights of the drive include seeing Roosevelt elk and the many vivid shades of green in the Hoh Rain Forest.

1 Olympia

Welcome to Olympia, city of weird contrasts, where streetside buskers belt out acoustic grunge, and stiff bureaucrats answer their ringtones on the lawns of the expansive state legislature. A quick circuit of the **Washington State Capitol**, a huge Grecian temple of a building, will give you a last taste of civilization before you depart.

The Drive: Your basic route is due west, initially on Hwy 101, then (briefly) on SR-8 before joining US-12 in Elma. In Grays Harbor, enter the twin cities of Aberdeen and Hoquiam. Here, swing north on Hwy 101 (again!) to leafier climes at Lake Quinault, 88 miles from Olympia.

2 Lake Quinault

The thickly forested Quinault River Valley is one of the park's least-crowded corners. Clustered on the south shore of deep-blue glacial Lake Quinault is the tiny village of **Quinault**, complete with the luscious Lake Quinault Lodge, a USFS office and a couple of stores.

The Drive: West from Lake Quinault, Hwy 101 continues through the Quinault Indian Reservation before entering a thin strip of national-park territory protecting the beaches around Kalaloch (klay-lock). This is some of the US' wildest coastal scenery accessible by road; various pullovers allow beach forays. After a total of 40 miles you'll reach Ruby Beach.

3 Ruby Beach

Inhabiting a thin coastal strip that was added to the national park in 1953, **Ruby Beach** is accessed via a 0.2-mile path that leads down to a large expanse of windswept coast embellished by polished black stones and wantonly strewn tree trunks. To the south toward Kalaloch, other accessible beaches include Beach One through to Beach Six. At low tide, rangers give talks about the tidal-pool life at Beach Four and the Olympic coastal strip's ecosystems.

The Drive: North of Ruby Beach, Hwy 101 swings sharply northeast and inland, tracking the Hoh River. Turn right off 101 onto the Hoh River Rd to explore one of the national park's most popular inner sanctums, the Hoh Rain Forest.

4 Hoh Rain Forest

Count yourself lucky if you arrive on a day when it isn't raining! The most popular detour off Hwy 101 is the 19-mile paved road to the Hoh Valley, a dense, wet, green and intensely surreal temperate rainforest. The essential hike here is the short but fascinating **Hall of Moss Trail**, an easy 0.8-mile loop through the kind of weird, ethereal scenery that even JRR Tolkien couldn't have invented.

The Drive: Rejoining Hwy 101, motor north to the small and relatively nondescript but handy settlement of Forks. Hwy 101 bends north then east through a logging area before plunging back into the national park on the shores of Lake Crescent, 66 miles from the Hoh Rain Forest.

5 Lake Crescent

The scenery shifts again as the road winds along the glittering pine-scented shores of glacial-carved **Lake Crescent**. The lake looks best from water level, on a rental kayak, or from high above at its eastern edge on the **Storm King Mountain Trail** (named after the peak's wrathful spirit), accessible via a steep, 1.7-mile ascent that splits off the **Barnes Creek Trail**.

The Drive: From Lake Crescent take Hwy 101 22 miles east to the town of Port Angeles, a gateway to Victoria, Canada, which is reachable by ferry to the north. Starting in Race St, the 18-mile Hurricane Ridge Rd climbs up 5300ft toward wildflower meadows and mountain vistas.

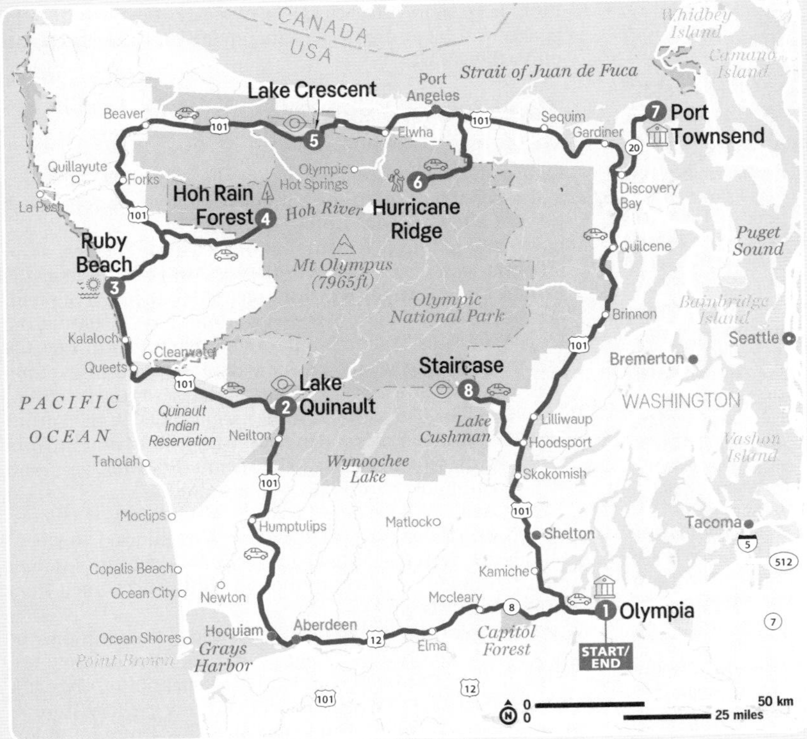

6 Hurricane Ridge

Up above the clouds, stormy **Hurricane Ridge** lives up to its name with fickle weather and biting winds made slightly more bearable by the park's best high-altitude views. Hurricane Ridge Visitor Center burned down, but the parking lot at its former location is the starting point of various hikes. **Hurricane Hill Trail** and the **Meadow Loop Trails** network are popular and moderately easy. The first half-mile of these trails is wheelchair accessible.

The Drive: Wind back down the Hurricane Ridge Rd, kiss the suburbs of Port Angeles and press east through the retirement community of Sequim (pronounced 'squwim'). Turn north on SR-20 to reach another, more attractive port, Port Townsend.

7 Port Townsend

Ease back into civilization with the cultured Victorian comforts of **Port Townsend**, whose period charm dates from the railroad boom of the 1890s, when the town was earmarked to become the 'New York of the West.' That never happened, but you can pick up a historic walking tour map from the visitor center and wander the waterfront's shops, galleries and antique malls.

The Drive: From Port Townsend, head back to the junction of Hwy 101, this time heading south past Quilcene, Brinnon, with its great diner, and the Dosewallips park entrance. You'll get more water views here on the park's eastern side. At Hoodsport, signs point west off Hwy 101 to Staircase, 67 miles from Port Townsend.

8 Staircase

It's drier on the park's eastern side and the mountains are closer. The Staircase park nexus, accessible via Hoodsport, has a ranger station, campground and a decent trail system that follows the drainage of the North Fork Skokomish River, and is flanked by some of the most rugged peaks in the Olympics. Nearby **Lake Cushman** has a campground and water-sports opportunities.

SEATTLE PRESS EXPEDITION HIKE

One of the most popular cross-park treks follows the pioneering route taken by James H Christie. A former Arctic explorer, he answered the call of the *Seattle Press* newspaper in 1889 to 'acquire fame by unveiling the mystery which wraps the land encircled by the snow-capped Olympic range.' Starting at the Whiskey Bend trailhead on the Elwha River, the route tracks south and then southwest through the Elwha and Quinault River Valleys to Lake Quinault, covering 44 moderately strenuous miles. It commonly takes walkers five days to complete.

Hikers should always take stock of weather conditions, rules and regulations, and bring necessary equipment. Stop in at the Olympic National Park Visitor Center in Port Angeles before setting out.

From here, more adventurous hikers can sally forth into the backcountry. The area's sparkling highlight is the **Enchanted Valley Trail**.

The Lure of Lake Crescent

RELAX ON AND AROUND THE WATER

Luminous Lake Crescent is a popular boating and fishing area and a departure point for a number of short national-park hikes. **Lake Crescent Lodge** is the oldest of the park's trio of celebrated lodges – it first opened in 1916. The best stop-off point is in a parking lot to the right of Hwy 101 near the **Storm King Ranger Station**, open May through September. A number of short hikes leave from here, including the Marymere Falls Trail, a 2-mile round trip to a 90ft cascade that drops over a basalt cliff. For a more energetic hike, climb the side of Mt Storm King, the peak that rises to the east of Lake Crescent. The steep, 1.7-mile ascent splits off the Barnes Creek Trail. Even more adventurous is the 17-mile Aurora Ridge Trail, which involves significant elevation gain and some route-finding through open meadows.

Trout fishing is good here – Lake Crescent is deep, with steep shorelines – though only artificial lures are allowed. Rowboat rentals are available at Lake Crescent Lodge in the summer months, or you can bring your own kayak and launch from either end of the lake.

After exploring, weary hikers can bed down in rooms or cabins at Lake Crescent Lodge, at Barnes Point off Hwy 101, or at the **Log Cabin Resort**, on East Bench Rd off Hwy 101. There's also a large **campground** and tiny grocery store in Fairholme. All facilities are typically closed in winter, but the lake is less than 20 miles from Port Angeles, which has a range of hotels and restaurants.

GETTING AROUND

You'll need your own car here. It's also a good idea to carry a decent map, as the distances between points on the peninsula are longer than they seem. Stop by the Olympic National Park Visitor Center in Port Angeles: the park's most comprehensive information center, it not only has great maps of the area but also children's exhibits, a bookstore, a replica of a prehistoric Makah seal-hunting canoe and shows a 25-minute film. Pick up a (free) 'Wilderness Trip Planner' with backcountry trails as well as campgrounds marked – although be aware that most of these will need to have been reserved ahead of time.

DENALI NATIONAL PARK & PRESERVE

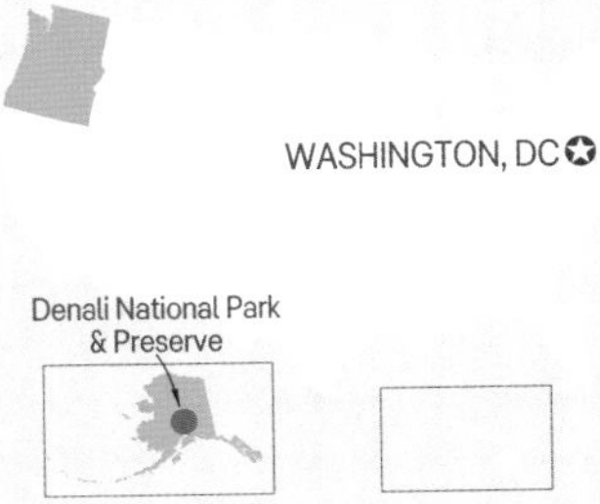

Denali encapsulates the great wonder of the Alaskan wilderness. Here you'll discover nature at its rawest and most fierce. With over 6 million acres of intact wilderness, this massive park offers remarkable views and insights into the flora, fauna and active ecosystems of Alaska's immense interior. Hovering above it all is 20,237ft Denali – the name means 'The Great One' in Athabascan, which is apt for the highest mountain in North America.

Whether you take just a day to head up the Denali Park Rd or plan a 10-day tromp across the virgin spaces of tundra, taiga forest, meadows, streams and hillsides that make this park so unique, a visit to Denali will not disappoint. With even the shortest of adventures, you're likely to see bear, moose and caribou. Stay a while longer and you might spot foxes and even wolves, plus numerous avian species.

FACTS

Great For Wildlife, scenery, walking
State Alaska
Entrance Fee 7-day pass adult/under 15 $15/free
Area 9492 sq miles

Moose, Denali National Park

DENALI NATIONAL PARK & PRESERVE

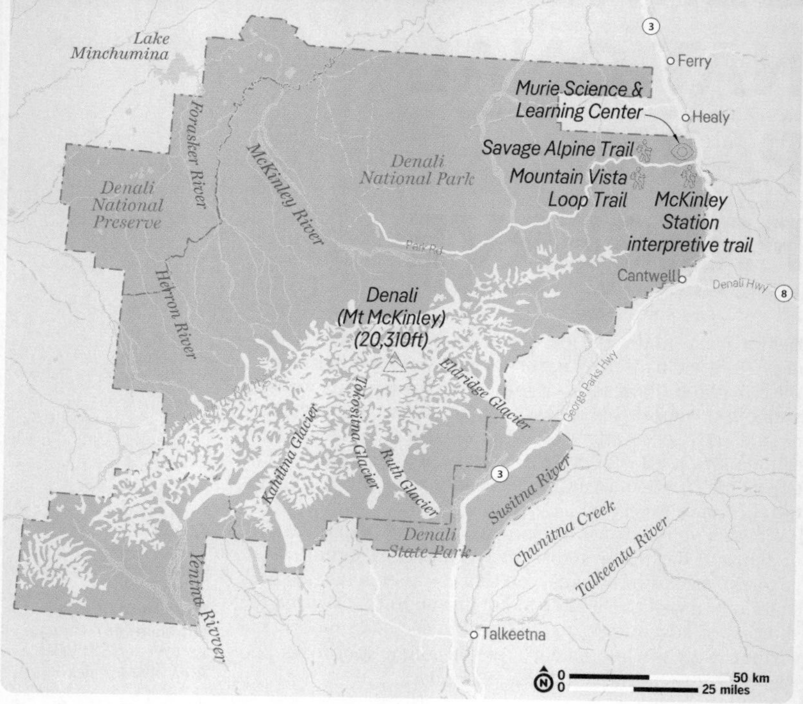

BEAR SENSE

Bears are no small consideration when hiking just about anywhere in Alaska. For tips on traveling safely amid some of the world's largest land predators, see p32.

Board a Bus & Go Deeper Into the Park

HISTORY AND WILDERNESS

For those wanting to learn more about the history, flora and fauna of Denali, tour buses feature a trained naturalist who both drives the bus and narrates during the trip.

The five-hour **Denali Natural History Tour** travels from the entrance area to Primrose Ridge at Mile 15. The bus stops at several points along the way, with an hour of free time to explore. The tour begins at the Denali Bus Depot with the film *Across Time and Tundra*, explaining the natural history of this

ACTIVITIES FROM THE VISITOR CENTER

Denali Sled Dog Kennels
Your chance to meet the only canine ranger force in the entire National Park Service (NPS) system.

Ranger Programs
Hosted by knowledgeable rangers and held at campground amphitheaters or led from the visitor center.

Fishing
Smaller waterways, including Riley Creek and streams flowing into Savage River, are best for fishing.

unique environment. Buses then stop at the historic Savage Cabin. Finally, at Primrose Ridge, there's a memorable Native Alaska presentation describing how the First Peoples have used this land for nearly 10,000 years.

The 5½-hour **Tundra Wilderness Tour** travels along the open sections of the Park Rd corridor, looking for wildlife and seasonal shifts in landscapes. A highlight is a stop at the Murie Cabin near the East Fork River (Mile 43) to experience where Adolf Murie lived while conducting his famous research inside what was then known as Mt McKinley National Park.

All Denali bus trips begin and end at various locations around the entrance of the park, and are not designed for passengers to disembark and reboard. Transit buses are a better option for getting off the bus to hike, picnic or explore on your own.

The daily schedule for each bus tour varies depending on demand, so visit the bus company booking page for more details, via the Denali National Park website.

Hikes in the Park

EXPLORE DENALI NATIONAL PARK ON FOOT

The hiking and backpacking in Denali is on par with other wilderness destinations around Alaska, especially given the enormous expanse of backcountry easily accessed from the Park Rd.

To hike maintained trails, the best bet is to drive or catch a shuttle bus to either Mountain Vista day-use area at Mile 13, or Savage River at Mile 15. **Mountain Vista Loop Trail** is a level, short (0.6-mile) trail perfect for catching a view of Denali on a clear day. Enjoy panoramic views of the entire area as well, with Savage River Valley to the south and Mt Healy to the north, and several spur trails leading to the rushing Savage River itself. This beautiful ecosystem passes through an area known as a 'transition zone', found at elevations sandwiched between taiga or boreal forests and tundra. Only brushy shrubs and smaller trees grow here, and the open landscape creates great views. Note that during the summer months, the Mountain Vista parking lot fills up quickly, so the Savage River Shuttle is the best bet for accessing the popular trailhead. There are also restrooms and several picnic tables available.

The Savage River parking area is a trailhead for two popular hikes: the **Savage Loop Trail** and **Savage Alpine Trail**. For the loop portion, hike along either side of Savage River through a scenic canyon between Healy Ridge and Mt Margaret. The trail winds along meadows and scrub brush for about a mile before crossing the river at a bridge (an excellent spot

PARK BUSES AT A GLANCE

Narrated Tour Buses
A reservation-only experience with a certified driver-guide providing commentary as you drive the Park Rd and stop at various locations.

Non-Narrated Transit Buses
Available by reservation, transit buses provide service between various locations within the park beyond Mile 17. All depart and arrive at the Denali Bus Depot near the park entrance.

Camp Buses
For accessing a campground or backcountry unit deeper in the park.

Free Shuttle Buses
The Savage River Shuttle, Riley Creek Loop Shuttle and Sled Dog Demonstration Shuttle are free.

WHERE TO EAT IN DENALI

The Overlook
High on a bluff, Denali's fanciest place has top-notch seafood, steaks and a wine list. **$$$**

Moreno Grill
The only restaurant on park property features sandwiches, soups, salads and snacks. Can get crowded. **$$**

Moose-AKa's
A delightful surprise in the Nenana Canyon area, featuring Serbian cuisine and fine wines. **$$**

DENALI IN WINTER

For the adventurous traveler, visiting Denali in winter can be unforgettable, with snow-shrouded spruce trees, vibrant northern lights and myriad opportunities for skiing, snowshoeing and fat-biking. Visitor services switch over to the Murie Science and Learning Center, and rangers patrol by dog sled. Stop by the Denali Sled Dog Kennels for a glimpse of the canine rangers at work.

Plan to be totally self-sufficient. Interior Alaska's winters are unforgiving, so be prepared. Rent a 4WD vehicle, and know how to drive it in icy conditions. Pack the vehicle with a winter emergency kit (often provided by rental companies – ask). Camping is available for free at Riley Creek Campground. There is no water, but pit toilets are provided.

MELISSAMN/SHUTTERSTOCK ©

Savage Loop Trail

for photos) and continuing on the other side. The 4-mile Savage Alpine Trail is tougher, traveling between Savage River Campground (next to Mountain Vista) at Mile 13 and the Savage River Canyon, traversing a high section of what's called the Outer Range. It's worth the climb, though, for the sweeping views of the valley, surrounding peaks and Park Rd. In the summer, use the Savage River Shuttle for transit between these two trailheads.

Denali is unique in that off-trail hiking is permitted within the park's backcountry, but there are occasional restrictions due to wildlife kills, animal dens or bird nesting sites. It is imperative that backcountry hikers check in with park rangers at the visitor center prior to embarking on a non-trail adventure. Additionally, for those seeking to overnight outside of campgrounds in Denali's wild spaces, a backcountry permit is required. From May 12 to September 21, these free backcountry permits are issued in person at the Backcountry Information Center on the Denali Bus Depot campus, no more than one day prior to travel. You will need this permit to get Camper Bus tickets, as well. This permit designates the region in which you'll be staying, and hikers can find a map on the Denali National Park website's Backcountry Unit Guide.

WHERE TO CAMP IN DENALI

Riley Creek
Near the main entrance, the park's largest campground has a small store, showers and post office. **$**

Savage River
Near Mile 17, this campground gives excellent access to hiking at Savage River or Mountain Vista. **$**

Teklanika River Campground
This distant campground has 53 sites and evening programs; three-night stay required if you drive. **$**

Additionally, all members of the party will need to watch the park's backcountry video series, either ahead of your visit or on arrival; and obtain a bear-resistant food container from the National Park Service (NPS).

Get to Know Denali

ALASKA'S MOST POPULAR NATIONAL PARK

Thanks to the well-oiled machine that is the National Park Service, visitors to Denali are provided with an abundance of printed and online materials to help plan activities once they arrive. Thus, the first stop should be at the main visitor center, located a few miles from the George Parks Hwy. Here, pay your park admission fees, get maps, learn of ranger-led programs and wander the many exhibits about the park's history, wildlife and mountaineering. Across the courtyard is a gift shop operated by Alaska Geographic, with excellent books, art and other memorable souvenirs.

Murie Science and Learning Center is across the parking lot from the visitor center, and focuses on the natural-science side of Denali National Park. Travelers can try their hand at mapping, learn sustainable recreation practices, or settle in by the fireplace if it's a rainy day. This facility also serves as the winter visitor center, and a popular activity is checking out snowshoes for a bit of free fun during the slower season.

Ringing the entire entrance is a network of fully accessible trails winding through lush birch, aspen and spruce forests. During the summer months, listen for an abundance of songbirds and keep an eye out for wildflowers, particularly lupines, which grow in open areas and along roadways. Try the **McKinley Station interpretive trail** toward Riley Creek Campground, noting original sites for the railroad station, a hotel and other buildings from the park's early days.

DRIVING INTO THE WILDERNESS

Try other road-accessible national parks such as **Wrangell-St Elias** (p252), southeast of Fairbanks and northeast of Valdez, or **Kenai Fjords** (p245), near the city of Seward, about three hours south of Anchorage.

ORIGINS OF THE PARK

Hunter and naturalist Charles Sheldon was lured to the Denali area by Dall sheep in the early 1900s. He had traveled the world hunting subspecies of sheep and had heard about Alaska's only specimen. As he spent the winter of 1907–08 in the interior, Sheldon observed hundreds of sheep taken by commercial hunters. Concerned about ecological devastation, Sheldon lobbied Congress to establish a wildlife reserve. His efforts paid off nearly a decade later when Mt McKinley officially became a national park. The name was a sore point for years (President McKinley never even visited Alaska), until the national park was renamed in 1980. The mountain itself remained McKinley until 2015, when Denali was finally returned to its proper Athabascan name.

GETTING AROUND

Reach Denali National Park via the George Parks Hwy, north or south from Anchorage or Fairbanks, respectively. The Alaska Railroad offers service daily during the summer and weekly in the winter. Motorcoach transportation is available from Seward or Anchorage, and van transfers are available from Fairbanks.

GATES OF THE ARCTIC NATIONAL PARK & PRESERVE

Gates of the Arctic National Park and Preserve is not a simple place to reach. Located above the Arctic Circle, 200 miles north of Fairbanks, the park is in the center of the rugged Brooks Range and stretches across more than 8 million acres. With all of the space available, visiting Gates of the Arctic is arduous and sometimes dangerous. There are no roads, no cell-phone coverage and a population of precisely zero. Traveling here requires serious outdoor skills, and its remoteness is the stuff of legends.

That said, those who make the journey will experience some of the most beautiful landscapes on the planet, from rugged peaks that seem to touch the sky, to glaciated valleys of tundra and braided rivers stretching for hundreds of miles. And there's wildlife everywhere, from caribou herds to brown bears and wolves, all surviving in a place some call Alaska's ultimate wilderness.

FACTS

Great For Wildlife, scenery, walking
State Alaska
Entrance Fee Free
Area 13,238 sq miles

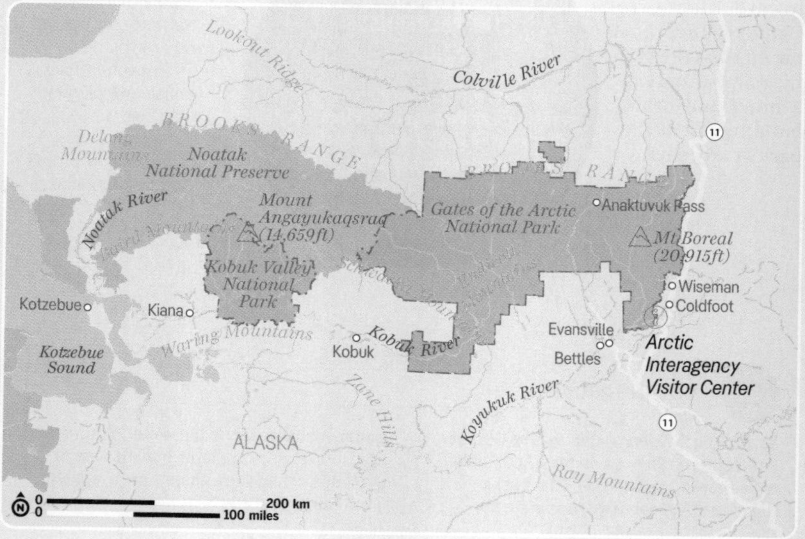

Noatak River, Gates of the Arctic National Park & Preserve

Backcountry Adventures

MULTIDAY WILDERNESS TREKS

Most backpackers enter the park by way of charter air taxis, which can land on lakes, rivers or river bars. Once on the ground, they often follow the long, open valleys for extended treks, or work their way to higher elevations where open tundra provides good hiking terrain.

While this appears to make planning an impossibly vague task, the landscape limits the areas in which aircraft can land or pick you up, as well as where you can hike. Park staff suggest consulting flight and guide companies, as well as topographic maps, for possible routes and then running it by rangers to make sure the area is not overused. If it is, they can suggest alternatives.

The only treks that don't require chartering a plane are those beginning from the Dalton Hwy (near Wiseman), or from the village of Anaktuvuk Pass. For hikes from the highway, which lead into several different areas along the eastern border of the park, stop at the Arctic Interagency Visitor Center in Coldfoot for assistance and advice on trip planning.

Hiking into the park from Anaktuvuk Pass is surprisingly one of the more economical options, as you only need to pay for a regular scheduled flight to the village from Fairbanks. From the airstrip, it's just a few miles' hike into the northern edge of the park. You can camp for free by the airstrip if needed, but elsewhere get permission until you enter the park.

If your wilderness experience in Alaska is limited, it's wise to go with a guide. Arctic Wild (arcticwild.com) leads a range of highly recommended backpacking, canoeing and packrafting trips.

DETOURING TO KOBUK VALLEY NATIONAL PARK

If you've come this far, it's worth tacking on a visit to Kobuk Valley National Park, which lies west of Gates of the Arctic. Here you'll find some extraordinary landscapes, including the largest collection of sand dunes in Arctic North America. The landscape is so otherworldly it's been used by NASA as an analogue for the environment on Mars.

The park is also home to the watershed of the Kobuk River, which runs through a dramatically beautiful valley in the shadow of the Baird Mountains. But you have to get here first, and that's the trick. As with Gates of the Arctic, there are no roads into the park, and no trails inside it, and visitors must possess a high level of wilderness savvy.

GETTING AROUND

Cessnas flown by Wright Air Service can take you to the gateway villages of Bettles (where you'll find the park headquarters) and Anaktuvuk Pass, from where you can get bush planes to drop you at remote sites in the park.

You can also walk out from these villages, but be prepared for river crossings. Another option is to hike in (or charter a plane) from Coldfoot on the Dalton Hwy.

GLACIER BAY NATIONAL PARK & PRESERVE

Glacier Bay is the crowning jewel of the cruise-ship industry and a dreamy destination for anybody who has ever paddled a kayak. Seven tidewater glaciers spill out of the mountains and fill the sea with icebergs of all shapes, sizes and shades of blue, making Glacier Bay National Park and Preserve an icy wilderness renowned worldwide.

Apart from its high concentration of tidewater glaciers, Glacier Bay is a dynamic habitat for humpback whales. Other wildlife seen at Glacier Bay includes sea otters, puffins, porpoises, brown and black bears, wolves, moose and mountain goats.

The park is an expensive side trip, even by Alaskan standards. Plan on spending at least $500 for a trip from Juneau. There's more to the area than just the boat trip to the glaciers, with good hiking, fishing and camping, and the tiny but charming settlement of Gustavus making for a rewarding base for exploring the national park.

Humpback whale, Glacier Bay

FACTS

Great For Wildlife, photo ops, scenery
State Alaska
Entrance Fee Free
Area 5156 sq miles

GETTING TO GLACIER BAY

It's a short but scenic flight between Juneau and Gustavus, with Alaska Airlines (once daily) and Alaska Seaplanes (four to five daily) making the 25-minute journey.

If you're not in a hurry, the Alaskan Marine Hwy ferry is a great way to travel as whales and other marine life are frequently spotted along the way. The boat travels three times a week during the summer (twice weekly in winter), typically departing Juneau at 7am and arriving at 11:30am. From Gustavus, boats sail at 12:30pm or 1:30pm, reaching Juneau 4½ hours later.

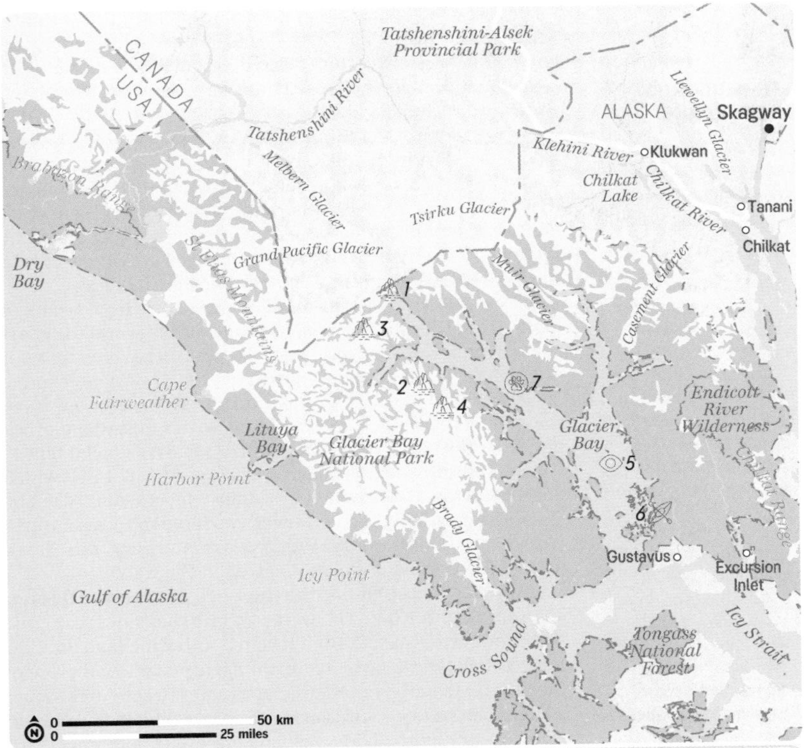

SIGHTS
1 Grand Pacific Glacier
2 Lamplugh Glacier
3 Margerie Glacier
4 Reid Glacier
5 South Marble Island

ACTIVITIES, COURSES & TOURS
6 Beardslee Islands
7 Gloomy Knob

Boating into the World of Ice

DAY TRIP IN THE NATIONAL PARK

One of the best ways to experience the national park is on a classic all-day boat trip. The seven-hour excursion departs in the morning from Bartlett Cove and makes a 130-mile journey through Glacier Bay before its return in the late afternoon. National park rangers on board bring the place to life, describing key features of the landscape and giving insight into the region's abundant wildlife.

WHERE TO STAY NEAR GLACIER BAY

Glacier Bay Lodge
Essentially a national-park lodge with cozy, wood-paneled rooms in a magnificent setting at Bartlett Cove. **$$$**

Cottonwood Lodge
Attractive rooms and several freestanding cabins set amid forest about a mile west of Four Corners. **$$**

Glacier Bay Country Inn
All-inclusive packages (fishing, wildlife watching, kayaking) in lodge rooms and cabins amid 160 forested acres. **$$$**

THE ONBOARD EXPERIENCE

Glacier Bay Lodge and Tours (visitglacierbay.com), which is the only operator (apart from cruise ships) leading day trips, heads out every morning in the summer on a 150-passenger high-speed catamaran. The vessel is designed for stability and has comfortable seating, large windows and outdoor decks on two levels. Onboard are several national park staff, who can answer questions about the region and give more insight into the flora and fauna. There are even kids' activities, such as watercolor painting using liquid from glacial ice retrieved during the trip.

Free coffee, tea and hot chocolate are available throughout the day, and there's also a counter where you can purchase snacks and drinks (including beer and wine). A sack lunch is included with the tour.

The first good viewing spot is the birding paradise of **South Marble Island**, where tufted and horned puffins, pigeon guillemots, surf scoters and pelagic cormorants are often seen. Near the shoreline, Steller sea lions bask on rocky ledges and watch idly as boats glide past.

Further along, the captain will slow the boat when sailing alongside **Gloomy Knob**, a barren rock face with steep cliffs where mountain goats are frequently spotted. You might see them grazing on shrubs, taking a dirt bath or gathering in small groups. Brown bears are occasionally seen walking along the shoreline. It's worth spending time out on the deck and studying the seas, coastline and sky. Binoculars come in handy.

The excursion offers dramatic views of the high peaks of the Fairweather Range, home to some of the world's highest coastal mountains, including Mt Fairweather, which tops out at 15,266ft. The landscape changes as you draw nearer to the icefield, with steeper mountains and sparser vegetation. Soon, the color of the water changes as well, with a milky blue-green hue from the silt and sediment of the massive glacial flows.

Boats typically take the narrow passage of Tarr Inlet, which dead-ends near one of the park's most spectacular glaciers. Well before you get there, however, you'll see the obvious presence of these frozen rivers, with growlers and bergy bits (small and medium-sized icebergs) floating in the water.

At the northwest end of the inlet lies **Margerie Glacier**, a stunning and iconic tidewater glacier that's nearly a mile wide and towers over 250ft above the waterline (and another 100ft below the surface). Its terminus is just a small piece of the 21-mile-long river of ice that originates in the Fairweather Range. The snowy, white surface appears blue in places, and its colors are more vivid on cloudy days. The boat lingers for the chance to possibly see calving, when huge icebergs sheer off the glacier and plunge into the water.

Apart from the striking backdrop – icebergs in the foreground, the wide glacier and chiseled mountains in the distance – the inlet is also a good place to spot wildlife. Look for harbor seals stretched out on the ice, sea otters in the water and black-legged kittiwake gulls flying past. Adjacent is the **Grand Pacific Glacier**, which is thickly covered by debris and lies just a mile south of the Canada border.

You'll pass other glaciers as you make the return journey, including **Lamplugh Glacier**, a photogenic formation reaching down from the ever-shrinking Brady Icefield. Nearby stretches small, slow-moving **Reid Glacier**, which was once the backdrop to a cabin built by the Ibachs, a pioneering family who, in the 1920s, searched for gold in the nearby mountains. The foundations are still there, along with several trees they planted.

WHERE TO EAT NEAR GLACIER BAY

Glacier Bay Lodge
Big windows (and outdoor tables) make the lodge a prime spot for halibut, rib eye or chowder. **$$$**

Sunnyside
In Gustavus, Sunnyside has breakfast burritos, sandwiches and canned craft beer, best enjoyed by the lawn. **$**

Fireweed
Stop in this Gustavus cafe, gallery and shop for crepes, biscuit sandwiches and good coffee. **$**

NICK STARICHENKO/SHUTTERSTOCK ©

Kayaking, Glacier Bay

Paddling Adventures in Glacier Bay

KAYAKING, CAMPING AND WILDLIFE

Glacier Bay offers an excellent paddling opportunity for people who have some experience on the water, even if not necessarily as kayakers, because the boat trip run by Glacier Bay Lodge and Tours drops off and picks up paddlers at two spots – usually at the entrance of the Muir Inlet (East Arm) and inside the West Arm. By using the tour boat, you can skip the long and open paddle through the bay and enjoy only the well-protected arms and inlets where the glaciers are located. The most dramatic glaciers are in the West Arm, but either arm will require at least four days of paddling to glaciers if you're dropped off and picked up. With only a drop-off, you'll need a week to 10 days to paddle from either arm back to Bartlett Cove.

Paddlers who want to avoid the tour-boat fares but still long for a kayak adventure should try the **Beardslee Islands**. While there are no glaciers to view, the islands are a day's paddle from Bartlett Cove and offer calm water, protected channels and pleasant beach camping. Wildlife includes black bears, seals and bald eagles, and the tidal pools burst with activity at low tide.

Alaska Mountain Guides and Climbing School (alaskamountainguides.com) runs guided kayak trips in Glacier Bay that range from five to eight days. The most active trip is the eight-day excursion up the East Arm, paddling 10 to 15 miles per day and changing campsites nighty. The seven-day West Arm excursion uses the day boat as a shuttle and requires a little less paddling.

NATURE & TRADITIONAL CULTURE IN BARTLETT COVE

On the Bartlett Cove waterfront, an open-sided pavilion contains one of the largest humpback whale skeletons on display in the United States. Known as Snow, the 45ft whale had been a regular visitor to Glacier Bay since 1975 when she was tragically struck by a cruise ship in 2001. After her death, the national park decided to preserve her skeleton for posterity.

Follow the shoreline northeast to reach Tuna Shuká Hit (Huna Ancestors' House), with its elaborate interior screen referencing the four main Huna Tlingit clans in Glacier Bay. The clan house is still a gathering spot for tribal members and is also used for presentations by the NPS, which manages it jointly with the Huna Tlingit.

GETTING AROUND

Some lodges provide free transport to/from the airport or the ferry terminal. Be sure to inquire when making a reservation. If not, TLC taxi (907-697-2239) can carry up to 10 people, gear and kayaks. There's also Strawberry Point Courier (907-697-2150). These two transportation providers are also the best options for reaching Bartlett Cove. If you have access to a bike, it's a mostly pleasant, easy-going ride with just a few moderate hills at the end (allow an hour to make the 8.5-mile ride from Four Corners to Bartlett Cove).

KATMAI NATIONAL PARK & PRESERVE

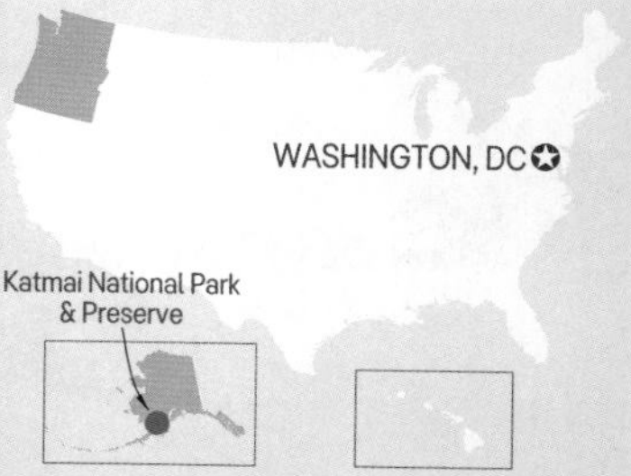

A national monument since 1918 and a national park since 1980, Katmai is famous for its salmon-trapping brown bears, epic sport-fishing potential and unusual volcanic landscapes. Unconnected to the main Alaskan road network and covering an area the size of Wales, the park is, for most people, a once-in-a-lifetime experience involving meticulous planning and quite a lot of cash.

Nearly all park visitors fly in by floatplane to the main tourist area of Brooks Camp, 35 miles east of King Salmon. Here they will stand spine-tinglingly close to formidable 1000lb brown bears pawing giant salmon out of the river (some bears even catch the fish clean in their chops). It's the most heavily visited section of the park, equipped with a rustic lodge plus a couple of short trails. Beyond the bears, Katmai has an astonishing archaeological record, with evidence of humans in the Brooks River area more than 5000 years ago.

FACTS

Great For Wildlife, photo ops, scenery
State Alaska
Entrance Fee Free
Area 6395 sq miles

OKSANA.PERKINS/SHUTTERSTOCK ©

Bears, Brooks Falls

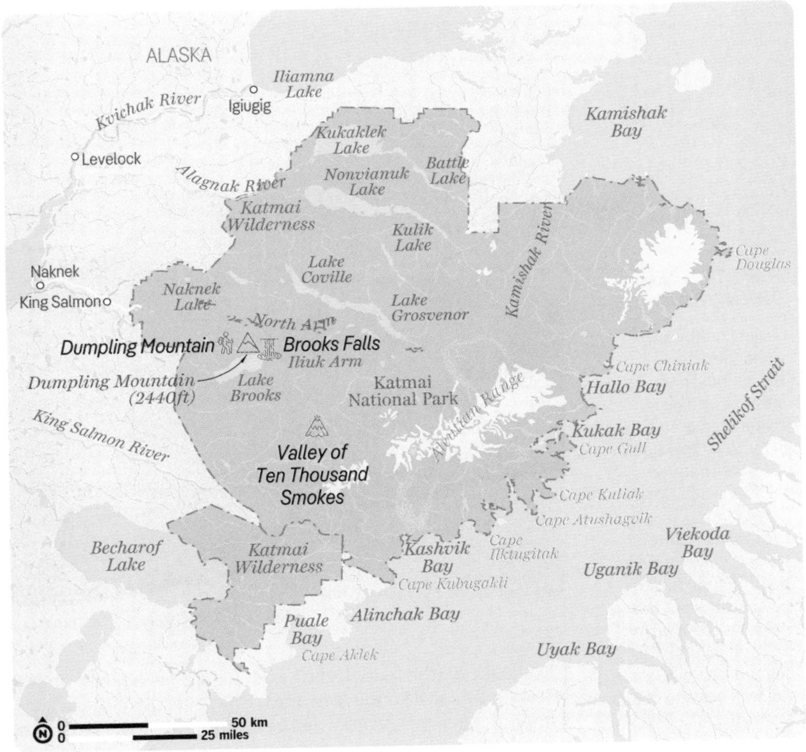

Bear Watching at Brooks Camp

SALMON-FEASTING GIANTS

Katmai supports a healthy population of 2200 brown bears. Many of the bears arrive with instinctual punctuality at **Brooks Falls** on July 1 for the annual salmon spawning, which lasts until the end of the month. The bears return in September for a second showing to feed on the dead salmon carcasses.

Brooks Camp has three established bear-watching areas. From the lodge, a dirt road leads to a floating bridge over the river and the first observation deck at the river's lower section. From here you can see the bears feeding in the mouth of the river or swimming in the bay.

GETTING TO KATMAI NATIONAL PARK

Katmai Air
An air charter flying floatplanes between the town of King Salmon and Brooks Falls (around $500 round trip).

Katmai Water Taxi
Boating between King Salmon and Brooks Falls is slower but more scenic than flying ($400 round trip).

Rust's Flying Service
Travel from Anchorage to Brooks Falls by floatplane with this highly experienced family-run business.

KNELSON20/SHUTTERSTOCK ©

Valley of Ten Thousand Smokes

PERMITS & BEAR ORIENTATION

Owing to growing visitor numbers, the national park introduced new visiting requirements in 2022. All travelers to Katmai between mid-June and October 31 must apply for a Brooks River Corridor Permit. Valid for seven days for groups of up to six people, the permit is required for any activities along the Brooks River (namely viewing bears from the platforms). Reserve a permit online through recreation.gov.

All visitors begin their stay with a mandatory bear-safety talk given by a park ranger. Despite Katmai's dense bear population (two bears per 1 sq mile in places), only two serious human-bear incidents have been recorded in 100 years – a testament to fine park management.

Continue on the road to the Valley of Ten Thousand Smokes, and in half a mile a marked trail, lined with two more viewing platforms, winds another half mile to Brooks Falls. The first platform sits above some shallows that occasionally draw sows trying to keep their cubs away from aggressive males at the falls.

The last deck at the falls is the prime viewing area, where salmon make spectacular leaps and hungry bears at the top of the cascade wait with open jaws to catch a fish. At the peak of the salmon run, there might be eight to 12 bears here, with two or three of them atop the falls themselves. The observation deck holds 40 people, and in early to mid-July it will be crammed with photographers, forcing rangers to rotate people on and off.

Brooks Camps' bear season is relatively short, but more adventurous visitors can charter floatplanes and guides to take them out to other bear-viewing areas on the coast between June and October.

WHERE TO STAY NEAR KATMAI NATIONAL PARK

Brooks Camp Campground
Summer reservations open 8am, January 5 for this coveted national park campground and fill within hours. **$**

Brooks Lodge
Reservations for these cabins are awarded by lottery; apply in December for the year after next. **$$$**

Antlers Inn
Friendly, easygoing place with simply furnished rooms and suites near the airport in King Salmon. **$$$**

Otherworldly Views at the Valley of Ten Thousand Smokes

RANGER-LED BUS TOUR

Katmai's only road is a scenic, 23-mile traverse of the park that leads from the lodge, past wildlife-inhabited meadows and river valleys, ending at the Robert F Griggs Visitor Center, which has a sweeping view of the **Valley of Ten Thousand Smokes**. It also has displays on the area's natural history and photographs from the past.

The peculiar landscape of this surreal valley is the result of the massive 1912 Novarupta volcanic eruption. Over three days, pumice and ash rained down and countless smoke vents jetted hot steam skyward. It was the largest volcanic eruption in the 20th century and after the magma stopped flowing, some 40 sq miles of forested wilderness had been transformed into a landscape of smoking valleys, blackened mountains and small holes and cracks fuming with steam and gas.

The easiest way to see the volcanic valley is on the daily tour operated by Katmailand. The day-long excursion leaves at 9am and returns around 4pm. Each bus carries a ranger who gives talks during the trip and answers any questions. Arriving at the visitor center and overlook, the views take in almost 12 miles of barren, moonlike valley where the lava once oozed down, with snowcapped peaks beyond. After a break for lunch, the ranger leads an optional hike down to the valley floor, where you can get an up-close look at the volcanic landscape. Though not particularly long (3.4 miles round trip), it's all uphill on the way back (about a 1000ft elevation gain).

The bus is filled most of the summer, and you often can't get a seat without making a reservation well in advance though Brooks Lodge.

Backcountry Adventures

BACKPACKING AND KAYAKING

Hiking and backpacking are the best ways to see Katmai's unusual backcountry. Like Denali National Park, Katmai has few formal trails. Backpackers follow river bars, lakeshores, gravel ridges and other natural routes. Some hiking trips begin with a ride on the park bus along the dirt road to the Robert F Griggs Visitor Center, on the edge of the Valley of Ten Thousand Smokes. The bus will also drop off and pick up hikers and backpackers along the road, or you can walk its full 23-mile length.

The only developed trail from Brooks Camp is a half-day trek to the top of **Dumpling Mountain** (2440ft). The trail leaves

FISHING AMONG BEARS

Fishing trips are popular and rainbow trout are plentiful in Katmai's large lakes. In fact, most park facilities were first built to accommodate anglers. Fishing populations are carefully managed by Katmai National Park & Preserve and Alaska Department of Fish and Game. Sport-fishing licenses are required for nonresidents aged 16 and older and most residents aged 16 to 59. Further regulations exist depending on where anglers cast their reels.

Because fishers and brown bears are often attracted to the same catch, anglers must be careful when fishing in Katmai and follow safe bear-country practices such as maintaining bear awareness, cutting the line if a bear approaches and safe catch storage.

SCENIC FLIGHTS & CRUISES

Alaska Ultimate Safaris
Has a range of once-in-a-lifetime adventures from Homer, including bear viewing by helicopter.

Adventure Kodiak
Runs a luxury six-day cruise visiting coastal Katmai and the Kodiak archipelago (from $6000).

Northwest Odyssey
Multiday luxury boat tours that visit both Katmai and Lake Clark National Parks.

TIPS FOR SAFE TRAVEL IN BEAR COUNTRY

Making Noise
Travel in a group and make noise to avoid surprising a bear. The human voice is effective, so speak loudly.

Bear Encounters
Don't run – bears can easily outrun you and will instinctively pursue a fleeing animal. Instead, back away slowly, talking soothingly to the bear while avoiding direct eye contact.

Bear Charges
A bear may charge if it views you as a threat. Use your pepper spray when the bear is within 30ft. If the bear attacks, lie face down and protect your neck and face. Once a bear no longer perceives you as a threat, it will stop attacking.

the ranger station and heads north past the campground, climbing 1.5 miles to a scenic overlook. It then continues another 2.5 miles to the mountain's summit, from where there are superb views of the surrounding lakes.

If you're backpacking, you'll need to camp at least 1.5 miles outside of the Brooks Camp Developed Area. The national park recommends campers set up an electric fence around their tent as a bear deterrent.

Katmai also has some excellent paddling, including the Savonoski Loop, a big adventure for more experienced kayakers. Other popular trips include a 30-mile paddle from Brooks Camp to the Bay of Islands and a 10-mile paddle to Margot Creek, which has good fishing and lots of bears.

Kayaks are a much better choice than canoes due to high winds blowing across big lakes and possible rough water. Accomplished paddlers should have no problem, but the conditions can sometimes get dicey for novices.

Kayaking the Savonoski Loop

EPIC MULTIDAY WILDERNESS TRIP

One of the legendary paddling adventures in the area is the 80-mile Savonoski Loop, a moderately difficult kayaking trip lasting five to 10 days. The adventure begins and ends at Brooks Camp and takes paddlers into remote sections of the park, offering the best in wilderness adventure without expensive bush-plane travel.

Although there's no white water, the trip is still challenging, with the hardest section being the 12-mile run of the Savonoski River, which is braided and has many sandbars and fallen trees. The Savonoski is also prime brown-bear habitat and for this reason park rangers recommend paddling the river in a single day and not camping along it.

The first section through Naknek Lake is especially scenic and well protected at the end where you dip in and out of the Bay of Islands. You're then faced with a mile-long portage trail (often a muddy and insect-laden trek) that begins at Fure's Cabin and leads to Lake Grosvenor and the Grosvenor River. It then heads down the Savonoski River, which brings you to the last leg: a 20-mile paddle along the south shore of the Iliuk Arm back to Brooks Camp.

Paddlers should be aware that Katmai is famous for its sudden and violent storms, some lasting days. The preferred mode of travel here is a kayak, due to the sudden winds and the rough nature of the big lakes. As far as gear goes, most visitors either fly in with a folding kayak or rent a kayak from Brooks Lodge inside the national park. For a guided nine-day trip, get in touch with Arctic Wild (arcticwild.com).

GETTING AROUND

There are few roads in the park, so the majority of visitors fan out over Katmai's 6395 sq miles by means of chartered floatplanes, backcountry hiking or paddling.

KENAI FJORDS NATIONAL PARK

The nearly 40 glaciers that carve their way through stone and rock to the rugged fjords are the crown jewels of this popular national park on the Kenai Peninsula south of Anchorage. Atop it all is the Harding Icefield, a majestic, otherworldly landscape sprawling across some 700 sq miles of Alaska's Kenai Mountains.

The quintessential experience here is taking a boat tour from the captivating fishing village of Seward out to see fjords, glaciers and a remarkable tapestry of marine wildlife. This is a place ruled by sea otters, porpoises, harbor seals and Steller sea lions, with humpbacks and other whales slicing through the waters.

For another perspective on this aquatic kingdom, get close to nature on a kayak tour – paddling between icebergs is magical. By land, the Exit Glacier draws hikers on day trips, which can be extended to more ambitious treks all the way up to the Harding Icefield.

FACTS

Great For Wildlife, photo ops, scenery
State Alaska
Entrance Fee Free
Area 1047 sq miles

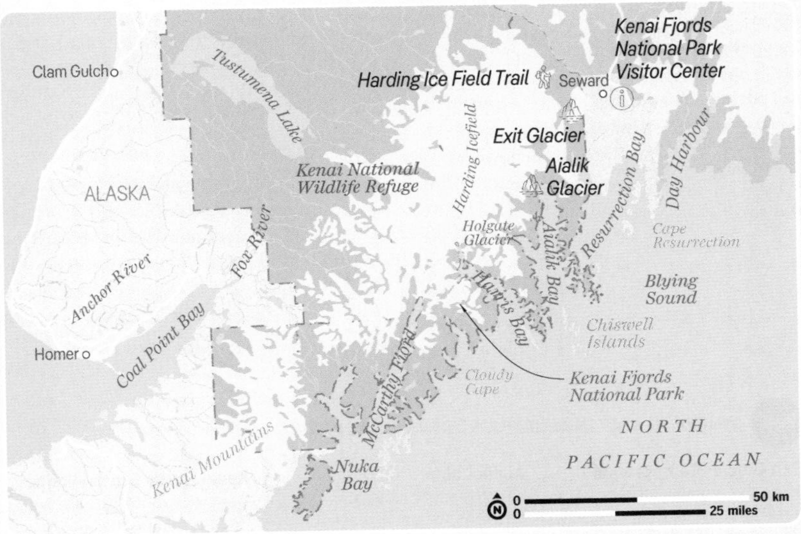

CHOOSING A TOUR

While a variety of operators offer small-group wildlife cruises out of Seward, the larger boats operated by Major Marine Tours and Kenai Fjords Tours give on-water stability and less chance of seasickness. The tour options, park sites and wildlife visited by the two companies are very similar, but they each offer distinct amenities. For example, while Kenai Fjords Tours has free off-site parking, a meal included in your ticket price and open seating onboard, some users will prefer Major Marine's assigned seating model with free coffee and tea. Regardless of which company you choose, book the full-day experience if possible. You won't tire of the endless wildlife encounters. A half-day tour will only leave you wishing for more.

Boating into the Fjords

SNOWCAPPED MOUNTAINS AND WILDLIFE

Kenai Fjords National Park encompasses 545 miles of coastline and steep, narrow inlets known as fjords that were created by glaciers long ago. From gigantic whales to adorable tufted puffins, the most efficient way to absorb this park is to head out on a full-day wildlife cruise.

After boarding your boat in Seward's harbor, stand on deck as it moves slowly through the bay, passing the stunning, snowcapped mountains. As the boat pauses at various coves and rocky outcroppings, witness nesting common mures, watch for colorful puffins bobbing along the water and catch a view of seals basking in the sun.

Head inside for lunch and a view out the window, but don't get too comfortable. Your captain will be in constant contact with other boats in the area as they all watch for signs of humpback whales and orcas. The'll take you where they've been spotted so you, too, can see these creatures rise from the water.

Hang on as your cruise goes from the relatively calm waters of the bay out into the bumpy open ocean. You're headed now to Aialik Bay and the stark blue tidewater **Aialik Glacier** descending into the ocean. Bundle up against the cold air here, watching ancient glacial ice float through the water near the boat. As you return towards port, linger over the magnificent landscape surrounding the boat.

Kayak Resurrection Bay & Its Nearby Glaciers

PADDLE PAST GLACIERS AND CLIFFS

The ocean and coastline of Kenai Fjords National Park are best experienced from the water, and touring by kayak is the most immersive way to do it. Kayak travel offers the most direct contact with this place and its deep beauty. Two different guided day trips are worth your time, and which you pick depends on what you value more: time near a glacier or time journeying on the water.

Glacier enthusiasts should join Liquid Adventures for a two-hour trip on a private catamaran to Aialik Bay and its active tidewater glacier. After whale-watching and seabird spotting from the shuttle boat, you'll land on a beach with your guide to start your 3½-hour kayaking journey, navigating around ice floes and experiencing the glacier. Pulling onto a rocky beach for a lunch break, take in the stunning views around you before your pick-up and trip back to Seward.

WHERE TO STAY IN KENAI FJORDS NATIONAL PARK

Exit Glacier Campground
The only formal campground has 12 great walk-in sites (free) that are first-come, first-served. **$**

Aialik Cabin
A rustic, public-use cabin set on a remote beach, reachable by chartered plane or boat. **$**

Kenai Fjords Glacial Lodge
Cabins overlook picturesque Pedersen Lagoon at this impressive place with all meals and activities included. **$$$**

Aialik Glacier

If you want more time on the water, join Sunny Cove Kayaking to paddle around Fox Island in Resurrection Bay. After a one-hour shuttle to the island, follow your guide around the island's perimeter on your seven-hour adventure, visiting a magical array of coves and cliffs. Pause on the shore for lunch, explore a waterfall, then land at a petrified forest to walk among the ghostly natural history created by the 1964 tsunami. Eat dinner at the lodge on Fox Island before your boat ride back to the harbor.

Glacial Discoveries

EXPLORING EXIT GLACIER

A visit to the Exit Glacier section of Kenai Fjords National Park is a striking journey into the clear impacts of global climate change. While the vast majority of this national park is on the coast and in the water, its 680,000 acres also include the Harding Icefield and the 40 glaciers it feeds, including **Exit Glacier**. Few other places in Alaska offer such clear, visual and experiential evidence of the rate of glacial retreat in the face of a warming planet.

PARK INSIGHT

The Kenai Fjords National Park visitor center, just off Seward's harbor, offers an in-depth view of the park's wildlife, fjords, coastline, Harding Icefield and Exit Glacier. Combining immersive static displays with a 20-minute educational video, the center and small gift shop are an ideal start for any Kenai Fjords adventure. It's no replacement for actually visiting the fjords on a tour, but the center does offer an excellent perspective on the area's wide variety of flora, fauna and history. If you're headed out on an all-day wildlife cruise or kayak trip and want to stop by, carefully check the opening hours – it can be easy to accidentally miss them entirely.

KAYAKING & SCENIC FLIGHTS

Miller's Landing
Rents kayaks and leads a wide range of day-long and multi-day paddling adventures.

Kayak Adventures Worldwide
Its many tours include a wildlife-watching boat trip combined with kayaking at Aialik Glacier.

Scenic Mountain Air
See Kenai's spectacular landscapes on a floatplane flight or book Scenic for drop-offs at USFS cabins.

HIKING THE HARDING ICEFIELD TRAIL

This difficult, 8.2-mile round-trip hike moves through forest, meadows and high alpine terrain, across avalanche chutes, icefall zones and river outwashes, and it's important to be prepared. As you hit the trail, climb 3000ft over steep terrain to the edge of the 700-sq-mile Harding Icefield, peering down onto striking views of the Exit Glacier's terminus zone and watching for mountain goats peeping out from the vegetation around you. As you trek over the narrow trail to the icefield, feel the air cool as you near the ice, which is as much as 1850ft deep. Take in the seemingly never-ending field of white ice and its periodic rocky points called nunataks – it's a window into ice ages long past.

Exit Glacier (p247)

As you drive the 10 miles to the visitor center from the Seward Hwy, feel how the air temperature drops as you wind towards the glacier's toe. See your first view of the glacier as you round a bend, noting where it ends today, far in the distance.

The story of climate change is unavoidably real for you here. A brown sign on the side of the road indicates the point to which the glacier extended in 1815. Encounter more of these year markers as you drive on to the glacier and, later, as you walk the **Glacier View Loop** path.

For more insight into this icy world, join a ranger-led glacier hike. These depart from the Exit Glacier visitor center and take you on a 1½-hour walk that travels over the Glacier View Loop and up a mile to the Glacier Overlook trail. The distance and pace of this walk down the wheelchair-accessible trail isn't high energy, but you'll get a deeper understanding of the glacier's past and present.

GETTING AROUND

Seward is the nearest town to the park. If you don't have a car, various shuttles, including Exit Glacier Shuttle, make the scenic 20-minute drive to Exit Glacier. To reach the coastal fjords, you'll need to take a tour or catch a water taxi with Miller's Landing.

LAKE CLARK NATIONAL PARK & PRESERVE

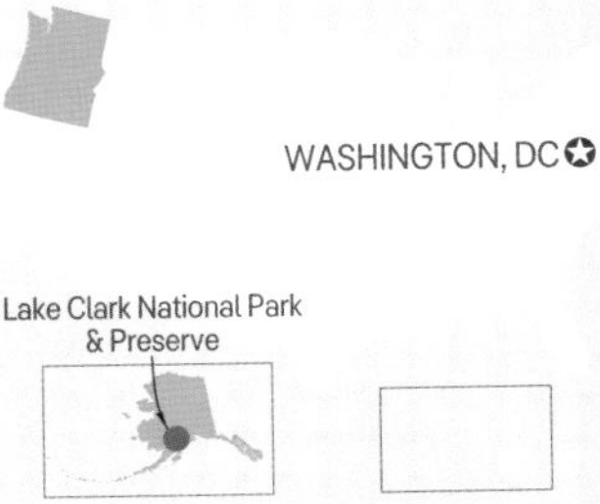

Lake Clark National Park and Preserve features spectacular scenery that is a composite of Alaska: an awesome array of tundra-covered hills, mountains, glaciers, coastline, the largest lakes in the state and two active volcanoes.

The centerpiece of the park is a 45-mile shimmering body of turquoise water fringed by the snowy summits of glacier-tipped peaks. The park is also where the Alaska Range merges into the Aleutian Range to form the Chigmit Mountains, and is home to two volcanoes: Mt Iliamna and Mt Redoubt.

Ancestors of the Dena'ina Athabascan people have been fishing Lake Clark for 12,000 years. In the early 20th century, the Dena'ina abandoned their village of Kijik, which they had occupied for almost 1000 years. Today, the ghost town is the largest Athabascan archaeological site in Alaska.

Despite its overwhelming scenery and close proximity to Anchorage, fewer than 20,000 visitors a year make it to this vast preserve.

FACTS

Great For Wildlife, scenery, walking
State Alaska
Entrance Fee Free
Area 6297 sq miles

Mt Iliamna

LAKE CLARK NATIONAL PARK & PRESERVE

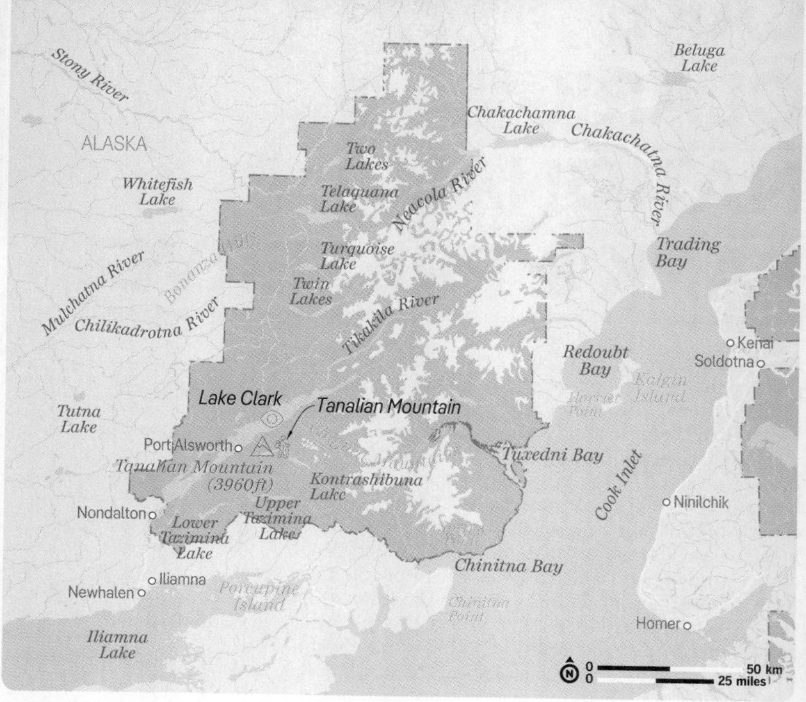

Adventures on Water & Land

KAYAKING AND HIKING

Kayaking and canoeing are popular ways to explore **Lake Clark** itself, the shores of which range from craggy horizons to low tundra. In the park's main town, Port Alsworth, Tulchina Adventures will rent out kayaks or set up an unguided kayaking/camping trip. It can also provide water-taxi service, taking you and your gear to your destination of choice.

The hiking is phenomenal, but Lake Clark is best suited to the experienced backpacker. For any trip planning, visit the park website (nps.gov/lacl), which has the latest guidance on traveling in the backcountry. Port Alsworth has a visitor center with displays and videos on the park. There you'll find information on the **Telaquana Trail Route**, a historic Dena'ina Athabascan route running from Telaquana Lake to Kijik Village, and **Twin Lakes**, where dry tundra slopes provide easy travel to ridges and great views.

WILDERNESS CONNECTIONS

Air taxis connecting Port Alsworth in Lake Clark National Park and Preserve to other locations such as Kenai and King Salmon can be arranged – useful for hopping straight over to other national parks in Alaska, like **Katmai** (p240).

KEVIN F BEASLEY/SHUTTERSTOCK ©

Fishing, Lake Clark National Park

The hike up **Tanalian Mountain** is another memorable outing. It may be only 4.1 miles to the top, but the trail climbs more than 3700ft through spruce and birch forests from Port Alsworth to the summit. It's a bit of a scramble at the end, but worth the effort to reach a lookout with exhilarating views of Lake Clark. You might also see bighorn sheep at the top.

If you prefer not to head out on your own, you can book a trip with various tour operators that run rewarding excursions in the park. Alaska Alpine Adventures leads a one-week paddling trip as well as several seven- to 10-day backpacking trips.

BEST PLACES TO SPEND THE NIGHT

Redoubt Mountain Lodge
This six-cabin lodge spread over 5 acres overlooks Crescent Lake, a glacially fed body of water in the shadow of Redoubt Volcano. There's legendary fishing, kayaking and wildlife watching, and a sauna and hot tub awaiting at day's end. **$$$**

Silver Salmon Creek Lodge
Set between volcanic peaks and tidal marshes beside Cook Inlet, this cozy lodge is a wilderness oasis. Its tent camp, 10 miles to the south, is an angler's paradise and operates late July to early September, which coincides with the salmon run. **$$$**

GETTING AROUND

To reach the park, you will need to arrange with a charter pilot for a drop-off and pick-up at the start of your adventure. Six different operators make the trip from Anchorage, including Lake Clark Air, which also runs a lodge on Lake Clark. Most lodges offer package deals that include flights from Anchorage.

WRANGELL-ST ELIAS NATIONAL PARK & PRESERVE

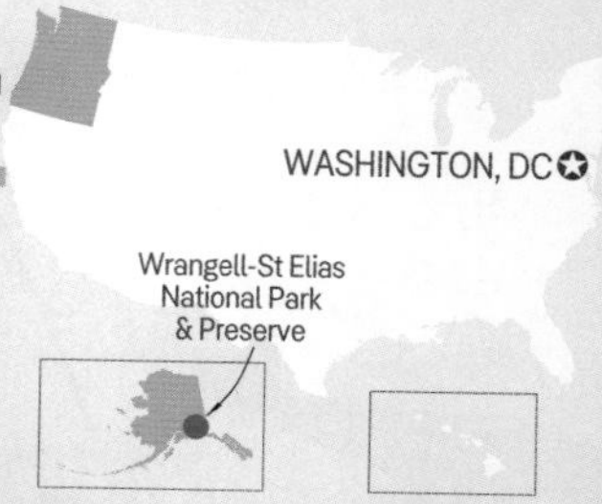

Enormous in scale, the United States' largest national park encompasses more than 13 million acres, making it larger than 70 of the world's independent nations. Getting to this remote place is a challenge, but what the park lacks in dedicated road access, it makes up for with adventure-laden activities, history and rich culture, thanks to a thriving Upper Tanana and Ahtna Athabascan Native community.

Logistics aside, visitors to Wrangell-St Elias must be prepared to explore mostly independently, with few resources other than what is self-provided, and be ready to overstay or understay in a particular location should weather or road conditions change. Guide services are available, however, and it makes sense not to go it alone. You're much more likely to learn about a place under the tutelage of an experienced glacier, river or naturalist guide, and enjoy more of what this stupendous park offers.

FACTS

Great For History, wildlife, scenery
State Alaska
Entrance Fee Free
Area 20,587 sq miles

TRAVIS J. CAMP/SHUTTERSTOCK ©

Ice climbing, Root Glacier

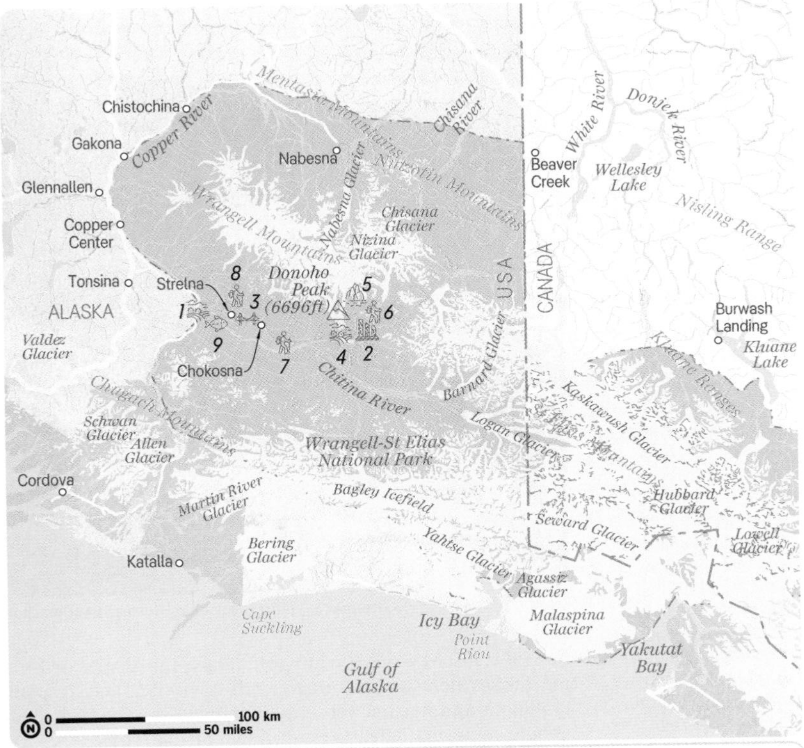

SIGHTS
1 Chitina
2 Kennecott Mines National Historic Landmark
3 Kuskulana Bridge
4 McCarthy
5 Root Glacier

ACTIVITIES, COURSES & TOURS
6 Bonanza Mine Trail
7 Crystalline Hills Trail
8 Dixie Pass Route
9 Silver Lake

Glacial Adventures

BIG ICE ABOVE AND BELOW YOUR FEET

Root Glacier is the closest glacier to the handy park villages of McCarthy and Kennecott, and the most accessible of the myriad rivers of ice dotting the landscape of Wrangell-St Elias National Park. St Elias Alpine Guides (steliasguides.com) offers half-day, full-day and overnight excursions onto the glacier, including ice climbing and the chance to belay into an ice cave to witness the

WHERE TO EAT IN WRANGELL-ST ELIAS NATIONAL PARK

Kennicott Glacier Lodge
Open to non-guests by reservation, this family-style restaurant serves up 'wilderness gourmet.' $$$

Glacier View Grill
This restaurant serves hearty post-hiking fare, including burgers 'as big as the Wrangell mountains.' $

Roadside Potato Head
The Potato, as it's commonly called, whips up fabulous burritos, fries and salads using locally grown ingredients. $

SUMMIT VIEWS FROM THE TRAIL

The tough but rewarding Bonanza Mine Trail leads past waterfalls, glaciers and mining ruins, and offers sweeping panoramic views of the mountains. Bring plenty of water for this strenuous 8.3-mile (round trip) uphill slog that includes more than 3900ft of elevation gain. Begin on the Root Glacier Trail and turn off to the right at the clearly marked junction. The first few miles are fairly buggy, so bring repellent. Once you get above the tree line, the bugs disperse (a bit) and you'll have stunning views of the confluence of the Root and Kennicott Glaciers.

Allow yourself six to eight hours to complete the hike, including some downtime at the summit. Snow lingers higher up until June.

Kennecott Mines National Historic Landmark

powerful forces of nature at work. Reach the glacier by hiking 2 miles along a trail from the mill-town site, then strap on crampons and step out onto the creaking ice surface, learning about the dramatic features of glacial formations.

Need more adventure? Learn to scale the vertical walls of Root Glacier on an ice climb, complete with all the instruction necessary to ascend and descend safely. It's even possible to view a moulin, a hole made by water reaching down hundreds of feet below the ice, where the bluest blues can be seen beneath.

It's worth noting that while anyone able to hike has the potential to be comfortable exploring on ice, kids under eight and those with mobility issues may find the experience overwhelming and difficult. Inquire about other opportunities when booking an ice trek or climb.

If the ice-trekking bug has caught up with you, St Elias Alpine Guides also offers multiday courses and backcountry trips deeper into the wilds of the park, with all the equipment necessary for a safe and memorable adventure.

WHERE TO STAY IN WRANGELL-ST ELIAS NATIONAL PARK

Ma Johnson's Hotel
A former boarding house and part living-history museum full of interesting exhibits and artifacts. **$$$**

Kennicott Glacier Lodge
A large historic hotel, with stunning views of Root Glacier, Kennecott Mine and surrounding mountains. **$$$**

Kennicott River Lodge and Cabins
Five quaint cabins and one suite room inside an attractive lodge, with shared kitchen. **$$**

Kennecott Mines National Historic Landmark

THRIVING COMMUNITY IN THE MOUNTAINS

Surprising for its unbelievable architecture and location, the former mill town of Kennecott Mines is an extraordinary example of 20th-century industry and technology. Kennecott Mines National Historic Landmark includes the land and mining claims for the Kennecott Copper Corporation and, later, the Kennecott Minerals Company. The whole operation had two sections: the mines where ore was extracted from craggy mountainsides, and the adjacent mill town where the ore was actually processed. During its heyday between 1911 and 1938, nearly $200 million worth of copper was processed at Kennecott.

Perhaps most interesting (mechanics of the mining process aside) was that entire families lived, worked and played in the mill town as a self-contained community with a hospital, general store, school, skating rink, tennis court, recreation hall and dairy. Work was six days a week, with Sunday off, and many miners sought refuge from the long hours by retreating to McCarthy, where alcohol and gambling were legally permitted, for a bit of self-inflicted recreation (or wildness). Dozens of old wood and log buildings have been restored, stabilized or purposely left in a state of decrepitude. You're welcome to wander around the outside of the buildings at will, or you can join daily tours.

Unless you have a penchant for uphill hiking or biking, the 4 miles between McCarthy and Kennecott should be taken by the provided shuttle service for a small fee. If staying at Kennicott Glacier Lodge – the only accommodations near the mill town – transportation is included. Once on the site, stop by the National Park Service visitor center for a map and a schedule of ranger talks and walks of the area. St Elias Alpine Guides offers in-depth walking tours of the mill town and adjacent buildings, providing an excellent look at life so far away from major centers of commerce.

If you'd like to take a look at some of the mines themselves, hike one of the many trails switchbacking up hillsides to Jumbo or Bonanza mines. For a lower-elevation experience, and a way to reach McCarthy from the mill town, take the Wagon Rd and Toe of Kennicott Glacier trail, which is also suitable for mountain bikes.

For a delightful look at past publications, notes and other written artifacts about Kennecott Mill Town, stop by the Kennicott Glacier Lodge for a meal and wander through the

PARK VISITOR CENTERS

Wrangell-St Elias Visitor Center
The main center for all things Wrangell-St Elias is 10 miles from Glennallen. It houses the Ahtna Cultural Center, and there's a short nature trail with views of the Copper River Valley.

Chitina Ranger Station
A charming log cabin in the town of Chitina has artifacts and exhibits about the Edgerton Hwy, McCarthy Rd and Kennecott Copper Mine.

Kennecott Visitor Center
The hub for information on Kennecott Mines National Historic Landmark. Sign up here for ranger-led walks and talks.

Slana Ranger Station
On the park's northern side, this is a must-stop for anyone traveling off-road (permits required). It's also a good place for camping and hiking information.

Glacier View Campground
Tent and RV sites, with a grill and cafe next door. No water or sewer hookup for RVs. $

Ultima Thule
One of Alaska's finest luxury wilderness lodges puts bush planes at your disposal for memorable adventures. $$$

Currant Ridge
Ecofriendly spot with attractive, well-equipped log cabins with decks boasting stunning mountain views. $$$

buildings that house hundreds of items salvaged by owner Rich Kirkwood during the town's renovation that began in 1998.

Motor the McCarthy Road

THE JOURNEY IS THE DESTINATION

Today's McCarthy Rd is actually yesterday's rail bed of the Copper River and Northwestern Railway (also known as the 'Can't Run and Never Will' railroad by skeptics). At just under 60 miles from Chitina to the town of McCarthy, the road has long been the subject of lore regarding old ties, spikes and metal bits that were known to pop out of nowhere and puncture the tires of unsuspecting motorists. Thankfully, those days are mostly over, thanks to crews who dug up the railway's remnants over the past decade and made the road a smoother traveling experience.

Start the drive in **Chitina**, a small town on the banks of the Copper River and the former stage-line terminus for workers and families living at Kennecott Mine and McCarthy. The passage for trains ended in 1938, but it took until 1950 for the line to be pulled up in the hopes of establishing a permanent auto route, and while driving the road today is decidedly better than it was, travelers should be wary of potholes, washouts and other potential hazards. Note that there are no services between Chitina and McCarthy, so packing food, water and a spare tire (with tools) is a must. Allow at least three hours for the drive to McCarthy, and allow for stops at waysides for interesting snapshots of history or a bit of recreation before arriving at the road's end.

The Copper River is a highlight at the beginning of the drive. Fishing for sockeye and chinook salmon here is popular and families from the Ahtna tribe have spinning wheels in the silty water to capture their allotment of subsistence fish. Eagles also frequent the beaches, feasting on remnants from the filleting process of human fishers.

At Mile 10.8, those interested in a bit of fly fishing for rainbow trout will enjoy the walk to **Van Lakes** or **Silver Lake** for uncrowded shorelines. Carry bear and bug spray, and be aware of your surroundings at all times.

At Mile 17.2, the **Kuskulana Bridge** towers above the adjacent roadway as a testament to the engineering that went into the trestle's construction. Stop at the wayside for a picnic, but be aware of steep cliffs that drop down to the Kuskulana River.

Pulling into Mile 34.6, the **Crystalline Hills** trailhead starts a 2.5-mile loop with lush forests and amazing views of surrounding mountains and the Chitina River valley.

HIKING THE DIXIE PASS ROUTE

The 24-mile (round trip) Dixie Pass Route provides the best wilderness adventure that doesn't require a bush-plane charter. Plan to camp at the pass at least one or two days to take in the alpine beauty and investigate the nearby ridges. Such an itinerary requires three or four days and is moderately hard.

You reach the Dixie Pass trailhead by hiking 2.5 miles up Kotsina Rd from Strelna and then another 1.3 miles along Kotsina Rd after the Nugget Creek Trail splits off to the northeast. The trailhead is on the right-hand side of Kotsina Rd; look for a marker.

Stop at the park headquarters in Copper Center to complete a backcountry trip itinerary and pick up USGS quadrangle maps.

WHERE TO EAT & DRINK IN WRANGELL-ST ELIAS NATIONAL PARK

The Meatza Wagon
Serves excellent meaty, or non-meaty, dishes such as fish tacos and the signature meatball sub sandwich. **$**

As the Glacier Melts Cafe
Need coffee or ice cream? This is the (only) place for the best of both. **$**

Uncle Tom's Tavern
A long-running classic, this friendly dive serves up cold drinks and the occasional live band. **$**

Kennicott River bridge

Stop at the McCarthy Ranger Station kiosk at Mile 58.4 for the latest information regarding Wrangell-St Elias National Park, Kennecott Mines National Historical Landmark and the McCarthy area conditions.

At Mile 58.8, the McCarthy Rd comes to an end at Kennicott River bridge, a suspension bridge only for pedestrians and bikes that welcomes visitors to a definitely unconventional community. If you're staying overnight, utilize the hand carts for gear.

Walk another quarter mile to the heart of McCarthy for a meal, perhaps some live music and a dash of local personalities.

ADVENTURES BY PACKRAFT

Packrafts are small, inflatable boats that fit in a backpack, and are becoming a popular way to hike then float the rivers and lakes of Alaska's backcountry. Kennicott Wilderness Guides offers several trips for new packrafters, including a float on Kennicott Glacier Lake, where a packraft's maneuverability comes into play as paddlers circle small 'bergy bits' coming off the glacier's toe.

If a hike and raft experience sounds more appealing, the same company runs a full-day experience, starting with a trek through forests and along ridges to Upper Kennicott Lake. There, rafts are inflated and a paddle through ever-changing landscapes begins.

GETTING AROUND

The best bets for transiting around and between McCarthy and Kennecott are under one's own power. Mountain bikes and sturdy hiking shoes are the equipment of choice to fully experience the outdoorsy atmosphere of both communities. Even the most hardy adventurers can be in need of a ride, however, so the McCarthy Shuttle fulfils the need. Look for its kiosk and stops at Kennicott Glacier Lodge and near the footbridge in McCarthy.

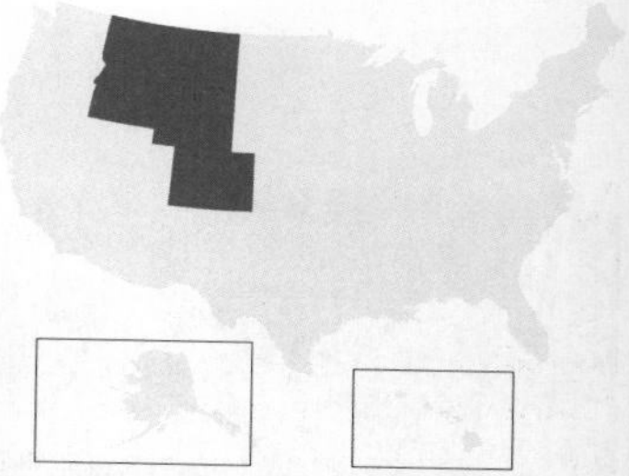

ROCKY MOUNTAINS

SOARING SUMMITS AND WILDLIFE-WATCHING

Chiseled peaks, topaz lakes and wildlife-rich valleys make a magnificent backdrop to hiking, climbing, boating or simply reconnecting with nature.

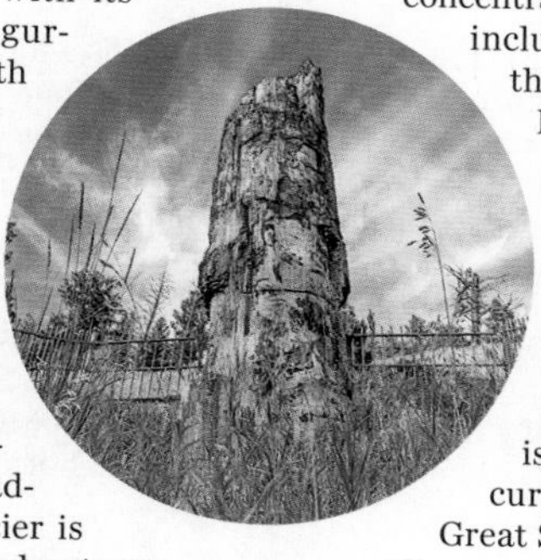

Awe-inspiring in their grandeur, the Rockies have captivated the imagination from the moment humans laid eyes on them. Yellowstone, the world's first national park, is the superstar, with its primordial geysers and gurgling mud pots, along with thundering herds of bison, roaring waterfalls and a stunning grand canyon of its own. Just south of there, the Grand Tetons have glacier-carved peaks and alpine lakes, with vestiges of a pioneering past hidden among its serene meadows. Farther north, Glacier is the gateway to wilderness adventures in summer and winter, with extraordinary hikes, cycling and cross-country skiing.

Colorado has three national parks in this swath of mountain country. Its oldest and most famous destination, Rocky Mountain, has drawn adventure seekers for over a century. Today, alpine lovers come from across the globe to experience the dense concentration of inspiring summits, including over a dozen peaks that stretch above 13,000ft. Lesser known Black Canyon of the Gunnison serves as a fine counterpoint to the sky-high landscape, with its multihued rock walls – some over a billion years old – that delve into the earth. Far to the south is one of the Rockies' most curious sites: the mirage-like Great Sand Dunes.

All are memorable places to experience the power of wild places, whether you're intent on climbing a cloud-scraping peak or spotting animals from the roadside.

THE MAIN AREAS

BLACK CANYON OF THE GUNNISON NATIONAL PARK
Hikes along the rim.
p264

GLACIER NATIONAL PARK
Grand views and scenic drives.
p266

GRAND TETON NATIONAL PARK
Adventures amid soaring peaks.
p277

MARGARET.WIKTOR/SHUTTERSTOCK ©

eft: Petrified Tree (p303), Yellowstone National Park; Above: Rocky Mountain National Park (p288)

GREAT SAND DUNES NATIONAL PARK
Sand-boarding and dramatic photos. **p286**

ROCKY MOUNTAIN NATIONAL PARK
Climb summits over 13,000ft. **p288**

YELLOWSTONE NATIONAL PARK
Watch bears, bison and geysers. **p291**

Find Your Way

The Rocky Mountains are home to some of the highest peaks in the lower 48. Though a rugged wilderness, these six national parks are all accessible by handy gateway towns.

Glacier National Park, p266
Mountain wilderness offering wide-ranging adventures: waterfall hikes, boat trips, as well as cycling a legendary road.

Yellowstone National Park, p291
The famed destination for geysers and other geothermal wonders also has breathtaking scenery and unrivaled wildlife watching.

Grand Teton National Park, p277
Chiseled peaks form the backdrop to hikes around lakes, through canyons and up steep mountain passes.

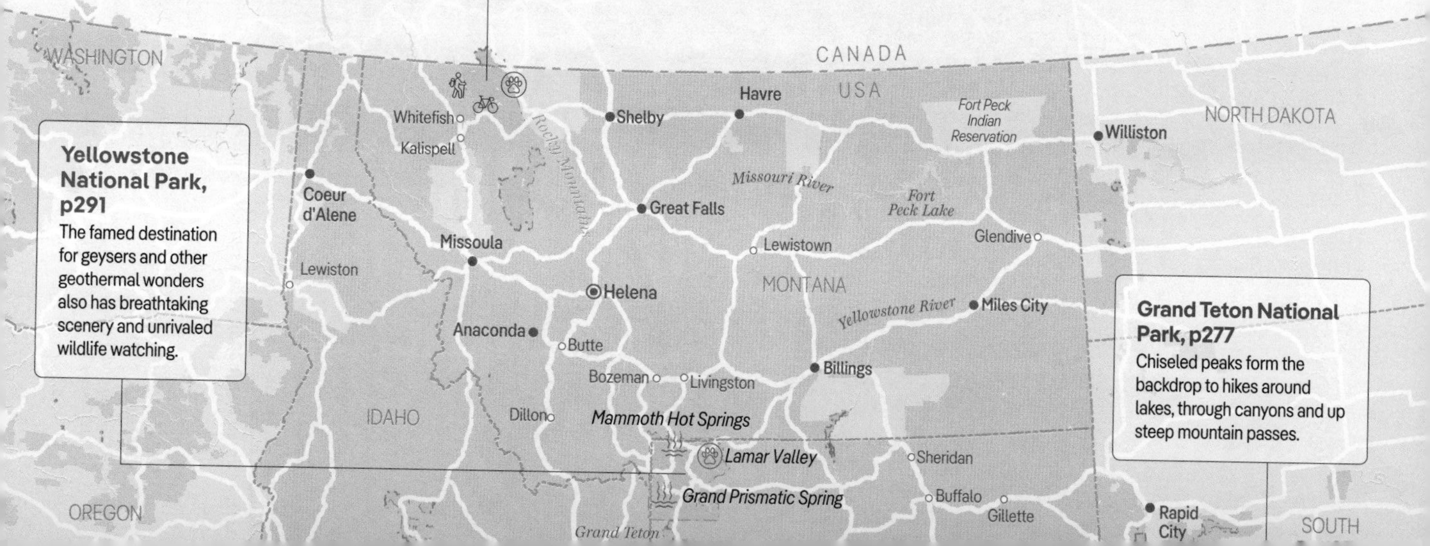

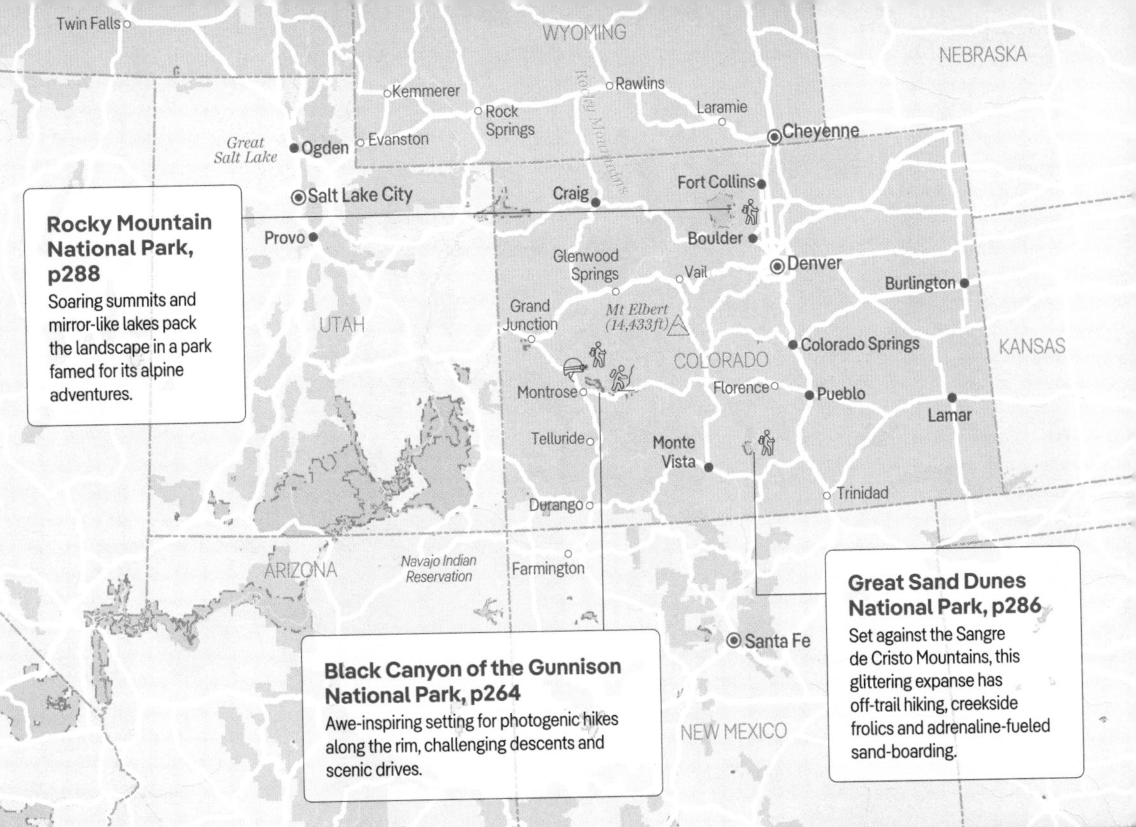

Rocky Mountain National Park, p288
Soaring summits and mirror-like lakes pack the landscape in a park famed for its alpine adventures.

Black Canyon of the Gunnison National Park, p264
Awe-inspiring setting for photogenic hikes along the rim, challenging descents and scenic drives.

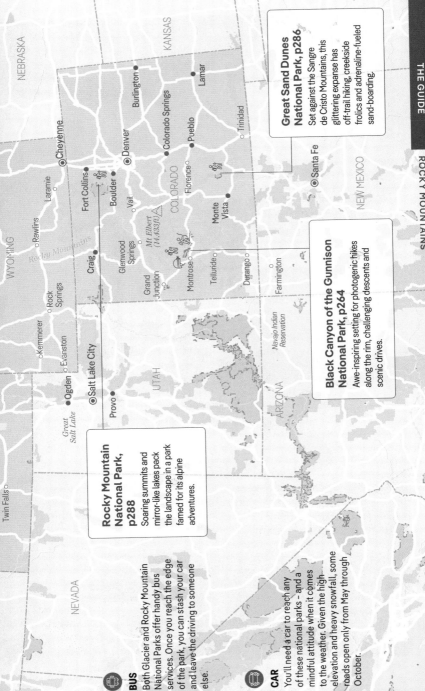

Great Sand Dunes National Park, p286
Set against the Sangre de Cristo Mountains, this glittering expanse has off-trail hiking, creekside frolics and adrenaline-fueled sand-boarding.

BUS

Both Glacier and Rocky Mountain National Parks offer handy bus services. Once you reach the edge of the park, you can stash your car and leave the driving to someone else.

CAR

You'll need a car to reach any of these national parks – and a mindful attitude when it comes to the weather. Given the high elevation and heavy snowfall, some roads open only from May through October.

Castle Geyser (p295), Yellowstone National Park

Rocky Mountain National Park (p288)

Plan Your Time

You could spend weeks exploring the Rocky Mountain parks. If time is limited, focus on a scenic drive and a key hike to give you a taste of each place.

Pressed for Time

Focus on America's oldest national park: **Yellowstone** (p291). Spend the morning taking in geysers and fumaroles. Later, check out the views of thundering falls through the **Grand Canyon of the Yellowstone** (p303). Before dark, look for wildlife in the **Lamar Valley** (p299). If you have another day, drive south to **Grand Teton** (p277) for a look at jagged peaks and shimmering lakes.

A Weeklong Road Trip

Enjoy a bit of sand-boarding in **Great Sand Dunes** (p286) followed by a splash in **Medano Creek** (p287). Drive northwest to gaze across the formations of **Black Canyon of the Gunnison** (p264). Hike amid lofty trails and wildflower-filled meadows of **Rocky Mountain National Park** (p288). Head to Wyoming for a grand finish in **Grand Teton** (p277) and **Yellowstone** (p291).

SEASONAL HIGHLIGHTS

SPRING

Many trails are still snowbound in the springtime, so spend your days looking for emerging wildlife.

SUMMER

High season brings heavy crowds to the roadways and trails, so plan on early-morning excursions and visits.

FALL

Early fall is an ideal time to explore the parks amid the blazing colors of aspens, cottonwoods and willows.

WINTER

Strap on those skis or snowshoes and hit the forested trails. Seeing the parks under heavy snowfall is pure magic.

BLACK CANYON OF THE GUNNISON NATIONAL PARK

The Colorado Rockies are known for their mountains, but the Black Canyon of the Gunnison National Park is the inverse geographic feature – a massive yawning chasm etched out over millions of years by the Gunnison River and volcanic uplift. Here a dark, narrow gash above the Gunnison River leads down a 2000ft chasm as eerie as it is spectacular.

No other canyon in America combines the narrow openings, sheer walls and dizzying depths of the Black Canyon, and a peek over the edge evokes a sense of awe (or vertigo). In just 48 canyon miles, the Gunnison River loses more elevation than the entire 1500-mile Mississippi. This fast-moving water, carrying rock and debris, is powerfully erosive. Without the upstream dams, the river would carry five times its current volume. Historically, this massive canyon has presented a formidable barrier. The Ute people settled the rim, but there's no evidence of human habitation within the chasm itself.

FACTS

Great For Family travel, scenery, walking
State Colorado
Entrance Fee 7-day pass per vehicle/pedestrian $30/15
Area 48 sq miles

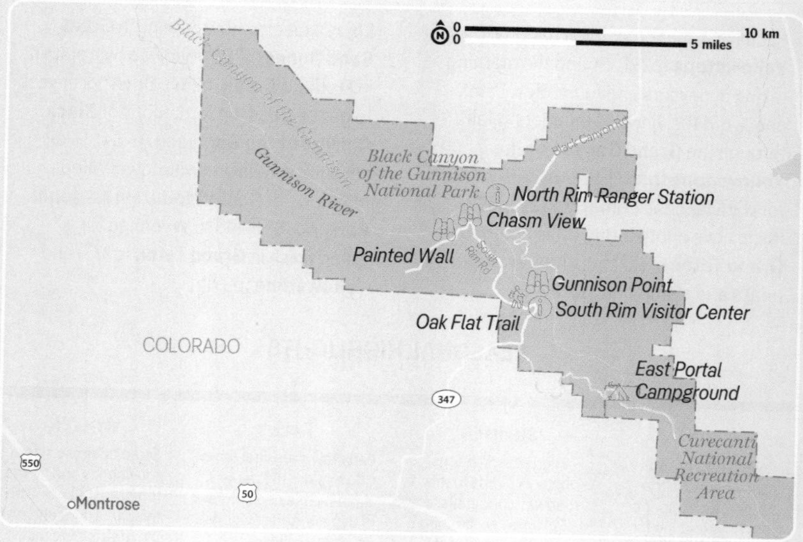

Painted Wall

Grand Vistas from the Road & Trail

HIKES AND SCENIC DRIVES

Before setting out, stop at the visitor center for the exhibits on resident wildlife and watch the short film that describes how this chiseled landscape was formed. The deck from the **South Rim Visitor Center** offers a staggering view over the canyon. From there, you can make the short walk out to **Gunnison Point**, which puts you right on the edge of the plunging sheer walls.

For something a little more strenuous, make the 2-mile round-trip loop along the **Oak Flat Trail** that takes you exploring below the rim. Start near the visitor center and turn right, which will take you on a descent through a grove of aspen before reaching Gambel oak scrub and some great views.

There are plenty of other rewarding overlooks. You can get the lay of the land on a scenic drive along the South Rim Rd.This 6-mile road visits 11 overlooks at the edge of the canyon, some reached via short trails up to 1.5 miles long (round-trip). At the narrowest part of Black Canyon, **Chasm View** is 1100ft across yet 1800ft deep. Rock climbers are frequently seen on the opposing North Wall.

You can get a less lofty view by following the East Portal Rd, a steep route (at 16% grade in places) with hairpin turns that takes you right down to the edge of the Gunnison River. There you'll find a small **campground** with 15 sites shaded by box elder trees. There's also a short trail that traces the edge of the Gunnison River and offers a tranquil picnic area.

WORLD-CLASS ROCK CLIMBING

Experienced rock climbers with their own equipment can get their kicks in Black Canyon. Most of the climbing in the park occurs on the North and South Chasms, which measure 1820ft. Black Canyon is also home to Colorado's tallest vertical cliff, **Painted Wall** – measuring 2300ft from the bottom of the canyon and named for its fabulous marble stripes – with a number of different climbing routes to the top.

Check the park's excellent website for information on specific routes and difficulty levels, as well as climbing updates – some routes close due to nesting raptors. You can book a climbing trip with **Irwin Guides**, a pro outfitter that takes you up legendary multi-pitch routes.

GETTING AROUND

The park is 12 miles east of the US 550 junction with US 50. Exit at Hwy 347 – well marked, with a big brown sign for the national park – and head north for 7 miles. In winter, the South Rim Rd stays open to Gunnison Point. The rest of this road and the North Rim Rd closes from November to mid-April.

GLACIER NATIONAL PARK

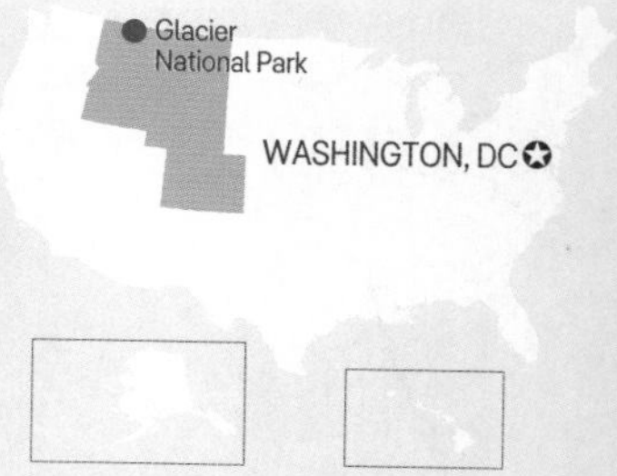

Few places on earth are as magnificent and pristine as Glacier. Protected in 1910 during the first flowering of the American conservationist movement, Glacier ranks with Yellowstone, Yosemite and the Grand Canyon among the United States' most astounding natural wonders.

The glacially carved remnants of an ancient thrust fault have left a brilliant landscape of towering snowcapped pinnacles laced with plunging waterfalls and glassy turquoise lakes. The mountains are surrounded by dense forests, which host a virtually intact pre-Columbian ecosystem. Grizzly bears still roam in abundance, along with grazing moose and fat-bellied marmots. Smart park management has kept the place accessible and authentically wild.

Glacier is renowned for its historic 'parkitecture' lodges, the spectacular Going-to-the-Sun Rd and 740 miles of hiking trails. These all put visitors within easy reach of some 1489 sq miles of the wild and astonishing landscapes found at the crown of the continent.

FACTS

Great For Wildlife, scenery, walking
State Montana
Entrance Fee 7-day vehicle pass $35
Area 1583 sq miles

SEAN XU/SHUTTERSTOCK ©

Two Medicine Lake (p272)

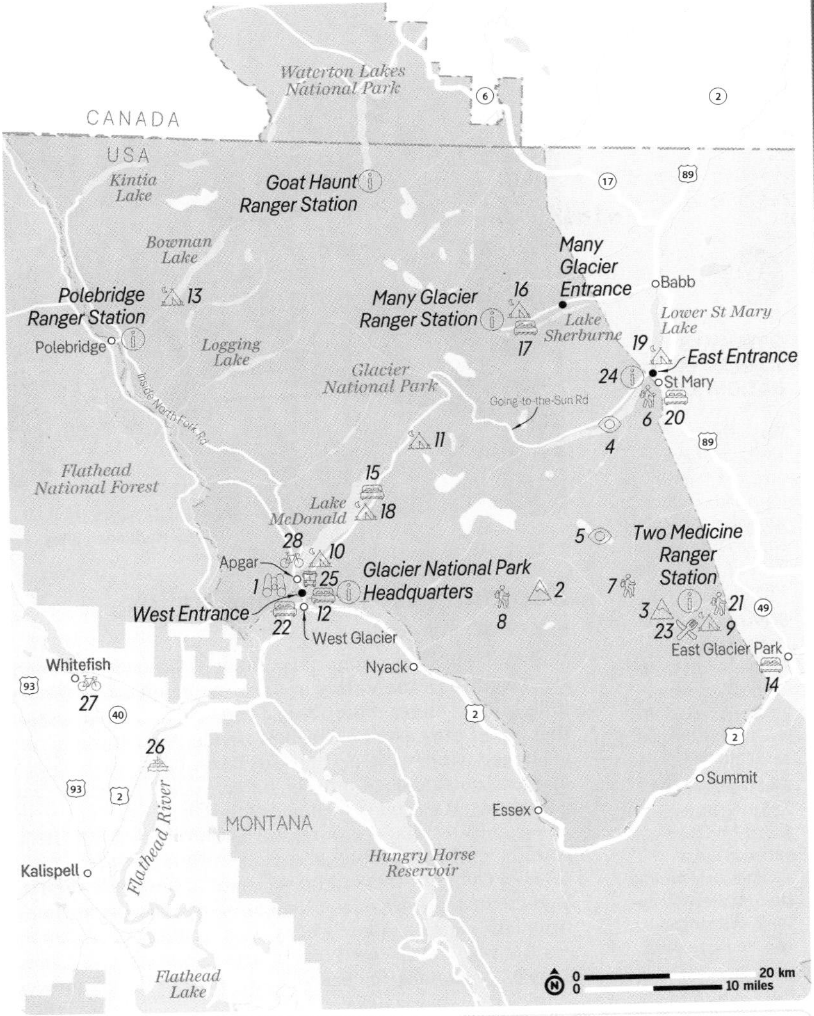

SIGHTS
1 Apgar Lookout
2 Mt Stimson
3 Rising Wolf Mountain
4 St Mary Lake
5 Triple Divide Peak

ACTIVITIES, COURSES & TOURS
6 Beaver Pond Trail
7 Cut Bank Pass
8 Nyack Creek
9 Two Medicine Valley

SLEEPING
10 Apgar Campground
11 Avalanche Creek Campground
12 Belton Chalet
13 Bowman Lake Campground
14 Brownies
15 Lake McDonald Lodge
16 Many Glacier Campground
17 Many Glacier Hotel
18 Sprague Creek Campground
19 St Mary KOA Campground
20 St Mary Village
21 Two Medicine Campground
22 West Glacier Village

EATING
23 Two Medicine Campstore

INFORMATION
24 St Mary Visitor Center

TRANSPORT
25 Apgar Transit Center
26 Flathead River
27 Glacier Cyclery
28 Go Glacier Outfitters

DANIEL DRSW/SHUTTERSTOCK ©

Two Medicine Valley

GATEWAYS TO GLACIER NATIONAL PARK

West Glacier
The park's most pleasant gateway town and the base for white-water rafting and kayak trips. Also has an Amtrak train station.

St Mary KOA Campground
A motel and a lodge on the Blackfeet Indian Reservation just outside the park's east entrance.

East Glacier Park
Good dining and accommodation options, plus a summer-only Amtrak stop, located 10 miles south of spectacular Two Medicine Valley.

Whitefish
Equal parts rustic and hip, Whitefish has an attractive stash of restaurants, a historic train station and an underrated ski resort.

Exploring Two Medicine Valley

HIKES AND HYDROLOGIC WONDERS

With no hotels, no restaurants and only one dead-end road, the **Two Medicine Valley** is a favorite haunt for ambitious hikers intent on reaching one of a trio of high-altitude passes that guard the gusty Continental Divide. More intrepid hikers forge further west, beyond **Cut Bank Pass**, where faintly marked trails descend into the barely visited **Nyack Creek** wilderness. It's a rough mélange of fordable rivers and primitive campsites that surround the isolated hulk of **Mt Stimson**, the park's second-highest peak at 10,142ft.

Before Going-to-the-Sun Rd was built in the 1930s, the Two Medicine Valley was one of the park's most accessible hubs, situated a mere 12 miles by horseback from the Great Northern Railway and the newly inaugurated Glacier Park Lodge. Famous for its healthy bear population and deeply imbued with Native American legends, the region is less visited these days, though it has lost none of its haunting beauty. Hikers can grab a picnic at the historic **Two Medicine Campstore**, once the dining hall for the now defunct Two Medicine Chalets and the venue for one of President FD Roosevelt's famous 'fireside chats.' Towering authoritatively over sublime Two

WHERE TO PITCH A TENT

Bowman Lake Campground
Spacious sites in forested grounds, and beautiful Bowman Lake is only steps away. **$**

Two Medicine Campground
A picturesque area with nicely wooded sites and easy lake and creek access. **$**

Sprague Creek Campground
A smaller, more intimate park option on the shoreline of Lake McDonald. **$**

CRUISING ALONG GOING-TO-THE-SUN ROAD

The spectacular 53-mile Going-to-the-Sun Rd starts at the park's western entrance before tracking northeast along **1 Lake McDonald**. Characterized by the famous Lake McDonald Lodge, the valley here is lush and verdant, though a quick glance through the trees will highlight the graphic evidence of the 2003 Robert Fire on the opposite side of the water.

After following McDonald Creek for about 10 miles, the road begins its long, slow ascent to Logan Pass, with a sharp turn to the southeast at **2 The Loop**, a famous hiking trailhead and the start of an increasingly precipitous climb toward the summit. Views here are unfailingly sublime as the road cuts precariously into the **3 Garden Wall**, a 8999ft granite ridge that delineates the west and east regions of the park along the Continental Divide. Look out for Bird Woman Falls, stunning even from a distance, and the more in-your-face **4 Weeping Wall**, as the gaping chasm to your right grows ever deeper.

Descending eastwards, keep an eye out for majestic Going-to-the-Sun Mountain, omnipresent to the north. At the 36-mile mark, you can pull over to spy one of only 25 remaining park glaciers at the **5 Jackson Glacier Overlook**, while a few clicks further on, you can sample narrow **6 Sunrift Gorge** near the shores of St Mary Lake. **7 Wild Goose Island**, a photogenic stub of land, is situated in the center of the lake. The 2015 Reynolds Creek fire, which thinned out much of the east side's tree cover, has also revealed new vistas and perspectives not previously accessible.

The **8 St Mary Visitor Center** on the lake's eastern shore is journey's end. The plains on this side of the park stretch east from St Mary to Minneapolis.

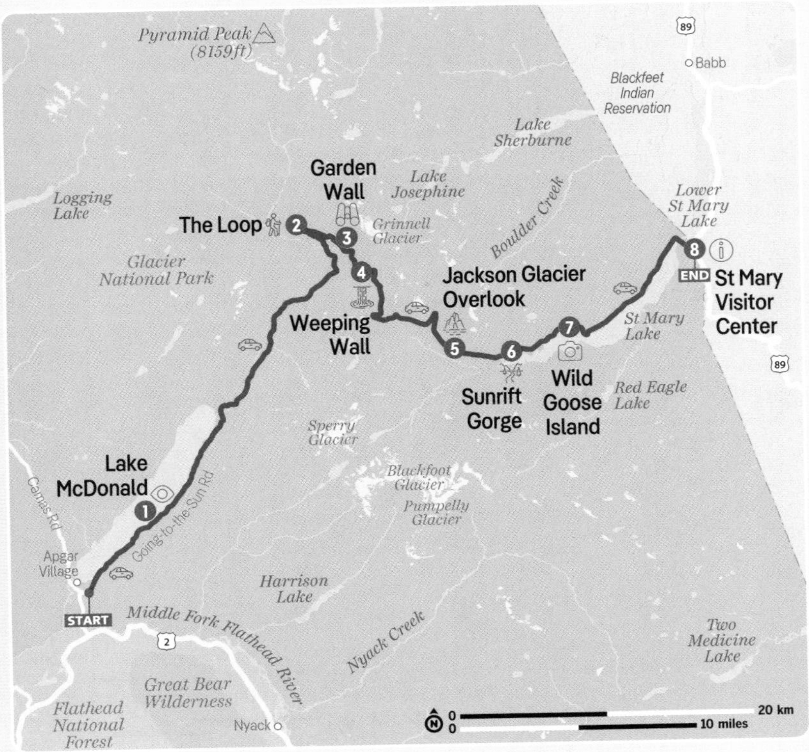

EXPLORING HIDDEN LAKE OVERLOOK TRAIL

One of Glacier's best-known hiking spots, the three-mile (round-trip) Hidden Lake Overlook Trail is justly famed for its great views coupled with the chance to see wildlife. You can beat the crowds by getting an early-morning or late-afternoon start. Minimal elevation gain (just 494ft of climbing) make this a fairly easy outing, which can be completed in around two hours.

From the busy **1 Logan Pass Visitor Center**, the hike ascends gradually along a raised boardwalk (with steps) through expansive alpine meadows replete with monkey-flower and pink laurel. Slippery melting snowfields add a challenge for those who decided to wear flip-flops, but, rain or shine, this trail is a hit with everyone – from adventurous toddlers to spry septuagenarians.

After a bit over half a mile, the boardwalk gives way to a gravelly dirt path. If the snow has melted, the diversity of grasses and wildflowers in the meadows around you is breathtaking. Resident trees include Engelmann spruce, subalpine fir and whitebark pine. Hoary marmots, ground squirrels and mountain goats are not shy along this trail. Up-close mountain views include **2 Clements Mountain** north of the trail and **3 Reynolds Mountain** in the southeast.

About 300yd before the overlook, you will cross the Continental Divide – probably without realizing it – before your first stunning glimpse of the otherworldly, deep-blue **4 Hidden Lake** (and a realization of what all the fuss is about), bordered by mountain peaks and rocky cliffs. Look out for glistening Sperry Glacier visible to the south.

Hearty souls can continue on to Hidden Lake via a 1.5-mile trail from the overlook, steeply descending 765ft.

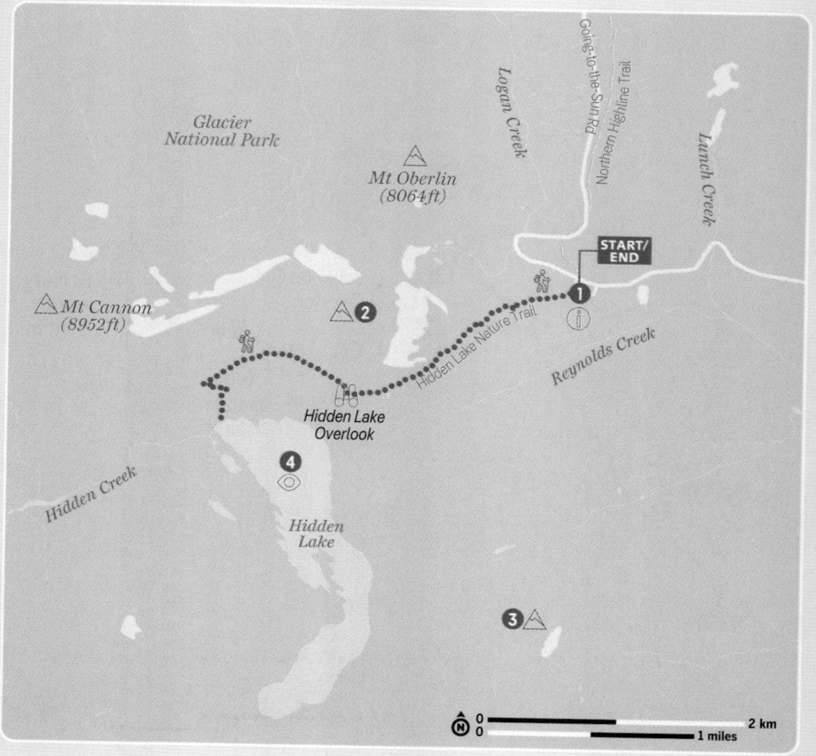

Medicine Lake is the distinctive hulk of **Rising Wolf Mountain**, named for Canadian-turned-Piegan-Native-American Hugh Monroe, who was the first white person to explore the region in the mid-19th century.

Located around 3 miles to the northwest, 8020ft **Triple Divide Peak** marks the hydrologic apex of the North American continent. Empty a bucket of water on its summit and it will run into three separate oceans: the Pacific, the Atlantic and the Arctic.

Visiting St Mary Lake

DRAMATIC PANORAMAS

Located on the park's dryer eastern side, where the mountains melt imperceptibly into the Great Plains, **St Mary Lake** lies in a deep, glacier-carved valley famous for its astounding views and ferocious winds. The 2015 Reynolds Creek fire dramatically thinned the northern slopes from the lake shore to Going-to-the-Sun Rd, but the valley views – overlooked by the tall, chiseled peaks of the Rockies – are still spectacular and punctuated by numerous trailheads and viewpoints.

St Mary's gorgeous turquoise sheen, easily the most striking color of any of Glacier's major bodies of water, is due to the suspension of tiny particles of glacial rock in the lake's water that absorbs and reflects light. The landscape-altering effects of the 2006 Red Eagle Fire is still very much visible on the southern slopes of the lake.

A good place for learning more about the park is at the **St Mary Visitor Center**. Here you'll find intriguing exhibits on wildlife, geology and Native American culture and history, as well as an auditorium featuring slideshows and ranger talks. For over 35 years, the **Native America Speaks program** has connected visitors with the stories, history and culture of the Blackfeet, Salish and Kootenai tribes. Check the seasonal schedule for days and times.

Various hiking trails stretch along the south side of the lake. For a short walk with the chance to see wildlife, head along the **Beaver Pond Trail**, a 3.3-mile loop that passes through meadows and old-growth conifer forest. Keep an eye out for the trail's namesake when you reach the beaver pond. Moose are also sometimes spotted in the area.

Aquatic Activities

BOAT RIDES, KAYAKING AND RAFTING

The loaded-up school buses ferrying groups from outfitters in and around West Glacier and Hwy 2 give you an idea of **rafting**'s popularity. All tours take place on or outside the

PARK REGIONS AT A GLANCE

North Fork (northwest)
A seldom-visited area with the isolated settlement of Polebridge.

Lake McDonald Valley (west)
The park's largest lake has Apgar village, Lake McDonald Lodge, and the west end of Going-to-the-Sun Rd.

Two Medicine (southeast)
A less-visited lake area that was once the center of east-side activity.

St Mary (east)
The eastern end of Going-to-the-Sun Rd has multiple hiking trails.

Many Glacier (northeast)
Towering peaks box in a lake and the park's most dramatic lodge location.

Goat Haunt (north)
A hikers' paradise, accessible via boat from Canada.

WHERE TO PITCH A TENT

Many Glacier Campground
With access to phenomenal trails, this heavily wooded campground is one of the most popular. **$**

Apgar Campground
This wooded campground, the park's largest, lies near the conveniences of Apgar Village and West Glacier. **$**

Avalanche Creek Campground
Lush campground abutting the park's old-growth cedar forest close to Lake McDonald. **$**

FREEBILLY PHOTOGRAPHY/SHUTTERSTOCK ©

St Mary Lake (p271)

BEST BOATING & HIKING COMBOS

One of Glacier Park Boat Company's best excursions leaves from the Many Glacier Hotel twice daily (July to September), chugging across Swiftcurrent Lake. Groups disembark on the southern shore and stroll to Lake Josephine, where another boat whisks you to another landing; from here your guide leads you a further 1.5 miles overland to Grinnell Lake for wondrous glacial views.

A similar boat-hike combo can be undertaken on Two Medicine Lake, which marries a 45-minute cruise with a 2-mile walk to double-flumed Twin Falls.

Reserve your excursion online through glacierpark boats.com.

park's boundaries, primarily on the North and Middle Forks of the **Flathead River**. The best water flow is from May to September, with the rapids ranking an unterrifying class I to III. All of the operators can customize highly recommended overnight adventures on the North Fork from near the Canadian border (tents and sleeping gear are provided). Or you can float down McDonald Creek on your own inner tubes. Glacier Raft Company or Glacier Guides and Montana Raft are two highly recommended outfitters.

McDonald, Bowman, Swiftcurrent, Two Medicine and St Mary lakes have launching ramps available for boats. Sailors might find St Mary Lake's winds to their liking. Stand-up paddleboarding is popular on Lake McDonald, and you can rent gear from Flathead Outdoors, located at Eddie's Cafe, and from Glacier Outfitters in Apgar. Another great spot for paddling adventures is at Bowman Lake in the North Country.

For scenic boat rides, check out the offerings of Glacier Park Boat Company. Six historic boats – some dating back to the 1920s – ply five of Glacier's attractive mountain lakes, and some of them combine the float with a short guided hike led by interpretive, often witty, ranger guides. For those looking for a bit of a workout, it also rents rowboats, kayaks and paddleboards at Lake McDonald, Many Glacier and Two Medicine.

WHERE TO SPEND THE NIGHT

Many Glacier Hotel
A massive, Swiss chalet–inspired lodge in a wondrous lakefront setting in the park. $$$

Belton Chalet
Elegant rooms, arts-and-crafts-style furnishings and a celebrated taproom in West Glacier. $$$

Lake McDonald Lodge
Comfortably rustic rooms and cottages fronting Lake McDonald and built in classic US 'parkitecture' style. $$$

CLIMBING THE HIGHLINE TRAIL

A Glacier classic, the Highline Trail cuts across the famous Garden Wall, a sharp, glacier-carved ridge that forms part of the Continental Divide. The stupendous views here are some of the best in the park and, with little elevation gain throughout its course, the treats come with minimal effort.

The moderately challenging, 11.6-mile (one-way) trail starts at **1 Logan Pass Visitor Center**, and kicks off with a bang. Cutting immediately into the side of the mountain (a garden-hose-like rope is tethered to the rock wall for those with vertigo), the trail presents stunning early views of the **2 Going-to-the-Sun Rd** and snowcapped Heavens Peak. Look out for the toy-sized red 'jammer' buses motoring up the valley below and the white foaming waters of 500ft **3 Bird Woman Falls** opposite.

After its vertiginous start, the trail is flat for 1.8 miles before gently ascending to a ridge that connects **4 Haystack Butte** with **5 Mt Gould** at the 3.5-mile mark. From here it's fairly flat as you bisect the mountainside on your way toward the Granite Park Chalet.

After approximately 6.8 miles, with the chalet in sight, a spur path on your right offers the option of climbing up less than 1 mile to the **6 Grinnell Glacier Overlook** for a peek over the Continental Divide. The **7 Granite Park Chalet** appears at around 7.6 miles, providing a welcome haven for parched throats and tired feet.

From here you have three options: retrace your steps back to Logan Pass; head for Swiftcurrent Pass and the Many Glacier Valley; or descend 4 miles to **8 The Loop**, where you can pick up a shuttle bus to all points on the Going-to-the-Sun Rd.

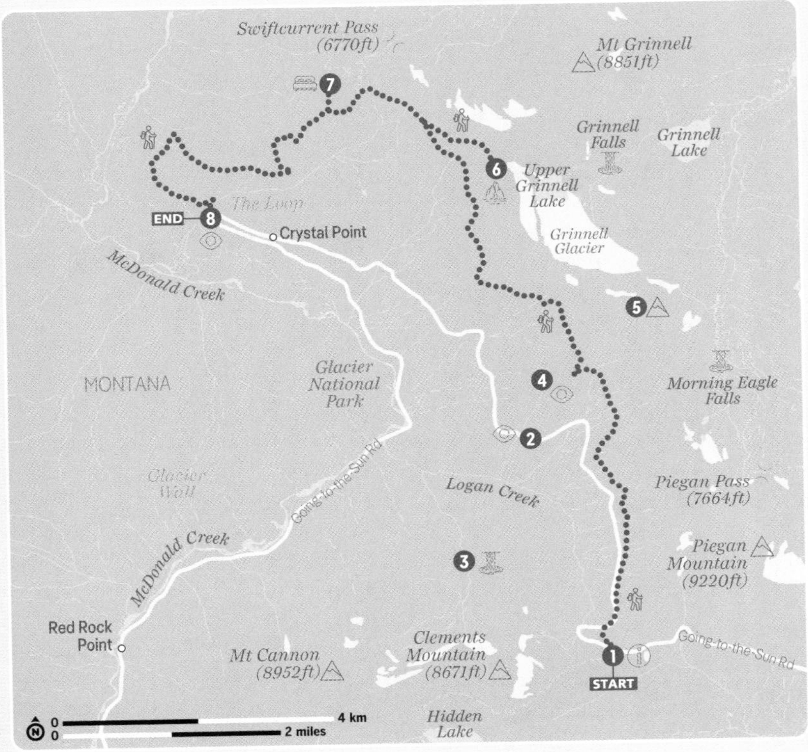

EXPERIENCE THE SUN POINT TO VIRGINIA FALLS HIKE

Handily served by the free park shuttle, the myriad trailheads along the eastern side of Going-to-the-Sun Road offer plenty of short interlinking hikes, a number of which can be pooled together to make up a decent morning or afternoon ramble. Post-fire, wildflowers are beginning to flourish and new vistas, once obscured by foliage, are now available.

This particular variation takes you on a seven-mile (round-trip hike), which takes you to a tempestuous trio of waterfalls, all amid the burned-out timber of the 2015 Reynolds Creek Fire. You'll start at the **1 Sun Point** shuttle stop, where you can track down a quarter-mile trail to a rocky (and often windy) overlook perched above sparkling St Mary Lake. In the 1910s, the Great Northern Railway built some of Glacier's earliest and showiest chalets here in an accommodation chain that stretched from Many Glacier to the Sperry and Granite Park Chalets. Falling into neglect after WWII, the Sun Point chalets were demolished in 1949, though the view remains timeless.

Take the path west through sun-flecked forest along the lake toward **2 Baring Falls**, at just past the half-mile mark, for a respite from the sun and/or wind. After admiring the gushing cascades, cross the river and continue on the opposite bank to link up with the busy **3 St Mary Falls** Trail that joins from the right. Undemanding switchbacks lead up through the trees to the valley's most picturesque falls on the St Mary River. Beyond here, the trail branches along Virginia Creek, past a narrow gorge, to mist-shrouded (and quieter) **4 Virginia Falls** at the foot of a hanging valley.

Retrace your steps to Sun Point for the full-length hike or, if your legs start to tire, shortcut to the St Mary Falls or Sunrift Gorge shuttle stops (follow the signs) and hop on a bus.

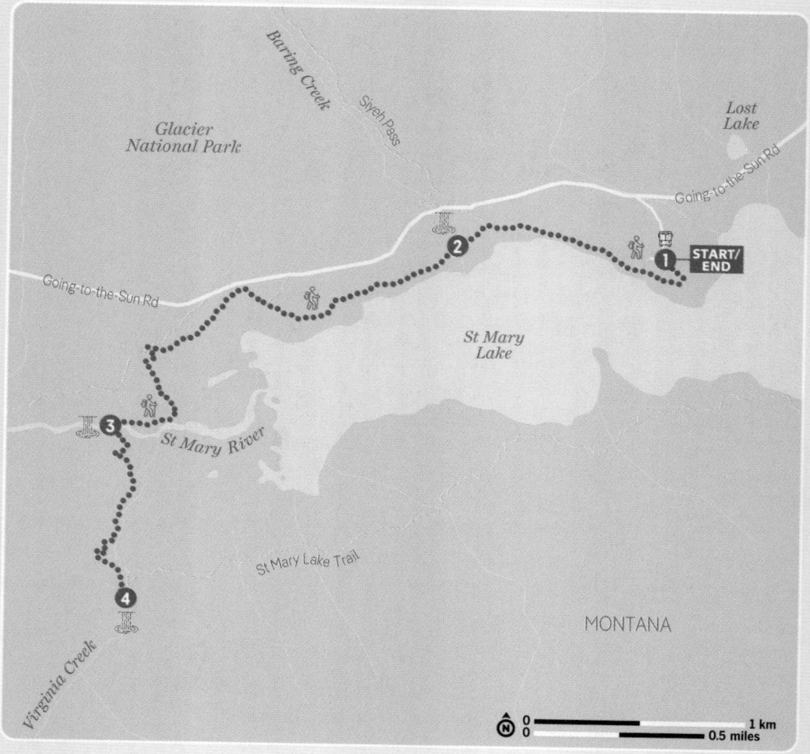

Going-to-the-Sun Road

Cycling in Glacier National Park

CHALLENGING ASCENTS AND REWARDING VIEWS

Despite the limitations, committed cyclists can be spied daily throughout summer attempting the 53-mile Going-to-the-Sun Rd, where the spectacular vistas and copious twists and turns are befitting of a challenging Tour de France stage. The best time to go is early in the season, when sections of the road are open to cyclists only (typically weekends from May to mid-June).

For safety and congestion reasons, the upper stretches of the road are officially shut to cyclists between 11am and 4pm daily (mid-June to Labor Day), so you'll need to be flexible with your schedule. If you do decide to go, start early, pack plenty of water and take extreme care on the long and potentially precarious descents. From a physical point of view, it's easier to start your ride in St Mary and tackle the climb east–west.

The closest thing to a mountain-biking venture in the park is the Inside North Fork Rd (Glacier Rte 7) to Kintla Lake. Cyclists craving trail rides should consider heading across the border into Canada to visit Waterton Lakes National Park, which has five trails.

VINTAGE EXCURSIONS

Glacier's stylish red 'jammer' buses (so-called because drivers had to 'jam' hard on the gears) are iconic park symbols. Guided tours take visitors along eight different routes, on three- to eight-hour journeys. The open-roof buses were introduced on the Going-to-the-Sun Rd between 1936 and 1939. They have been serving the park loyally, save for a two-year sabbatical in 1999 when the fleet was reconfigured by the Ford Motor Company. After an extensive makeover, they are safer, sturdier and more environmentally friendly. The drivers provide excellent information about what you are seeing during the drive, though the four-person seats can be cramped and you may not have the best views from the middle.

WHERE TO SPEND THE NIGHT

Brownies
Above a bakery, this nicely designed hostel has both dorms and small rustic private doubles. $

St Mary Village
This expansive place has a wide array of rooms and cabins, with ample dining options. $$

West Glacier Village
No-frills motel and cabins that offers good value for its location near the park entrance. $$

You'll encounter plenty of colorfully clad cyclists just outside the park's eastern boundary, plying Hwys 49 and 89, on the edge of the Blackfeet Indian Reservation. Inclines here are gentler, although the stiff winds off the adjacent prairies can be punishing.

You can find cruisers, mountain bikes, road bikes and e-bikes at **Go Glacier Outfitters** on the west side of the park in Apgar Village, and a stash of basic bikes (including e-bikes) in the **St Mary KOA Campground** on the east side. Top-quality bicycles are available at **Glacier Cyclery** in Whitefish, 45 miles southwest.

Wintertime Adventures

SKIING AND SNOWSHOEING

From October to May, when Going-to-the-Sun Rd is snowed under, most services in Glacier close, leaving the park to wildlife and intrepid, self-sufficient cross-country skiers and snowshoers, most of whom base themselves in Whitefish or Kalispell.

Cross-country skiers can choose from a number of popular marked but ungroomed trails in the park itself, the bulk of them emanating from Apgar Village and Lake McDonald. A well-used favorite is to ski along an unplowed section of Going-to-the-Sun Rd from the (closed) Lake McDonald Lodge to Avalanche Creek. The road is always plowed as far as the lodge, allowing easy access by car. Another regularly tackled trail is the 11.5-mile **McGee Meadow Loop** heading up the unplowed Camas Rd and back down the Inside Fork Rd to Apgar Village. Far more difficult is the steep 5.2-mile ascent to the **Apgar Lookout**.

Other, lesser-used park penetration points are St Mary for the Red Eagle Lake Trail, Polebridge for the Bowman Lake Trail, and Two Medicine for the unplowed Two Medicine Rd as far as Running Eagle Falls.

Although all hotels and restaurants stay closed, and the park registers only a handful of visitors, Glacier's mountains and valleys remain gloriously open all winter to those intrepid enough to breach them. For ultimate safety, organize a guided backcountry tour by skis or snowshoes with **Glacier Adventure Guides**, which operates out of Columbia Falls, MT. Day rates hover at around $200 per person, including the use of equipment.

VEHICLE RESERVATIONS

In an effort to cut down on the heavy traffic on park roads, Glacier officials launched a vehicle reservation system in 2021. A vehicle reservation is now required for both cars and motorcycles when visiting four areas of the park during the following times:

- Going-to-the-Sun Road (May 26–September 10)
- North Fork (May 26–September 10)
- Many Glacier (July 1–September 10)
- Two Medicine (July 1–September 10)

Reservations ($2) are valid for one day only and don't include the park admission fee. Reservations are not required if you enter the park before 6am or after 3pm.

GETTING AROUND

From July 1 until Labor Day, Glacier National Park runs a free hop-on, hop-off shuttle bus from **Apgar Transit Center** to St Mary over Going-to-the-Sun Rd; it stops at all major trailheads. Xanterra concession operates the classic guided Red Bus Tours.

If driving a personal vehicle, be prepared for narrow, winding roads, traffic jams, and limited parking at most stops along Going-to-the-Sun Rd. You'll also need to make a vehicle reservation.

GRAND TETON NATIONAL PARK

Awe-inspiring in their grandeur, the Tetons have captivated the imagination from the moment humans laid eyes on them. Some 12 imposing glacier-carved summits frame the singular Grand Teton (13,775ft). Many of the mountains consist of gneiss, formed some 2.7 billion years ago. Ironically, the mountain range itself is one of the continent's youngest, uplifting for less than 10 million years.

While the view is breathtaking from the valley floor, it only gets more impressive on the trail. It's well worth hiking the dramatic canyons of fragrant forest to sublime alpine lakes surrounded by wildflowers in summer. Aside from hiking and taking in scenic views, the lake-filled national park is a prime spot for kayaking, cycling along vehicle-free paths, and visiting historic sites left behind by early pioneers. In winter, the Tetons make a magical setting for snowshoeing and cross-country skiing.

FACTS

Great For Wildlife, scenery, walking
State Wyoming
Entrance Fee 7-day pass per vehicle/pedestrian $35/20
Area 485 sq miles

Grand Teton National Park

GRAND TETON NATIONAL PARK

SIGHTS
1 Inspiration Point
2 Jackson Lake
3 Leigh Lake
4 String Lake

ACTIVITIES, COURSES & TOURS
5 Cascade Canyon
6 Jenny Lake Trail
7 Moose Pond
8 String Lake Trailhead

EATING
9 Blue Heron
10 Dornan's Pizza & Pasta Company
11 Leek's Marina
12 Ranch House
13 Trapper Grill

INFORMATION
14 Jenny Lake Visitor Center

TRANSPORT
15 Colter Bay Marina
16 Jenny Lake Boating
17 Signal Mountain Marina
18 Solitude Float Trips
19 Triangle X Ranch

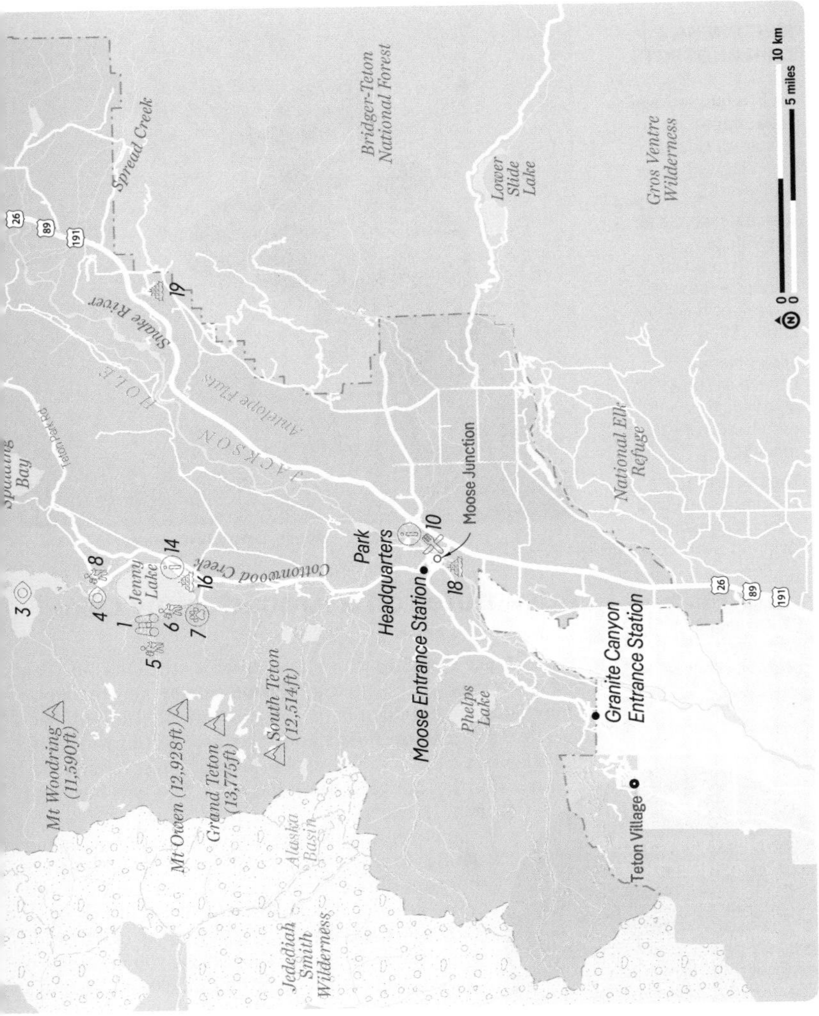
Bridger-Teton National Forest
Spread Creek
Lower Slide Lake
Gros Ventre Wilderness
Snake River
Antelope Flats
JACKSON HOLE
Teton Park Rd
Spalding Bay
National Elk Refuge
Moose Junction
Park Headquarters
Moose Entrance Station
Cottonwood Creek
Jenny Lake
Mt Woodring (11,590ft)
Mt Owen (12,928ft)
Grand Teton (13,775ft)
South Teton (12,514ft)
Alaska Basin
Jedediah Smith Wilderness
Phelps Lake
Granite Canyon Entrance Station
Teton Village
26
89
191
1
3
4
5
6
7
8
10
14
16
18
19
0
10 km
5 miles

BEST DINING & DRINKING SPOTS

Blue Heron, Jackson Lake Lodge
A must for sunset cocktails, with huge windows. $$

Ranch House, Colter Bay Village
Comfort fare, with vegetarian options, and a huge breakfast buffet. $$

Leek's Marina
End the day on a high note with pizza and draft beer on the patio. $$

Trapper Grill
Tuck into pan-seared trout while enjoying lakefront views from the deck. $$

Dornan's Pizza & Pasta Company
Satisfying food, craft beers and impressive views. $$

Moose, Grand Teton National Park

THE YELLOWSTONE CONNECTION

Yellowstone (p291) lies just north of Grand Teton, and you can drive from one to the other without leaving national park territory. It's 40 miles (an hour's drive) from Colter Bay Village to West Thumb.

Adventures on & Around Jenny Lake

BOATING AND LAKE STROLLS

Jenny Lake Boating runs shuttles across the lake between the east-shore dock near the **visitor center** and the west-shore dock near Hidden Falls, offering quick (12-minute) access to **Inspiration Point** and the Cascade Canyon Trail. Shuttles run every 15 minutes but expect long waits for return shuttles between 4pm and 6pm. You can buy your tickets at the dock.

If you prefer to walk, from the visitor center it's about 2.5 miles to reach Hidden Falls, then continues for a short uphill run to fine views at Inspiration Point. If you've come this far, it's worth continuing up to **Cascade Canyon** with a good supply of water for more excellent views. From here, you can return the way you came or continue clockwise 1.5 miles to the **String Lake Trailhead** to make a 3.8-mile circle around the lake. If you're walking the **Jenny Lake Trail** in the early morning or late afternoon, detour approximately 15 minutes (about 0.5 miles) from the visitor center to **Moose Pond** for a good chance of spotting moose.

PARK LODGES & CABINS

Jackson Lake Lodge
Attractive hotel-style rooms, some with mountain views, as well as comfortably furnished cottages. **$$$**

Jenny Lake Lodge
Jenny Lake's rustically elegant cabins are a short walk from String Lake and Jenny Lake. **$$$**

Colter Bay Village
This busy but forested area has inviting log cabins, tent cabins and a campground. **$$$**

This scenic loop with its fantastic views begins 8 miles north of Jackson at **1 Moose Junction**. Follow Hwy 191 north past Blacktail Ponds Overlook and Glacier View Turnout. Seven miles after Moose Junction, **2 Snake River Overlook** has views of the braided channels of the Snake River. Dense cottonwoods, willows and Engelmann spruce provide an excellent habitat for moose and deer. Stop at **3 Cunningham Cabin**, the site of an 1892 shoot-out when a band of self-deputized locals sought to root out rumored horse thieves. Now the historic spot is overrun with homesteading ground squirrels. At Moran Junction bear left, continuing on 191. The hulking peak of Mt Moran looms to the west, bearing five glaciers. Stop about 3.5 miles later at **4 Oxbow Bend** to look for fishing eagles, ospreys and trumpeter swans. Long-legged great blue herons stalk the shallows. Head south along Teton Park Rd at Jackson Lake Junction. The rustic 1930s **5 Log Chapel of the Sacred Heart** follows. On your left, you will see a sign for **6 Signal Mountain Rd**, a 5-mile climb. You can detour here or continue straight ahead. Turn on the one-way **7 Jenny Lake Scenic Dr**, twisting through a forested area with the tantalizing spires of the Tetons just across the lake. It will deposit you back on Teton Park Rd. On the left just before Moose Junction, you will see **8 Menor's Ferry Historic District**. The brainchild of Bill Menor, the ferry provided the only transportation across the river. In the same area, the log **9 Chapel of the Transfiguration**, built in 1924, still holds church services. Return to the main road and follow it until it exits the park at Moose Junction.

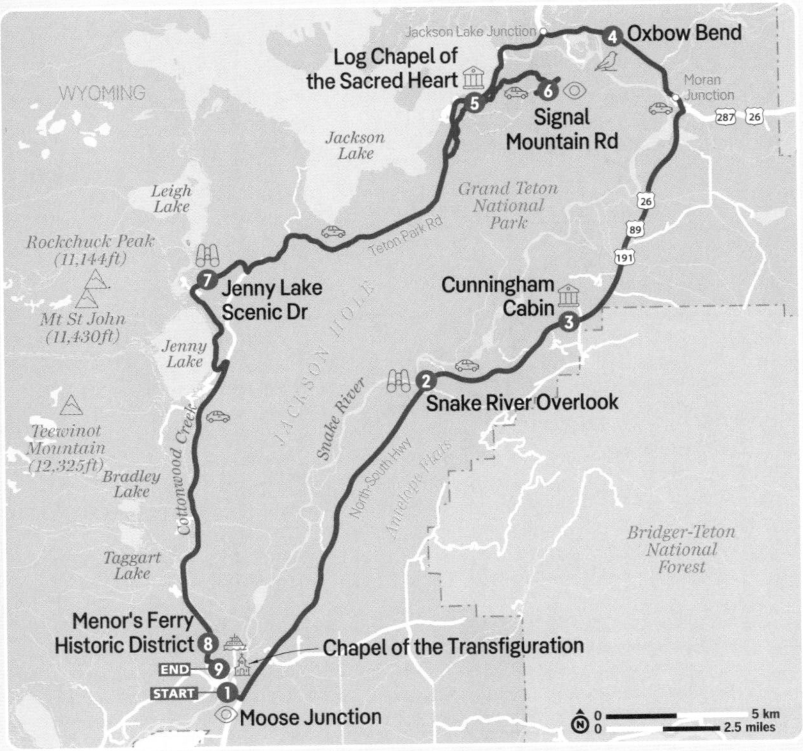

HIKING TAGGART & BRADLEY LAKES

One of the best options for a relatively easy 6-mile hike for the whole family is to head to Taggart and Bradley. This pair of glacial lakes sits at the base of the Tetons, surrounded by grassy areas thick with summer wildflowers and fragrant pine forest. The terrain is open from earlier fires, so it's a bit easier to spot wildlife, particularly moose. The trails here offer several easy loop options ranging from around 3 to 5 miles. Plan an early start in summer since much of the trail lacks shade. Don't forget your swimsuit. The **1 Taggart Lake Trailhead** is just off Teton Park Rd, 5 miles north of Moose. Follow the trail northwest, past horse corrals, and take the first left at a **2 marked signpost** after 0.2 miles. Although this trail is only slightly longer, it receives far less traffic than the other option. After another 1.4 miles, turn right and climb open slopes to a point on the **3 moraine wall** overlooking the jewel-like waters of **4 Taggart Lake**. Descend the short distance to the lakeshore and use a wooden footbridge to cross the outlet creek. A small, rocky outcropping makes a fine point to swim from. The views of the Tetons are fantastic. Follow the trail as it winds around the east shore of Taggart Lake before climbing steadily to the **5 moraine wall** separating Taggart and Bradley Lakes. Descend through the trees to reach the thickly forested shores of Bradley Lake. You'll reach a **6 junction** just before the trail reaches the shore. Turn right to begin the trip back to the parking area or forge ahead to explore the **7 perimeter** of the lake before returning to this junction.

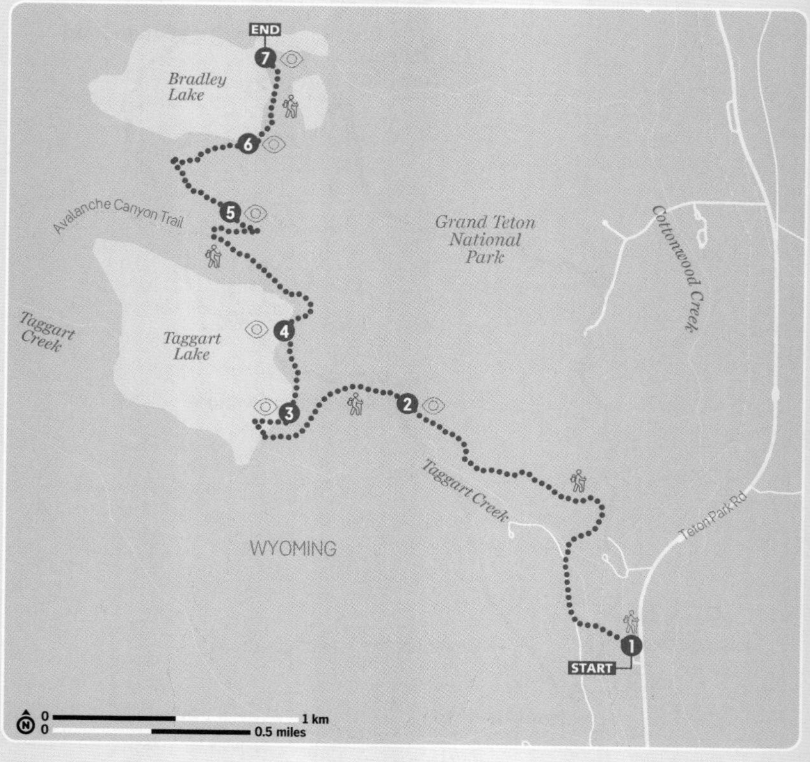

Canoeing, Jackson Lake

Canoes, kayaks and boats with motors less than 8HP are allowed on Jenny Lake. The put-in is by the east-shore boat dock, accessed by a separate road that branches off the Lupine Meadows Trailhead road. Jenny Lake Boating rents kayaks and canoes. It also offers hour-long scenic Jenny Lake cruises throughout the day. Inquire at the dock or call to reserve.

Jenny Lake also offers good fishing and is stocked with lake, brown, brook and Snake River cutthroat trout.

Boating in Grand Teton

CRUISES, KAYAKS & FLOAT TRIPS

A fun, mellow activity for families or groups is to rent a motorboat for a day and explore **Jackson Lake**, stopping to picnic and swim at uncrowded inlets and islands. Though they cover less terrain, canoes and kayaks are also wonderful. Rent them at **Colter Bay Marina** or **Signal Mountain Marina**.

String and Leigh Lakes are other perfect destinations for a family canoe trip, stand-up paddleboarding or just splashing around. Start on **String Lake** and make a 120ft portage before Leigh, which offers the most scenic day and overnight paddles. Six beautiful backcountry campsites flank the lakeshore, three of which (16, 14A and 14B) are only accessible by

SADDLING UP IN GRAND TETON

Horseback riding is possible at Jackson Lake, Colter Bay and the Flagg Ranch area. Children are charged the same as adults and must be at least eight years old and over 4ft tall.

The Colter Bay Corral offers short rides around Swan Lake. Families with small children can check out the 10-minute wrangler-led pony rides. Make reservations at the activities booth next to the Colter Bay grocery store a few days in advance.

Over at the Jackson Lake Lodge Activities Desk, you can sign up for a two-hour guided horseback ride that loops around the local trails departing in the mornings, or afternoon one-hour rides that are perfect for first-timers.

WHERE TO CAMP IN THE PARK

Jenny Lake Campground
The popular tent-only campground sits among the evergreens and glacial boulders but lacks lake views. $

Gros Ventre Campground
Sizable, attractive campground has tall cottonwoods for shade and a pretty nearby river (moose spotting). $

Lizard Creek Campground
Pleasantly shaded sites set amid spruce and fir forest on the shores of Jackson Lake. $

HIKING DEATH CANYON

In the southwestern corner of the park off Moose–Wilson Rd, the lesser-known Death Canyon takes you on a 9-mile journey through a dramatic canyon beneath sheer cliffs towering overhead. You'll find the **1 trailhead** about five miles southwest of Moose. The trail starts off with a climb to **2 Phelps Lake Overlook** (7200ft) and then descends through lovely aspen forest, passing a springtime waterfall. Shortly after, you'll enter the towering **3 gorge**. This is when the real ascent kicks in – a relentless uphill climb over rocky switchbacks that quickly joins the river, which cascades over large boulders. After a hard slog of about 1.5 miles, the path flattens out. Devoid of the river's roar, the valley seems impressively serene. The trail hits a junction by an **4 old patrol cabin**, 4.5 miles from the trailhead. The right branch climbs steeply to Static Peak Divide (10,792ft); if you have the energy, switchback up the trail to the treeline for great views of the peaks and plains (a two-hour detour). Alternatively, continue straight on the main trail up **5 Death Canyon**, through riverside willows in prime moose habitat. The trail crosses a log bridge and enters a lush forest filled with berries, which indicate bear territory. The **6 campsites** of the Death Canyon Camping Area pop up occasionally, as do views of the Death Canyon Shelf, an impressive layer of sedimentary rock atop harder granite and gneiss. To exit, retrace your steps. Consider descending to the pine-rimmed **7 Phelps Lake** for a dip before the final grind, a 1.6-mile hike that includes climbing back up the moraine hill, which somehow seems a lot longer at the day's end.

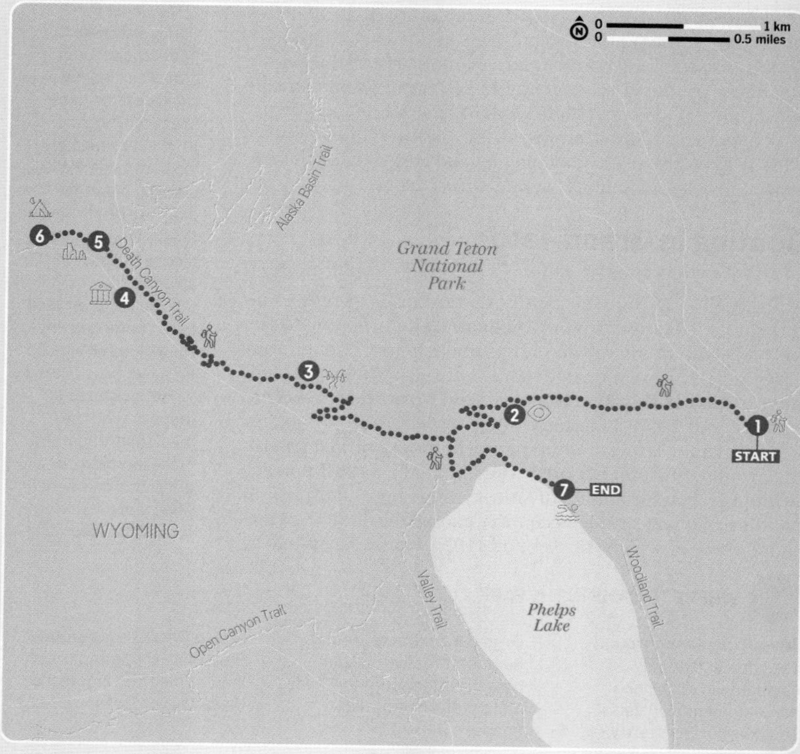

boat. It's 3 miles one way from the portage point at the outlet of **Leigh Lake** to the farthest campsite (16). String Lake's canoe-only put-in is just before the Leigh Lake Trailhead parking lot. Leigh Lake also offers quality fishing.

If you prefer to leave the planning to someone else, various operators run float trips in the national park. The **Triangle X Ranch** offers dawn, daytime and sunset floats, plus a four-hour early-evening float and cookout. Trips run out of Moose. **Solitude Float Trips** is another recommended rafting company that runs Deadman's-Bar-to-Moose trips and sunrise trips, plus shorter 5-mile floats.

On the east side of Jackson Lake, **Colter Bay Cruises** runs 1½-hour cruises three times daily, as well as longer breakfast, lunch and dinner cruises in the shadow of Mt Moran.

Embracing Winter

SKIING AND SNOWSHOEING

With the crowds gone, bears tucked away in their dens and powdery snow blanketing the pines, the Tetons make a lovely winter destination. Teton Park Rd is plowed from Jackson Lake Junction to Signal Mountain Lodge and from Moose to the Taggart Lake Trailhead. The outer park road (Hwy US 89/191) is plowed and open for winter travel from the town of Jackson to Flagg Ranch just south of Yellowstone National Park.

Cross-country skiers hit the trails between mid-December and mid-March. The park grooms 15 miles of track right under the Tetons' highest peaks, between the Taggart and Bradley Lakes parking area and Signal Mountain. Lanes are available for ski touring, skate skiing and snowshoeing.

For an easy 8-mile, round-trip, cross-country ski trip, start from the Taggart Lake parking area and follow the Jenny Lake trail parallel to Cottonwood Creek. Return via Teton Park Rd. There are great views of the Tetons throughout.

A slightly more challenging route begins at the same spot. The Taggart Lake to Beaver Creek excursion is a moderate-to-difficult trail with some climbing. It's a 3-mile round-trip to Taggart Lake or 4 miles to do the Beaver Creek loop, climbing through a glacial moraine. Use care on the return descent, as the trail may be icy.

From late December through to mid-March, rangers lead free two-hour, 1.5-mile snowshoe hikes from the Taggart Lake trailhead two times per week. Traditional wooden snowshoes are available for rent. The tour is open to those aged eight years and up.

ASSINIBOINE HERITAGE

Dani Bahnsen, an artist from the Assiniboine tribe, shares memories from her childhood. *@buffalo.sister*

As a kid, I spent summers with my grandparents to learn. They had a big ranch in Montana on the reservation. And so during the week I was a cowgirl, and on the weekends I was an Indian, and we would go to powwows.

At gatherings and ceremonies, the elders, holding their peace pipes, would tell stories. Some of them were funny and would be lighthearted. And at other times the stories were very serious. It was really inspiring. I didn't realize at the time how lucky I was to have that culture.

GETTING AROUND

The small town of Jackson is just a short drive to the park. At popular destinations (like Jenny Lake) parking lots fill by 9am, so get an early start. Biking into the park is also a possibility, thanks to the multiuse vehicle-free trail that runs from Jackson to Jenny Lake (20 miles).

GREAT SAND DUNES NATIONAL PARK

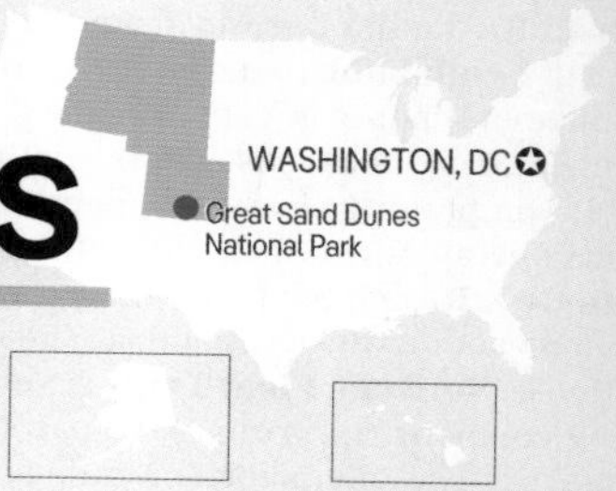

For all of Colorado's striking natural sights, the surreal Great Sand Dunes National Park – a veritable sea of sand bounded by jagged peaks and scrubby plains – is a place of stirring optical illusions where nature's magic is on full display.

From the approach up Hwy 150, watch as the angles of sunlight make shifting shadows on the dunes. The most dramatic time is the day's end, when the hills come into high contrast as the sun drops low on the horizon. Hike past the edge of the dune field to see the shifting sand up close; the ceaseless wind works like a disconsolate sculptor, constantly amending the landscape.

Most visitors limit their activities to the area where Medano Creek divides the main dune mass from the towering Sangre de Cristo Mountains. The remaining 85% of the park's area is designated wilderness: not for the unfit or fainthearted.

FACTS

Great For Family travel, photo ops, walking
State Colorado
Entrance Fee 7-day pass per vehicle $25
Area 234 sq miles

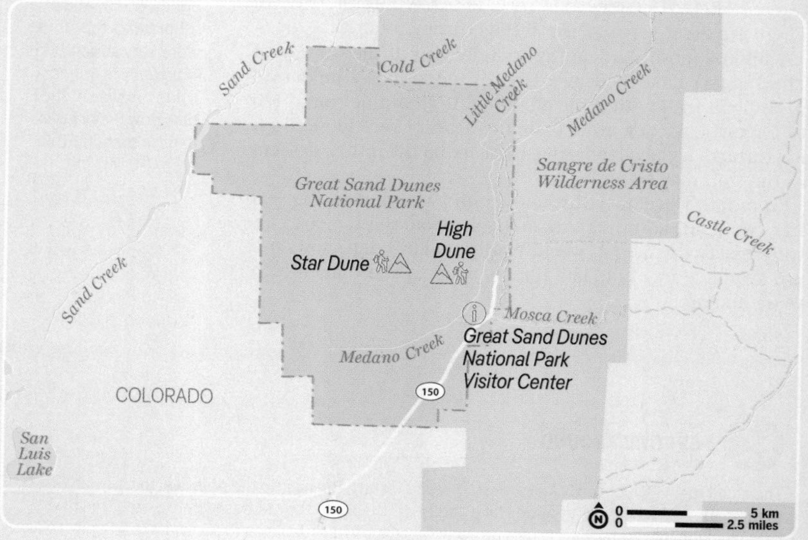

Sand boarder

Adventures on the Sands

HIKING & SAND-BOARDING

There are no trails through this expansive field of sand, but it's the star attraction for hikers. Two informal hikes afford excellent panoramic views of the dunes. The first is a hike to **High Dune**, which departs from a parking area just beyond the visitor center. It's about 2.5 miles out to the peak and back, but be warned: it's not easy. As you trudge along up the hills of sand, it feels like you're taking a half-step back for every one forward. If you're up for it, try pushing on to the second worthy goal: just west of High Dune is **Star Dune** (750ft), the tallest in the park.

From the **Great Sand Dunes National Park Visitor Center,** a short trail leads to the Mosca Picnic Area next to ankle-deep Medano Creek, which you must ford (when the creek is running) to reach the dunes. Across the road from the visitor center, the Mosca Pass Trail climbs up into the Sangre de Cristo Wilderness.

Sand-boarding and sledding are great fun especially for kids – who often zip down much more quickly than adults. The heavy wooden sled may seem like a bad idea when you're trudging out to the dunes, but the gleeful rush down the slopes is worth every footstep. Sand conditions are best after a recent precipitation; when it's too dry you'll simply sink. During the winter days when snow covers the dunes, the sledding is excellent. To rent a board, visit Kristi Mountain Sports in Alamosa or the Great Sand Dunes Oasis at the edge of the park.

SPLASHING AMID THE DUNES

One of the most curious spectacles in the entire park, the snowmelt Medano Creek flows down from the Sangre de Cristos and along the eastern edge of the dunes. Peak flow is usually in late May or early June, and the rippling water over the sand creates a temporary beach of sorts, which is extremely popular with families. In years when the water is high enough (check the park website for daily water-level reports), children can even float down the creek on an inner tube, right along the dunes. The combination of the creek's appeal and the end of the school year means that this is the park's peak season.

GETTING AROUND

To get to some of the more remote trailheads in the park, you will need a high-clearance 4WD. Most people just park and walk out to the dunes. Biking is prohibited in the wilderness-designated sections of the park.

ROCKY MOUNTAIN NATIONAL PARK

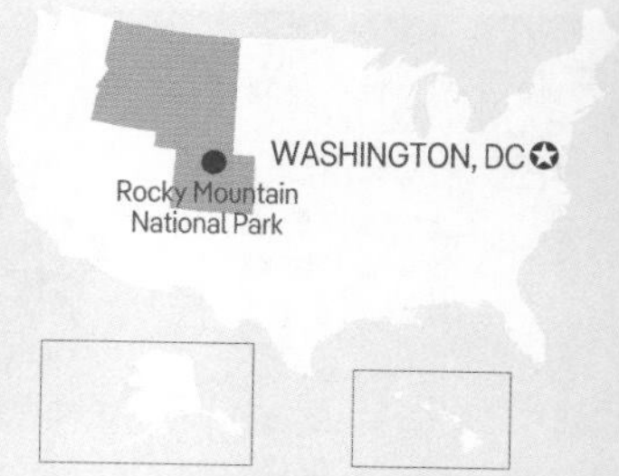

The crown jewel of Colorado's national parks is a natural spectacle on every scale: from hulking 12,000ft granite formations that developed over 1.3 billion years ago, to delicate yellow glacier lilies, one of the dozen alpine wildflowers that burst to life at the edge of receding snowfields every spring.

Wonders of the natural world are the main attractions here: huge herds of elk and scattered bighorn sheep, pine-dotted mountain slopes and blindingly white alpine tundra. However, there are a few museums and historic sites within the park's borders that are worthy of a glance and good for families. Rocky Mountain National Park is surrounded by some of the most pristine wild areas in the west: Comanche Peak and Neota Wilderness Areas in the Roosevelt National Forest to the north and Indian Peaks Wilderness to the south. The jagged spine of the Continental Divide intersects the park through its middle.

FACTS

Great For Family travel, scenery, walking
State Colorado
Entrance Fee 7-day pass per vehicle/person $35/20
Area 415 sq miles

SKOSTEP/SHUTTERSTOCK ©

Rocky Mountain National Park

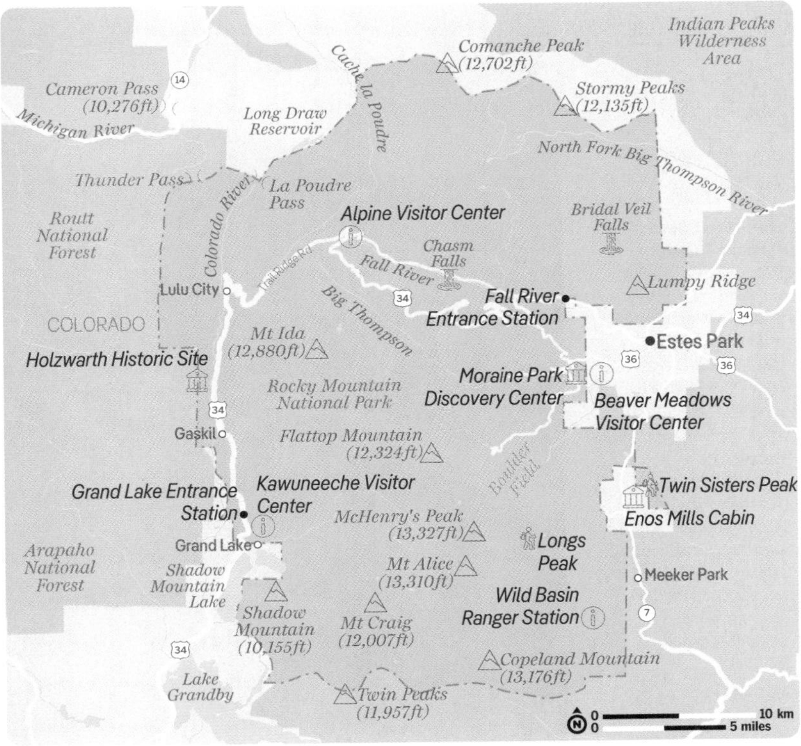

Sweeping Mountain-Filled Vistas

SCENIC DRIVES AND HIKES

Travel through the sky on the remarkable 48-mile road between Estes Park and Grand Lake. The road is only open summers, and can be jam-packed. But it is really worth it – by car, 4WD or bicycle. About 11 miles of the road sits above the tree line. Along the way, you might sight elk, moose, marmots and plenty of birds and plant species.

After getting a lay of the land, get off the pavement and into the backcountry. With more than 350 miles of trails, traversing all aspects of its diverse terrain, the park is suited to every hiking ability. Those with kids in tow might consider the easy hikes in the Wild Basin to Calypso Cascades, or to Gem Lake in the Lumpy Ridge area, while those with unlimited ambition, strong legs and enough trail mix will be lured by the challenge of summiting **Longs Peak** (elevation 14,259ft). Regardless, it's best to spend at least one night at 7000ft to 8000ft prior to setting out to allow your body to adjust to the elevation. Be-

ECHOES FROM THE PAST

Enos Mills Cabin Museum & Gallery Naturalist Enos Mills (1870–1922) led the struggle to establish Rocky Mountain National Park. His passion for nature lives on in his tiny cabin (1885).

Holzwarth Historic Site When Prohibition was enacted in 1916, a Denver saloonkeeper started a new life as a subsistence rancher. This site houses several original buildings.

Moraine Park Discovery Center Built in 1923 and once the park's proud visitors lodge, this renovated building hosts exhibits on geology, glaciers and wildlife.

Longs Peak and Gem Lake (p289)

fore July many trails are snowbound and high water runoff makes passage difficult.

A good warm-up to more grueling ascents (like Longs Peak) is the climb up **Twin Sisters Peak** (elevation 11,428ft). Erosion-resistant quartz caps the oddly deformed rock at the summit, and delicate alpine flowers (plenty of mountain harebell) fill the rock spaces near the summit's stone hut. One of Twin Sisters' best features is the unequaled views of Longs Peak. Bring plenty of water. You'll gain 2300ft in just 3.7 miles.

GETTING AROUND

During summer, the park operates three shuttle buses. Reserve ahead for the Hiker Shuttle ($2), which runs from Estes Park Visitor Center to Moraine Park, where you can transfer to two other free shuttles that stop at various trailheads. If driving your own vehicle, you'll need to reserve a timed entry permit.

YELLOWSTONE NATIONAL PARK

Yellowstone National Park deserves all its accolades. Its real showstoppers are the geysers and hot springs, but at every turn this land of fire and brimstone breathes, belches and bubbles like a giant kettle on the boil. Geothermal features aside, Yellowstone has numerous other highlights, from towering waterfalls that plunge into a multihued canyon to a vast alpine lake skirted by forested overlooks. Yellowstone has few rivals when it comes to wildlife watching. The pristine northern range is home to herds of bison and elk, fleet-footed pronghorn as well as moose, grizzlies and wolves.

And yet, Yellowstone is much more than the sum total of its wild, disparate parts. There's the park's extraordinary volcanic past and the scientific anomalies continually being uncovered, not to mention a human history that encompasses Native American tribes, explorers and landscape artists. You could spend a lifetime here and still have things to discover.

FACTS

Great For Family travel, wildlife, scenery
State Wyoming
Entrance Fee 7-day pass per vehicle/pedestrian $35/20
Area 3472 sq miles

Grand Prismatic Spring (p294)

YELLOWSTONE NATIONAL PARK

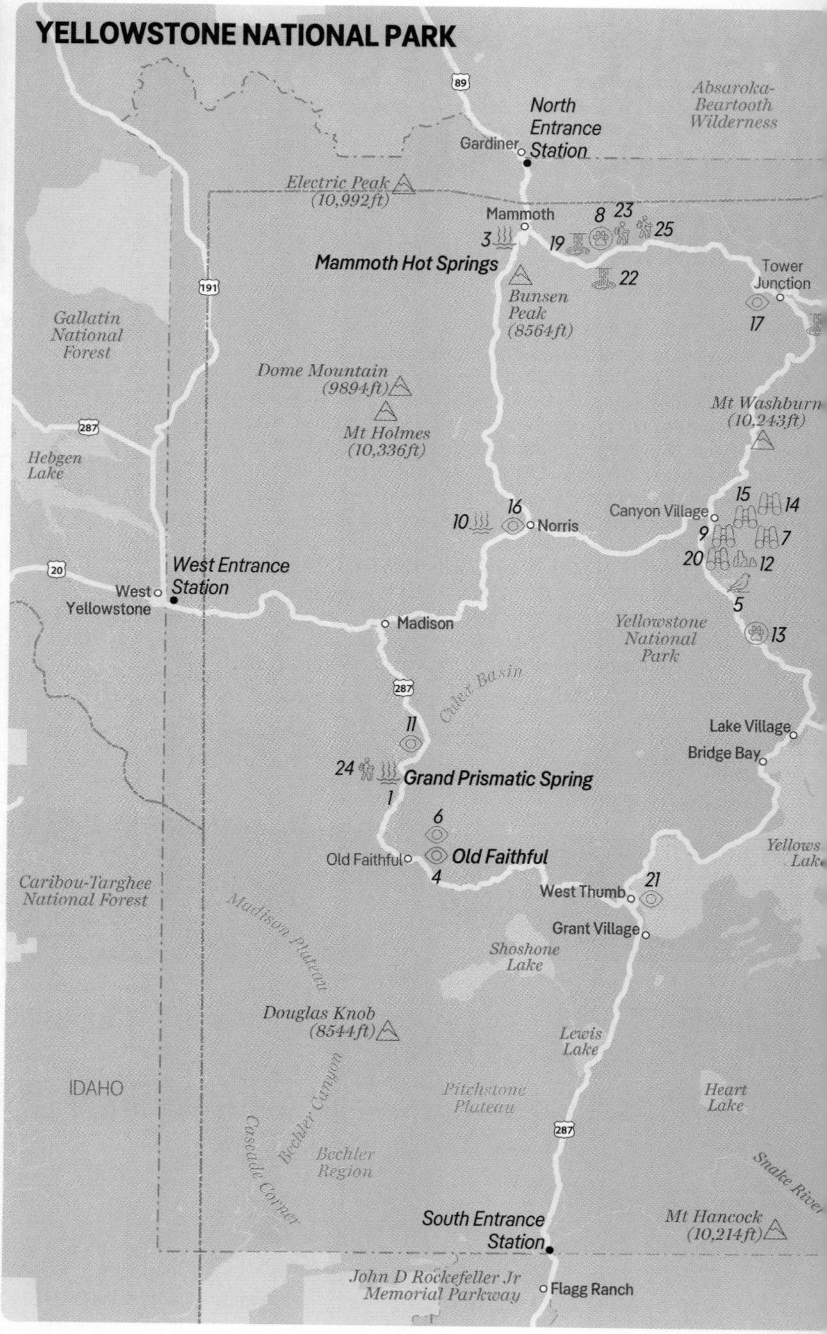
89
North Entrance Station
Gardiner
Absaroka-Beartooth Wilderness
Electric Peak (10,992ft)
Mammoth
8
23
3
19
25
Mammoth Hot Springs
22
Bunsen Peak (8564ft)
Tower Junction
17
191
Gallatin National Forest
Dome Mountain (9894ft)
Mt Holmes (10,336ft)
Mt Washburn (10,243ft)
287
Hebgen Lake
10
16
Norris
Canyon Village
15
14
9
7
20
12
5
20
West Entrance Station
West Yellowstone
Madison
Yellowstone National Park
13
287
Culex Basin
11
Lake Village
Bridge Bay
24
Grand Prismatic Spring
1
6
Old Faithful
Old Faithful
4
Yellows Lak
Caribou-Targhee National Forest
West Thumb
21
Madison Plateau
Grant Village
Shoshone Lake
Douglas Knob (8544ft)
Lewis Lake
IDAHO
Bechler Canyon
Pitchstone Plateau
Heart Lake
287
Cascade Corner
Bechler Region
Snake River
South Entrance Station
Mt Hancock (10,214ft)
John D Rockefeller Jr Memorial Parkway
Flagg Ranch

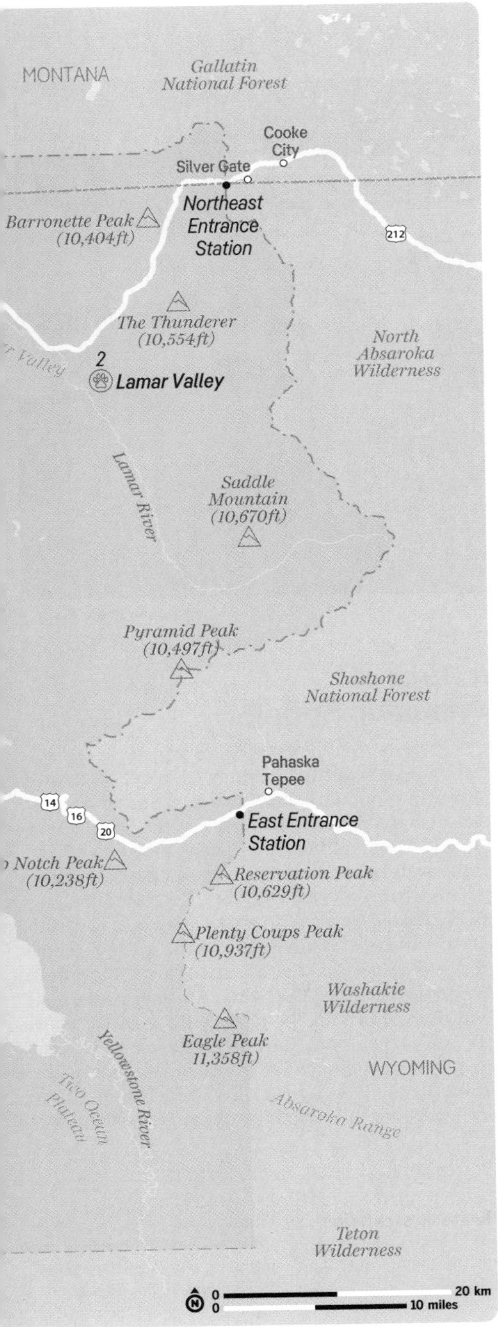

HIGHLIGHTS
1 Grand Prismatic Spring
2 Lamar Valley
3 Mammoth Hot Springs
4 Old Faithful

SIGHTS
see 21 Abyss Pool
5 Alum Creek
6 Anemone Geyser
7 Artist Point
see 6 Aurum Geyser
see 6 Beehive Geyser
see 21 Big Cone
see 16 Black Growler Steam Vent
see 21 Black Pool
8 Blacktail Ponds
9 Brink of Lower Falls
see 11 Clepsydra Geyser
see 16 Crackling Lake
see 6 Doublet Pool
see 16 Echinus Geyser
10 Emerald Spring
see 21 Fishing Cone
see 11 Fountain Geyser
11 Fountain Paint Pot
see 6 Giantess Geyser
12 Grand Canyon of the Yellowstone
13 Hayden Valley
see 6 Heart Spring
14 Inspiration Point
see 6 Lion Geyser Group
15 Lookout Point
see 11 Morning Geyser
16 Norris Geyser Basin
see 1 Opal Pool
17 Petrified Tree
see 6 Plume Geyser
see 16 Porcelain Basin
see 11 Red Spouter
see 11 Silex Spring
see 11 Spasm Geyser
see 16 Steamboat Geyser
18 Tower Fall
see 1 Turquoise Pool
19 Undine Falls
20 Upper Falls Viewpoint
see 6 Vault Geyser
21 West Thumb
see 10 Whale's Mouth
22 Wraith Falls

ACTIVITIES, COURSES & TOURS
23 Blacktail Deer Creek Trail
24 Fairy Falls Trailhead
25 Forces of the Northern Range Trailhead

Bison, Firehole River

GATEWAYS TO YELLOWSTONE

Latched onto Yellowstone Park's northern boundaries, the three gateway towns of Gardiner, West Yellowstone and Cooke City serve as functional visitor hubs, good for a bed and a bite to eat, but it's the four corridors that radiate out from the park that offer the real scenic draws. It's worth planning your itinerary around the spectacular drives in the area. The Paradise Valley route takes you from Bozeman or Livingston down into Gardiner, while the Beartooth Hwy is a dramatic alpine approach from Red Lodge into the Lamar Valley. The Chief Joseph Scenic Hwy and Buffalo Bill Cody Scenic Byway connect the park's east side with the Wild West town of Cody.

Brilliant Hues of Grand Prismatic Spring

YELLOWSTONE'S MOST FAMOUS SPRING

One of the park's most beautiful geothermal features, **Grand Prismatic Spring** is not only the park's largest and deepest hot spring, it's also the biggest hot spring in the US. It spans some 330ft in width and, although it doesn't look like it from the surface, the waters reach a depth of over 120ft. However, the colors are what make this spring so extraordinary.

The drama begins as soon as you park the car (in the Middle Geyser Basin) and walk the bridge spanning the Firehole River. You'll notice waves of steam wafting over the water. This comes from the Excelsior Pool, a huge former geyser that blew itself out of existence in the 1880s with massive 300ft explosions of water. The pool continually discharges some 4000 gallons of boiling water a minute into the Firehole River.

Follow the boardwalk loop, and you'll soon reach the Grand Prismatic Spring. Under full sun, the water appears an intense

FREE PARK ACTIVITIES

Guided Walks
Take a guided ranger-led hike, walk or snowshoe excursion.

Amphitheater Presentation
Get new insights into geology or wildlife, the cosmos during an evening talk.

Films
Gain deeper insight while watching films screened in the Old Faithful Visitor Education Center.

blue color, while the edges of the spring glimmer in shades of yellow, orange and ocher. The steaming waters look all the more striking against the backdrop of pine-covered hills in the distance. After taking in the spring, the boardwalk continues past several other smaller features including **Opal Pool**, which is something of a miniaturized version of Grand Prismatic, with its bright colors fringing the waters. Aptly named **Turquoise Pool** lacks the rich shoreline hues, though its waters glow a deep blue on sunny days.

For a panorama of the spring, make the easy hike up to the overlook along the **Fairy Falls Trail**. Find the trailhead by driving 1.3 miles south of the Grand Prismatic Spring.

Exploring Geyser Hill

EYE-CATCHING ERUPTIONS NEAR OLD FAITHFUL

From Old Faithful, follow the inner boardwalk counterclockwise and take the bridge across the Firehole River. This leads to the 0.6-mile loop that passes a diverse array of simmering pools and steaming fountains.

Seepage from **Giantess Geyser** and **Vault Geyser** has created geyserite terraces that look like scaled relief maps. Giantess springs to life between two and six times a year, though when active the geyser erupts twice hourly for up to 40 hours.

Doublet Pool is known for its deep-blue color, thin scalloped geyserite border and the occasional thumping that emanates from collapsing steam and gas bubbles deep underground. **Aurum Geyser** has some lovely disc-shaped formations, and it erupts to 20ft every 2½ to five hours.

The **Lion Geyser Group** is a gathering of four interconnected geysers – their eruptions are preceded by a roar, hence the name. **Heart Spring** is said to resemble the shape of a human heart.

Beehive Geyser erupts twice a day, rising up to 200ft through its 4ft-high cone-shaped nozzle, with a jet engine–like whoosh. It's the second- or third-tallest regularly active geyser in the park and is a regular crowd-pleaser. The park will make announcements inside the visitor center when it's about to go off.

Erupting every 20 minutes, **Plume Geyser** is one of the easiest geysers to catch. It's also one of the basin's youngest geysers, created by a steam explosion in 1922.

Nearby **Anemone Geyser** erupts every 10 minutes or so, and offers the chance to see the full cycle of an eruption, from the pool filling, overflowing, bubbling up and finally shooting skyward, 6ft into the air. Afterward, the water rushes back underground with a gurgling sound.

MORE GEOTHERMAL FEATURES

Before or after you explore Old Faithful and Geyser Hill, head northwest along a boardwalk trail that leads past numerous other unique features. Here are a few highlights:

Castle Geyser
Huge cone resembling a bleached sandcastle. Erupts every 14 hours or so.

Crested Pool
Near constantly boiling, with water thrown up to 6ft in the air.

Grand Geyser
The world's tallest predictable geyser (150ft to 180ft) bursts roughly every eight hours.

Chromatic Pool & Beauty Pool
Strikingly colorful features.

Riverside Geyser
Photogenic eruptions of a 75ft column of water arcing into the Firehole River, often capped by a rainbow.

Daisy Geyser
Lets loose every three hours or so. Can be predicted to within 45 minutes.

WHERE TO EAT & DRINK NEAR OLD FAITHFUL

Old Faithful Inn Dining Room
Expansive buffets (lunch and dinner) served in an elegant log cabin–style interior. **$$$**

Old Faithful Snow Lodge Geyser Grill
Counter-service spot with burgers (veggie too), bison bratwurst, salads and soup. **$**

Bear Pit Lounge
Hidden behind the fireplace, the welcoming bar is a cozy spot for an après-geyser cocktail.

PRACTICALITIES

Scan this QR code for predicted eruption times.

TOP SIGHT

Old Faithful

DON'T MISS

- Watching the spectacular eruption
- Strolling the looped boardwalk
- Exhibits in the Old Faithful Visitor Center
- Ranger-led walks in the area
- Native American culture in the Yellowstone Tribal Heritage Center
- Views from the Old Faithful Inn Observation Deck
- Guided tour around the Old Faithful Inn

Though it's neither the tallest nor even the most predictable geyser in the park, Old Faithful is the poster child for Yellowstone and a consistent crowd-pleaser. Every 90 minutes or so the geyser spouts some 8000 gallons of water up to 180ft in the air. If you're around long enough, it's worth viewing the eruption from several locations for the complete experience.

Timing

For more than 75 years, the geyser faithfully erupted every hour or so – one reason for the name the Washburn expedition gave it in 1870. The average time between shows these days is 90 minutes and getting longer, though it has historically varied between 45 and 110 minutes. The average eruption lasts around four minutes, though the duration can range from 90 seconds to five minutes. The water temperature is normally 204°F (96°C), and the steam is about 350°F (177°C). The longer the eruption, the longer the recovery time. Rangers correctly predict eruptions to within 10 minutes about 90% of the time. And no, Old Faithful has never erupted on the hour.

Old Faithful Visitor Center

Get insight into the inner works below the earth's surface while perusing the exhibitions at the visitor center. You can also find out predicted eruption times for both Old Faithful and other prominent geysers in the park. Park rangers are on hand to answer questions about the area, and they often make announcements when other eruptions are imminent. During the summer, rangers lead guided walks around Old Faithful.

Old Faithful Historic District

A 0.7-mile boardwalk loops around Old Faithful, which is overlooked by a handful of buildings off in the distance. These make up the so-called Old Faithful Historic District, with old-fashioned wooden structures dating back to the 1920s.

Don't miss the Old Faithful Inn. Designed by Seattle architect Robert C Reamer and built in 1904, this building has log rafters above a seven-story lobby that rises over 65ft. The chimney of the central fireplace (actually eight fireplaces combined) contains more than 500 tons of rhyolite rock. Grab a seat in the lobby and take in the finely crafted log and wood-frame structure. You can also climb the gnarled log staircase to various levels overlooking the main floor. The Crow's Nest, a top-floor balcony where musicians once played for dancers in the lobby below, is wonderful (but unused since 1959). Look also for the huge popcorn popper and fire tools at the back of the fireplace. For more insight into the building, take one of the free guided tours that happen throughout the day.

The 2nd-floor observation deck offers the chance to enjoy fine views of Old Faithful geyser while enjoying a bit of fresh air (the covered deck also keeps out the rain and snow on dreary days). The lobby hosts local artists and authors. Free 45-minute Historic Inn tours depart from the fireplace at various times throughout the day, with animated guides bringing the past to life.

Yellowstone Tribal Heritage Center

One of the newest features (opened in 2022 on the park's 150th anniversary), just off the Old Faithful boardwalk, pays homage to the region's 27 associated tribal nations. From mid-May through mid-October, indigenous artists, historians and craft makers give presentations and demonstrations. You might see an exhibition of beadwork, photography or moccasin making. There are also performances – storytelling, drumming, dancing – as well as food demonstrations and other activities. It's a great place to learn more from people with a deep connection to Yellowstone.

HIKE TO MALLARD LAKE

If you need a break from the crowds, immerse yourself in nature on one of several memorable hikes in the area. The out-and-back trail (7-miles round-trip) climbing steadily to Mallard Lake leaves from the southeast side of the Old Faithful Lodge cabins and takes you across the Firehole River and past Pipeline Hot Springs up to peaceful views of the pine-fringed lakeshore.

TOP TIPS

- You can access the geyser 24 hours a day. Go early in the morning or late in the afternoon to see Old Faithful with fewer crowds.
- For an alternative view of Old Faithful and a fine perspective over the basin, make the short hike up to Observation Hill.
- You can make a full day of visiting Old Faithful by visiting the many other geysers in the area, starting with Geyser Hill and following the boardwalk trail out to other distant geothermal features (like Morning Glory).
- Get the lowdown on the day's predicted eruptions at geysertimes.org, or by calling 307-344-2751.

THE COEUR D'ALENE

Photographer **Teresa White** sheds light on the origin of her tribe's name.

French fur traders called us 'Coeur d'Alene' (meaning 'heart like an awl') because they found us difficult to trade with. And so we took that as a point of pride, of honor, but our traditional name is Schitsu'umsh. It means 'those who are found here.' We lived right there on the edge of Coeur d'Alene Lake in (present-day Idaho). We weren't real nomadic. We did travel into the park once a year for hunting, so that's how our tribe used the park. Now we just come hunting for animals to see and take photos of them.

Otherworldly Stroll at Fountain Paint Pot

DYNAMIC GEOTHERMAL AREA

Yellowstone's still active volcano manifests itself in many ways, and the power lurking beneath the earth's surface is particularly evident along this half-mile boardwalk trail. The first feature you'll see is **Silex Spring**, a smoke-spewing pool whose waters hover just below the boiling point. Note the strips of yellow, orange and russet-colored bacterial mats along the pool's runoff. These are created by thermophiles, or heat-loving microorganisms.

Just past Silex Spring, **Fountain Paint Pot** is a huge bowl of plopping goop that ranks as one of the biggest in the park. The action is sloppiest in spring, with some mud pots drying up by August. The area around the thermal features is slowly being drowned in deposits, while a grassy basin beyond supports the park's largest bison herd.

You'll hear the hiss of fumaroles as you continue along. The sounds come from steam as well as gases of carbon dioxide and hydrogen sulfide as low-volume water comes into contact with hot rocks far below. Nearby, **Red Spouter** is particularly fascinating, since it acts like a muddy hot spring or even a low-erupting geyser in early summer, only to become a mud pot and then a fumarole later in the year.

The next stretch of boardwalk takes you to surprisingly different features. Before descending the stairs, you can take in the view across this geyser area and perhaps spot a handful of eruptions happening simultaneously. **Morning and Fountain Geysers** are impressive but infrequent gushers. The latter drains into **Spasm Geyser**, which has shorter but more frequent eruptions, peaking about 20ft high. **Clepsydra Geyser** has erupted almost constantly since a 1959 earthquake.

Steamy Sights in Norris Geyser Basin

THE BUBBLING, PULSING EARTH

The **Norris Geyser Basin** is North America's most volatile and oldest continuously active geothermal area (in existence for around 115,000 years). A good place to see the action is along the boardwalk path that loops through **Porcelain Basin** – named for the area's milky deposits of siliceous sinter, also known as geyserite. The bleached basin boils and bubbles like some giant laboratory experiment, and the ash-white ground actually pulsates in places.

As you enter, veer left before the continually blowing fumarole of **Black Growler Steam Vent**, said to be the park's hottest. Going clockwise, the boardwalk heads left past

WHERE TO STAY NEAR OLD FAITHFUL

Old Faithful Inn
Variety of rooms in historic log-walled inn with a frenetic lobby that quiets by night. **$$$**

Old Faithful Snow Lodge
Modern but cookie-cutter rooms as well as pine-walled Frontier cabins with showers only. **$$$**

Old Faithful Lodge Cabins
A 1920s-era design, with a mix of modern and rustic cabins, some with private bathrooms. **$$$**

MATTHIEU GALLET/SHUTTERSTOCK ©

Pronghorns, Yellowstone National Park

Crackling Lake, which bubbles like a deep fryer, and the **Whale's Mouth**, a gaping, blue hot spring.

Nearby, 2 miles of boardwalks and gentle trails snake through Norris' forested Back Basin. The main show here is **Steamboat Geyser**, the world's tallest active geyser, which infrequently skyrockets to an awesome 380ft.

Heading into Back Basin, you'll soon reach **Emerald Spring** which combines reflected blue light with yellow sulfur deposits to create a striking blue-green color. For a shorter loop, take the right branch at Cistern Springs; otherwise, continue clockwise around the basin.

Past the eroded runoff channel of Steamboat Geyser, you'll come to dramatic **Echinus Geyser**, the park's largest acidic geyser. It erupted every couple of hours until around 2018, with spouts reaching up to 60ft and sometimes continuing for more than an hour, but these days it's pretty quiet.

Wildlife Watching

DISCOVERING YELLOWSTONE'S FAMOUS VALLEYS

Sometimes referred to as America's Serengeti, the **Lamar Valley** contains great herds of bison and elk, along with pronghorn, mule deer, moose and bighorn sheep. They come

SACRED LAND

According to legend, the Dragons' Mouth Spring is where it all began for the native Kiowa people. Doh Ki, the great deity, created the world and promised the Kiowa a homeland if they traveled through a harsh, volcanic place. They crossed the land and discovered the bubbling hot spring. Doh Ki told them the land would be theirs if anyone would enter. Only one great Kiowa warrior answered the call, and dove into the spring. He was badly burned and soon lost consciousness. Fellow Kiowa pulled him out, and when he opened his eyes, the barren earth had been transformed into a verdant place of forests, streams and abundant game, and the land was theirs.

WHERE TO CAMP IN YELLOWSTONE

Indian Creek Campground
Forested sites near hiking trails and a pretty stream some 8 miles south of Mammoth. $

Norris Campground
One of Yellowstone's best campgrounds, with forest-fringed sites overlooking the Gibbon River. $

Madison Campground
Forests, meadows and wildlife make this well-located campground (14 miles from Norris) an enticing prospect. $

to feed in the lush river valley against the sagebrush steppe, which seems to glow in incandescent hues in the golden morning light.

The great number of ungulates draw predators, including some of the park's most famed residents, its wolf packs. At all hours of the day, you'll find wildlife lovers parked at pullouts on the roadside, watching the action unfold as wolves, along with the odd coyote, bobcat and bear, pass through the valley. The best viewing is along the northeast entrance road between Slough Creek Campground and Soda Butte.

South of the Lamar, the **Hayden Valley** is another premier wildlife-viewing area. Take your time as you drive the 16-mile road from Canyon Village south to Lake Village. With patience you're likely to see coyotes, springtime grizzlies, elk and lots of bison, plus one of the largest autumn ruts. Bison, in fact, are usually here year-round, and if you visit in the spring, you might see the year's first calves, which are born in late April or May.

Bird-watching is equally impressive. The region is home to white pelicans and trumpeter swans, sandhill cranes, ospreys, bald eagles and Canada geese. There are popular viewing areas 1 mile north of Sulphur Cauldron and 1.5 miles north of Trout Creek. At prime spots like **Alum Creek**, you'll want to set up your spotting scope early, as the pullouts fill with cars an hour or two before dusk.

MOUNTAIN LEGENDS

Writer and historian **Jeff Henry** describes the tough life of early explorers.

Jim Bridger guided some of the official explorations in the later part of the 1800s, but in his early life, he knew people like Andrew Henry, who in turn had known Lewis and Clark. Bridger got to the mountains in 1822 when he was just a 17-year-old kid. One time he got two Blackfoot arrows stuck in his back. His buddies could pull one out, but not the other one, since the arrowhead was lodged under a bone. He had to wait four years till a doctor who came along, gave him a lot of whiskey and maybe a stick to bite on.

Discovering Mammoth Hot Springs

ORNATE POOLS AND TERRACES

Northern Yellowstone's major thermal feature, **Mammoth Hot Springs**, is a graceful collection of travertine terraces and cascading hot pools. Some terraces are bone dry, while others sparkle with hundreds of minuscule pools, coral-like formations and a fabulous palette of colors that could come from an impressionist painting.

An hour's worth of boardwalks wind their way between the sights. Near the parking lot is the dormant 37ft-high hot-spring cone called Liberty Cap. Around the corner, Palette Spring has steep terraces in varying tones, from snow white to oranges, browns and yellows. Thermophiles continue to create the rich palette of seemingly flowing watercolors.

The famously ornate travertine formations that characterize the lower terraces of Minerva Spring have dried over the years due to earthquake activity but are still among the area's most picturesque. Nearby Mound Spring has some of the most beautiful colors and abstract patterns on the terraces. The landscape is so otherworldly that it provided the

YELLOWSTONE NATIONAL PARK LODGES WINTER TOURS

Wake Up to Winter Wildlife
Look for bison, elk, coyotes and wolves on a sunrise tour to the Lamar Valley.

Grand Canyon Day Tour
See the dramatic ice formations around the canyon and waterfalls on a full-day excursion.

Tower Ski Tour
Make an afternoon tour through the Blacktail Plateau, with views at the Tower Fall Overlook.

CLIMBING MT WASHBURN

One of Yellowstone's most popular day hikes offers unsurpassed 360-degree mountaintop views, with the chance of spotting bighorn sheep and black bears. Though you'll ascend some 1400ft during the 6.8-mile round-trip hike, it's a fairly gradual rise.

The hike begins at **1 Dunraven Pass** (8859ft) on the Grand Loop Rd, just a bit under 5 miles north of Canyon. The wide trail follows a rough, disused road (dating from 1905) following a series of long, ribbon-like loops through a forest of subalpine firs. After 20 minutes the views start to open up. Continue northeast up broad switchbacks to a viewpoint, then follow a narrow ridge past a few stunted whitebark pines (look out for bears). At the **2 Mt Washburn Trail** junction, the road curves up to the three-story **3 fire-lookout tower**, about two hours from the trailhead.

Mt Washburn is all that remains of a volcano that erupted around 640,000 years ago, forming the vast Yellowstone caldera. Interpretive displays in the lookout tower point out the caldera extents, making this a memorable place to get a sense of the awesome scale of the Yellowstone super-volcano. The peak is named after Montana surveyor-general Henry Washburn, who rode up the peak to see the view during the Washburn, Langford and Doane expedition of 1870.

The majestic panoramas (when the weather is clear) stretch over three-quarters of the park, across the Yellowstone caldera south to Yellowstone Lake, Canyon, the Hayden Valley and even the Tetons, and north to the Beartooth and Absaroka Ranges. Below you are the smoking Washburn Hot Springs. Keep your eyes peeled for bighorn sheep basking near the summit. From the top, return the way you came.

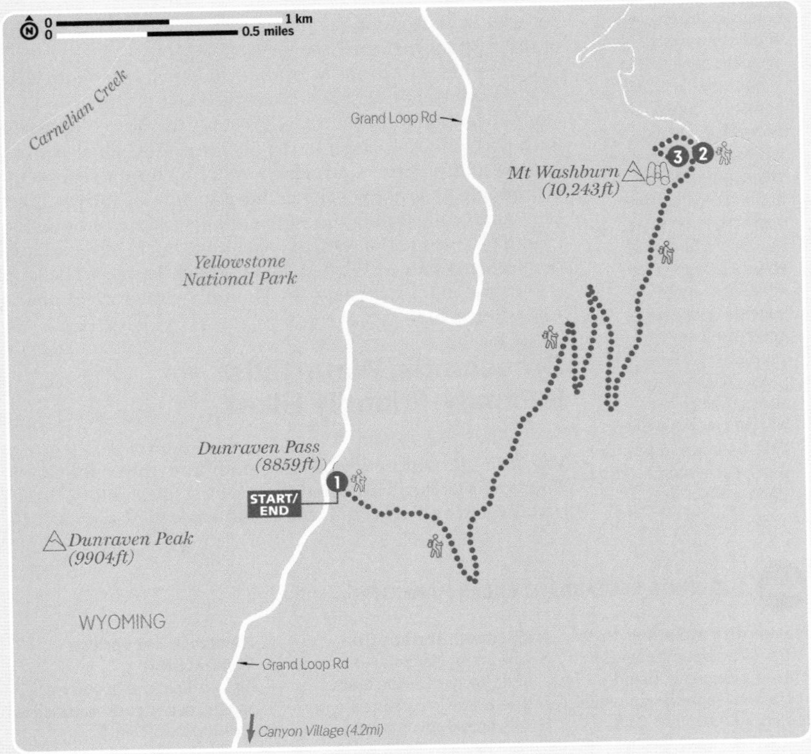

YELLOWSTONE-POWERED SCIENCE

A huge variety of microbes and bacteria thrive in these extreme waters, tolerating heat, extremely acidic or alkaline conditions and toxic minerals. One such species has yielded an important enzyme crucial to DNA fingerprinting tests. Other research is revealing important clues about the origins of life on earth and the survival of life in outer space.

Much of this activity occurs on a microscopic scale, but visitors can still appreciate the brilliant colors these microorganisms produce in bodies of water. Each species inhabits a highly specific temperature and chemical zone, so each layer produces the rings and patches of vibrant color that give Yellowstone's waters their psychedelic signature.

ALEXANDER OGANEZOV/SHUTTERSTOCK ©

Petrified Tree

pre-CGI backdrop for the planet Vulcan during the filming of the 1979 movie *Star Trek*.

A 1.5-mile, paved one-way road loops counterclockwise around the Upper Terraces. Near the start of the drive, you can pull over and take in the views over the Lower Terraces, with Fort Yellowstone off in the distance. You can also stroll out to Canary Springs, which was once a vibrant yellow color, though its craggy terraces have mellowed into orange, brown, green and pink tones. Highlights further around the road loop include the spongelike Orange Spring Mound and the perfectly named White Elephant Back Terrace. The loop rejoins the main road near the looming white formations of Angel Terrace.

Grasslands, Waterfalls & Family-Friendly Hikes

HIGHLIGHTS IN THE NORTH

The 18-mile road between Mammoth and Tower-Roosevelt Junction is packed with scenic spots. First up, is pretty, three-tiered **Undine Falls**. You can get up-close views of the falls

LODGING & RESTAURANTS NEAR MAMMOTH

Mammoth Hot Springs Hotel
Attractive modern rooms and cabins, plus an ecofriendly restaurant serving up mostly locally sourced fare. **$$$**

Mammoth Terrace Grill
Line up for MacYellowstone-style burgers, bison brats, salads and ice cream, along with breakfast options. **$**

Mammoth Hot Springs General Store
Pick up groceries or order snacks: pulled pork sandwiches, chili and ice cream. **$**

by continuing another half mile down the road and taking the Lava Creek Trail. It's less than a half-mile walk to the falls.

Back in the car, it's 0.4 miles farther along the road to reach the trailhead for **Wraith Falls**. This easy-going 1-mile round-trip walk is a good family hike through pretty meadows, fire-burn patches and mixed conifer forest. As you near the end, you'll cross rushing Lupine Creek and soon get a view of the 79ft falls high up in the hillside.

The **Blacktail Ponds** are another mile along the road. Early or late in the day, this treeless watering hole is a fine spot to look for muskrats and waterfowl. A good trail nearby is **Blacktail Deer Creek Trail**, an 8-mile out-and-back hike that goes through rolling grass-covered hills, fir forest and across a suspension bridge over the Yellowstone River.

Another few minutes' drive takes you to a pullout for the **Forces of the Northern Range Trailhead**. Overlooking a vast stretch of grasslands, this fully accessible boardwalk loop has signposts that give insight into the animal and plant life in this part of the park.

Just before you reach Tower-Roosevelt Junction is the 0.25-mile turnoff to the **Petrified Tree**, surrounded by a fence like a priceless work of art.

A few miles south of Tower-Roosevelt Junction, Tower Creek plunges over 132ft **Tower Fall** before joining the Yellowstone River. Though it's a busy area, stroll out to the viewpoint overlooking Tower Falls.

Sweeping Views of Yellowstone's Grand Canyon

SOUTH & NORTH RIM LOOKOUTS

Nature's majesty comes into clear focus in the breathtaking, wind-whipped **Grand Canyon of the Yellowstone** near the center of the national park. It's also the backdrop to Yellowstone's most impressive waterfalls.

A little over one mile south of Canyon Junction, a one-way road leads along North Rim Dr, which is dotted with lofty viewpoints above the Grand Canyon. The first parking area you'll reach gives access to **Brink of the Lower Falls**. Here a steep 0.75-mile trail descends 600ft for exciting close-up views of the tumbling white water.

Continuing along the road, stop for the astonishing panorama from **Lookout Point**. Here you'll get a majestic view of the thundering Lower Falls. If you seek closer canyon encounters, make the 500ft descent along the half-mile-long Red Rock Points trail. Next up is Grandview Point, which offers views of the canyon's colorful smoking walls. Keep going

WHY I LOVE THE GRAND CANYON OF THE YELLOWSTONE

Regis St Louis, writer

For witnessing the staggering power of nature, I love going to the lookout at Brink of the Lower Falls and leaning out over the railing as Yellowstone's mightiest waterfall roars past. It feels like therapy: the mist against my face while watching this endless thundering stream against the backdrop of cliffs and forest. After the close-up, I like to head over to the Lower Rim trail for a walk on the edge of the canyon, with every step yielding yet a new angle on the magnificent sweep of canyon stretching beneath me. The canyon's magic continues in the backcountry, with a hike to Clear Lake, past gurgling, steaming geothermal features seen by so few visitors.

LODGING & RESTAURANTS IN CANYON VILLAGE

Canyon Lodge Rooms
Huge variety of options, from standards with shower-only to plush suites with forest-facing decks. **$$$**

Western Cabins
Comfortably set: two queen beds in each and full bathrooms, plus a shared front porch. **$$$**

Canyon Lodge Eatery
Diner-esque setting with lunchtime wok/noodle bowls; and chicken, veg items or roasted salmon for dinner.

CANYON VIEWS ON THE YELLOWSTONE RIVER OVERLOOK HIKE

A short drive from Tower-Roosevelt junction, this hike offers fantastic views into the eroded towers and basalt formations of the Narrows and Calcite Springs sections of the Yellowstone Valley. With an elevation gain of only 350ft, the 4-mile round-trip hike is popular with families, but be mindful of the sheer drop-offs.

The **1 trailhead** is at the picnic site on the left side of the vault toilets. As you ascend, you'll pass several large **2 erratic boulders**, deposited in the valley more than 10,000 years ago from the Beartooth Mountains by slow-moving glaciers.

The hike soon puts you on the astonishing **3 canyon rim**. More features come into sight, giving unobscured views down past the crooked canyon walls to the Yellowstone River, and north and east beyond rolling ridges to the peaks of the Absaroka Range.

About one mile from the trailhead, you may smell sulfur, a sign that you are about to pass 180-degree views of the **4 Calcite Springs** thermal area across the canyon. Just above the river, you may even see steam spilling from the cliff walls.

As you continue tracing the canyon, you'll have fine views of the breccia spires of **5 the Narrows**. These basalt columns were formed some 1.3 million years ago from rapidly cooling lava flows. Look out for bighorn sheep on the cliffs above.

The trail ends abruptly at a **6 Bald Overlook**, offering views down on the site of the Bannock Indian ford, used by the Bannock to cross the Yellowstone River during their annual hunting trips across the park. You can also see the Tower Fall region (but not the falls themselves) to the right, and the fire tower atop Mt Washburn in the distance.

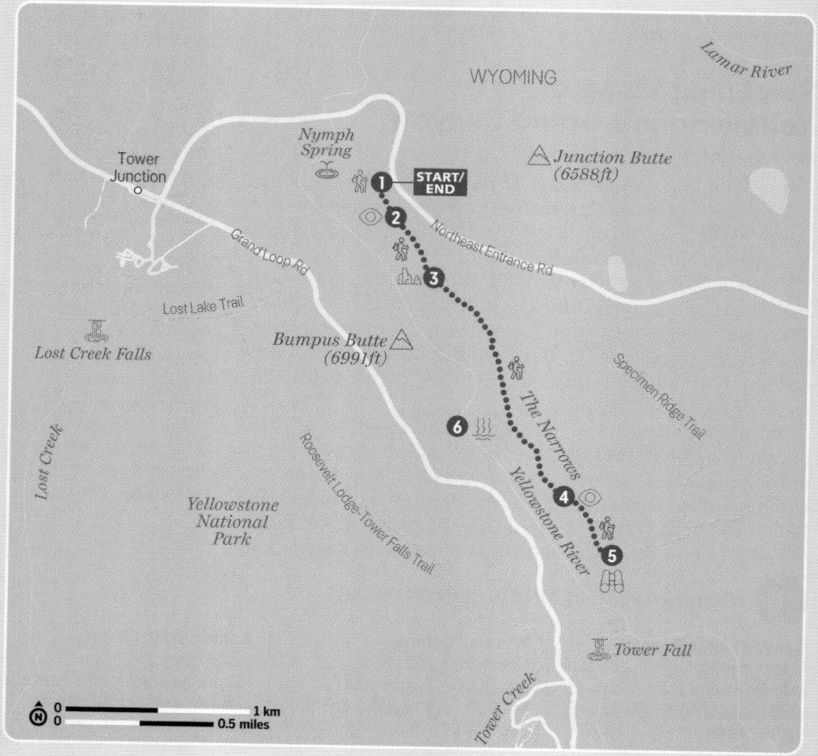

to reach **Inspiration Point**, which gives an overview of the length of the canyon.

Afterwards, continue down to South Rim Dr. Cross the Chittenden Bridge, and pull over at the large parking area for the Upper Falls Viewpoint, where overlooks provide fine vantage points through the pine trees of the fast-flowing white water churning over the **Upper Falls**.

From here you can head off on foot for views of waterfalls from the trail, or continue by car one mile farther to the west. The road ends near **Artist Point**. This is probably the most famous of the canyon's viewpoints, offering a long panorama of the Lower Falls and canyon.

Exploring West Thumb

THE STEAMING, SPOUTING LAKESHORE

Named for its location in the hand-shaped Yellowstone Lake, **West Thumb** is a small volcanic caldera spawned 150,000 years ago inside the much larger Yellowstone caldera. Yellowstone Lake filled the crater, creating West Thumb Bay, a circular inlet at the lake's western end. The geyser basin pours more than 3000 gallons of hot water into the lake daily.

Back in the early days of the park, visitors would take a steamboat from West Thumb to the Lake Hotel, stopping at Dot Island en route to gawk at the captive elk and bison that were in pens there. Although West Thumb is not one of Yellowstone's prime thermal sites, its half-mile shoreline boardwalk loop (with a shorter inner loop to finish with) passes more than a dozen hot springs. At famous **Fishing Cone**, anglers once used the infamous 'hook 'n' cook' method to prepare their catch, casting fish into the boiling water – a practice now prohibited.

Fluctuating lake levels in spring and early summer sometimes submerge Fishing Cone and Lakeshore Geyser, but you can still see **Big Cone**. You can spot the underwater features by looking for slick spots or a slight bulge in the water.

Abyss Pool is one of the park's deepest springs, and during high season rangers typically give short talks here several times a day. Nearby **Black Pool** is one of the prettiest lakeside features, with stunning amber-colored runoff, though it's now sapphire blue after years of lower temperatures supported mats of black thermophiles. Thumb Paint Pots are struggling to regain the energy that once catapulted boiling mud 25ft into the air.

BEST LODGING & DINING NEAR YELLOWSTONE LAKE

Lake Lodge Cabins
Comfortable Western cabins and smaller, shower-only Frontier cabins. **$$$**

Lake Yellowstone Hotel
Classy rooms, some with lake views and internet access (a rarity in Yellowstone). It also serves upscale breakfast buffets and reservation-only French-inspired dinners. **$$$**

Wylie's Canteen at Lake Lodge
Serves food all day with breakfast bowls and English muffin sandwiches, burgers and milkshakes. **$$**

Grant Village Lake House Restaurant
Satisfying tacos, churros and margaritas served on a covered deck overlooking the water. **$**

GETTING AROUND

There's no bus system through the park, so you'll have to drive. Long lines entering the park can make for tedious waits, so get an early start to beat the crowds.

PAUL BRADY PHOTOGRAPHY/SHUTTERSTOCK ©

Above: Gateway Arch National Park (p317); Right: Rankin Ridge (p330), Wind Cave National Park

THE MAIN AREAS

BADLANDS NATIONAL PARK
Explore a weirdly wonderful landscape.
p312

CUYAHOGA VALLEY NATIONAL PARK
Hike through history in Ohio.
p314

GATEWAY ARCH NATIONAL PARK
Climb the gateway to the West.
p317

ISLE ROYALE NATIONAL PARK
Walk across the Great Lakes.
p320

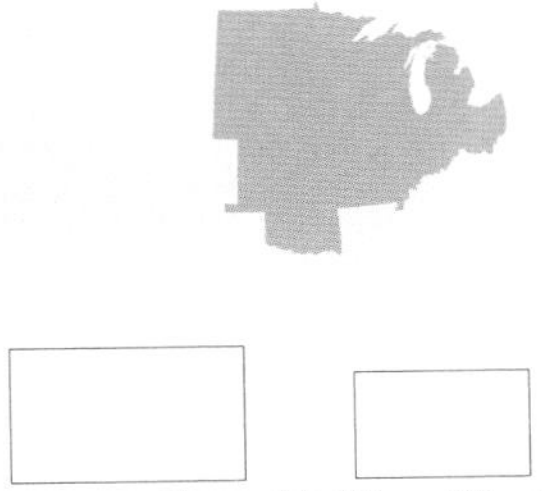

GREAT LAKES & GREAT PLAINS

EXPLORE THE AMERICAN HEARTLAND

From Missouri, Minnesota and Michigan to the Dakotas, enjoy unique national parks that showcase the best of the lakes and plains.

Surprisingly few national parks pepper the Great Plains and Great Lakes – perhaps both are such great wilderness destinations in their own right that it takes something special to stand out. The national parks you'll find here include some of America's least known, but the breadth of experiences they offer are like a cross-section of the American experience. Together they serve as a reminder of why national parks are still celebrated as America's best idea.

RACHAEL MARTIN/SHUTTERSTOCK ©

Take North and South Dakota, for example. While everyone else is heading for Mt Rushmore, travelers in the know make a beeline for Theodore Roosevelt, Badlands and Wind Cave. Badlands protects one of the truly special landscapes of the American West, Theodore Roosevelt celebrates a time when a US president was molded by a stirring wilderness that's still ripe for exploration, and Wind Cave protects a subterranean world that has few rivals anywhere in the US.

Not to be outdone, the Great Lakes showcase their best and wildest side in Isle Royale, while Voyageurs, hard up against the Canadian border in Minnesota, offers a fantastic houseboat experience in summer and all manner of activities and fun in winter. History and nature exist side by side in Cuyahoga Valley, Ohio's only national park. And then there's tiny Gateway Arch in Missouri, an urban national park unlike any other park in the country.

THEODORE ROOSEVELT NATIONAL PARK
Follow in a president's footsteps.
p323

VOYAGEURS NATIONAL PARK
Houseboats and winter sports in Minnesota.
p327

WIND CAVE NATIONAL PARK
Discover South Dakota's subterranean world.
p329

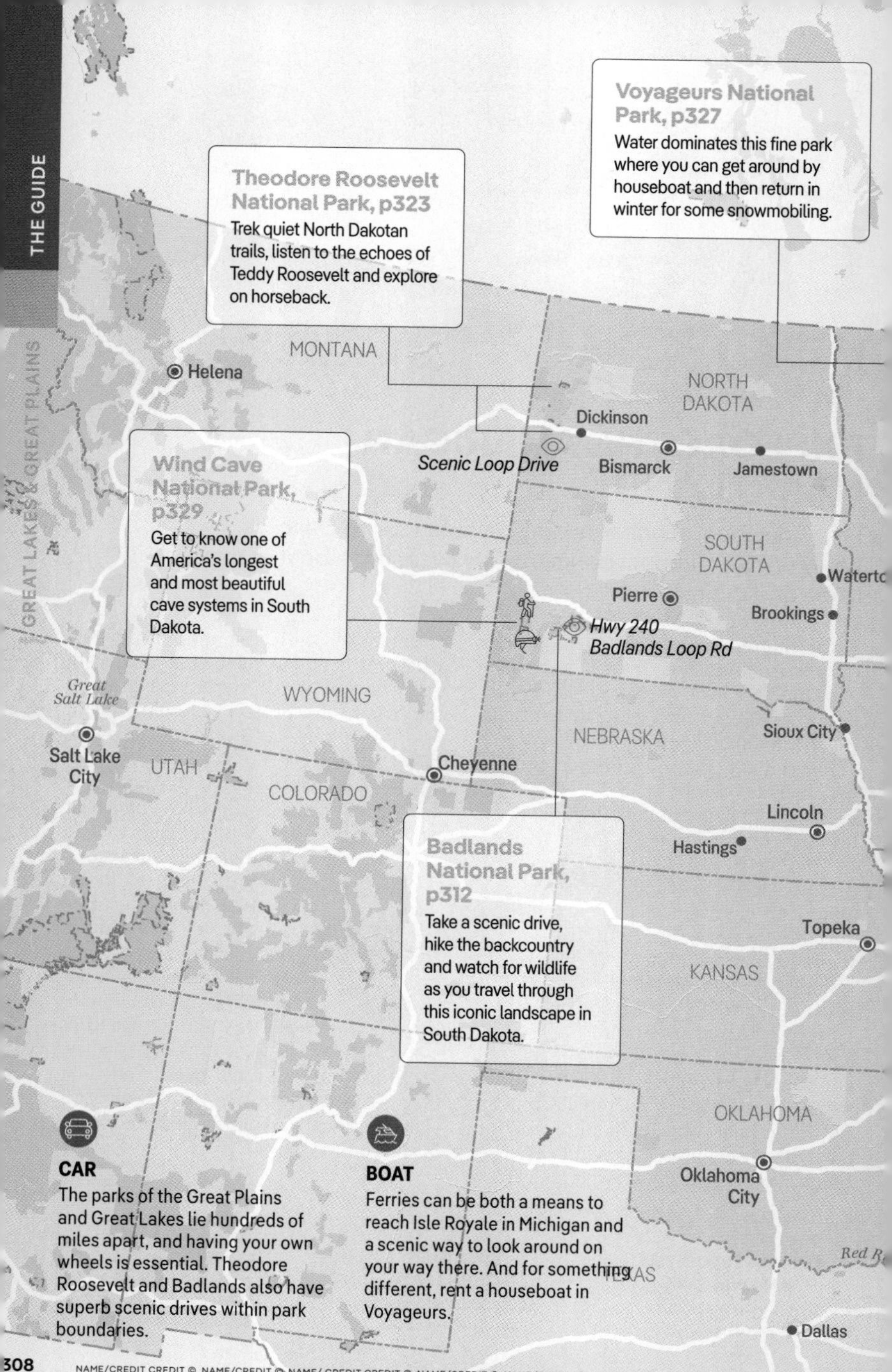

Theodore Roosevelt National Park, p323

Trek quiet North Dakotan trails, listen to the echoes of Teddy Roosevelt and explore on horseback.

Voyageurs National Park, p327

Water dominates this fine park where you can get around by houseboat and then return in winter for some snowmobiling.

Wind Cave National Park, p329

Get to know one of America's longest and most beautiful cave systems in South Dakota.

Badlands National Park, p312

Take a scenic drive, hike the backcountry and watch for wildlife as you travel through this iconic landscape in South Dakota.

CAR

The parks of the Great Plains and Great Lakes lie hundreds of miles apart, and having your own wheels is essential. Theodore Roosevelt and Badlands also have superb scenic drives within park boundaries.

BOAT

Ferries can be both a means to reach Isle Royale in Michigan and a scenic way to look around on your way there. And for something different, rent a houseboat in Voyageurs.

Find Your Way

Having your own wheels is essential for getting to and around many of these parks. You'll need a boat here and there, and walking is best for exploring a little deeper.

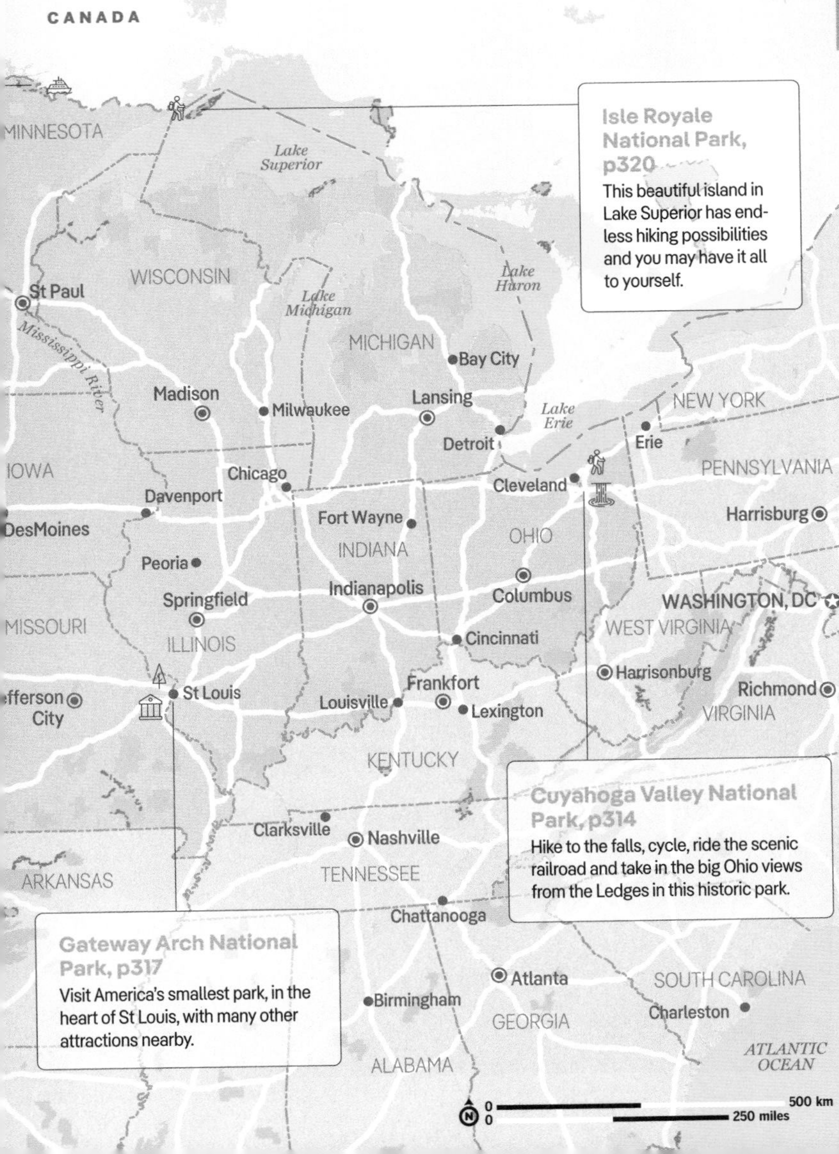

WIRESTOCK CREATORS/SHUTTERSTOCK ©

Badlands National Park (p312)

Canoeing, Voyageurs National Park (p327)

Plan Your Time

These parks cover much of the US interior, so it makes sense to link the Dakotan parks into a single trip, with the rest saved for a different itinerary.

A Dakotan Detour

North and South Dakota are a long way from anywhere, so if you're this far out onto the Great Plains, make the most of it. Begin with two days hiking and horseback riding in **Theodore Roosevelt National Park** (p323), then head south for a couple more days driving around beautiful **Badlands National Park** (p312). If you've only got one day left, take a cave tour in **Wind Cave National Park** (p329).

Lakes & Rivers

Begin by the Mississippi River in St Louis for a unique park experience at **Gateway Arch National Park** (p317). Trace the river's path north for two days of wilderness hiking in Michigan's **Isle Royale National Park** (p320), and follow it up with either houseboats or snowy fun – depending on the season – in **Voyageurs National Park** (p327) in the far north of Minnesota.

SEASONAL HIGHLIGHTS

SPRING

A nice balance between baking summers and icy winters. Visitor numbers are fewer. Watch for wildflowers.

SUMMER

Head for the parks where water dominates, such as Voyageurs and Isle Royale.

FALL

Another great time to visit, with often clear, mild weather conditions and fall colors.

WINTER

Winters can be fiercely cold out on the Great Plains, but it's the perfect time to explore Voyageurs National Park.

BADLANDS NATIONAL PARK

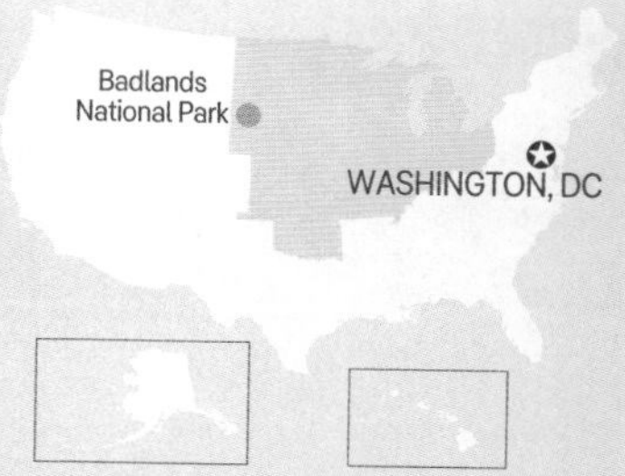

The otherworldly landscape of Badlands National Park, oddly softened by its fantastic rainbow hues, is a spectacle of sheer walls and spikes stabbing the dry air. It was understandably named *mako sica* ('badland') by Native Americans. Looking over the bizarre formations from the corrugated walls surrounding the park is like seeing an ocean someone boiled dry.

The North Unit of the park is easily viewed on a half-day drive for those in a rush, though there are a number of short hiking trails that can get you right out into this earthen wonderland, including the surreal Door Trail near the Ben Reifel Visitor Center. The less-accessible Stronghold Unit is in the Pine Ridge Indian Reservation and sees few visitors. Bisecting the two is Hwy 44, which makes a scenic alternative route between the Badlands and Rapid City: it's the main thoroughfare through the park, with lookouts, vistas and animal sightings aplenty.

FACTS

Great For Wildlife, photo ops, scenery, walking
State South Dakota
Entrance Fee 7-day pass per car/person on foot, motorbike or bicycle $30/15
Area 379 sq miles

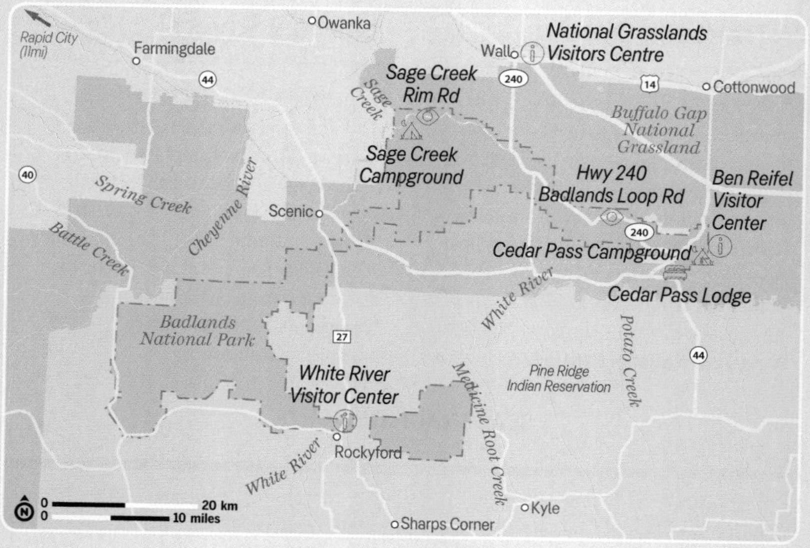

Drive the Scenic Badlands

EXPLORE THE PARK BY CAR

Badlands National Park's North Unit gets the most visitors; the stunning **Hwy 240 Badlands Loop Rd** is easily reached from I-90 (exits 110 and 131) and you can drive it in an hour if you're in a rush (and not stuck behind an RV). But why hurry? There's so much to see along the way that you'll want to pull over regularly for photos.

The portion of the Badlands west of Hwy 240 along the gravel **Sage Creek Rim Rd** is much less visited than the sights of the Badlands Loop Rd. There are scenic overlooks and stops at prairie dog towns; this is where most backcountry hikers and campers go to escape the crowds. As there is almost no water or shade here, don't strike out into the wilderness unprepared.

Look for Wildlife in Buffalo Gap National Grassland

SHARE TRAILS WITH BISON

This nature reserve surrounds Badlands and together they protect the country's largest prairie grasslands, several species of Great Plains mammal (including bison and black-footed ferrets), prairie falcons and lots of snakes.

The **National Grasslands Visitors Center** has good displays on the wealth of life in this complex ecosystem. Rangers can map out back-road routes that will let you do looping tours of Badlands National Park and the grasslands without ever touching I-90.

Stay Overnight in Badlands

SLEEP UNDER THE STARS

Most visitors to Badlands drive right on through, so staying overnight assures you of a much more soulful experience. The park has two campgrounds – **Cedar Pass** (with its windbreaks and shaded picnic tables) and more primitive **Sage Creek** – and **Cedar Pass Lodge**, which opens from mid-April to mid-October. There are also campgrounds and inns near the southern entrance at Interior.

WORTH A TRIP: THE BLACK HILLS

The Black Hills, south of Badlands, are known as an evergreen island in a sea of high-prairie grassland. This stunning region on the Wyoming–South Dakota border lures scores of visitors with its winding canyons and wildly eroded 7000ft peaks. The region's name – the 'Black' comes from the dark ponderosa-pine-covered slopes – was conferred by the Lakota Sioux. With the signing of the 1868 Fort Laramie Treaty, they were assured that the hills would be theirs for eternity, but the discovery of gold changed that and the Sioux were shoved out to low-value flatlands only six years later. The 1990 film *Dances with Wolves* covers some of this period.

GETTING AROUND

Badlands National Park is about 70 miles east of Rapid City. You can access the park at several points north and south. There is no public transportation to (or within) the park, so you'll need your own wheels.

CUYAHOGA VALLEY NATIONAL PARK

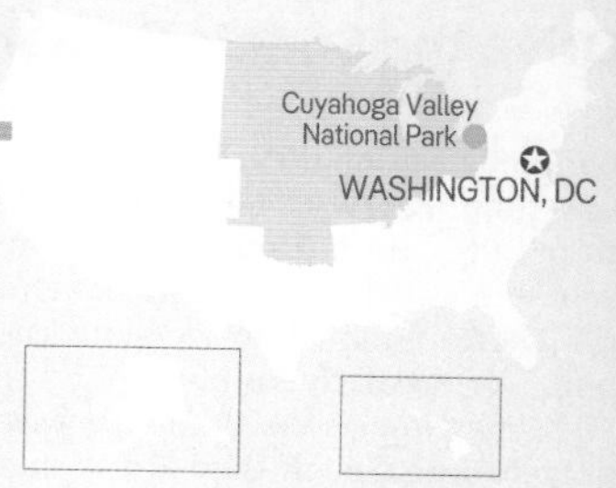

Like a great, cold serpent, the Cuyahoga River snakes through a forested valley, earning its Native American name of 'crooked river' (or possibly 'place of the jawbone'). Either name is evocative, and hints at the mystical beauty that Ohio's only national park engenders on a cool morning, when mists thread the woods and all you hear is the honk of Canadian geese and the 'fwup-fwup-whoosh' of a great blue heron flapping over its hunting grounds.

There was a time, early in the history of the USA, when this was the frontier for those settlers huddled in the Eastern colonies; at the same time it was already home for vast confederations of Native Americans. Today, a mere 20 miles from Cleveland and 18 miles from Akron, you can walk trails that sneak past white waterfalls and dark hollows to find the frontier still, along with traces of a great indigenous nation.

FACTS

Great For Cycling, Family Travel, Walking
State Ohio
Entrance Fee Free
Area 51 sq miles

OLEG KOVTUN HYDROBIO/SHUTTERSTOCK ©

Waterfall, Brandywine Creek

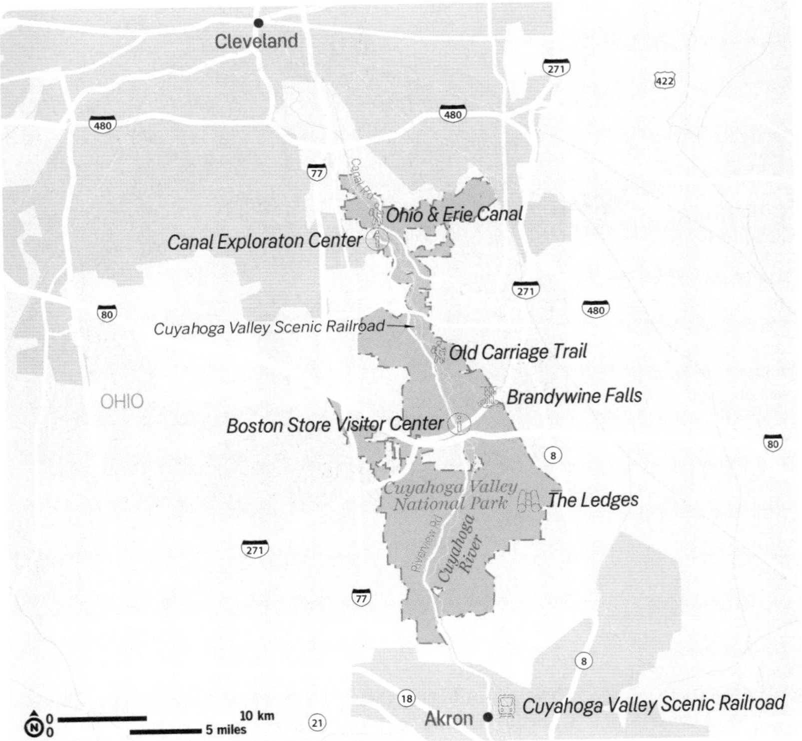

Visit Brandywine Falls

STROLL TO CUYAHOGA'S MAIN ATTRACTION

Long considered one of the main attractions within the park, **Brandywine Falls** is a pretty spill of ice-cold water nestled in a wooden idyll, and can be accessed via a 1.5-mile round-trip hike that features some light elevation gain (160ft). A small bridge and a boardwalk lookout make this a visitor favorite.

Go Hiking & Cycling

ENJOY THE GREAT OUTDOORS

The park's main trail follows the old **Ohio & Erie Canal**, which once served as one of the primary historical arteries into the American West. Boats pulled by mules ran adjacent to this trail, now an ideal thoroughfare for hikers and cyclists. Many of the park's main trails intersect the towpath.

The Ledges, which offers a sweeping view of the Cuyahoga, is probably the most photographed place in the park, with an unobstructed vista looking west over the valley to eternity. There's a moderately difficult loop trail nearby, a little over 2 miles in length, that's a nice leg stretcher.

CUYAHOGA ESSENTIALS

Boston Store Visitor Center
The main visitor center (nps.gov/cuva) for the park was originally a 19th-century warehouse and boarding house. Inside you'll find helpful park rangers, interpretive displays and a ton of park-trail maps.

Inn at Brandywine Falls
This 1848 Greek Revival country home (brandywinefallsinn.com) is situated in a gentle sweep of pastoral prettiness that's easy to fall in love with. The six rooms are individually differentiated, but all nicely put together.

Fischer's Cafe
Burgers, steaks, fish and chips and other spins on pub food, plus a good beer menu, are the name of the game at this bar-restaurant. There's a nice outdoor area for good weather.

Cycling the towpath (p315)

The 5.3-mile **Old Carriage Trail** is one of the longer loop trails in the park, but it's not particularly difficult. Along the way you'll pass forested ledges, running streams and a 500ft ravine. The eponymous overlook is fine, but sight lines get a little blocked when there are leaves on the trees.

Ride a Scenic Railroad

SIT BACK AND ENJOY THE RIDE

The old-school iron carriage of the **Cuyahoga Valley Scenic Railroad** chugs along a pleasant course from Akron to Independence, OH, through the heart of the park. The most expensive tickets score you seating in the glass-topped dome, offering nice roundabout views. A full round trip takes around 3½ hours.

GETTING AROUND

The park is easily accessible by car from Cleveland (20 miles) or Akron (18 miles), and lies just off I-77. Once here, to get around the park you can either walk or take the scenic railroad.

GATEWAY ARCH NATIONAL PARK

As a symbol for St Louis, the Gateway Arch has soared above any expectations its backers could have had in 1965 when it opened. Now the centerpiece of its own recently christened national park, the silvery, shimmering arch is the Great Plains' own Eiffel Tower. It stands 630ft high and symbolizes St Louis' historical role as 'Gateway to the West.' It's the design of the legendary Finnish American architect Eero Saarinen (1910–61).

The park may seem like a far cry from the likes of Yellowstone, Yosemite or the Everglades: Gateway Arch rises from the heart of big-city St Louis, with all the noise and clamor that entails. But the park is proof of the adaptability of the national-park idea, and as far as symbols go, there are few more powerful than the American West and the Mississippi River. Throw in some great surrounding museums and attractions, and it's a fantastic urban-park experience.

FACTS

Great For History, Family Travel, Photo Op
State Missouri
Entrance Fee Free
Area 0.14 sq miles

Gateway Arch National Park

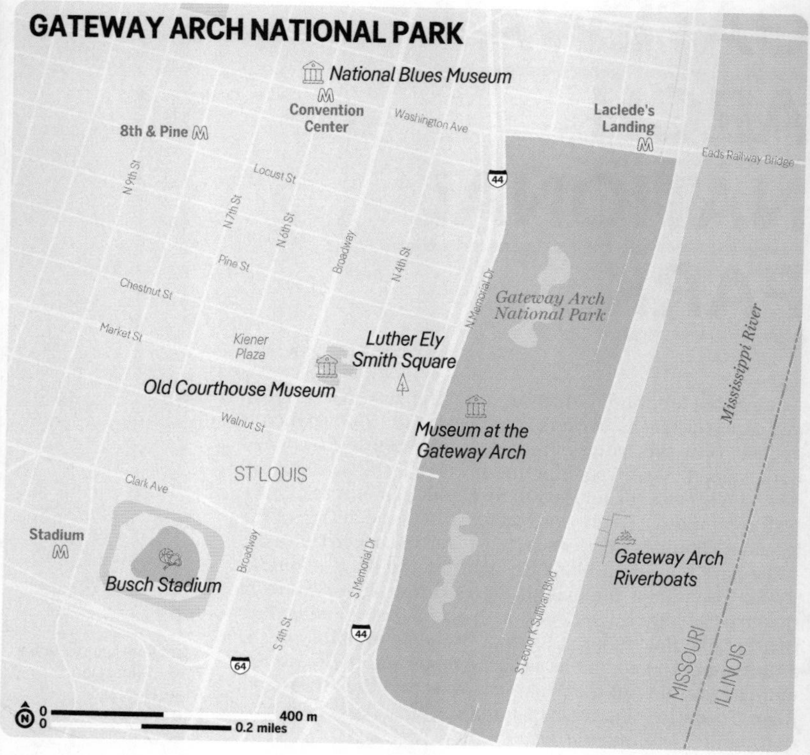

Explore America's Smallest National Park

DISCOVER MUSEUMS AND MORE

Before entering the park, pause long enough to explore the **Old Courthouse Museum**. Free to enter, this historic structure was the site of two trials in the Dred Scott case, now considered among the very worst US Supreme Court decisions. Scott, an enslaved man who attempted to sue for his freedom, was denied standing to bring the suit. Now a museum, the courthouse's galleries deal with the ignominious history of slavery and the fight for emancipation.

It's a short walk across **Luther Ely Smith Square** to the park. This elegant new space was built to commemorate the Arch's 50th birthday and covered the traffic-choked I-44. Previously the road formed a forbidding moat, separating the Arch from the rest of St Louis. There's lush landscaping, wide lawns and plenty of sitting areas.

Time for another museum, the **Museum at the Gateway Arch**. It not only offers high-tech interactive exhibits but an updated

Old Courthouse Museum and Museum at the Gateway Arch

historical view of westward expansion, with displays acknowledging that the West was either 'won' or 'stolen,' depending on your perspective. Visitors can also learn about the innovative engineering behind the Arch monument.

From the museum, take the **tram ride** to the tight confines at the top of the Arch and take in the extraordinary views out over the Mississippi River. Book tickets in advance online or by phone. At busy times, same-day tickets may be sold out. Some of the many money-saving combo tickets include rides on the Gateway Arch Riverboats. And when you're back down, the **parkland** around the Arch is a great place to escape the crowds and relax by the river.

NEARBY ATTRACTIONS

Gateway Arch Riverboats
Churn up the Big Muddy on replica 19th-century steamboats (gatewayarch.com). A park ranger narrates the midday cruises in season, and those after 3pm sail subject to availability. There are also numerous dinner and drinking cruises.

National Blues Museum
This flashy museum (nationalbluesmuseum.org) explores blues legends like hometown hero Chuck Berry. There are interactive exhibits from the likes of Jack White, and interesting stories about the early years of blues and its (almost exclusively female) pioneers.

Busch Stadium
The St Louis Cardinals baseball team (stlcardinals.com) play in this fun, retro stadium, opened in 2006. The Cardinals have 11 World Series wins, second only to the New York Yankees, and they last won the Series in 2011.

GETTING AROUND

To reach Gateway Arch from elsewhere in St Louis, take the MetroLink (metrostlouis.org) light-rail system. The Old Courthouse Museum is accessible on foot from Kiener Plaza. The only way to get around the actual site is by walking.

ISLE ROYALE NATIONAL PARK

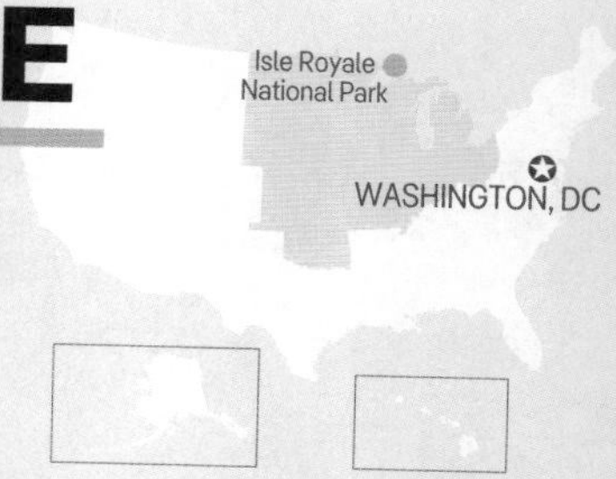

Totally free of vehicles and roads, Isle Royale National Park – a 210-sq-mile island in Lake Superior – is certainly the place to go for peace and quiet. Its appeal is summed up in one remarkable statistic: Isle Royale gets fewer visitors in a year than Yellowstone National Park gets in a day, which means the 2000 moose roaming through the forest are all yours.

The island is laced with 165 miles of hiking trails that connect dozens of campgrounds along Lake Superior and inland lakes. You must be totally prepared for this wilderness adventure, with a tent, camping stove, sleeping bag, food and water filter. You can also take a seaplane scenic flight or explore by using the ferries that ply the waters of Lake Superior.

One last thing to remember: the park is only open from mid-April through October, then it closes due to the possibility of extreme winter weather.

FACTS

Great For Scenery, Wildlife, Walking
State Michigan
Entrance Fee 1-day pass per person $7
Area 210 sq miles

BRYNN DELANGE/SHUTTERSTOCK ©

Backpacker, Isle Royale National Park

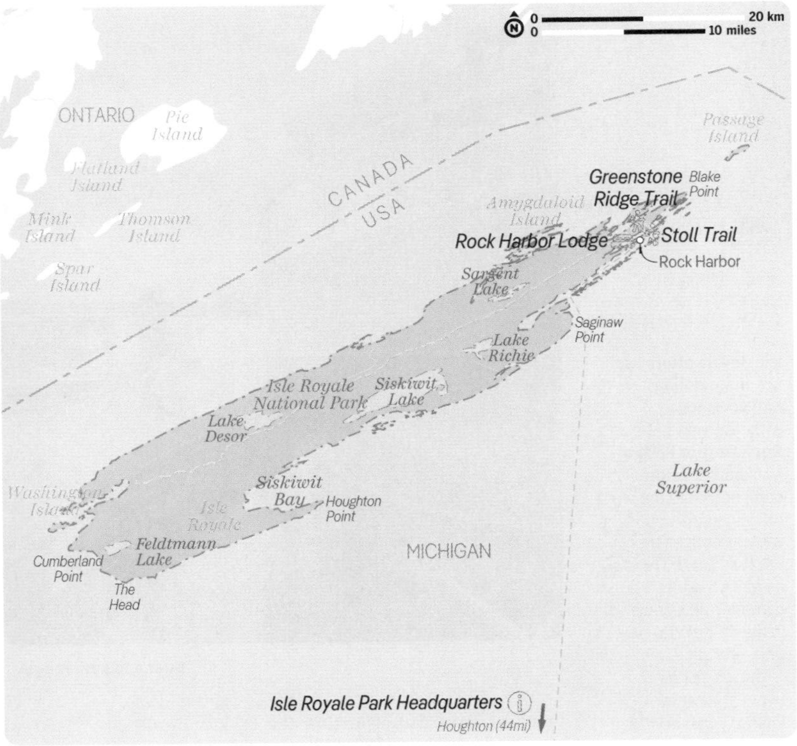

Hike Isle Royale's Quiet Trails

WALK AMONG THE WILDLIFE

At a length of 42 miles, the **Greenstone Ridge Trail** is the longest trail on Isle Royale. It is a grand backpacking adventure that spans the entire length of the island, from Rock Harbor in the east to Windigo in the west. You can hike it in either direction, but most people start in Rock Harbor and take five to seven days to complete this epic wilderness trek.

The moderately difficult route pays off big time with forest solitude, fab lookouts over the coast and abundant moose and red fox sightings. The only accommodations along the way are primitive campgrounds with pit toilets, so you'll have to carry all your food and gear. Whether you finish your trek in Windigo or Rock Harbor, it's easy to arrange boat transportation back to your starting point.

The easier 4.4-mile **Stoll Trail** loop begins at Rock Harbor Lodge and meanders through old-growth forest and along shoreline bluffs to Scoville Point, an outcrop that unfurls dramatic

ISLE ROYALE SLEEPING & EATING OPTIONS

Isle Royale offers two accommodations options: snooze with lake views at **Rock Harbor Lodge** (rockharborlodge.com) or hike to the rustic campgrounds with outhouses that dot the island. There's no extra fee for camping – it's covered in the $7-per-day park-entrance fee.

The lodge has two restaurants: a dining room serving American fare and a more casual cafe. The Dockside Store at Rock Harbor stocks a small array of groceries and there's another small store in Windigo. Prices are steep.

KELL CREATIVE/SHUTTERSTOCK ©

Boat and park ranger

views of Lake Superior and the craggy landscape. Keep an eye out for moose and osprey.

Before setting out on your hike, pay a visit to **Isle Royale Park Headquarters** (nps.gov/isro), which is located in Houghton. They have detailed information on ferries, camping and, yes, hiking routes throughout the park. They even have some maps on hand. They can also provide you with information on scenic flights and all-important ferry timetables.

GETTING AROUND

From the dock outside the park headquarters in Houghton, the *Ranger III* departs at 9am on Tuesdays and Fridays for the six-hour boat trip to Rock Harbor, at the east end of the island.

Isle Royale Seaplanes (isleroyaleseaplanes.com) is quicker, flying from the Portage Canal Seaplane Base in Hancock to Rock Harbor or to Windigo (at the island's west end) in 35 minutes, with fabulous views on the way. They operate from mid-May to late September.

Or head 50 miles up the Keweenaw Peninsula to Copper Harbor and jump on the *Isle Royale Queen* (isleroyale.com) for its daily 3½-hour crossing, from late July through August.

Reserve all transportation well in advance. Check at the visitor center or online (nps.gov/isro) for more information, including departure times and the latest fares.

THEODORE ROOSEVELT NATIONAL PARK

Future president Theodore Roosevelt retreated from New York to this remote spot in his early 20s after losing both his wife and mother in a matter of hours. It's said that his time in the Dakota badlands inspired him to become an avid conservationist, and he set aside 360,000 sq miles of federal land while in office, a quantity of land larger than Texas. His North Dakota legacy is this 110-sq-mile national park, one of the most underappreciated stars of the park system.

Wildlife abounds in these surreal mounds of striated earth, from mule deer to wild horses, bison, bighorn sheep and elk. There are also around 200 bird species, and innumerable prairie dogs in sprawling subterranean towns. Sunrise is your best time for animal encounters, while sunset is particularly evocative as shadows dance across the lonely buttes, painting them in an array of earth tones before they fade to black.

FACTS

Great For Walking, Wildlife, Scenery
State North Dakota
Entrance Fee 7-day pass per car/motorbike/person on foot or bicycle $30/25/15
Area 110 sq miles

Buffalo

HIGHLIGHTS
1 Scenic Loop Drive

SIGHTS
2 Oxbow Overlook

ACTIVITIES, COURSES & TOURS
3 Achenbach Trail
4 Buckhorn Trail
5 Coal Vein Trail
6 Maah Daah Hey Trail
7 Wind Canyon Trail

INFORMATION
8 South Unit Visitor Center

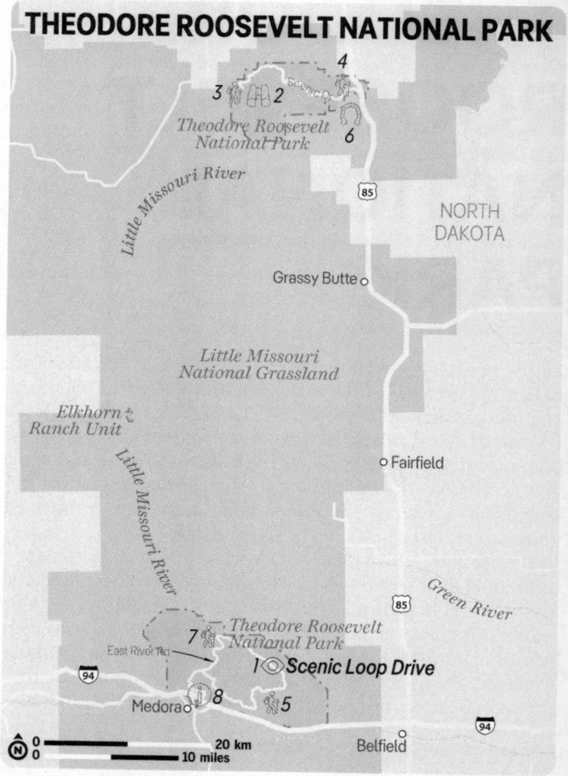

Hike in Teddy's Footsteps

TREK TRAILS, LONG AND SHORT

Hiking opportunities range from paved nature trails to rugged multiday backcountry treks. In the park's South Unit, the 0.4-mile **Wind Canyon Trail** leads to a dramatic viewpoint over the Little Missouri River, which is especially scenic at sunset. The slightly more strenuous 0.6-mile **Coal Vein Trail** explores the badlands' multilayered geology, tracing the history of an ancient coal vein that spontaneously caught fire and burned for 26 years in the mid-20th century.

In the less-visited North Unit, the 1.5-mile **Buckhorn Trail** leads to Prairie Dog Town, a favorite spot for observing these animated little critters. The challenging but spectacular 18-mile **Achenbach Trail** offers a true backcountry experience, crossing the Little Missouri River twice as it climbs and dips through the heart of American bison habitat. Here you'll get grand perspectives on the rolling North Dakota grasslands and see the well-trodden wallows where bison roll around on their backs for a dust bath. Other wildlife that you might

Maah Daah Hey Trail

see along the way on this and some of the other trails includes wild horses, elk, white-tailed deer and mule deer, as well as many of the different bird species that have been recorded in the park.

For a good adventure, hike or cycle the 96-mile **Maah Daah Hey Trail** between the two park units.

Go Horseback Riding

CHANNEL YOUR INNER COWBOY

History buffs and adventurous spirits will find it hard to resist seeing these landscapes as Teddy Roosevelt himself once did, on horseback. The **Maah Daah Hey Trail** passes through a dauntingly rugged but awe-inspiringly scenic stretch of badlands. Travel through this area is facilitated by a network of campsites spaced roughly 20 miles apart. How long it takes you to ride the full 96 miles, or even whether it's possible, will depend on your level of riding expertise.

For information about planning a trip on horseback, check in with the **South Unit Visitor Center**. They can fill you in on everything from where to make the arrangements to possible routes with a Teddy Roosevelt story.

THE ENCHANTED HIGHWAY

Southeast of Theodore Roosevelt National Park, and boasting huge whimsical metal sculptures of local folks and critters by artist Gary Greff, the **Enchanted Highway** runs for 32 miles straight south to Regent from I-94's exit 72. Once there, you can stay in a themed motel, the Enchanted Castle, which is an elementary school remodeled with crenelations. The roadside artworks include the world's largest scrap-metal sculpture, the 110ft-tall *Geese in Flight*.

WHERE TO STAY & EAT IN THEODORE ROOSEVELT NATIONAL PARK

Cottonwood Camping
The most popular campground: 76 sites and plenty of shade, 6 miles from the South Unit Visitor Center. $

Amble Inn
This comfortable five-room inn in Medora is like your friend's Western-themed vacation home. Rooms have fridges. $

Little Missouri Saloon
This old-timey Medora saloon with red wallpaper and door handles made of pistols serves burgers and pizzas. $$

ROOSEVELT'S MALTESE CROSS CABIN

For a glimpse of how Teddy Roosevelt lived during his first North Dakota sojourn, visit this classic frontier log cabin where the 25-year-old future president spent the winter of 1883–84. Faithfully reconstructed using its original ponderosa pine logs, the cabin houses a few artifacts belonging to Roosevelt, including a writing desk and a traveling trunk inscribed with his initials.

The cabin was originally sited several miles to the south, but in 1903 it embarked on a whirlwind tour of the United States, making appearances at the World's Fair in St Louis, Missouri and the Lewis and Clark Centennial Exposition in Portland, Oregon, before returning to North Dakota. It currently sits behind the park's South Unit Visitor Center.

Oxbow Overlook

Take a Scenic Drive

DRIVE AWAY FROM THE CROWDS

The most popular way for visitors to appreciate the park is via the South Unit's 36-mile-long **Scenic Loop Drive**. It takes in the most dramatic scenery, plus crowd-pleasers like Prairie Dog Town, which is signposted and easily reached just off the road.

The North Unit, which is off US 85, gets few visitors. However, it's well worth the journey for the 14-mile drive to the **Oxbow Overlook**, with its wide views into the vast and colorfully striated river canyon. The verdant surrounds are protected as the Little Missouri National Grassland.

Like all roads out west, these see their fair share of vehicles (with slow-moving convoys of RVs, overcrowded roadside stops and campgrounds) in the peak summer months, and again during Christmas and the New Year. Visiting during less busy fall or spring can make a huge difference to your experience.

GETTING AROUND

The park is divided into North and South Units, which are 70 miles apart. The South Unit is in Medora, 135 miles west of Bismarck along I-94. It houses the park's main visitor center and receives more traffic due to its proximity to I-94. The more remote North Unit is 15 miles south of Watford City, accessed via US 85. You'll need your own wheels to get here. Medora is a four-hour drive north from Rapid City, SD.

The nearest airports are Theodore Roosevelt Regional Airport in Dickinson (42 miles east of the South Unit), with direct flights to Denver, and Williston Basin International Airport in Williston (61 miles north of the North Unit), with services to Minneapolis and Denver.

VOYAGEURS NATIONAL PARK

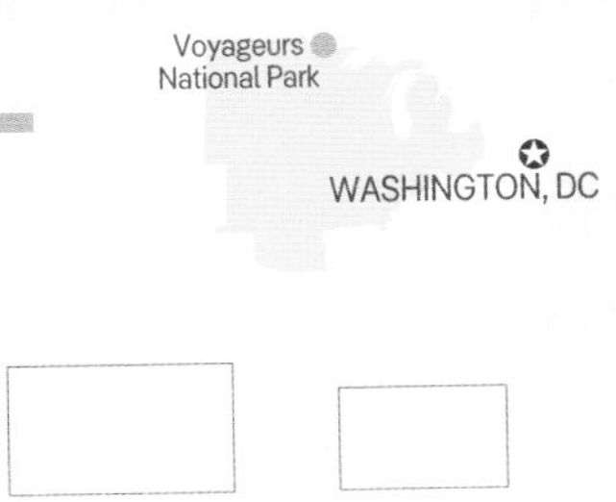

Voyageurs National Park, which marks the border between the USA and Canada, is a wet wilderness of some 341 sq miles. It's almost 40% water and only accessible by hiking or motorboat – the waters are mostly too wide and too rough for canoeing. In summer, people come to boat, swim and fish in the park's five main lakes: Kabetogama, Namakan, Sand Point, Crane and Rainy Lake. In winter, visitors can cross-country ski or snowmobile on specially marked trails. In addition to offering waterborne fun, the park is filled with wildlife, including large populations of deer, moose, black bears and white pelicans.

The park traces its roots to the 17th century, when French-Canadian fur traders, called voyageurs, began exploring the Great Lakes and northern rivers by canoe. Though the idea of establishing a national park here was formed in the early 20th century, the park was only formally founded in the 1970s.

FACTS

Great For Scenery, Walking, Winter Travel
State Minnesota
Entrance Fee Free
Area 341 sq miles

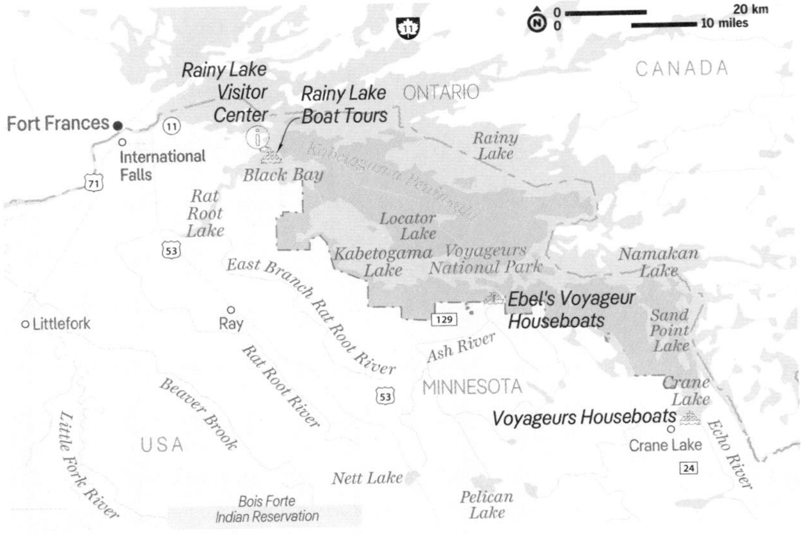

BEST PLACES TO STAY & EAT

Kettle Falls Hotel
This 12-room, shared-bath hotel is inside Voyageurs National Park and accessible only by boat. **$**

Nelson's Resort
The 27 pine-log cabins fringing Crane Lake are a winner for hiking, fishing and relaxing under blue skies. **$$**

Rocky Ledge
Dig into walleye sandwiches, fish tacos, wild-rice casserole and other Minnesota specialties, along with burgers and pizzas. **$$**

Take to the Water in Summer

HOP ON A HOUSEBOAT

From May to September, the main activities at Voyageurs National Park include berry-picking, boating, fishing and swimming. Some nature trails and walks lead off from the park's three visitor centers. In winter, Voyageurs is prime territory for snowmobiles and cross-country skiing.

The park operates **Rainy Lake Boat Tours** to see eagles, an 1890s gold-mining camp and more. It's best to reserve in advance, but you can try for same-day tickets at the Rainy Lake Visitor Center (218-286-5258), from where the boat departs. The park also offers free 1½-hour jaunts in mighty voyageur canoes from late June to mid-August.

One of the best ways to experience the lake is on board a houseboat. Novice boaters are welcome (and receive instruction on how to operate the vessels) at family-run **Ebel's Voyageur Houseboats** (ebels.com), which launch from Ash River. The pricier houseboats have air-conditioning, DVD players and hot tubs. Another option is **Voyagaire Houseboats** (voyagaire.com), based at Crane Lake.

Enjoy the Winter Action

SKIS AND SNOWMOBILES

When the boats get put away for the winter, the snowmobiles come out. Voyageurs is a hot spot for the sport, with 110 miles of staked and groomed trails slicing through the pines. **Rainy Lake Visitor Center** provides maps and advice. It also lends out free snowshoes and cross-country skis for local trails, including a couple that depart from outside the center. To the south, an ice road for cars spans the boat launches of the Ash River and Kabetogama Lake Visitor Centers. There's also a fun sledding hill near the Kabetogama center.

Houseboat
REBECCA SCHWARTZ/SHUTTERSTOCK ©

GETTING AROUND

Hwy 53 is the main highway to the region. It's about five hours' drive from the Twin Cities (or a three-hour drive from Duluth) to Crane Lake, Ash River or Lake Kabetogama. International Falls, near the park's northwest edge, has the closest airport. It also has a busy border crossing with Canada.

WIND CAVE NATIONAL PARK

Wind Cave National Park, protecting 44 sq miles of grassland and forest, sits just south of Custer State Park. The central draw is, of course, the cave, which contains 148 miles of mapped passages. The strong wind gusts that are felt at the entrance, but not inside, give the cave its name. The visitor center has details on the variety of tours that are offered, from one-hour candlelit walks to four-hour crawls.

The cave's foremost feature is its 'boxwork' calcite formations (95% of all that are known exist here), which look like honeycomb and date back 60 to 100 million years. Hiking is a popular activity in the park, where you'll find the southern end of the 111-mile Centennial Trail to Sturgis. The campground usually has space, and backcountry camping (free with permit) is allowed in limited areas.

FACTS

Great For Scenery, Walking, Wildlife
State South Dakota
Entrance Fee Free
Area 44 sq miles

'Boxwork' calcite formations

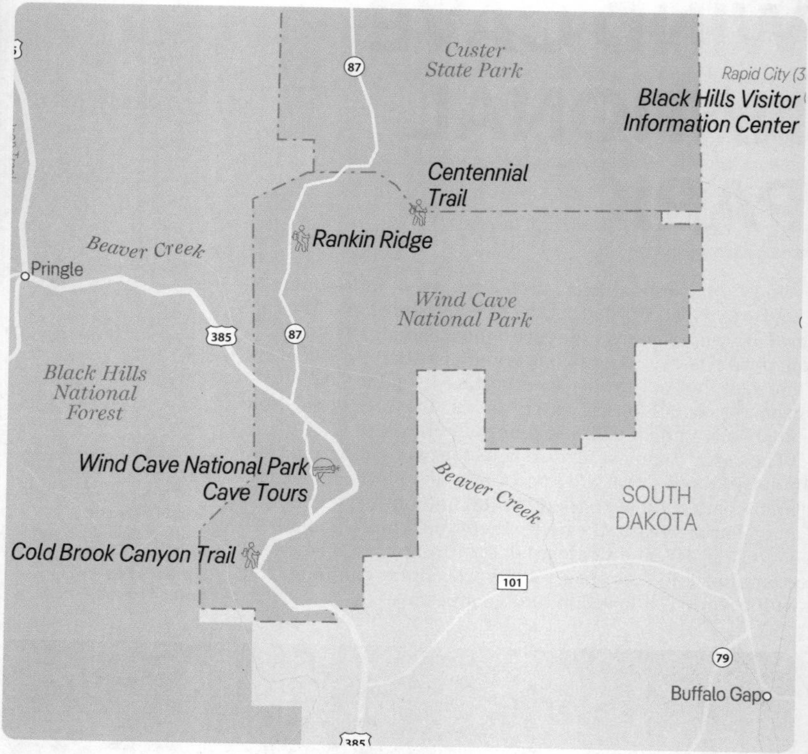

Go on a Cave Tour

EXPLORE UNDERGROUND

It's a fascinating world that you're about to enter, and several tours plunge you into the scene. The easiest is the hour-long **Garden of Eden Tour**, a 0.33-mile walk. The most strenuous is the four-hour **Wild Cave Tour**, where you crawl and climb through farther-flung passages. The moderate **Natural Entrance Tour** is the most popular, while the romantic **Candlelight Tour** dips into less-developed sections of the cave, lit only by – that's right – candles. Reserve cave-tour tickets by calling 605-745-4600.

Hike in Search of Wildlife

EXPLORE ABOVE GROUND

The park unfurls 30 miles of unspoiled trails. **Rankin Ridge** is an easy walk, where you amble up a 1-mile path to an old fire tower, the park's highest point. The **Cold Brook Canyon Trail** is a moderate 2.8-mile hike that takes in meadows, a prairie dog town and falcon-laden cliffs. The **Centennial Trail** is a bit

Rankin Ridge

more difficult, meandering 6 miles one way through patches of prairie and along Beaver Creek.

Whenever you're out exploring, keep an eye out for large herds of bison, elk and pronghorn antelope that wander the plains munching fresh grass. Prairie dog towns see lots of action, and not just from the cute main characters, but also from sneaky coyotes and slithering black-footed ferrets. The town at the intersection of Hwys 385 and 87 provides a good peek at the scene.

For more information on hiking trails and the wildlife you might see along the way, check in at the **Black Hills Visitor Information Center** (blackhillsbadlands.com).

WORTH A TRIP FROM WIND CAVE NATIONAL PARK

Custer State Park
Not only does this park boast some of the best American wildlife viewing outside Yellowstone, it also promises curvaceous mountain drives, serene lakeside retreats and plenty of open range.

Jewel Cave National Monument
Jewel Cave lies 13 miles west of Custer and is another fabulous cave excursion. It's so named because calcite crystals line much of its walls. Some 187 miles have been surveyed so far (3% of the estimated total), making it the third-longest known cave in the world. Tours vary in length and difficulty, and can be reserved three to 90 days in advance (605-717-7629).

GETTING AROUND

There is no public transportation to (or within) Wind Cave National Park, or to (or around) anywhere else in the Black Hills, so it's best to visit the region with your own wheels. Once here, you explore the caves on foot.

NEW ENGLAND & THE MID-ATLANTIC

WILD COAST AND GENTLE MOUNTAINS

Nature is barely tamed in Acadia, a glacier-carved park on the rugged Maine coast, while Virginia's Shenandoah offers gentler charms: waterfalls, wildflowers and roadside wildlife.

When it comes to national parks, the New England and Mid-Atlantic states were definitely ripped off. Two? Just two? Yep, that would be Acadia National Park, representing New England; and Shenandoah National Park, a vision of mountain perfection in the Mid-Atlantic.

Acadia and Shenandoah are exemplars of beauty and adventure, thanks to the visionary politicians and philanthropists who helped create them a century ago. But the natural charms of New England and the Mid-Atlantic are spread well beyond the two parks. In fact, you may want to think of them as gateway parks – compelling introductions to the many amazing national seashores, federal recreation areas and state parks that stretch from the Appalachian Mountains in the west to the Atlantic Ocean in the east.

SHOSHANA WEISSMANN/SHUTTERSTOCK ©

For outdoor adventure, New England undulates with the rolling hills and rocky peaks of the northern Appalachians. Along the Maine coast, waves crash against glaciated mountain-scapes and rocky shores. Beaches are less dramatic along the Mid-Atlantic coastline, but their wide, sandy shores are quite beautiful. The Blue Ridge Mountains, also part of the Appalachians, ripple gently in the west – worn by erosion over the millennia. Scenic roadways anchor both parks: the Park Loop Rd in Acadia, and Skyline Dr in Shenandoah. And both parks are hiking hubs. Multiuse carriage roads bring recreational oomph to Acadia while Shenandoah delivers 105 miles of mountaintop views along Skyline Drive.

THE MAIN AREAS

ACADIA NATIONAL PARK
Rugged coastal mountains.
p336

SHENANDOAH NATIONAL PARK
Waterfalls, summits and scenic drives.
p345

Left: Precipice Trail (p342), Acadia National Park;
Above: Skyline Drive (p348), Shenandoah National Park

Find Your Way

New England and the Mid-Atlantic are neighbors in the eastern United States, and both regions are tucked between the Appalachians and the Atlantic. The two national parks – Acadia and Shenandoah – are 800 miles apart.

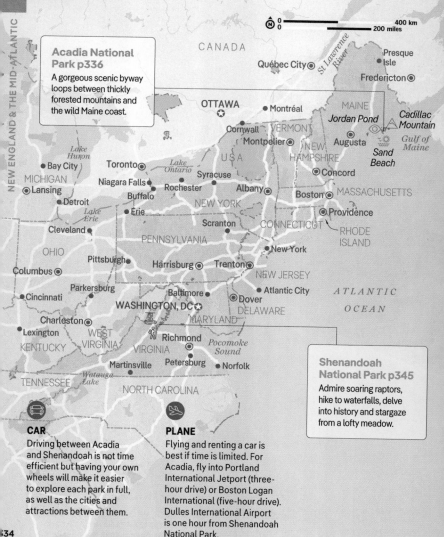

Acadia National Park p336
A gorgeous scenic byway loops between thickly forested mountains and the wild Maine coast.

Shenandoah National Park p345
Admire soaring raptors, hike to waterfalls, delve into history and stargaze from a lofty meadow.

CAR
Driving between Acadia and Shenandoah is not time efficient but having your own wheels will make it easier to explore each park in full, as well as the cities and attractions between them.

PLANE
Flying and renting a car is best if time is limited. For Acadia, fly into Portland International Jetport (three-hour drive) or Boston Logan International (five-hour drive). Dulles International Airport is one hour from Shenandoah National Park.

Acadia National Park (p336)

Plan Your Time

Mountains are the backdrop at both national parks, but only Acadia borders the coast. Shenandoah earns bragging rights, thanks to its ancient history – Old Rag Mountain dates back one billion years.

Pressed for Time

If you've only got one day, drive to **Shenandoah** (p345). Follow **Skyline Dr** (p348) south, puling over to hike to the summit of **Hawksbill** (p347) – the highest point in the park – for views and a picnic. Learn park history at the **Byrd Visitor Center** (p347) then hike to **Dark Hollow Falls** (p349). Soak up sunset views of the Shenandoah Valley from your cabin at **Skyland** (p348).

Three Days to Travel

Follow the loop road through **Acadia National Park** (p336) to appreciate its well-planned infrastructure. Climb a **ladder trail** (p337) then explore **Bar Harbor** (p343). Enjoy the **Cadillac Mountain sunrise** (p337) and spend the next two days biking carriage roads, strolling the shore, exploring the **Schoodic Peninsula** (p344) and savoring **Jordan Pond House** (p341).

SEASONAL HIGHLIGHTS

SPRING

Wildflowers bloom beside trails in Shenandoah. Trails are less crowded in Acadia, though may be chilly.

SUMMER

Join a ranger-led stroll in Shenandoah and enjoy Night Sky Festival in August. Weather is pleasant in Acadia.

FALL

Bring the kids to Acadia in October (in costume!) for the Eek of Ecology nature program.

WINTER

Many facilities close across both parks. Locals cross-country ski the carriage roads in Acadia.

ACADIA NATIONAL PARK

The only national park in New England, Acadia offers unrivaled coastal beauty and activities for both leisurely explorers and adrenaline junkies. The park, which incorporates both coastline and mountains, protects a remarkably diverse landscape. Spend the morning checking out tidal pools and watching the sea crash against the cliffs down by the waterfront, then head into the interior for a walk through dense forest up past a boulder-filled ridgeline with osprey and the occasional bald eagle soaring overhead.

Drivers and hikers alike can thank John D Rockefeller and other wealthy landowners for the aesthetically pleasing bridges, overlooks and stone steps that give the park its artistic oomph. Rockefeller in particular, before donating the lands, worked diligently with architects and masons to ensure that the infrastructure – for both carriage roads and motor roads – complements the surrounding landscape. Three days will cover the park highlights, but you could easily spend a week.

FACTS

Great For Cycling, scenery, walking
State Maine
Entrance Fee 7-day pass per car/motorcycle/ person on foot or bicycle $35/30/20
Area 74 sq miles

View from Cadillac Mountain

A Morning on Cadillac Mountain

FIRST SUNRISE & MOUNTAIN TRAILS

From October 7 through March 6, **Cadillac Mountain** is the first place in the US to see the sunrise. Brave the predawn chill to climb the most famous mountain in Acadia and the tallest peak on the eastern seaboard at 1530ft. You can drive the twisty, 3.5-mile Cadillac Summit Rd to the top or hike one of the view-filled summit trails. The rocky 4.4-mile round-trip **North Ridge Trail** climbs through the forest to exposed granite rocks overlooking Bar Harbor and Frenchman Bay. Time your arrival for one hour before sunrise.

After sunrise, stretch your legs and soak up views of the bay and coast along the partially paved, 0.5-mile **Cadillac Summit Loop Trail**. You'll also find interpretive signage and restrooms. For a memorable breakfast, make your way to the quirky **Cafe This Way** in Bar Harbor. In a sprawling white cottage, it serves plump Maine blueberry pancakes, organic oatmeal, and eggs Benedict with smoked salmon.

To manage traffic and crowds, the park now requires a vehicle reservation ($6) for a trip up Cadillac Mountain from late May through late October. Visit recreation.gov for details about online reservations, which can be made up to 90 days in advance.

If you're not an early riser, take heart. Sunset is always a good bet too.

Exploring the Park on Park Loop Road

BUILT FOR SCENIC DRIVING

The fabulous 27-mile **Park Loop Rd** takes you past some of Acadia's great natural treasures, including Sand Beach, Thunder Hole and Jordan Pond. Numerous trails start just off this road. If you're visiting for several days, drive the entire loop road when you arrive to get oriented. The road is largely one-way; in summer you can cover the route on the **Island Explorer** bus system (shuttle route 4; explore acadia.com). Try to drive it early in the morning to avoid large crowds. Note that the loop road is closed in winter, typically form December through mid-April, though its opening may be delayed by heavy snow.

Climbing Ladder Trails

IRON RUNGS AND LOFTY VIEWS

Acadia has a handful of hikes where you'll be ascending stretches of the trail with the help of iron ladder-like rungs.

ACADIA NATIONAL PARK: ORIENTATION

Acadia National Park covers about two-thirds of Mount Desert Island (MDI). Formed by glaciers some 18,000 years ago, the 108-sq-mile island offers vast geographical variety, with freshwater lakes, thick forests, stark granite cliffs and voluptuous river valleys. The 27-mile Park Loop Rd is the main roadway through the park and MDI. The island has four townships. Bar Harbor, on the northeast side, functions as the gateway to the park for most travelers. Jutting into the Atlantic Ocean from the mainland, the southern tip of the Schoodic Peninsula is a quiet, less-visited section of the park. It is a 42-mile drive, or 45-minute ferry ride, between Bar Harbor and the Schoodic Peninsula park entrance.

WHERE TO CAMP IN ACADIA NATIONAL PARK

Blackwoods Campground
Open year-round, 5 miles south of Bar Harbor. Access to trail up Cadillac Mountain. **$**

Seawall Campground
Four miles south of Southwest Harbor with 200 sites. Open late May through September. **$**

Schoodic Woods Campground
Around 90 wooded sites, all within 15 minutes' walk of the waterfront. **$**

ACADIA NATIONAL PARK

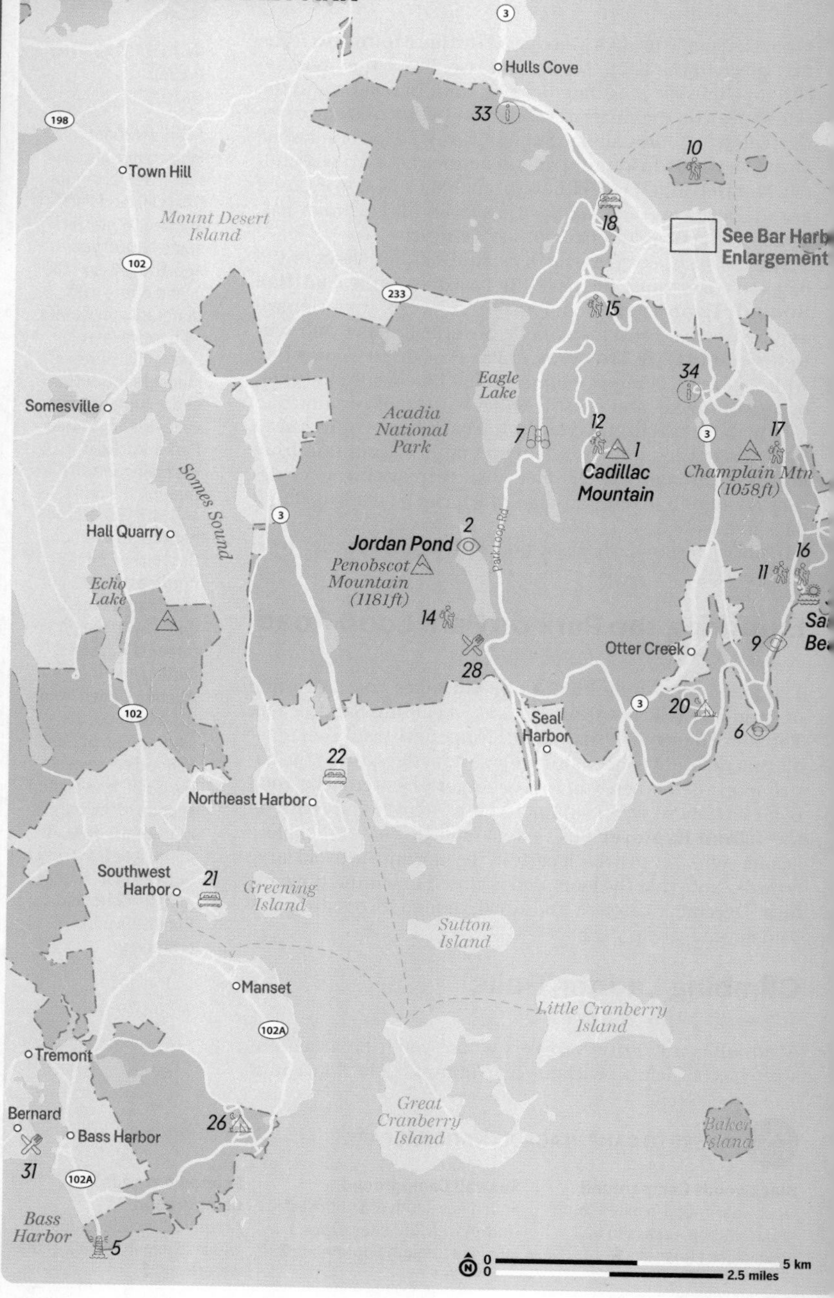

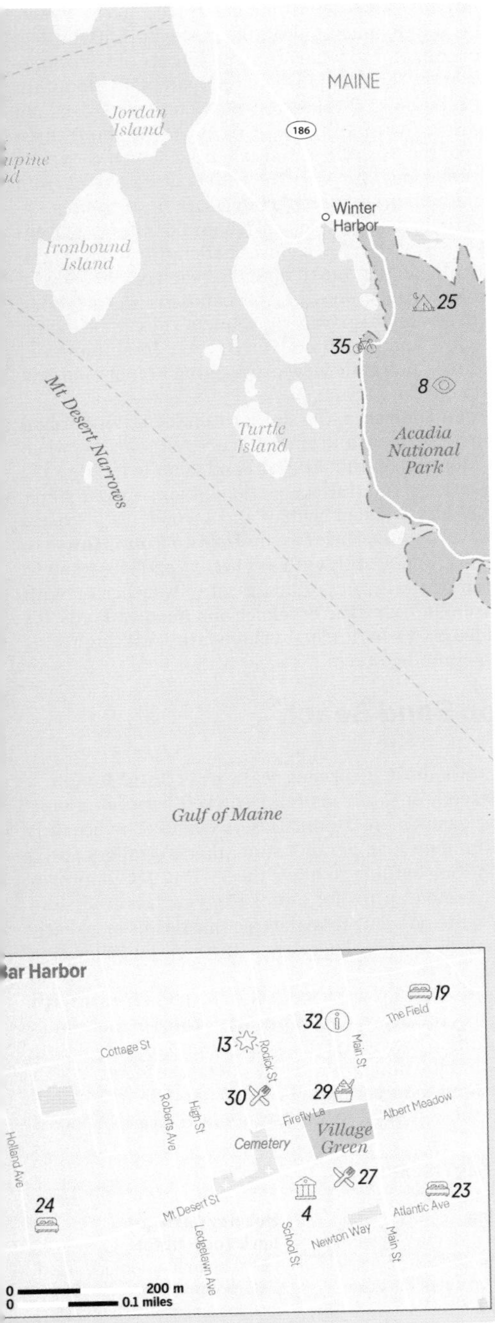

HIGHLIGHTS
1 Cadillac Mountain
2 Jordan Pond
3 Sand Beach

SIGHTS
4 Abbe Museum
5 Bass Harbor Head Lighthouse
6 Otter Point
7 Park Loop Road
8 Schoodic Peninsula
9 Thunder Hole

ACTIVITIES, COURSES & TOURS
10 Bar Island
11 Beehive Trail
12 Cadillac Summit Loop
13 Coastal Kayaking Tours
14 Jordan Cliffs Loop
15 North Ridge Trail
16 Ocean Path Trail
17 Precipice Trail

SLEEPING
18 Acadia Inn
19 Bass Cottage Inn
20 Blackwoods Campground
21 Claremont Hotel
22 Harbourside Inn
23 Moseley Cottage Inn & Town Motel
24 Primrose Inn
25 Schoodic Woods Campground
26 Seawall Campground

EATING
27 Cafe This Way
28 Jordan Pond House
29 Mount Desert Island Ice Cream
30 Side Street Cafe
31 Thurston's Lobster Pound

INFORMATION
32 Bar Harbor Chamber of Commerce
33 Hulls Cove Visitor Center
34 Sieur de Monts Nature Center

TRANSPORT
35 Schoodic Loop Rd

PARK SHUTTLES

The **Island Explorer** is a free bus service that operates along 10 different routes, linking hotels, inns and campgrounds to destinations within Acadia National Park. Route maps are available at local establishments and online. Most of the routes converge on the Village Green in Bar Harbor. The shuttle runs from late June to mid-October. All shuttle buses have wheelchair lifts and bike racks. Buses do not travel on Cadillac Summit Rd, but they will drop you off at the North Ridge Trailhead to the summit.

If you want speedy transport to the carriage roads for cycling, take the free **Bicycle Express**. This takes cyclists and their wheels from Bar Harbor's Village Green to Eagle Lake.

The iron rungs are hammered into a cliff face on the **Precipice Trail**, a tough, much-loved hike in the park. Definitely not recommended for anyone afraid of heights (nor for inexperienced hikers), this scenic ascent up Champlain Mountain along the Park Loop Rd takes you along narrow ledges, up granite stairs and straight up cliff faces. Allow about three hours to make the 3.2-mile round-trip hike, which vertically ascends 1000ft along the way. The trail is often closed from April to August to protect peregrine falcon nesting sites.

Just south, though short in length (about 1.6 miles), the **Beehive Trail** is one of the park's more challenging hikes. Starting at the trailhead just north of Sand Beach, you'll soon be climbing steep sections along narrow exposed cliffs. At times, you'll have to scramble up iron-rung ladders along the mountain. After a few tough sections, you'll reach the summit and its outstanding panoramic view overlooking Frenchman Bay, Great Head and Sand Beach.

In the Jordan Pond area, the similarly challenging **Jordan Cliffs Loop** gets you up and across a sheer cliff face between Penobscot Mountains and Jordan Pond. The five-mile hike serves up a series of fun trail navigation options – stone steps, iron-rung ladders, wooden bridges and a wooden staircase – along the way. Post-hike, head to the **Jordan Pond House** to enjoy popovers (hollow rolls with egg batter) and lobster stew.

Don't attempt these trails during rainy weather or with small children. If hiking the Precipice and Beehive Trails, it's recommended that you descend via a nearby walking route, rather than climbing down.

Relax on Sand Beach

SUNBATHE, STROLL AND STARGAZE

One of Acadia's most surprising features is **Sand Beach**: a beautiful stretch of sandy shoreline tucked between mountains on the east side of Mount Desert Island. The beach is around 300m long and attracts sunbathers, strollers and a few intrepid souls willing to brave the 55°F/12.7°C (summertime) water temperatures for a dip. The beach is well signposted and quite popular. Take the free shuttle bus or go early or late for a parking spot. There are bathrooms and changing areas just above the beach.

Several trails link up with Sand Beach. The **Ocean Path Trail** connects the beach with **Thunder Hole** – which emits an intimidating roar when strong incoming tides hit just the right way – and the pink granite walls of **Otter Point**, which seem to rise from the sea. This area is popular with rock climbers. Several times a week in warmer months, the park hosts

WHERE TO SLEEP ON MOUNT DESERT ISLAND

Primrose Inn
Sweet, simple 10-room motel in Bar Harbor with kind hosts and bright, well-maintained rooms. **$$**

Acadia Inn
Traditional 95-room hotel with smart, comfortable rooms; a mile or so out of the town center. **$$**

Moseley Cottage Inn & Town Motel
Large, charming, antique-filled B&B rooms in traditional 1884 inn plus motel-style units. **$$**

Sand Beach

ERIC URQUHART/SHUTTERSTOCK ©

Stars over Sand Beach, a free guided star-viewing session. During these one-hour talks, lie on the beach, look up at the sky and listen to rangers share stories and science about the stars. Dress warmly and bring a blanket for stretching out on. Check at one of the visitor centers for days and times. Even if you miss the talk, the eastern coastline along Ocean Dr is worth checking out at night, when you can watch the Milky Way slip right into the ocean.

Enjoying the Good Life: Jordan Pond

AFTERNOON TEA, NATURE WALK

Afternoon tea at the lodge-like **Jordan Pond House** has been an Acadia tradition since the late 1800s. From 3pm to 5pm steaming pots of Earl Grey come with hot popovers and strawberry jam. Eat outside on the broad lawn overlooking the adjacent **Jordan Pond**. On clear days, the glassy waters of this 176-acre pond reflect the image of Penobscot Mountain like a mirror. A stroll around the pond and its surrounding forests and flower meadows is one of Acadia's most popular and family friendly activities. (Sorry, no swimming allowed.)

The lunch menu at the teahouse includes lobster stew, gnocchi mac and cheese and a bison meatloaf sandwich. Wine, beer and cocktails are also served. The dinner menu includes elevated entrees, from mussels in white wine sauce to beef tenderloin. Reserve ahead for tea and all meals at this extremely popular place (open mid-May to early Sep).

PARK & MDI VISITOR CENTERS

The informative **Hulls Cove Visitor Center** (open early June to October) anchors the park's main Hulls Cove entrance, which is three miles northwest of Bar Harbor via ME 3. Buy your park pass and pick up maps and information here. The Park Loop Rd, which circumnavigates the eastern section of Mount Desert Island, starts nearby. When Hulls Cove is closed, head to the **Bar Harbor Chamber of Commerce** (2 Cottage St) for information. The park moves its visitor operations here in the winter. You can also find information at the **Sieur de Monts Nature Center** (open late May to mid-October) within the park.

WHERE TO EAT ON MOUNT DESERT ISLAND

Mount Desert Island Ice Cream
Bar Harbor cult hit for innovative ice-cream flavors, such as stout beer with fudge. **$**

Side Street Cafe
Pub food with some quirks in Bar Harbor – think mac 'n' cheese with gourmet toppings. **$$**

Thurston's Lobster Pound
Super-fresh lobster and crab are the headliners at yellow-roofed Thurston's, overlooking Bass Harbor in Bernard. **$$**

ROAD TRIP

Acadia National Park

John D Rockefeller Jr and other wealthy landowners gave Acadia its bridges, overlooks and stone steps. Travelers can admire Rockefeller's aesthetic touches – not to mention Mother Nature's – by touring the park on the wonderful Park Loop Rd, which links the park's highlights in the eastern section of MDI. Begin this 33-mile drive at Hulls Cove Visitor Center, where you can get the lay of the land and pay the admission fee.

1 Sieur de Monts Spring

At Sieur de Monts Spring you'll find a nature center and the summer-only branch of the Abbe Museum, which sits in a lush, nature-like setting and hosts a fascinating collection of natural artifacts related to Maine's Native American heritage. Acadia's many biospheres are displayed in miniature at the Wild Gardens of Acadia.

The Drive: The park road crosses ME 3, which leads into Bar Harbor, and rolls toward the ocean before swinging south. You'll pass Beaver Dam Pond on the way.

2 Precipice Trail

The Precipice Trail and the Beehive Trail, which is accessed a short drive south, are two 'ladder trails' that cling to the sides of exposed cliffs along the northeastern section of Park Loop Rd, dubbed Ocean Dr.

The Drive: Continue south. You can access Sand Beach and the Beehive Trail from the same parking lot.

EQROY/SHUTTERSTOCK ©

Jordan Pond House

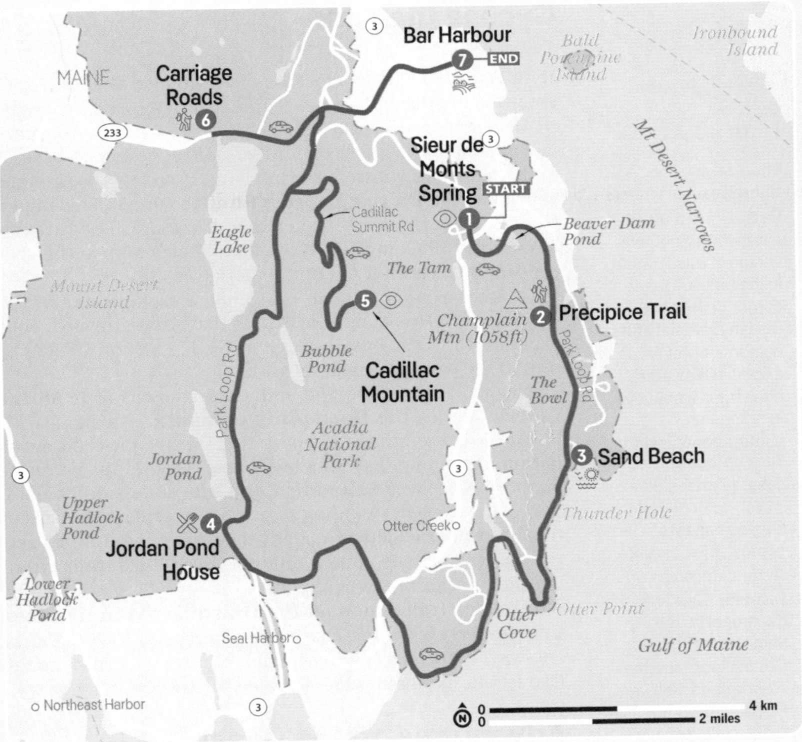

3 Sand Beach

Sand Beach is home to one of the few sandy shorelines in the park, and it links to the Beehive Trail and the Ocean Path.

The Drive: Swoop south past the crashing waves of Thunder Hole. Pass Otter Point, then follow the road inland past Wildwood Stables.

4 Jordan Pond House

Share hiking stories and views of scenic Jordan Pond with other nature lovers over a traditional afternoon tea.

The Drive: Look up for the rock precariously perched atop South Bubble from the pull-off almost 2 miles north. Continue north to Cadillac Mountain Rd.

5 Cadillac Mountain

The 1530ft summit of Cadillac Mountain is the first spot in the US to see the sunrise between October 7 and March 6. Drink in the views of Frenchman Bay and walk the 0.5-mile Cadillac Mountain Summit Loop.

The Drive: You could complete the loop road and exit the park, or continue driving so you can stroll the pretty walking trails, accessed from various parking lots.

6 Carriage Roads

Car-free and made from crushed stone, the 45 miles of crisscrossing carriage roads in the park are popular for hiking and cycling. Several carriage roads branch out from Jordan Pond House. You can also join them further north by Eagle Lake.

The Drive: Continue north then follow ME 233 to Bar Harbor.

7 Bar Harbor

Tucked on the rugged coast in the shadows of Acadia's mountains, Bar Harbor is a busy gateway town. Restaurants, taverns and boutiques are scattered along Main St, Mt Desert St and Cottage St.

BASS HARBOR HEAD LIGHTHOUSE

There is only one **lighthouse** on Mount Desert Island, and it sits in the somnolent village of Bass Harbor in the far southwest corner of the park. Built in 1858, the 36ft lighthouse still has a Fresnel lens from 1902. It's in a beautiful location that's a photographer favorite. The lighthouse is a coastguard residence, so you can't go inside, but you can take photos. You can also stroll to the coast on two easy trails near the property: the Ship Harbor Trail, a 1.2-mile loop, and the Wonderland Trail, a 1.4-mile round-trip. These trails are spectacular ways to get through the forest

Cycling the Park

CARRIAGE ROADS AND SCHOODIC PENINSULA

John D Rockefeller Jr, a lover of old-fashioned horse carriages, gifted Acadia with some 45 miles of crisscrossing carriage roads. Made from crushed stone, the roads are free from cars and are popular with cyclists, hikers and equestrians. Several of the roads fan out from Jordan Pond House. If you brought your bike, the **Bicycle Express Shuttle** runs to Eagle Lake from the Bar Harbor Village Green from late June through late August. Pick up a Carriage Road User's Map at the visitor center or check it out on the park website.

If you're driving, you can try to nab a parking spot at the Jordan Pond House parking lot. If that's too crowded, continue north to the parking area at Eagle Lake on US 233 to link to the carriage-road network.

Attached to the mainland and across the bay from Mount Desert Island, the **Schoodic Peninsula** is a beautiful, less-crowded section of the park that's also a pleasant destination for cycling. Part of a larger loop around the peninsula, the park's paved **Schoodic Loop Rd** runs six miles along the western coast, swinging past the wave-splashed rocks of the atmospheric Schoodic Point then traveling up the eastern coast. You'll also find 8 miles of linked bike trails crossing the interior of the peninsula.

To reduce traffic, hop on the **Downeast Windjammer Cruises** ferry with your bike in Bar Harbor (adult/child $18/14 one-way) to travel to Winter Harbor. Here you can pick up the free Island Explorer Schoodic Shuttle (Route 8).

Adventures off the Coast

KAYAKING AND A DISAPPEARING TRAIL

You can explore the jagged Maine coast near Acadia by kayak. Sign up for a half-day or sunset kayaking trip in Bar Harbor. Both **Maine State Sea Kayak** and **Coastal Kayaking Tours** offer trips. Intrepid hikers should consider a walk to **Bar Island**, a 157-acre island that lies directly offshore, north of Bar Harbor. It can be reached on foot at low tide. For two hours on either side of low tide, a gravel bar is exposed, connecting the town to the island. A trail continues to its summit, providing great views. It's just under two miles out and back.

GETTING AROUND

Driving inside the park can be a nightmare during the summer. Expect heavily congested roads and no ease in finding parking. Go early if you're driving. Better yet, ditch the vehicle and take one of the free Island Explorer buses (p000) that zip around the island. Hiring a bike in nearby Bar Harbor is a breeze, and a good way to avoid traffic snarls and parking problems. All park buses accommodate bikes (from four to six per bus), but if you want speedy transport to the carriage roads, take the free Bicycle Express (late June through late August). This takes cyclists and their wheels from Bar Harbor's Village Green to Eagle Lake.

SHENANDOAH NATIONAL PARK

A road trip through Shenandoah National Park on Skyline Dr is a drive with just the good parts. Views of cloud-snagging mountains and pretty valley farms interrupt the forest backdrop with perfect cinematic pacing. Seventy overlooks and a string of trailheads line the route, which travels the crest of the Blue Ridge Mountains between Front Royal in the north and Waynesboro in the south. You'll likely see rabbits and whitetail deer as your car eats up the miles. Seasonal charms – wildflowers in spring, colorful foliage in autumn – keep views engaging year-round. Sunsets are sublime.

The park draws hikers and backpackers with more than 500 miles of trails, including 101 miles of the Appalachian Trail. Waterfalls and mountain summits are abundant and easily reached. President Roosevelt said the park was a work of conservation built for 'enriching the character and happiness of our people.' That mission succeeds to this day.

FACTS

Great For Wildlife, Scenery, Walking
State Virginia
Entrance Fee 7-day pass per car/motorcycle/ person on foot or bicycle $30/25/15
Area 310 sq miles

Hawksbill trail (p347)

SHENANDOAH NATIONAL PARK

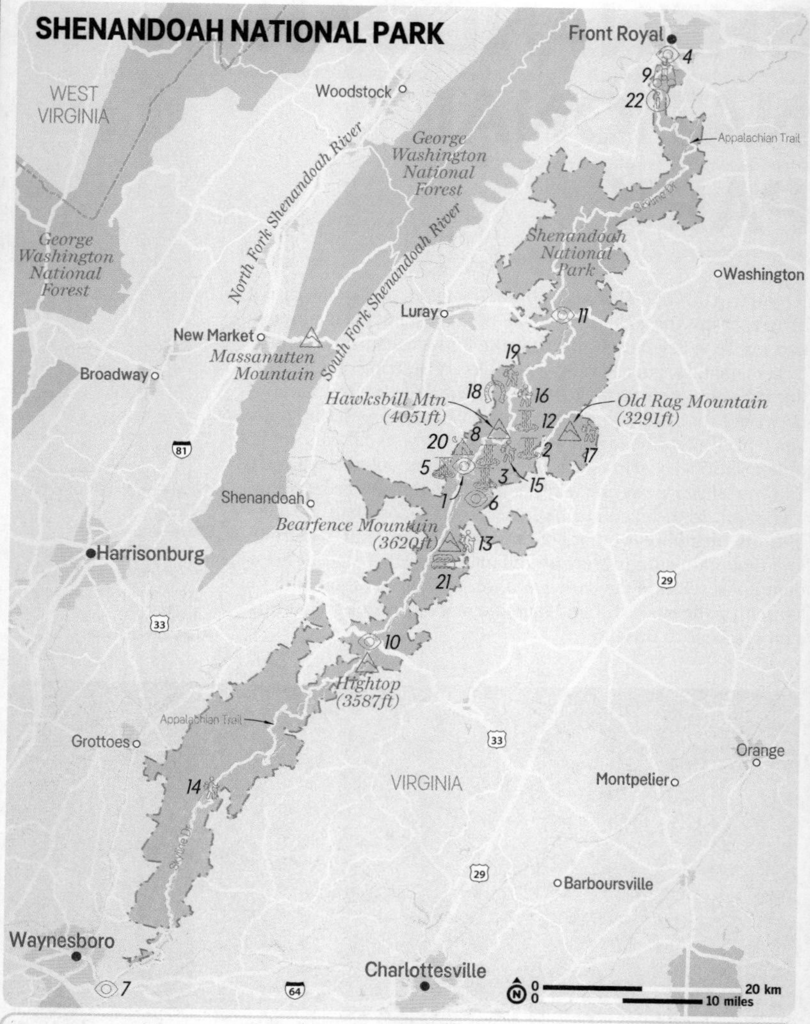

SIGHTS
1 Big Meadows
2 Cedar Run Falls
3 Dark Hollow Falls
4 Front Royal Entrance
5 Lewis Spring Falls
6 Rapidan Camp
7 Rockfish Gap Entrance
8 Rose River Falls
9 Skyline Drive
10 Swift Run Gap Entrance
11 Thornton Gap Entrance
12 Whiteoak Canyon Falls

ACTIVITIES, COURSES & TOURS
13 Bearfence Mountain
14 Blackrock Summit
15 Hawksbill Mountain
16 Limberlost Trail
17 Old Rag Mountain
18 Skyland Stables
19 Stony Man Trail

SLEEPING
20 Big Meadows Campground
see 20 Big Meadows Lodge
21 Lewis Mountain Cabins
see 21 Lewis Mountain Campground
see 18 Skyland Resort

INFORMATION
see 1 Byrd Visitor Center
22 Dickey Ridge Visitor Center

Old Rag Mountain trail views

Summit Hikes: Hawksbill & Old Rag

LOOP HIKES TO LOFTY VIEWS

The hike to the summit of **Hawksbill**, the highest point in the park at 4051ft, is a rewarding half-day adventure. Highlights on this popular 2.8-mile loop include: a short climb on the Appalachian Trail (AT), a fun scramble across boulder fields and a 360-degree view of farm-dotted valleys and rolling mountains from the summit observation platform. Begin at the Hawksbill Gap parking lot (Mile 45.6), then link with the AT, the Salamander Trail and the Lower Hawksbill Trail along the way. Several other trails intersect in this area, so longer loop hikes are possible.

The 9.4-mile loop hike to the 3291ft summit of **Old Rag Mountain** is generally acknowledged to be the most challenging day hike in Virginia. It's also a ton of fun for hikers in reasonably good shape and up for a bit of adventure. The best part? A mile-long jumble of exposed granite boulders that must be navigated before reaching the top. Expect scrambling, climbing, leaping and the occasional tight squeeze.

A freestanding mountain on the eastern fringe of the national park, Old Rag is an erosion-resistant monadnock. It

SHENANDOAH NATIONAL PARK: GETTING ORIENTED

The primary road through the park is the 105-mile Skyline Dr. There are four entrance stations. The **Front Royal entrance** is at the northern end while the **Rockfish Gap entrance** is at the southern end. The **Thornton Gap entrance** is east of Luray, and **Swift Run Gap** is east of Elkton. **Big Meadows** is the epicenter of the park, sitting in the middle of Skyline Drive at Mile 51. Here is the year-round Byrd Visitor Center plus a gas station, campground, lodge and restaurants. Skyland Resort is ten miles north of Big Meadows, along mileposts 39 through 42. **Dickey Ridge Visitor Center** (mid-March to November) at Mile 4.6 is near the northern entrance.

WHERE TO CAMP IN SHENANDOAH NATIONAL PARK

Big Meadows Campground
This 217-site campground can feel crowded but has good facilities and is centrally located for exploring. $

Lewis Mountain Campground
Secluded campground with 31 first-come, first-served spots, plus a camp store, bathroom and coin-operated showers. $

Backcountry Camping
Obtain a permit – currently free. The park website lists routes and camping areas. No campfires. $

PHOTO SPIRIT/SHUTTERSTOCK ©

Whiteoak Canyon Falls

SKYLINE DRIVE

A 105-mile road running along the spine of the Blue Ridge Mountains, Shenandoah National Park's **Skyline Dr** is one of the most scenic drives on the East Coast. You're constantly treated to an impressive view, but keep in mind the road is bendy, slow-going (35mph limit) and congested in peak season. It's best to start this drive just south of Front Royal, VA; from here you'll snake over Virginia wine and hill country. Numbered mileposts mark the way; there are lots of pull-offs. One favorite is near Mile 51.2 in the Big Meadows area, where you can take a moderately difficult 3.6-mile-loop hike to Lewis Spring Falls.

was formed more than one billion years ago from molten rock that crystallized after the collision of continents. Flat spots on the many boulders provide inviting picnic areas at the summit, and the best are backdropped by the rolling beauty of the forested Blue Ridge Mountains.

To manage the crowds here, the park has implemented a day-use ticket requirement (March to November), and hikers must purchase the permit, either online or by phone, before they reach the park. Visit nps.gov/shen for details. The trailhead is one-hour from Big Meadows, and it is not located on Skyline Dr. Many hikers arrive from Charlottesville.

Relaxing at Rapidan Camp

EXPLORING A PRESIDENTIAL RETREAT

Sitting on the deck of the Brown House, which is surrounded by forest and flanked by two mountain creeks, it's easy to understand why President Herbert Hoover and First Lady Lou Henry Hoover enjoyed their escapes to this presidential retreat during the Great Depression in the early 1930s. Built in a thickly forested hollow on the eastern flanks of the Blue Ridge, about a 3½-hour drive from DC, **Rapidan Camp** doubled as the summer White House during Hoover's presidency. Today, three of the original 13 camp buildings remain, and interpretive markers tell the story of the camp. The moderate Mill Prong Trail drops from the Milam Gap parking lot (Mile 52) to the camp (4 miles round-trip). There's a stream

WHERE TO SLEEP IN SHENANDOAH NATIONAL PARK

Big Meadows Lodge
There are 29 lodge rooms and cabins in woods near waterfalls, a visitor center and namesake meadow. $

Lewis Mountain Cabins
Pleasantly furnished cabins with hot showers. Smaller cabins: bunk beds, but no linens or bathrooms. $

Skyland Resort
Enjoy grand views of the Shenandoah Valley from premium hotel-style rooms and small cabins. $$

crossing that kids will love – across an oversized log – along the way. Guided ranger tours of the camp, with a 30-minute van ride, are available in summer, typically late May through early September (Thursday to Sunday).

Waterfalls Everywhere

PRETTY CASCADES NEAR BIG MEADOWS

Anticipation builds as you drop through the forest to **Dark Hollow Falls**. Slick rocks and thick moss slowly overtake the scene and the sound of splashing cascades becomes your soundtrack. Even with the inevitable crowds – the trail is near the Byrd Visitor Center – the pathway feels like a place of enchantment. And the creek-fed falls, dropping 70ft, are a beautiful sight.

For waterfall fans, the Central District holds an impressive collection of cascades, and you can view several on loop hikes on the district's interconnecting trails. In spring, wildflowers line the path to **Rose River Falls** (Mile 49; 2.6-miles round-trip), which expands into several parallel falls after a rainstorm. This is a good alternative if crowds are heavy at Dark Hollow. A steep, rocky trail behind Big Meadows Campground drops 1 mile to the 81ft-high **Lewis Spring Falls**. For solitude and a workout, head into the wilderness for a view of 34ft-tall **Cedar Run Falls** (Mile 45; 4 miles round-trip). A 2.3-mile trail descends to the 86ft-high **Whiteoak Canyon Falls** (Mile 42), the second highest in the park and probably its most well-known.

For a handy overview, buy the *Hike to Waterfalls* booklet sold at wayside shops and visitor centers ($3). Keep in mind that you'll be climbing back up to the parkway after viewing the falls, an endeavor that will likely take longer than your descent. Pick up picnic supplies in Big Meadows.

Horseback Rides

SADDLE UP FOR A RIDE

Two hundred miles of trails are open to equestrians in the park, but you don't have to own a horse to explore by horseback. A short walk from Skyland Lodge, **Skyland Stables** (Mile 42.5) offers one-hour guided horseback rides from early May through October. Rides are offered several times per day, passing an old apple orchard in the Limberlost area. Book ahead online or simply walk up and check availability. Pony rides are available for younger kids between noon and 1pm.

BEST FAMILY HIKES

Stony Man Trail (Mile 41)
Easy climb to a cool rock outcrop with views across the Shenandoah Valley (1.6 miles round-trip).

Limberlost Trail (Mile 43)
Fully accessible 1.3-mile loop though mountain laurel. Also a kid-minded TRACK Trail with nature brochures.

Bearfence Mountain (Mile 56)
This 1.2-mile loop includes an adventurous rock scramble and a 360-degree view.

Blackrock Summit (Mile 84)
Short loop hike to a talus slope with view of Massanutten Mountain. Interactive TRACK Trail with brochures and information kiosk.

GETTING AROUND

Driving your own car is the best way to reach Skyland and Big Meadows in the Central District of the park. From Washington, DC, it's a 95-mile drive west to the Thornton Gap Entrance Station. From I-81, your best bet for accessing the Central District is by entering the park at either Thornton Gap or Swift Run Gap – efficiency will depend on your location. There are no shuttles within the park, and trailheads and overlooks can be miles apart along Skyline Dr. There is one gas station, located at Big Meadows.

FLYING PIG STUDIOS/SHUTTERSTOCK ©

Above: BASE jumper (p375), New River Gorge Bridge; Right: Mammoth Cave (p373)

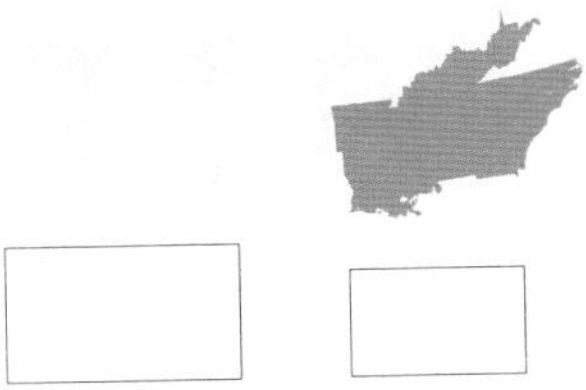

THE SOUTH

ADVENTURES ABOVE GROUND AND BELOW

Paddle a swamp, climb a mountain, explore subterranean passages and ride wild rapids. Or simply soak in a hot spring tub. One guarantee? Gorgeous backdrops.

Don't be deceived by the gentle beauty of the South. The mountains and rivers may be among the oldest on earth, but active travelers have their pick of adventures across five national parks, which stretch east from Arkansas' Ouachita Mountains to Kentucky, the Appalachian Mountains and central South Carolina. Their locations are historically important, all having played a role in the story of the South. Some were hunting grounds and burial spots for Native Americans. European settlers once farmed the fertile valleys. And several parks were hubs of industry – home to vast logging and coal-mining operations.

The five parks today are marked by superlatives. Paddlers run some of the wildest rapids in the country in New River Gorge National Park, the 63rd national park in the US and its newest. The world's largest cave system snakes beneath central Kentucky – spooking visitors with a bottomless pit and shadow-filled lantern tours. Things stay moody on a paddle through Congaree, home to soaring 'champion trees' and roaming alligators. The most-visited national park in the country, Great Smoky Mountains, has the pull of an enchanted forest, with emerald groves of green, misty waterfalls and a mountaintop observation platform that surely fell to earth from the future. And Hot Springs? This special place is likely the oldest federally protected park in the country, with a protected status dating back to the 1830s.

THE MAIN AREAS

Find Your Way

The South is not as compact as you might think, and driving times between the parks vary from a half-day to 12 hours. Hot Springs and Congaree are 800 miles apart.

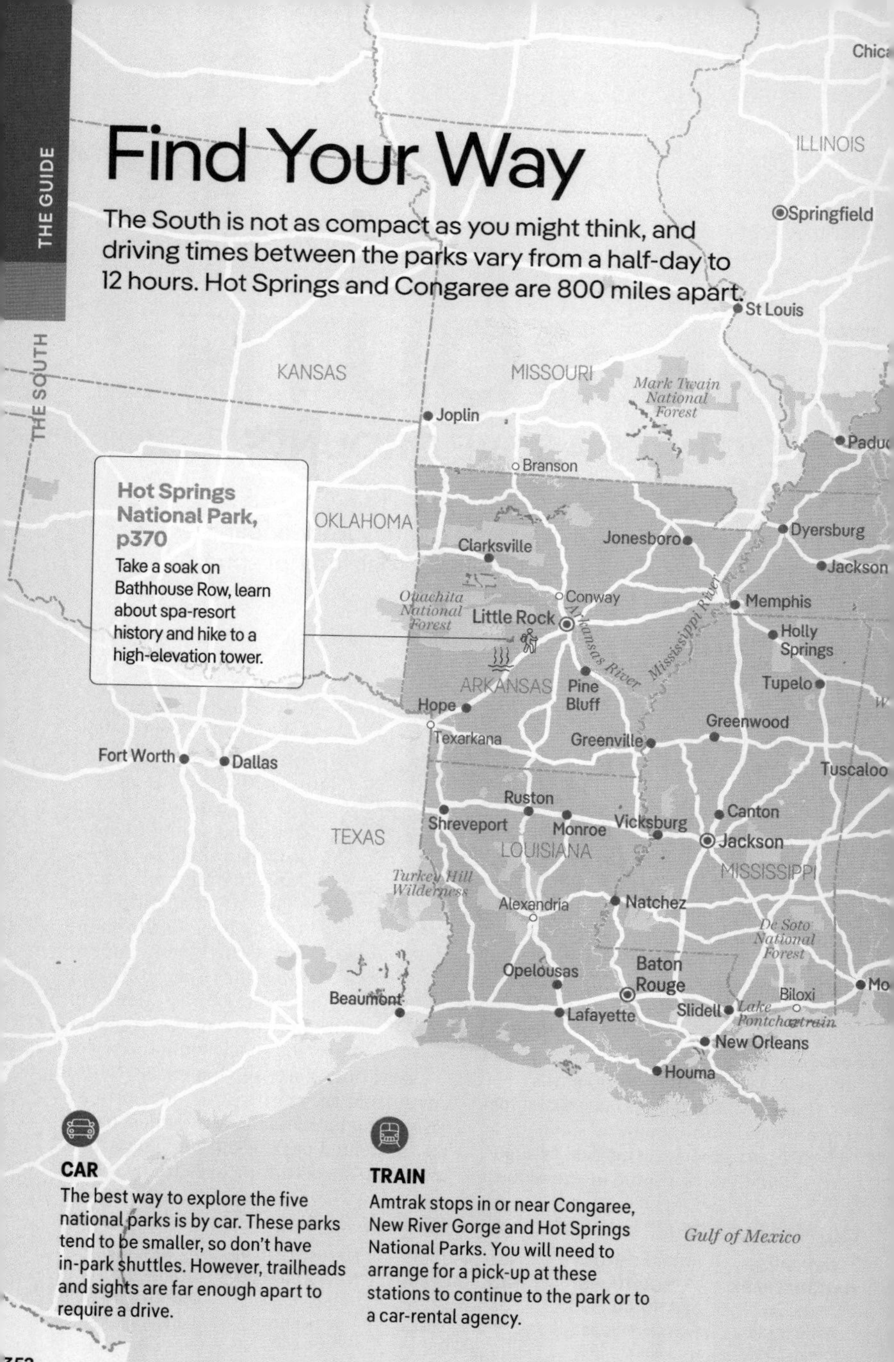

Hot Springs National Park, p370

Take a soak on Bathhouse Row, learn about spa-resort history and hike to a high-elevation tower.

CAR

The best way to explore the five national parks is by car. These parks tend to be smaller, so don't have in-park shuttles. However, trailheads and sights are far enough apart to require a drive.

TRAIN

Amtrak stops in or near Congaree, New River Gorge and Hot Springs National Parks. You will need to arrange for a pick-up at these stations to continue to the park or to a car-rental agency.

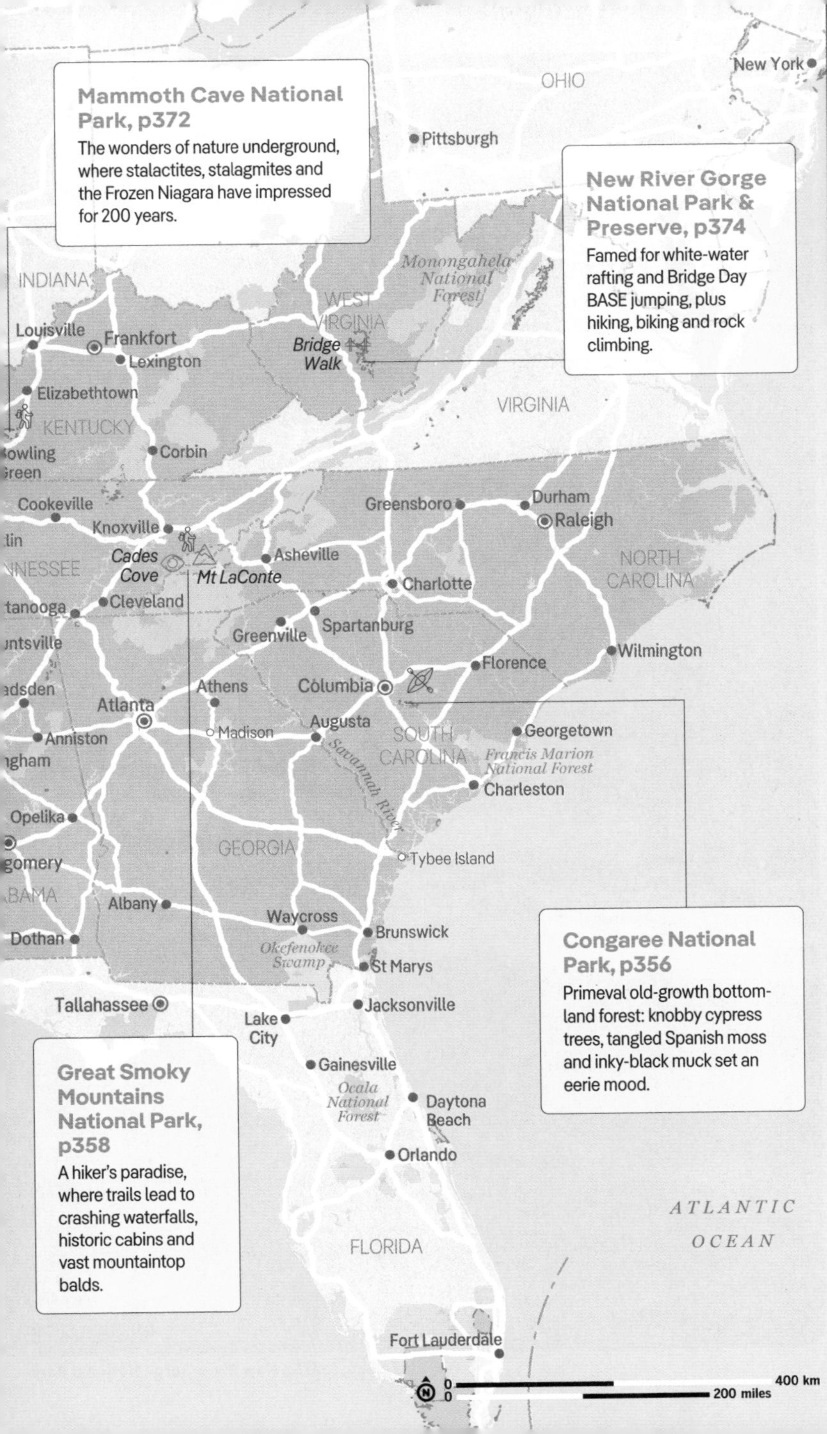

Mammoth Cave National Park, p372

The wonders of nature underground, where stalactites, stalagmites and the Frozen Niagara have impressed for 200 years.

New River Gorge National Park & Preserve, p374

Famed for white-water rafting and Bridge Day BASE jumping, plus hiking, biking and rock climbing.

Congaree National Park, p356

Primeval old-growth bottomland forest: knobby cypress trees, tangled Spanish moss and inky-black muck set an eerie mood.

Great Smoky Mountains National Park, p358

A hiker's paradise, where trails lead to crashing waterfalls, historic cabins and vast mountaintop balds.

Rafting (p375), New River Gorge National Park

Clingmans Dome viewing platform (p359), Great Smoky Mountains National Park

Plan Your Time

If you have a week, you can visit two, maybe three, national parks in the South. However, your best bet is digging into the wonders of just one.

If You Only Do One Thing

Drive south from Gatlinburg directly into **Great Smoky Mountains National Park** (p358), where the transformation is instantaneous. Get oriented at Sugarlands Visitor Center. Set up camp at **Cades Cove** (p365) then explore the loop road. The next day hike to a waterfall then soak up sprawling, high-elevation views of the Smokies from **Clingmans Dome** (p359).

A Weeklong Stay

Paddle into the heart of **Congaree National Park** (p356) then head to the Oconaluftee Visitor Center. From Newfound Gap explore the **Appalachian Trail** (p359) before ascending Clingmans Dome, admiring a waterfall and watching wildlife in **Cades Cove** (p365). Drive to **New River Gorge National Park** (p378) for white-water rafting and hiking in an ancient gorge.

SEASONAL HIGHLIGHTS

SPRING

Check out the firefly display in Great Smoky Mountains and Congaree National Parks.

SUMMER

High season in the parks, with a list of tour options in Mammoth Cave and rafting adventures on the New River.

FALL

Bridge Day brings BASE jumpers to New River Gorge Bridge, and white-water rafting is intense on the Gauley River.

WINTER

Ideal time to visit Hot Springs National Park, where the waters remain toasty for a soak.

CONGAREE NATIONAL PARK

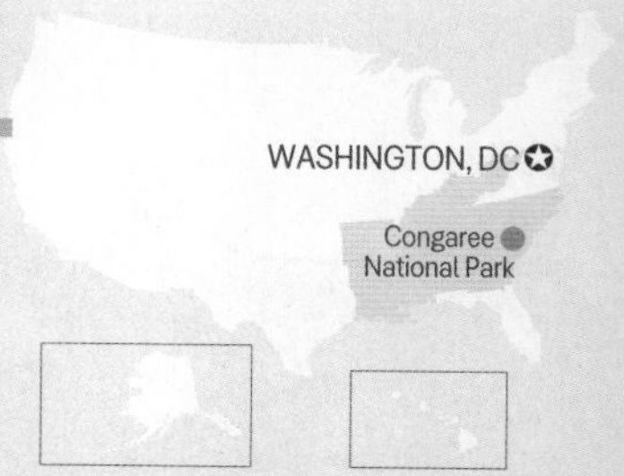

Thick with knobby bald cypress trees, moss-covered tupelos and tangled drapes of Spanish moss, the dark and swampy interior of Congaree National Park is a Southern Gothic setting at its most elemental. Home to the largest old-growth forest in southeastern USA, the park is fed by the floodwaters of the Congaree and Wateree Rivers. This eerie wonderland is just 20 miles southeast of Columbia, South Carolina, the state's capital and home of the University of South Carolina. A boardwalk trail meanders through the heart of the primeval muck as does a 15-mile canoe trail, both introducing adventurous travelers to the floodplain's unique and diverse inhabitants, which include turtles, salamanders, alligators and the occasional feral pig. The park is also home to numerous 'champion trees': record holders, based on their immense size. The champion loblolly pine here soars nearly 17 stories. The park has two primitive campgrounds and a visitor center.

FACTS

Great For Scenery, walking, wildlife
State South Carolina
Entrance Fee Free
Area 41 sq miles

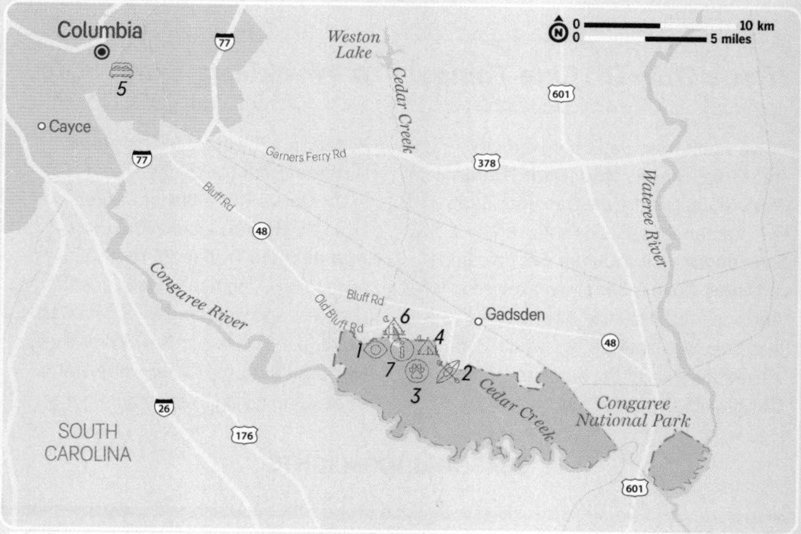

SIGHTS
1 Boardwalk Loop Trail

ACTIVITIES, COURSES & TOURS
2 Cedar Creek Canoe Trail
3 Firefly Trail

SLEEPING
4 Bluff Campground
5 Graduate Columbia
6 Longleaf Campground

INFORMATION
7 Harry Hampton Visitor Center

Boardwalk Loop Trail

Stroll the Boardwalk Trail

MUCK AND MINIMAL LIGHT

The most efficient way to explore the floodplain is to walk on the 2.4-mile **Boardwalk Loop Trail**, an elevated walkway that loops through the park's old-growth bottomland forest. The trail passes beneath loblolly pines, water tupelos and bald cypresses, and it provides up-close views of the dark Dorovan muck, an 8ft-deep mix of clay and dead leaves. Due to minimal sunlight, few plants grow at the base of the trees, but you might see turtles and snakes or hear a pileated woodpecker pecking away for insects at the base of a dead tree, known in these parts as a snag.

The trail begins and ends at the **Harry Hampton Visitor Center** and is open to wheelchairs, strollers and pets. Pick up a self-guided boardwalk tour pamphlet at the visitor center or check it out on the park website. Ranger-led Nature Discovery Walks along the boardwalk are offered the second Saturday of the month.

Paddle the Cedar Creek Canoe Trail

PRIMEVAL LANDSCAPE AND ABUNDANT WILDLIFE

For an even more immersive experience, join a half-day guided paddling trip on the 15-mile **Cedar Creek Canoe Trail**, which meanders through the park's old-growth forest. Look for otter, deer and even alligators while kayaking or canoeing along the marked trail. Guided trips take three to four hours and cost about $80 to $100 per person. Check the park website for a list of approved outfitters. You can also plan your own paddling adventure; just be aware you may have to carry your kayak or canoe around the occasional log or downed tree in the waterway.

SYNCHRONOUS FIREFLIES

For two weeks between mid-May and mid-June, synchronous fireflies light up at night while searching for a mate within the park. Visitors can view this annual mating ritual along the **Firefly Trail**. Synchronous firefly displays occur in very few places in the US, and viewing events have become extremely popular in the last few years. To view them in Congareee, you will need to enter a park-sponsored lottery and hope you score a ticket. The lottery typically opens in early April.

WHERE TO STAY IN CONGAREE NATIONAL PARK

Longleaf Campground
Leafy, sometimes crowded, campground, easily accessed by car from the entrance road. **$**

Bluff Campground
Relaxing, secluded campground accessed by a 1-mile hike on the Bluff Trail. Six sites. **$**

Graduate Columbia
Upbeat hotel with a decor tribute to the University of South Carolina and its Gamecocks. **$$**

GREAT SMOKY MOUNTAINS NATIONAL PARK

America's favorite national park is a lush green wonderland, abundant with mossy streams, glorious wildflowers, venerable wildlife, massive old-growth trees and waves of misty mountains. Recognized as a Unesco World Heritage Site and International Biosphere Reserve, Great Smoky Mountains is the most biologically diverse national park in the US, with over 19,000 plant and animal species and the densest concentration of black bears in North America. Its 522,427 acres feature some of the East Coast's highest peaks and most gorgeous river valleys, traversed by 850 miles of hiking trails – including almost 72 miles of the Appalachian Trail. The Cherokee called these mountains Shaconage, or 'place of blue smoke,' a phrase later adapted by white settlers. Watch elk graze in the gauzy dawn light of Oconaluftee, or hike the slopes of Mt LeConte, with wisps of mist hanging in the valleys below, and it's hard to think of a more fitting name.

ZAKZEINERT/SHUTTERSTOCK ©

Sunrise, Clingmans Dome

FACTS

Great For History, wildlife, hiking
State North Carolina & Tennessee
Entrance Fee Free
Area 816 sq miles

PARK IT FORWARD

With visitation at over 13 million per year, Great Smoky Mountains National Park sees more tourists than the Grand Canyon, Yosemite and Yellowstone combined. However, these other parks charge entrance fees. GSMNP cannot charge an entrance fee. From March 2023, the park began requiring parking tags on all vehicles. This new initiative, dubbed Park It Forward, provides a means to raise much-needed funds. Visit the park website for details about where to purchase your parking tag (day/week $5/15).

Greet the Dawn at Clingmans Dome

SENSATIONAL MOUNTAINTOP VIEWS

It will be dark. A little chilly. And you might be breathing hard from the steep climb up the parking lot. But watching the sun lift above the eastern Smokies, with mists hanging in the valleys below, is unforgettable. At 6643ft, **Clingmans Dome** is the highest point in Great Smoky Mountains National Park. It's topped by a space-age viewing platform, completed in 1959, which has become one of the park's best-known attractions. Elevating visitors another 45ft above the ground, the platform affords 360-degree views of the Smokies' grandeur.

Plaques placed at the four corners of the viewing platform identify major regional landforms, from Mt Mitchell (6684ft) in the east to Thunderhead Mountain (5527ft) in the west. Below you, the **Appalachian Trail** rolls over the dome on its 14-state journey between Georgia and Maine. If you're enjoying the lofty views, follow the **Andrews Bald Trail** from Clingmans Dome to a high-elevation meadow. It's 3.6 miles round trip.

A 7-mile spur road leads from Newfound Gap to Clingmans Dome. At the Clingmans Dome parking lot, look for the paved trail at the far end.

Watch Fireflies at Elkmont

NATURE'S MESMERIZING LIGHT SHOW

Each year in late May/early June, *Photinus carolinus* fireflies light up the forests around **Elkmont** in a rare display of entomological magic. Also known as the synchronous firefly, the males synchronize their flashing as part of the mating display. For several seconds at a time, the fireflies fill the forest with pulsating light. Like a human 'wave' at a sporting event, the pattern builds as each firefly joins the cloud of twinkling light. The effect is eerie and stunningly beautiful. The synchronized twinkling begins at nightfall and continues till around midnight. Adding a whimsical sideshow are Elkmont's 'blue ghosts,' a separate species that cruises around the forest's edge glowing for up to 40 seconds at a stretch.

Just before dusk, a parade of campers armed with red headlamps (white light disrupts the fireflies) walk south from their campsites towards **Little River** and **Jakes Creek** trails. Great Smoky Mountains National Park is one of the few places in the US – and the world – to witness this spectacle.

The easiest way to participate is to snag a campsite at **Elkmont Campground** (p362). Savvy campers reserve months in advance, but you can sometimes get in on a last-minute cancellation at recreation.gov. Alternatively, join the annual

NEED TO KNOW: GREAT SMOKY MOUNTAINS NATIONAL PARK

The park is open year-round, but summer and autumn are the most popular seasons. Some facilities are closed from late autumn through early spring, and roads may close in inclement weather. Newfound Gap Rd/Hwy 441 is the only thoroughfare that crosses the park, winding through the mountains from Gatlinburg, TN to the town of Cherokee, NC, passing en route the **Sugarlands Visitor Center** in the northwest and **Oconaluftee Visitor Center** in the southeast. There are 10 developed campgrounds in the park and one rustic, hike-in lodge. There are no restaurants, and food and beverage services are limited to snacks and some grocery items.

BEST VIEWPOINTS FOR HIKERS

Charlies Bunion
The quintessential Great Smokies photo op: rocky promontory on the Appalachian Trail commands astounding views.

Myrtle Point
At 6500ft, a classic vantage point for sunrise after an overnight on Mt LeConte.

Gregory Bald
Feast your eyes on flame azaleas and expansive panoramas at this iconic high-mountain meadow.

GREAT SMOKY MOUNTAINS NATIONAL PARK

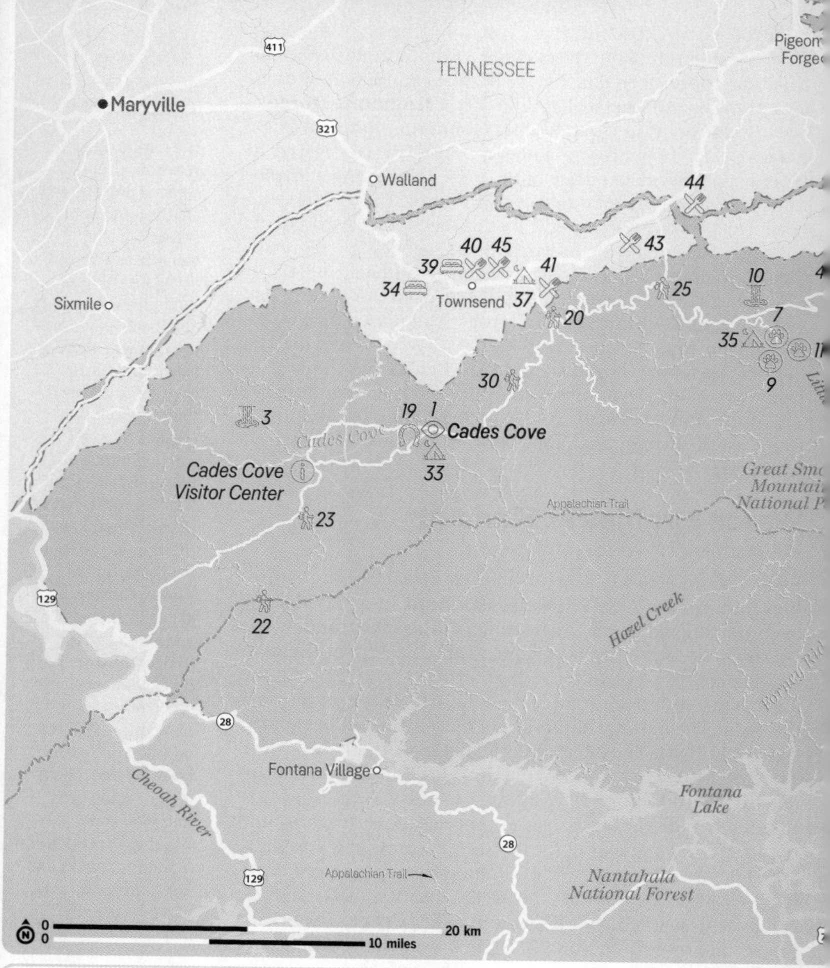

HIGHLIGHTS
1 Cades Cove
2 Mt LeConte

SIGHTS
3 Abrams Falls
4 Charlies Bunyon
5 Cliff Tops Viewing Point
6 Clingmans Dome
7 Elkmont Nature Trailhead
8 Grotto Falls
9 Jakes Creek Trailhead
10 Laurel Falls
11 Little River Trail
12 Myrtle Point
13 Rainbow Falls

ACTIVITIES, COURSES & TOURS
14 Alum Cave Trail
15 Andrews Bald Trail
16 Appalachian Trail
17 Big Creek Trail
18 Bradley Fork Trail
19 Cades Cove Riding Stables
20 Chestnut Top Trail
21 Deep Creek
22 Gregory Bald
23 Gregory Ridge Trail
24 Little Cataloochee Trail
25 Metcalf Bottoms Trail
26 Noah 'Bud' Ogle Place Nature Trail

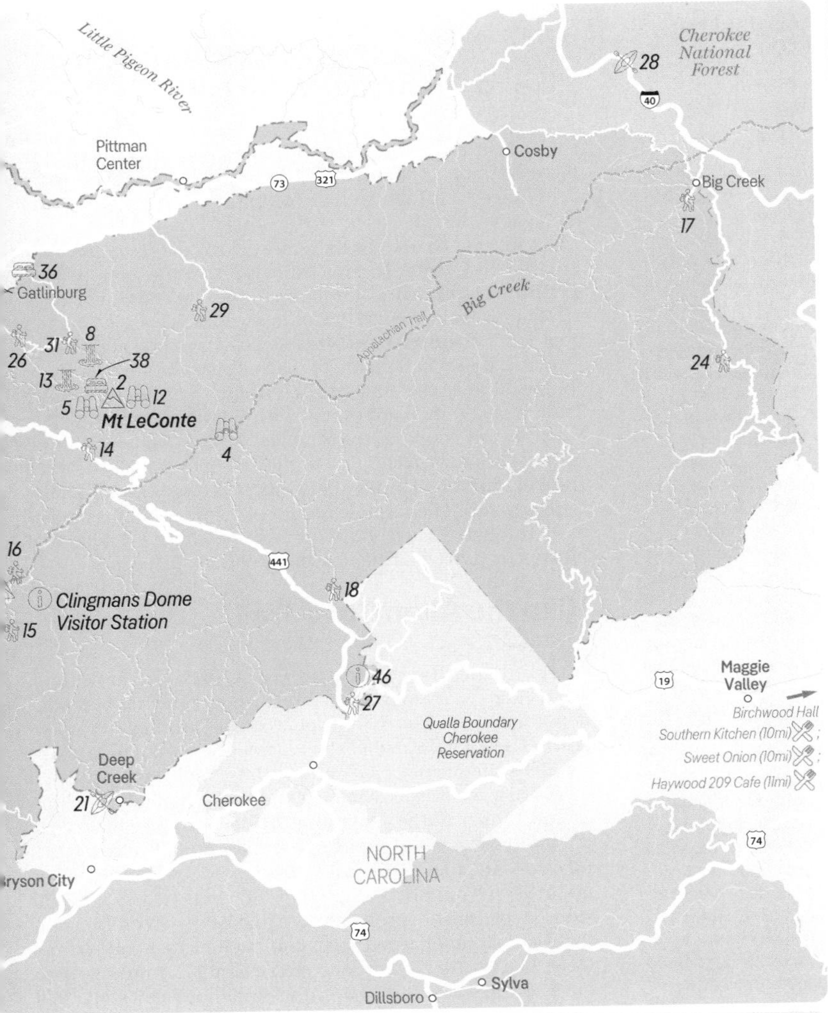

27 Oconaluftee River Trail
28 Pigeon River
29 Porters Creek Trail
30 Schoolhouse Gap Trail
31 Trilium Gap Trail

SLEEPING
32 Bearskin Lodge
33 Cades Cove Campground
34 Dancing Bear Lodge
35 Elkmont Campground
36 Ely's Mill Cabins
37 KOA Kampground & Kabins
38 LeConte Lodge
39 Strawberry Patch Inn

EATING
40 Abbey
41 Burger Master Drive-In
42 Crockett's Breakfast Camp
43 Elvira's
44 Hillbilly's
45 Peaceful Side Social

INFORMATION
46 Oconaluftee Visitor Center
47 Sugarlands Visitor Center

Firefly Viewing Lottery in late April. Peak display lasts about eight days.

Hike to Dramatic Waterfalls

THE SMOKIES' MOST POPULAR FALLS

You've heard about the waterfalls, now it's time to check out three of the best – all located near the Sugarlands Visitor Center near Gatlinburg. To avoid the crowds, arrive as close to dawn as possible.

Picturesque **Grotto Falls** is most easily accessed from the Roaring Fork Motor Nature Trail via a 1.4-mile section of the **Trillium Gap Trail**. Enjoy the scenic beauty of the falls themselves then walk behind the 25ft cascades (a classic Smokies photo op!). **Rainbow Falls** is the most dramatic of the three – and the most challenging to reach. From the Rainbow Falls trailhead, near the start of the Roaring Fork Motor Nature Trail, it's a 2.8-mile uphill trek with 1600ft of elevation gain. Your reward is one of the Smokies' highest waterfalls, cascading 90ft down a cliff face immersed in forest. Multi-tiered **Laurel Falls** sits halfway between Sugarlands and Elkmont Campground. The 1.3-mile out-and-back trail climbs moderately through a laurel-dotted forest, reaching a bridge that crosses the falls near the midpoint of their 75ft drop.

Hike the Alum Cave Trail

EVERYONE'S FAVORITE GREAT SMOKIES HIKE

After crossing the rushing waters of Walker Camp Prong, you'll enter a gorgeous green forest where canopies of rhododendrons await. This is your photogenic introduction to the **Alum Cave Trail**, one of the Smokies' most popular trails, thanks to its scenic beauty and variety. You're guaranteed a memorable experience, whether you walk a half mile or climb its full 5 miles to the summit of **Mt LeConte**.

Wide and flat at the outset, the trail's first mile is a delightful stroll. At 1.4 miles, the trail crosses a log bridge and spirals up through Arch Rock, a striking cleft navigated by graceful stone steps. A more pronounced climb begins, with frequent flights of stone or wood steps punctuated by breathtaking views of the valley. At the end of one climb (2.3 miles), Alum Cave appears, a dramatic overhang of sandy-hued stone that contrasts with the forest and serves as a convenient umbrella during rainstorms.

Most people retrace their steps from here, but you can continue 2.7 miles on the steep trail to the summit. The views keep getting better, while strategically placed cables serve as

TAKE A WILDFLOWER HIKE

For spring wildflowers (March–May), experts recommend:

- Bradley Fork Trail
- Noah 'Bud' Ogle Place Nature Trail
- Porters Creek Trail
- Chestnut Top Trail
- Schoolhouse Gap Trail (connects with Chestnut Top)

In May, mountain laurel blooms throughout the park. There are also 11 species of rhododendron blooming, and stunning displays of flame azaleas can be found beginning in mid- to late June at:

- Gregory Ridge Trail and Gregory Bald
- Andrews Bald

Rosebay and catawba rhododendrons bloom from June to July, but prefer different elevations. Rosebays prefer lower elevations and can be found along many creeks and trails. The catawba prefers higher, exposed ridges. Good spots to see them include Andrews Bald, Alum Cave Trail, above the Chimney Tops Trailhead.

WHERE TO STAY NEAR SUGARLANDS VISITOR CENTER

Elkmont Campground
The soothing sounds of Little Creek are omnipresent at this delightful, family friendly NPS campground. $

Ely's Mill Cabins
Two kitchen-equipped cabins adjacent to historic mill near the end of Roaring Fork Motor Nature Trail. $$

Bearskin Lodge
Enjoy the pool and prime location at this river-facing Gatlinburg hotel on the national park's doorstep. $$

ROARING FORK MOTOR NATURE TRAIL

This short one-way driving loop just south of Gatlinburg is an excellent introduction to the Great Smokies' natural and historic attractions, especially for visitors with limited mobility. Named for one of the park's biggest and most powerful mountain streams, Roaring Fork was designed to be taken slowly (the speed limit is 10mph, so allow at least an hour). The undulating route weaves along rushing creeks, rising and dipping through gorgeous green forest. Parking spots and pullouts offer opportunities to stop and explore on foot, with short trails leading to historic homesteads and longer paths climbing to some of the park's most beloved waterfalls. The road can get crowded, so for maximum enjoyment, consider visiting midweek or early in the day.

The Motor Nature Trail begins about 5 miles outside of Gatlinburg; follow Cherokee Orchard Rd south from town. First up is the **1 Bud Ogle Cabin**, where a short jaunt leads to a mountain farmstead with a streamside tub mill (a primitive contraption for grinding corn) followed by the **2 Rainbow Falls trailhead**. You'll next reach the official entrance to the narrow one-way section, which follows one of the park's most tempestuous streams. The road passes though an impressive stand of old-growth eastern hemlocks, some soaring 100ft. Worthwhile stops over the next 5 miles include an easy, short hike on the **3 Grotto Falls Trail**, the hardscrabble 19th-century **4 Ephraim Bales Cabin**, and the 'saddlebag house' and another tub mill at **5 Alfred Reagan Homestead** (painted with all three colors that Sears and Roebuck had). The last stop is the **6 Place of a Thousand Drips**, a wet-weather waterfall. Pick up a booklet covering these and several other stops at park visitor centers.

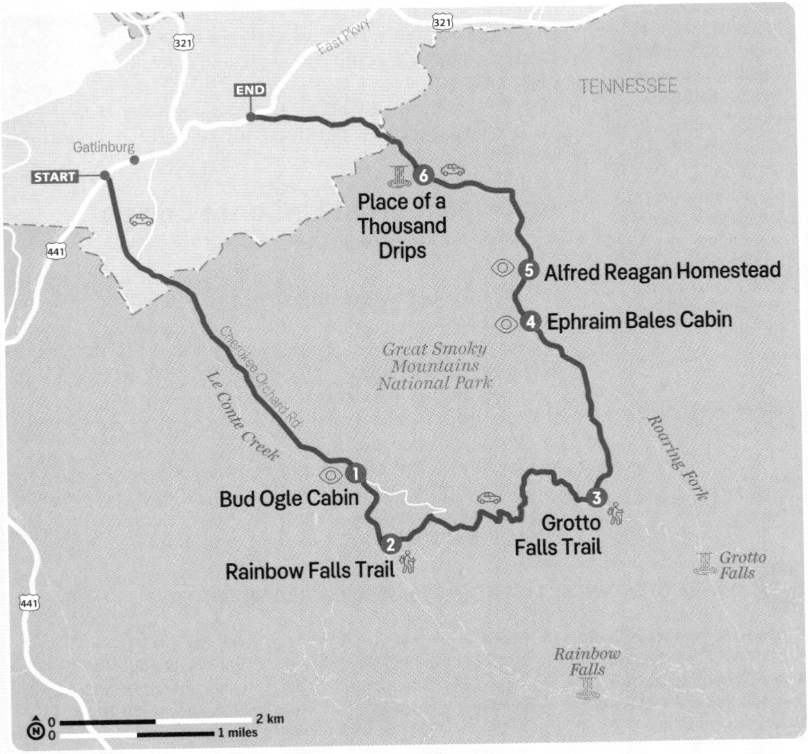

Rainbow Falls (p362)

BEST EASY HIKES FOR FAMILIES

Metcalf Bottoms Trail
Splash in river and hike to 19th-century schoolhouse on 0.7-mile trail from Metcalf Bottoms picnic area.

Little River Trail
Explore rocky pools and the ruins of former vacation homes on this out-and-back ramble.

Oconaluftee River Trail
See nature through the eyes of Cherokee storytellers on this interpretive nature trail near the Oconaluftee Visitor Center.

Big Creek Trail to Midnight Hole & Mouse Creek Falls
Follow Big Creek's banks 2 miles upstream to a swimming hole and waterfall.

handholds for navigating slippery stretches of rock. At the end of the trail, turn right on Rainbow Falls Trail to reach Le-Conte Lodge, Mt LeConte summit, and a pair of classic viewpoints, Cliff Tops and Myrtle Point.

Arrive at the trailhead as early as possible (before 8am) for the best shot at a parking spot, or reserve a shuttle in Gatlinburg.

An Overnight at LeConte Lodge

SLEEP NEAR A MOUNTAIN SUMMIT

For a memorable adventure, spend the night in the legendary, sky-high **LeConte Lodge**. The 10 rustic cabins here, clustered at 6400ft near Mt LeConte's summit, are the only place to sleep indoors within the national park. While the accommodations are simple – bunk beds, kerosene lamps, a wash basin, an outhouse and rockers on every front porch – the effort required to snag a spot makes the memory even sweeter for those who succeed.

Reservations are accepted beginning October 1 each year, and rooms fill up almost instantly. The lodge is accessible only by foot, via the Alum Cave, Rainbow Falls, Trillium Gap or Boulevard Trails. Breakfast and dinner are included in the

WHERE TO EAT BREAKFAST NEAR SUGARLANDS VISITOR CENTER

Crockett's Breakfast Camp
Challenge yourself to the world's largest cinnamon roll at Gatlinburg's favorite breakfast spot. $

Elvira's
Hearty Southern breakfast fare served on a wraparound porch in Wears Valley. $

Hillbilly's
Convenient option for breakfast without the Gatlinburg crowds, 20 minutes from Elkmont in Wears Valley. $

price and served in the lodge's dining room overlooking the Smokies, with supplies brought in by helicopter and llama. Popular guest activities include twilight treks to watch the sun rise and set over waves of misty mountains from two of the park's most stunning viewpoints: **Cliff Tops** and **Myrtle Point**. If you come up shorthanded during the brief early October booking window, it's worth trying again in early November, as reservations not paid for within the first 30 days are automatically cancelled and made available again to the general public. It's also worth checking the lodge's social-media feed, where last-minute cancellations are announced on an ongoing basis.

Camping in Cades Cove

CAMPING AND WILDLIFE WATCHING

Cades Cove is one of the Smokies' most bewitching landscapes, a vast open valley encircled by mountains, dotted with historic structures and roamed by bears, wild turkeys and deer. At dawn, as the sun's rays pierce the fog and the cove's lush verdancy comes into focus, you feel you've unexpectedly entered another time, another place. With its abundant wildlife, the cove is believed to have been inhabited as early as 8000 BCE, and long served as hunting grounds for the Cherokee. White settlers began arriving around 1820, building log cabins, churches and gristmills, clearing forests and farming; modern-day visitors traveling the Cades Cove Loop see the preserved remains of this bygone culture.

With 164 sites (including 11 that are ADA accessible), **Cades Cove Campground** is the ideal jumping-off point for the Cades Cove Loop Rd. Campers get special 24-hour rates at the on-site bike rental shop. There's a ranger station and a store selling ice, firewood, a few groceries and souvenirs. RVs find easy parking in Loops A and B – so expect your mornings to be interrupted by the roar of generators, or opt for a quieter site in generator-free Loop C. This can be a friendly campground, so don't be surprised if your neighbors walk over to say hello – maybe bringing some moonshine to share! The closest gas, restaurants and other services are in Townsend, about 20 minutes away.

Hike to Abrams Falls

THE PARK'S MOST VOLUMINOUS WATERFALL

With wildflowers along the way, a few big rocks well-suited for picnics, and a gorgeous waterfall as your payoff, the **Abrams Falls Trail** is a perfect half-day hike – and undeniably a

THE SMOKIES BY LAND & WATER

Andy Gallatin is a Master Guide for the Nantahala Outdoor Center and an Appalachian Trail through hiker. @river_weasel

Hike

Anything on the **Appalachian Trail**!

Standing on the highest peak of the entire park, **Clingmans Dome**, gives you a top-of-the-world feeling.

The beauty of this tower that was sourced from **Mt Cammerer** nearly a century ago takes you back in time.

Max Patch Bald is the prettiest bald on the entire trail. The 360-degree views will take your breath away.

Raft

I love the **Upper Pigeon** because it's friendly for first-timers and splashy for experienced thrill seekers. The first class III rapid, **Powerhouse**, will have you hooked!

WHERE TO STAY IN TOWNSEND

KOA Kampground & Kabins
The closest non-NPS campground to Cades Cove, offering both camping and cabins. $

Strawberry Patch Inn
Kitchen-equipped apartments with log-cabin aesthetic, plus shared deck and garden spaces overlooking the Little River. $$

Dancing Bear Lodge
Townsend's cushiest sleeping option, with luxurious cabins and a high-end bistro on a forested hillside. $$$

ROAD TRIP

Exploring the Cades Cove Loop Road

Thanks to its history, wildlife (especially bears) and pastoral scenery, the Cades Cove Loop has become one of the Smokies' most sought-after tourist destinations. Set off at dawn or in late afternoon. Better yet, come on Wednesdays, when motor vehicles are prohibited and cyclists and walkers rule the road. To shorten the loop, turn left on Sparks or Hyatt Lanes (1.1 or 3.1 miles from the start, respectively).

1 Cades Cove Campground

Start at the Cades Cove Campground Store, where you can rent bikes for the journey and park your 'other' vehicle.

The Drive: Exit the campground and turn left onto Cades Cove Loop, which soon becomes one-way. The idyllic, tree-lined route rolls through open meadows to your first stop.

2 John Oliver Place

Take the 0.3-mile footpath off the main road to this historic homestead, tucked into a clearing at the edge of the forest. Dating to the early 1820s, this is the oldest surviving log home in Cades Cove.

The Drive: Continue 1.2 miles west on the main road, then take the signposted 0.4-mile detour on your left for the Primitive Baptist Church.

3 Primitive Baptist Church

An evocative park sight, this simple Baptist church down a side road has a serene adjoining graveyard. Deer sometimes come to graze at the cemetery's edge in early

DANIEL KORZENIEWSKI/SHUTTERSTOCK ©

John Oliver Place

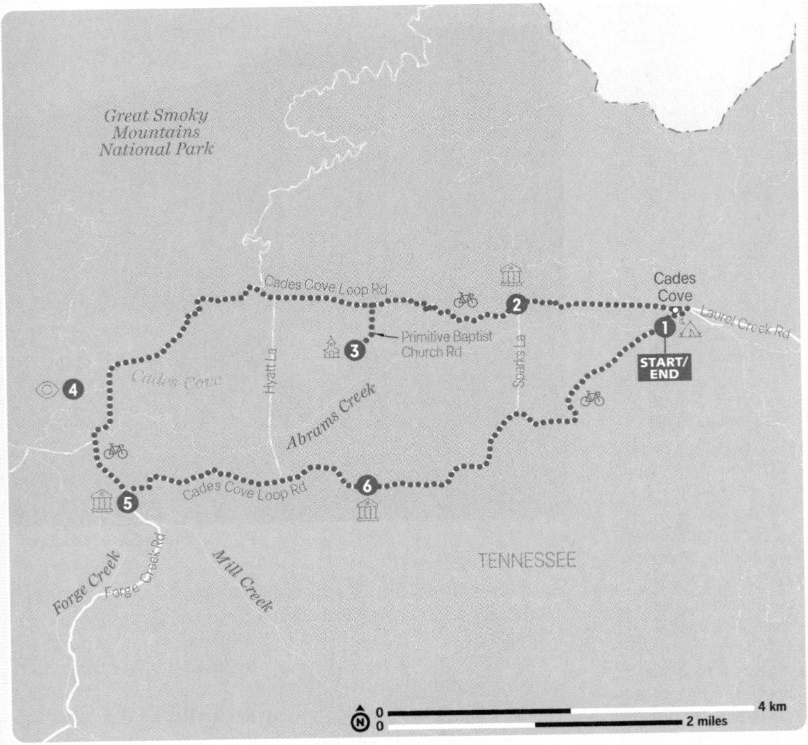

morning, and many familiar Cades Cove names are chiseled on the tombstones here.

The Drive: Return to the main road and bear left, enjoying long views of mountain-backed meadows before a steep descent to the Elijah Oliver parking area (2.3 miles further west).

4 Elijah Oliver Place

Park your bike or car and walk the lovely 0.5-mile path to this old homestead, complete with smokehouse (for preserving hams), springhouse (for chilling dairy products) and corncrib (for storing corn).

The Drive: It's an easy 1-mile jaunt south to your next stop; en route is an optional turnoff for Abrams Falls Trail, one of the Smokies' prettiest waterfall hikes.

5 Cable Mill Area & Cades Cove Visitor Center

This attractive streamside assemblage of historical buildings beside the Cades Cove store and visitor center makes the perfect midway picnic stop. The star attraction here is the Cable Mill, a historic gristmill flanked by a pretty mill race, a blacksmith shop, a cantilever barn and other 19th-century structures.

The Drive: Your return trip begins here! You'll be following the southern edge of the cove the rest of the way. Continue 2 miles east to your next stop.

6 Tipton Place

The most attractive of several homesteads on your return route, the Tipton Place features a shingle-roofed clapboard 1870s home with a collection of outbuildings straddling both sides of the road.

The Drive: Complete the loop, riding 2.9 miles past another historic cabin and the Cades Cove Stables to return to your starting point.

RAFTING THE PIGEON RIVER

Many winding creeks and crystal-clear streams in the Smokies find their way to the Pigeon River. When they converge they create a fantastic setting for white-water adventures on churning rapids amid a gorgeous forest backdrop. Families with small kids can enjoy a peaceful paddle on the Lower Pigeon, while those seeking more thrills should opt for Upper Pigeon, with its Class III and IV rapids. Near the Pigeon River, the teeny town of Hartford off I-40 is the center of a vibrant rafting community, and a dozen different rafting companies operate along the riverbank off Exit 447. Excursions take place from May through Labor Day, with schedules dependent on water releases from the dam upstream.

Cades Cove (p365)

Smokies' classic. Total walking time for this 5-mile round-trip hike, which is easily accessed from the Cades Cove Loop Rd, is about 2½ hours. However, allow half a day to make the most of the beautiful setting at the base of the falls, where many people linger to picnic or sun themselves on the rocks.

From the trailhead, the path crosses a log bridge and hugs Abrams Creek. Around the 1-mile mark, the creek disappears from sight as it makes a big horseshoe bend around a promontory, which the trail crosses via a low pass. After descending back to the creek, you'll continue another mile or so to reach the falls.

The falls are not high (only 20ft, or so), but they carry a greater volume of water than any other cascades in the park. The surrounding rock shelves are more spacious and welcoming than at many of the park's other waterfall hot spots. One caveat? The crowds, which can be quite heavy in summer.

Horses & Hayrides

TRAIL RIDES, CADES COVE CIRCUIT

A staggering 550 miles of hiking trails are open for horseback riding in the park. If you're not towing your own horse, reserve a trail ride with one of the park's four stables (Cades

WHERE TO EAT & DRINK NEAR TOWNSEND

Peaceful Side Social
Haven in Townsend with draft beers, taco truck, sandwiches, pizza, kids' playground and indoor-outdoor seating. **$$**

Abbey
Chilled-out Townsend spot for beer, cider, sandwiches, salads and daily specials, with delightful riverside patio. **$$**

Burger Master Drive-in
In business since 1967, luring locals and tourists with burgers, shakes and ice cream. **$**

Cove, Smokemont, Smoky Mountain, Sugarlands), all open between mid-March and late November. It's best to call ahead to make reservations. One-hour trail rides cost $40 to $45 per person. For more saddle time, you can sign up for a longer ride, ranging from 2½ to four hours. Among the horse outfitters, **Cades Cove Riding Stables** stands out for its 1½ to three-hour tractor-drawn hayrides, which make a full circuit of Cades Cove Loop Rd. It's a romantic way to experience one of the park's prettiest landscapes, seated on hay bales, enjoying open-air views and refreshing breezes.

Escape to Cataloochee Valley

SOLITUDE, HISTORY AND WILD ELK

For travelers seeking a peaceful refuge, the eastern outposts of Cataloochee is a little slice of heaven. A century ago, Cataloochee was among the most heavily settled places in the Smokies, but with the advent of the national park, the valley has reverted to a more natural state. Roads are still mostly hard-packed dirt or gravel; elk, wild turkeys and occasional bears wander peacefully among the ghostly remnants of early settlers' homesteads; and campsites feel more intimate. Hiking the **Little Cataloochee Trail** and stopping by its historic structures feels like stepping into another century, where the phantoms of an earlier time and place still roam.

Go Tubing at Deep Creek

FLOATING FUN FOR THE FAMILY

For low-cost family fun, you can't beat a day **tubing** on beautiful **Deep Creek**, near the eponymous ranger station and campground just 2 miles north of Bryson City. Several tubing outfits line Deep Creek Rd, the main conduit leading north from town into the national park. Rentals are generally less than $10 per person and good for the whole day. Grab your tubes, drive up to the Day Use parking area just inside the park boundary, and walk up the Deep Creek Trail as far as you like before plunging into the creek.

ELK REINTRODUCTION

On February 25, 2001, 13 male and 12 female elk were brought to Cataloochee Valley from Land Between the Lakes, Kentucky. For two months they were held in a 3-acre pen, as they acclimated to their new surroundings. On April 2, they were released. Elk had returned to the Smokies. Before European settlement, an estimated 10 million elk ranged across America, including southern Appalachia. By the mid-1800s this region's elk were gone – extirpated by habitat loss and overhunting. Reputedly, the last elk in eastern Tennessee was shot in 1849.

Today the herd's population has risen to 200, and elk now range throughout the park; look for them in Cataloochee and Oconaluftee Valleys.

GETTING AROUND

The closest airports are McGhee Tyson Airport near Knoxville (40 miles northwest of the Sugarlands Visitor Center) and Asheville Regional Airport , 58 miles east of the Oconaluftee Visitor Center. There's no public transportation to the park or within the park. There is a wide variety of car-rental companies at each of the airports. A handful of shuttle companies offer private transport inside the park. The following shuttle companies can take you to, or pick you up from, trailheads:

In Tennessee:

AAA Hiker Shuttle 865-322-0691
A Walk in the Woods 865-436-8283
Great Smoky Mountains Eco Tours 865-900-5979
RockyTop Tours 865-429-8687
Smoky Mountain Rides 865-562-2833

In North Carolina:

Bryson City Outdoors 828-342-6444
Carolina Bound 828-569-6699

HOT SPRINGS NATIONAL PARK

Famed for its warm geothermal waters, this small national park is a hot spot for relaxation and low-key adventuring. Thanks to the 47 steamy springs found here, Native Americans called this region the Valley of the Vapors. Those attracted to their alleged healing powers included the Caddo, Choctaw and Cherokee tribes, and Spanish conquistador Hernando de Soto. American explorers William Dunbar and George Hunter visited in 1804 after the Louisiana Purchase. Twentieth-century resort crowds followed. During its 1930s heydays, Hot Springs was a hotbed of gambling, bootlegging, prostitution and opulence.

Today, the appeal is less the actual springs than the tourism infrastructure that commemorates them, although two restored bathhouses in the park offer spa treatments. Note that Hot Springs is the name of the park as well as the inviting town that surrounds it.

FACTS

Great For Family travel, history, scenery
State California
Entrance Fee Free
Area 8.7 sq miles

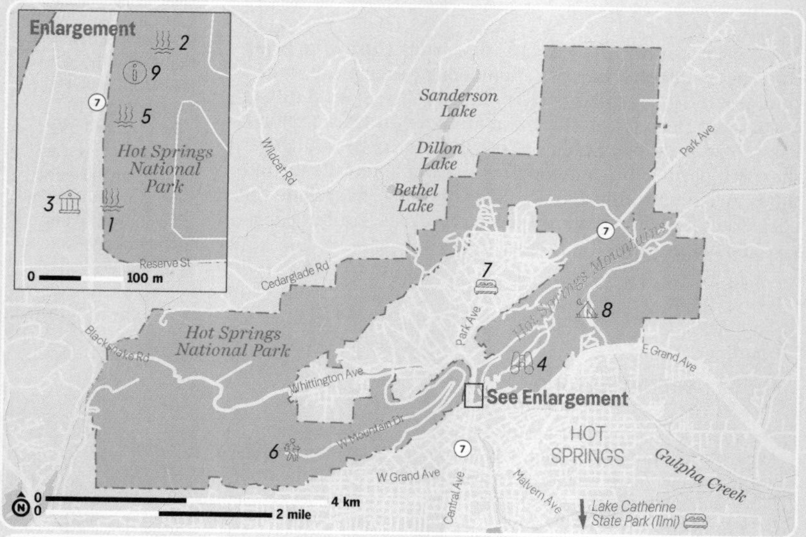

SIGHTS
1 Buckstaff Bathhouse
2 Display Spring
3 Gangster Museum of America
4 Hot Springs Mountain Tower
5 Quapaw Bathhouse

ACTIVITIES, COURSES & TOURS
6 Sunset Trail

SLEEPING
7 Gold-Inn
8 Gulpha Gorge Campground

INFORMATION
9 Fordyce Bathhouse

Healing Waters

SOAK IN THE HISTORY

You can enjoy the waters 1930s-style at the **Buckstaff Bathhouse**, where visitors have taken to the waters in the bathhouse since 1912.

You can also soak in the waters with Quapaw Baths & Spa in the **Quapaw Bathhouse**, but most of the other old bathhouses have been converted into art galleries and offices affiliated with the National Park Service (NPS). The **Fordyce Bathhouse**, built in 1915, houses the park visitor center. You can learn about the sinful glory days of Prohibition at the **Gangster Museum of America** – this small town in the middle of nowhere was a hotbed of lavish wealth, thanks to Chicago bootleggers like Al Capone and his New York counterparts.

A promenade runs through the park around the hillside behind Bathhouse Row, where some springs survive intact. Outdoor springs are not open for soaking. Look for **Display Spring**, sometimes called Open Spring, directly behind Maurice Bathhouse. With a temperature of 143°F (62°C), it is too hot for a dip!

TIMELINE: HOT SPRINGS VS YELLOWSTONE

President Andrew Jackson signed legislation for the creation of the Hot Springs Reservation in 1832 – a good 40 years before Yellowstone National Park was established in California. Various buildings have held bathing tubs in Hot Springs since the creation of the reservation, and Bathhouse Row was completed in 1922 – the year after Hot Springs became an official national park.

Hike the Trails

SUNSET AND A MOUNTAIN TOWER

The park has 26 miles of trails; many of them are short and scenic and they link up to form a network across the town's mountains. The 10-mile **Sunset Trail** (one way) ribbons through a hardwood forest and crosses three mountains – West, Sugarloaf and Music – before linking to **Gulpha Gorge Campground**. From the campground, you can also climb trails to the **Hot Springs Mountain Tower** atop Hot Springs Mountain. The 216ft commercially run tower (adult/child $13/9) has spectacular views of the city as well as surrounding mountains covered with dogwood, hickory, oak and pine – lovely in the spring and autumn.

Buckstaff Bathhouse
KIT LEONG/SHUTTERSTOCK ©

WHERE TO STAY IN HOT SPRINGS NATIONAL PARK

Gulpha Gorge Campground
Beautifully positioned on a creek near hiking trails. Only place to stay in the park. $

Gold-Inn
Former old roadside motel upgraded into a boutique hotel; 1 mile from Bathhouse Row. $

Lake Catherine State Park
Contains 20 cabins built by the Civilian Conservation Corps; also tent camping and yurts. $

MAMMOTH CAVE NATIONAL PARK

The names of the guided tours at Mammoth Cave are highly evocative – Gothic Avenue, Frozen Niagara – priming visitors for otherworldly underground adventures. The longest cave system in the world, this national park in central Kentucky holds 400 miles of surveyed passageways. It spans five distinct levels and is at least three times longer than any other known cave, with vast interior cathedrals, bottomless pits, and strange, undulating rock formations – all created by water dripping through the porous limestone over the millennia.

Native American remains discovered in the cave suggest a human presence here about 4000 years ago. According to lore, European settlers discovered the cave in the late 1700s after a hunter chased a wounded bear to the entrance. The interior later served as a saltpeter mine and as a tuberculosis hospital. Tourism began in the early 1800s. Do bring a sweater; the temperature inside remains a chilly 54°F (12°C) year-round.

FACTS

Great For Hiking, family travel, scenery
State Kentucky
Entrance Fee Free; cave tours $8 to $66
Area 82.6 sq miles

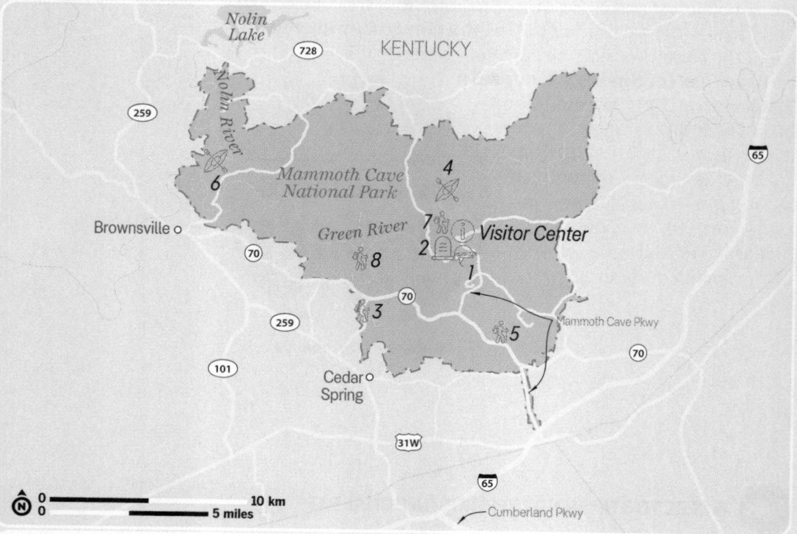

SIGHTS
1 Mammoth Cave
2 Old Guide's Cemetery

ACTIVITIES, COURSES & TOURS
3 Cedar Sink Trail
4 Green River
5 Mammoth Cave Railroad Trail
6 Nolin River
7 River Styx Spring Trail
8 Turnhole Bend Trail

Cave Tours

NUMEROUS UNDERGROUND ADVENTURES

Tours of **Mammoth Cave** vary slightly by season, but you'll have numerous options for viewing the rock formations and learning more about the history and geology of the cave. Options range from an hour-long subterranean stroll to strenuous day-long spelunking adventures. The **Frozen Niagara Tour** is the easiest, offering glimpses of groovy formations in large caverns. The popular **Dome and Dripstones Tour** takes in several dramatic deposits, though you must walk up and down 500 stairs and squeeze through tight areas. The magical **Violet City Tour** is a walk through the passageways by candlelight. In the months of June and July you can buy a ticket for the **self-guided Discovery Tour**. You cannot enter the cave without a ticket.

Tickets do sell out in summer and in early autumn, so book ahead to avoid disappointment. Tickets can be purchased on recreation.gov or by calling 877-444-6777. The visitor center also sells tickets.

Above-Ground Adventures

HIKING AND PADDLING

Eighty-five miles of hiking trails twist through the park's forested hills. Seven miles from the visitor center, the **Cedar Sink Trail** passes trees, wildflowers and cliffs on its way to a limestone sinkhole surrounded by rock outcroppings. The hike to the sinkhole is 2 miles round trip.

The **Green River** runs through the park for 25 miles as does the 6-mile **Nolin River**. They're prime for canoeing and kayaking, carrying paddlers on slow-moving currents past dramatic cliffs, soaring trees and wildlife – you might see beavers, foxes and wild turkeys. Check the park website for a list of outdoor outfitters who can get you on the water for half-day and full-day trips.

Mammoth Cave National Park
ZACK FRANK/SHUTTERSTOCK ©

THE STORY OF STEPHEN BISHOP

One of the most famous tour guides at the park was Stephen Bishop, an enslaved African American who arrived at the cave in 1817. He began exploring the cave and mapping its passageways, and he lead tours in the park's earliest days as a tourist attraction. He and a visitor were the first to cross the Bottomless Pit, apparently over a ladder, which opened up new sections of the cave system to tourism. Bishop is also credited with discovering Mammoth Dome and the Ruins of Karnak. His knowledge of the cave system was well-known and many visitors requested him as their guide. He is buried in the park in the **Old Guide's Cemetery**.

WHERE TO HIKE IN MAMMOTH CAVE NATIONAL PARK

Turnhole Bend Trail
Winds through old-growth stands of oaks and hickories and past secluded bluffs. Seven miles round trip.

River Styx Spring Trail
Short trail ribbons through thick forest to the spot where River Styx leaves the cave.

Mammoth Cave Railroad Trail
Nine-mile (one-way) trail follows a railroad line through hardwood forest. Great during foliage season.

NEW RIVER GORGE NATIONAL PARK & PRESERVE

Famed for its white-water rafting and breathtaking beauty, this rugged sliver of Appalachia is the nation's newest national park, earning its official designation in 2021. The narrow park protects a stretch of the New River as it carves through an ancient forest gorge, dropping 750ft over 50 miles. Rapids, some designated Class V, cluster in the northernmost end of the park. Hiking trails along the rim and within the gorge share views of the river, while mountain-biking trails rip through the forest. For outdoor gear, good eats, craft beer and lodging options, stop in Fayetteville, a fun mountain town just south of the bridge.

FACTS

Great For Walking, cycling, scenery
State West Virginia
Entrance Fee Free
Area 114 sq miles

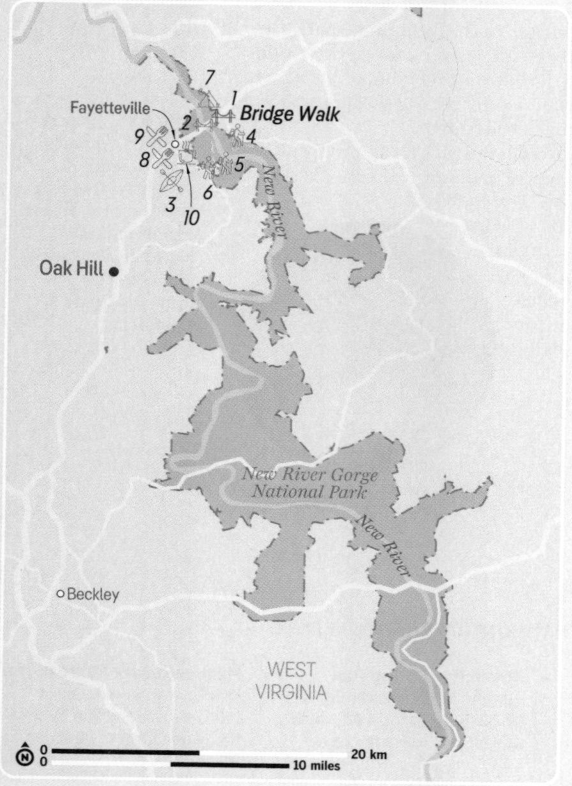

HIGHLIGHTS
1 Bridge Walk

SIGHTS
2 New River Gorge Bridge

ACTIVITIES, COURSES & TOURS
3 Cantrell Ultimate Rafting
4 Endless Wall Trail
5 Kaymoor Miners Trail
6 Long Point Trail

SLEEPING
7 Adventures on the Gorge

EATING
8 Pies & Pints
9 Tudor's Biscuit World

DRINKING
10 Cathedral Cafe

White-Water Thrills

RAFTING GAULEY AND NEW RIVERS

Dropping into a raft on the Lower Gauley River during 'Gauley Season' is a test of personal courage. On dam-release weekends in September and October, the Summersville Dam releases extra water into the river, triggering epic waves. From the drop-in point below the dam, the river looks unrunnable. But the rafting guides always seem undaunted. One of the wildest white-water rafting trips in the country, with three Class Vs along 25 named rapids, a dam-release trip will earn you lifetime bragging rights. Trips begin just north of the national park.

You'll also find big rapids (rising up to Class IV) on the Lower New River, the most popular section of the New River for rafting season, which typically begins in May. Many rafting companies provide camping and lodging. Standouts include **Cantrell Ultimate Rafting** and **Adventures on the Gorge**. The latter runs a base camp near Fayetteville, complete with campsites, cabins, restaurants and guided adventures.

Celebrate the Bridge

BRIDGE WALKS AND BASE JUMPING

Slip into a harness and clip onto a cable before following a catwalk across the river – from a height of 886ft! **New River Gorge Bridge** – one of the longest single-span arch bridges in the world – is the most iconic sight in West Virginia and an epicenter of regional adventure. Half-day **Bridge Walk tours** are guided and very informative. Grab lunch and a craft beer at **Pies & Pints** afterwards. The bridge closes to vehicles on the third Saturday in October for **Bridge Day**, when hundreds of BASE jumpers parachute from its ledge, and pedestrians are allowed to stroll from one end of the gorge to the other.

For an easy, tree-framed view of the bridge and the gorge, walk to the Upper Bridge Overlook behind the Canyon Visitor Center.

New River Gorge Bridge
STEVE HEAP/SHUTTERSTOCK ©

BEST HIKES IN NEW RIVER GORGE NATIONAL PARK

Long Point Trail
Three-mile round-trip hike to a rock outcrop with expansive views of the New River Gorge Bridge.

Endless Wall Trail
You may pass rock climbers on this moderate 2.4-mile out-and-back hike with high-elevation views of the gorge.

Kaymoor Miners Trail
This strenuous trail drops a mile into the gorge, passing an old coal-mine site before ending at an abandoned mining community on the riverbank.

WHERE TO EAT IN FAYETTEVILLE

Cathedral Cafe
Coffee shop serving pastries, salads and sandwiches in a former church. **$**

Pies & Pints
The flagship location of a popular regional pizza-and-craft-beer chain. **$$**

Tudor's Biscuit World
A statewide West Virginia institution, this fast-food joint specializes in delicious biscuits. **$**

FLORIDA

EXPERIENCE FLORIDA'S WILD SOUTH

Florida's three national parks have wilderness and pristine waters at the heart of their appeal.

Florida and its three national parks will surprise you. Biscayne, Dry Tortugas and the peerless Everglades are poster children for the wild beauty of the US coast, and each lies where you'd least expect to find it.

High-rise towers of Miami loom on the near horizon, but this takes nothing away from the magnificence of what's on offer at Biscayne. Here, islands might dot a turquoise sea, but it's all about what's beneath the ocean. Plunge below the surface and in an instant you'll be transported into another world, of shipwrecks and coral gardens animated by an astonishing array of marine life.

Dry Tortugas is as remote as Biscayne is close to the city. It lies out beyond Key West, that enduring symbol of the end of the American road, as far from Miami as from Havana. Surrounded by ocean and adorned by an isolated fortress that tells stories of the great battles of the American South, Dry Tortugas is a remarkable place to spend a few days staring at the stars and soaking up the isolation.

BLUEBARRONPHOTO/SHUTTERSTOCK ©

And then there are the Everglades, a watery world of alligators and abundant birdlife, of 10,000 islands and countless channels where you canoe and camp far from the noisy world. Immerse yourself in its many hidden corners and you'll never look at Florida in the same way again.

THE MAIN AREAS

BISCAYNE NATIONAL PARK
Explore a magical underwater world.
p382

DRY TORTUGAS NATIONAL PARK
A remote outpost of US history.
p385

EVERGLADES NATIONAL PARK
Hike, paddle and watch wonderful wildlife.
p387

Left: Pelican, Dry Tortugas National Park (p385); Above: Boca Chita lighthouse (p383)

CAR

Unlike elsewhere in the US, a car can only take you so far in Florida's parks. Well-maintained roads run to the trailheads of hikes, as well as to piers from where boats depart.

BOAT

It could be a ferry to Dry Tortugas, a boat cruise to explore the islands of Biscayne, or a canoe you need to paddle yourself through the Everglades: boats are essential for exploring here.

Everglades National Park, p387

Vast wilderness with wildlife and extensive trails that can be impossible to resist.

Dry Tortugas National Park, p385

Far out in the Gulf of Mexico, with a historic fort, deserted beaches, stargazing and snorkeling.

Find Your Way

All three of Florida's national parks are in Florida's south. You'll need your own wheels to reach the gateway to each of these parks. From there, take a boat.

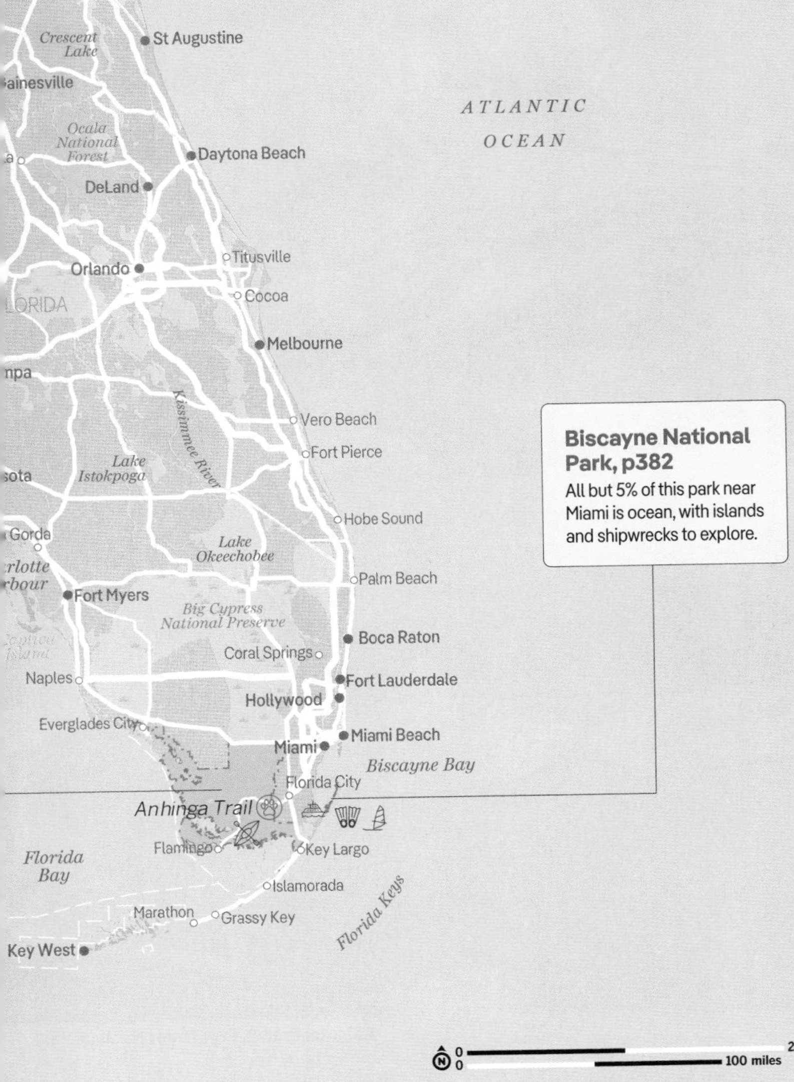

Biscayne National Park, p382
All but 5% of this park near Miami is ocean, with islands and shipwrecks to explore.

FRANCISCO BLANCO/SHUTTERSTOCK ©

Alligator (p389), Everglades National Park

Fort Jefferson (p386), Dry Tortugas National Park

Plan Your Time

You could build an itinerary around Florida's three parks, but you could equally dip into the parks as part of a wider exploration of Florida's south.

If You Only Do One Thing

In three days you can hike the **Anhinga Trail** (p386), take a boat cruise out into the **10,000 Islands** (p389) or **paddle through the Everglades backcountry** (p390). You can even **drive a loop** (p390) through the park. You could, of course, take longer if you fall in love with the wildlife and wild landscapes you encounter along the way.

Five Days to Explore

Begin with a **boat cruise** (p383) through **Biscayne National Park** (p382), then return in your own boat for some **diving and snorkeling** (p384), not to mention exploring the islands. Then drive out to Key West and take the ferry to **Dry Tortugas** (p385) – stay overnight to explore **Fort Jefferson** (p386), stare at the stars and explore the waters.

SEASONAL HIGHLIGHTS

SPRING

Expect clear skies and milder temperatures; escape to the parks while spring-breakers fill Florida's beaches.

SUMMER

The weather can be hot and humid, parks are busy with visitors, and hurricane season begins in June.

FALL

Hurricanes are possible until November. Florida's three parks see fewer visitors in fall.

WINTER

Positively balmy compared to elsewhere in the US, winter can be a quieter (and excellent) time to visit.

BISCAYNE NATIONAL PARK

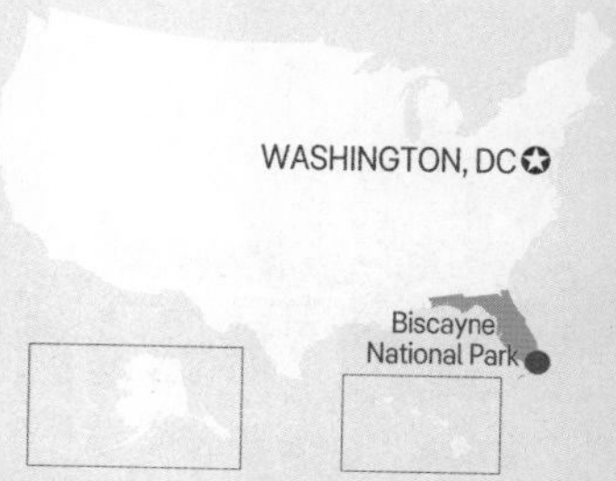

Just to the east of the Everglades, Biscayne National Park protects a portion of the world's third-largest reef. Barely 5% of the park is on land, consisting of the islands that sit here off the coast of Florida. The park also has mangrove forests and the northernmost Florida Keys.

Biscayne National Park may not be far from Miami, but that only adds to the park's unlikely appeal, to the feeling of a world removed from cities and their clamor. Encompassing a vibrant swath of biologically rich coral reef, this park is teeming with life – though you'll have to head on a boat tour or, better yet don a snorkel and mask to see it firsthand. Manatees, dolphins and sea turtles are just a few inhabitants of this diverse ecosystem; there are also over 500 species of reef fish, neotropical waterbirds and migratory species.

FACTS

Great For Beaches, family travel, wildlife
State Florida
Entrance Fee Free
Area 270 sq miles

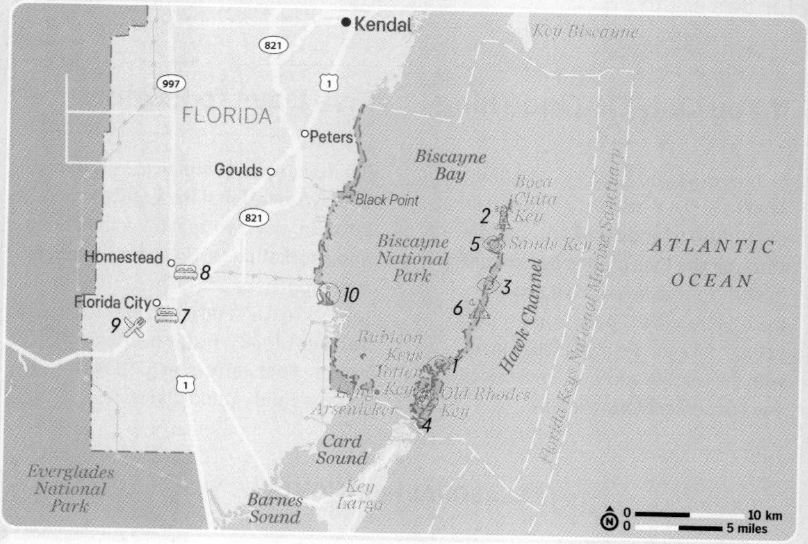

SIGHTS
1 Adams Key
see 2 Boca Chita Key
2 Boca Chita Lighthouse
3 Elliott Key
4 Jones Lagoon
5 Sands Key

SLEEPING
6 Elliott Key Campgrounds
7 Hoosville Hostel
8 Hotel Redland

EATING
9 Everglades Gator Grill

INFORMATION
10 Dante Fascell Visitor Center

Kayaking, Biscayne Bay

Explore Biscayne by Boat

TAKE A GUIDED BOAT CRUISE

In a park where 95% of the national park's surface area is water, it makes sense to explore by boat. For an introduction to the park and its most beautiful corners, take one of the boat tours offered by the park, with a ranger giving an overview of the wildlife and history of the area as you go. Cruises depart from the **Dante Fascell Visitor Center** (305-230-7275) in Homestead. Among the options is a 3½-hour Heritage Cruise.

Longer trips cruise along the bay, stopping at Boca Chita or Adams Key, followed by lunch (which is not included – bring your own), then snorkeling or paddleboarding in a peaceful spot, and then the homeward journey, arriving around 4pm. Although somewhat pricey, the tour gets rave reviews from those who've made the trip.

Call to confirm times and book your spot, or book online through biscaynenationalparkinstitute.org.

If you're keen for a little more freedom, you can rent your own boat, or even a kayak. And if you're planning your own boat

SIGHTSEEING IN BISCAYNE

Long **Elliott Key** has picnicking, campsites and hiking among mangrove forests; tiny **Adams Key** has only picnicking; and equally tiny **Boca Chita Key** has an ornamental lighthouse, picnicking and campsites. These little islands were settled under the Homestead Act of 1862, which gave land freely to anyone willing to spend five years turning a scratch of the tropics into a working pineapple and key-lime farm. If you end up on Boca Chita Key, allow time to walk part of the 6-mile trail and look for the 65ft-high **lighthouse**. Other highlights include **Jones Lagoon**, with its rich marine life and bird rookeries, and **Sands Key**, another rarely visited lagoon.

WHERE TO STAY & EAT AROUND BISCAYNE

Hoosville Hostel
Good-value dorms and rooms with a creatively configured backyard. Small pool with waterfall and gazebo. $

Hotel Redland
On the edge of Homestead, occupying a 1904 building with a warm, cozy feel. $

Everglades Gator Grill
Enjoy gator tacos, gator stir-fry, gator kebabs and straight-up fried alligator served in a basket. $

PARK HEADQUARTERS

Located at Convoy Point near Homestead, the **Dante Fascell Visitor Center** (nps.gov/bisc) shows a great introductory film for an overview of the park. It also has maps, information and excellent ranger activities.

trip, make sure you have your paperwork in order. Pick up a tide chart from the park (or from nps.gov/bisc/planyourvisit/tide-predictions.htm). Make sure you comply with local slow-speed zones, designed to protect the endangered manatee.

Dive & Snorkel off Miami

EXPLORE UNDERWATER BISCAYNE

Biscayne is one of the best places to dive and snorkel in Florida: the park has shipwrecks, more than 500 different kinds of fish (including parrotfish, angelfish, wrasses and butterfly fish), as well as sea cucumbers and the gloriously named Christmas tree worm.

The **Maritime Heritage Trail** (nps.gov/bisc/learn/historyculture/maritime-heritage-trail.htm) takes visitors through one of the only trails of its kind in the US. If you've ever wanted to explore a sunken ship, this may well be the best opportunity in the country. Six ships are located within the park grounds; the trail experience involves taking visitors out, by boat, to the site of the wrecks where they can swim, snorkel and dive among derelict vessels and clouds of fish.

There are even waterproof information site cards placed among the ships. Three of the vessels are suited for scuba divers, but the others – particularly the *Mandalay*, a lovely two-masted schooner that sank in 1966 – can be accessed by snorkelers.

Biscayne National Park Institute also offers guided snorkeling opportunities – check out the possibilities at biscaynenationalparkinstitute.org.

Windsurfing, Biscayne Bay
RICHARD PROSS/SHUTTERSTOCK ©

Camping & Windsurfing

STAY OVERNIGHT & SURF THE WIND

Biscayne National Park's two **campgrounds** are both located on islands – **Elliott Key** and **Boca Chita Key**. These are lovely settings, but you need a boat to get there. You pay on a trust system, with exact change on the harbor (rangers cruise the Keys to check your receipt). Bring all supplies, including water, and carry everything out.

The water around Convoy Point is regarded as prime **windsurfing** territory. Windsurfers may want to contact outfits in Miami.

GETTING AROUND

South of Miami and west of the Everglades, Biscayne National Park is easy to reach: drive about 9 miles east of Homestead; the way is pretty well sign-posted on SW 328th St (North Canal Dr) and leads into a long series of green-and-gold flat fields and marshes. Exploring the park itself requires a boat – either on your own or a rented vessel, or on boat cruises organized by the park authorities.

DRY TORTUGAS NATIONAL PARK

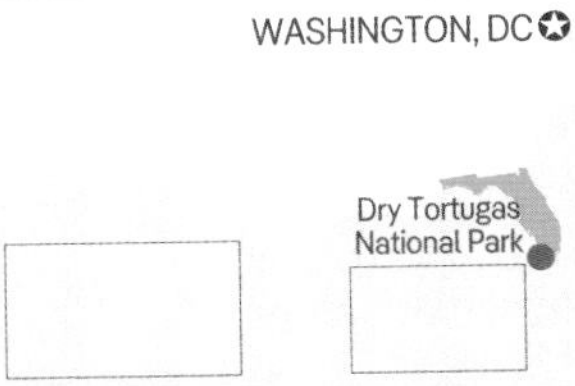

Out beyond the Florida Keys, the nicest islands in the archipelago require a little extra effort. Ponce de León named them Las Tortugas (The Turtles) for the sea turtles that roamed here. A lack of freshwater led sailors to add a 'dry' to the name. Today the Dry Tortugas are a national park accessible only by boat or plane. They're also America's most remote national park experience.

The park is open for day trips and overnight camping, which provides a rare phenomenon: a quiet Florida beach. Reserve months in advance through the *Yankee Freedom III*, which provides ferry service to the island. The sparkling waters offer excellent snorkeling and diving opportunities. A visitor center is located within fascinating Fort Jefferson.

In March and April, there is stupendous bird-watching, including aerial fighting. Stargazing here is mind-blowing any time of the year. The silence after the day-trippers leave is golden.

FACTS

Great For Beaches, Wildlife, Scenery
State Florida
Entrance Fee $15 per person
Area 100 sq miles

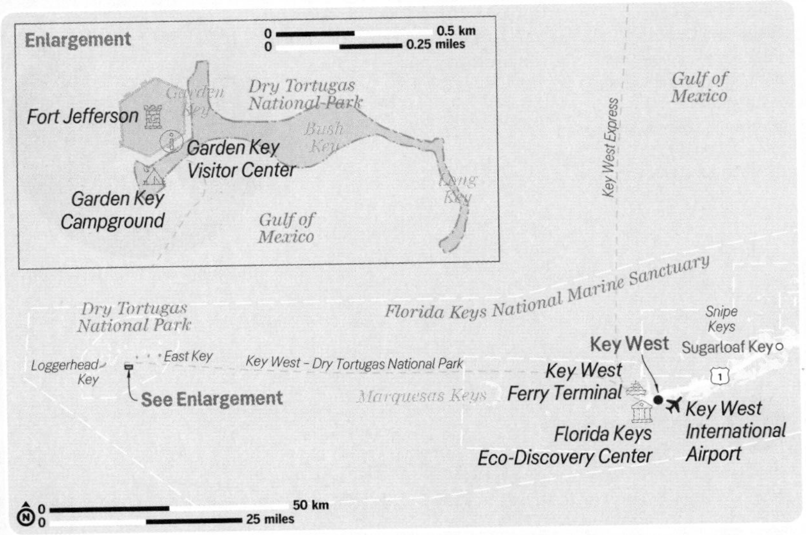

DRY TORTUGAS: THE ESSENTIALS

Camping
There's no lodging on the island, but **Garden Key** has 10 **campsites** ($15 per person per night, maximum three nights) on a first-come, first-served basis. Reserve eight to 12 months ahead on the ferry *Yankee Freedom III* (drytortugas.com), which takes only 10 campers per day to and from the island. There are toilets, but no freshwater showers or drinking water; bring everything you'll need.

Garden Key Visitor Center
Located within fascinating Fort Jefferson, with a video presentation, bookstore and information.

Florida Keys Eco-Discovery Center
Interactive exhibits on the human and natural history of the park, with some fascinating information on the area's unique wildlife.

Explore Fort Jefferson

DISCOVER A STORIED FORTRESS

For many years, Dry Tortugas was a barely inhabited outpost thanks to a lack of freshwater. But its strategic location – equidistant between Miami and Havana – saw the US Navy build a fort here in 1847. By the Civil War, **Fort Jefferson**, the main structure on the islands, had become a prison for Union deserters and at least four other people, among them Dr Samuel Mudd, who had been arrested for complicity in the assassination of Abraham Lincoln. Hence a new nickname: Devil's Island. The name was prophetic: in 1867 a yellow fever outbreak killed 38 people, and after an 1873 hurricane the fort was abandoned. It reopened in 1886 as a quarantine station for smallpox and cholera victims, was declared a national monument in 1935 by President Franklin D Roosevelt, and was upped to national park status in 1992 by George Bush Sr.

Wander the ramparts and learn a little of its fascinating history. And one look out to sea is a reminder of the lonely isolation that enveloped those who were posted (or imprisoned) here.

Get Active in Dry Tortugas

SWIM, SNORKEL AND STARGAZE

Just getting to Dry Tortugas is quite the adventure, but the rewards are many. Activities on offer include diving and snorkeling just offshore from the main beach. The bird-watching here is also unlike anywhere else, with Gulf seabird species drawn to the islands. And, perhaps best of all for those who stay overnight, the spray of stars in the night sky is perspective-altering.

Visit nps.gov/drto/ for more information.

Camping near Fort Jefferson
MATT A. CLAIBORNE/SHUTTERSTOCK ©

GETTING AROUND

The fast ferry (drytortugas.com) leaves Key West's Historic Seaport (at the northern end of Margaret St) at 8am and takes 2½ hours to reach Garden Key in Dry Tortugas. It sets out at 3pm for the return trip, arriving at Key West around 5:30pm.

Key West Seaplane Adventures (keywestseaplanecharters.com) can take up to 10 passengers (flight time 40 minutes each way). The half-day tour is four hours, allowing 2½ hours on the island. The eight-hour full-day excursion gives you six hours on the island.

EVERGLADES NATIONAL PARK

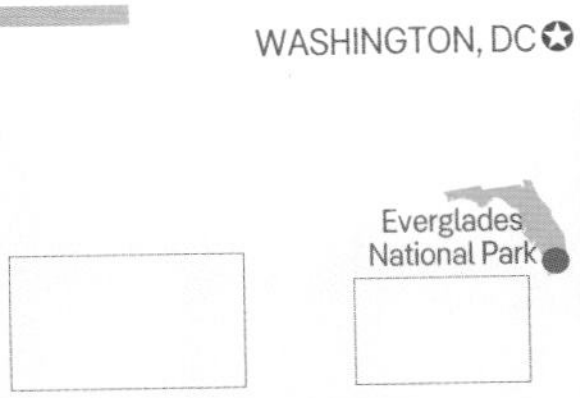

This vast wilderness, encompassing 2358 sq miles, is one of America's great natural treasures and certainly the best place to see wildlife in Florida. Utterly unlike anywhere else in the state, the Everglades is where the natural world takes over, with a vast network of islands and watery channels sheltering alligators, abundant birdlife and a sense of being far from the world and its buzz. There's much to see and do – from hiking past floating manatees as herons stalk patiently through nearby waters in search of prey, to kayaking through mangrove canals and on peaceful lakes.

There are sunrise strolls on boardwalks amid the awakening of birdsong, and moonlit glimpses of gators swimming gracefully along narrow channels in search of dinner. Backcountry camping, bicycle tours and ranger-led activities help bring the magic of this place to life. The biggest challenge is really just deciding where to begin.

FACTS

Great For Family Travel, Wildlife, Scenery
State Florida
Entrance Fee 7-day pass per vehicle/pedestrian $30/15
Area 2358 sq miles

Alligator (p389)

WHY I LOVE THE EVERGLADES

Anthony Ham, Writer

The Everglades is not just the largest subtropical wilderness anywhere in the US, it's also one of the best places to see wildlife anywhere in the country, from alligators to birds and a whole lot more in between. I love the diversity of experiences on offer here, from short strolls along a boardwalk to deep backcountry immersion in the 10,000 Islands in a kayak. In a state known for its overdeveloped coastline, the Everglades is a soul-enriching antidote.

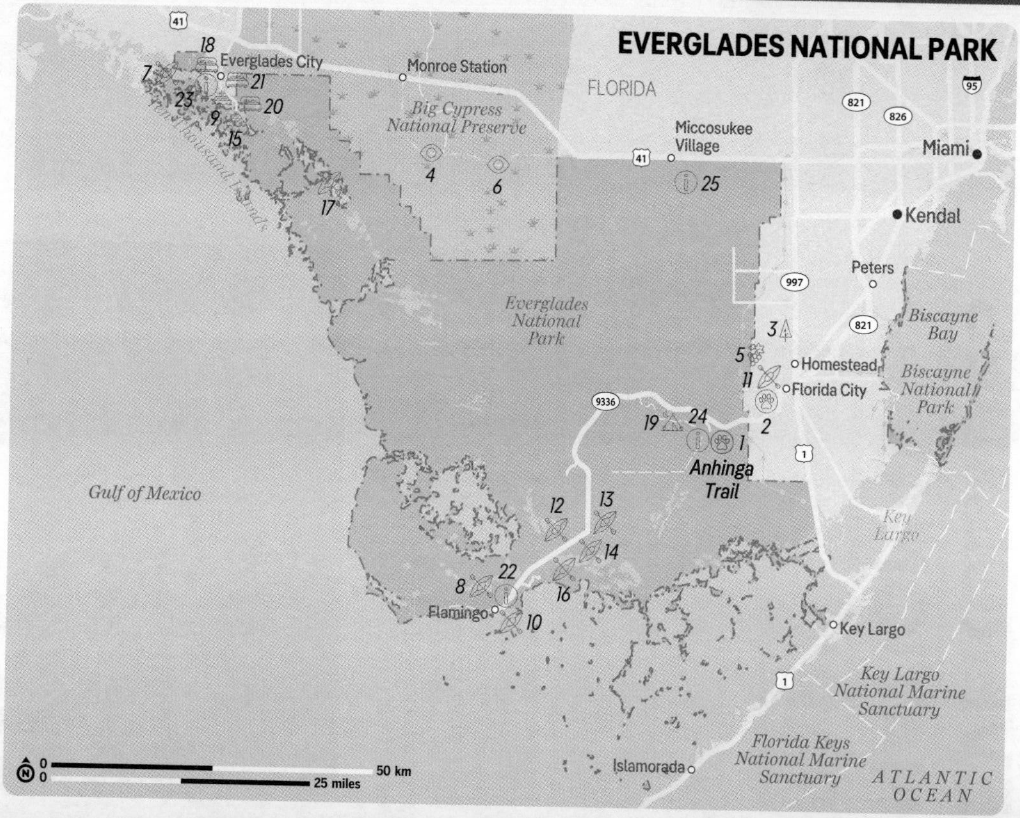

HIGHLIGHTS
1 Anhinga Trail

SIGHTS
2 Everglades Outpost
3 Fruit & Spice Park
4 Loop Road
5 Schnebly Redland's Winery
6 Tree Snail Hammock Nature Trail

ACTIVITIES, COURSES & TOURS
7 10,000 Islands
8 Bear Lake
9 Everglades Florida Adventures
10 Flamingo at Everglades
11 Garls Coastal Kayaking Everglades
12 Hell's Bay
13 Nine Mile Pond
14 Noble Hammock
15 Smallwood Store Boat Tours
16 West Lake Trail
17 Wilderness Waterway

SLEEPING
18 Ivey House Everglades Adventures Hotel
19 Lone Pine Key Campground
20 Outdoor Resorts of Chokoloskee
21 River Wilderness Waterfront Villas

INFORMATION
22 Flamingo Visitor Center
23 Gulf Coast Visitor Center
24 Royal Palm Visitor Center
25 Shark Valley Visitor Center

Hike in Search of Alligators

WALK THE ANHINGA TRAIL

If you do just one walk in the Everglades, make sure it's on the **Anhinga Trail**. Gators sun on the shoreline, anhinga (also known as the snake bird) spear their prey, and wading birds stalk haughtily through the reeds. You'll get a close-up view of wildlife on this short (0.8 mile) trail at the **Royal Palm Visitor Center**. There are various overlooks, where you can sometimes see dozens of alligators piled together.

Come back at night (be sure to bring a flashlight) for a view of the gators swimming along the waterways – sometimes right beside you. The park offers periodic ranger-led walks along the boardwalk at night, though you can also do it yourself. Seeing the glittering eyes of alligators prowling the waterways by flashlight is an unforgettable experience.

Explore the 10,000 Islands

PADDLE INTO THE WILDERNESS

One of the best ways to experience the serenity of the Everglades – somehow desolate yet lush, tropical and forbidding – is by paddling the network of waterways that skirt the northwest portion of the park. The **10,000 Islands** consist of many (but not really 10,000) tiny islands and a mangrove swamp that hugs the southwestern-most border of Florida.

The **Wilderness Waterway**, a 99-mile route between Everglades City and Flamingo, is the longest canoe trail in the area, but there are shorter trails near Flamingo. Most islands are fringed with narrow beaches with sugar-white sand, but note that the water is brackish, and very shallow most of the time. You can camp on your own island for up to a week.

Getting around the 10,000 Islands is pretty straightforward if you're a competent navigator and you religiously adhere to National Oceanic & Atmospheric Administration (NOAA) tide and nautical charts. Going against the tides is the fastest way to make a miserable trip. The **Gulf Coast Visitor Center** sells nautical charts and gives out free tidal charts. You can also purchase charts prior to your visit – call 305-247-1216 and ask for charts 11430, 11432 and 11433.

To join a boat tour into the 10,000 Islands, try **Smallwood**

Roseate spoonbills

FINE ART PHOTOS/SHUTTERSTOCK ©

BEST FREE GUIDED TOURS

Starlight Walk
Walk along the Anhinga Trail looking for creatures by nightfall.

Bike Hike
Bikes and helmets are provided for this 2½-hour bike ride, departing Ernest Coe Visitor Center.

Canoe the Wilderness
Three-hour morning paddle. Meet at Flamingo Visitor Center and Gulf Coast Visitor Center.

Early Bird Walk
Morning hike looking for some of the Everglades' feathered species. Meet at Flamingo Visitor Center.

Glades Glimpse
Daily talk given by rangers at Royal Palm Visitor Center and Shark Valley Visitor Center.

WHERE TO CAMP IN THE EVERGLADES

Backcountry Camping
Wilderness camping in the Everglades ranges, from ground sites to *chickees* (wooden platform). Permits required. $

Flamingo Campground
There are over 200 campsites at the Flamingo Visitor Center, some of which have electrical hookups. $

Lone Pine Key Campground
Just west of Royal Palm Visitor Center, 108 sites on a first-come basis (no reservations). $

DETOUR: DRIVE THE LOOP ROAD

The 24-mile-long **Loop Road**, off Tamiami Trail (Hwy 41), offers some unique sites. One: great pull-offs for viewing flooded forests, where egrets that look like pterodactyls perch in the trees, and alligators lurk in the depths below. Two: houses with large 'Stay off my property' signs; these homes are as much a part of the landscape as the swamp. And three: the short, pleasantly jungly **Tree Snail Hammock Nature Trail**. Though unpaved, the graded road is in good shape and fine for 2WD vehicles. True to its name, the road loops right back onto the Tamiami; expect a leisurely jaunt on the Loop to add an hour or two to your trip.

Kayaking Nine Mile Pond

FRANCISCO BLANCO/SHUTTERSTOCK ©

Store Boat Tour (smallwoodstoreboattour.com) and **Everglades Florida Adventures** (evergladesfloridaadventures.com).

Canoe the Southern Everglades

EXPLORE THE EVERGLADES BACKCOUNTRY

The real joy in this part of the park is paddling into the bracken-filled heart of the swamp. There are plenty of push-off points, all with names that sound like they come from Frodo's map to Mordor in JRR Tolkien's *Lord of the Rings*, including Hell's Bay, the Nightmare, Snake Bight and Graveyard Creek.

If you plan to camp along any of the following trails, you'll need to pick up a backcountry permit from any park visitor center.

Nine Mile Pond (3- or 5.2-mile loop) takes you through grassy marshes and mangrove islands; follow the numbered white poles. For the shorter version, take the cut-through from marker #44. Allow four hours for the full loop. It's good for spotting alligators, wading birds and turtles.

Noble Hammock (2 miles return) is a short loop with some challenging tight corners. In the dry season, check water levels before setting out.

Despite the frightening name (and terrible mosquitoes), **Hell's Bay** (5.5 miles one way) can be a magnificent place to kayak. 'Hell to get into and hell to get out of' was how this sheltered launch was described by old Glades aficionados. Once inside you'll find a capillary network of mangrove creeks, saw-grass islands and shifting mudflats, where the brambles form a green tunnel and all you can smell is sea salt and the dark organic breath of the swamp. Three *chickee* (wooden platform above the waterline) sites are spaced along the trail. Allow six to eight hours for the return trip.

West Lake (7.7 miles one way) crosses open lakes linked by narrow creeks to Alligator Creek; good for alligators and crocodiles.

Mud Lake (7 miles return) takes you through mangroves between Coot Bay Pond and Mud Lake.

Bear Lake (11.5 miles one way) is a classic Everglades trail, close to the Flamingo Visitor Center. The park authorities are not maintaining the trail while they work out a conservation plan for threatened local fauna, although the trail remains open.

For operators and canoe or kayak rentals, try **Garls Coastal Kayaking Everglades** (garlscoastalkayaking.com) or **Flamingo Everglades** (flamingoeverglades.com).

WHERE TO STAY IN THE EVERGLADES

Ivey House Everglades Adventure Hotel
Family-run inn with well-appointed rooms overlooking a courtyard, with a pool. **$$**

Outdoor Resorts of Chokoloskee
Good-value basic rooms, pools, hot tubs, tennis and fitness center, boat rentals. **$$**

River Wilderness Waterfront Villas
Large one- and two-bedroom villas on stilts with prime river-frontage and great location. **$$**

Wine & Wildlife

BEYOND THE EVERGLADES

The southern Everglades region may feel like a world away from Miami. In fact, it can be one of the more unusual flying experiences of a lifetime to fly in over the Everglades wilderness where nature is very much in the ascendancy, only to emerge from Miami Airport into one of America's most boisterous cities. Homestead, on the cusp of both Miami and the Everglades, lies between both. It's where many visitors base themselves for visiting the park, but remember that there are some fun things to do in and around Homestead in between park visits.

In Homestead itself, **Everglades Outpost** (evergladesoutpost.org) houses, feeds and cares for wild animals that have been seized from illegal traders, abused, neglected or donated by people who could not care for them. Residents of the outpost include a lemur, wolves, a black bear, a zebra, cobras, alligators and a majestic tiger (who was bought by an exotic dancer who thought she could incorporate it into her act). Your money goes toward helping the outpost's mission.

Set on the edge of the Everglades, the 35-acre **Fruit & Spice Park** (miamidade.gov/fruitandspicepark) grows the great tropical fruits you usually have to travel to far-flung corners of the globe to enjoy. The park is divided into 'continents' (Africa, Asia etc) and it's a peaceful experience to wander past various species bearing (in total) around 500 different types of fruits, spices and nuts. Unfortunately, you can't pick the fruit, but you can eat anything that falls to the ground (go early for the best gathering!).

Something completely different awaits at **Schnebly Redland's Winery** (schneblywinery.com), which has the distinction of being the southernmost winery in the US. Given the climate, you won't find malbec, pinot noir or zinfandel – wines here are made of mango, passion fruit, lychee, avocado, coconut and other flavors from the tropics, and are surprisingly good. It's tucked along a quiet farm road west of Homestead, and you can stop in for tastings, available any time, or for a tour (weekends only, hourly 1pm to 5pm). There's also a good restaurant, and a pretty back garden next to a small gurgling waterfall.

AIRBOATS & SWAMP BUGGIES

You can't visit the Everglades without being aware of the airboat, a flat-bottomed skiff that uses powerful fans to propel it through the water. The environmental effect has not been determined, but one thing is clear: airboats can't be doing much good, which is why they're not allowed in the park. Swamp buggies are enormous balloon-tired vehicles that can go through wetlands, creating ruts and damaging wildlife.

Airboat and swamp-buggy rides are offered all along US Hwy 41 (Tamiami Trail). Think twice before going on a 'nature' tour. Loud whirring-fan boats and marsh jeeps are the antithesis of the Everglades' quiet serenity.

GETTING AROUND

You need a car to properly enter and explore the Everglades, or at least to get as far as the hiking trailheads or kayak jumping-off points. Once you're in, wearing a good pair of walking boots is essential to penetrate the interior. Having a canoe or a kayak helps as well; these can be rented from outfits inside and outside the park, or you can seek out guided canoe and kayak tours. Bicycles are well suited to the flat roads of Everglades National Park, particularly in the area between Ernest Coe and Flamingo Point. Road shoulders in the park tend to be dangerously small.

By road, the Tamiami Trail leads all the way from the southeast out to Everglades City at the park's northwestern corner. Or you can head south to Florida City, which gives access to the southern reaches of the Everglades.

CHERI ALGUIRE/SHUTTERSTOCK ©

Above: Waimoku Falls (p399), Haleakalā National Park; Right: Lava, Kilauea Iki (p402)

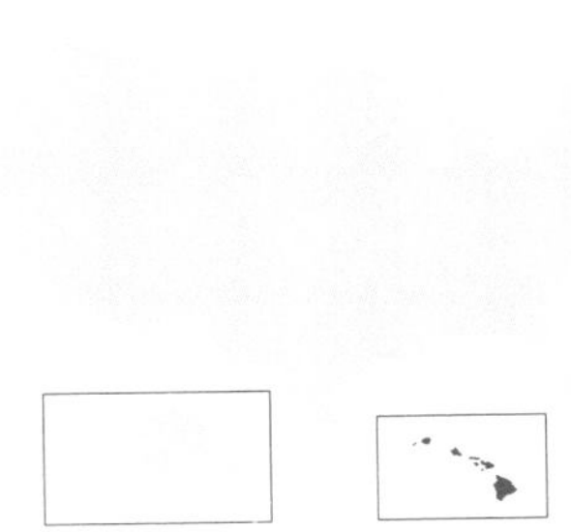

HAWAII

BIG LANDSCAPES AND EPIC HIKES

Hawaii's two national parks, Haleakalā and Hawai'i Volcanoes, rank among the grandest natural spectacles anywhere in the US.

Hawaii isn't built like other US states. More than anywhere else in the country, nature rules supreme. And this is nature at its most exciting. For a start, the islands' high volcanic summits and wild coastline pile drama upon natural drama. It's about more than the views: from the wild waves shaping the shore to the steam vents that suggest that the next eruption may not be far away. And, above all, this world in motion is a very beautiful place.

Admire it all, by all means. But this is a landscape that demands exploration. Both Haleakalā and Hawai'i Volcanoes offer the kind of summit-to-sea experience – from picturesque day hikes to waterfalls and freshwater pools to strenuous, multiday expeditions – that take you into some of Hawaii's most beautiful and most spectacular corners.

The trails that traverse both parks are many and varied, and a visit here requires careful planning. Warm up with a few shorter hikes, move up into daylong walks, then head into the high and backcountry with a multiday trek that takes in Hawaii's most glorious landscapes. And even if you don't hike, you can still get a taste along paved roads – the Chain of Craters Road in Hawai'i Volcanoes National Park, for example – that run to some of the most astounding viewpoints anywhere in the country.

THE MAIN AREAS

HALEAKALĀ NATIONAL PARK
Hike amid the volcanoes.
p396

HAWAI'I VOLCANOES NATIONAL PARK
Hawaii at its elemental best.
p400

Find Your Way

Although you *could* reach the two parks by public transport, you'll need your own wheels to explore in any depth, even if it's just to get you to where the trails start.

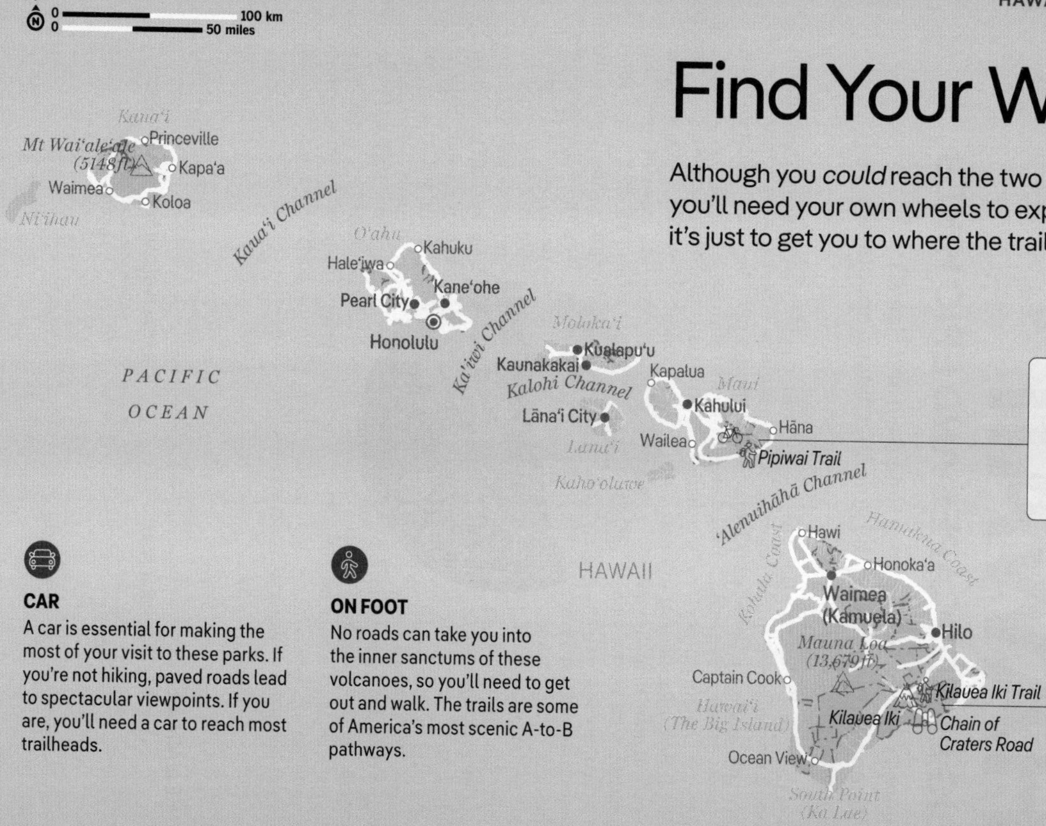

Haleakalā National Park, p396
Whether it's the high summits or deep craters, the hiking trails of Haleakalā are breathtaking.

Hawai'i Volcanoes National Park, p400
The world of Mauna Loa can feel like it's being created before your very eyes.

CAR

A car is essential for making the most of your visit to these parks. If you're not hiking, paved roads lead to spectacular viewpoints. If you are, you'll need a car to reach most trailheads.

ON FOOT

No roads can take you into the inner sanctums of these volcanoes, so you'll need to get out and walk. The trails are some of America's most scenic A-to-B pathways.

Mauna Loa (p403)

Plan Your Time

You could combine Haleakalā with Hawai'i Volcanoes; getting between the two is easy. But it makes sense to explore each park in its own right.

With One Week

Focus on **Haleakalā National Park** (p396), beginning with warm-up hikes in the **Kipahulu region** (p398), enjoying waterfalls, freshwater pools and amazing views. Then head for summit country along the **Skyline Trail** (p399), followed by the day-long **Halemau'u Trail** (p399) and **Kaupo Trail** (p399). Rest then take two glorious days to walk the **Keonehe'ehe'e Trail** (p399).

If Time is Tight

Begin your exploration of **Hawai'i Volcanoes National Park** (p400) with the utterly spectacular **Kilauea Iki Trail** (p402). Rest weary legs by driving the **Chain of Craters Road** (p402) and paying a visit to the park's remarkable collection of rock art at the **Pu'u Loa Petroglyphs** (p402). Then trek the superb, two-day **Mauna Loa Trail** (p403), which really is the state's crowning glory.

SEASONAL HIGHLIGHTS

SPRING

An agreeable time to explore the parks; a spring visit avoids the peak visitor numbers of summer and winter.

SUMMER

Busiest time of year, with mostly clear skies. Don't miss the Hawai'i Volcanoes National Park Cultural Festival.

FALL

Early autumn is excellent; September and October often quiet and dry before the rains arrive in November.

WINTER

Rain can disrupt your visit in winter, and clouds can obscure the views. The Christmas–New Year period is busy.

HALEAKALĀ NATIONAL PARK

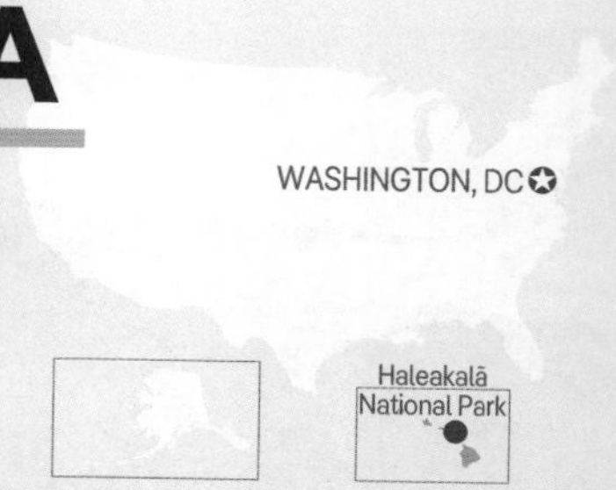

To peer into the soul of Maui, climb to the dormant summit of Haleakalā volcano. Below the rim, mists caress a vast crater, which glows ethereally in the early light of sunrise. Lookouts provide breathtaking views of the moonscape below and the cinder cones marching across it.

The rest of this amazing park, which is divided into two distinct sections, is all about interacting with this mountain of solid lava and its rare life-forms, some of them found only here. You can hike down into the crater, follow lush trails on the slopes, or put your mountain bike through its paces. For the ultimate adventure, get a permit, bring a tent and camp beneath the stars. The experience will stick with you for a lifetime.

Even if you don't hike, perched on the crater rim at 9745ft, the visitor center is the park's main viewing spot.

FACTS

Great For Cycling, walking, scenery
State Hawaii
Entrance Fee 7-day pass per vehicle/pedestrian $30/15
Area 60 sq miles

STEVEN PHRANER/SHUTTERSTOCK ©

Haleakalā National Park

HIGHLIGHTS
1 Pipiwai Trail

SIGHTS
2 Makahiku Falls
3 'Ohe'o Gulch
4 Waimoku Falls

ACTIVITIES, COURSES & TOURS
5 Haleakalā Ridge Trail
6 Halemau'u Trail
7 Hosmer Grove Trail
8 Kaupo Trail
9 Keonehe'ehe'e (Sliding Sands) Trail
10 Kipahulu 'Ohana
11 Kuloa Point Trail
12 Polipoli Trail
13 Skyline Trail

SLEEPING
14 Holua Cabin & Campground
15 Hosmer Grove Campground
16 Kipahulu Campground
17 Polipoli Spring State Recreation Area

INFORMATION
18 Kipahulu Visitor Center

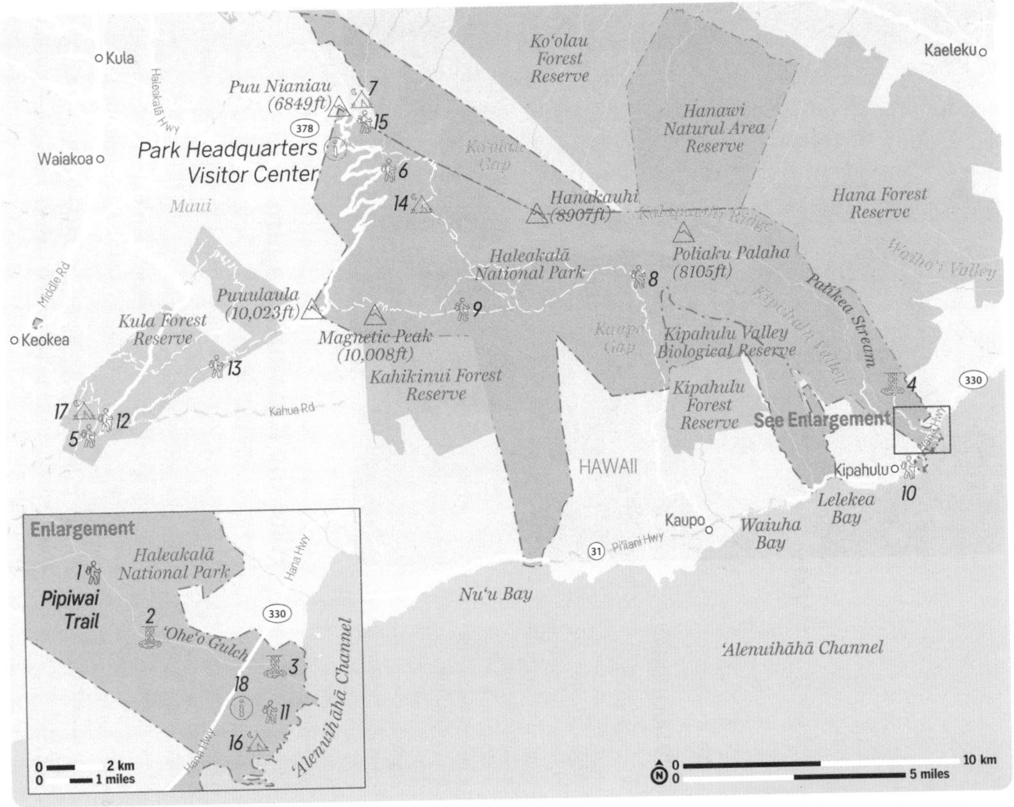

Pipiwai Trail (p399)
EVA HAWKER/SHUTTERSTOCK ©

KIPAHULU 'OHANA

Kipahulu was once a breadbasket or – more accurately – a poi bowl, for the entire region. For fascinating insights into the area's past, join the ethnobotanical tour led by **Kipahulu 'Ohana** (kipahulu.org/whatwedo/kapahufarm/hiketour), a collective of Native Hawaiian farmers who have restored ancient taro patches within the national park. The two-hour outing includes about 3 miles of hiking and concentrates on the farm activities, such as sampling Hawaiian foods and intriguing details about the native plants and ancient ruins along the way. Reservations required, and the tour meets outside the Kipahulu Visitor Center.

TRACY IMMORDINO/SHUTTERSTOCK ©

'Ohe'o Gulch

Hike the Kipahulu Region

WARM UP FOR THE MAIN EVENT

There's more to Haleakalā National Park than the cindery summit. The park extends down the southeast face of the volcano all the way to the sea. The crowning glory of the Kipahulu section of the park is **'Ohe'o Gulch**, with its magnificent waterfalls and wide pools, each one tumbling into the next one below.

In the Kipahulu area, the **Kuloa Point Trail** is an unmissable 20-minute (0.5-mile) stroll. The path runs from the **visitor center** to the lower pools and back. A few minutes down, you'll reach a broad grassy knoll with a gorgeous view of the Hana coast. On a clear day you can see Hawai'i (the Big Island) 30 miles away across 'Alenuihaha Channel. The large freshwater pools (no swimming) along the trail are terraced one atop the other and connected by gentle cascades.

WHERE TO STAY IN HALEAKALĀ NATIONAL PARK

Kipahulu Campground
Basic campground, incredible setting on oceanside cliffs amid stone ruins of an ancient Hawaiian village. **$**

Hosmer Grove Campground
The Summit Area's only drive-up campground. Camping is free on a first-come, first-served basis. **$**

Holua Cabin & Campground
Easiest cabin to reach, 3.7 miles down the Halemau'u Trail at an elevation of 6940ft. **$**

Just as memorable, the fun **Pipiwai Trail** is one of Maui's best. It ascends alongside the 'Ohe'o streambed, has gorgeous waterfalls and includes an otherworldly trip through a bamboo grove. The trail starts on the *mauka* (inland) side of the visitor center and leads up to **Makahiku Falls** (0.5 miles), a long bridal-veil waterfall that drops into a deep gorge. With a name meaning 'water that recognizes no friend,' this cascade crashes from a height of 200ft through a cathedral-like jungle setting into the 'Ohe'o Gulch stream (otherwise known as the Seven Sacred Pools). Further on, spectacular **Waimoku Falls** (2 miles) is one of the tallest waterfalls on Maui, tumbling dramatically 400ft down a jungle-lined lava-rock face into a boulder-dotted pool.

Trek the Haleakalā High Country

HIKE THE FAMOUS SKYLINE TRAIL

The otherworldly **Skyline Trail** rides the precipitous spine of Haleakalā. It begins just beyond the summit at a lofty elevation (9750ft) and leads down to the campground at **Polipoli Spring State Recreation Area** (6200ft). It covers a distance of 8.5 miles and takes about four hours to walk. Get an early start to enjoy the views before clouds take over.

The Skyline Trail starts in barren open terrain of volcanic cinder, a moon walk that passes more than a dozen cinder cones and craters. The first mile is rough lava rock. After three crunchy miles, it reaches the tree line (8500ft) and enters native māmane forest. In winter, māmane is heavy with flowers that look like yellow sweet-pea blossoms. There's solitude on this walk. If the clouds treat you kindly, you'll have broad views all the way between the barren summit and the dense cloud forest. Eventually, the trail meets the Polipoli access road, where you can either walk to the paved road in about 4 miles, or continue via the **Haleakalā Ridge Trail** and the **Polipoli Trail** to the campground.

If you prefer treads to hiking boots, the Skyline Trail is also a wild and exhilarating mountain-bike ride from Science City Access Rd down to Polipoli Spring State Recreation Area. Look out for hikers! The trail may occasionally close due to weather damage. Check its status at hawaiitrails.hawaii.gov/trails or at one of the local bike shops.

HALEAKALĀ'S BEST HIKES

Halemau'u Trail
(7.4-mile round trip; seven to eight hours) Views of crater walls, lava tubes and cinder cones; this is a memorable day hike.

Keonehe'ehe'e (Sliding Sands) Trail
(17.8-mile round trip; two days) High-altitude (9740ft) start at Haleakalā Visitor Center to crater floor to Paliku campground (permit needed).

Kaupo Trail
(8.6 miles one way; one day) The most extreme of Haleakalā's hikes: from Paliku campground to Kaupo on the southern coast.

Hosmer Grove Trail
(0.5-mile loop; 20 minutes) Shaded woodland walk, also popular with birders.

GETTING AROUND

Getting to Haleakalā is half the fun. Snaking up the mountain, all of Maui opens up below you, with sugarcane and pineapple fields creating a patchwork of green on the valley floor. The highway ribbons back and forth, and in some places as many as four or five switchbacks are in view all at once.

To explore the park in depth and on your own schedule, you'll need to rent a car. There is no public bus service to either district of the park. The summit is 40 miles from Kahului, just over an hour's drive. Kipahulu is 55 miles from Kahului via the Road to Hana. Expect the drive to take at least two hours. Guided tours also stop at both sections of the park.

The Kipahulu area is on Hwy 31, 10 scenic miles south of Hana. There's no direct road access from here to the rest of Haleakalā National Park; the summit must be visited separately.

HAWAI'I VOLCANOES NATIONAL PARK

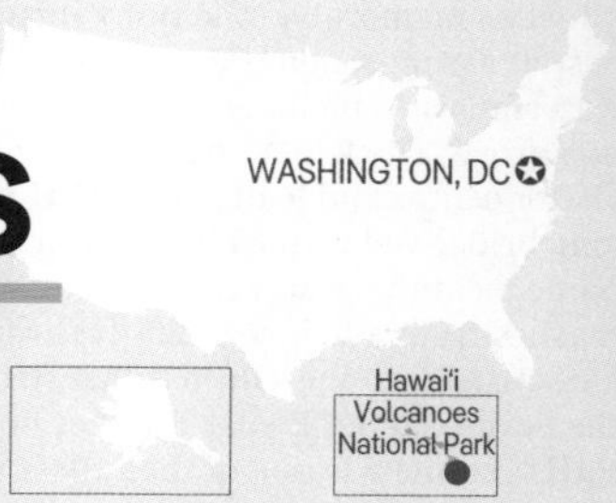

From the often-snowy summit of Mauna Loa, the world's most massive volcano, to the boiled coastline where lava poured into the sea for decades, Hawai'i Volcanoes National Park is a micro-continent of thriving rainforests, volcano-induced deserts, high-mountain meadows, coastal plains and plenty of geological marvels in between.

At the heart of it all is Kilauea – the earth's youngest and most active shield volcano. While Kilauea's monstrous crater brings photo opportunities, the real magic of Hawai'i Volcanoes National Park can only be found while exploring its 150 miles of trails. It is entirely possible to hike from a lonely beach to the summit of Mauna Loa – passing grasslands, rainforest oases, lava deserts and steaming craters – with only a brief stint on pavement. While that feat is best reserved for a few extraordinary souls, many shorter journeys will reveal complex and magnificent details that are impossible to see from behind a windshield.

FACTS

Great For Photo ops, S\ scenery, walking
State Hawaii
Entrance Fee 7-day pass per vehicle/pedestrian $30/15
Area 505 sq miles

Kilauea Iki's crater (p402)

HIGHLIGHTS
1 Chain of Craters Road
2 Kilauea Iki
3 Kilauea Iki Trail

SIGHTS
4 Holei Sea Arch
5 Kilauea Overlook
6 Mauna Loa Lookout
7 Moku'aweoweo Caldera
8 Steam Vents
9 Steaming Bluff

ACTIVITIES, COURSES & TOURS
10 Mauna Loa Observatory Trail
11 Mauna Loa Trail
12 Napau Crater Trail

SLEEPING
13 Aloha Junction Guesthouse
14 Mauna Loa Cabin
15 Pu'u'ula'ula (Red Hill)
16 Volcano House
17 Volcano Rainforest Retreat

DRINKING
18 Pu'u Loa Petroglyphs

INFORMATION
19 Backcountry Permit Office
20 Kilauea Visitor Center

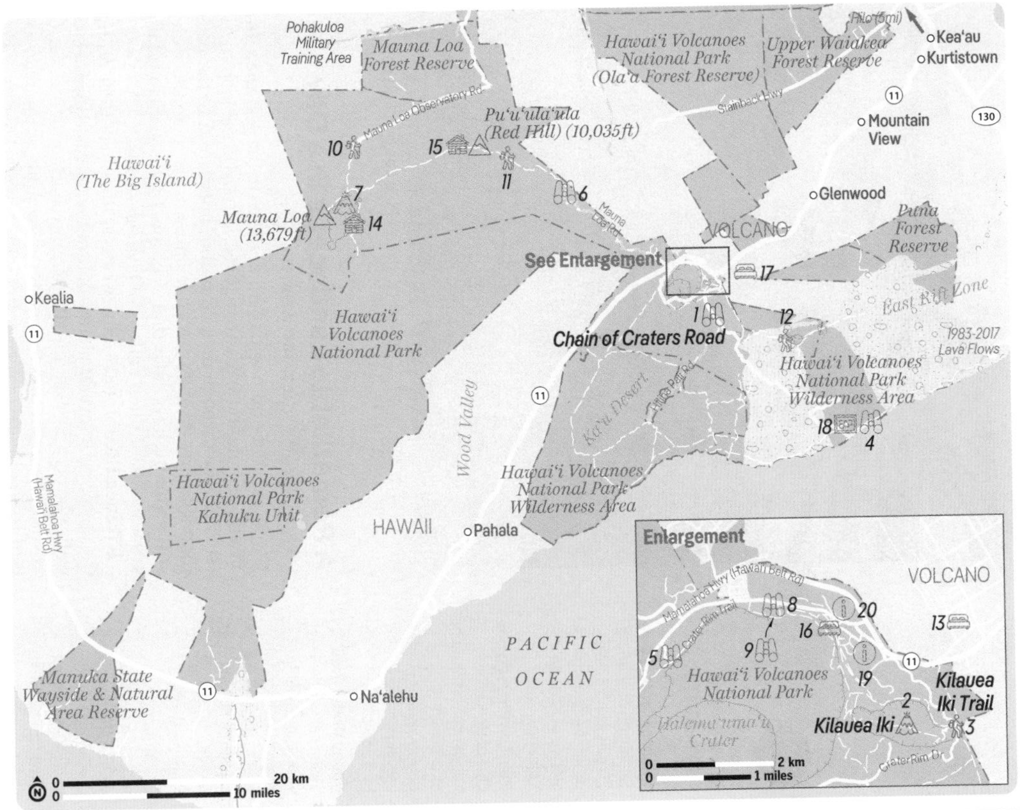

OTHER PARK HIGHLIGHTS

Chain of Craters Road
Scenic drive winding 20 miles and 3700ft down the southern slopes of Kilauea Volcano.

Pu'u Loa Petroglyphs
One of Hawai'i's largest concentrations of ancient petroglyphs: 23,000 carvings, some over 800 years old.

Napau Crater Trail
Seven-mile (one-way) undulating hike from Mauna Ulu Eruption Trail to edge of the mile-long Makaopuhi Crater.

Puna Coast Trails
Experience secluded snorkeling, white-sand beaches, soaring cliffs and savagely beautiful landscapes on these remote backcountry trails amid the wilder side of Hawai'i Volcanoes.

GEORGE BURBA/SHUTTERSTOCK ©

Pu'u Loa petroglyphs

A Remarkable Landscape in a Day

HIKE THROUGH A VOLCANIC WORLD

If you can only do one day-hike, make it the **Kilauea Iki Trail** (4.5 miles return, two to three hours). Do the loop counterclockwise through an astounding microcosm of the park that descends through fairytale ohia forests to a mile-wide, still-steaming lava lake that was filled by a fiery fountain spewing 403 million gallons of lava per second.

Kilauea Iki erupted for five weeks at the end of 1959, filling the crater with several meters of lava that washed against its walls like ocean waves and then drained back into the fissure. The lava fountain that formed the cinder pile above reached 1900ft, the highest ever recorded in Hawaii. This awesome sight turned terrifying when boulders blocked the passage like your thumb on a garden hose, sending a jet of lava shooting across the crater toward crowds of visitors.

To fully appreciate this hike, first watch the excellent vintage film, *Eruption of Kilauea 1959–1960* at **Kilauea Visitor**

WHERE TO STAY AROUND HAWAI'I VOLCANOES NATIONAL PARK

Volcano House
Perched on Kilauea Caldera's rim, this is the park's only hotel. Pay up for a volcano view. **$$**

Aloha Junction Guesthouse
At this historic plantation-executive's vacation home, modern rooms are cozy and upscale. **$$**

Volcano Rainforest Retreat
These four artistically decorated, big-windowed cottages are well-secluded among dense rainforest. **$$$**

Center (or online at youtube.com/watch?v=WpQyjVEfx5c), then grab a very informative brochure ($2, or download it from the park's website).

Hit the trail before 8am to beat the crowds. The faint footpath across the crater floor is marked by *ahu* (stone cairns) to aid navigation. Follow them; the crust can be thin elsewhere.

Walk the Two-Day Mauna Loa

TAKE A BUCKET-LIST WALK

One for your bucket list: the relentless (though nontechnical) 19.6-mile **Mauna Loa Trail** ascends 7000ft through surprisingly diverse lavascapes. Enjoy epic views, unmatched solitude and a profound sense of accomplishment. Take at least three days, although four or five is better for a summit bid. Get your required permit from the **Backcountry Office** a day before you start.

The first day climbs 3400ft over 7.5 miles of ancient *pahoehoe* (smooth-flowing lava) and collapsed lava tubes to **Pu'u'ula'ula (Red Hill)**, where a historic cabin with bunk beds (bring your own bedding) gets you out of the elements. Collected rainwater is usually available, but treat it before drinking. Fill your water bottles before bed; the spigot often freezes, and you'll want an early start in the morning.

The next day, tackle the grueling, but sublimely rewarding, 11.6-mile march up another 3200ft to the **Mauna Loa Cabin** (13,250ft; also with bunk beds and untreated water). Lava flows seemingly pour out of red, serrated fissures to cover technicolored cinder fields. This marvelous dreamscape can also become a nightmare if you lose the trail – easy to do when the *ahu* disappear in rain, fog or snow. It is impossible to distinguish between solid rock and thin crust over a bottomless lava tube.

Note that the actual summit (13,677ft) is on the other side of **Moku'aweoweo Caldera** from the cabin. The trail splits at Mile 9.5, and while some hikers do the additional 5.2-mile round-trip Summit Trail on their way to the cabin, most elect to tackle their 16.8-mile day on the way down. Or, better yet, spend two nights on top of the world. Of course, there's the option of summiting via the **Mauna Loa Observatory Trail**, but that's cheating.

BEST VIEWPOINTS

Holei Sea Arch
Coastal section of Chain of Craters Road: lava-rock *pali* (cliffs) and ephemeral high rock arch.

Kilauea Overlook
Drive to this overlook to view the spectacular mile-wide crater formed in 1959.

Mauna Loa Lookout
Epic spot (6662ft) looking out over the world's most massive active volcano.

Steam Vents
Creating impressive billowing plumes in the cool early morning; a convenient drive-up photo opportunity.

Steaming Bluff
Evocative and striking natural phenomenon, a short walk out to the rim.

GETTING AROUND

The park is 30 miles (45 minutes) from Hilo and 95 miles (2¾ hours) from Kailua-Kona via Hwy 11. The turnoffs for Volcano village are a couple of miles east of the main park entrance. Hwy 11 is prone to flooding, washouts and closures during rainstorms. Periods of drought may close Mauna Loa Rd and Hilina Pali Rd due to wildfire hazards.

Five daily (none Sunday) Hele-On Bus services travel in from Hilo, with one continuing on to Ka'u. There is no public transportation once you get inside the park, and hitchhiking is illegal in all national parks. You'll need your own wheels.

Cyclists are permitted on paved roads, and a handful of dirt ones, including the Escape Rd but not on any trails – pavement or no.

TOOLKIT

The sections in this chapter cover the most important topics you'll need to know about in USA's national parks. They're full of nuts-and-bolts information and valuable insights to help you understand and navigate USA's national parks and get the most out of your trip.

Inspiration Point (p138), Bryce Canyon National Park
MARGARET.WIKTOR/SHUTTERSTOCK ©

Arriving

When you arrive at a national park, your first port of call should be the visitor center. They offer a lay of the land through museum exhibits and films, and you can ask rangers questions, check weather reports and trail conditions, and purchase books and maps.

Resources

At parks with entrance stations, rangers offer maps and a park newspaper on entry. all packed with useful information. If you arrive before the stations are staffed, check outside visitor centers.

Picking Up Permits

If you've bought a permit online for a hike or to explore the backcountry, you'll often need to check in with rangers at visitor centers before you set off. Double-check the details.

Camping

If you're hoping to snag a first-come, first-served campsite, head straight to the campground. Try to arrive no later than mid-morning to secure a spot – they can go quickly.

America the Beautiful Pass

Save time at the national-park entrance stations with an America the Beautiful Pass ($80; store.usgs.gov/pass). Simply show your pass and ID, and you're in.

Nearest Airports

GREAT SMOKY MOUNTAINS NATIONAL PARK	McGhee Tyson Airport (Tennessee), Asheville Regional Airport (North Carolina)
GRAND CANYON NATIONAL PARK	Flagstaff Pulliam Airport, Phoenix Sky Harbor International Airport (Arizona)
ZION NATIONAL PARK	St George Regional Airport (Utah), Las Vegas Airport (Nevada)
ROCKY MOUNTAIN NATIONAL PARK	Denver International Airport (Colorado)
ACADIA NATIONAL PARK	Hancock County–Bar Harbor Airport, Bangor International Airport (Maine)

TIMED-ENTRY TICKETS

Visitor numbers to the national parks have skyrocketed, and some parks have implemented mandatory timed-entry systems during peak periods. In 2023 a handful of national parks required the purchasing of tickets in advance to visit during certain months or times of day: Arches (7am to 4pm April through October), Glacier (6am to 3pm from the end of May to mid-September), Haleakalā (3am to 7am year-round) and Rocky Mountain (9am to 2pm from the end of May through October).

Some of these systems are still in the trial phase and could change significantly or be scrapped, so check before you visit.

Getting Around

The appeal of the USA's national parks is leaving civilization behind. Remote and rugged locations come with the territory, meaning you'll need to find your own way there.

TRAVEL COSTS

Rental
From $35/day

RV rental
From $100/day

Gas
Approx $3.65/ gallon

EV charging
$10–30

Car

Having a car is the most convenient way to travel around and between the national parks. Most of the roads are paved, but some are gravel, and others require 4WD. Traffic inside some parks can be horrendous, and parking places are few.

RV

Recreational vehicles (RVs) solve your transportation, accommodation and cooking needs in one package, but they guzzle gas and their use is restricted in some areas of the national parks. RV rental options are better in larger cities.

TIP

Gas can be comically expensive inside the parks and gateway towns. Fill up elsewhere if possible.

TRAINS & THE NATIONAL PARKS

Riding the rails has always been intertwined with US national parks, and the potential of trains to bring huge volumes of tourists drove a flurry of development in the early 20th century. Today, getting to most national parks by train is challenging, but some have well-placed stations. Amtrak's Empire Builder runs along Glacier National Park's southern edge, stopping at East Glacier and West Glacier stations. The Pacific Surfliner and Coast Starlight stop in Oxnard and Ventura, where you can get a boat to Channel Islands National Park.

Shuttle Bus

Ditch the traffic and take a shuttle bus. Some national parks have shuttle systems with stops at major points of interest and trailheads. At Zion National Park, visitors are required to ride the shuttle when it's running (March through November), but these services in most parks are optional.

Scenic Drives

The main road through many national parks is a scenic drive, with plenty of places to pull over and read interpretive panels and enjoy the views. These drives are a great option if you're short on time or if you want to get an overview of the park before diving deeper.

4WD Roads

A handful of national parks, including Canyonlands in Utah and Big Bend in Texas, have rugged backcountry roads that are suitable only for 4WD vehicles. These routes promise solitude and an entirely different perspective on the park if you have the proper know-how.

DRIVING ESSENTIALS

Drive on the right

.08

Blood alcohol limit is 0.08%, except in Utah, where it's 0.05%.

Yield to pedestrians at crossings and intersections.

Wearing a seatbelt is the law in all national parks.

Money

CURRENCY: **US DOLLAR ($)**

Cash & ATMs

Have some cash on hand to pay fees at trailheads, state parks and campgrounds. ATMs are available in gateway towns and at some accommodations. Expect a surcharge of at least $2 per transaction on top of any fees applied by your bank.

Credit Cards & Contactless Payments

Credit cards are almost universally accepted and given the COVID-19 pandemic, often preferred. In fact, you'll find it next to impossible to rent a car or book a hotel room without one. The number of businesses offering contactless or digital card payment is growing but isn't ubiquitous.

HOW MUCH FOR...

Entry to individual national parks
Free–$35

Ranger-led tours
Free–$15

A half-day tour or an activity
From $50

HOW TO... Save Money

Buy an America the Beautiful Pass if it makes sense for your travel plans – many of the most popular parks cost $35 to enter, meaning that visiting just three in a year makes the pass worth it. Pack a picnic to eat instead of dining at the park restaurants, which are often scenic and historic but occasionally bland and overpriced.

Tipping

Tipping in the US is *not* optional. Only withhold tips in cases of outrageously bad service.

Bartenders Tip 10% to 15% per round.

Guides Not required in this case but recommended. A good start is $20 per day.

Restaurant servers Tip 15% to 20%, unless a gratuity is already added to the bill.

LOCAL TIP

Single-use plastics will be banned in all national parks by 2032, and many parks have already stopped selling disposable water bottles. Fill up your reusable bottle for free at visitor centers.

AMERICA THE BEAUTIFUL PASS

If you're headed to at least three national parks, buy an America the Beautiful Pass ($80; store.usgs.gov/pass). It's valid for a year and gives you access to all national parks across the country, as well as national monuments and other federal recreation sites.

Seniors, travelers with disabilities and members of the US military get discounted or free passes with the same benefits. Park visitors who are 62 and older can pay just $20 for the Senior Pass (or $80 for a lifetime pass). Kids in fourth grade in the US also get a free pass.

Accommodations

Camping

The national parks are dream destinations for campers. Reserve months ahead of your trip, particularly for sites in the national parks themselves and if you're in an RV. Use recreation.gov for federal lands and reserveamerica.com for state parks. Show up early in the day at campgrounds that are first-come, first-served. Free dispersed camping is allowed in some areas managed by the US Forest Service (USFS) and the Bureau of Land Management (BLM).

Park Lodges & Cabins

Some national parks have historic lodges, often built in the early 20th century in a style called National Park Service Rustic or 'Parkitecture.' Located in unbeatable spots mere steps from iconic landscapes and major trailheads, the lodges are unsurprisingly in high demand. Some offer both cabins and motel-style rooms – if you have a choice and the budget, opt for the pricier cabins, which have more personality. Rates are steep, and rooms are booked out far in advance. Check for cancellations to snag something last minute.

Hotels & Motels

Major hotel brands have outposts in many gateway towns. Hotel choices are often limited in rural areas, but motels line the roadsides everywhere. The decor might be outdated and the buildings have seen better days, but most are still comfortable options for travelers on tighter budgets.

B&Bs

B&Bs in family-run homes generally offer good value and a heaping helping of personality. Hosts are eager to dispense helpful advice and assist with your onward travel plans. Rates often include a home-cooked breakfast. Minimum stays are common in the high season and on weekends.

HOW MUCH FOR A NIGHT IN...

A national-park lodge
$130–600

A hotel outside the parks
From $200

A campground
Free–$40

Glamping

More glamping spots are popping up across the country, including canvas tents, tiny homes and geodesic domes. Most lean high-end, with luxury linens and organic bath products, but a few are simply a small step up from camping. Check listings at **Under Canvas** (undercanvas.com), **GlampingHub** (glampinghub.com), **HipCamp** (hipcamp.com) and **AutoCamp** (autocamp.com).

NO RESERVATIONS

Accommodations around the national parks go fast, so it pays to reserve a place to stay as far in advance as possible for the widest selection and best price. If you're set on staying at in-park lodges and campgrounds, mark your calendar and book as soon as reservations open (13 months in advance for lodges and six months for campgrounds). The parks' gateway towns fill up in summer, but travelers on a budget and those making up their itinerary as they go will find rooms in towns a little further from the entrance gates.

CLOCKWISE FROM TOP LEFT: QUANG HO/SHUTTERSTOCK ©, AYMAN ALAKHRAS/SHUTTERSTOCK ©, BILL OXFORD/GETTY IMAGES ©

Family Travel

The national parks feature mind-blowing landscapes that seem like one ginormous playground, with wildlife to see, rock formations to run around, rivers to ride, waterfalls to marvel at and a variable level of adventure that can be tailored to every family's needs. A trip to the national parks promises priceless family memories and might start a lifelong love of the outdoors.

Junior Ranger Programs

All of the national parks offer junior ranger programs for kids aged four and up. Pick up an activity book at park visitor centers – kids can then complete some of the pages during their visit and attend a ranger program. Upon completion, a ranger solemnly swears them in as junior rangers, and they receive a certificate and a badge.

Timing Your Trip

Summer is the most popular time to visit the national parks, but the crowds, hot sun and potentially high temperatures can quickly turn into sunburn, dehydration and fatigue. Try not to squeeze too much in. Endless hours in the car can result in grumpy, tired kids and frustrated parents. After a while the views start to look alike and the trip can become a blur. Stop often and stay flexible.

KID-FRIENDLY PICKS

Yellowstone (p291)
Watch gushing geysers, spy on wildlife and take magnificent hikes.

Cave Tour, Mammoth Cave (p373)
Explore vast interior cathedrals, bottomless pits and strange rock formations in the world's longest cave system.

Sand-sledding, Great Sand Dunes (p287)
Race down the dunes in this shifting sea of sand.

Zion (p193)
Splash your way through the Narrows and get dripped on by the unique hanging gardens at Weeping Rock and Emerald Pools.

Camping

No trip to a national park would be complete without at least one night in a tent – most kids love it. Look for a campground with fire rings so you can have the obligatory campfire and s'mores.

Plan Ahead

Some small national-park gateway towns do not have large grocery stores. Stock up on supplies for babies and toddlers at the start of your trip in larger urban areas, or bring what you'll need with you.

SAFETY

It's easy to forget, as you're waiting in line for a shuttle or walking a trail with hundreds of other visitors, that the national parks are still wilderness. Many areas and viewpoints do not have guardrails, and even when they are present, small children could easily slide through. Secure toddlers in backpacks, always clutch young children's hands and do not let anyone get close to ledges.

Children are particularly vulnerable to the heat: they dehydrate faster and symptoms can turn severe more quickly. Make sure they drink plenty of water at regular intervals. A wide-brimmed hat, sunglasses and sunscreen are essential.

LANYCH/SHUTTERSTOCK ©

JAANA ELEFTHERIOU/SHUTTERSTOCK ©

Grand Canyon National Park (p166)

HOW TO... Travel with Pets

It's only natural to want to explore the great outdoors with your pet, but the national parks have lots of rules that make bringing your doggo a challenge. While some parts are open to pets, other federal lands (such as those administered by the USFS and the BLM) and state parks might be a better bet if you want to spend time on the trails together.

Pets in the Park

Pets are allowed in parts of the national parks, but with specific restrictions (exceptions are made for service animals; emotional support animals are not considered service animals). These rules are in place to protect the park's flora and fauna. Pets are allowed in developed areas of many national parks, including paved trails, viewpoints and campgrounds. Dogs must remain on a leash no longer than 6ft and be accompanied by a person.

Check the specifics of the parks you're visiting on the National Park Service (NPS) website (nps.gov/subjects/pets/visit.htm).

BARK Rangers

Some national parks let your pups be part of the fun as BARK Rangers. Individual parks set up their own programs, which might include walks with a ranger or taking a pledge to get a treat. The acronym stands for the first letter of each of the four principles to keep in mind when visiting with pets: bag your pet's waste, always leash your pet, respect wildlife and know where you can go.

Pet-Friendly Accommodations

Pets are allowed to join you at developed in-park campgrounds and at some lodges. Day-care and overnight boarding options are available in some gateway towns. Be aware that even if you're staying in a pet-friendly hotel, most don't allow pets to stay in the room unaccompanied.

Do not leave pets unattended, especially in vehicles, which can heat up quickly to deadly levels.

Safe Hiking

The environment of some national parks can be harsh on pets, and wildlife is often prevalent. Prepare for weather and temperature extremes. Think twice before taking pets on desert hikes in the summer; surfaces can burn tender paws. Always bring a portable water bowl.

Remember that dogs, like humans, need to be in good shape before taking off on extended hikes, and they are also susceptible to altitude sickness and dehydration.

BEST NATIONAL PARKS TO VISIT WITH PETS

Acadia (p336)

Walk 100 miles of hiking trails and 45 miles of carriage roads with your pet.

Grand Canyon (p166)

Admire the country's most iconic natural feature along the 13-mile pet-friendly Rim Trail. The park also operates its own kennel for day and overnight stays on the South Rim.

White Sands (p191)

Leashed pets and their humans can roam around this otherworldly dunescape.

New River Gorge (p374)

Pets are permitted on all of the trails at the country's newest national park.

Responsible Travel

Climate Change & Travel

It's impossible to ignore the impact we have when traveling and the importance of making changes where we can. Lonely Planet urges all travelers to engage with their travel carbon footprint. There are many carbon calculators online that allow travelers to estimate the carbon emissions generated by their journey; try resurgence.org/resources/carbon-calculator.html. Many airlines and booking sites offer travelers the option of offsetting the impact of greenhouse gas emissions by contributing to climate-friendly initiatives around the world. We continue to offset the carbon footprint of all Lonely Planet staff travel, while recognizing this is a mitigation more than a solution.

Stay Local

Skip the hotel chains and stay in B&Bs, motels and other locally run accommodations. Hosts often dish out helpful advice and hearty breakfasts, and the buildings are characterful instead of cookie cutter.

Get Off the Interstate

To take the road less traveled, exit the interstate and drive the country's scenic byways and backways. Support local economies by stocking up on supplies at mom-and-pop shops and stopping for a meal in small towns and lesser-visited areas.

Travel Slower

Water is precious everywhere, but especially in the western US. Hotels use nearly 400 gallons of water per day per room, so stay in one place longer to cut down on the amount used for washing sheets and towels.

Round Up

Nonprofit partners run the gift shops and bookstores at the national parks. When you make a purchase, staff will ask if you'd like to round up to the nearest dollar and donate your change to help preserve the parks.

Use bear canisters on overnight hikes. Never store food or scented products in your car.

Wildfires burn millions of acres across the West each summer. Always observe campfire restrictions.

YOSEMITE FACELIFT

The biggest volunteer event annually – in Yosemite or any other national park – sees climbers and other travelers arrive in September for a major cleanup. The weeklong event includes free campsites for volunteers and evening activities.

FRENCH FRY EXPRESS

Locomotive 4960 of the Grand Canyon Railway runs on recycled vegetable oil collected from restaurants in Williams, Arizona. Over the course of a year, the train's passengers reduce the park's vehicle traffic by as much as 70,000 cars.

Volunteer

Sign up with organizations like the Student Conservation Association and American Conservation Experience, which partner with the NPS and offer dozens of extended volunteer opportunities in restoration and conservation work.

Rent an Electric Vehicle

More national parks are adding EV charging stations, as are the gateway towns near their entrances. Check the map of charging stations on the NPS website to plan your national parks EV road trip (nps.gov/subjects/sustainability/electric-vehicle-charging-map.htm).

Fish for Invasive Species

At Yellowstone National Park, the invasive lake trout pose a dire threat to the native cutthroat trout population. You can do your part by fishing for lake trout, and they also make a tasty meal.

Practice the principles of Leave No Trace: plan ahead and prepare, respect wildlife and be considerate of other visitors. Pack out your trash, including fruit peels, which can take years to biodegrade in some environments.

Know what to do when nature calls and restrooms aren't available. In the backcountry, come prepared with a disposable toilet system, such as a WAG bag that neutralizes pathogens and breaks down waste.

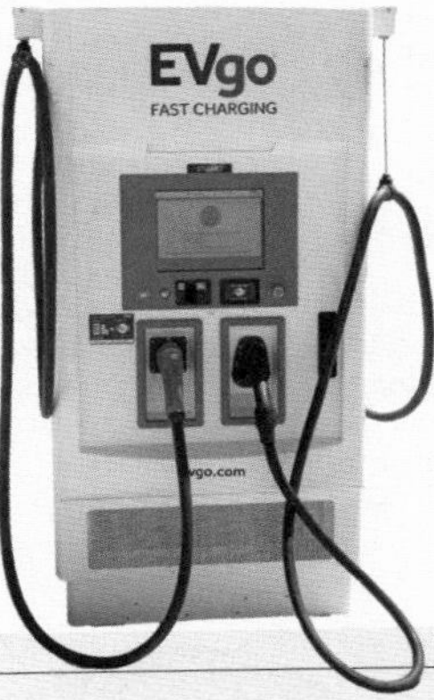

26%

The top eight NPS-administered parks see 26% of all recreation visitors. That's almost the same percentage as the total visitor numbers for the 331 least-visited NPS sites (25%).

RESOURCES

nationalparks.org
Official nonprofit partner of the National Park Service (NPS).

npca.org
Nonpartisan organization advocating for the national parks.

lnt.org
Useful insights into no-impact travel.

Accessible Travel

The national parks exist for the enjoyment of all. That said, most of them have few accessible trails, but it's still possible for travelers with disabilities to experience the country's most epic landscapes.

Best Parks for Wheelchair Users

A 2022 study by Aging in Place found that Badlands National Park in South Dakota is the most accessible in the country, with three of its 17 trails suitable for wheelchairs.

Airport

All US airports are required to comply with the Americans with Disabilities Act (ADA), providing accessible facilities and assistance to those who need it. Companies like Thrifty and Wheelchair Getaways offer wheelchair-accessible van rentals.

Accommodations

Accommodations are required to have at least one wheelchair-accessible room, though few are fully ADA-compliant. More often, these are ground-floor rooms with wider doorways and handles around the tub and toilet. Always ask exactly what 'accessible' means when making reservations.

RESOURCES

The **National Park Service** (nps.gov/aboutus/accessibility.htm) has detailed accessibility information about each park online. State parks and the Bureau of Land Management also have webpages on their accessibility efforts.

Popular hiking app **AllTrails** (alltrails.com) includes a filter for wheelchair-friendly trails in the national parks and beyond.

Travelability (travelability.net) offers state-specific information about accessible travel, including informative articles and a list of specialized travel companies.

SHUTTLES

National-park shuttle buses are wheelchair accessible, but most motorized scooters won't fit on board. If you're not able to ride the shuttles, you can request a personal vehicle permit from visitor centers.

Service Animals

Service animals may accompany visitors on park shuttles, inside museums and visitor centers, and on hiking trails. Ensure your service animal wears its official vest at all times to avoid misunderstandings with park rangers or other visitors.

Visitor Centers

Visitor centers are wheelchair accessible, and some have tactile maps of the park for travelers who are blind. Film screenings include subtitles, and museum exhibits sometimes have audio recordings.

ASL INTERPRETERS

If you're deaf or have hearing loss, you can request an American Sign Language interpreter for ranger programs. The NPS recommends submitting your request at least a week before your visit.

Access Pass

Visitors with disabilities can obtain a free access pass to national parks, wildlife refuges, national forests and Bureau of Land Management sites. The pass can be obtained at any park entrance or online. You must sign a form confirming eligibility.

Nuts & Bolts

DAYLIGHT SAVING TIME

Two states do not observe daylight saving time (March to November): Arizona and Hawaii. Arizona is a particularly tricky case because the neighboring states and the Navajo Nation do change their clocks. Keep the time difference in mind if you're going to or from the Grand Canyon from March to November.

Marijuana

Be aware of the patchwork of laws around recreational marijuana, especially if you're crossing state lines. It's legal in 23 states for recreational use, plus 14 more states for medical use, but elsewhere it remains illegal.

Phone Reception

Expect poor phone reception in most national parks. Some visitor centers have free wi-fi.

Toilets

Visitor centers, campgrounds and picnic areas often have flushing toilets. Pit toilets are stationed near trailheads.

GOOD TO KNOW

Time zone
Eastern (GMT-5)
Central (GMT-6)
Mountain (GMT-7)
Pacific (GMT-8)
Alaska (GMT-9)
Hawaii (GMT-10)

Country code
+1

Emergency number
911

Population
332 million

Electricity 120V/60Hz

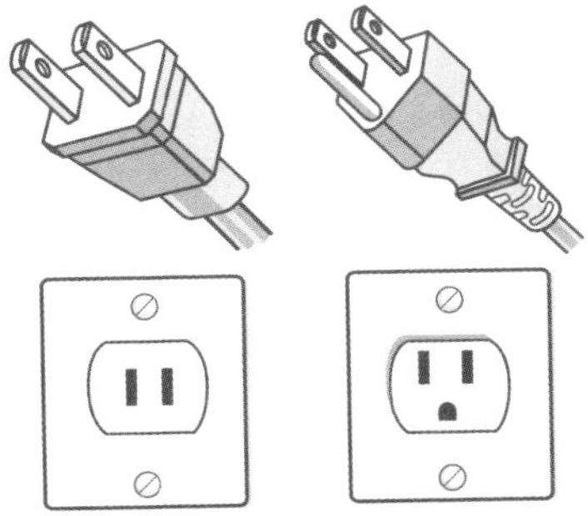

Type A 120V/60Hz

Type B 120V/60Hz

PUBLIC HOLIDAYS

Many national parks are open 365 days a year, though visitor centers and some other facilities close on federal and state holidays. Peak holiday periods include times when students of all ages are out of school, such as spring break (March and April).

New Year's Day January 1

Martin Luther King Jr Day Third Monday in January

Presidents' Day Third Monday in February

Memorial Day Last Monday in May

Juneteenth June 19

Independence Day July 4

Labor Day First Monday in September

Columbus Day Second Monday in October

Veterans' Day November 11

Thanksgiving Fourth Thursday in November

Christmas Day December 25

THE USA'S NATIONAL PARKS

STORYBOOK

Our writers delve deep into different aspects of National Park life

A History of USA's National Parks in 15 Places

The story of America's national parks goes to the heart of Americans' relationship with their country's wild places.

p418

Meet the Rangers

Learn about the rangers from five of the USA's National Parks.

p422

The First Peoples

The Grand Canyon has a compelling human history, coming from the stories and cultures of those who have lived here for millenia.

p430

This Land Is Your Land: Public Land & Politics

More than 70% of Utah is owned by the federal or state government – but how should it be used?

p434

A Changing Sierra

Climate change in the Sierra Nevada has led to catastrophic wildfires, drought, floods, storms and bark beetle infestations.

p437

The Yellowstone Supervolcano

Yellowstone has seen momentous change over time, from a primordial landscape to epicenter of geothermal energy.

p441

The Narrows (p195), Zion National Park

A HISTORY OF USA'S NATIONAL PARKS IN 15 PLACES

The story of America's national parks goes to the heart of Americans' relationship with their country's wild places. It's a story of the US at its best, from its leaders' long road to protecting so many places of astonishing beauty to its people's passion for exploring their own country. By Anthony Ham

THE US HAS always been considered the cradle of the national-park idea and it could just be the country's greatest gift to the world, not to mention to its very own people. From early imaginings in the mid-19th century to a large portfolio of protected areas that go to the heart of how Americans experience their country, US national park history is a long and noble story, albeit one with humble origins.

American portrait artist George Catlin (1796–1872) is credited as the first person to conceptualize a 'nation's park.' He envisioned a 'magnificent park' to protect the country's remaining Indigenous people, buffalo and wilderness from the onslaught of western expansion. More than three decades would pass before anything remotely resembling that vision existed. But nearly 200 years later, it's remarkable how much of that original idea continues to guide the country's approach to its 63 national parks.

If anything has changed dramatically over the years, it's the extent to which Americans have embraced the idea. In 1950, some 32 million people visited America's national parks. The figure now tops 325 million. There are now more than 400 protected areas under the administration of the National Park Service (NPS). And the number just keeps on growing.

1. Yosemite National Park

THE BIRTH OF AN IDEA

In 1851, members of an armed militia accidentally rode into a massive granite valley in California's Sierra Nevada. They called it 'Yosemity,' possibly a corruption of the Miwok word Oo-hoo'-ma-te or uzumatel, meaning 'grizzly bear.' The name stuck, and word of the valley and its waterfalls got out. In 1864, President Abraham Lincoln signed into law a bill that put Yosemite Valley, and the nearby Mariposa Grove of giant sequoias, under California's control. Although it wasn't a national park, it was the first time any government had mandated the protection of a natural area for public use.

For more on Yosemite National Park, see page 71

2. Yellowstone National Park

THE FIRST NATIONAL PARK

In 1868, an expedition bankrolled by Northern Pacific Railroad headed into the Wyoming wilderness to investigate reports of thermal pools and geysers. Among their discoveries were the Great Fountain Geyser and another geyser they would name Old Faithful. Soon, lobbyists at Northern Pacific, with their eyes on tourist dollars, rallied alongside conservationists for a public park like Yosemite. In 1872 Ulysses S Grant signed the landmark Yellowstone National Park Act, creating the country's first national park. In 1926, the last wolves in Yellowstone were killed as a result of the federal predator control program, which also targeted mountain lions, bears and coyotes; wolves only returned in 1995.

For more on Yellowstone National Park, see page 291

3. Sequoia National Park

THE FATHER OF AMERICA'S PARKS

Often considered the father of the US national park system, Scottish-born John Muir (1838–1914) was a writer, naturalist and arguably the greatest defender of wilderness areas in the late 19th century. He was pivotal in the creation not just of Yosemite, but also introduced many Americans to the existence of giant sequoias – he was instrumental in the creation of America's second national park, Sequoia, in 1890. Yosemite followed a month later. Muir's writings also cemented the now widely held belief that national parks should remain as close as possible to their natural state.

For more on Sequoia National Park, see page 59

Old Faithful (p296), Yellowstone National Park

4. Mesa Verde National Park

THE ANTIQUITIES ACT AND CULTURAL HERITAGE

In 1906 Congress passed the Antiquities Act, which gave the president the authority to protect public land by designating it a national monument. It was originally designed to protect Native American archaeological sites out West, but Theodore Roosevelt quickly realized he could use the Act to protect any tract of land for any reason – and without opposition from lobbyists or political opponents in Congress. A year later, Mesa Verde, including Cliff Palace, the largest cliff dwelling in North America, became the country's seventh national park and the first dedicated to protecting cultural heritage.

For more on Mesa Verde National Park, see page 181

5. Theodore Roosevelt National Park

A PRESIDENT'S VISION

Although this land wouldn't become a national park until 1978, its origins stretch back nearly a century. In the 1880s, future president Theodore Roosevelt retreated to North Dakota to hunt bison after losing both his wife and mother. An avid hunter, birder, far-sighted thinker and lover of the outdoors, Roosevelt's time out West profoundly shaped his life and legacy. By the time he left office in 1909, he had signed off on five national parks, 18 national monuments, 51 federal bird sanctuaries and 100 million acres of national forest.

For more on Theodore Roosevelt National Park, see page 323

6. Grand Canyon National Park

AMERICA'S FINEST

In 1903, President Theodore Roosevelt undertook a two-month-long campaign tour of the United States. Along the way, he spent two weeks exploring Yellowstone and three nights camping with John Muir in Yosemite. But the greatest legacy of that trip – which was to have a lasting impact on the degree of protection afforded to national parks – arose from time spent at the Grand Canyon. Upon seeing the canyon for the first time, Roosevelt famously opined that the mystical natural wonder could not be improved by any human intervention: it should be left exactly as it was. Grand Canyon National Park was established in 1919.

For more on Grand Canyon National Park, see page 166

7. Hawai'i Volcanoes National Park

THE BIRTH OF THE NATIONAL PARK SERVICE

The number of national parks may have been increasing, but there existed no effective protection or management of the parks until President Woodrow Wilson created the National Park Service (NPS) in 1916. The NPS was the brainchild of industrialist and conservationist Stephen Mather, who became the first NPS director and initiated so many NPS practices – the ranger system, campfire talks, museums – that we know today. The first to benefit were Hawaii's two newly minted parks, Hawai'i Volcanoes and Haleakalā, which became symbols of the expanding geographical spread of the park system.

For more on Hawai'i Volcanoes National Park, see page 400

8. Denali National Park & Preserve

OLD LAND, NEW PARK

The Athabascan people used what is now Denali National Park and Preserve in Alaska as hunting grounds. But gold was found near Kantishna in 1905 and the big-game hunters followed the stampede. Stunned by the destruction, noted hunter and naturalist Charles Sheldon mounted a campaign to protect the region. From this, Mt McKinley National Park was born in 1917. In 1980, the park was enlarged by 4 million acres and renamed Denali National Park and Preserve.

For more on Denali National Park & Preserve, see page 229

9. Great Smoky Mountains National Park

CARVING OUT A PARK

As America's population grew, it became more and more complicated to carve national parks from an increasingly human-dominated landscape. With huge swaths of forest in the Great Smoky Mountains being felled by lumber companies, more and more locals were beginning to notice the devastation left by clear-cutting. In the early 1920s, a few key figures from Knoxville, TN, and Asheville, NC, began to advocate for conservation of the Smokies. It took more than a decade, negotiations with over 6000 property owners and massive fund-raising campaigns to buy the land before the park finally became reality in 1934.

For more on Great Smoky Mountains National Park, see page 358

10. Joshua Tree National Park

FDR'S GREAT LEAP FORWARD

With the Great Depression, national parks went through significant changes. President Franklin Delano Roosevelt created the Civilian Conservation Corps (CCC) and put thousands of young men to work improving national-park roads, visitor shelters, campsites and trails. In 1936, FDR created the Joshua Tree National Monument, and it's a fine example of how many current national parks began as FDR-decreed national monuments – during his presidency, FDR founded not just Joshua Tree, but also Capitol Reef and Channel Islands national monuments (both of which would become national parks), and Olympic and Kings Canyon National Parks.

For more on Joshua Tree National Park, see page 103

11. Everglades National Park

THE IMPORTANCE OF WILDERNESS

Post-war prosperity allowed more Americans to travel – and hordes of them headed to the parks. With burgeoning populations in places such as Florida, the need to lock away wilderness areas became ever more urgent. In 1947, the Everglades – the largest subtropical wilderness in the US and the largest of any kind east of the Mississippi River – became a national park. One million people now visit the Everglades every year, which is more people than live in nearby Miami.

For more on Everglades National Park, see page 387

12. Redwood National Park

MISSION 66

The number of travelers descending on parks put tremendous pressure on them. In 1956, NPS director Conrad Wirth created Mission 66, a 10-year plan to improve park infrastructure and dramatically increase visitor services. The plan established the first park visitor centers, more staff and

Blue Mesa (p186), Petrifi ed Forest National Park

improved facilities, with the number of protected areas constantly growing. During the 1960s, Petrified Forest (1962), Canyonlands (1964), North Cascades (1968) and Redwood (1968) were added to the expanding portfolio. Redwood was especially significant, securing an icon of the American wild and reminding Americans of the importance of formally protecting its natural treasures.

For more on Redwood National Park, see page 93

13. Alaska

THE NEW FRONTIER

In 1980, with a flourish of Jimmy Carter's presidential pen, the Alaska National Interest Lands Conservation Act doubled the amount of land under control of the NPS, with an additional 100 million acres added to the state's portfolio of protected land. As a direct consequence, and against the wishes of many in the pro-development and pro-mining lobbies, seven new national parks appeared on maps of Alaska: Gates of the Arctic, Glacier Bay, Katmai, Kenai Fjords, Kobuk Valley, Lake Clark and Wrangell-St Elias. It wasn't only national parks that were added, with national wildlife refuges, wilderness areas, the Iditarod National Historic Trail and conservation areas also announced.

For more on Alaska, see page 203

14. Bears Ears National Monument

NEW BATTLEGROUNDS

The fragility of America's national park system is highlighted by the fight over Bears Ears, in Utah. In December 2016, President Barack Obama designated Bears Ears as a national monument, protecting 1.35 million acres of land filled with ancient cliff dwellings, ponderosa forests, 4000-year-old petroglyphs, mesas, canyons and glorious red-rock formations. In December 2017, President Donald Trump countered Obama's move, reducing the monument's size by a whopping 85%. One of President Biden's first acts was to order a review of the site: in 2021 his administration restored Bears Ears to its 2016 boundaries.

For more on Bears Ears National Monument, see page 435

15. New River Gorge National Park & Preserve

AMERICA'S NEWEST PARKS

Since Yellowstone was created in 1872, the national park system has grown to encompass over 400 sites and more than 84 million acres. The parks today protect many of the continent's most sensitive ecosystems, some of the world's most remarkable landscapes, and America's most important historical and cultural landmarks. And the list of parks continues to rise. In 2019, White Sands National Park in New Mexico became the 62nd US national park. A year later, one of America's oldest rivers became the centerpiece of America's 63rd national park, New River Gorge National Park and Preserve in West Virginia.

For more on New River Gorge National Park & Preserve, see page 374

MEET THE RANGERS

Learn about the rangers from five of the USA's National Parks.

Grand Canyon National Park

Carmen Kraus works as a Visual Information Specialist at Grand Canyon National Park.

What draws you to nature?

I remember vividly the first time I saw the Milky Way. I was 10 years old, staying with my parents in a cabin near Hawai'i Volcanoes National Park. Just as we finished cooking, the power went out in our campground. It was incredible – we went outside to marvel at the multitude of stars stretched above us, without a single streetlight for miles. Like many people, my first thought was that my view of the sky was marred by clouds, but I was actually seeing the extreme density of stars in the Milky Way core.

Closer to home in the southeastern US, I observed the progression of the seasons, looked for salamanders in the streams, and eagerly awaited the first fawns of spring. I've traveled internationally and met close friends hiking in the mountains of South America and along the coasts of Europe.

And I remember visiting Grand Canyon National Park for the first time in my teens, feeling the immensity of the canyon walls towering above as my dad and I hiked down the Bright Angel Trail. The juxtaposition of proximity and distance left a powerful impression – the ancient rock mere feet from the trail while the wide expanse of the canyon stretched into the hazy horizon.

How did you come to work for the National Park Service?

To get where I am today, I followed my curiosity. During school I started out in the sciences, and then added art. It was a reasonable combination since both involve observation and study of the natural world. Although I had initially anticipated a career in lab research, I found my way to communication and interpretation. The opportunity to share nature and stories with people was something I couldn't resist.

People come to work for the National Park Service through many different paths. For some, it's a dream they've worked toward since high school. For others, it's a career shift or a second career. I have col-

Pictured clockwise from top left: Carmen Kraus, Grand Canyon National Park (p166); Sonja Schwartz, Yosemite National Park (p71); Emily Davis, Great Smoky Mountains National Park (p358); Rich Jehle, Yellowstone National Park (p291)

leagues who studied forestry, education, accounting, history and music. There are many career paths within the park service.

What drew me is the feeling of being able to make a difference, to the plants and animals, the people passing through and the people who call this place home. I started with an internship in interpretation on the North Rim of the Grand Canyon National Park. High on the Kaibab Plateau, surrounded by the rustling sounds of wind through the aspens and pines, I learned from my supervisors and companions. I spent one winter season at Death Valley National Park (which was hotter than my summer season) working in education. I returned for another beautiful season on the North Rim in interpretation, presenting programs to people and designing signs. Working in this park sometimes feels like I'm traveling while standing still, since I get to interact with people from all over the world. I love hearing people's stories and impressions of their trips. People come to national parks looking for beauty or adventure and find connections – with the area, with each other, with people they've just met.

Connection is why I keep returning to Grand Canyon National Park. I currently work on the South Rim in graphic design and communications, but my job is a combination of service, art and science. I share stories and information online and through signs. The message I hope to get across is one of respect. For this region – which has been home to tribes since time immemorial. For the land – which is home to rocks that date back 1.8 billion years and unique species that live here and nowhere else. For yourself – to honor your body and listen to what it is telling you, especially on hot days and strenuous hikes. And for each other – what stories do your companions and fellow travelers have to tell?

Great Smoky Mountains National Park

Emily Davis is a ranger and public affairs specialist at Great Smoky Mountains National Park. In this Q&A, she shares some visiting tips and ranger info, and tells us about the park's most famous residents: bears.

What skills does someone need to become a park ranger?

The ranger 'field' is pretty wide. We have law-enforcement rangers, we have search and rescue rangers, and we also have education and interpretive rangers.

So are rangers specialized, or do they help out as needed across the park?

We are very fortunate at the Smokies that we have people who are experts in their fields, and we also have a number of staff who have collateral duties, or help out when needed. For instance, we have a number of members on our search and rescue team who are not full-time search and rescue rangers but who, if their daily duties allow and there's an emergency, will be released to go help.

Is there an interesting fact about the park that isn't well known?

One of the coolest things I learned recently is that this park is one of the most studied and researched of all the national parks.

Bear, Great Smoky Mountains National Park (p358)

Why is so much research going on here?
This place is beyond measure in terms of its biodiversity. We work closely with one of our partners, Discover Life in America (DLIA). The DLIA group and a lot of our researchers and park staff work to discover just how many plants, animals and living things are found in the park. They discovered many new species in the last 25 years – new to the park and some new to science as well.

Any recent discoveries that stand out?
Salamanders that bioluminesce under black light. It's just something that's come up very recently – in the last couple of years at most.

Any helpful tips for visitors that you can share?
A lot of our visitors tend to go to the 10 hot spots in the park, and those are all wonderful places, but... there are other places in this park that, even on the busiest day, visitors can go, that are equal or sometimes even better.

Any examples of hot spots?
Laurel Falls. It's great, it's easy to get to, but there are other waterfalls in the park and other hikes of equal distance and equal difficulty, or ease, that are really great places to discover.

What are good alternatives to hiking to Laurel Falls?
Middle Prong Trail is a really good one. Baskins Creek Trail is another.

Any other ways to avoid congestion and parking problems at popular trailheads?
We have been working a lot with some local businesses who have been offering shuttle services (nps.gov/grsm/planyourvisit/shuttles.htm) to some of those really popular spots in the park. To have that as an option to driving is really nice; it takes some of the pressure off visitors who don't want to try to find a place to park.

Just how many bears are there in Great Smoky Mountains National Park? And what should you do when you see one?
There are something like 1900 black bears in Great Smoky Mountains National Park. The best thing to do is observe from a distance. It's really a joy to see a bear in its natural habitat doing natural bear things. So if you see a bear, remain watchful. Don't approach it. Don't let it approach you. Just let it do its thing; 50 yards or greater is a safe distance.

Always make sure, especially if you're in a campground, to secure your food in a vehicle. In backcountry campsites, there is a set of cables where you put your food in a bin and put it up in the air to remove it from a bear's reach.

Park Visitation

Great Smoky Mountains National Park recorded 12,937,633 visits in 2022 – it's second-busiest year, ever. But how does this compare with other parks? According to Emily, the park sees 'more people here every year than go to Grand Canyon, Yosemite and Yellowstone National Parks combined.'

Yellowstone National Park

Diverse landscapes, wildfires and uninvited dinner guests: it's all part of the Yellowstone experience for Rich Jehle, a ranger with the national park for more than 35 years. As told to Regis St Louis.

What makes Yellowstone so different from other national parks?
All this spectacular stuff is just crammed into a relatively small area. There are many parts of this park that if nothing else existed they would be worthy of being their own national park: the geyser basins, the Grand Canyon of the Yellowstone, and the northern range – called the Serengeti of North America for its huge concentrations of wildlife.

What do you love most about working in Yellowstone?
The goal of the National Park Service is a very noble endeavor. We're trying to help preserve Yellowstone in as much of a natural condition as we can, so we can pass that on to future generations. Just that in and of itself gives meaning to the work for me. It inspires me to think that I'm doing behind-the-scenes work that's contributing to a much bigger cause.

Apart from that, work here is never dull. There are events that require your immediate attention: from fires to wind storms to changing geyser patterns. After the big flood in 2022 washed out roads, the entire park, in an incredible team effort, responded and very quickly did some amazing work to allow visitors to get access to Yellowstone.

I understand you were here during the devastating fires of '88. Did you ever think Yellowstone would recover?

This was probably the biggest fire event that Yellowstone had in 200 years. I thought to myself, 'The landscape is destroyed. It's never going to look the same again.' And yet, fire is a part of the ecosystem here. Just like wind, rain and running water, fire has shaped the landscape for tens of thousands of years. Now I can go back to some of those same badly burned spots and see new growth – trees that are 35ft or 40ft tall.

Do you have any memorable wildlife encounters?

Some years ago I lived in a small one-story staffing complex across from the Madison Campground. One night in late October, I was cooking dinner in my apartment when I heard a knock out front. I went over and opened the door, and it took me a second to realize what I was looking at. But when I came to my senses there was a bear, a black bear, standing up, leaning against the glass screen door. Literally I was no more than 6in from his face. It was so surprising that the image didn't quite register. It took me a few seconds for me to realize, 'Wow, I should probably shut the door.' So I shut the door. Later we set a trap that was baited with elk meat, but that bear was too smart, and we never caught it.

WHILE THE MOST VISITED SITES ARE IN THE VALLEY, IT COMPRISES LESS THAN 5% OF THE PARK.

Do you have any favorite places?

I have lots of favorite spots. One of the things I used to love doing was going to the geyser basins at night. When there are no crowds and the moon is out, that's an eerie, otherworldly experience.

Castle Geyser (p295), Yellowstone National Park

GJ-NYC/SHUTTERSTOCK ©

How has Yellowstone affected your life?

Yellowstone has been a huge part of my life. In the summer after college, I came up here and worked a seasonal job in a general store in Grant Village. Pretty quickly this place got its hooks in me and filled a lot of things I was looking for in my life: spectacular outdoor landscapes with endless opportunities to enjoy this environment. One thing led to another, and I just stayed. On a personal level, I met my wife here. We even got married in the historic chapel that is part of Fort Yellowstone.

We've raised a family here – we have two daughters, one of whom is out of college and has also worked for the National Park Service here in Yellowstone. I've been incredibly lucky in that I've been able to live and work in a place as spectacular as Yellowstone, which is a very inspiring place to be.

Yosemite National Park

Originally from New Jersey, Sonja Schwartz first moved to California when she was in college and fell in love with the mountains. Today she is a Wilderness Education Ranger in Yosemite National Park.

What made you want to become a ranger in Yosemite?

After a career in wildlife biology, tech and project management, I decided to come back to the place I love. To be able to help share that love with other people and encourage them to experience the tranquil beauty of the wilderness.

What's a usual day like on the job?

About half the time, you can find me in the Wilderness Center in Yosemite Village. There we issue wilderness permits to visitors for their backpacking trips, educate them about Leave No Trace principles and help folks looking for information on our vast network of wilderness trails. The rest of the time, you can find me in the backcountry out on patrol. On patrol,

I'm maintaining our wilderness resources by checkingto see that hikers and backpackers are following our rules and regulations, checking on conditions and doing trail maintenance.

What are some of your favorite spots in the park and why?

I'm a sucker for a good lake or river hang. In the spring when the waterfalls are all still going, I love heading up the Panorama Trail to the Illilouette Basin and hanging by Illilouette Falls. In the summer, when it heats up at lower elevations, you can find me up at May Lake enjoying the views of Mount Hoffman or over on North Dome looking down on the Valley below.

What are some things you wish more park visitors knew about Yosemite and going into the wilderness?

Yosemite National Park is not just Yosemite Valley! While the most visited sites are in the Valley, it comprises less than 5% of the park. There are many amazing areas out of Hetch Hetchy, Wawona and Tuolumne to explore with their own share of amazing waterfalls, alpine lakes and big trees.

Got any good stories about wildlife encounters you've had in the park?

I once woke up when I was camping to find a ringtail curled up with me on my sleeping bag taking a nap. It was adorable, but I managed to convince it that it was probably best for both of us if it found its own bed.

What crucial item do backpackers seem to forget most often?

I always tell people to double-check for a water filter, a lighter/matches, a headlamp, sun protection, bug protection and an extra pair of socks.

Do you have any advice for first-time visitors?

Take a look at a map and get yourself oriented before you come here, including the best place to park if you're arriving by car. Expect a range of conditions including, but not limited to, cold and snow in the winter, flooding in the spring, heat and crowds in the summer and wildfire smoke in the fall. Take the time to check the weather and road, trail and park conditions on the park website so you can better prepare for your visit. Lastly, be flexible about your plan. You might not be able to do everything on your list, but there are so many amazing and interesting spots to explore in Yosemite if you're open to the experience, you'll be able to have a great time.

What are a few important things visitors can do to help protect the park for future generations?

Stay on trail when possible and don't make new social trails. Be sure to carry out all of your trash, including toilet paper. Follow established guidelines for fires and pooping in the wilderness. Let wild animals be wild and don't feed or approach them.

NO MATTER WHO YOU ARE, YOU CAN COME HERE AND BE MOVED BY THE LAND

Zion National Park

Having worked for the National Park Service for more than a decade, Ashley Dang is now a ranger at Zion. In this Q&A, she dishes on her background and favorite parts of the park.

How long have you been a ranger at Zion National Park?

I've been a ranger at Zion National Park for a noncontinuous 2½ years. I started here as a seasonal Fire Effects Monitor some years ago and then came back as an Emergency Dispatcher for two years. I am relatively new in my current position as an Education Technician.

Have you been a ranger at other national parks?

I've worked for the National Park Service since 2011. In that time, I've had the privilege to work at more than a dozen different sites, and all of them have been unique experiences.

What is your favorite part of being a ranger at Zion?

As a ranger, I get to meet people from all over the world. It's fun and eye-opening to hear how Zion (and the national-park system as a whole) compares to natural and

ASHLEY DANG ©

Ashley Dang, Zion National Park (p193)

cultural landscapes around the world, as well as how Zion has changed as a park over time. Some of the most interesting stories come from people who have been visiting the park for decades or whose families have lived in the area for even longer.

What prompted you to become a national-park ranger?

The National Park Service offers opportunities to do almost anything, almost anywhere within the US and its territories. I became a park ranger because I believe in protecting the places that are naturally and culturally meaningful; I stayed because of the many ways it's possible to carry out that mission.

When did you visit Zion for the first time?

I first visited Zion in October 2011. It was rainy and overcast, and the most striking memory I have from that visit is an image of the Court of the Patriarchs surrounded by a beautiful moody mist.

What makes Zion such a special place?

Zion National Park is a place that means different things to different people, and I think that's what makes it special. Many people come here to find awe and wonder in the sweeping scenery, while others come to test their physical and mental limits on our challenging trails and technical canyoneering or climbing routes. Visitors with keen observation skills can witness first-hand the natural and physical sciences in motion or discover some truly compelling stories of human history. For some, Zion may be an unforgettable first outdoor experience: a first camping trip, wilderness hike, outdoor rock climb or canyoneering adventure. No matter who you are, you can come here and be moved by the land.

What are your favorite parts of Zion National Park?

I love the park's east side, the area from the historic Zion–Mt Carmel Tunnel eastward toward the park's East Entrance. The scenery feels simultaneously grand and intimate out there, and you can enjoy it in so many different ways. On low-energy days, I like to enjoy the sights directly from the comfort of my vehicle or find a quiet spot to hang out in the shade and look for wildlife. On days that I want an adventure, I bring a good map and explore some of the many routes the east side has to offer.

What do you wish more people knew before visiting Zion?

Many people think of Zion National Park as Angels Landing and the Narrows. While those are beautiful areas with amazing views and opportunities to challenge yourself physically (and mentally!), there is so much more to Zion. With some good planning, it's possible to have a unique, rewarding adventure. Remember to pack appropriately for your day (water, food, sun protection, extra clothing layers, appropriate technical gear etc), understand what current conditions are like in the park, and exercise situational awareness always

What are your favorite outdoor activities?

Good old-fashioned hiking.

Havasupai medicine man, Arizona

BILL GOZANSKY/ALAMY STOCK PHOTO ©

THE FIRST PEOPLES NATIVE AMERICANS OF THE GRAND CANYON

There are 11 local tribes that have historical ties to the Grand Canyon. These are the Havasupai, the Hopi, the Hualapai, the Navajo, the Paiute (Kaibab Band, Las Vegas Band, the Mopa Band, the Paiute Tribe of Utah, and the San Juan Southern Paiute Tribe), the Yavapai-Apache, and the Zuni.

It would be a mistake to generalize about Native Americans in the region: each nation has its own traditions, sacred lands and specific relationships to other tribes.

Havasupai (Havsuw 'Baaja)

Well known for their beadwork and basketry, the Havasupai ('People of the Blue-Green Waters') share the Yuman language with the Hualapai. Both tribes are together referred to as Northeastern Pai. Their legends tell how humankind originated on a mountain near the Colorado River. They left their Mojave relatives behind and headed to Meriwitica, near Spencer Canyon (a tributary of Grand Canyon). The Hualapai stayed near Meriwitica, but one story explains that a frog, enticed by the stream and lush vegetation, led the Havasupai east to Havasu Canyon. Archaeological records indicate that the Northeastern Pai arrived at the Grand Canyon around 1150 CE, and the Havasupai have occupied Havasu Canyon since that time.

Hualapai (Hwal'bay)

The Hualapai trace their origins to Kathat Kanave, an old man who sometimes took the form of a coyote and lived in Mada Widita Canyon (also known as Meriwitica), on the canyon's westernmost edge. He taught the Pai ('the People') how to live in the canyon, explaining what herbs cured which ailments and how and what to plant. The Hualapai and Havasupai developed complex systems of irrigation and spent summers farming within the canyon, at places like Havasu Canyon and Havasupai Gardens. During the winter, they hunted on the plateau. Through trade with other tribes, they acquired peaches, figs, wheat, melons, cattle and horses.

Nowadays the Hualapai Reservation, bordering a large section of the western Grand Canyon, stretches as far south as Route *66*. The Hualapai ('People of the

Tall Pines') count themselves among the few tribes in the Southwest that do not generate revenue from gambling; instead, they've tried their hand at tourism, most successfully through motorized rafting tours on this section of the Colorado River, and through tourism on the scenic West Rim (known as Grand Canyon West). If you plan to travel off Route 66 on the Hualapai Reservation, you must purchase a permit in Peach Springs. Like the Havasupai, the Hualapai are renowned for their basketry.

Hopi (Hopituh)

East of the Grand Canyon lies the 2410-sq-mile Hopi Reservation, which is completely surrounded by the Navajo Reservation. The Hopi are Arizona's oldest tribe and are known for their distinctive, rich culture, whose intricacies remain closely guarded.

In the Southwest, certain Pueblo tribes believe that the universe consists of several worlds stacked one upon the other. In one telling of the story, in order to pass from one world to the next, Spider Grandmother gave her people a reed, which they used to climb up through the dying world's ceiling and into the new world.

For the Hopi, this place of emergence is not just a myth but an actual location: the Sipapuni, a domed mineral spring located in the Grand Canyon, near the confluence of the Colorado and Little Colorado Rivers. If you have the chance to look into an Ancestral Puebloan kiva, you'll probably see a *sipapu* – a small round hole in the floor that symbolizes the original Sipapuni.

Navajo (Diné)

The Navajo Reservation is the largest and most populous in the US, covering more than 27,000 sq miles in Arizona and parts of New Mexico and Utah; its western edge borders Grand Canyon National Park. The Navajo call themselves the Diné (dee-nay; 'the People') and their land Dinétah. The word Navajo comes from the Tewa (a Pueblo tribe); the Spanish began referring to the Diné as 'Navajo' in the 1600s to distinguish them from their kin the Apache.

Nationwide, there are nearly 400,000 Navajo. The Navajo's Athabascan tongue

Navajo riders, Arizona

is the most spoken Native American language, with 170,000 speakers, despite its notorious complexity. In the Pacific Theater during WWII, Navajo 'code talkers' sent and received military messages in Navajo; Japan never broke the code, and the code talkers were considered essential to US victory.

Like the Apache, the Navajo were feared nomads and warriors who both traded with and raided the Puebloans, and who fought settlers and the US military. They also borrowed generously from other traditions: they acquired sheep and horses from the Spanish, learned pottery, farming and weaving from the Puebloans and picked up silversmithing from Mexico. Today, the Navajo are renowned for their woven rugs, pottery and inlaid silver jewelry. Their intricate sandpainting is used in healing ceremonies.

THE HOPI ARE ARIZONA'S OLDEST TRIBE AND ARE KNOWN FOR THEIR DISTINCTIVE, RICH CULTURE, WHOSE INTRICACIES REMAIN CLOSELY GUARDED.

Zuni Pueblo clothing, New Mexico

FROM LEFT: THEPALMER/GETTY IMAGES ©, SHIZUKO ALEXANDER/GETTY IMAGES ©

Paiute (Nuwuvi)

The Southern Paiute occupy land north of the Colorado River in what is known as the Arizona Strip, and have traditionally used the canyon for hundreds of years. After contact and conflict with the Navajo and Ute, Spanish explorers, Mormon settlers and the US government, the Southern Paiute now live in scattered settlements and reservations in California, Utah, Nevada and Arizona.

One branch of this tribe, the Kaibab band, occupies a reservation in northern Arizona, just west of Fredonia and south of Kanab, Utah. The tribe is largely involved in both agriculture and tourism and runs a visitor center and campground at Pipe Spring National Monument.

Zuni (A:shiwi)

The Zuni, like the Hopi, are one of 21 Puebloan tribes, located in New Mexico and Arizona. These tribes are as different as they are alike; nevertheless, the term 'Pueblo' (Spanish for 'village') is a convenient shorthand. All are believed to be descended from the Ancestral Puebloans – formerly known as the Anasazi and whose ruins you will see throughout the Grand Canyon – and to have inherited their architectural style and their agrarian, village-based life, often atop mesas.

Pueblos are unique among Native Americans. These adobe structures can have up to five levels, connected by ladders, and are built with varying combinations of mud bricks, stones, logs and plaster. In the central plaza of each pueblo is a kiva, an underground ceremonial chamber that connects to the spirit world.

The Zuni trace their origins to Ribbon Falls, off the North Kaibab Trail in the Grand Canyon. Eventually settling in what is today western New Mexico, the Zuni refer to the Little Colorado River, which connects them with the Grand Canyon, as their umbilical cord.

THIS LAND IS YOUR LAND: PUBLIC LAND & POLITICS

More than 70% of Utah is owned by the federal or state government – but how should it be used? By Lauren Keith

WHEN PRESIDENT BARACK Obama created Bears Ears National Monument in 2016, Utah found itself back at the center of a long-simmering controversy: how should the vast tracts of public land in the West be managed? Should they be set aside for recreation and environmental and cultural preservation, or sold off to private interests to promote economic growth in local communities?

With so much public land – Utah ranks second in the country for the most government-owned acres, after neighboring Nevada – it's no surprise that land use and stewardship is a continually contentious issue in the state. As administrations come and go, the political ping-pong carries on unresolved.

Buying – & Taking – the West

The federal government owns nearly half of the land in the West. As the 19th-century idea of 'manifest destiny' pushed Euro-American settlers to spread and stake their claims, the US government bought or took land, including from Native people,

Pictured clockwise from top left: Saguaro National Park (p188); The Narrows (p195), Zion National Park; Petrified Forest National Park (p185); Grand Staircase-Escalante National Monument

to fuel its expansion. Homesteading and land grants brought land into the private hands of farmers, and ranchers were often permitted the free use of 'unclaimed' areas.

While this method worked in the Midwest, with flat landscapes and fertile soil, the mountain-filled and arid stretches of the West were not always well suited for agriculture. Over time, environmental conservation became a higher public priority, and some of the land became protected wilderness and parks.

National Park Versus National Monument

The difference between a national park and a national monument is simply to do with how the site is established. An act of Congress designates a national park, while a national monument can be created by presidential proclamation (as well as by Congress). National monuments established by a president can become national parks with congressional approval.

The 1906 Antiquities Act, brought into law by conservationist president Theodore Roosevelt, authorized presidents to create national monuments. The act was passed in response to concerns about the looting of Native archaeological sites in the West, and it permitted the president to preserve 'historic landmarks, historic and prehistoric structures, and other objects of historic or scientific interest' as national monuments, 'the limits of which in all cases shall be confined to the smallest area compatible with the proper care and management of the objects to be protected.'

A few months after the act passed, Roosevelt created the first national monument, Devils Tower in Wyoming, and the Petrified Forest and Grand Canyon in Arizona soon joined its ranks. Even then, the protection of the Grand Canyon was contentious – a mining claimant sued in federal court, arguing that Roosevelt had overstepped his power by setting aside the entire canyon. The Supreme Court ruled unanimously in Roosevelt's favor.Since then, seven Republican and nine Democratic presidents have used the Antiquities Act to create more than 140 national monuments across the country, including four of Utah's five national parks.

Slot Canyon, Grand Staircase-Escalante National Monument

The Controversy of Grand Staircase-Escalante & Bears Ears

Bill Clinton created Grand Staircase-Escalante (GSENM) in 1996. It was the country's second-largest national monument at the time, covering nearly 2 million acres. In 2017, just a year after Bears Ears was established, the Trump administration shrank the new monument by 85%, the biggest cutback of federal land protection in US history, further fanning the flames of national discord. And no wonder – Bears Ears has come to represent many hot-button topics in US political debates: federal versus state power, the influence of industry lobbyists among politicians, racism and Indigenous rights, and climate change versus natural-resource extraction. GSENM was downsized by almost half at the same time.

Within hours of Trump's proclamation, five Native American tribes, environmental groups such as the Natural Resources Defense Council and the Southern Utah Wilderness Alliance, and outdoor outfitter Patagonia filed lawsuits in federal court. The cases remain in court, but one of President

Angels Landing (p200), Zion National Park
APINBEN4289/SHUTTERSTOCK ©

Joe Biden's first acts in office was ordering a review of these national monuments, and later in 2021, both were expanded back to their original boundaries.

This move launched a new wave of court cases. In 2022, the state of Utah, a mining company and recreationalists sued the Biden administration, and Native tribes have been granted motions to intervene. The federal government asked the court to dismiss Utah's lawsuit in 2023.

Are Tourists Loving Utah to Death?

Regardless of the political battle, one thing is clear: everyone loves Utah's parks. Visitation hit record highs in 2021, when 11.2 million people traveled to the state's five national parks. Zion leads the way, breaking records with more than five million visitors in 2021, becoming the fourth national park to ever reach that number.

While more visitation means more awareness of the need to protect Utah's wild lands and more funds for the National Park Service, the challenges are numerous and have put considerable strain on popular destinations. In Zion, for example, traffic jams to enter the park in summer can be up to an hour long. There are only 1200 parking spots, but some 10,000 daily visitors.

Finding a solution to increased visitation has not been easy: proposals have included increasing entrance fees by more than 100% during peak season, mandating a reservation system for park entry or installing a permit system for hiking certain trails. Some of these initiatives have been put into action: since 2022, hikers to Angels Landing are required to have a permit, and travelers to Arches National Park must have timed-entry tickets from 7am to 4pm from April through October. Both the National Park Service and many visitors say these restrictions are working.

In a region where life hangs by a slender thread, the heavy trampling of human feet leaves lasting impressions. Desert crusts, wet meadows, and riverside campsites are slow to recover from such use, and repeated visits can cause permanent damage. Other effects may accumulate so gradually that they almost go unnoticed: scientists at Bryce Canyon estimate that 3% of the vegetation disappears each year as people wander off-trail among the hoodoos.

The first paintings of Western landmarks such as Zion Canyon were instrumental in sparking the US conservation movement during the late 19th century, which in turn brought about the establishment of the National Park Service. But who owns Utah's land and how its beautiful spaces should be enjoyed are enduring questions with no easy answers.

A CHANGING SIERRA

Over the last decade, human-caused climate change in the Sierra Nevada has led to catastrophic wildfires, drought, floods, severe storms and bark beetle infestations. By Ashley Harrell

A DRIVE THROUGH the Sierra Nevada's national parks is not what it once was. Sizeable stretches of the landscape are defined by dead and dying trees that have succumbed to wildfire, drought and bark beetle infestation. It's hard to look at, frankly. But at the same time, when taking into consideration what the future of the planet looks like if we don't curb climate change, what could be a more important thing to see?

Visiting the nation's parks is about enjoying yourself outdoors, of course, but you can make your trip an educational one as well. Understanding what's in front of you matters, be it a fire-charred giant sequoia, a pine forest annihilated by bark beetles or a wildfire burn scar stretching over hundreds or even thousands of miles. Before venturing into the wilderness, here's a primer on how climate change has been impacting the Sierra Nevada's parks and what you can do to help.

Shifting Weather Patterns

The western part of the Sierra Nevada has a Mediterranean climate with cool, wet winters and warm, dry summers. This area receives more precipitation due to moisture and warm air coming off the Pacific Ocean. In contrast, the eastern part of the region lies in a rain shadow and receives less precipitation. Temperatures are cooler in the southern part of the Sierra Nevada, and more precipitation falls as snow due to higher elevations.

Like the rest of California, the Sierra Nevada has historically seen high variability in annual precipitation. However, human-caused climate change is leading to perceptible shifts in the region's climate. Temperatures have been increasing, resulting in more precipitation falling as rain instead of snow. This has led to reduced snowpack in many areas and earlier snowmelt. Warmer temperatures have also been linked to increased wildfire activity.

Rising Temperatures

Recent reports out of the University of California, Berkeley have found that human-caused climate change has increased the annual temperature in Yosemite National Park by about 2°F since 1895. That's higher than the global rate, and unfortunately, the park's ecosystems are especially vulnerable to such shifts. Namely, warmer temperatures can reduce snowpack and increase the length of summer droughts, posing a threat to high-elevation mountain streams and their aquatic biodiversity.

Rising temperatures coupled with drought have led to the weakening of

millions of Yosemite's trees, leaving them vulnerable to invading bark beetles. A dry, dying tree is also a highly flammable tree. Throw in woody debris left over from a century of fire suppression and Yosemite starts to look like a tinderbox, with fires burning hotter and faster than ever before.

Worsening Wildfires

Fires in the Sierra Nevada are igniting more often and burning hotter than ever before. Climate change is part of that, but there are other factors, too: fuel loads in forests are sky-high thanks to a century of fire suppression, meanwhile, drought and a bark beetle epidemic are weakening the trees and high winds are carrying embers into bone-dry vegetation.

Before all this happened, fires swept through the Sierra's forests regularly. But they didn't usually burn hot enough to do long-term damage, and certainly, the giant sequoias (which are incredibly resilient trees) were able to withstand them. Sequoias just don't die very often, but in the last several years hotter fires started to change that.

The Castle Fire

The Castle Fire started in August 2020 in Sequoia National Forest and grew to become one of the most devastating wildfires for giant sequoias in history. It burned through 174,000 acres, including areas within the Alder Creek Grove, home to the world's fifth-largest giant sequoia, Stagg Tree. Despite efforts to protect the ancient giants, the fire caused significant damage to the grove, scorching the lower trunks of many trees and threatening their long-term survival. When the smoke cleared, an estimated 7500 to 10,600 large giant sequoias were dead, demonstrating for the first time the vulnerability of these ancient trees to increasingly severe wildfires fueled by climate change.

KNP Complex and Windy Fires

In September 2021, a lightning storm ignited two fires: the KNP Complex Fire in Sequoia & Kings Canyon National Parks, and the Windy Fire in Sequoia National Forest to the south. The KNP Complex Fire quickly became a grave threat to giant sequoias, burning through more than 88,000 acres, including the vicinity of the famous General Sherman Tree, the world's largest tree by volume. The Windy Fire took out an additional 1250 acres, and the two fires together destroyed an estimated 3000 giant sequoias. In 2020 and 2021, lightning-sparked wildfires killed nearly a fifth of the giant sequoias on Earth, underscoring the urgent need for proactive measures to safeguard the trees and their habitat.

The Washburn Fire

The human-caused Washburn Fire began in Yosemite National Park in July 2022 and burned into the park's iconic Mariposa Grove. Due to the historical significance of the grove, the fire gained national attention as it destroyed the air quality in the Sierra National Forest and prompted the evacuation of nearby communities. When it was fully contained and extinguished on August 1, a total area of 4886 acres had burned, but the grove's giant sequoias had come through unscathed. The reason, say fire ecologists, is that the grove has been receiving fuel reduction treatments for some 50 years. So the fire simply couldn't burn as fast or hot.

These days, park officials across the Sierra Nevada are scrambling to do prescribed, or deliberate, burns when possible, and allowing fires to burn naturally if they don't threaten lives or infrastructure. The idea is to thin the forests to prevent catastrophic fires, but some environmentalists take issue with the practice, and in some cases they've been able to stall efforts with lawsuits.

When Snow Turns to Rain

The Sierra Nevada has experienced extraordinary conditions over the last several years. From 2018 to 2022, an extended drought stressed natural resources and altered the rhythm of the seasons in an unprecedented way. Then in the winter of 2022–23, snow buried the mountains to a degree not seen in decades, providing momentary respite from cascading environmental dangers from lack of precipitation.

Burnt sequoia trees, Sequoia National Park (p59)

Still, evidence shows a general shift in precipitation from snowfall to rainfall, particularly at lower elevations. This has profound implications for the region's hydrological cycle, as the snowpack acts as a natural reservoir, gradually releasing water during the warmer months. With less snow accumulation and earlier snowmelt, water availability during the dry season is reduced, posing challenges for ecosystems that depend on a steady flow.

Changing Ecosystems

The ecological composition of the Sierra Nevada is undergoing significant transformation due to climate change. As temperatures rise and precipitation patterns shift, plant and animal communities must adapt or perish. Species that are accustomed to specific temperature ranges and habitats may need to migrate to more suitable areas. Alpine ecosystems (where pikas make their homes) are particularly vulnerable as higher elevations warm at a faster rate. These changes in ecosystems can have cascading effects on food webs, species interactions and ecological processes, altering the overall functioning and resilience of the Sierra Nevada's natural systems.

CLIMATE CHANGE HAS INCREASED THE ANNUAL TEMPERATURE IN YOSEMITE NATIONAL PARK BY ABOUT 2°F SINCE 1895. THAT'S HIGHER THAN THE GLOBAL RATE.

Flooded Merced River (p80)

BRET J. UNGER/SHUTTERSTOCK ©

What to Do

Curbing climate change in the Sierra Nevada and beyond requires concerted efforts from humans to mitigate their impacts. Here are some actions individuals and communities can take to make a difference.

First, we must reduce our carbon emissions, advocating for the expansion of renewable energy sources to reduce dependence on fossil fuels, and supporting policymakers to prioritize clean energy initiatives. One small thing you can do in the Sierra Nevada to minimize your use of fossil fuels is to opt for cleaner transportation methods, such as carpooling, biking, or using public transportation. In addition, it helps to embrace energy-efficient practices in homes and businesses, such as improving insulation.

Protecting our wild spaces, and particularly our forests, is also a big one. One way to get involved is to support local reforestation initiatives and participate in community tree-planting programs. While you're at it, might as well aim to reduce your water usage wherever possible and practice responsible outdoor recreation, following the Leave No Trace principles to minimize your impact on the environment. Respect wildlife, stay on designated trails and properly dispose of waste to preserve the region's delicate ecosystems.

Finally, talk to others about these issues. Engage in discussions, organize community events and support educational programs. Who knows, you might inspire some collective action.

THE YELLOWSTONE SUPERVOLCANO

Yellowstone has seen momentous change over the eons, from a flat primordial landscape to a mountainous epicenter of geothermal energy nestled atop one of the foremost hot spots. By Regis St Louis

IT'S HARD TO IMAGINE a time when the soaring mountains of Northwest Wyoming did not exist. But some 570 million years ago, present-day Yellowstone was nothing more than a stark, featureless plain, sitting at an elevation at or even below sea level. Over the next several hundred million years, shallow seas covered the area and stretched from present-day Canada all the way down to Mexico. These great bodies of water teemed with early forms of life, including trilobites (a type of marine arthropod), some of which are now preserved as fossils in the region's Cambrian rock deposits.

Around 75 million years ago, the days of flat horizons came to an end. Forces deep within the earth began uplifting and contorting the ground, deforming sedimentary rock on the surface and pushing up and exposing deeper Precambrian rocks – some of which first formed around 2.7 billion years ago (these astonishingly old rocks can still be seen in the steep walls of Lamar Canyon).

The Volcanic Past

Fire played a prominent role in reshaping this corner of the continent as large volcanoes around Yellowstone erupted some 50 million years ago. Huge explosions of volcanic rock covered large swaths of the landscape, with solidified magma making up a key part of the present-day Absaroka Range. Vast flows of lava and ash swept across the landscape, burying trees, some of which became petrified wood (as is visible in the stumps hidden along the Fossil Forest Trail in the Lamar Valley). Mt Washburn and Eagle Peak – Yellowstone's highest summit at 11,372ft – are remnants of this early Absaroka volcano. Elsewhere, the steady flow of lava created extraordinary formations, like the basalt columns and volcanic breccia in Tower Fall.

More dramatic movements occurred 10 million years ago, with tensional forces pushing up mountain blocks along faults while causing other areas to drop, creating the steep and jagged east face of the Tetons.

All of these events were mere preludes to the dynamic changes that transpired around two million years ago. That's when molten rock surging from deep within the earth produced the first of three gargantuan volcanic eruptions – in fact, one of the largest eruptions known to science. It covered over 5000 sq miles with ash and was an estimated 6000 times more powerful than the 1980 eruption of Mt St Helens in Washington. Another great eruption occurred around 1.3 million years ago.

This was followed by a third around 631,000 years ago that created the 1000-sq-mile Yellowstone caldera at the center of the park. The explosion spat out magma and clouds of 1800°F (982°C) liquid ash at supersonic speeds, vaporizing all in its path and suffocating the land in blisteringly hot ash flows. Billowing ash traveled thousands

of square miles in minutes, landing as far away as the Gulf of Mexico. The crater roof and floor then imploded and dropped thousands of feet, creating a smoldering volcanic pit 45 miles long and 30 miles wide. Ash circling the globe caused a volcanic winter by reducing the amount of solar heat reaching the earth.

Visitors sometimes wonder why Yellowstone lacks the dramatic peaks found in places like the nearby Grand Tetons. The reason is simply that the mountains were either blown away by the explosion or they sank into the caldera.

Since this last massive eruption, at least 80 smaller eruptions have occurred, including one some 174,000 years ago that created West Thumb in Yellowstone Lake. Ensuing lava flows have filled in and forests have reclaimed the area, making it difficult to see the entirety of the Rhode Island–sized caldera. However, parts of the park still bear the scars of this great eruption. The steep southern slopes of the Washburn Range stand just beyond the northern end of the caldera and remain tall because they were not involved in the collapse. Some of the caldera's outline can, in fact, be seen from the summit of Mt Washburn.

Yellowstone's Hot Spot

The many eruptions did not exhaust Yellowstone's fuel source. Yellowstone sits atop two enormous magma chambers – one that lies 3 to 10 miles below the surface, and below it an even larger reservoir – big enough to fill the Grand Canyon 11 times with molten rock. This great underground furnace fuels Yellowstone's geothermal features – all 10,000 of them, which is more than all other geothermal areas on the planet combined.

Heat is only one part of the equation. Essential to Yellowstone's thermal features is the addition of water, falling onto the park as rain or, more commonly, snow. This surface water may seep as deep as 2 miles over long periods of time before it drains through the side channels of geysers, hot springs and underground aquifers. This means that the burst from a geyser may have fallen as snow or rain up to 500 years ago.

With Yellowstone's geothermal activity constantly in flux, what seem like permanent features are mere blips on the geologic timescale. Geysers suddenly erupt, or dry up; hot springs gradually appear, or explode so violently that they destroy themselves.

Scientists are still making sense of the complicated plumbing beneath the supervolcano. In 2022 new research using a decade worth of seismic data was published which showed that there was far more liquid magma than previously thought found in the upper reservoir. The more liquid the molten rock, the more likely an eruption is imminent. However, an explosion isn't likely to happen in the near future given the current composition of roughly 20% liquid material. Around 35% to 50% is the threshold for eruptions.

Yellowstone is rising or falling as much as an inch a year, moving 65ft with each slow-motion 'breath,' particularly at Mallard Lake Dome just east of Old Faithful, and Sour Creek Dome, east of the Hayden Valley. These movements in the earth's crust are probably due to the withdrawal of molten rock from twin magma chambers on the rim of the Yellowstone caldera.

No one knows for sure what will happen if (or when) Yellowstone's slumbering giant awakens. The last major Yellowstone eruption dwarfed every other volcanic eruption on the earth's surface for the past several million years, and such an explosion remains beyond human experience. But don't bet on Armageddon just yet. According to the US Geological Survey (USGS), a supereruption is not imminent. If there is an explosive event, it is likely to be hydrothermal, involving a rock-hurling geyser eruption or lava flow.

More pressing are the threats facing Yellowstone from climate change. The park anticipates the years ahead will bring more severe weather – like the heavy rains and flooding that wiped out a major park entrance road in 2022. With rising temperatures, officials also expect more frequent and destructive wildfires, along with droughts that can impact the park's geothermal features; recent studies found that Old Faithful stopped erupting for several decades owing to a mega-drought in the 13th century. Yellowstone's southern neighbor, Grand Teton, also faces grave threats from climate change, including longer fire seasons and the disappearance of its glaciers.

Grand Prismatic Spring (p294)

INDEX

Map Pages **000**

D

E

F

G

H

Map Pages **000**

I

J

K

Map Pages **000**

S

NOTES

"I love the diversity of experiences on offer [in the Everglades] (p387), from short strolls along a boardwalk to deep backcountry immersion in the 10,000 Islands in a kayak."

ANTHONY HAM

"For me, the trip is infused with a sense of mischief, from the swift blast of wind that rips off your cap at the roadside overlook to the knowledge that your last stop is, literally, Road's End (p50)."

AMY C BALFOUR

Mapping data sources:
© Lonely Planet
© OpenStreetMap http://openstreetmap.org/copyright

THIS BOOK

Commissioning Editor
Darren O'Connell

Production Editor
Kathryn Rowan

Book Designer
Clara Monitto

Cartographer
Alison Lyall

Assisting Cartographer
Dorothy Davidson

Assisting Editors
Andrew Bain, Nigel Chin, Barbara Delissen, Karyn Noble, Charlotte Orr, Gabrielle Stefanos

Cover Researcher
Kat Marsh

Thanks Allison Killilea, Graham O'Neill

MIX
Paper from responsible sources
FSC™ C021741

Paper in this book is certified against the Forest Stewardship Council™ standards. FSC™ promotes environmentally responsible, socially beneficial and economically viable management of the world's forests.

Published by Lonely Planet Global Limited
CRN 554153
4th edition – February 2024
ISBN 978 1 83869 975 8

10 9 8 7 6 5 4 3 2 1
Printed in China